ALSO BY JAMES L. HALEY

Fiction

Final Refuge

The Lions of Tsavo

The Kings of San Carlos

Nonfiction

Stephen F. Austin and the Founding of Texas

Sam Houston

Texas: From Spindletop Through World War II

*Most Excellent Sir: Letters Received by Sam Houston,
President of the Republic of Texas, at Columbia, 1836–1837*

Texas: An Album of History

Apaches: A History and Culture Portrait

*The Buffalo War: The History of the Red River Indian
Uprising of 1874*

PASSIONATE NATION

THE EPIC HISTORY OF TEXAS

JAMES L. HALEY

FREE PRESS

NEW YORK LONDON TORONTO SYDNEY

FREE PRESS

A Division of Simon & Schuster, Inc.
1230 Avenue of the Americas
New York, NY 10020

First Free Press trade paperback edition April 2009

FREE PRESS and colophon are trademarks
of Simon & Schuster, Inc.

For information regarding special discounts for bulk purchases,
please contact Simon & Schuster Special Sales at 1-866-506-1949
or business@simonandschuster.com.

The Simon & Schuster Speakers Bureau can bring authors to your live event.
For more information or to book an event contact the Simon & Schuster
Speakers Bureau at 1-866-248-3049 or visit our website at
www.simonspeakers.com.

Manufactured in the United States of America

1   3   5   7   9   10   8   6   4   2

The Library of Congress has cataloged the hardcover edition as followed:
Haley, James L.
Passionate nation : the epic history of Texas / James L. Haley.
p.   cm.
Includes bibliographical references and index.
1. Texas—History.   I. Title.
F386.H2355 2006
976.4—dc22   2005058062
ISBN-13: 978-0-684-86291-0
ISBN-10:   0-684-86291-3
ISBN-13: 978-1-4391-1018-8 (pbk)
ISBN-10:   1-4391-1018-2 (pbk)

To Kelley and Dana,

with love

Like most passionate nations, Texas has its own private history based on, but not limited by, facts.

—JOHN STEINBECK

CONTENTS

CONTENTS

ACKNOWLEDGMENTS

Because this is the first general trade book overview of Texas history under-taken in nearly forty years, it has given me the happy opportunity to make a fresh assessment of the state's journey. I drew from the outset on the sug-gestions, even if only in a curbside chat, of an amplitude of historians, archivists, librarians, museum curators, and other scholars. To all of them my sincere thanks.

Likewise in recent years I have had the chance to meet, at formal lectures and casual luncheon talks, hundreds of members of the Sons and Daughters of the Republic of Texas and other historical interest groups, virtually all of whom have lively opinions of the state of Texas history to share along with ancestral memories. Each of them shaped this book in some subtle way.

I owe more particular thanks to my usual crowd of suspects for their long-standing interest, advice, and encouragement, including my buddy Jane Karotkin at the Friends of the Governor's Mansion; Carl McQueary during his tenure at the Republic of Texas Museum; Jean Carefoot, Donaly Brice, and John Anderson at the Texas State Archives; Ron Tyler at the Texas State Historical Association; and Al Lowman, a past president of that august body. And for a work as much of writing as of historical recitation, I need to acknowledge the help, support, and occasional beer from my cabal of writer friends who understand the madness of the craft.

Further assists are gratefully acknowledged from Jack Nokes, Joy Bar-nett, and Sandy Page at the Texas Association of Museums, and Kit Neu-mann at the Texas Historical Foundation. For various hints, suggestions, and signposts, to say nothing of stories told, I am indebted to Roger Olien and Bill Kirchner of Austin; Galen Moore of Round Rock; Bill Bandy of Amarillo; Don Richardson of Lufkin; and the Honorable William P. Hobby Jr. of Houston. Thanks are finally extended to Ann Hodges and Cathy Spitzen-berger at the University of Texas at Arlington for help in finding Mirabeau Lamar's "Birthday Acrostic."

Finally, while this volume did not require the fifteen years consumed by my biography of Sam Houston, a deep bow is made to my editor, Bruce Nichols at Free Press, for allowing me the extra time to see it through properly.

PREFACE

It is now nearly forty years since anyone has produced a sizable, single-volume interpretation of Texas history for the general reading audience. There have been a few small occasion-pieces, such as Joe B. Frantz's cheeky but facile *Texas: A History* in 1976 and the *Texans* segment of the Time-Life series; textbook publishers regularly bring out new works consisting of sanitized passion plays for the schoolchildren. But T. R. Fehrenbach's *Lone Star,* published in 1968, marks the last time the mainstream book market has seen a general history of Texas. Before Fehrenbach, Rupert Richardson's *Texas: The Lone Star State* appeared sixty-three years ago, in 1943. It is a textbook, but because of the dearth of trade titles it has done service in bookstores for decades, and is now in its ninth edition, regularly updated and politically corrected by editorial committees since Richardson's death. The genre of textbook crossover attained a new standard with the very able *Gone to Texas,* by Randolph B. Campbell of the University of North Texas (2003), and with a new college-level text, *Texas: Crossroads of North America,* by Jesús F. de la Teja, Paula Marks, and Ron Tyler (2004). But where are the books written by writers, for people to enjoy rather than to study?

This dearth of new work is at once unsurprising and very surprising. It is unsurprising because of the intimidating scope of the subject, but it is surprising because Texas history is a field that has long been popular. Every year sees several score of new books and articles interpreting and presenting some facet or other of the Texas experience. Despite this, much of the Texas story has yet to be written; most of Texas' seven hundred museums, and its one thousand municipal and college libraries, have caches of papers and memoirs and photographs, yet many of them have never been cracked open. And that is in addition to troves still stashed in the closets and attics of our older families. Though Texas history surrounds us, it remains, as Sam Houston loved to say, concealed behind the veil of futurity.

Some years ago, I put together a book containing about two hundred old photographs, many of which had not been published before. I was particularly proud of having located an early daguerreotype of Jane Long, the so-called Mother of Texas. Signing copies at a bookstore in Tyler, in Northeast Texas, I looked up and beheld two stocky, rural-looking women glowering at me from the door and hefting several shopping bags heaped with yellowing papers. They marched over to my table, and as one pulled out an antique derringer and held it on me, Sisterwoman spread their documents on the table. I had, they said, made a mistake in my book: Jane Long was not the mother of the first white baby born in Texas. That honor belonged to their great-great-great-great-grandmother, Helena Dill Berryman. Under the watchful barrel of the derringer, and as other store patrons were torn between edging closer and calling the police, I looked over their papers. The signatures they bore comprised a galaxy of early Texas figures, including Houston and Stephen F. Austin. It appeared that the ladies, who had driven up fifty miles from their farm outside of Nacogdoches, had a pretty good case, and I asked them why they didn't write, or commission, an article about their family, or at least get these documents copied and in safekeeping. They were too busy running their farm to do that, they said, but they just wanted me to know I didn't know it all.

Texans are bonded more tightly to their history than are the people of any other state. First, this is because it is a relatively recent history. Its Spanish antecedents extend back to the early sixteenth century, but the Anglo period is still less than two hundred years old. In many places in Texas, people live on land that their family has owned since the Indians were killed or driven away. Arrow points aren't something you see in a museum, they are something you pick up after you plow the south forty.

Second, Texas history is unique among the United States. Texas is not the only state that can claim at least nominal independence before becoming part of the United States, but it is the only state whose nationality was maintained, both by diplomacy and by force of arms, over many years, and that was recognized and courted by the world's great powers. It is a history whose romance has captured the imagination of the rest of the country, indeed of the world, as that of no other region has. Any Texan who has traveled abroad can testify to this.

Third, Texas is a place where our social and political processes were accelerated perhaps faster than anywhere else—from wilderness to independent nation in only a decade and a half. In the study of Texas history we have one advantage over older nations: there are no mists of time into which to disappear. Much documentation exists of Texas even from its earliest days. This doesn't mean the facts are always easy to discern, however, for our

Texas national story has also made the journey from fact to myth in record time.

This hints at the fourth reason why Texans maintain such an energetic interest in their history: the tug-of-war over which history to tell. A while ago I delivered a luncheon talk about Sam Houston to a local chapter of the Sons of the Republic of Texas, which is made up of descendants of early settlers and soldiers who fought in the Texas Revolution. During their business meeting, it was reported with some approval that they had won a more recent skirmish: the museum at Goliad, which had been under pressure from Hispanic advocacy groups to stop referring to the 1836 incident there as a "massacre" and refer to it instead as an "execution," demurred. For the time being, at least, the shooting of James Walker Fannin and up to four hundred of his captive men will continue to be a "massacre."

For the first two-thirds of the twentieth century, Texas history by and large became codified into a generally accepted canon, which was Anglocentric and not overly welcoming of other points of view. During the 1960s, concomitant with the academic upheaval all over the country, that facade was battered by a new generation of revisionist historians, sensitive to old racial injustices and suspicious of long-recited mythologies. Old assumptions were challenged and often shown to be lacking in substance. The revisionist movement gained credibility as well as momentum, breaking the rose-colored glasses through which the past had often been seen. But with revisionism more recently entering the era of "political correctness," and even engaging in some of the excesses of earlier historical study, those who take a more conservative view of the past have found themselves more often in dissent. Academic history has, to an extent, gone the way of classical music: written by professionals to challenge or perhaps annoy or even outrage other professionals, with the general public largely irrelevant. Politically correct history has reached such a state that more than one professor has muttered to me, over a late-night beer, a confidence he would never own up to in the classroom: the emperor, though not yet stark naked, is getting a little threadbare.

Where, then, can one turn to uncover the "real" history, if indeed there is one? The operative principle of this book is that the history lies with the people, with the distinct flavor of the experiences of the rank and file. That has often been neglected while the deeds of the high and mighty have been recited. History is made by people, who have passions, and foibles, and a spark of the eternal in both good and evil.

In reducing a rich and varied history to a single volume, a process of selection is inevitable. Complex issues must be explained succinctly, and many illuminating sidelights cannot be detailed. The most I can hope for is that people can say of this book that it is accurate as far as it goes, and that they enjoyed reading it. If it stimulates their curiosity to read further and look closer, then I will have done my job.

BOOK ONE

GOLD AND SOULS

ONE

SMILING CAPTORS

IN LIGHT OF THE SUBSEQUENT HISTORY, IT IS ONLY RIGHT that European contact with the area that became Texas began with jealousy and intrigue. In 1518 Diego Velásquez, the Spanish governor of Cuba, caved in to pressure from an ambitious retainer named Hernán Cortés and allowed him to form an expedition to explore and conquer that portion of the interior of New Spain that lay directly westward of Cuba. Velásquez believed that any riches plundered from the steaming mainland jungles should be his, and he was naturally suspicious of Cortés' thirst for power.

It was a time in which political stewardship meant control of wealth—only in later eras would this be called corruption—and just a quarter century after the landings of Columbus, Spanish governors in the New World were already snapping at each other like wolves over a kill. Velásquez soon thought better of the commission and revoked it, but Cortés sailed anyway, with ten cannons and six hundred men, landing in Mexico in March 1519. Cowing coastal Indians, he hacked his way into the heart of the Aztec empire, where he was welcomed as a god in fulfillment of prophecy and he became the *conquistador* he had always dreamed of being. As Velásquez suspected, Cortés threw over his allegiance and established his own government. Not all of Cortés' men were in agreement, and Cortés burned his fleet to keep loyalists from carrying word of his coup back to Cuba.

Late in the year, at Cortés' coastal headquarters of La Villa Rica de la Vera Cruz, there appeared the ships of Alonso Álvarez de Pineda, who had just mapped the whole curve of the Gulf of Mexico for the first time, proving that Florida was not an island; he had sailed west through the great freshwater discharge of an enormous river, certainly the Mississippi, then southwest and finally south, until he dropped anchor at Villa Rica. Álvarez de Pineda, however, was sailing in the service of the governor of Jamaica, and Cortés arrested his envoys as soon as they came ashore. Álvarez quickly weighed anchor and withdrew back to the north, seeking shelter and starting his own colony near the mouth of the Pánuco River, in the vicinity of later Tampico. Sending his ships back to Jamaica for supplies, Álvarez stayed at Pánuco with several dozen of his men. Local natives, who thanks to Cortés had seen all they needed to see of the Spanish, devastated the settlement. Returning ships ferried the survivors to Cortés' Villa Rica; Álvarez was not among them, but his map, the first to show the coast of Texas, still exists, with its imprecise squiggles of speculative rivers.

Back in Cuba, Velásquez finally learned that Cortés' actions justified his earlier apprehension, and he sent an army under his lieutenant governor, Pánfilo de Narváez, to arrest the recreant and bring him home. Narváez reached Mexico in April 1520; Cortés learned of his arrival, and after entering his camp at night, talked most of the invaders into defecting, and captured Narváez. There was a fight, in which Narváez got an eye put out, and that was the end of Velásquez' ambition to control Cortés, who three years later was confirmed as governor and captain general of New Spain. (He did have his own downfall, later.) Narváez returned to Spain to recover, where he became a favorite of that country's young King Charles I, the grandson of Ferdinand and Isabella. Tired of being a pawn serving greater men's games, Narváez began angling for his own expedition to explore and conquer. The king, feeling perhaps that the immensity of the New World must be capable of embracing at least one more breastplated egomaniac, commissioned him to explore "Florida," a name that then covered the entire curve of the Gulf north and east of Cortés.

Narváez returned to Cuba and in April 1528 crossed the Straits of Florida with about three hundred men, including his treasurer, another young noble who had gained the king's favor, Álvar Núñez Cabeza de Vaca. His name derived from a maternal ancestor, who saved the day in a thirteenth-century battle by marking a strategic pass with a cow's skull. In dignity-conscious Spain, he chose to live by his mother's name, which carried higher rank than his father's. He was soon, however, to begin measuring dignity by very different standards.

Narváez' leadership skills were negligible. He landed his men on the west coast of Florida, and made it clear to the local natives that he was seeking gold. Establishing a pattern that held for decades, the Indians realized they could get rid of the invaders by pointing to some place over the horizon and promising all the gold they desired. Narváez took the bait and split his command, leaving the ships to find a secure anchorage, and leading the men off to collect the gold; he soon got them hopelessly lost. Even more stupidly, he believed they were only a jaunty sail from Pánuco on the east coast of Mexico. By the time he reached what is now the Florida Panhandle, fifty of his men had died or been killed, and he had the remainder construct five crude barges with the intention to sail west, hugging the coast, until they should reach the settlements. A month into their voyage, they crossed the discharge of the Mississippi, still looking for civilization, a lark turned desperate. Their boats separated in a storm, the food was almost gone, and they were numb from exposure. On the evening of November 5, 1528, the officer of Cabeza de Vaca's boat passed command to him, "as he was in such condition," wrote de Vaca, "that he believed he should die that night."

Shortly before sunrise he thought he could hear surf. He awakened the master, and "near the shore a wave took us, that knocked the boat out of water the distance of the throw of a crowbar." The violent jar roused the nearly insensible survivors. Finding themselves near the shore, they crawled through the surf on hands and feet, reaching the shore and finding shelter in some ravines. "There we made fire, parched some of the maize we brought, and found some rain water."

The strongest of the survivors, Lope de Oviedo, climbed a tree and descried that they were on an island, probably Galveston or one of the small islands just to the west of it. He found an Indian village, apparently deserted, and helped himself to some mullets and a pot. Regaining the Spanish camp, the castaways saw that he was followed at a distance by what they took to be a hundred warriors armed with bows. Defense was impossible, for as Cabeza de Vaca related, "it would have been difficult to find six that could rise from the ground." Rummaging in their stores, he gave the warriors beads and hawkbells, receiving arrows in exchange as a sign of amity. The natives signed that they had no food with them, but would return in the morning.

"At sunrise the next day . . . they came according to their promise, and brought us a large quantity of fish with certain roots, some a little larger than walnuts, others a trifle smaller, the part got from under the water and with much labor." More food arrived that evening, along with native women and children to have a look at the strangers. The Spaniards gave them more beads and hawkbells, thus ensuring their hospitality for a time longer.

Somewhat recovered and with no sign of survivors from the other four barges, the Spaniards began digging their boat out of the sand where the surf had largely buried it. With enormous effort they got it back into the water and made to resume their journey toward Pánuco and safety, but "at the distance of two crossbow shots in the sea we shipped a wave that entirely wet us. As we were naked, and the cold was very great, the oars loosened in our hands, and the next blow the sea struck us, capsized the boat." Three men drowned, and the rest were cast back on the shore, "naked as they were born, with the loss of all they had." No wonder they named the place Isla de Malhado, the isle of misfortune.

With no other recourse, Cabeza de Vaca appealed to the Indian benefactors to take them to their village for shelter. This alarmed the other survivors, who feared that they were pushing hospitality too far. To their surprise, the Indians "signified that it would give them delight." Moreover, the natives asked the Spaniards to wait a short time while preparations were made. Along the trail to their village they made several large fires at which the freezing Europeans warmed themselves, and on reaching the village, they discovered that the Indians had built them their own large hut, with numerous fires in it.

The Spaniards—or as they referred to themselves, the Christians—took up life with these natives, eventually encountering other survivors of the Narváez expedition until they numbered some eighty. Again they tried to sail away but the boat, Cabeza de Vaca noted laconically, sank simply from its unfitness to float. The Indians among whom they found themselves were Karankawas, a tribe now extinct. They were a people surprisingly tall and powerful to have lived in an environment that was so poor of sustenance that they had to move camp constantly to find seasonal foods in turn—turtles, shellfish, fish, roots. The men were skilled warriors, their principal weapon a longbow of cedar as tall as themselves. They were cannibals, although there was a religious element to their human consumption that rendered their cannibalism somewhat less orgiastic than that of natives farther inland. (In point of fact, Karankawas would eat only enemies; when they learned that other survivors of the Narváez disaster had turned to cannibalism to keep from starving, the Indians expressed their mortification and declared that if they had known the Spanish were capable of such an abomination, they would have been slaughtered on the beach.)

Karankawa men wore simple skin breechcloths, or just as often nothing at all. Protected from mosquitoes by a smear of alligator grease, their bodies were decorated with spikes of cane pierced through the lower lip and one or both nipples. Families traveled from camp to camp in enormous dugout canoes of cypress logs, suitable for negotiating the bayous and lagoons, but nothing like seaworthy. They communicated with distant family groups by using smoke signals. Their territory along the Texas coast extended as far south as the mouth of the Guadalupe River, and they maintained limited trading relations with other tribes along their borders.

At first they welcomed the Europeans with open-handed generosity and shared their meager existence, but then the Indians began dying—cholera, pox, the host of European maladies to which the natives had no immunity. When half of the entire village was dead, the belief was expressed that it was the strangers who brought the death with them, and the castaways should be killed. Medical science was centuries away from proving them right, but a council, called a *mitote*, was convened to decide on the Spaniards' fate. There more deliberate advice prevailed before Cabeza de Vaca and his companions could be slaughtered. The warrior who was to some degree their keeper said that if the white men had power to kill in this way, they would have used that power to save themselves. In the preceding months so many of them had died—from an original eighty castaways, only fifteen survived—that it was silly, he argued, to believe they had such power.

Two of that fifteen, Alonso Castillo Maldonado, a noble captain from Salamanca, and Andrés Dorantes de Carranza, a fortune-hunter and also a captain, in spring of 1529 determined to strike out on foot for Mexico with a dozen of the survivors, and they took Dorantes' servant, a slave Moor called Estevanico, with them. The remaining castaway, Lope de Oviedo, prevailed upon Cabeza de Vaca to remain behind with him. They lived for three years with their hosts as virtual slaves, trying to do for themselves as traders but having to devote time first to satisfy the increasingly unfriendly Karankawas. Their station improved somewhat when Cabeza de Vaca fell into dire illness, and having been given up for dead, upon his recovery gained celebrity among the local tribes as a medicine man. He had observed that much of Karankawa life revolved around the *mitotes* and ceremonies of various kinds, and he copied the forms of healing rituals that he saw, breathing on the patients and interspersing his improvised cures with Christian prayers. It was a scam and he knew it, but enough of the sick and injured recovered to keep him in business—and alive. His reputation as a healer also gave him a tiny prosperity as a trader, gathering mesquite beans and mussel shells along the coast, exchanging them among inland tribes for red ochre body paint and animal skins that his host-captors prized.

The names that Cabeza de Vaca gave to these various Indian groups are meaningless today, for the array of native societies in Texas in the sixteenth century was vastly different from the large and well-organized tribes of the nineteenth-century frontier. Spanish explorers named several hundred tribes, some no larger than a few families, living independently and connected only by basic cultural affinities to similar small tribes. They formed large, vague areas of cultural identity that anthropologists are still trying, with little success, to reconstruct.

In 1532 de Vaca finally convinced Lope de Oviedo to set out for Mexico with him. They made good their escape and proceeded southwest along the coast. Bands in the area where they had been located were familiar with his reputation as a healer, and at virtually every camp he was required to perform. By a stroke of providential fortune, soon after escaping Cabeza de Vaca prayed over the body of a man he believed had already died, only to discover the next day that he had merely been in a deep stupor, had awakened, and was eating and talking. More famous than ever, the two white men continued down the coast, trading and healing and extemporizing new relationships with different Indians, all the way to the mouth of the Guadalupe River.

The tribes in that region began to be of a different cultural stock, the Coahuiltecan, whose structure and divisions are even murkier than those of the Karankawas. But farther now from the scene of their fame, the native practice of greatest relevance to the Spaniards was their warlike bearing and their delight in enslaving the Europeans. The trek became a gauntlet of servitude, with each new village of captor hosts assigning camp drudgery to the Spaniards. Frequently they were forced naked out into the thornbrush to collect fuel for the fires. "At times," Cabeza de Vaca wrote, "when my turn came to get wood, I collected it at heavy cost in blood. . . . My only solace in these labors was to think of the sufferings of our Redeemer, Jesus Christ, and the blood He shed for me. How much worse must have been his torment from the thorns than mine here!"

A keen observer of native cultures, Cabeza de Vaca noted that many of the tribes reveled in a stupor from smoking what was surely peyote, which, like addicts, they would trade anything they owned to secure. The Karankawas from whom they had escaped lacked peyote and so obtained a hallucinogen from a tea. The natives burned yaupon leaves in a pot, added water before the fire burned down, then boiled it twice until it formed a froth. But a strange superstition went with it: from the moment the cry went out to the camp that the brew was ready, every woman within earshot had to freeze in her tracks, stock still, until the beverage was consumed. For a woman to move during the tea drinking rendered the liquid a medium for evil; the batch had to be thrown out, those men who had already partaken forced themselves to vomit, and the woman was beaten fiercely. Among the same people, perhaps predictably, the men would not eat food prepared by a woman during her monthly "indisposition," as Cabeza de Vaca called it.

He found many tribal customs shocking. The practice of routine female infanticide (girl babies being fed to camp dogs) meant that wives had to be stolen from outside the group. Even more demoralizing was his discovery that, among some of these natives, it was perfectly acceptable and a common practice for a warrior to live conjugally with another man who had been rendered a eunuch. These latter would go about "partly dressed, like women, and perform women's duties." While calling the practice diabolical, the fair-minded healer also allowed that the eunuchs were skilled bowmen. "They are more muscular and taller than other men and can lift tremendous weight."

Eventually Cabeza de Vaca and Lope de Oviedo were taken up by other truculent natives, who responded to the usual inquiries of whether they knew of more Christians with yes, they did, and they had killed them. "They commenced slapping and batting Oviedo and did not spare me either. . . . They would stick arrows to our hearts and say they had a mind to kill us the way they had finished our friends." Oviedo, who could not swim, and who had just nerved fording a shallow bay, lost his courage, turned back across the water with the women of the previous tribe, and was never heard from again.

Cabeza de Vaca now believed himself alone, but presently encountered, to his surprise, Dorantes, Estevanico, and Castillo, all that survived of those who left Galveston Island in 1529. He joined them in servitude to these Mariame Indians—another name of limited utility. More watchful than the Spaniards' previous owners, the Mariames kept the four white men in slavery for two years before the men succeeded in another escape and struck off westward, overland, into the cactus-studded brush country of South Texas. They crossed the Rio Grande and turned north into the desert, crossing it again near the present location of Presidio.

On what was probably the upper Pecos River, the Spaniards saw evidence of the scope and sophistication of the native trading network. The tribes in this locale—belonging to another of those large, vague collections of villages, and called the Jumanos—possessed cotton shawls from tribes far to the west, turquoise from the north, shells from the unknown Pacific Northwest, and large copper rattles fashioned from metal mined in the interior of New Spain. Cabeza de Vaca's trumped-up reputation as a healer almost got him in trouble here, as the natives brought him a man who had been shot in the back with an arrow, which had pierced deep, with the point lodged above the man's heart. "With a flint knife," he recalled of the first known surgery in Texas, "I opened the fellow's chest until I could see that the point was sideways and would be difficult to extract. But I cut on and, at last, inserting my knife-point deep, was able to work the arrowhead out with great effort. It was huge." Stanching the copious flow of blood with a swatch of hide, Cabeza de Vaca sutured the wound with a deer-bone needle.

Miraculously, the patient recovered without infection. The Indians demanded the arrowhead, which they examined in amazement and sent on a tour through neighboring villages. "This cure," wrote Cabeza de Vaca, "so inflated our fame all over the region that we could control whatever the inhabitants cherished." The Spaniards took full advantage of the Indians' awe, intending to turn their journey into an almost royal progress westward to civilization. Soon, however, as often happened when European met Native American, the Indians around them began to sicken and die. Afraid that they would be killed or abandoned, the Spaniards saw instead the Indians coming to them and begging for their lives; one baby was taken away and cut with mouse teeth for daring to cry in Cabeza de Vaca's presence.

Slowly they made their way west, accompanied by several hundred attentive retainers. They occasionally spoke of God, but proselytizing was hardly a priority in their struggle to survive. Only as they neared civilization did Cabeza de Vaca finally remember the reason other than gold for the Spaniards' voyage to the New World. "We taught all the people by signs, which they understood, that in Heaven was a Man we called God, who had created the heavens and the earth; that all good came from Him, and that we worshipped and obeyed him and called him our Lord; and that if they would do the same, all would be well with them. . . . From then on, at sunrise, they would raise their arms to the sky with a glad cry, then run their hands down the length of their bodies. . . . They are a substantial people with a capacity for unlimited development."

In May 1536, having been away from civilization for seven and a half years, Cabeza de Vaca, his three companions, and their Indian throng approached Culiacán, near the Pacific coast of Mexico. They were presented to the local authority, Captain Diego de Alcaraz, who happened to be on a slaving expedition but was frustrated that his men had found no quarry. Prevailing on Cabeza de Vaca to coax his six hundred adoring Indians out of the woods, Alcaraz moved to capture and enslave them, but Cabeza de Vaca protested with such fury that Alcaraz backed down—or seemed to. In fact he began executing a more subtle plan that hinged upon separating leader from retainers. Cabeza de Vaca ended his New World odyssey as he began it, under the smiling arrest of those who welcomed him—this time his own people—but not before he managed with great difficulty to convince his Indians to return to the east, rebuild their towns, and live in peace. "And I solemnly swear," he wrote the king, "if they have not done so, it is the fault of the Christians."

TWO

THE CITIES OF GOLD

FROM THE TIME THAT CORTÉS CONQUERED THE AZTEC empire, the Spaniards had been lured deeper and deeper into North America by the rumors of ever greater treasure, expressed not least in tales of the Seven Cities of Cíbola. Upon his redemption to civilization, Cabeza de Vaca described walled cities that were widely interpreted to be the fabulous place.

Actually the origin of "Cíbola" was a complicated case of life imitating legend. There had long been an Iberian tale that in the eighth century a group of Christian bishops and their parishioners fled the Moorish conquest of Portugal by sailing west to a place called the Antilles. The seven bishops founded seven cities that became fabulously wealthy. Seven centuries later, the islands of the Caribbean were called the Antilles because, it was believed, that must have been the place. When the islands proved not to be so, the legend was not destroyed, but merely moved west again. When Cabeza de Vaca described walled cities in the high desert of interior New Spain, the hearts of the adventurous swelled. The new country had already yielded wealth beyond measure; how much more must there be now that the ancient cities had been sighted?

The viceroy of New Spain, Antonio de Mendoza, proceeded with a circumspection admirable for his times. To make this first contact he sent not an army, but a priest, Marcos de Niza. He also purchased Estevanico, the slave Moor, from his master, Andrés Dorantes de Carranza, who had accompanied Castillo and Cabeza de Vaca on their epic journey. He turned Estevanico over to Fray Marcos as a guide to the cities. Departing in spring of 1539, the party trekked north along the western Sierra Madre into present Arizona and New Mexico. Exasperated at their crawling pace, the light-traveling Moor took to preceding them by days. Having accompanied Cabeza de Vaca, he was used to being welcomed like a god, and he dressed the part in flash and feathers. He also acted the part with arrogant hauteur. When he reached what is now believed to have been the Zuñi Indian village of Hawikuh, he brazenly entered, demanding women and tribute, and the thoroughly unimpressed Indians killed him on the spot. Learning of this, Fray Marcos reported that he saw the great metropolis from a distance and judged it greater than Mexico City, but fearing for the safety of his party, he turned back.

This news finally won Mendoza over, and he turned to his protégé, the governor of the New World province of Nueva Galicia, Francisco Vázquez de Coronado, who had accompanied him from Spain. Between Mendoza's wealth and the dowry of Coronado's wife—an aggregate equivalent of several million dollars—they financed the expedition themselves, ever an important consideration in the frugal administration of the Spanish empire. Correctly referred to as Vázquez, but universally known in subsequent history as Coronado, the governor was thirty years old and the father of five. He organized quickly, and was ready to move by February 1540, assembling his force at Compostela for Mendoza to review. It was to be a mighty entrada: a thousand men, fifteen hundred mules and horses, guides, servants, camp followers, and thousands of head of stock for provisions. With Fray Marcos among their number, the force marched north from Culiacán in April, and on July 7 assaulted and took the "city" where Estevanico had been killed. It was not a city of gold. It, and the string of native towns conquered in turn, were mud-walled pueblos, impoverished and squalid. Smoldering at having been duped, Coronado sent Fray Marcos back to civilization, with the priest bearing in his own hand the dispatches that branded him, in short, a liar and an idiot.

Coronado in his turn, however, soon proved no less gullible. The expedition reached the southern rim of the Grand Canyon before turning east, sacking pueblos as they went. It was a thorough exploration, as Coronado split his army to search different areas for the cities of gold. Although Coronado finally reported that the Pueblo Indians had been "pacified," his reduction of them had been ruthless. In an incident that presaged much of the Spanish conquest, both in brutality and in native attempts at revenge, a Spanish soldier forced himself on an Indian woman. Natives began killing the Spaniards' horses, which Coronado answered by dispatching a lieutenant and soldiers to make an example of the village. After its "pacification," two hundred men were to be burned at the stake before their families. The lesson went awry, for the prisoners bolted the instant they saw what their fate was to be. Many were killed during the escape, but eventually only thirty were consigned to the flames. Once it was clear to the native elders that armed resistance was suicidal, they decided upon a little trickery. At the Rio Grande pueblo of Cicúique, the "pacified" chiefs provided Coronado a guide, a Pawnee Indian captive whose complexion was so dark that the Spaniards, who were happy to have him, called him El Turco, "The Turk."

It was too late in the year to proceed, so the expedition wintered at Tiguex, an Indian village near the present location of Albuquerque. While feeding off the Indian larders they learned of an alien world. The Indians brought them presents of hides of a large beast they could not identify, until one of Coronado's exploratory probes became the first Europeans to see one. With no word for bison in the European lexicon, the Spaniards simply called them cattle, but after gaining some firsthand experience with them, Coronado acknowledged that "they are the most monstrous beasts ever seen or read about. There are such quantities of them that I do not know what to compare them with, unless it be the fish in the sea. . . . Should we have wished to go some other way we could not have done it, for the fields are covered with them. The bulls are large and fierce, although they do not attack very often. However, they have mean horns and they thrust and rush well. They killed several of our horses and wounded many."

The captain who led the patrol that discovered the buffalo, Hernando de Alvarado, was guided by El Turco, who spun them a fabulous story of a rich province he called Quivira, in which gold and silver were commonplace, far to the east. Alvarado hustled back to Coronado's winter quarters, where El Turco repeated his story. Too deeply bitten by the gold bug to resist, Coronado determined to see for himself. They set out eastward again in late April 1541, crossing the Rio Grande to the Pecos and then downstream, then east again, where they came up against an escarpment, steep and rock-buttressed, that reminded them of the stakes of a palisade. Upon reaching the top they beheld a landscape unlike anything they had seen before, a vast, treeless prairie, as flat as a table, and so became the first Europeans to traverse what later became the Texas Panhandle. Virtually swallowed by the trackless soft grassland, they found it an unnerving experience.

As Coronado's diarist, Pedro de Castañeda, committed to paper, "Who could believe that 1,000 horses and 500 of our cows and more than 5,000 rams and ewes and more than 1,500 friendly Indians and servants, in traveling over those plains, would leave no more trace where they had passed than if nothing had been there—nothing—so that it was necessary to make piles of bones and cow dung now and then, so that the rear guard could follow the army. The grass never failed to become erect after it had been trodden down, and, although it was short, it was as fresh and straight as before."

Coronado himself was equally nonplussed, writing in his report to the king that the plains had "no more landmarks than if we had been swallowed up in the sea. . . . There was not a stone, not a bit of rising ground, nor a tree, nor a shrub, nor anything to go by." Either because of the palisaded escarpment that bounded the high prairie, or because of the cairns of bones and dung they erected to mark their course, the region became known as El Llano Estacado: the Staked Plains. Here Coronado saw for himself the fearsome large "cattle" that roamed by the millions.

Lured on by El Turco's tales of Quivira, Coronado continued to the eastern edge of the weird prairie, which fell away in an escarpment even higher than where they entered. The feature that later became known as the Cap Rock fell away more than a thousand feet beneath them. Of the gold that was of such importance to his mission, and which had been promised in such abundance, there was no sign. Eventually growing discouraged, but unwilling to abandon the enterprise, the practical Coronado sent the bulk of his army back to the pueblos of the Rio Grande to wait for him, while he kept a smaller column to make a last sweep in search of the golden land. He struck out north, arriving at the river that was represented as leading to Quivira, almost certainly the Arkansas, on July 29, 1541—Sts. Peter and Paul's Day, in Spanish parlance—and they proceeded downstream.

The Quivira that he reached was, to his dismay and disgust, a village or series of villages of impoverished Indians of another of those large cultural delineations encompassing several tribes. These called themselves Kitikitish, meaning Raccoon's Eyes, from the men's traditional facial tattoo designs, and were known to later history by their French name, the Wichitas. They were prairie farmers, not particularly warlike, the men mostly stout and not described as handsome. They were more swarthy than other natives (some French later called them Panis Noirs, the black Pawnees) and they tattooed themselves into great decoration. The women, however, were noted then and later for being attractive, if dark, and for their ample barechestedness, endowments of which they were rather proud, and they tattooed their breasts and nipples extensively with circles and radiating lines, a practice that was believed to ward off sagging in old age.

Coronado found the Wichitas on the upper Arkansas, but within a few generations the tribe began a southerly migration that carried them deep into the Brazos Valley of central Texas. They were not one unified tribe, but a landscape of related bands with different names, such as the Waco and the Tawakoni, who after their arrival in Texas bequeathed a variety of place-names to the geography. They were pushed out of the Arkansas River country, not by Europeans, but first by hostile and expansion-minded Osage Indians, and then by hostile and expansion-minded Comanches. It was from those tribes that they learned something of the arts of war; otherwise, in

Texas they continued their previous mode of living, in villages surrounded by fields of corn and beans and melons. They were frugal and provident, drying and plaiting pumpkins into edible sheets that were efficient to store. The fact that their round houses were covered with grass did not mean that they were fragile. They were constructed around a core of cedar poles and might be thirty feet across, separated into rooms by hanging skins and providing shelter for up to ten persons. Their social life was rich and complex; villages were arranged by maternal residence, and relationships were governed by strict custom, including the avoidance-respect of a man for his mother-in-law, offset by approved rapid-fire joking between cousins, who roared over witticisms about sex and bodily functions.

Typically, the Wichitas welcomed the Spanish strangers. They lived well enough on their stores of dried beans and pumpkin jerky, but there was no gold. "The natives here gave me a piece of copper which a chief Indian wore hung around his neck," wrote Coronado. "I sent it to the viceroy of New Spain, because I have not seen any other metal in these parts except this and some little copper bells which I sent him, and a bit of metal which looks like gold." He did not know where the gold came from, but thought the local natives must have obtained it from Indians in his own service, because "I cannot find any other origin for it, nor where it came from. . . . What I am sure of is that there is not any gold nor any other metal in all that country."

His lesson had finally been hard learned. But without gold, there was still that other goal of Spanish exploration. Of the Indian souls which were of concern to His Most Catholic Majesty, Coronado reported, "I have treated the natives . . . as well as was possible, agreeably to what Your Majesty had commanded, and they have received no harm in any way from me or from those who went in my company." Except for El Turco. Under pressure (a sixteenth-century euphemism for torture) he admitted that Quivira did not exist. Coronado's brutality in conquering the pueblos had prompted those chiefs to commission El Turco to get the invaders thoroughly lost. El Turco had apparently then compounded his crime by conspiring with some of the Wichitas to kill the Spaniards, and Coronado "reluctantly" had him garroted. Hoping to save himself at the last, El Turco claimed desperately that there truly were cities of gold—farther to the east. This time, it didn't work.

With dramatically lowered expectations, Coronado hired Wichitas as guides, and continued to explore into what is now southwestern Kansas before returning circuitously to Tiguex to spend the winter of 1541–42. There he was partially disabled by a head injury from falling off his horse. After reuniting with the columns he had sent out to explore separately, in the spring they returned whence they came, having solidified Spain's claim to a vast area of the interior of North America. Coronado later survived attacks on his gubernatorial administration—including a charge of cruelty against the natives. Though demoted, he lived out his remaining dozen years as a councilman in Mexico City.

THREE

SO BESET WITH HARDSHIPS

THIS SPANISH EAGERNESS TO BELIEVE IN THE WONDER-
ful and the magical seems as pathetic today as it was plausible in the middle
of the sixteenth century. During the pillage of the Aztec and Inca empires
farther south, Spanish treasure galleons creaked, and sometimes sank, beneath their cargoes of silver and gold and emeralds. Why might there *not* be
entire cities yet undiscovered whose streets were paved with precious
metal? The native cultures yielded foods theretofore unimagined, from potatoes to chocolate, nutritious and delectable. Why might there *not* be, say, a
spring of water that held the power of eternal life? Finding these magical
waters was the goal of Juan Ponce de León in the exploration of Florida in
1513. He thought then that Florida was the island of Bimini; by 1539 the
Spanish knew that Florida was a peninsula, and they had given up on the
Fountain of Youth, but they still clung to the dream of a vastly wealthy inland empire to conquer. In 1537 one Hernando de Soto approached King
Charles—now elevated to Charles V, Holy Roman Emperor, thanks to some
strategically placed bribes—for permission to revisit Florida and extend
Spanish dominion over who and what might be there. De Soto was a soldier
of fortune; in Peru he had marched under Pizarro and returned to Spain with
a fortune in Inca gold. Like Mendoza and Coronado before him, he offered to
finance the new Florida expedition himself, to which the frugal Charles,
who had borrowed some of De Soto's Inca gold, happily agreed.

Shortly after De Soto was given his commission, there arrived at court
one of the four survivors of the Narváez expedition, to seek the king's permission to return to North America at the head of a conquering force.
Cabeza de Vaca arrived just an eyelash too late. His disappointment that his
years of privation and uncertainty would not be rewarded with his own expedition can only be imagined, but De Soto was no fool. He knew that
Cabeza de Vaca's experience would be invaluable to him. "Don Hernando de
Soto was desirous that Cabeza de Vaça should go with him, and made him
favorable proposals," wrote De Soto's chronicler, a Portuguese known to
history as the Fidalgo (knight or gentleman) of Elvas, but after they struck a
bargain they quarreled over their financial arrangement and quit company.

Texas' first explorer, first merchant, and first surgeon took a consolation job, as governor of Paraguay, only later to be toppled by enemies and charged with mismanagement, convicted, and briefly exiled to north Africa. Shortly before his death, however, Cabeza de Vaca gained one more distinction: his *Relación*, a memoir of seven years in the Texas wilderness, accorded him status as Texas' first author.

De Soto's expedition left Cuba May 18, 1539, with more than six hundred men and two hundred horses. As the massive column trekked northward through present Florida, Georgia, and into North Carolina, they found no new empire to rival that of Montezuma or Atahualpa. They turned west through the thick forest, eventually reaching—indeed, "discovering"—the Mississippi River. Traversing the mighty stream, they penetrated as far as the Ozark Mountains before despairing of conquering an empire—only a few hundred miles, had they but known it, east of the equally dejected Coronado. They turned back, descending the Quivira-less Arkansas River to where it joined the great stream that split the continent. There De Soto took ill, and as he lay dying he called his officers before him, knowing that without his unifying presence, the strong and contentious personalities of his captains could bring the expedition to disaster. He asked them to choose a successor whom they all could swear to obey; they discreetly returned the prerogative to him, and De Soto made a remarkable choice: Luís Moscoso de Alvarado, a shiftless playboy who had gained note during the expedition only once, fourteen months earlier, when his inattention allowed the camp to be overrun by Chickasaw Indians, costing a dozen Spanish dead and the loss of most of their horses. Now thirty-seven, Moscoso began his career as a soldier when he followed a more famous uncle to Peru and returned home with a fortune, which he squandered in worldly pleasures. Adroit in using his family connections, he secured a place in De Soto's enormous Seville household, which transferred almost in toto to court, where De Soto dazzled the emperor with his lavish spending. Moscoso then attached himself to De Soto's Florida expedition, hoping to amass a second fortune.

His mind eased that his captains had given their allegiance to a successor, De Soto died May 21, 1542, three years and three days out of Cuba, and just at the same time that Coronado returned from his disappointing entrada in the west. De Soto and his men had filled the local Indians with dread of their power and magic, but when the natives noticed De Soto's absence they began to inquire more closely, and were told, somewhat nervously, that he had gone into the sky to talk to God. Rather than risk having his buried body discovered by the Indians, Moscoso had him dug up and committed to the middle of the Mississippi. Of all available options, he decided to try to reach New Spain by going west, overland.

This party entered what later became Texas from the northeast, through dense mixed forests of pine and hardwood, and encountered another broad cultural grouping of natives, the Caddoan Indians, actually a confederacy of related bands and part of North America's Eastern Woodlands culture. Of all the conquistadors who entered Texas, Moscoso was the least interested in converting the natives to Christianity, but had any energy been expended in that direction at this early time, the results might have been surprising. The Caddoes were a vastly different entity from the desperately foraging Karankawas and Coahuiltecans of the coast, or the hard-farming Wichitas of the Plains. While the Spaniards were revolted by their appearance—heavily tattooed, with skulls flattened in infancy—the Caddoes were already familiar with the concept of one god, or at least a chief god whom they called Caddi Ayo, who was approached through the intercession of a priest termed a xinesi—suggesting aspects of Catholicism to which they could have readily adapted. Their matrilineal kinship system might even have prepared them for the veneration of Mary. All of this potential went unexplored, however, for the Caddoes showed Moscoso a very different face, and one in which cultural misunderstanding played heavily.

The richness of their territory led the Caddoes into a more sedentary life of advanced agriculture than their neighbors to the west, living in large timber-and-thatch houses located in permanent or semipermanent settlements. They were capable weavers and thatchers, and expert potters whose functional and decorative stoneware was not just used locally but traded widely. They lived a richly complex social life and recited a complicated and meaningful mythology; in fact some scholars have speculated that they were a culture past their prime, for their spiritual centers were great flat-topped earthen mounds built centuries before, but which were no longer constructed. They had been settled long enough to develop not just chiefs but a functioning government and bureaucracy. As they prospered they could have expanded westward onto the prairies, but they were too well settled in their agricultural life to have much disposition to challenge the Plains Indians for more territory. They were, however, skilled and cunning warriors, and the bows they made were so superior that the French named the Osage orange tree from which the bows were crafted the bois d'arc. Prisoners were tortured hideously before being eaten—their cannibalism was ritualistic, but not dainty. In one fate most dreaded by their captives, the victim was strung on a frame and slowly bled over a period of three or four days, the blood being cooked and consumed before his eyes. When he finally died the entire corpse was roasted and eaten.

Caddo warriors lacked the reckless defiance of death later famous among the Plains Indians; war was for survival or sustenance, and victory by guerrilla tactics or even treachery was not dishonorable. When De Soto first skirted their domain the Spanish were repeatedly attacked but could not bring the Caddoes to pitched battle. When Moscoso approached their heartland at the great bend of the Red River around the last of July it was also after repeated harassment. Moscoso sent mounted patrols out to find a ford across the surging stream, and the Caddoes sent a deputation that called on him. They were weeping. Unaware that this was the customary Caddo greeting of strangers, Moscoso took it as a sign of guilt and contrition, and acted like a disdainful victor. It was midsummer, Moscoso had an army to feed, and the Caddoes had plenty. He rested his men two or perhaps three weeks at the Caddo town, which he called Naguatex, before he cleaned out the foodstuffs, and impressed guides to lead him onward.

Early scholars conjectured his route primarily westward, but almost certainly he trekked more to the south before turning southwest, following trails that were well known and well worn among the many related Caddo tribes. He encountered a succession of settlements, all of them poorer than Naguatex. Their conscripted guides—usually acquired by riding down some hapless native—tried to get them lost, leading them off the road to the east. The first ones who did this Moscoso hanged before spending three days finding the route again, led by a female captive. In contrast to Coronado, who only "reluctantly" had his guide El Turco strangled, Moscoso slashed through the countryside in the most appalling way, treating native guides as expendable. As his column penetrated deeper southwest into the pine forests, Moscoso became annoyed at thinking another guide was leading them astray. He had the Indian "put to the torture" until he confessed that his chief ordered him to get them lost. That guide, according to the chronicler, "was commanded to be cast to the dogs, and another Indian guided us." Taking his cue from conquistadors farther south, Moscoso maintained a pack of huge war dogs who could tear apart an Indian on command, which was believed helpful in maintaining order in the countryside. The Indian guides, however, repeatedly tried to decoy the Spaniards away from their towns; doubtless there was communication among the different Caddo bands behind Moscoso's back, for a guide captured from the Nondacao Indians led them into an ambush by Ayish Indians during the first week of September, in the vicinity of present San Augustine. The Spaniards also noticed the towns becoming poorer the farther they traveled, even though the land seemed no less fertile, until it occurred to them that the Indians, with advance warning, were hiding their stores of food in the forest.

In the trek south and west, Moscoso habitually inquired of resident natives whether they had seen other Christians, not hesitating to "order them put to the torture" until they screamed that yes, yes, there were Christians farther on. Probably they just wanted to end the pain, for it is doubtful that any of these Indians had seen or heard of Coronado. Some may have remembered Cabeza de Vaca, who had perhaps ventured this far inland to obtain wares to trade to his Karankawa masters. Eventually, perhaps in the middle course of the Trinity River, Moscoso encountered Indians whom it was useless to torture because none of his guides could understand their language. "So wretched was the country, that what was found everywhere, put together, was not half an alquiere of maize." That amounted to a few handfuls of corn. It was then October, and Moscoso did not relish wintering his hungry army in such a poor and hostile land.

Moscoso, even as De Soto had done, called a conference of his officers to hear their advice. Winter was coming on, and if it was severe they could neither proceed nor turn back. There was no prospect of enough food for the army. Travel farther west would be more difficult because they had no interpreters for the tribes that lay ahead. Besides, they believed that they were at the threshold of a country, according to the chronicler, of which "Cabeza de Vaca had said . . . the Indians wandered like Arabs, having no settled place of residence, living on prickly pears, the roots of plants, and game." All things considered, Moscoso, "who longed to be again where he could get his full measure of sleep, rather than . . . go conquering a country so beset for him with hardships," followed his officers' advice to return to the great river, use the winter to build boats, and try to reach civilization by sea.

De Soto's original force of six hundred was now barely half that number, but remarkably, Moscoso and his survivors retraced their route all the way back to the Mississippi. As they passed through the Caddo capital at Naguatex they discovered that the stores of grain had been completely replenished in their absence. Back at the place where De Soto had died they built seven small brigantines, and set off down the Mississippi on July 3, 1543. They reached the Gulf of Mexico and steered west, but were forced to put into a bay on the eastern coast of Texas to make repairs. Presaging the discovery of oil by more than three and a half centuries, they caulked their leaky vessels with tar balls collected from the beaches. Without further casualty, they reached the safety of Pánuco on September 10, having been absent four and a half years, and having extended Spanish claims farther into the northeastern interior than ever before.

FOUR

IMPERIAL COMPETITION

OF THE TWIN SPURS OF SPANISH EXPLORATION, GOLD
for the king and souls for the Church, it is not altogether fair to allege that
the Europeans cared all for the former and nothing for the latter. The brutality of the conquistadors requires no amplification in the retelling, but it is
equally true that there were many priests of conscience who protested the
treatment of the natives. Having given such men their due, though, the fact
remains that efforts to Christianize the Indians were concentrated in those
provinces where Spain realized the greatest return in precious metal.

Once the destitution of what became called the Eastern Interior
Provinces, including later Texas, became a matter of record, little happened
there. There were a few further entradas. One was led by Antonio de Espejo,
a dark character in the history of New Spain, who would doubtless be even
more fascinating if more were known about him. He was from Córdoba, his
birthdate unknown, and he came to Mexico as a soldier of the Inquisition in
1571. Once in the New World he turned his abilities to ranching, and soon
became a major landholder around Querétaro. After his involvement in the
murder of two ranch hands, he removed toward the eastern frontier to avoid
paying a fine. Meanwhile, during the summer of 1581 a group of Franciscans
under Padre Agustín Rodríguez undertook the first missionary journey to
natives on land later included in Texas. From a northern base at Santa Barbara, on the present-day border between the Mexican states of Chihuahua
and Durango, they explored northward until they encountered a powerful
stream that Rodríguez called the Río del Norte. There they encountered
friendly Indians susceptible to conversion; continuing up the desert canyons
of the great river, they discovered a new pass into the pueblo country traversed by Coronado. The Pueblo Indians were less welcoming, understandably, than they had been to Coronado, but when recalcitrant natives killed
some Spanish horses, the Franciscans showed themselves smarter than
Coronado had been at the same challenge. Instead of carrying out a mass execution, the priests arranged with the soldiers to prepare a block for behead-
ing the guilty, and then as the astonished Indian assemblage looked on, the
priests stormed the scaffold and "rescued" the condemned from the army.

The ruse bought continued goodwill toward the clergy, but cemented the natives' hatred of the military.

The bulk of the party returned to Mexico in the spring of 1582, having left Rodríguez and another priest behind to proselytize the Indians. The former was soon martyred, however. When the expedition returned to their Mexican base at Santa Barbara, they told, like most explorers before them, fine tales of the wealth of the country, but also reported that some of their number became separated from the main body and disappeared. When the disgraced Espejo encountered the remnant of Rodríguez' expedition, he followed the dual scent of riches and dramatic rescue, both of which could help resuscitate his standing, and he obtained permission to search for the missing priests.

Espejo departed civilization in November 1582, riding at the head of fourteen soldiers and their servants, guided by one of the Franciscans. They retraced the route north along the Río del Norte, contacting the large and amicable tribe that Rodríguez first encountered; Espejo named them Jumanos, and some of them could recall Cabeza de Vaca and his three companions. This contact with the Jumano Indians introduces a deep mystery in the history of New Spain, for in the late sixteenth century they were numerous and apparently prosperous, but by the late eighteenth century they were extinct, and today no one knows exactly who they were. Ethnologists now call it the "Jumano Problem." The name was over time applied to at least three different tribes of Indians, some sedentary and some hunter-gatherers; different linguists believe they have found linguistic roots in various irreconcilable peoples. The most pragmatic view is that they were a tribe in active cultural change, but whoever they were, they inhabited a large territory in the Rio Grande Valley that they eventually lost to raiding Apaches; the surviving Jumanos found refuge among other tribes and were assimilated.

Espejo continued north toward Coronado's pueblos, eventually learning that the missing padres had been killed by other, presumably non-Jumano natives. He found the place where the river coursed through a gap in the mountains that Rodríguez had described, and named it El Paso del Norte, and then revisited Coronado's sites on the far side of it. Like Coronado, he found no precious metals. Espejo on his return nevertheless repeated the Franciscans' tales of great silver mines, and of advanced Indians ready for conversion. The sanguine nature of his report likely had something to do with his proposing himself to be the governor of the new territory. The royal administration turned him down, for the job of bringing the pueblo country under permanent control required more deft consideration. The faces had changed, but the game remained essentially the same. Spain had a new king now, Philip II, the son of Charles the emperor; he was preparing a mighty (and expensive) naval armada for the invasion of England. After that fleet was obliterated by a combination of English sea dogs and savage weather in 1588, Spain's treasury lay in serious need of a recharge, and squeezing further wealth from New Spain was a more palatable alternative than peace with England's heretic Elizabeth. For taming the pueblo country, King Philip needed a good and constant soldier, and one who was rich enough to pay for his own expedition.

Espejo did not fit the bill, but he was not alone in his disappointment. In fact the viceroyalty occasionally had its hands full trying to keep private interlopers from seeking Cíbola on their own. The worst was Gaspar Castaño de Sosa, the lieutenant governor of Nuevo León and a longtime trafficker, to the horror of the Crown, in illegal Indian slaves. His party of 170 ascended the Río del Norte in 1590 before diverting up the Pecos and turning north into the pueblo country. After murder and mayhem, they were overtaken and arrested, and Castaño was sentenced to six years' exile in the Philippines. Still the lure of Quivira worked its magic, and in 1599 Francisco Leyva de Bonilla, a soldier on a punitive Indian expedition, went on an unauthorized detour to have a look at the buffalo plains explored by Coronado. This time, internal quarrels and Indian attacks finished the expedition before agents could even be sent out after them.

As the issue of organizing the eastern interior became more urgent, Philip II settled on Don Juan de Oñate, son of the owner of the Zacatecas silver mines, a descendant of both Cortés and Montezuma and, significantly, native-born in the New World. Spain had now occupied Mexico just short of eighty years, and it was a vastly different world than the one Cortés beheld when he landed. As the sixteenth century closed, there were great cities of Spanish architecture and cathedrals, a thriving economy, and an evolving class system.

Oñate, much like the very religious new king, had also shown interest in Christianizing the Indians, making him, in addition to his wealth, doubly fit to bear the commission. Not just a conquistador but a genuine colonizer, Oñate had in tow 130 men who brought families, in addition to the 270 men who did not, 83 carts and wagons, and more than 7,000 head of stock. They departed Santa Barbara in January, and instead of following the usual safe route down the Río Conchos and up the Río del Norte, Oñate struck north into the desert to explore a new route to the Paso del Norte. It was a harrowing trek—his scouts reached the place after enduring four days without water. When the whole column joined them Oñate proclaimed a feast in gratitude for their safe arrival. It took place at the later town site of San Elizario, which locals still commemorate as the real first American Thanksgiving, pre-dating the English Plymouth colony by a generation. On April 30, 1598, he claimed for Spain the drainage of the great Río del Norte, and renamed it the Río Grande; he then traversed the Paso del Norte and established his colony in the pueblo country.

The subjugation of the Pueblos was effected, or perhaps reeffected, but in the hills surrounding them Oñate discovered another, far more dangerous tribe of Indians, the Apaches. They were Athapaskan-speaking insurgents, not related to the Pueblo tribes, and their appearance was part of a kaleidoscopic sea change of native dominance on the continent that began during the sixteenth century and would in time bring the Comanches and Kiowas down onto the southern Plains. Ferocious mountain warriors who had adapted to survival in the deserts, the Apaches soon expanded their range deep into Texas, dominating the trans-Pecos and extending as far east as the later site of San Antonio—and in the process playing a key role in the extinction of the Jumanos. During eight years, Juan de Oñate sent expeditions in all directions but discovered no more precious metal; he even bit again on the Quivira story and sent men as far as present Kansas, but they returned as empty-handed as Coronado had. Oñate was eventually recalled, and like his predecessors tried for mistreatment of natives and banished, yet it was he who had established the Spanish presence on the Rio Grande in a permanent way.

East of the Rio Grande, in the vast land where Cabeza de Vaca had lived out his mussel-digging years along the coast; north, to where Moscoso de Alvarado had cast his dissembling guides to the dogs; and west, up to the weird flat buffalo plains that nearly unnerved Coronado, little was spoken or cared of the place, and generations passed. It was finally accepted that there was no gold in it. The neglect was broken only a couple of times. Jumano Indians east of the Rio Grande claimed they had been transfixed by the visitation of a beautiful lady, cloaked in blue, who preached the gospel to them in their own language. Investigation revealed a Franciscan nun, María de Jesús, who dreamt of making such a visit from her convent cell in Agreda, Spain. As a result, the Jumanos were visited by priests, in 1629, on the Middle Concho River. The padres made a favorable report of the country, including freshwater pearls obtained from mussels in the river. After a century without gold, pearls would do, and a couple of commercial expeditions soon scoured the area.

At the Paso del Norte on the Rio Grande a mission was established at Juarez in 1659, and a second one nearby at Ysleta a couple of decades later; El Paso del Norte thus technically became the first permanent settlement on territory that was later part of Texas. However, it was mainly considered an important station on the route north to the pueblos; another couple of centuries would have to pass before El Paso was connected in anyone's mind to the vast country east of the Rio Grande. In 1680, a century and a half of Spanish rule led a Pueblo chief named Popé to organize a grisly rebellion that threw the Spanish cause on the upper Rio Grande back to the lower river; there was little attention to spare for the wasteland east of the river.

There were other minor entradas; one explored the Edwards Plateau and another threaded its way through the brush country between the Rio Grande and the Nueces. Again it was the Jumano Indians who provided the impetus for the greatest activity when they asked for a mission in their country. One of the leading figures in Spanish combat of the Popé rebellion, Juan Domínguez de Mendoza, in company with Father Nicolás López, probed east from the Rio Grande in December 1683, and in early spring of 1684 founded the San Clemente Mission, whose exact location has long been disputed but was probably on the San Saba River not far from present Menard on the Edwards Plateau. A sturdy stone fort was constructed, and over two thousand Jumano Indians showed up for instruction and baptism, but the mission's remote location and the relentless attacks of the expanding Apaches forced its abandonment after only a couple of months. This first attempt at proselytizing the natives east of the Rio Grande was not a success. It did net the Spanish some important information, in a rude shock: the friendly Jumanos were found in possession of a flag, on which were emblazoned the golden fleurs-de-lis of the king of France. Mendoza and López pressed to establish a permanent settlement on the San Saba, but governmental consternation over learning that the French were afoot caused the project to be postponed.

In fact, Spain had hardly ever been alone in her colonial ambitions. Shortly after its discovery, the New World was probed and sounded by ships of the French, English, Dutch, and Portuguese. While each nation carved out its presence, Spain remained secure in its possessions. As the seventeenth century began to wane, however, that situation changed, through the agency of René Robert Cavelier, Sieur de la Salle.

The scion of a wealthy merchant family in Rouen, he immigrated to Canada with a small patrimony in 1666, and through the effort of his brother, a priest, obtained a grant of land from the Church and went into fur trading.

With an explorer's wanderlust, he discovered the Ohio River, returned to France, was ennobled, and was given a trade concession. His great passion was to explore the Mississippi, and after three years of preparation, he floated all the way down to its mouth, claiming the river and all lands drained by it for Louis XIV, and actually naming the stream, rather pointedly, the Rivière Colbert, for the longtime finance minister. That was in 1682, and possibly the source of the French flag that found its way to the Jumano Indians. Delighted to have a superior claim that severed the Spanish possessions east from west, the Sun King sent La Salle back to "Louisiana" with ships and colonists to establish a permanent presence. The fleet billowed out of La Rochelle in June 1684, and the various mischances of the journey culminated in La Salle's sailing right on by the Mississippi and landing instead in Lavaca Bay, the western thumb of the much larger Matagorda Bay, in present Texas, in February 1685. It had not been a pleasant voyage. Like most Frenchmen who gained a title for an occasion, he was resented by those of the expedition who had more genuine claims to nobility. Most of his three hundred or so "settlers" had been impressed from dockside stews, and the few who actually wanted to be there were fortune-hunters not interested in the glory of France. The female settlers were not ladies of gentility, either, and had joined the enterprise, as it was delicately phrased, "in search of husbands." La Salle responded to the situation with coldness, hauteur, and severe discipline, creating even worse feeling; one recalled La Salle referring to them as the lice in his gown. Dining in his cabin, he indulged himself and favored priests and retainers with full meals of meat and wine while, in one accusation, keeping the others alive literally on bread and water. Ill will increased further as La Salle forced his attentions on some of the younger and more handsome of the men. As a doomed venture, the fix was already in.

The Spanish quickly learned what was afoot by capturing one of La Salle's vessels, and as soon as the French landed they began salvaging timber from the other ships and building their Fort St. Louis on Garcitas Creek near present-day Vanderbilt. They did so not a moment too soon, since according to the expedition's chronicler, Henri Joutel, "about the beginning of April we were alarmed by a vessel which appeared at Sea, near enough to discern the sails, and we supposed they might be Spaniards, who had heard of our coming and were ranging the Coast to find us out." The ship passed on, however, "without perceiving us."

Speculation has been written for years whether La Salle had secret orders to sail past the Mississippi to challenge Spain farther down the coast. Most historians acknowledge this possibility before concluding that he was probably just lost. An examination of court politics, however, does not allow such a fast dismissal. La Salle was a man who made enemies readily, and during his absence from Canada that government passed to a scheming foe who began undermining La Salle's trade concessions and writing inflammatory letters about him home to the new finance minister, the Marquis de Seignelay. The ministerial wing at Versailles was crawling with intrigue, and Seignelay and others succeeded in turning the king against La Salle. "I am convinced," Louis XIV conceded to the marquis, that La Salle's traversal of the Mississippi "is very useless, and that such enterprises ought to be prevented in the future." Back in France to press for the Gulf expedition, La Salle counterattacked fiercely. France and Spain were at war, and the Mississippi, he argued ingeniously, emptied into the Gulf tantalizingly close to the rich silver mines of New Spain. A French force operating from there could easily seize them. The mines, La Salle insisted, "are very rich . . . they adjoin the Rivière Colbert—they are far removed from succour—they are open everywhere on the side on which we should attack them, and are defended only by a small number of persons, so sunk in effeminacy" that they could never defend them. By moving the mouth of the Mississippi six hundred miles to the west, La Salle resurrected his fortunes with the king and won the fleet that sailed from La Rochelle in 1684, under sealed orders to a secret destination, and accompanied, through special order of the king, by an engineer named Minet who would know how to operate the Spanish mines once they were secured.

La Salle did not just read maps; he was the explorer who gave the information upon which the maps were made. One map of the time shows the Mississippi emptying into the Gulf barely fifty miles from the Rio Grande; another actually depicts the Mississippi as a tributary of the Rio Grande. La Salle may very well have been lost, but he might have gotten lost by relying on his own artful disinformation. If there was any man in the seventeenth century who could coldly calculate himself into an irretrievable disaster, it was he. And once aground on Matagorda Bay, with most of his ships either captured, sunk, or turned for home with a large part of his men, that was exactly what he faced. Rather than attacking the silver mines of New Spain, La Salle was reduced to trying to discover just where in the New World he was, and how to get out of there.

Three of his ships were now gone: one was sunk by the Spanish, and the other two were wrecked. The spring crop had failed, and the local Karankawas had turned hostile after numerous mean and unnecessary

provocations by La Salle, which he committed to the bewilderment of his officers and men. On the one remaining ship La Salle, rather than sending for
aid, herded those whom he considered the most disloyal, including the engineer Minet, with whom he'd had a falling out, and sent them back to
France. Having arrived at La Rochelle, authorities read a scathing indictment of Minet by La Salle and clapped him into the St. Nicolas Tower, where
Minet in his defense composed a list of questions that needed to be put to
La Salle when the occasion should offer itself:

—Having found some savages, why, out of malicious convictions,
did he quarrel with them . . . when with kindness he could have done
with them whatever he wanted?
—Why go steal their food, canoes, and nets to have war with
them?
—Why starve the soldiers to death by giving them only flour
while he stuffed himself with wine and meat with the monks and did
not let the officers eat with him, giving them only a little corn?
—Why have young and handsome valets and make them sleep
with him?
—Why forbid his surgeon to help the ones on board care for the
sick?

His interrogatories went on for pages, concluding, "Everything I have
put here a hundred people will sign," and some of them must have offered
corroboration, for Minet was released to go on his way six weeks later.

Back in the New World, La Salle opened explorations to discover just
where he was. In his first expedition he struck westward, "very far up into
the Country, including toward the Northern part of Mexico," where he
found the land good and the natives friendly. After six months he returned
to the encampment, in August 1686, with five horses he had purchased from
the Indians, only to find his colony in total disarray. Only forty-five people
remained at Fort St. Louis. He soon struck out east with another party to try
to find the real Mississippi, but turned back after having gone perhaps as far
as the Sabine River. By the time he set out on a third journey, northeast, the
dissatisfaction among his surviving colonists had reached the boiling point.
He left the sick and the women at Fort St. Louis, taking the healthy men on
a determined effort to reach the Mississippi and help. La Salle probed east
almost to the territory of the Woodland Indians, probably near the Trinity
River. There, as food on this journey became scarce, a fierce quarrel erupted

when one of La Salle's lieutenants, who was also his nephew and named Moranget, rashly deprived the rankers of meat they had prepared. A plot to kill him and La Salle's footman, whom they also hated, soon expanded to include the leader himself.

La Salle, according to Joutel, "seemed to have some Presage of his Misfortune." Those who objected to his leadership, a ring led by one Pierre Duhaut and a man named Larcheveque, stayed in a camp of their own, where they murdered Moranget with an ax. Learning that there was trouble, La Salle set out for their camp to investigate. "The first of [the rebels] spying Monsier de la Salle at a distance . . . advanced and hid himself among the high Weeds. La Salle saw Larcheveque at a good Distance from him, and immediately asked for his nephew Moranget, to which Larcheveque answered, That he was along the River. At the same Time the Traitor Duhaut fired his Piece and shot Monsr. de la Salle thro' the Head, so that he dropped down dead on the Spot, without speaking one word."

The rebellion ended badly as the conspirators soon fell upon each other, and at least four who took command were murdered by their successors, until Indians and the wilderness claimed the rest. The handful of La Salle's expedition who were not involved in his assassination, including chronicler Joutel, eventually made their way to Canada. Back at Fort St. Louis, overwork and disease decreased their numbers to perhaps two dozen as they vainly awaited La Salle's return. During the winter of 1688–89, Karankawa Indians entered the fort under signs of friendship, but knowing its weakness, slaughtered all the adults and took five children as captives. It was the Karankawa women who saved the children, and they also took pity on Madame Barbier, widow of the garrison chief. As related by a rescued captive, "they were moved with tenderness at the sight of the three-month-old baby she had at her breast, but the savages returned to their cabins after the massacre, killed her first, and then her child, which one of them dashed against a tree while holding it by a foot."

FIVE

SOULS WITHOUT GOLD

HENRI JOUTEL'S CONSTERNATION AT SIGHTING A SPANISH
sail, followed by relief once it passed on, displayed French nervousness that
their game of colony poaching was about to be discovered. In truth, the
Spanish tried no fewer than eleven times to descry where the French had secreted themselves. Five of the attempts were by sea, the most determined in
the spring of 1687 and summer of 1688 by two ships, the *Esperanza* and the
Rosario, which had been specially built with shallow draughts for the job.
They probed the bays and barrier islands so closely that Indians ran along
the dunes to keep up with them. They examined Matagorda and Lavaca
bays, sent canoes up coastal creeks, and even discovered the wreck of
La Salle's supply vessel, *La Belle*, but they failed to find the colony. What they
did gain was the most accurate set of maps yet produced of the Texas coast.

Of the six land expeditions sent after the French, the one that got lucky
was headed by the governor of Coahuila, Alonso de León, in 1689, as he
made his fourth foray into Texas. De León was fifty, and near the end of his
career and his life. He was born in Mexico and sent to school in Spain at ten;
he enlisted briefly as a naval cadet before returning to Mexico. He chose a
hale life of exploring and prospecting, and he made a success of himself as a
salt producer. When the government first heard of the French incursion,
they turned to De León as a man who could stand the rigors of journeying
through unexplored country. Of his two sallies to find the French, the first
did not extend beyond the Rio Grande and the second only barely so. Unsur-
prisingly, he saw no sign of them, but he became governor on his return
from the second sortie. His third entrada carried him as far north as Baffin
Bay, where he discovered a partly demented old Frenchman, Jean Jarry, living as a sort of king over a small tribe of Coahuiltecan Indians. Jarry was
often incoherent in his answers, but maintained that he was a deserter from
La Salle's colony, which De León accepted. The governor induced Jarry to return to civilization with them, and persuaded him to serve as a guide on a
fourth entrada.

De León set out again late in March 1689 and crossed the Rio Grande
with 114 men, guided by Jarry and chaplained by Damián Massanet of the

College of the Holy Cross in Querétaro. Intending this time to make a longer coastal sweep, they encountered Indians on April 16 who claimed to have seen the Frenchmen. As they neared Matagorda Bay, Jarry became more lucid and helpful, and guided further by Indians to a native village, the Spaniards prepared to apprehend the interlopers. But then they were told that most of the French had moved on east, into the land of a tribe of Indians called the Tejas. The French houses, they learned, were nearby, but the remaining inhabitants had been killed by other Indians three months before. De León's men reached Fort St. Louis, and "we found all the houses sacked, the boxes all broken, and the bottle cases also . . . more than 200 books (it seemed) in the French language, broken, and the pages thrown in the patio were rotten." The Karankawas had had the presence of mind to destroy the French arsenal, carrying away the barrels and hammers of more than a hundred flintlock arquebuses. "We found three bodies strewn in the field, one of which seemed to be a woman by the clothes that still clung to the bones, which we gathered and gave burial to with a Mass."

The discovery of Fort St. Louis rattled Spain right out of her 150-year complacency of New World hegemony. The failure of the French colony would certainly not mean the end of French ambitions, and Spain moved with unaccustomed speed to meet the threat. After returning home, Governor de León and Father Massanet each submitted reports praising the country's fertility and potential. The priest related that he had met with a chief of the Tejas, that tribe of Indians from the pine forests beyond the Karankawas, and found him friendly, intelligent, and eager for religious instruction. Together, governor and padre pressed the viceroy so energetically on the suitability of establishing a mission in the far east of the province that De León was turned right back around in a fifth expedition. The twin goals of gold and souls were now to be compressed, and this time De León rode at the head of a column of soldiers to man a fort of their own, with three priests under Father Massanet planning to open a mission for the Indians. They left—sort of—on March 28, 1690, but their haste created confusion, as Father Massanet noted: "When we left, the twenty soldiers from Vizcaya had not yet arrived. The forty from Zacatecas were for the most part tailors, shoemakers, masons, and miners—in short, none of them could catch the horses on which they were to ride that day, for when they had once let them go they could manage them no longer."

Retracing the previous route, they paused at Fort St. Louis just long enough to torch what remained of it, and then they did the French one better at their own game. Instead of founding their own mission there at Fort

St. Louis, De León pushed his column north and east more than two hundred miles, well into country that the French were sure to claim, taking in tow two young French boys whom natives had captured at Fort St. Louis. Well beyond the reach of the hostile Karankawas, they arrived in the territory of the Tejas—or in their flexible spelling, the Texas, which in the native tongue meant "friend" or "ally." Tejas was a generic name for any of the several small tribes comprising the Hasinai Confederacy, a highly advanced people of Southern Woodland stock, cousins of the Caddoan Confederacy further north. The chief of a Tejas tribe called the Nabedache greeted and fêted the Spaniards at the Trinity River, and after some scouting for a suitable location the missionaries began the settlement of San Francisco de los Tejas, in present Houston County, west of the Neches River. A makeshift chapel was erected for the Feast of Corpus Christi, with first Mass said on May 24, 1690; the Tejas chief, who seemed amenable to the new religion, was given a staff and named governor. While exploring the countryside, the Spaniards were shown some last evidence of Gallic detritus: the remains of two Frenchmen who had shot each other—probably two of the La Salle's mutineers.

The priests would have been happy to be left there among the Tejas, but de León insisted that a garrison remain to protect them—not the last time that church and military clashed on the Texas frontier. "It was at no time necessary for the safety of the priests to leave soldiers among the Tejas," complained Father Massanet, "for from the very first they welcomed us with so much affection and good will, that they could hardly do enough to please us. Yet, in the face of all this . . . De León made arrangements to leave fifty men, under the command of Captain Nicolas Pretti, an incapable and undeserving old man." Massanet talked De León into leaving only three soldiers, and returned with the governor to Coahuila and began rounding up supplies and support for the new mission.

De León's route into the Tejas country, and back again, blazed the trace that became El Camino Real, or later the San Antonio Road, the principal east-west thoroughfare through the province. Worn out by his travels, Governor de León expired soon after returning from this fifth entrada, on March 20, 1691. During their absence, back among the Tejas, a second mission was started near the first, called Santísimo Nombre de María, but no sooner was it dedicated than things went downhill. Massanet returned the following year with a new governor, Domingo Terán de los Ríos, and with ten more priests and huge herds of stock to start still more missions. When they regained San Francisco de los Tejas, he found the whole enterprise near collapse. One of the three priests had died, crops that once promised ample bounty withered in a drought, and once again, the Indians who began to be decimated by disease associated their mortality with the presence of the foreigners. The once-friendly Tejas had turned into skulking stock thieves. At the end of 1691 Massanet turned his attention to Caddo Indians farther north, but he found them so truculent, and they stole so many horses, that he gave up the idea of starting more missions. It had been 150 years since the entrada of Moscoso de Alvarado, but the Caddoes still wanted nothing more to do with the Spanish. As he had with De León, Massanet had a falling out now with Terán, and he remained in East Texas with his priests when the governor returned to Mexico. He even refused to provide the governor and his troops with horses from the mission, forcing Terán to requisition them.

Affairs at the mission continued to decline. The Tejas soon equated the waters of the baptistry with death, and no more progress with them was possible. By the time the surviving friars burned their buildings and buried their vestments in October 1693, the garrison had deserted them. The missionaries walked, alone, through gesticulating crowds of angry Indians, and then all the way back to Coahuila. They had long overstayed their welcome, and the Tejas had long outgrown their famous friendliness.

SIX

LOVE AND BOOTY

IT TOOK MASSANET AND HIS BROTHERS MORE THAN
three months to walk the breadth of Texas; when they regained Monclova on
February 17, 1694, the great Massanet's zeal was finally spent. The viceroy
himself contacted him with a request that he suggest the location of future
missions in the north, but Massanet refused. Over the years, he said, trying
to get the government to support his missions adequately had cost him
more effort than civilizing the Indians, and until that battle was won, he believed that the establishment of future missions was a waste of time. He returned to the Franciscan College of the Holy Cross in Querétaro and passed
from history.

The failure of the Tejas mission, while a sore point with the church, was
greeted by the Spanish government with something like relief, because it
was dangerous for its inhabitants and remote from help. Like most governments that rule by crisis-response, the Spaniards were content to relax their
grip on the remote pine forests after several years of quiet from the French.

This complacency lasted for two decades, but it was not shared by the
more conscientious of the priests, especially Francisco Hidalgo, Spanish-
born and a Franciscan since the age of fifteen. He was one of the fathers who
had walked with Massanet all the way back to Mexico after the abandonment of San Francisco de los Tejas; in the intervening years his efforts to return to East Texas came to naught, but he did help establish the very
important Mission San Juan Bautista, near the Rio Grande about thirty
miles downstream from present Eagle Pass, in 1700. It quickly became a
road hub and trading center, and a staging area for entradas into Texas.
Eventually fed up with Spanish inertia, Hidalgo took matters into his own
hands, and in an astonishing display of nerve wrote a letter to the French
governor of Louisiana, Antoine de la Mothe, Sieur de Cadillac, requesting
his assistance in maintaining a Christian influence in East Texas.

As far as Hidalgo knew, this scheme also amounted to nothing, but then
on July 18, 1714, there arrived at San Juan Bautista a forty-year-old French
Canadian named Louis Juchereau de St. Denis, with a load of goods to trade,
some of which were illegal under existing agreements. No warning, no no-

tice; he just rode in out of the desert, from the east, with bargains to offer. Cadillac had received Hidalgo's letter, and thinking that Spanish-French cooperation and perhaps trade were in the offing, commissioned St. Denis to contact the Spanish. He was a shrewd choice, a southern Voyageur who had commanded a fort and explored up the Red River, learning wilderness survival and the ways of the Indians. In Mexico St. Denis was seized as an intruder, but as Father Hidalgo's role became known, San Juan Bautista's nonplussed commandant, Diego Ramón, placed the merchant under polite house arrest until a decision could be made what to do with him. The Sun King's grandson was now king of Spain, the two Catholic countries might now be allies, and St. Denis might not actually be an intruder any more. Not one to waste time, St. Denis used the delay and confusion to woo, and win, Ramón's granddaughter, Manuela Sánchez. In company with Father Hidalgo, St. Denis was eventually sent to Mexico City to explain himself.

Not knowing how long he would be detained in the capital, St. Denis sent word back for most of his party to return to Louisiana, which they accomplished after a journey of two months. The French, since their settlement of Louisiana, had cultivated a more amicable relationship with the Tejas than Father Massanet had managed. Back among the Tejas, St. Denis' traders beheld a spectacle that unnerved them, and placed the need for a mission in a rather different complexion. The Tejas were genuinely glad to see the Frenchmen, but they had been waging a war against nearby Kichai Indians. St. Denis' partners arrived in time to see two Kichai captives tortured hideously and eaten, and they learned that four other prisoners had already met the same fate.

Facing a rather less dire interrogation in Mexico City, St. Denis talked his way out of his difficulty so smoothly that when he returned to San Juan Bautista, it was with a commission as Ramón's commissary supplier. For a man who could bring a whole caravan of contraband safely all the way from Mobile, keeping a garrison fed and equipped would be an easy job.

The Spanish government finally acquiesced in the need to establish a permanent presence in East Texas, and mounted an expedition commanded by Domingo Ramón, son of Diego, and guided by St. Denis, who easily stepped into Spanish service. The column that left San Juan Bautista on April 27, 1716, consisted of three Frenchmen, including St. Denis; nine priests, including Father Hidalgo; thirty civilians; and a couple dozen soldiers, seven of whose wives became the first Spanish women to colonize into Texas. As with the founding of San Francisco de los Tejas in 1690, they did not position their new settlements conservatively. Their first business was the reestablishment of San Francisco de los Tejas, which was accomplished on July 3, with Father Hidalgo, appropriately, left to preside. Then, penetrating almost to the estimated border of French territory, Ramón and the Franciscan friars started the Mission Nuestra Señora de Guadalupe de Nacogdoches at the site of the later city of that name, and then farther east founded a cluster of missions at the later town site of San Augustine, Texas. Finally, still farther east they founded the Mission San Miguel de Linares de los Adaes, east of the Sabine River, where the French could not possibly ignore it.

As Domingo Ramón stayed in East Texas with soldiers to protect the new missions, St. Denis returned to San Juan Bautista in April 1717 with even more bargains to offer. There he learned, however, that while he had been away, France had fought the War of the Spanish Succession, and his wares were no longer wanted. He was again arrested and hauled to Mexico City, where he learned that he was destined for a prison in Guatemala. Padre Hidalgo interceded with the viceroy himself, arguing that the Frenchman was indispensable in pacifying the Tejas. It was Hidalgo, of course, whose meddling letter to Cadillac had forced Spain's hand into the whole chain of events, and his advice now was less than welcome. St. Denis looked to his own aid, stealing a horse and circuitously returning to the French outpost at Natchitoches, Louisiana, by 1719, where he was made commander. The Spanish allowed Manuela to join him in 1721, and St. Denis occupied himself with continued "trading" to the Spanish settlements, whether his merchandise was legal or not.

For the next twenty years the Spanish had to keep an eye on him, although he always avowed his amity toward his wife's country. They were jealous of his influence over the Indians, among whom St. Denis retained his popularity long after the Tejas came to loathe the Spanish. Typically for a Frenchman in North America, he was pragmatic and adaptable in his Indian dealings, desiring only trade and mutual profit. He didn't claim dominion over their souls like the Spanish did, and he wasn't particularly interested in hegemony over their land. If commerce required an occasional bribe and some discreet smuggling, then no harm done; his business was simply business—so much so that even Cadillac sometimes wished that St. Denis would show more nationalistic loyalty. Indeed, when St. Denis retired aged near seventy, and sought permission to live in Mexico, the French government denied it. Yet the Spanish viceroy, upon learning of St. Denis' death in 1744, was said to have involuntarily uttered, "Thank God!" Distrusted by all, St. Denis established both the first regular trade route across Texas and the long-standing principle that banned goods, which were nevertheless of practical use and in demand, would not be interdicted with any great vigor.

During these years, the contest between the French and Spanish for control of the land extended also to competition for the allegiance of the Indians. These natives were not stupid people, and some quickly learned to play both sides of the table. A minor Hasinai tribe on the lower Trinity River, the Akokisa, had a chief the Spanish called Calzones Coloradas (Red Breeches), whom they gifted with supplies seized from unlicensed French traders. St. Denis sent two Bidai Indians to Red Breeches with a bribe of ammunition to use against the Spanish. The Spanish in turn upped the ante with an allowance to the chief of five *fanegas* (about eight bushels) of corn a week and two cows to settle peaceably at a mission. In subsequent centuries, the practice of bribing Indian chiefs to bend to a government's will came to be harshly judged by history. In the early years, however, when power was more equally balanced, it was a more open question of who was using whom.

SEVEN

THE EMPTY QUARTER

ONLY AFTER THE EAST TEXAS MISSIONS WERE SET IN place did the Spanish turn their attention to areas closer to home. The vast distance between San Juan Bautista and the missions of the east made necessary a kind of halfway rest stop. In a government reshuffle, the viceroy appointed Martín de Alarcón governor of the Eastern Interior province that now included Texas, with broad powers to pacify Indians, investigate St. Denis, resupply Ramón and the East Texas missions, and promote the settlement of this vast new empty quarter. In April 1718 Alarcón made his own entrada into Texas, traversing the now better-worn El Camino Real. On the first of May he assisted in the dedication of the needed halfway mission, on the San Antonio River at the eastern edge of a range of limestone hills, naming it San Antonio de Valero, whose chapel later became known as the Alamo. Just to the north he established its protective presidio, San Antonio de Béxar, and the settlement, the Villa de Béxar, quickly became the locus of the Spanish occupation of Texas.

No one believed that the French would ignore the Spanish encroachment into their realm, even though the location of Los Adaes had been selected at the suggestion of St. Denis, who was as usual figuring the trade angle. Then the European kaleidoscope rolled again. France, Spain's recent ally, was now fighting Spain in the War of the Quadruple Alliance. In the New World it was the French who learned before the Spanish that they were now not just rivals but enemies. The Spanish target nearest to the French fort at Natchitoches was Los Adaes, which was watched over by one soldier and one lay brother. France attacked in June 1719 with an overwhelming army of seven led by Lieutenant Philippe Blondel, who captured the Spaniards and their supplies, including a few chickens, which Blondel tied to his saddle. As he mounted his horse, the chickens' terrified squawking caused the horse to throw him, and during the ensuing fracas the brother escaped. He reached the San Augustine missions on June 22 and informed Captain Ramón that the French had told him a force of one hundred was en route to take the remaining Spanish establishments. The San Augustine missions withdrew to Nacogdoches, and Ramón, having nowhere near sufficient force to carry on, withdrew to the western limit of Tejas country and camped while a messenger was sent to San Juan Bautista for reinforcements. By October it was clear that no help was coming, and Ramón rounded up all the East Texas Spaniards and withdrew to San Antonio de Béxar.

The "Chicken War," although it sounds vaguely comical, resulted in the abandonment of the entire eastern theater of Spanish missions and exposed what a tenuous grip that nation had on the territory. Once Spain understood that the war was in earnest, keen humiliation was felt over the precipitate abandonment of East Texas. One José de Azlor, who had married into the fortune of his better-known title, the Marqués de San Miguel de Aguayo, informed the viceroy that he could end the French menace in Texas, and pay the cost of the expedition for the privilege. The viceroy quickly accepted, and appointed Aguayo governor and captain-general of Coahuila and Texas. He entered the troubled province with an army of five hundred on March 20, 1721. When on April 4 he reached San Antonio—a name that came to be used interchangeably with the Villa de Béxar—he discovered that the refugee padres had founded a second establishment and named it, flatteringly, Mission San José y San Miguel de Aguayo, which over time became a kind of flagship of the Texas missions. Inclement weather and floods caused Aguayo to detour north as far as present Austin before heading to East Texas, where he quickly reestablished the vacated missions. St. Denis, with his commercial eye, welcomed the sight of so many men who would need supplies, but was displeased when the no-nonsense Aguayo left a garrison of one hundred, with cannons, to see that the laws were observed. To make a point to the French, Los Adaes was declared the capital of the province.

Returning to San Antonio, Aguayo established a third mission, San Francisco Xavier de Nájera. Only after all this did the Spanish finally plant their standard near the original site of La Salle's Fort St. Louis, at the Mission Nuestra Señora del Espíritu Santo de Zúñiga at La Bahía, later adjusted inland to the site of Goliad, with an accompanying presidio to vouchsafe a sea route between Texas and lower Mexico. The Marqués de Aguayo was by far the most successful commander yet to enter Texas, and he left the province dotted with ten missions and four presidios garrisoned with more than 250 soldiers, connected by El Camino Real, which was now a well-trod thoroughfare from San Juan Bautista, through San Antonio and Nacogdoches, to Los Adaes. It was enough to permanently quash French mischief. Before he returned to Mexico to retire to his vast estates as an honored field marshal, Aguayo promoted an aggressive colonization plan for the province, advocating the settlement between San Antonio and Los Adaes of some four hun-

dred immigrant families from elsewhere in the empire, along with loyal Indians. His grand scheme was never completed, but some fifteen families,
comprising fifty-five settlers from the Canary Islands, did reach Béxar in
March 1731 and became a sort of rootstock of San Antonio aristocracy.

Over the subsequent decades, an informal boundary came to be recognized
between Louisiana and New Spain, marked by the Arroyo Hondo, a wash located suitably between Los Adaes and Natchitoches. Meanwhile, the population and material wherewithal of Mexico grew to the point that, by
midcentury, new attention to better organizing Texas was possible. One effort, to colonize the lower Rio Grande Valley, was led by José de Escandón.
Between 1748, when the region was made a separate province under his
governorship, and 1755, Escandón was responsible for founding numerous
towns, including Camargo, Reynosa, Mier, and most successfully, Laredo.
    During these years the makeup of the local native tribes changed consid-
erably. The hundreds of tiny wandering family groups that greeted the first
Europeans had been wiped out by disease or war, or had become assimilated
into larger and more powerful tribes, like the Apaches, who were gaining in
the western desert, and a new presence, fierce prairie warriors called Comanches, who had been pushed down off the Northern Plains by the Sioux.
Indians who now asked for the establishment of missions generally did so
more with a view toward protection from native enemies than to draw near
the cross. Such was the case with the Tonkawa Indians of the Central Plains.
They were a small, hard-luck central Texas tribe, difficult to classify. Their
language was unrelated to that of any of the surrounding natives; they may
in fact have been still evolving as a tribe, for they seem to have comprised
several unrelated splinter groups; even their name meant simply, "We stay
together." What culture they had bore several features in common with the
Apaches, who had forced them from the buffalo plains down into central
Texas before being themselves forced west into the desert by the Comanches. Once in central Texas they began to develop a Plains Indian
culture, but never very successfully. They failed at farming, and lived by subsistence hunting and gathering. At first they allied themselves with the
Comanches in their enmity with the Apaches, but the Comanches later
turned on them and became the Tonkawas' bitterest enemies. Several missions were set up for them between 1745 and 1757, but the Tonkawas were
more interested in protection than conversion.

More sinister was a scam devised by the Apaches. The southernmost band of that tribe, the Lipanes, had fought desultory wars against the Spanish since their arrival, but they also carried on almost as bloody a strife with the Comanches, who were proving as effective in displacing the Apaches from southwestern Texas as the Apaches had once been effective in eliminating the Jumanos. Eventually the Apaches got tired of fighting on two fronts. They asked the good padres in San Antonio for a mission to be established out in their own country, northwest on the San Saba River. Their plea won the support of Pedro Romero de Terreros, the *alcalde* (mayor) of Querétaro who had made a fortune in mining and become a philanthropist. He pledged a hundred thousand pesos to support such a mission for three years, provided his cousin, Father Alonso Giraldo de Terreros, be selected to head it. Father Terreros had been a Franciscan for thirty-six years and had risen to the post of guardian of the College of Santa Cruz de Querétaro. He had been pursuing the conversion of the Apaches for many years, most recently at a mission in Coahuila for about fifty Texas Apaches, who burned the mission when he left to try to raise money.

The viceroy approved the new San Saba mission, and Father Terreros, with five Franciscan friars and a military escort, arrived at their station in April 1757. They established Mission Santa Cruz de San Saba, with the soldiers quartered in the nearby Presidio San Luís de las Amarillas. What the Apaches did not tell the Franciscans was that the Comanches had driven them out of the San Saba country several years before. While pretending in a desultory way to be interested in conversion, the Lipan Apaches also carried out some clever raids on Comanche villages, leaving Spanish goods lying around for the survivors to find, and they kept their lookouts on the San Saba alert. On the morning of March 16, 1758, the Apache tenants vanished, shortly before the mission was swarmed by as many as two thousand shrieking Comanches, Taovayas, Wichitas, and warriors from many other tribes. Two of the priests, including Father Terreros, and six civilians were butchered, but the Comanches were smart enough not to attack the presidio. Back in Querétaro the other Terreros, grief-stricken, had his cousin's martyrdom memorialized with a commission for the first professional historic painting of a Texas subject.

The following year, the commander of the San Saba garrison, Colonel Diego Ortiz Parrilla, led a force of 500, with Apache "allies," all the way to the Red River to exact some revenge. Instead he suffered a disastrous defeat at the hands of the Plains Indians, whom they discovered, to their surprise, fighting under a French flag. The Comanches were not in any formal alliance with the French; rather the incident demonstrated France's perennial success as traders. St. Denis had been made commander at the French outpost of Natchitoches, from where he continued his trading efforts with the natives. He then married his daughter off to a man of similar abilities, Athanase de Mézières, who carried French trade far up the Red River, almost to the breaks below the Cap Rock escarpment in North Texas.

Once again, European great-power politics altered Texas history. Spain and France fought as allies in the Seven Years' War, and shortly before they lost, France ceded Louisiana to Spain in recognition of the latter's sacrifices. Spain had long maintained the East Texas missions almost entirely as a buffer against French expansion, and that threat was now removed. Spain was also aware that her imperial fortunes were in serious decline, and in 1766 King Charles III sent a kind of inspector plenipotentiary, the Marqués de Rubí, to tour the region and decide what to do.

Rubí—in full, Cayetano María Pignatelli Rubí Cordera y St. Climent—was forty years old. His father was a Spanish ambassador to France and his mother a multiple grandee: the Baronesa de Llinas and Marquesa de Rubí, from whom he inherited his titles. A highly competent soldier, he was a field marshal, knight commander of the Order of Alcántara, and accepted his duty with a withering thoroughness. It took nearly two years for him to traverse the entire frontier of New Spain, from the Gulf of California eastward, traveling over 7,500 miles, with an engineer as consultant. His Texas entrada was in July 1767, and the first place he visited, significantly, was San Luís de las Amarillas and its destroyed mission. He turned south to San Antonio, and then east all the way to Los Adaes. He left Texas late in the year at Laredo, and by February 1768 was back in Mexico City, writing a series of stunning recommendations. What he saw in the mission system struck him as a litany of failure that Spain in her reduced circumstances could no longer support. With the French threat evaporated, he suggested the total abandonment of East Texas and the withdrawal of all settlers to San Antonio. He also suggested that a more interior line of presidios be established in an area small enough for Spain to defend; fifteen forts, averaging one every hundred miles from the lower Guadalupe in Texas west to the Gulf of California. All settlements outside that line were to be abandoned, except Santa Fe and San Antonio (the subsequent decree also exempted La Bahía). Finally wise to the Apaches' trickery, he saved his harshest words for them: "This vile nation of Lipanes . . . whose injuries directly and indirectly occasioned the treasure of the King, enticing us with their false friendliness and supposed desire for conversion and settlement never realized," led him to recommend that Spain switch sides in the Indian conflict, befriend the Comanches and their allies, and attempt the extermination of the Apaches by making them again fight a war on two fronts.

The suddenly smarter government recognized that the French had always been better at dealing with Indians, and so they hired French emissaries to do their talking for them. For a time, Comanches and other Plains warriors rode with Spanish soldiers in attacks on the Apaches. Rubí's recommendations were in the main approved, yet in the case of the settlement that grew up around Nacogdoches, its evacuation proved to be a cruel displacement indeed to its residents. The community had begun finally to thrive, and when the order was executed in summer of 1773, more than five hundred people were forced to move to San Antonio, leaving their ripening crops unharvested. One leader of that group, Antonio Gil y Barbo, petitioned to be allowed to return. The governor, the Baron de Ripperdá, was sympathetic, and the viceroy allowed them to move back east, but ordered that they stay at least a hundred leagues east of Natchitoches, Louisiana. Many of Nacogdoches' former inhabitants followed Gil y Barbo to a five-year sojourn on an East Texas plot approved by the viceroy, probably in present Marion County, where floods, Indian attacks, and crop failures caused extreme hardship. In 1779, with Ripperdá out and Domingo Cabello in, and with a new viceregal administration that probably wouldn't remember what the whole commotion had been about anyway, they resettled Nacogdoches illegally. Gil y Barbo addressed himself to the real authority in the region, Commandant General Teodoro de Croix, and explained their actions, begging "your lordship to be pleased to take pity on us for the hardships that we have been suffering since the suppression of Los Adaes, where we so obediently abandoned our belongings and our houses. . . . Your most attentive and grateful subject kisses your lordship's hand." De Croix did not have the heart to oust them again.

The capital of the province, which was once located defiantly at Los Adaes, was pulled back to San Antonio de Béxar in 1773, in another of Rubí's recommendations. Strengthened by this consolidation and by further immigration, in 1783 colonial officials could report a population at San Antonio of 331 men, 311 women, 321 boys, and 284 girls, plus clergy, comprising nearly half of the entire population of the province of Texas. Another 554 souls clustered about the five San Antonio missions. In all the remainder of the vast province, according to the single-sheet census with Governor Cabello's tidy rubricked signature at the bottom, Europeans lived in only two other places: Nacogdoches had recovered to a population of 349, and La Bahía held on with 668. The total population enumerated 2,819 people—not much to show for two and a half centuries of ownership.

EIGHT

MISSION LIFE

THE ECONOMY OF A MISSION COMMUNITY WAS PREDOMI-
nantly agricultural. There was some local manufacture of needed goods—
blacksmiths and cobblers, for instance—but almost to the end of the eighteenth century a professional class was nonexistent.

The lack of sanitation around the mission settlements, with the attendant disease and death, was made the more melancholy for lack of medical
attention. From the time that Alonso de León determined to plant the Spanish flag for good in 1689, nearly a century passed before a doctor resided in
Texas. The mission community was presided over by the senior padre, but in
the civil settlements a start was made at rudimentary democracy. Local officials, the town council or *ayuntamiento*, presided over by an *alcalde*, a sort of
mayor and marshal, were elected by secret ballot. In some cases this even
extended to the Indians, who were taught to elect their own leaders. (In a
way this was a very odd exercise. Most unreconstructed Indians freely followed whatever chief they chose; it was only after submitting to Christian
servitude that they had to be taught about "democracy.")

Society was basic. Men outnumbered women, but only by about 10 percent after the towns became established. While native indenture sustained
the ecclesiastical community, the common citizen's time was mostly consumed with his own subsistence labor. Leisure consisted of fiestas at weddings or other special occasions, and occasional fandangos. For sport there
were bullfights, horse races, cockfights, and the *carrera de gallo,* in which a
rooster was buried up to its neck in the ground. The prize was won by the
first rider to snatch off its head at full gallop.

San José, just south of San Antonio and named to flatter the Marqués de
Aguayo in 1720, became the most successful operation in Texas and earned
the sobriquet "Queen of the Missions." Government inspectors were repeatedly charmed that "the church and the sacristy, because of their architecture, are the most beautiful structures to be seen anywhere this side of
Saltillo" (today the capital of Mexico's Coahuila state). The church with its
famous sacristy window was the focal point of a large walled campus lined
with houses ("with a kitchen for each family," noted one impressed Church

official), ample quarters for the priests, and granaries. Outside the complex, fields of crops were watered by a web of *acequias*, cleverly constructed irrigation channels. The plantings of corn, beans, pumpkins, and melons were augmented by peach orchards, sugarcane, and even cotton. The exemplary success of San José was, as the Church was painfully aware, an exception to the rule, and was occasioned "because the Indians are less indolent in the cultivation of the fields and the care of the herds."

"Herds" meant cattle, because sheep and goats, while brought along with virtually every entrada, did not thrive. They were difficult to herd in the thick brush, especially by Indians who thought shepherding an exceptionally stupid labor, and they were helpless against predators. The lanky, longhorned, and often vicious Iberian cattle, on the other hand, could take care of themselves in the wild. In fact, stocking the countryside with feral cattle had long been a Spanish priority. Many animals simply wandered away from expeditions as early as Coronado's, but by the time Alonso de León entered Texas in search of the French in 1689, he deliberately loosed a breeding pair at every stream he crossed. The Marqués de Aguayo brought nearly five thousand. The rawboned cattle increased with stunning rapidity; St. Denis had no trouble trading illegally for meat and hides from early in the eighteenth century. The mission at La Bahía estimated that the number of cattle in its environs more than quintupled, from 3,000 to 16,000, in the decade ending in 1768. The San Antonio missions claimed about 5,000 cattle.

Most of them, of course, were *mesteños*, unbranded feral animals not provably belonging to anyone. This led to acrimonious disputes of ownership, with the government eventually declaring them Crown property and levying a fee of four reales to kill one. This in turn led to bitter recrimination from the Church, which was itself strapped for money and dependent on the king for support of the missions. Cattle that belonged to the government could not be given by the Church as rations to natives, who "are moved more by gifts than by the clearest reasoning . . . to conversion into the ranks of the Holy Church." The dispute between priests and civil authorities continued for generations, until a peace was arranged in spring of 1787 that called for a massive roundup and allocation of wild cattle.

This was only one conflict in the settlement of Texas, and in retrospect there is no shortage of other reasons why the overall mission system in Texas was such a failure. In the first part, the Spanish system of development in the New World, from the *encomiendas* of Central America to the later *haciendas* of Mexico, was dependent upon the labor of large numbers of tamed, Christianized Indians—often slaves in all but name and referred to with sympathetic contempt as *reducidos,* the reduced ones. Indians in Texas were at least an order of magnitude more wily and fierce than any the Spanish encountered earlier. Most of them would not tolerate such a life, and those who could be broken to mission labor seldom lasted. A report on the status of the missions in 1785 lamented that many mission Indians "have died on account of the plague of buboes . . . a kind of leprous venereal disease (which has become common in the country) and many others from smallpox." Faced with sickness and death, other Indians fled, or in the estimation of the Church, left "impelled by their inclination to the wild, lazy life of the woods." Then too, they were not infrequently driven away by raiding Comanches, Apaches, and others.

In his report, the Marqués de Rubí noted the same flaw, with the additional carp that what native laborers could be obtained at Texas missions were not even local Indians. Rather, they were "those brought from the coast of the colony of Nuevo Santander, and from other districts farther to the interior, where the missionaries go to get their spiritual recruits." Rubí's unconcealed hostility was not lost on the Church, which cited military and civil obstacles deliberately placed in the way of Christianizing the natives. The worst governor in this category was Franquis de Lugo; from the beginning of his administration in 1736 he lost no opportunity to undermine the padres and shoo the natives back into the wilderness. The Church managed to get him recalled the following year, but not before he inflicted a serious setback on the mission effort. The abuse of native women by Spanish soldiers was a separate and contentious issue, and sometimes led priests to limit contact between the presidio garrisons and the Indians they were trying to convert. The bad blood between Massanet and Terán a century before only got worse in their successors, and it often made for administrative chaos that hindered Texas' development.

Life for the common soldiers in the presidios presented its own problems. For their isolation and dangerous duty they were paid on average about four hundred pesos a year—a very livable wage, but from it they not only had to support their families but also purchase their arms and supplies, which were not furnished by the Crown. Even worse, in an all-too-frequently accepted invitation to corruption, it was the captains of the presidios who supplied their own garrisons, and grossly overcharged them for their equipment. Soldiers who were unable to pay might then work off the debt with labor on the captain's own estate.

It was also true that the rigid class system, imported from Spain and fractured into novel gradations in the New World, complicated the effort to turn

Texas into an economically viable province. Native-born Spaniards, *peninsulares*, comprised the top social class in Mexico, followed by *criollos*, pure-bred Spaniards who happened to be born here, and so on down the line to the lowest caste of mixed-breed Indian slave. An object lesson was afforded by the importation of Canary Islanders, Spanish political exiles whom the Crown induced to emigrate by paying their expenses and even ennobling the families with the title of *hidalgos*. It was a minor elevation, but it gave them the expectation that when they came to Texas, they would not have to work. Their airs created hard feelings among colonists who had no such pretensions. The shrewd Rubí saw through this, too. In fact, his recommendation that San Antonio be allowed to remain outside the picket line of frontier presidios was made not because the *villa* was so mighty or self-sustaining, but because to suppress it would waste the "many expenditures . . . from the royal Treasury in the movement of the families from the Canary Isles, [and] in the gratuities distributed among the settlers, to provide the necessaries for their fields, which they do not take care of." What efforts the government did make to induce Mexican Europeans to move to San Antonio amounted to little, for its isolation fifty leagues east of San Juan Bautista, and the litany of hardships and Indian attacks, left the average citizen with no heart to attempt such a life.

It took a decade for all of Rubí's recommendations to be studied and acted upon, by which time it was clear that the course he advocated did indeed make the most sense for the Spanish empire. But then history rounded a corner from which there could be no going back: in 1783, the year of Cabello's census, the British colonies on the Atlantic coast of North America gained their independence as the United States of America, after the Spanish had been in Texas for a quarter of a millennium.

NINE

AMERICANS

LOUISIANA'S PASSING TO THE SPANISH CROWN IN 1763 did not altogether erase the border with New Spain. Texas was a province of the latter; Louisiana was ruled from Cuba. And just as early Spanish governors in the New World eyed rival colonies with suspicion, Texas and Louisiana remained separated by restrictions on trade and travel.

Fuzzy frontiers at the edge of empire have always attracted adventurers out for the main chance, and in 1787 there materialized in Louisiana an American army general, James Wilkinson, who could have served as an archetype. Commissioned a captain in the Continental Army in 1776, Wilkinson served with Benedict Arnold and Horatio Gates, high schooling indeed in the arts of double dealing and self-interest. He was also involved in the Conway Cabal, which attempted to replace George Washington with Gates as commander in chief. After that failure he was forced, briefly, from the military. He was back in uniform at the time he entered New Orleans, where he had acquired business interests, and he swore his allegiance and his services, for a fee, to the king of Spain. What exactly he meant to accomplish for the king was less clear than the fact that after he arrived, strange episodes piled one atop another.

In 1791 a Wilkinson protégé, Philip Nolan, obtained a passport from the governor of Louisiana to enter Texas on a "mustanging" expedition—rounding up wild horses with the intent to drive them back to Louisiana and sell them. The twenty-year-old Irishman was Wilkinson's boarder, clerk, and bookkeeper. He obtained his passport through Wilkinson's favor, and apparently obtained leave from somebody to introduce trade goods into Texas, which even though Texas and Louisiana were now governed by the same Crown, was still illegal. Authorities in Texas confiscated his merchandise, and Nolan sojourned for about two years with various Texas Plains tribes, including Comanches. He finally returned home with fifty mustangs for sale. Nolan returned to Texas in early summer of 1794 with a new passport, and seeking to avoid the earlier trouble, visited the capital at San Antonio de Béxar. He won the support of that governor, Manuel Muñoz, who obtained for him permission from his superior, the commandant general of the Interior Provinces, to capture and export horses for the military in Louisiana. This trip passed without incident and Nolan rode home with some 250 horses to sell about a year and a half later.

During Nolan's months in Texas, however, his suspiciously close interest in the geography and features of the prairie country led the authorities to eye him askance. Spanish suspicions were heightened when Nolan was later seen in Natchez in company with a United States boundary commissioner, and they would have increased exponentially had the Spanish known he was passing geographical information on Texas to Wilkinson, who was preparing a map. As Nolan made his third mustanging foray into Texas, he was denounced by authorities in Louisiana, which prompted the Texas military commandant to withdraw his support, and only the intercession of Governor Muñoz allowed Nolan to escape the province, this time with some 1,200 horses, in 1799.

Under the disastrous King Charles IV, Spain joined the European powers against revolutionary France, was humiliated, and ceded Louisiana back to France in 1800, which reactivated the question of the old Arroyo Hondo quasi-boundary. As Louisiana reverted to France, Nolan desired to make a fourth expedition, but the Spanish government was so alert to him that he was unable to obtain a passport. He then foolishly entered Texas on his own, with a couple dozen heavily armed companions, to hunt mustangs somewhere on the central prairie in the vicinity of present Waco or Hillsboro. A Mexican column dispatched from Nacogdoches discovered the party in a well-fortified horse camp in March 1801, and attacked. Nolan was killed after about ten minutes, and the Spanish began firing grapeshot from a swivel gun strapped to the back of a mule. In midafternoon the Spanish approached under a flag of truce, and through an interpreter said they only required the Americans to return to their own country, and would allow them to keep their arms while escorting them to the border. The surviving Americans agreed. The whole party was compelled to cross the flooding Trinity River, shuttling from bank to bank in a cottonwood canoe. After the soldiers had crossed, one of the Americans, Peter Ellis Bean, pointed out "that we had it in our power to throw all their guns in the river, take what ammunition we wanted, and return. Some of them were willing; others said it would be very wrong now we were to be sent home. These last were unfortunate men who put confidence in Spanish promises." Bean's suspicions were well founded since, instead of being escorted to the border, the remainder of Nolan's party were held in Nacogdoches for a month before being sent, in irons, first to San Antonio and then to San Luís Potosí in Mexico, where they were imprisoned as a deterrent to future American incursions. They were also sentenced to decimation, and drew lots to see which one of them would hang—the first piece of a long chain of evidence that, as Bean wrote, "these are a people in whom you should put no trust or confidence whatever."

The United States was now secure enough in its national identity that some people, especially in the South, were thinking of territorial expansion, and the fate of the Nolan party inflamed their sentiments against the Spanish regime. For his unexplained activities and his violent end, Philip Nolan is often described as the first of a generation of American "filibusters," expansionist-minded adventurers who entered Mexico with the purpose to destabilize the government and claim the huge province for the United States. There is evidence for this, but it is circumstantial and rests principally on Spanish suspicions and Nolan's association with the scheming Wilkinson. Either he was merely a greedy and reckless mustanger, or he was the first of Wilkinson's pawns to enter a Texas grave.

From the time Cabeza de Vaca washed ashore on Texas in 1528, it took the French a century and a half to mount a challenge to Spanish control of New Spain. From the independence of the United States, it took that brash new nation less than a decade and a half before it began to flex its expansionist muscles. With the accession of Thomas Jefferson to the presidency of the United States, vast and vexsome Louisiana changed hands again. When Napoleon needed to raise cash for his military campaigns, he sold the huge territory to the United States for $15 million. With brilliant draftsmanship, the agreement conveyed the tract not with specific boundaries, but to the extent that France had owned it. And Jefferson, while writing that the province of "Techas," if it could be acquired, would become a crown jewel of the Union, seized upon the explorations of La Salle to claim that Texas should be and was included in the Louisiana Purchase. Thus as the nineteenth century opened, Spain's monarchy had never been weaker nor more ineffectual, and the bureaucracy in New Spain was often without instructions or oversight from Madrid, which left ample room for corruption. And then suddenly, there was the United States, looking right over their eastern border, with Jefferson claiming Texas, with Wilkinson appointed governor of the Louisiana Territory, and with men like Nolan (in Spanish minds) trying to pluck the ripe fruit before it even fell. It was an extremely troubling scenario for the royal government of New Spain, especially after Jefferson sent a column of troops that forced the Spanish out of Los Adaes.

The Spaniards answered as best they could. When the president who took such pride in dispatching Lewis and Clark to explore upper Louisiana sent a smaller and less heralded column under Thomas Freeman to probe the limits of lower Louisiana, Spanish troops blocked them at a place called Spanish Bluff, near present-day Texarkana. Another American, Zebulon Pike, penetrated as far as the northern reaches of the Rio Grande before he was stopped. But then came a far more dangerous American filibuster in the person of Aaron Burr, a former vice president, who had been advocating ouster of the Spanish from the Southwest since 1796 and, now out of office, was thought to be organizing forces in the Western U.S. for the purpose of striking into Texas. Wilkinson was confederate with Burr in these plans to some unknown degree, but when Burr's plan changed into perhaps taking some American territory for his own, Wilkinson lost his nerve and preserved his standing with the American government by reporting Burr and turning state's evidence. Burr was acquitted in a trial for treason, but disgraced, and Jefferson sent Wilkinson with troops to uphold American boundary claims along the Arroyo Hondo.

With so much confusion emanating from contending but far-removed capitals, it fell to local military commanders to finally exercise some common sense. Both the United States and Spain had pushed troops into the border area, and for once Wilkinson performed an act of smart statecraft. To keep fighting from breaking out, he took a huge risk, and sent a personal letter to the Mexican governor, Antonio Cordero y Bustamante. "Your excellency is sensible," he wrote on October 29, 1806, "to the extreme delicacy with which a military man may exercise his discretion." Yet, without yielding any diplomatic points, he said, "the subject of our test is scarcely worth the blood of one brave man." He would, he proffered, withdraw his troops to Natchitoches, if the Mexican force would withdraw to Nacogdoches, and decline to open hostilities until their governments settled the border question.

Cordero gave the job of responding to Wilkinson to his commander on the scene, the experienced and successful Simón de Herrera. "Your Excellency manifesting by these operations, the peaceful ideas that possess you," wrote Herrera on November 4, "I wish to preserve the reciprocity of good Harmony." Thus was struck the Neutral Ground Agreement. The opposing forces marched away from each other, and the principal governments, shamed by the pact's abundant good sense, allowed it to stand. Further boundary negotiations broke down the following year and were not resumed for over a decade, but the Neutral Ground Agreement held. The no-man's-land between the two fixed positions created a lawless zone, however, where even the most extreme characters could find refuge and plot their mischief.

TEN

GREEN FLAG, RED BLOOD

A COUPLE OF YEARS AFTER THE NEUTRAL GROUND DEAL was struck, it became apparent that the United States was not the only problem confronting New Spain's beleaguered viceroy, José de Iturrigaray. Far from the people and everyday affairs of the colonies, the Napoleonic Wars in Europe continued to play hell with colonial administration. Charles IV abdicated in favor of his son, Ferdinand VII, but the transfer was not recognized by Napoleon, who invaded Spain in 1808 and forced the abdication of Ferdinand in favor of Joseph Bonaparte, the emperor's brother.

In New Spain, the French puppet king was taken seriously by virtually no one, but in Mexico the two important upper classes, the Spanish-born peninsulares and the slightly less haughty criollos, disagreed on how to respond to Madrid's increase of taxes, secularization of church holdings, and general milking of the colony for war funds. And in a stratum underlying all those considerations, Mexico's vast peonage of Indians and mestizos were sick of being trampled on by apparently everyone. When they finally found a champion in an activist priest, Miguel Hidalgo y Costilla, the real Mexican Revolution began, on September 16, 1810. Mexican provinces went into rebellion one by one.

It took a few months for the revolt to reach Texas. The governor there, who had replaced Bustamante, Manuel María de Salcedo, was a clear-eyed pragmatist. Son of a previous governor of Louisiana, he had tried for years to suppress the smuggling operations that had thrived since the days of St. Denis, and understood that Spain could not hold Texas without settling the land with her own colonists. Yet, after assuming his duties in 1808 and leading an expedition into the Neutral Ground to evict American squatters, he mollified his draconian instructions to drive them out by force, and instead counseled them to try to gain title to the land from the Spanish government. The sudden Hidalgo rebellion left him in a quandary. The priest had sent one of his aides, Bernardo Gutiérrez de Lara, to round up recruits in the Rio Grande Valley, and Salcedo needed to lead troops to restore order there, but the soldiers in the presidio were unwilling to leave, since their families in San Antonio would have no protection from Indian raids. Salcedo also didn't feel he could trust a local militia while he was gone, for he knew Hidalgo had support among many Bexareños. In fact he had already arrested two revolutionary agents who had been proselytizing his garrison.

The issue was soon taken out of his hands. Local alcaldes, who had the job of raising the militia, persuaded a retired captain, Juan Bautista de las Casas, to assume command. On January 22, 1811, five days after Hidalgo's own forces suffered a decisive defeat deep in Mexico, Casas raised the revolutionary standard, arrested Salcedo and the garrison commander, and released the two agents. In sympathy with Hidalgo's goals, Casas ordered the arrest of all peninsulares in Texas and the seizure of their lands, and dispatched eighty soldiers with one of Hidalgo's agents, Antonio Saenz, to Nacogdoches, which quickly fell under their banner. The leaders of that column kept some of the confiscated wealth for themselves, for which the idealistic Casas arrested them. With a web of lies and cleverly planted rumors, the guilty men allied themselves with the remaining royalists, and saved themselves by betraying Casas into their hands. As Salcedo was restored to his office, Casas was sent to Monclova for trial. On August 3, two days after Hidalgo's own execution, he was shot in the back—the penalty for traitors—and his head returned to Béxar as an example.

The failure of the Casas revolt was not the end of revolutionary sentiment in Texas, but thereafter matters took on a peculiarly—and suspiciously—American flavor. Shortly before the revolt collapsed, Hidalgo commissioned Gutiérrez de Lara to go to the United States and seek aid for the revolution. He was warmly received in Washington, where he was presented to a galaxy of foreign ministers, and he also met Cuban revolutionary José Álvarez de Toledo, with whom he began preparations for an organized invasion of Texas.

Secretary of State James Monroe dispatched a special "observer" to Natchitoches, William Shaler, with funds to distribute for the effort. Monroe also arranged for Gutiérrez de Lara to meet the governor of Louisiana, who connected him with Shaler. Another brought into the scheme was a young former U.S. Army lieutenant who had left the service in a huff over being snubbed for promotion. Augustus W. Magee was instrumental in raising American volunteers; grandly calling themselves the Republican Army of the North and flying a banner of bright green, 130 men splashed across the Sabine on August 8, 1812, brushed aside royalist units, and entered Nacogdoches in triumph four days later. Such initial success soon swelled the insurgent army to more than three hundred, and they headed west. To defend San Antonio, Salcedo deployed his forces along the Guadalupe, but

Magee shrewdly bypassed them and took La Bahía on November 7. Salcedo laid siege to the place through the winter, slowly gaining in strength until he commanded about eight hundred men. Magee died of a fever on February 6, 1813, and command passed to Major Samuel Kemper, a Virginian who had already tried to lead one filibuster, in West Florida in 1804. Where Magee, faced with Salcedo's increasing forces, had begun negotiating a surrender, Kemper defeated the Mexican army in sharp engagements on February 10 and 13.

Kemper stayed on at La Bahía for a month, gaining strength from American adventurers and royalist deserters, before moving on San Antonio with an army of about eight hundred. Salcedo moved south to meet them with a force of over a thousand and the assistance of the capable Simón de Herrera, who had made the Neutral Ground Agreement with Wilkinson in 1806. As the "Green Flag" army approached the San Francisco de la Espada mission, Salcedo and Herrera prepared an ambush, which was discovered by Kemper's flankers. It was the royalists instead who were surprised at the Battle of Rosillo, and in an hour of severe fighting Salcedo lost over a hundred dead and most of his mounts and materiel, including six cannons. When the rebels appeared at the gates of San Antonio on April 1, Salcedo was compelled to surrender the city. The transfer of power was civilized; Kemper dined with Herrera and Salcedo that evening, and the royalist troops were disarmed the next day.

Those Mexican provinces still in rebellion quickly recognized Gutiérrez de Lara's Texas regime, which promulgated a Declaration of Independence on April 6: "Governments are established for the good of communities of men," it proclaimed, "and not for the benefit and aggrandisement of individuals. When these ends are perverted to a system of oppression, the people have a right to change them for a better."

Gutiérrez de Lara talked of democracy, but came the critical hour and he proved no more able to break the pattern of repression and revenge than others who grasped for the reins of power. A week and a half after his noble Declaration of Independence, Gutiérrez promulgated a constitution declaring Texas to be "inviolably joined" to the Mexican Republic, which of course did not exist, and confirming Catholicism as the established religion. Government was to be by a ruling junta, without reference to free elections. The American volunteers who had set Gutiérrez on the chair of authority were shocked, but then came worse. Gutiérrez tried Salcedo for treason, a remarkable charge to be brought against the royal governor by an insurgent backed by foreign interventionists. He was convicted, but at least sentenced only to exile. There was an officer serving under Gutiérrez, however, whose father had been executed by Salcedo, and it was to this Captain Delgado that the prisoners were consigned for deportation. Instead of conducting Salcedo and his aides—fourteen men in all, including Herrera—safely to New Orleans, Delgado marched them to the site of the Rosillo battle, bound them feet and hands, scourged and humiliated them, and cut their throats as if they were so many hogs. It was both charged and denied that Gutiérrez de Lara was complicit in the act.

Major Kemper quit the scheme in disgust, and most of the American contingent followed him back to Louisiana. Monroe's "observer" Shaler, meanwhile, had along with the Cuban Álvarez de Toledo established and edited a Spanish-language, single-sheet newspaper, the *Gaceta de Texas,* whose masthead bore the location of Nacogdoches but was probably printed in the safety of Natchitoches. While disseminated to proclaim and justify the Green Flag rebellion, it is still usually counted as the first newspaper to be published in Texas. With news of Gutiérrez de Lara's sudden overturning of American interest in Texas, Shaler and Álvarez de Toledo used their news sheet to discredit him, and convinced the junta in San Antonio to replace Gutiérrez with the friendlier Álvarez. Gutiérrez de Lara was packed off to Louisiana, where he lived to fight another day, and Álvarez de Toledo assumed command of the forces in San Antonio on August 4 in a gold-braided general's uniform.

A new royalist army of nine hundred under Colonel Ignacio Elizondo attempted to retake San Antonio late in June, but the Green Flag revolutionaries and remaining Americans defeated them soundly in a battle at Alazán Creek on June 20. Royalist help was on the way, however. Deeper in Mexico, this first phase of the Mexican Revolution was gradually suppressed by the frighteningly formidable ability of the commandant of the Eastern Interior Provinces, Joaquín de Arredondo. A peninsulare and career soldier, born in Barcelona and the son of the viceroy of Buenos Aires, he was brutal and wily. As Arredondo marched north to reinforce Elizondo, Álvarez de Toledo tried desperately to meet and fight him before those two forces could link. He was prevented from doing so by the intrigues of disaffected Bexareños, who couldn't stand him, first because he was himself also a peninsulare, and second because they perceived him as an American puppet. The fact that Álvarez de Toledo shared their republican sentiments only nourished their disgust.

Nevertheless, Álvarez de Toledo led his force of 1,400 south from the city, hoping to ambush Arredondo on the Laredo road near the Medina

River. In a reversal of the Battle of Rosillo, this time it was the royalist forces, 1,850 strong, who discovered the ambush and responded with one of their own. In the four-hour Battle of the Medina River, fought in stifling heat on August 18, 1813, Arredondo lost just over fifty men while obliterating the rebel force. Those not killed in the fight were executed after they surrendered—a gruesome demonstration not lost on one of Arredondo's junior officers, nineteen-year-old Antonio López de Santa Anna, who was commended for gallantry in the action. Álvarez de Toledo himself escaped back to Louisiana, but only perhaps a hundred of his army survived the day. Over the next two years he involved himself in two more filibustering plots against Texas, one by land and one by sea, but neither scheme bore fruit. A consummate survivor, he then reversed course and sought a pardon, gained by squealing on other filibusters. He returned to Spain, counseled King Ferdinand VII, served in various European diplomatic stations, and died on a pension forty years later.

Arredondo, by contrast, upon assuming power in Béxar, rounded up by one count 327 of the former republicans and their sympathizers, including Salcedo's murderer. They were marched by tens to the edge of pits and shot. Their property was seized, and their families forced into camp drudgery for the royalist troops. Elizondo too gained a measure of revenge for his defeat at Alazán Creek, pursuing scattering republicans eastward across Texas all the way to Nacogdoches, catching and summarily executing about a hundred of them before he was himself killed by one of his own officers.

It had been a chaotic year, but Texas' first experience with independence was ended, and the king once again ruled those who were left in the province.

ELEVEN

STRANGE BEDFELLOWS

EVEN WITH THE FIRST FLUSH OF THE MEXICAN REVOLU-
tion suppressed, Texas was simply too porous a sieve, and the residents too
accustomed to placing their practical interests ahead of Crown policy, to
keep more foreigners out of the province. Of course, it helped the foreigners
to operate if they behaved themselves.

Whereas Philip Nolan's earlier "mustanging" expeditions were probably
a cover for geographical intelligence, and earned him an unmarked grave
somewhere in the central prairie, others fared better. An Irish-born American resident, later a citizen of Spanish Louisiana, named William Barra was
allowed to trade profitably between the two provinces, and he left an estate
valued at over $150,000 when he died in 1810. Five years later, Americans
William Hensley and William Lawrence used the ambiguity of the Louisiana
boundary to poke into Northeast Texas and establish an agrarian community called Jonesborough, near present Clarksville. The couple dozen Indian
traders and farm families who joined them there and at a second village
downstream at Pecan Point lay low, worked hard, and were tolerated by
Spanish officials unwilling to provoke the boundary question. This gained
Jonesborough the distinction of being the first permanent Anglo-American
settlement in Texas.

During 1818 a second "agrarian" settlement, of rather more dubious
dedication to the plow, camped itself in Texas and caused international consternation. After the final fall and exile of Napoleon to St. Helena in 1815, a
cabal of Bonapartist officers coalesced in the United States and made plans
to start over in an isolated corner of Texas. Under the leadership of General
and Baron Charles Lallemand, they doggedly raised money and supplies in
Philadelphia, while Lallemand tendered his service to the Spanish Crown.
Ferdinand, once again seated on his precarious throne, wouldn't have anything to do with him. Lallemand won instead American approval to begin a
French colony in Alabama, which turned out to be only a staging area for
their launch into Texas. The baron sailed to Galveston Island to seek the
help of the pirate Jean Lafitte, who wined him and dined him, and aided
the French in planting their colony about thirty miles up the Trinity River,

somewhere near the present town of Liberty in the early spring of 1818. Lafitte then reported all to the Spanish authorities.

While proclaiming to the world that they desired naught but "peace and friendship from all those who surround us," the Bonapartist officers and their servants and camp followers made scant effort at actual farming. They named their establishment Champ d'Asile—the Plain of Refuge. They probably never numbered more than a hundred at any one time, but they divided themselves into Napoleonic "cohorts," drilled, built a fort, and manufactured ammunition. The baring of a plot in Spain to invade Mexico and place Joseph Bonaparte on a New World throne made their presence even less tolerable to the royal administration. Collateral opposition was also forming. Rumors that their ultimate aim was to free Napoleon himself made the English edgy, and the last thing that the United States wanted was a French sideshow in the Neutral Ground that could complicate eventual settlement of the boundary question.

By the time the Monroe administration sent an agent to gather hard facts about the Champ d'Asile colony, it had already broken up. Lallemand had learned that a Spanish column was on its way to evict his colonists, and they returned to the dubious hospitality of Lafitte on Galveston Island. About half the Frenchmen had died of disease, starvation, or exhaustion; some were murdered or killed in duels, and two were eaten by cannibals. The decision by both Spain and the United States that Lallemand and his followers were unwelcome only hammered the final nail in the Champ d'Asile coffin. Lafitte assisted in transporting the melancholy Bonapartists back to New Orleans by late November. Oddly, however, the failed colony was lionized in the French press, mostly to annoy Louis XVIII, the restored but unpopular Bourbon monarch. The mystery of the true nature of the Champ d'Asile colony only deepened when Napoleon bequeathed Lallemand a hundred thousand francs in his will, most of which inheritance went to pay his debts. Lallemand became an American citizen, but only until the 1830 revolution placed Louis-Philippe on the French throne. Restored to his rank, Lallemand returned to France as governor of Corsica and died in 1839.

Not all filibustering during these years was carried out by foreigners. Peninsular Spain herself had her share of liberals, one of whom, Francisco Xavier Mina, fell out with Ferdinand VII over the constitution of 1812 and spent four years raising money, ships, and supplies for an invasion of Mexico. He was encouraged in this, probably informally and certainly without authority, by General Winfield Scott, whom Mina met in England on his journey west. In the United States, Mina was backed by various business venturers, and finally landed a small fleet at Galveston, where he was joined by Henry Perry, a survivor of the Green Flag rebellion, and a hundred Americans. He also made a stormy alliance with the French pirate and Lafitte associate Louis Michel Aury. Mina invaded Mexico at the mouth of the Santander River, and won some initial victories before being captured and executed. Perry had already fallen out with him and led forty-three of his men overland back to Texas. On June 18, 1817, he failed to take La Bahía. In a battle with a royalist army the following day, most of the Americans were killed and Perry took his own life rather than surrender and face execution.

For three hundred years, European politics had had an inordinate impact on Texas, and it was far from over. Further fallout from Napoleon's meddling in Spain manifested itself in 1819. At the time of the Louisiana Purchase, President Jefferson had maintained that Texas was part of the deal, which Spain denied with sufficient determination to move troops into the Piney Woods in the east. The Neutral Ground Agreement formulated by General Wilkinson and Governor Cordero had held good since 1806; it provided a breather in international relations but created a lawless hell in the "Neutral Ground." Not until February 1819, and spurred partly by the Champ d'Asile flap, were Spain and the United States able to settle the matter in the Adams-Onís Treaty. The Americans never really had good title to Texas, but it was enough of a bargaining chip that they were able to win the cession of Florida in exchange for their Texas claims. The boundary was finally fixed at the Sabine River.

To American expansionists, particularly in the South, giving up one territory to gain the other was anathema. An angry mass meeting convened in Natchez, Mississippi, and resulted in the organization of an armed expedition, formed with the expressed aim of wrestling Texas from New Spain. Filibustering was now in earnest. Selected to command the private expeditionary force was James Long, a twenty-six-year-old doctor, planter, and merchant. He also happened to be married to the niece of the ubiquitous General Wilkinson, who now was furious that Texas had been given away. Financed by wealthy Southerners to the tune of as much as half a million dollars, recruits were attracted by the pledge of a league of conquered land. The Mississippi filibusters had it settled in their own minds that their pending invasion "was founded in neither private speculation nor a desire for personal aggrandizement. It was well known to the intelligent portion of the people . . . that its sole design and intention were to get possession of the country, to rescue it from the grasp of tyranny, and . . . to invite its settlement by North Americans." The fact that Texas didn't actually belong to them raised no obstacle.

A vanguard of 120 splashed across the Sabine on June 8, 1819; Long joined them there two weeks later, accompanied by his wife Jane and her babe in arms. Nacogdoches rallied to them, and the "Supreme Council" of eleven revolutionaries elected Long president. Texas was declared independent on June 23; the new government upped the land bounty for enlistment to ten leagues per recruit, and Long's numbers grew to 300. The invasion took on a more international character when it was joined by Bernardo Gutiérrez de Lara of the Green Flag rebellion, back to stir up some more trouble. Long also wrote to Jean Lafitte, and upon receiving a cordial answer, he departed for Galveston to seek aid. Then it all unraveled. In a way reminiscent of the Gutiérrez-Magee revolt before him, Long began publishing a newspaper, the *Texas Republican,* in Nacogdoches in August, hoping the journal would rouse more support, but promised additional supplies from Natchez never arrived, and Long had to break up his force into foraging parties. Lafitte had written that as a veteran of eight years' fighting against Spanish tyranny, he could not but welcome Long and his confederates, but he never came up with any actual help. While Long was absent from Nacogdoches, the local administration collapsed at the approach of a Spanish army of five hundred under Colonel Ignacio Pérez, who was intent on housecleaning. Long warned his wife to return to Natchitoches, while he continued his effort to bring Lafitte into the republic; the Supreme Council even named the pirate governor of Galveston Island, as though he needed their recognition. When Pérez entered Nacogdoches on October 28 he found it deserted, and within a month had chased the remaining filibusters back into Louisiana.

Long rallied in the safety of Natchitoches, and prepared to try again. Gutiérrez de Lara was still with him; he was aided by another Southern filibuster named Ben Milam, and then significantly he was joined by one of the Mexican liberal rebels, José Félix Trespalacios, who was planning his own invasion. Making common cause, the second Long invasion chose a more surreptitious route, erecting a fort on Point Bolivar, opposite Galveston. Jane was with him again, with a new babe in arms, and was soon expecting another, and she had with her a slave woman named Kiamatia. The Long force erected Fort Las Casas and planned the new campaign.

Long departed Point Bolivar by boat with fifty-two volunteers on September 19, 1821. On October 4 they captured the town of Goliad, but then were cut off by Pérez' army and forced to surrender four days later. Long was taken to prison, first in San Antonio and then to Monterrey, and finally to Mexico City. His execution might have been summary, but the Mexican Revolution had finally succeeded in toppling the royal administration, and it was the chaos of juntas that kept Long alive for six months. The revolutionary wheel of fortune in Mexico finally seemed to point to a winner in Agustín de Iturbide, who, democratic goals aside, soon became emperor. He seemed to offer some prospect of permanent government, and became a rallying point for ex-revolutionists. The clever Gutiérrez de Lara got on his good side and later became governor and commandant of Tamaulipas. Trespalacios, although he had broken with Long, needed to make his peace with the emperor, too, and Long knew too much about Trespalacios' involvement in the filibustering. Long was shot dead on April 8, 1822, by a guard on Trespalacios' payroll. The shooting was claimed to be accidental, and Trespalacios became the first Mexican governor of Texas that year. It was an inauspicious start for the new government of Mexico.

Jane Long, meanwhile, spent the frigid winter of 1821–22 on Galveston Bay, remaining behind with her daughter and Kiamatia after the remaining Americans grew discouraged and returned home. Alone against the elements and the Karankawas, she gave birth to another daughter, Mary James Long, December 21, 1821, for many years popularly reputed to be the first Anglo baby born in Texas (which she was not). Jane earned the nickname "Mother of Texas" from the ordeal. Emaciated but still game, she was picked up by a passing ship of suddenly legal American immigrants to Texas early in 1822. She traveled and camped with them until midsummer; when she learned that James was dead, she brazenly journeyed to San Antonio to obtain a pension from Governor Trespalacios, who kept her waiting ten months before turning her away.

In a graphic way, Gutiérrez de Lara and Félix Trespalacios demonstrated one quality, the animal instinct of self-preservation, that was lacked by American filibusters such as Nolan and Magee and Long. They were guided instead by a toxic combination of greed and ego and genuine, if self-righteous and misshapen, political idealism—forces that came to be synonymous with American intervention in Texas, and then with American Texas itself, for generations.

BOOK TWO

FROM EMPRESARIOS TO INDEPENDENCE

TWELVE

A CONNECTICUT YANKEE
IN KING FERDINAND'S COURT

INTO THIS LABYRINTH OF LACE AND INTRIGUE, OF GENU-flecting and firing squads, strode another American on the make, a businessman whose brash confidence masked the desperation of his circumstances.

Moses Austin was a native of Durham, Connecticut. He was nearly sixty, and had made and lost two separate fortunes. As a young man of twenty-two he went into the dry goods business with his brother Stephen in Philadelphia, then married into wealth in 1785 in the person of Maria Brown, with whom he established one of the finest households in Richmond, Virginia. The Brown family money was made in iron mining, and Austin thought he could duplicate the fortune in lead. He developed ore deposits in southwestern Virginia, modestly naming the primitive digs Austinville, where he relocated and where she gave birth to a son, Stephen, in 1793, and a daughter, Emily, in 1795. Austin took a contract to roof the new Virginia legislature with native lead; he ran a good operation with imported English smelters, but the deal was a loser and left him on the edge of bankruptcy. Learning of the presence of rich lead deposits in upper Spanish Louisiana (now Missouri), Austin journeyed to the province during the winter of 1796–97, and subsequently applied to the Crown for a concession to develop the resource. It wasn't gold, but the Spanish government took sufficient hope that metal of any kind could be extracted from its wasteland that it overcame its xenophobia and approved a one-league (4,428-acre) grant to Austin on land surrounding the mines. The Austins removed to the village of Potosi, about fifty miles southwest of present St. Louis, in 1798; Moses' Virginia experience led to quick success, and at full flush his new fortune approximated two hundred thousand dollars—an astronomical sum at the time. He built a rambling, porticoed mansion in Potosi which he named, triumphantly, Durham Hall, after the hometown where he began life as the son of an innkeeping tailor.

The location was still on the frontier—marauding Indians were shot from the windows—but the settlement stuck. His citizenship then followed the Louisiana ball toss from king to king, until he found himself once more a citizen of the United States, thanks to the Louisiana Purchase. When Maria gave birth that year to a second son, Brown, Austin thought he had finally reached his proper station in life. Ten-year-old Stephen was packed off to a boarding school in Connecticut for three years and then to Transylvania University in Kentucky, while the territorial governor, William Henry Harrison, appointed Moses Austin to a judgeship. Then with other financiers he founded the Bank of St. Louis, the first bank west of the Mississippi. Stephen was recalled from university to help run the family empire, and he also began making his own name with service in the militia and the territorial legislature. The entire idyll came crashing down in the financial panic of 1819, and for the second time, Moses Austin worried how to put food on the table. Stephen left the family fold to make his own way, and was soon sworn in as a judge in Arkansas. As the elder Austin had once recouped his losses by relocating beyond the national boundary, he conceived the notion of starting an American colony deep in Texas, and sent to Washington for a copy of his Spanish passport. Spain's difficulty in convincing their own people to settle there was well known, and Spain had done well by Austin's lead venture. If he brought good Catholics who swore allegiance to the Spanish king, Austin could recover his fortune as a colonial empresario, a recruiter and manager who would introduce settlers into the region.

With a Yankee's confidence—despite the fact that after his re-Americanization his lead mines had been foreclosed on and he himself had been jailed briefly for debt—Moses Austin set off for San Antonio de Béxar. At least he thought it prudent to stop and visit Stephen in Arkansas to seek some substance to put behind his brave front. Stephen was close to despair. He had spent most of the previous year trying to rescue his father's failing business ventures, even having vowed not to marry until he pulled the family back from ruin. He acquired an interest in land speculations in southwestern Arkansas, and spent time and labor trying to improve a farm at Long Prairie, where Moscoso de Alvarado had entered the Caddo heartland in 1542. By the autumn of 1819 young Austin was becoming rapidly disenchanted with the place. "The navigation of Red River is much more difficult than I expected," he wrote a friend from his Missouri militia days, Jacob Pettit, "and the country has proved to be *very sickly*. I have been sick nearly the whole summer, as indeed has almost every person around me. . . . These reasons induce me to wish for a *change* of situation." Stephen inquired into land prices and the availability of credit in Pettit's vicinity of Plaquemines Parish on the Mississippi Delta. "If there is no such property for sale, how can land be *rented?*" If he stayed where he was on the Red River, he would be reduced to raising hogs and farming peas and beans, and he inquired into their current market prices. He also asked how much cash he could expect to raise by selling his Negro, Richmond, whom he described as "young, stout, and healthy."

When Moses showed up, Stephen wanted nothing to do with the colonial venture. He knew that his father was a big dreamer whose schemes sometimes collapsed; all his life he had answered to Moses' ambitions—when he was only three years old, the elder Austin wrote him a thirty-page letter outlining how he had succeeded in winning the Spanish lead mining contract. During his lonely years in boarding school, which he loathed, every letter from his father, which he tore open in a search for encouragement and affection, badgered him about how to become a Great Man. Always he had been too dutiful to complain or resist, and even now in the paucity of his own circumstances, he anted up fifty dollars, plus the loan of a horse, and Richmond. Moses also visited his son-in-law, Emily's husband James Bryan, and obtained the loan of a mule.

Austin entered San Antonio de Béxar two days before Christmas in 1820. He strode into the presence of the provincial governor, Antonio María Martínez, and presented his colonial plan. Martínez was a peninsulare from Andújar who boasted a distinguished and highly decorated military career of thirty-five years, fought mostly in Europe. By the time of Austin's arrival he had been civil and military governor of Texas for nearly four years. He had witnessed the inexorable weakening of the Spanish grip on the New World, and it was a situation neither attractive nor simple. Peasant uprisings had been put to sleep with the executions of Hidalgo in 1811, and of his spiritual heir, José María Morelos, in 1815. Surprisingly, when a Mexican independence movement reemerged in 1820, it was led by conservative criollos who were alarmed by the advent of a liberal government in Spain, which might encourage the peons and *pobladores* to agitate for rights and social position. Agustín de Iturbide, the former royalist criollo officer from Michoacán who had played a part in crushing Hidalgo, appeared now to have won Mexico for the new conservative revolution, and now the James Long filibustering business was in full blow. Bringing more Americans into Texas was the last thing Martínez wanted to hear about. He didn't even read Austin's proposal, but ordered him out of the country with "all possible speed." The Yankee dealmaker left the audience a shattered man.

Even as he agonized over what to do, Austin saw a face along the street that he was sure he recognized, a Dutchman named Felipe de Neri, whom he had briefly met in New Orleans nearly twenty years before. They spoke; it was indeed he, only now he was a society swell known in San Antonio as the Baron de Bastrop. The man in question was not an aristocrat and Neri was not his surname. He was really a native of Dutch Guiana (Suriname) named Bögel—pronounced "burgle," which was not too bad a description of his previous occupation. He had settled in the Netherlands, become a minor bureaucrat, and fled the country before he could be prosecuted for embezzling taxes that he had collected. He came to Spanish Louisiana in 1795, and by 1806 had ensconced himself in San Antonio, where he discovered that his polished manners and plausibility gave him access to all the best families. He was among the first, but certainly not the last, loser to come to Texas to reinvent himself and emerge in prominence.

He is far better known to history as the Baron de Bastrop, and in this capacity he offered his help to the stricken Austin. Bastrop also had some experience with an undertaking similar to Austin's, having won approval, if not much actual settlement, of a colony of five hundred families on the Ouachita River as early as 1796. What was needed was to draw up a petition of the appropriately obsequious formality, which Bastrop would submit to Martínez with persuasions that he endorse it. The tactic worked, and two days later, Austin was summoned back into the governor's presence. Granting permission for the colony was beyond his power, but Martínez agreed to append his endorsement and send the proposal up the chain of command. Austin departed San Antonio jubilantly, but the return trip degenerated into a nightmare. It turned out that one of his traveling companions was a black marketeer named Jacob Kirkham. Fearful of being tainted by the association of traveling with him, Austin had no sooner determined to report him to the authorities than Kirkham absconded with all of Austin's materiel, leaving him and Richmond afoot and disarmed on the Trinity River. For the last week of the return journey the two men had nothing to eat but acorns and roots. He stumbled half frozen into McGuffin's inn near Natchitoches on January 15, 1821, having suffered, as he said, everything but death. He couldn't leave his bed for three weeks, before he was fetched home to Missouri by a nephew.

The "Baron" de Bastrop may have sweet-talked Governor Martínez into endorsing Austin's plan, but the final say was not his. The meaningful permission had to come from the military commandant, the bloody-handed old Joaquín de Arredondo. He had helped defeat Hidalgo, he had executed the 327 republican sympathizers in San Antonio in the wake of the Gutiérrez-Magee rebellion, and ordered the deaths of 100 more. In fact, his purge of disloyal elements in Texas had been so complete that when he received his copy of the new liberal constitution that King Ferdinand had been forced to approve, he had to admit he couldn't implement it because there weren't enough qualified men left alive in the province to fill the offices it created.

Yet, there were factors working in Austin's favor. The authorities had failed for generations to convince Mexicans from the interior to settle in Texas, far from their homes or help and squarely in the middle of savage natives. It was increasingly necessary to convince someone loyal to Spain to live there. Then too, one provision of that new liberal constitution specifically permitted foreign nationals who had once been loyal citizens of Spain to resettle. Ferdinand VII was an absolutist deep in his bitter heart, but the clause covered Moses Austin squarely on point. Certain that he must triumph, Austin, instead of resting to recover his health, began recruiting colonists with all the energy he could muster. With his fatally weakened constitution, however, the extended chill and exposure of the journey settled into pneumonia. In spring he received a stunning letter: Arredondo had indeed approved the colony. In a final manic burst Austin wrote to his son, "I hope and pray you will discharge your doubts as to the enterprise. Raise your spirits. Times are changing, and a new chance presents itself."

From his Arkansas judgeship, Stephen had moved on to New Orleans to try to land better employment, but found it slow going. "I offered to hire myself out as a clerk," he wrote his mother, "as an overseer, or anything else, but business here is too dull." The financial panic that had ruined the Austins also plagued New Orleans, and forgetting wages, other likely young men his age were taking jobs just for food and a bed. Then his luck appeared to improve. He obtained a position editing a newspaper, and he was befriended by one Joseph Hawkins, a former Kentucky congressman and the brother of a school acquaintance, who was rooming him and boarding him free of charge so Stephen could learn French and study law. "An offer so generous," Austin wrote in another letter to his mother, "and from a man who two months ago was a stranger to me, has almost made me change my opinion of the human race." This was not a time to go chasing after one of his father's pipe dreams. But Moses, anticipating Stephen's opposition, outflanked him. The elder Austin himself wrote to Hawkins, offering him a share of the colonial venture if he could convince Stephen to join in; he also convinced his son-in-law James Bryan that the scheme must succeed. Bryan had assumed much of Stephen's debt to enable him to obtain more credit, and his urging toward Texas, which might not be easily refused, brought nearly irresistible family pressure to bear.

Unable to combat such forces, Stephen at least consoled himself that Arredondo's approval, when it came, was for real. Governor Martínez dispatched a high-powered delegation to meet Moses Austin at Natchitoches, including the alcalde of San Antonio de Béxar, Josef Erasmo Seguín, and one of the town's leading citizens, Juan Martín de Veramendi, who later became governor. When Stephen received a letter from Missouri with the news that his father was too dangerously ill to travel, there was no help for it, but he must get on a riverboat and go to Natchitoches to meet them. He had barely left New Orleans when he was overtaken by another letter, from his mother. Moses Austin, in his last breaths, "drew me down to him an with much distress and difficulty of speech, told me it was two late, that he was going . . . he beged me to tell you to take his place dear Stephen that it is his dieing fathers last request to prosecute the enterprise he had Commenced."

In Natchitoches the Mexican officials graciously condoled with the twenty-seven-year-old Stephen, who accompanied them back to San Antonio to work out the details of the contract.

THIRTEEN

THE YOUNG EMPRESARIO

STEPHEN F. AUSTIN'S RELUCTANCE TO UNDERTAKE HIS
father's colonial scheme has long been part of the bedrock of Texas history.
And it was genuine—at first. Once he acquiesced to his fate, however, there
is evidence that he may have warmed to it. A letter discovered in recent
years from Austin to his friend Jacob Pettit talks up the adventure of the
project. "I am now on the eve of taking leave of my 'native land' for the first
time in my life," wrote the prospective young empresario. His father had
learned that Arredondo had approved the project, and the commander's
special envoys were awaiting Stephen in Natchitoches. "I shall return to St.
Antonio with him and mark out the tract of country for the settlement &c
. . . my father will be on in October. If you do not consider yourself settled
for life, you could not do better than to join us. The prospects are much better than they ever were in upper Louisiana for this country is much better
and will settle faster than that ever has—Should any families of your acquaintance wish to move with my Father and you will *recommend them*, to be
honest, moral, good Citizens, they will be provided for. . . . I have a party of
10 fine companions and think shall have a pleasant trip."

After news of the elder Austin's death, Veramendi and Seguín took the
solemn young man under their wing, and the party crossed into Texas on
July 16, 1821. The next day they stopped at the cabin of Josiah Bell, an illegal American squatter whose emotions at seeing a posse of mounted
Spaniards can easily be imagined—until he discovered Stephen Austin
among them. They were old friends, having served in the Missouri militia
together. The next day in Nacogdoches, this sudden Mexican amity was explained. Their continuing need to populate the wilderness, paired with their
continuing inability to prevent Americans from slipping across the border,
led them to conclude that that which they could not stop, they might control. Arredondo's housecleaning a few years before had virtually depopulated Nacogdoches, and Don Erasmo Seguín was able to round up only three
dozen locals to read them the government's fiat: they were welcome to stay,
but they had to relocate into the interior and live in Austin's colony. This
was received, in the main, as great news.

The 300-mile journey to San Antonio took three weeks, allowing for time to get lost in places where El Camino Real petered out and had to be re-blazed; time to recover stock that wandered off during the nights; and time to hunt in a land so thick with game that even Austin, a poor stalker, killed two deer for the campfire. Malarial swamps bordered the Neches and the Trinity, where Seguín and others took fevers, but gradually they gave way to more elevated hardwood forests and lush breezy meadows, and the younger Austin's impression of Texas improved in equal measure. They saw buffalo but no Indians, and by the time they approached San Antonio de Béxar, crossing the clear, cold Guadalupe River, Austin was emotionally trans-formed by journeying through a land he called "the most beautiful I have ever seen."

They were met by a welcoming committee at the edge of town on August 12, but Austin learned that his arrival was not the biggest news of the day. Texas, it seemed, was now part of an independent Mexico. In San Antonio, Martínez, peninsulare and soldier of the Crown, was also a realist who knew when a battle was done. Two days after Austin entered Texas, Martínez di-rected Spanish government officers to swear allegiance to Iturbide, and arranged an orderly transition of power to the incoming Mexican governor, Félix Trespalacios, the twice-condemned career rebel who probably had James Long killed. As Martínez was preparing to retire to Mexico City, Austin was presented to him, and the last royal governor of Texas was duly impressed. The young empresario was five feet seven or eight inches tall and slender, with large hazel eyes and curly brown hair. He displayed consider-ate speech and delicate manners; to his superiors Martínez pronounced him a youth "of high honor, of scrupulous regard for formality, and of desiring to learn how to faithfully discharge the duties proposed by his late father."

At first it appeared that all would proceed, by the usual Mexican reckon-ing, at breakneck speed. Also waiting for Austin in San Antonio was the "Baron" de Bastrop, who extended his services as aide and translator, which the young empresario was grateful to accept. Austin and Martínez, however, did much of their own talking in a scene of one of history's sweeter ironies: an American, who spoke no Spanish, negotiating in French with a royalist peninsulare, on the terms of a colonial contract in an independent Mexico. In ten days Austin secured permission to settle three hundred families, each man to receive at least a section of land, 640 acres, plus 320 acres of river-bottom farmland, and more if he brought his family. Martínez could not have helped but also be impressed that Austin avoided discussing what he himself might gain as profit from the venture. There was a kind of tacit un-

derstanding that Austin would get his own grant of land, and would be allowed to charge some fee for surveying and issuing titles to the other immigrants, but for Austin to have avoided that American stereotype of relentless
avarice certainly helped his cause. Martínez offered Austin the valley of the
Colorado River (a moderate-sized stream not to be confused with the great
Colorado of the Southwest) to explore to the coast as a likely location, and
before long, Austin, leaving Veramendi and Seguín behind, set off with his
American companions for the only other town in Texas' interior, La Bahía,
about eighty miles southeast, to obtain a guide.

Here inertia and confusion overtook the hopeful empresario. It took the
local authorities several days to decide who should guide them, until they
settled on Manuel Becerra, who sat on the town council. Austin tried to say
he was curious whether they might find the site of the original Presidio La
Bahía, which had been abandoned for many years. Becerra thought he
wanted to be shown Nuestra Señora del Refugio, which he refused to do because he was supposed to take them to the Colorado. Austin finally sent Becerra back to Goliad, as he and his traveling companions headed toward the
Colorado, living a high adventure as they hacked and tramped their way
through the valleys of the Guadalupe and Colorado rivers.

During this exploratory journey Moses Austin finally got his wish:
Stephen became seized with enthusiasm at the possibility of transplanting
American civilization into this tangled wilderness. They descended the Colorado, and on nearing the Gulf of Mexico encountered a band of natives of a
Karankawa subtribe called the Cocos. Austin parleyed with them while
warning his companions to be on guard. The Indians' peaceable intent was
known when the chief later entered Austin's camp, unarmed, with a boy and
five women. Austin, who was known for a lifetime of social, not to say sexual, repression, got an eyeful. The women wore panther skins around their
midriffs, but "above the waist they were naked," he recorded, "their breasts
were marked or tatooed in circles of black beginning with a small circle at
the nipple and enlarging as the breast swelled . . . one of them quite pretty."
The sight gave him pause enough to regret, but accept, their eventual extermination if they could not be civilized.

The Cocos informed them that a large band of Karankawas were camped
at the mouth of the Colorado, and they sensibly turned northeast, overland,
until on September 19 they topped an eminence overlooking the surging
Brazos River. "The bluff is about 60 feet high," Austin recorded. "The country back of this place and below for . . . as far as we went is as good in every
respect as a man could wish for, Land all first rate, plenty of timber, fine

water—beautifully rolling. . . . A most beautifull situation for a Town or set-tlement." To cover more ground Austin divided his party to explore both sides of the river, recording the abundance of game and wild cattle. They fol-lowed the Brazos northwest until they struck El Camino Real, and then turned east for Nacogdoches, which they reached on October 6.

In another week he was back in Natchitoches, where he found a hundred letters waiting for him from willing colonists. On October 12 Austin sent a detailed report of his exploration to Governor Martínez, which was un-doubtedly received with relief, because while he was exploring, Manuel Be-cerra sent Martínez a scathing letter. He was offended that Austin didn't speak Spanish, the Americans made no religious observances, and Austin had set off west instead of east. He appeared to be just another American fil-ibuster. It was the kind of incendiary missive that could have landed Austin in jail on his next visit, but his detailed report to Martínez, and his enthusi-asm that he could as easily settle fifteen hundred families as three hundred, allayed any qualms the governor may have had. In a second letter to Mar-tínez the following day, Austin further refined the terms of his proposed colony, and in his ardor also suggested that the valleys of the Trinity on the east, and the Guadalupe on the west, be added to the grant, which was never acted upon.

Austin, the former legislator, knew that reliance could be a key factor in a contract's enforceability, and it was important to get settlers into the colony as soon as possible. He himself had to get to New Orleans to make arrangements, so he tapped his Arkansas squatter friend, Josiah Bell, to lead the first contingent into Mexican Texas and wait for him at the mouth of the Colorado. To raise some fast cash he completed the sale of half-interest in the colony to his friend and mentor, Joseph Hawkins, for $4,000, using the funds to outfit a small ship, a schooner called the *Lively*, with supplies. He dispatched her to Bell, and then he trekked back into Texas, first to meet his colonists on the Colorado and then to San Antonio to finalize plans with Martínez.

It all seemed too good to be true, and indeed, fortune began to frown. The *Lively* was first blown off course and then missed the Colorado, landing its men and supplies at the mouth of the Brazos instead. Austin found his people on the Colorado, but in weeks of anxious waiting, there was no ship and no seed corn. Those who landed at the Brazos, meanwhile, waited until their food was gone, and hiked back to Louisiana. The *Lively* sortied again, but this time was wrecked off Galveston Island, stranding those immigrants until they were rescued by a passing ship. Worse yet, when Austin returned to San Antonio he received a shock: with a new government functioning in Mexico City, Austin's contract had been disallowed. The best Martínez could suggest was that Austin hurry to Mexico City and try to save the situation. The capital was more than a thousand miles distant, he didn't even speak Spanish, and he barely had money enough to cover the trip. He and his couple of companions dressed as beggars, which was shrewd, as they were pounced on by fifty Comanches at the Medina River. The Comanches had come to hate Mexicans, but had traded affably with Americans. Putting on a brave face, Austin upbraided the warriors for threatening their American friends, and the Comanches departed, after lightening their "friends" of their food, blankets, and assorted sundries—including, oddly, Austin's Spanish grammar, from which he was beginning to learn the language.

The party reached Laredo on March 21, San Luís Potosí a month later, and then on to the capital. Once in Mexico City, Austin was dismayed to find the city "in an unsettled state, the whole people and country still agitated by the revolution . . . Party spirit raging." It was April 1822; James Long had just been shot.

Still, there was nothing to do but begin. "I am the property of Esteban Austin," he wrote in crude Spanish on the flyleaf of a new grammar from which he started teaching himself the language. Even more important, he learned the culture—the importance of deference and formality, and above all of patience. His earnestness and politeness won him friends in the legislature, but they would not cross the new emperor. Austin lobbied Iturbide with respectful tenacity and finally won his point, only to see Iturbide deposed—he was later shot—and a new congress again threw out his contract.

Finally he earned enough sympathy from the new congress that they approved an empresario contract, far better than he ever dreamed of. It called for him to settle three hundred families, each of the family heads to receive not a section of land but a *league*—4,428 acres—for ranching, and a *labor*— 177 acres—for farming. The government was too distracted to oversee the colony's affairs, and Austin was given almost absolute power. He was allowed to charge his settlers twelve and a half cents per acre to survey the grants and provide for their defense, plus he could select a hundred thousand acres of his own. It was a victory almost beyond measure.

Back in San Antonio, the governor authorized the "Baron" de Bastrop to act as Austin's land commissioner. The empresario was back in his colony by August, having been gone a year and a half, and the two set to work filling the contract to settle three hundred families. Some of the original immigrants had grown discouraged and gone home, but once they heard the terms, they hustled back. And with the United States still suffering the aftershock of the Panic of 1819, plenty more followed. By September, land was granted to 272; some contracts were forfeited and new arrivals claimed them. The number eventually climbed to 297, partly helped by Austin's policy, in some instances, of recognizing partnerships between single men as constructive "families." In sum they became known as the Old Three Hundred, and they formed the rootstock of Texas' later Anglo aristocracy.

FOURTEEN

PELTS PASSED CURRENT

STEPHEN F. AUSTIN FOUNDED HIS CAPITAL OF SAN FELIPE de Austin on the west bank of the Brazos River about a hundred miles by boat above its mouth, or seventy miles as the crow flies, on the bluff he so admired during that first exploration. By 1827 San Felipe was home to perhaps two hundred, mostly men, in several dozen cabins scattered for a half mile down the riverbank in the town proper. Each lot owner built in a manner to suit himself, presenting no uniform front on anything like a street. Each building was a single-pen log cabin, or else a dogtrot, two log pens separated by a breezeway, with a one-room residence on one side and a one-room place of business on the other. This was the style of dwelling that became the standard in Anglo Texas. Roofs commonly leaked, and in the absence of firebrick and building stone, chimneys were constructed of wood chinked with clay—material that was discovered to be self-defeating if the fire got too hot. "We often held an umbrella over our bed when it rained at night," remembered one matron, and though they suffered from the winter cold, "we were afraid to light a fire."

The hotel was the largest structure, an ample dogtrot with rooms tucked in the attic eaves, and wood and clay fireplaces at either end. As the population began to grow such inns were chronically crowded; a common rate was a dollar a night for transient travelers, or one might board more permanently for four dollars per week; as one sojourner noted, "to place thirty men in a horizontal position, on a space about twenty feet square . . . required no small care and calculation." The only building of sawn lumber was Cooper and Chieves' saloon and billiard hall. There were two grocery mercantiles, one of which only sold alcoholic beverages, and the beginnings of a newspaper presided over by the man who, aside from Austin, was perhaps the dominant personality in the town. Godwin B. Cotten, jowly and jovial, regularly threw public stag dinners that he called "love feasts," requiring only that each of his guests contribute to the night's entertainment, whether or not he possessed any talent. He signed his name "G. B. Cotten," which he announced stood for "Great Big Cotton," and referred to his *Texas Gazette* newspaper as the "Cotton Plant." He shortly went into partnership with Gail Borden, a New York native who for a time became Austin's surveyor. They moved the printing operation downstream to Brazoria, a satellite settlement founded in 1828 on the Brazos about twenty miles up from the Gulf, where their newspaper became the official print medium of the colony.

Austin located his own home a half-mile west of the hubbub of the town, near the mouth of Palmito Creek on the Brazos. From here he conducted his administration; most of an average day for him was taken in land business—ordering and recording surveys, issuing titles. He also maintained a voluminous correspondence, much of it with prospective immigrants from the United States, and with Mexican officials to fine-tune the interpretation of the colonization law. In his isolated dogtrot, Austin had undergone a profound transformation. He began his Texas venture almost as the emotional hostage of his father's ghost, but now he was committed, heart and soul. Texas, he admitted, had become "the idol of my existence—it . . . assumed the character of a *religion* for the guidance of my thoughts and actions." Mexican officers and bureaucrats rewarded Austin's earnestness with trust and respect, but it wasn't long before they began to hear unfavorably of others in his colony. Typical was the account of one José María Sánchez, who was compelled to cross the Brazos as the water was rising. "The baggage was placed in the ferry boat, and . . . we started down the river in search of a landing. . . . A drunk American held the rudder and three intoxicated Negros rowed, singing continuously" until they encountered a landing where Sánchez could continue his journey.

While Austin gained a reputation for scrupulous honesty and hard work, he could be dour and was often depressed; his letters frequently revealed relentless self-pity, as though he was still about his father's business. He wished to send for his mother, who was living in poverty in Missouri, but the widow of Moses Austin died while preparations for her journey were still early. His much-beloved sister Emily settled in Texas with her husband and children, establishing a kind of family compound at Peach Point plantation near the mouth of the Brazos, where the empresario often stayed. For them he designed a large, clever house, appearing from the outside to be a single dwelling, but actually containing separate apartments. His younger brother, Brown, also settled in Texas, married, and with Stephen being a bachelor, fathered Stephen F. Austin Jr. before dying of yellow fever in 1829.

Austin's colonists found the terms of immigration easy to comply with: they had to become Catholic, someone had to swear to their good character, and they had to show improvement on the land within two years of receiving the deed. Still, some complained of the twelve and a half cents per acre that Austin was allowed to collect for survey fees, from which money he also had to provide some kind of militia for defense. There were no other civil revenues, for Mexico had exempted Texas from paying any kind of tax for a period of six years. Austin proved himself strict in administering his duties; those who desired shortcuts to getting their land were invariably disappointed, and their muttering was doubtless made more pointed by his studied aloofness from the conviviality of the town. But he also governed pragmatically when he could, if the colony would benefit. Horse racing he considered a vice, but he permitted it as an incentive for improved stock breeding. There was even a story, which cannot be authenticated, that when some colonists complained to him of the presence of two men living together and engaging in what was euphemistically known as the Unspeakable Vice of the Greeks, Austin left them undisturbed, perhaps aware that local Indians regarded such practices as powerful medicine, and would not attack a settlement where such a thing went on. Indian raids, principally by the dwindling number of Karankawas, were frequent, with isolated households pillaged and women and children hacked down while the armed menfolk were away. In 1823 Austin procured the services of ten experienced fighters as a "ranging" company, a unit that is sometimes singled out as the forebear of the more celebrated Texas Rangers.

Most of Austin's Old Three Hundred boasted professional qualifications—doctors, lawyers, surveyors—a class of pioneer that the Spanish had failed for two centuries to plant in Texas. Many were well educated; one traveler was thunderstruck to hear a farmer slopping his hogs while reciting a Latin lesson: Tacitus. Another, hearing what sounded like a speech late one night emanating from alcalde Jimmy Whitesides' residence, crept close enough to hear Whitesides' sixteen-year-old son "rehearsing the address of the Scythian ambassador to Alexander the Great to an appreciative audience composed of the Negro boy, Will." Austin petitioned the Mexican legislature to provide a regular school system for his classically alluding populace, but failed. Instead, it was a frail, twenty-five-year-old Baptist missionary from Connecticut with the singularly appropriate name of Tom Pilgrim who partially solved Austin's education difficulty, opening a boys' academy in San Felipe in 1829. (His concomitant effort to teach a Sunday school was broken up, however, Protestant worship being illegal.)

In furtherance of his utopia, Austin as empresario had the power to grant extra allotments of land to those who brought extraordinary benefit to the colony. When the wealthy Jared Groce of Alabama determined to relocate his empire in Texas, Austin awarded him ten leagues of prime land. He rumbled across the Sabine with ninety slaves in fifty wagons and did more than anyone else to establish the cotton culture in the new colony, including building the first gin. The Groce family home, Liendo Plantation, still stands.

The great distances between the households quickly led to universal adoption of a strong ethic of hospitality. Later famous Texas Ranger John Salmon "Rip" Ford took particular note of it. "A more candid, friendly and hospitable population never occupied any country," he wrote. "A stranger was not allowed to pass a house without being invited to stop. No difference how long a guest remained, provided he minded his own business, he was entertained free of cost. If he asked for his bill he was told a repetition of the inquiry would be taken as an insult. The coffee pot was on the fire in nearly every house in the country from day-light till bed-time. A visitor was invited to take a cup—a refusal was not taken in good part." Such open-handed hospitality was not completely altruistic, of course. Strangers brought news of the outside world, and for a simple outlay of pork, cornbread, coffee, and the ubiquitous buttermilk, lonely families gained conversation late into the night.

Some early Texans did become full-time innkeepers, and did expect payment, which sometimes left travelers in a quandary. "The uncertainty we had often been in," wrote one diarist, "whether to pay or not, we had found embarrassing, and we had resorted to different devices to ascertain the humor of our hosts. Sometimes we would put a piece of money into the hands of a child, to see how the parent regarded it, and if we found it not likely to be well received, we could easily reclaim it."

The empresario's beloved older cousin, Mary Austin Holley, came to Texas to visit and wrote a travelogue that became something of a bestseller in the United States. "People live too far apart," she explained, "to beg or borrow often, and few trouble themselves to send anything to market. . . . They had rather give to you of their abundance." And while Mary Holley quickly mastered the intricacies of frontier barter, "there is a peculiar feeling among them about game. No one will receive money for any thing taken by his gun, but will cheerfully give you as much as you will take, and feel insulted, if you offer money in return." Being from the East, Mary Holley found this discomfiting, and believed that it hindered the development of regular, currency-based commerce. "It would be better for the public," she claimed, "if this feeling did not prevail, as provisions of this sort, could be furnished at so easy and cheap a rate." In a way she was correct, because with so much available for free, little was for sale, and what was for sale even of common commodities was fiercely expensive. Sweet potatoes, of which the rich earth yielded up to a quarter of a ton per acre, were sold in the few markets at a remarkable seventy-five cents per bushel.

"Flour was ten dollars a barrel," recorded one settler. "Trading vessels came in sometimes but few people had money to buy anything more than coffee and tobacco, which were considered absolutely indispensable. Money was as scarce as bread. There was no controversy about 'sound' money then. Pelts of any kind passed current and constituted the principal medium of exchange." Corn was by far the prevalent food crop; in fact children born in early Texas often grew up having never seen wheat flour, and had no idea what to do with biscuits when they saw them. Early Texas blacksmith Noah Smithwick recalled one youngster who, seeing his first batch of biscuits, which were prepared without baking powder and "doubtless heavy as lead," took two from the table, inserted a stick through their centers, and made an axle for a toy cart. Smithwick's recollection of those frontier biscuits was that they were "capable of sustaining a pretty heavy load."

In settling his families on their land, Austin was careful to give each family frontage on a river. With roads few and often impassable, riverboats plying the Colorado, the Brazos, and associated bayous were the easiest transportation. Often they published handbills of their itineraries, with lists of what goods were on board for sale, and those wishing to engage in commerce waited on the bank on a certain day. If one had no hides to trade, corn or tallow was accepted. The latter was one of the most precious commodities on the frontier; candles were so husbanded that one locally crafted holder featured a movable bottom that could be pushed up as the candle burned, so no wax would be wasted. Boarding schools levied a stiff surcharge for candles used during a student's term. The source of the hides and tallow, the abundant wild longhorns, had required no maintenance since being turned out by the conquistadors centuries before. "Cows and horses get their own living," wrote one observer; all one had to do was catch them and pen them. The potential for stock raising, as confirmed by generations of Spanish ranching heritage, was noticed by others. "Texas is, perhaps, one of the finest portions of the world for raising cattle," wrote a visiting Methodist missionary. "Provided for in the rich pastures of nature . . . some are making fortunes in this way, who could do perhaps but little in any other."

The settlements were, of course, offshoots of the antebellum culture of the American South, so much of the labor of actually clearing land and

planting cotton fell to the slaves. And while most of Austin's settlers undoubtedly worked hard, the men did come to expect a certain amount of
leisure time to hunt, smoke out bee trees, chase Indians, and talk politics.
The work of beginning a household fell much harder on the women, for
when they came it was often with very little. One famous saw was not far
from wrong, that Texas was "heaven for men and dogs, but hell for women
and oxen." Travelogues offered guidance on what to bring: mosquito netting
was indispensable, because muslin could not be obtained on the frontier;
mattresses were not, because the moss that hung thick from the live oaks
made superior stuffing. Small kitchen utensils were especially recommended, because a family once settled, finding itself overstocked, could
barter them profitably. Furniture was best brought from home, but space
should be saved by bringing it disassembled; housekeepers should bring
with them as much common clothing as they could manage. Fancy dress,
however, "is not wanted." One observer, a Kentucky lady of good family,
found the situation salutary. "Delicate ladies find they can be useful, and
need not be vain. . . . They discover in themselves, powers, they did not suspect themselves of possessing." With most married women toiling on their
rural leagues, social life in San Felipe was almost exclusively a male affair;
one resident noted that he did not know of a single party between 1828 and
1831 at which ladies were present. There were women as heads of households among the Old Three Hundred, though, and not just the tough Jane
H. W. Long. One Louisiana widow named McNutt, who had lost her fortune, came to Texas, started over, and made good marriages for her three
daughters. Such weddings were the principal social activity for the colonists
for some years.

One sticking point between Austin and most of his colonists was religion. Landholders were baptized as Catholics, but went through it with a
shrug and a wink. The Old Three Hundred were mostly Protestants raised
with a distrust of the Catholic priesthood, and with daily provision and survival the main occupation, a majority of the people in Texas didn't care about
religion one way or another. Austin took their conversion as a serious element of his contract with the Mexican authorities, but oddly, found himself
unable to procure a priest to administer sacraments. The Mexican Revolution had been phobically secular and nearly all the political leaders in Mexico were Masons, but three hundred years of Catholicism was not so easily
stamped out in either the people or the law. Thus, while Catholic baptism
was mandatory, no priest was assigned to minister to the Texas flock until
the Diocese of Monterrey dispatched Father Michael (Miguel) Muldoon in

1831. An Irishman ordained in Spain, he had been in Mexico for some ten years and was popular and well connected. He was also an easygoing tippler, which ensured his acceptance among the Texans, for by the time he arrived, the days of Austin being able to vouch for the character of each and every colonist were long gone. Muldoon was sensitive to the spiritual handicaps of his parish—isolation, vast distances, no priest for nearly a decade—and he administered a mild brand of Catholic practice such as validating bond betrothals, some of whose partners had been cohabiting for several years.

Many Anglo settlers found this arrangement particularly congenial. As one of them noted, "When a couple concluded to join their fortunes they forthwith repaired to the alcalde's office and had him draw up a bond to avail themselves of the priest's services whenever he came around; both parties signed the bond and went on their way as man and wife. . . . Then if they changed their minds before the priest got around, they had only to go together to the alcalde and demand the bond, which they tore to pieces and were free again."

Just about the time Padre Muldoon trekked into Texas to bend the elbow and bless people, the Protestant denominations back in the United States began concluding, with some justification, that Texas was a spiritual wasteland in need of proper missionaries. This was a time of important religious ferment in America, as the "Second Great Awakening" of backwoods revivalism began sweeping down the Ohio and Mississippi valleys, reaching the Gulf shortly after the American settlement of Texas gained momentum. Those who came to spread the Gospel soon found, as did Muldoon, that Texas' circumstances required a flexible style of evangelism.

Some even came without formal appointment. Sumner Bacon was an illiterate Army private from New England, on surveying duty in Arkansas, when he was overcome by the spirit at a Cumberland (Presbyterian) revival meeting, and announced that he would be a preacher. The Arkansas Presbytery suggested he get an education before seeking a preaching license, but Bacon could barely write before entering Texas in 1829, preaching and holding meetings one jump ahead of both the Mexican and the Presbyterian authorities. He applied to Austin in 1830 to become the colony's chaplain, but the empresario would have nothing to do with him. Denied a preaching license a second time in 1832, Bacon was befriended by Benjamin Chase, a fellow Presbyterian and representative of the American Bible Society. Chase made him the society's Texas agent, and after Bacon distributed some two thousand Bibles, the Louisiana Presbytery found a way to bend the rules, and ordained him in 1835. He went on to become chaplain of Texas' revolutionary army and one of Sam Houston's confidential couriers, and later that year organized the Texas Presbytery of the Cumberland Church. Other Protestants preached in Texas before Sumner Bacon, but he was the first to cultivate an ongoing ministry, which he accomplished despite the hostility not just of the wilderness and a Catholic government, but of his own denomination as well.

FIFTEEN

GONE TO TEXAS

FOR A TIME STEPHEN F. AUSTIN WAS ABLE TO CONTROL the flow of settlers into his colony. The "Baron" de Bastrop was presently elected to the state legislature, and to replace him Austin settled on Samuel May Williams of Rhode Island as his secretary and land commissioner. A scribe of faultlessly Spencerian penmanship, he was two years younger than Austin and also something of an authority on the workings of Spanish commerce, having been apprenticed to a Yankee merchant uncle at fifteen and sent to Buenos Aires to learn business.

Sam Williams quickly made himself indispensable to the overworked and lonely Austin, whose attachment to him became personal and deeply emotional. While Williams performed a variety of services to the colony, from postmaster to tax collector, Austin's awarding him eleven leagues of land, nearly fifty thousand acres, was probably as much a testament of personal affection as compensation. It was a love that Williams, as Austin learned to his grief at the end of his life, did not return in equal measure.

The Mexican colonization law did not apply exclusively to Austin, by any means. From the very first, in fact—from the time that Moses Austin won the acquiescence of Joaquín de Arredondo to the idea of an American colony in Texas—other American entrepreneurs had been lining up to be the next. One reason that Stephen Austin finally succeeded in Mexico City was that he was not the only would-be empresario stalking the halls of the Mexican congress. There were any number of others, floating similar and sometimes competing proposals.

The government made no secret of its preference that Mexicans come forward to establish colonies in Texas, but in this it had no more success than before, with one exception. A likely and welcome proposal was received from Don Martín de León, vastly wealthy, himself born in Tamaulipas but the son of grandees from Burgos. He was nearly sixty, a six-foot-tall Indian-fighting equestrian, and strangely, his award of an empresario contract was the fulfillment of a life's dream. He first applied for such a colony as early as 1807, but was turned down because his loyalty to Spain was doubted. The suspicion was well founded, as De León opposed Arredondo and the royalists during the Green Flag rebellion. After a safe exile, he started a ranch on the lower Guadalupe, and in 1824 he contracted to settle forty-one Mexican families on a coastal tract southwest of Austin's colony. He founded his capital in a town named for the then president, Guadalupe Victoria—later shortened to just Victoria.

In 1825 a third colony, bordering Austin's on the west but much smaller, and mistakenly overlapping De León's, was awarded to Green DeWitt, like Austin a Missourian. He was to settle four hundred Americans on the Guadalupe River, and while he issued land to enough people for a settlement to take, he defaulted on the four hundred and his contract was not renewed. Although his handwritten scrips were the first paper money in Texas, the colony eventually broke him, partly due to Comanche Indian attacks, and partly because Mexican law, policy, and sympathy favored De León in their endless land disputes. Still, his settlement at Gonzales became a leading early town.

Very early in the colonial land race, a consortium of investors in Nashville, Tennessee, sent an agent, Sterling Clack Robertson, to Mexico to secure a grant for them across El Camino Real, northwest of Austin's colony, to settle eight hundred families. He succeeded in 1825, and the following year an Englishman named Wavell and his American partner, Ben Milam, won a contract to settle five hundred families in the northeast. After settling his Old Three Hundred, Stephen Austin was not out of the game by any means; he was given leave to settle some nine hundred additional families on his original grant, which was still the largest in the province. When Sterling Robertson ran into difficulties and his contract was declared in default, it was awarded to Austin as well. Robertson protested and got it back, only to later see it go to Austin again. The land dispute between the two has passionate advocates, especially among their descendants, to this day. In partnership with Sam Williams, Austin also won a contract to settle eight hundred families in vacant land in north-central Texas. Within five years, the map of Texas was carved into a patchwork quilt of some twenty-five empresario colonies, entitled to settle some 8,000 families, nearly all of them Anglo-American.

Many schemes were never realized, but more often, Americans spilled across the border to squat on empty land, assuming that in Mexico they would have the same freedom of movement that they enjoyed in the United States. The Neutral Ground between the Sabine and the Neches had been a den of cutthroats for twenty years anyway. In Austin's original colony, settlers were required to swear out witnessed character certificates and show the ability to support themselves. By 1825 or 1826, Americans were pouring into Texas in such numbers that no one could control them; many came without benefit of sponsorship from an empresario. Austin found the situation dangerous and terrifying, but he tried mightily to exercise that patience and understanding he was so famous for. "I have had a mixed multitude to deal with," he explained in a letter, "collected from all quarters. Strangers to each other, to me, and to the laws and language of the country, they come here with all the ideas of americans and expect to see and understand the laws they are governed by, and many very many of them have all the licentiousness and wild turbulence of frontiersmen. Added to this when they arrive here the worst of the human passions avarice is excited to the highest extent."

Austin's accurate analysis of the problem did not make it go away. Immigrants came on in numbers, in any way they could. About a quarter of them entered Texas by sea, which usually meant taking a coastal schooner from New Orleans, but an inshore voyage did not necessarily translate into a smooth sail. Big gulf rollers often rocked a boat every mile of the way, and Southern landlubbers soon discovered the meaning of seasickness. John W. Dancy, a colonist and early legislator who became one of Texas' first railroad boosters, was such a victim. "After passing the mouth of the Mississippi," recalled a companion, "the swell of the open sea, though not rough, made Dancy deathly sick, and he lay about . . . on the deck in perfect abandon. The sailors passing fore and aft on duty were compelled to step over him so frequently that one of them became fretted and said to him, 'Get out of the way, or I'll throw you overboard,' to which Dancy replied, 'I wish you would.' "

Some ships were lost in storms; others ran aground as they tried to get "over the bar" into the mouths of rivers. Every year a couple of massive northers—frigid Canadian cold fronts—made it all the way to the coast, and when they did the effect was not to be forgotten. One coastal schooner full of immigrants was blown onto her starboard beam and stayed there, spars touching the water, until the terrified crew managed to loosen the sails and right her.

Most newcomers trekked by land, families or friends traveling together to the ferry crossing on the Sabine. "They travel ten or fifteen miles a day," wrote one observer, "stopping wherever night overtakes them. The masters are plainly dressed, often in homespun . . . generally dogged, surly, silent. The women are silent, too, frequently walking to relieve the teams." Many families came with slaves, whom the whites could only view in the stereotypes of the day, "the active cheery prime Negroes, not yet exhausted, with a joke and a suggestion about tobacco . . . the black pickininnies, staring, in a confused heap, out at the back of the wagon, more and more of their eyes to be made out among the table legs and bedding."

Slavery became a source of chronic discord between the governing authorities in Mexico, where it was illegal, and the American immigrants who came to plant cotton, which required slave labor if it was to be economical. Stephen Austin himself agonized over the institution of slavery, and disliked it, but could not see how a Southern-style economy could function without it. He also knew that any attempt by the government to divest his colonists of their human capital would lead to serious trouble. Largely through his diplomacy, Mexico interpreted its antislavery laws loosely as they applied to Texas. At first the state legislature tried to work a cumbersome regimen of dates from when existing slavery would be recognized, but then found it more practical to recognize labor "contracts" drawn up in "foreign countries," i.e., the United States, but banning trading in slaves and limiting terms of servitude to ten years.

When enough cutthroats and fugitives from the law lived in any one location, life could be hell. While Rip Ford had been enchanted with what he found in early Texas, another immigrant who became no less famous a Ranger, William A. A. "Big Foot" Wallace, was mortified. When he arrived in Texas several years after Austin's Old Three Hundred, he wrote to his family in Virginia: "Such a sight I never saw. . . . The water is scarcely fit to drink and no timber scarcely worth naming. . . . And worse society could not be found on the globe people kill each other here every day. . . . I would not stay if all my relations were here and I beg of you never to come to Texas. . . . I would rather see a sister of mine in the grave than in Texas." He changed his mind about leaving, of course, and by the time the frontier closed this descendant and namesake of William Wallace the Highlander had left new legends to embellish his distinguished family name.

Back in the United States, so many people decamped ahead of the local sheriffs that it became axiomatic throughout the South that, when a cabin was found deserted, the initials G.T.T. scratched on the door meant "Gone to Texas." When Texas progressed enough to have newspapers, those back east who had in some way been stung by those who had Gone to Texas wrote west to warn future victims by having accounts published of their previous capers. One barely legible missive from Wayne County, Tennessee, gives some idea of the hard feelings that could be left in their wake:

Dr sir I take this moment to inform you of a little circumstance which hapened in this county not long since a man by the name of

John A. Crimes married a girl by the name of Marie and a Mr. James P. Gray married her sister then settled near each other in Wayne City & about 15 months since Crimes wife died & Grays wife agreed to keep his children for one of his children was only a few weeks old & Grays wife had one about the same age. Crimes soon after wards went to live there himself. Each of them had seven & not long since Crimes took Gray's wife & cut for Texas He was a man that had stood fair in our county also but such an act might not be countenanced Please show this to some of your editors and have it published so as to give society an oportunity of garding against such a villain. They stole away by night and left Gray & all 14 children fast asleep and they was both in the methodist church. Crimes was clerk of our county court before his elopement to Texas. I will describe him in part he is about 35 years of age very dark rather of a [illegible] dresses tolerable well & rather fond of his liquor. His woman tolerable fair, eyes rather large & appears to fly about so as to denote what she has turned out to be. They took with them one negro man three horses & their saddles & bridles.

Against the growing milieu of anti-Catholic, anti-Latin, frontier American arrogance, it was inevitable that some incident would arise to challenge the authority of the government in a direct way. It happened in Nacogdoches at the end of 1826. Haden Edwards was a fifty-five-year-old Kentuckian, a land speculator from a family of land speculators. In 1825 he was awarded an empresario contract to settle eight hundred families on a sprawling grant in East Texas that included the old town of Nacogdoches. He arrived in September to face a situation with the land titles that was even more complicated than Austin had to administer, for Edwards, assisted by his younger brother Benjamin, was required to respect the rights of settlers on Spanish grants, some of whom dated back to Gil y Barbo. His grant also took in the roughneck squatters in the old Neutral Ground, plus about thirty families bound for Austin's colony who stopped short, and also a branch of Cherokee Indians, who were being pushed out of their old homes in Tennessee and the Carolinas and were settling in the area north of Nacogdoches.

Where Austin would have begun with tactful inquiry, the Edwardses turned the colony into their cash cow, charging fees higher than the colonization law allowed, and browbeating old Spanish families to produce their papers or pay Edwards for the land anew. Complaints swiftly reached San Antonio, on to Saltillo, and on to Mexico City. The *jefe político*, the appointed chief civil administrator, in San Antonio invalidated many of Edwards' actions; Edwards sought to trump him by forcing an election for alcalde, one of whose legal functions was to settle land disputes, and running his son-in-law for the position. He won, but the authorities disallowed votes cast by nonfranchised squatters and awarded the election to the candidate favored by the old Spanish families. When he began hearing the cases, most were decided against Edwards. Edwards refused to comply. Old settlers were arrayed against the new, and in June the president declared the contract forfeit and ordered the Edwardses out of the country. Word of this did not reach Texas for months.

Setting up his colony had cost Haden Edwards about $50,000, and he would not give up easily. In November, he arranged for a little legal drama. He was to be arrested, along with his rivals, the alcalde and the militia chief. All were to be tried for corruption. Edwards was to be acquitted and the other two were to be condemned, but paroled on the condition that they resign. This little sideshow came to naught when word arrived that Lieutenant Colonel Mateo Ahumada was marching from San Antonio with 130 troops to clean house. With their colonial hopes fading, the Edwardses had one card left to play. On December 16, 1826, with Haden Edwards back in the United States to tend to business matters, Benjamin Edwards and about thirty ruffians rode into Nacogdoches, seized the Stone Fort, and unfurled a white-and-red banner reading INDEPENDENCE, LIBERTY, JUSTICE.

Five days later, Ben Edwards' cockamamie declaration of independence, which was modeled vaguely on the United States document, with a heavy dash of contractual drafting and survey notes, was penned with all the venom of an outwitted shyster. Claiming that they had endured "repeated insults, treachery and oppression [by] an imbecile, faithless and despotic government, miscalled a Republic," they declared into existence the Republic of Fredonia, stretching from the Sabine to the Rio Grande. The same document also contained a treaty with the Cherokee Indians—actually a disaffected splinter group who had no authority to deal—with whom the Edwards brothers agreed to split the new country fifty-fifty, Anglos south of a line and Indians north. The Edwards brothers made certain that newspapers in the United States heard of their doings, and frontier jingoes who thought they heard the ring of democracy published yards of newspaper columns in support—to the shock and consternation of Mexico.

Austin saw in the Fredonian Rebellion not just the ruin of the Edwards brothers and their empresario contract, but potentially the quashing of all Anglo settlement in Mexican Texas, and he was appalled. He was not, however, entirely without obligation to Haden Edwards. The rich old man had been working the congresses in Mexico City at the same time Austin had, and Austin in his poverty had sometimes turned to Edwards for money. When Austin first heard of the trouble brewing in Nacogdoches, he wrote both brothers patient and laborious letters, urging them to govern with a lighter hand and attempting to explain the complex colonization law to them. Benjamin Edwards answered brusquely that Austin had little understanding of human nature.

Once the Fredonians declared themselves in rebellion, Austin's course was clear. On the first day of 1827 he informed his colonists of the Nacogdoches rebellion fomented by a "small party of infatuated madmen." He admonished them of their responsibility to the Mexican government, and asked for volunteers to march with Ahumada to suppress the rebellion. When the Mexican force entered Nacogdoches on January 31, Austin and a hundred Anglo militia were at Ahumada's side, but the Edwards brothers and most of their backers had fled across the Sabine into the safety of Louisiana.

The Cherokees found and killed the two pretenders who attached them to the conspiracy; Ahumada was able to round up about twenty pro-Edwards Americans who had been involved in the insurgency and prepared to have them tried. Austin, however, now turned and exercised his influence to spare the lives of the guilty. He succeeded, except in the case of Adolphus Sterne, a twenty-five-year-old German Jewish draft dodger who had gone into the mercantile business in New Orleans. A recent émigré to Nacogdoches, he had not only sworn his oath of loyalty to Mexico, but had been awarded a contract to vend supplies to the sizable garrison there. Mexican agents in New Orleans had discovered Sterne smuggling lead, powder, and gunflints to the Edwards faction in barrels of coffee and packets of dry goods.

Sterne was tried and sentenced to death, but capital sentences had to be confirmed by the military commandant, General Manuel de Mier y Terán, in Saltillo. Sterne was imprisoned in the Stone Fort to await the decision, but as he already "enjoyed the friendship of his guards . . . his cheerful deportment satisfied them that he would not try to escape." His chain was clamped around one of his boots, which were so loose as to slip easily on and off. As Sterne's son recalled, "One evening his guards locked the doors of his room and went to a fandango. Left alone, he drew the boot off his chained leg and the chain with it. Then he arose and washed, went out through a window, proceeded to his store, dressed himself properly, and made his way also to the fandango. There he found his guards, who were much startled by his arrival; but he and they promised not to inform against each other and all were easy." After the dance, Sterne resumed his prison garb, entered the *cuartel* through the same window, and pulled on the shackled boot once more.

Sterne's joviality during confinement was not misplaced, for despite his undoubted guilt, there was one large factor working in his favor: he was a Mason, and his connections in New Orleans were already interceding for him with Mier y Terán, who was also a Mason. Old Texas hands claimed it was untrue that a Mason would never allow a brother to be punished when he could prevent it, but as one admitted, "in the case of purely political offenses, Masonry has frequently been the means of saving life." In Sterne's case, he was paroled on his honor never again to bear arms against Mexico or aid its enemies.

SIXTEEN

A FINGER IN THE DIKE

WHILE AUSTIN HIMSELF WAS ALMOST UNIVERSALLY RE-
spected in Mexico, the government viewed the growing unruliness in the
colonies with alarm. In the wake of the Fredonian uprising, Mexico sent one
of its premier officers to Texas to report on conditions. He was the same man
who had just paroled Adolphus Sterne. General Manuel de Mier y Terán,
thirty-nine, was a mining engineer by training but also a successful naviga-
tor of the revolutions and juntas that rose and fell. A man of conscience, he
was often gloomy and depressed but effective once he turned his mind to action. He had fought for independence from Spain as early as 1811, and supported the rise of Iturbide ten years later. Mier y Terán had been a brigadier
for three years, was a former minister of war, and was familiar with the
labyrinth of the colonization laws, having served on that committee as a
member of the first constituent congress. He knew Stephen Austin well and
they were on very good terms.

Every time the government in Mexico City sensed trouble in the distant
province, they sent someone to inspect and report. Mier y Terán, however,
came with the second specific assignment of ascertaining the northeast
boundary between Mexico and the United States, for at some place the
boundary of the Sabine River must cross in a surveyed line to the boundary
of the Red River. He was also to use the opportunity to conduct a geographical exploration of the region, and he was accompanied by a naturalist, a geologist, and an artist-mapmaker. Most importantly, he was to estimate the
actual numbers and assess the attitudes of the American colonists.

Traveling with his staff in an enormous, silver-inlaid coach, it took three
and a half months for Mier y Terán and his Boundary Commission to
progress from Mexico City to San Antonio, where they arrived on March 1,
1828. They were in Austin's capital at San Felipe by the 27th, and reached
restive Nacogdoches on June 3, and three weeks later he completed a devas-
tating letter to President Guadalupe Victoria. General Mier y Terán looked
deeply into the trouble that was Texas, and no more perceptive assessment
had ever been composed by anybody. "I must ask your forbearance for this
long letter," he wrote the president, "but I desire to forward you at once my

observations of this country and not withhold them until the day when I make full report to the government, for fear the time for remedy will be past."

One thing he noted was the dangerous chemistry of the mix of populations, composed of "strange and incoherent parts without parallel in our federation." There were Indians, just then at peace, but still warlike and threatening. The American colonists he found "more progressive and better informed than the Mexican inhabitants, but also more shrewd and unruly." There was a strong mutual respect between him and Austin, and his opinion of most American newcomers mirrored that of Austin. Of the empresario's own settlers, "they are for the most part industrious and honest, and appreciate this country." Among the flood of newcomers, however, "are fugitives from justice, honest laborers, vagabonds and criminals, but honorable and dishonorable alike travel with their political constitutions in their pockets," he sniped, and they were heedless of the fact they were no longer in the United States and did not enjoy the same political rights. Many of them, he said, were land speculators, dealing sharply and sometimes dishonestly. And the only thing that kept more of them from coming was that slavery was illegal in Texas. Those slaves that did come, under the loose rules of Texas, soon realized that the Mexican government would free them if it could. This made them restive at their labor, and thus subject to greater cruelty from their masters. He detailed cases of slaves who had been set on by dogs, had their teeth pulled, and been whipped until their backs were laid open. Terán was firm in his conviction that if slavery were legalized, "which God forbid—in a few years Texas would be a powerful state which could compete in productions and wealth with Louisiana."

And that, in turn, would poison the easygoing poverty of the Mexican population in Texas: the friction between them and the Americans he outlined in detail. In truth, he said, he could not blame the foreigners for looking down on the native Mexicans, because the only Mexicans in East Texas were "what is in all countries called the lowest class—the very poor and the ignorant," and were actually content to remain so. It made him ashamed, he wrote the president, that most Americans had never seen any Mexicans other than these. He noted conditions in the old Neutral Ground, populated by men who were "ready to cross and recross the [Sabine] as they see the necessity of separating themselves from the country in which they have just committed some crime."

Mier y Terán also scrupulously noted political reasons for growing discontent on the part of the legitimate colonists—the capital of the state was too far away, in Saltillo, to rely on for justice, leaving them prey to the "petty pickpocketing that they suffer from a venal and ignorant alcalde. . . . Neither are there civil authorities or magistrates; one insignificant little man—not to say more—who is called an *alcalde,* and an *ayuntamiento* that does not convene once in a lifetime."

Mier y Terán's assessment of the situation in East Texas was keen, right down to his conclusion: "Therefore I am warning you to take timely measures. Texas could throw the whole nation into revolution." He recommended several specific steps, the most important of which was to take every chance to encourage emigration from the interior of Mexico into Texas—a tack that had never worked in the past. To accomplish this he even suggested posting convict-soldiers in Texas, with encouragement to stay and settle after their time was served. He also suggested the Swiss and Germans as possible new sources of immigrants. Rather than depend solely on American labor and capital for development in Texas, he recommended that coastal trade between Texas and the rest of Mexico be encouraged. Consideration of Mier y Terán's recommendations was postponed due to another round of political turmoil. Guadalupe Victoria was out, replaced by the election of the centralist Gómez Pedraza. He never took office, however, since he was overturned in a coup d'etat by the federalist Vicente Guerrero. Guerrero just had time to re-outlaw slavery in Mexico and cause a new uproar in Texas, although he was finally talked into exempting the state of Coahuila y Tejas from the emancipation by fellow federalist José María Viesca, who believed Texas could best be saved by economic progress, for which some continuation of slavery was essential. Guerrero was soon toppled by the centralist Anastacio Bustamante, who was ruthless enough to last awhile, and it was his government that finally considered Terán's proposals. All were incorporated into *la Ley,* the Law, of April 6, 1830.

Its promulgation fell to Bustamante's foreign relations minister, Lucas Alamán y Escalada, who adopted Terán's recommendations virtually intact, but then went the general one better in a provision that fueled more fear and discontent in Texas than anything else up to that time. In Article Eleven, he suspended all empresario contracts not already fulfilled, and prohibited "emigrants from nations bordering on this Republic" from settling in Mexican states bordering their country of origin, "under any pretext whatever." Almost equally unpalatable, from the point of view of the American colonists, was the appropriation of half a million pesos to settle Mexican convict-soldiers and their families in Texas, to construct permanent military fortifications.

SEVENTEEN

ALMOST A BLACK COLONY

THE CHILL FELT THROUGHOUT THE AMERICAN COLONIES
in Texas by enactment of the Law of April 6 was quickly confirmed. Austin's
pernicious leatherstockings would ignore it entirely, but Mexico seemed
dead serious about enforcing it. Contemporaneously with its passage the
government constructed Fort Tenoxtitlán, at a strategic location on the Brazos River at the San Antonio Road crossing. Two more new posts were located on the coast, at Anahuac, near Galveston, and Velasco, at the mouth of
the Brazos. Existing garrisons at Nacogdoches, San Antonio, and Goliad
were beefed up; this included the importation of convict-soldiers.

Austin realized that he had to try to get at least the most offensive elements of the law repealed. Bustamante had not yet shown the rigor of his
centralism, and Austin enjoyed a cordial relationship with him. Ironically,
Austin learned of the Law of April 6 the very same day he received a letter of
support from the new president. He quickly wrote a diplomatically per-
plexed letter to Bustamante, wondering how to weigh a decree that seemed
"to destroy in one blow the happiness and prosperity of this colony which
Your Excellency has always protected."

Fortunately for Austin, and for Texas, enforcement of the Law of April 6
lay with a newly appointed commissioner, who proved to be Terán himself.
The able (and wily) general had refused the job of minister of war in Bustamante's government, to keep his post of commandant of the Eastern Interior. Austin could rely on Mier y Terán's friendship, but the terms of the
decree were so specific that he could do little to help the other colonies. He
did arrive at a saving interpretation of Article Eleven, to which he won
Terán's acquiescence. Instead of nullifying all empresario contracts that
were not completed, the term was softened to spare contracts under which
a hundred families or more had already been located. Only two Anglo
colonies qualified, his own and that of Green DeWitt. It wasn't much, but it
was something, and it allowed the population of Austin's colony to increase
from 4,248, just after passage of the decree, to 5,665 the following year.

Other American colonizers proved equally savvy at finding loopholes.
The prohibitions of the *Ley* did not extend to non-Anglo American foreign-

ers. To take advantage of that provision, the Galveston Bay and Texas Land Company brought prominent Mexican liberal Lorenzo de Zavala into their organization, hoping that his nationality would extend to the rest of their colony near Galveston. At first Mexico refused to recognize the evasion; the scale of speculation that attended this particular grant was probably a factor. Eventually the government relented, and more than 900 families were settled on the "De Zavala" grant. Further, the hard times wrought on most of the Anglo colonies encouraged settlement in those founded by non-Americans, particularly two Irish colonies started in the territory between Austin's grant and the Nueces River. The town of San Patricio—the Hispanicized version of St. Patrick—anchored settlement in that lonely section of the province. Austin and Sam Williams themselves tried to keep step with the times. When they were placed in receivership of the failed Sterling Robertson colony, they stated their intention to settle Mexican and European families on it. That scheme never took off, first, because most Mexicans were still not interested in settling in Texas and Austin lacked the contacts to attract European immigration, and second, because Robertson was mounting a furious counterattack to prove that he had, indeed, established a hundred families on his grant and deserved protection under the same artful interpretation that protected Austin and Green DeWitt.

Some Mexican authorities also came to suspect they may have acted with too great a sweep, for they received a late application for a new American colony that actually piqued their sympathy. It was from Benjamin Lundy, a Quaker abolitionist who sought land on which to settle freed American slaves. Lundy was born in New Jersey, but after he undertook his campaign to end slavery he was so peripatetic that he could hardly be pinned to a place of residence. In 1821 he began publishing the first emancipation journal in the United States, and he was instrumental in recruiting able younger people to the movement, including William Lloyd Garrison. Lundy opposed sending slaves back to the savagery of Africa, but he had traveled to study the possibility of starting colonies of freedmen in Canada and even Haiti, whose government responded with encouragement. Texas offered the most complete solution for his agenda: slavery was illegal, the black colonists would be living in a Southern climate where much of the land was richly suited to agriculture, and they would not be oceans removed from the roots and culture they had known. Also, a demonstration colony there would be more visible to his backers both moral and financial in the East.

Lundy arrived in Texas in spring of 1833 but immediately ran, barrier by barrier, into all the bureaucratic obstacles that Austin had confronted a dozen years earlier—with the added complication that he was so well known as an abolitionist that he felt obliged to travel incognito through the American settlements. His journey to Monclova was a nightmare; he had little money, and often had to take temporary employment—he was a skilled leatherworker—to earn money for the next leg of his journey. The only good news he received was that the *Ley* of April 6 would eventually be repealed. However, he was dismayed when the secretary of state of Coahuila y Tejas, Santiago del Valle, showed no warmth to Lundy's idea. Slavery might be illegal in Mexico, Lundy finally understood, but in the government's—or at least Del Valle's—view, the "degraded condition" of the Negroes made them poor candidates for citizenship. The benign neglect of the Negro, with its attendant hypocrisy, was a phenomenon that Lundy was intimately familiar with in the North. Stalemated, he returned home when his meager finances finally petered out.

With the stubbornness of the abolitionist, however, he returned the next year, and this time made an important ally in Colonel Juan Almonte, one of Mexico's ablest officers. Said but not proven to be the illegitimate son of the famous cleric Father José María Morelos and an Indian woman, he was thirty-one, spoke English that had been perfected on a diplomatic mission to Great Britain, and had taken active part in Mexico's political upheavals, always choosing the side on which he believed the higher principles lay. He accompanied Lundy west from San Felipe, eventually arriving at Monclova and receiving heartbreaking news. After well over a year's absence, the colonial application he had left with the governor still lay unacted upon. "After all my hardships and perils," he wrote a friend, "I am completely baffled in my attempts to establish colonies in Texas." All he felt now was "total disappointment, conscious poverty, and remediless despair." It was the resourceful Almonte who propped him up again with an ingenious solution. The governor had refused to act because the Mexican congress was considering a renewal of anti-American sanctions in Texas. Why bother with Texas at all, Almonte argued, when the sanctions would apply only there? Why not seek a grant of land in Tamaulipas, the next state to the south, still within reach of Texas but with greater political advantages? Lundy took his advice and traveled to the Tamaulipan capital of Matamoros, at the mouth of the Rio Grande, where he met a large number of resident American free Negroes who proved closely interested in his plan. With the help of Almonte and others, Lundy eventually won a colonial grant to settle 250 families on 138,000 acres in the Nueces Strip, that stretch of brush country north of the Rio Grande and south of the Nueces. Lundy was further elated to learn that as empresario, he would enjoy such financial advantages as would lift him out of his grinding poverty and even make him wealthy; he had two years to make the colony work. Financially broke and physically exhausted, but with renewed hope, he returned to the United States to raise money and settlers.

Lundy's eventual failure to do so was attributable in large part to infighting within the abolitionist movement. His erstwhile protégé, William Lloyd Garrison, came to oppose the establishment of any freedmen's colonies on any foreign soil, on the grounds that it undercut the movement to expeditiously emancipate slaves within the United States. If some of them had a place to go, the pressure would be lightened to free them all. Garrison worked effectively to cut off Lundy's support, and did it so successfully that Lundy served jail time for debt. That betrayal did nothing, however, to ameliorate Lundy's hatred for the slaveholding establishment in Texas, and when plans for a colony of freed slaves were permanently quashed by the success of the 1836 revolution, Lundy would rise to exact a revenge that made Texas' diplomatic life miserable for nearly a decade.

EIGHTEEN

FLASHPOINT DOUSED

AMONG THE LEGAL DIFFICULTIES FACING TEXAS WAS THE impending loss of a tax exemption that the Mexican republic had granted to Austin's and then the other colonies in recognition of the economic difficulties that came with starting from nothing. Economic conditions in Texas were suffocatingly bad, but pleas to extend the tax break fell on deaf ears. The only bright spot that Austin saw in the situation was that the man who must enforce the tax collection was, again, Manuel de Mier y Terán.

Sadly for Austin, and for Texas, Bustamante hardened into a centralist strongman. Mier y Terán was now serving in a government less sympathetic to the needs of Anglo colonies, and he was compelled to dispatch two collectors to Texas to begin levying port duties. His actions were perceived as a crackdown, which was a bit unfair, but the two men he sent to East Texas to do the job were Mexicanized adventurers grievously ill-suited to the delicate task.

George (Jorge) Fisher was really a Hungarian-born Serb named Djordje Ribar. A turbulent spirit, Ribar fought briefly in the Serbian revolution and sailed to America under indenture. Having no money there, he fled his bond, took his American name, and thought about joining the expedition of James Long. He visited Mexico in 1825, and although he was denied an empresario contract, he became a naturalized citizen four years later and eventually got a contract to reorganize the colonial mess left by Haden Edwards and the Fredonians at Nacogdoches. Terán had just made him administrator of the port of Galveston when enaction of the Law of April 6 compelled the commandant to close the port. Fisher then won appointment in Austin's colony as secretary to the ayuntamiento, but was soon run off under suspicion of being a spy for Guerrero. With the expiration of Texas' tax breaks, Terán sent him back to Galveston in November 1831. Fisher crossed the locals at every turn. He decreed that all ships leaving ports east of the Brazos had to clear through his new customs house at Anahuac, at the mouth of the Trinity. This placed an onerous burden on sea captains and merchants to either navigate an extra passage through treacherous and shallow Galveston and Trinity bays, or travel up to two hundred miles overland to pay their duties.

The owner of a small ship, the *Sabine,* was a local hothead named Edwin Waller. The vessel lay in port at Velasco, a settlement that was growing up around the customs house newly planted at the mouth of the Brazos. Waller refused the order to put in at Anahuac, although he did offer to pay a duty of fifty dollars to the commandant of the fort there at Velasco. That officer declined, but hinted that a duty of a hundred dollars might spring him out of the harbor. Furious, Waller put to sea, wounding a Mexican soldier in the exchange of fire as the vessel slipped over the bar. Fisher had ordered all traffic through Anahuac at Terán's direction, but his truculence and inflexibility led to further trouble with the Anglo Texans and he withdrew to Matamoros, where he began publishing a newspaper.

Greater trouble was caused by Fisher's superior, John (Juan) Davis Bradburn, a Virginian of forty-three at the time the Law of April 6 was promulgated. A career revolutionary, he was involved in the Green Flag revolt, fought with American insurgents in Mexico, served under Guerrero as a go-between with Iturbide, and in 1830 held the rank of lieutenant colonel. Terán tapped him for garrison commander at the new post of Anahuac. The principal object of his tenure was enforcement of the Law of April 6, under which guise he arrested the local land commissioner, Francisco Madero, and his surveyor, José María Carbajal, for continuing to issue land titles to immigrants. He also began issuing orders to the commandant of Nacogdoches, Colonel José de las Piedras, with dubious authority; he seized local slaves for labor without compensating the owners and confiscated supplies for use of the garrison. The latter two acts were not out of line with regular Mexican military practice, but they went down hard with American colonists who, as Terán had already noted, were prickly about the rights they claimed in their vest-pocket constitutions.

In May 1832, Bradburn arrested a local lawyer named William Barret Travis, who had been hired by the owner of the confiscated slaves to recover them. Bradburn was holding them in "protective custody" as runaways, and Travis attempted to inveigle Bradburn into releasing them with bogus letters alluding to an approaching armed force. When another prominent local, Patrick Jack, demanded Travis' release, Bradburn arrested him as well. Word spread like a grassfire, and before long 150 angry colonists were surging toward the Anahuac garrison. Unbowed, Bradburn sent out a squadron of cavalry to disperse them, but they were instead captured, and the Texans used them as bait to effect an exchange of prisoners. When Bradburn agreed, the colonists released the cavalry, only to discover that Bradburn had used the interlude to fortify his position and train his cannon on the town. He had no intention of releasing Jack and Travis.

One force of Texans, led by Stephen F. Austin's cousin John, headed to Velasco to seize a small armory there. That post's commander, Colonel Domingo de Ugartechea, refused, and in a sharp little action that became known as the "Lexington of Texas," five Texans and ten Mexicans fell before Ugartechea surrendered. Bradburn meanwhile sent for aid from the commandant at Nacogdoches, Colonel Piedras. The latter responded by leading a detachment swiftly down to the coast, but instead of reinforcing Bradburn, Piedras, sensibly believing the situation too volatile to be allowed to degenerate any further, negotiated with the colonists, persuaded Bradburn to resign and leave, and finally freed Travis and Jack.

The so-called Anahuac Disturbances displayed in detail all the weaknesses of Mexican administration in Texas. It was true that both Fisher and Bradburn had acted within the scope of their powers and discretion as Mexican officers. But their intemperate and ill-advised use of that power outraged Anglo Texans who would have had difficulty accepting that any government had such power. It was also true that Fisher and Bradburn were enforcing national decrees, but in a state, Coahuila y Tejas, whose government was often poised counter to national policy. Mexico's ongoing struggle between centralists and federalists made the situation in Texas even more confusing and volatile. Nevertheless, the Texans at Anahuac and Velasco had now committed themselves, firing on and killing Mexican soldiers. That could only be regarded as treason, and now they learned of the approach of a Mexican army of four hundred under command of Colonel José Antonio Mexía.

What saved the colonists was that at this juncture, the government in Mexico was about to change yet again. In opposition to the iron centralism of Bustamante there arose a federalist general, a national hero for defeating an attempted Spanish invasion in 1829: Antonio López de Santa Anna, the same man who as a cadet had been schooled in ruthless warfare under Arredondo in Texas. As news of the violence at Anahuac spread, Mexía with his federalist army was near Matamoros to engage a centralist army loyal to Bustamante. The two commanders agreed to a truce so that common cause could be waged against the Texas rebels.

Mexía had declared himself a Santanista, and as he marched northward he was accompanied by Stephen F. Austin, who did some fast talking to convince Mexía that the men at Anahuac and Velasco were not in rebellion but in sympathy with him. As he approached the scene of the trouble, Mexía offered the Texans a choice: if they were rebels or were contending for independence, they must be punished with all the force of the law. But, if they cared to also declare for Santa Anna, they would be welcomed as brothers in arms.

From Anahuac the Texans withdrew a distance up Turtle Bayou to consider what was best to do, which, thanks to further arm-twisting from Austin, was just long enough to draft the Turtle Bayou resolutions, declaring in pertinent part "that we view with feelings of the deepest interest and solicitude, the firm and manly resistance, which is made by the highly talented and distinguished Chieftain, General Santa Anna, to the numberless Incroachments and infractions, which have been made by the present administration, upon the constitution and law of our adopted and beloved country." Mexía was welcomed as a conquering hero at Brazoria, a town established in 1828 by John Austin on his land grant about fifteen miles above the mouth of the Brazos. With a dinner, a ball, and a salute boomed from the captured cannon, the Anahuac business was allowed to slide. The only American to be dismayed by the development was he who had engineered the events, and the only one who could see the larger picture: Stephen F. Austin. For ten years he had kept Texas scrupulously neutral in Mexico's violent intestine commotions, and now they had been forced to choose sides. He was pleased that Travis and Jack and the others had saved their skins, but no good could come from involving Texas in the fratricidal discord.

In an odd kind of tandem of emotion, dismay was also felt, though of a different nature, by General Mier y Terán. His instincts were as progressive as any in the Mexican army; he had shared Santa Anna's honors in the fight against the Spanish, but now he was serving a centralist government that was tottering. He knew Santa Anna better than the jubilant Texans, and while the two were still friendly, they were beginning to separate politically, and perhaps he knew what to expect of Santa Anna's enmity. Upon news of Mexía's victories and advance into Texas, General Manuel de Mier y Terán dressed in his full uniform, went to the churchyard where Iturbide had been shot, and fell, Roman-like, on his sword. He was only forty-three. "How could we expect to hold Texas when we do not even agree among ourselves," he wrote in a last letter. "What will become of Texas? Whatever God wills."

Events were not long in proving Austin's foreboding correct. Colonel Piedras, back in Nacogdoches, fearful that a repeat of the Anahuac Disturbances might flare there, issued an order for the townsmen to disarm. He should have known better; he himself had been a witness of Bradburn's intemperance and seen the result. Between July 28 and August 2, 1832, more than a hundred Anglo volunteers converged on Nacogdoches from all the surrounding settlements. They elected as their captain James W. Bullock, an American Army veteran who had fought under Andrew Jackson at New Orleans. Bullock sent Piedras an ultimatum to revoke his order, and as Mexía had done farther south, called for him to declare loyalty to Santa Anna. When Piedras, who had about 350 troops at his command, refused, Bullock's militia entered the town but were soon chased off by Mexican cavalry. The Americans then surrounded the town, following the directions of town merchant Adolphus Sterne to circle back via Lanana Creek and reenter behind the Mexican barricades. Mindful of his Fredonian parole, however, Sterne did not himself bear a gun.

Piedras stationed troops in his headquarters, known as the Red House, as well as in the Stone Fort and a church. In house-to-house combat during the afternoon of August 2, Piedras' troops suffered a severe beating; he evacuated his men during the night to retreat to San Antonio. Anglo Texans set out after them on the morning of August 3 and overtook them on the Angelina River; after a running battle Piedras' soldiers mutinied, and effected a surrender. Under the watchful eye of one of the Texans, an already-famous Mississippi frontiersman named Jim Bowie, the remnant of Piedras' force marched to San Antonio and disbanded. The centralist Piedras himself was put at the disposal of Austin, who issued him a parole and safe conduct back to Mexico. The Anglo Texans had lost three killed and five wounded, one mortally; Piedras had lost nearly fifty. In the August heat, no one wanted the detail of burying the bodies, and Mexican soldiers who fell in the town were thrown down wells, which were filled in. Sterne recognized Masonic brothers among the dead Mexican officers, though, and had them buried in the Spanish cemetery with some dignity.

Many Mexicans had been killed in the upper story of the Red House, and in later years, after the structure was incorporated into Nacogdoches University, an important student rite was to creep into the attic and look at the bloodstains, which were never cleaned. It was the locals' way of remembering an engagement that was in its way more important than the Anahuac Disturbances themselves, for it stripped Mexican military power from the whole eastern section of Texas.

NINETEEN

SAM HOUSTON, LATE OF TENNESSEE

AS DESTABILIZING AS THE ANAHUAC DISTURBANCES were, events far more incendiary for Texas were taking place in Washington, D.C., at exactly the same time. Andrew Jackson was sworn in as the American president in March 1829. Like his predecessors, he was alive to the issue of acquiring Texas; he had longed for years to add the potentially rich and geographically important province to the Union. Throughout his first term he sought by various means to purchase it, but his diplomatic style could be most charitably described as rustic, and his ham-handed attempts to snatch Texas had not only come to naught, but when paired with the nonstop incursions of filibusters, had also aroused Mexico's hostile suspicion. After three years of frustration, Jackson saw a fresh opportunity stride into the White House in the form of Sam Houston, his onetime Tennessee political protégé and heir.

Houston was already a frontier legend and one of the most famous men in America, although considered in respectable circles to be as unsavory as he was colorful. He was born in Virginia, but moved to Tennessee at thirteen when his mother was widowed. In the Appalachian foothill town of Maryville, Houston discovered that he hated working on the family farm, and hated clerking in the family store even worse; at sixteen he ran away to live with Cherokee Indians on an island in the Hiwassie River. He remained with them for three years, was adopted by their chief, and learned to speak the language and hunt with a bow, preferring, as he told siblings who came to fetch him home, to measure deer tracks instead of dry goods. He joined the army at twenty to fight in the War of 1812, and his valor gained the favor of Andrew Jackson during a campaign against Creek Indians, where Houston received three grievous wounds that bled and drained for the rest of his life.

As Jackson's protégé he rose through Tennessee state offices to serve two terms in Congress, during which he met two elder legends of the American Revolution, Thomas Jefferson and the Marquis de Lafayette, and became that most tragic of miscasts, a Southern Unionist. In 1827 he began a successful term as governor of Tennessee, recognized also as Jackson's chief political lieutenant, and was often mentioned as Old Hickory's successor to the White House—a destiny made the more promising by a brilliant wedding to a politically connected Tennessee belle named Eliza Allen. Disaster struck, and the course of American history changed, when she did the unthinkable: she rebelled at being married off to a man she did not love. Eliza deserted Houston after barely two months of marriage and returned to her family. Ruined both socially and politically, Houston resigned the governor's office and sought refuge with the Cherokees among whom he had lived as a boy. They were then living in the Verdigris River country near Fort Gibson, in what is now Oklahoma. He stayed with them for another three years, damaging his former social standing even more by taking a Cherokee wife, by native custom and without Christian sacrament. Suffering from malaria and alcoholism, his state of mind careened from being able to undertake useful diplomatic errands in their behalf to periods of such abject despondency that his wife, Diana Rogers, often had to carry him home from Fort Gibson slung over his horse. His adopted people stripped him of his Cherokee name, The Raven, and derisively addressed him (in Osage, insultingly) as Oo-tse-tee Ar-dee-tah-skee, meaning Big Drunk.

Houston's life was nearing its lowest ebb when he undertook a Cherokee mission to Washington in early 1832. There he assaulted an Ohio congressman for a slur uttered on the House floor; he was convicted in a trial that was a national sensation and worth far more than an acquittal. And so he was welcomed back into Jackson's circle at the White House. Rumors had circulated in the United States for years that Houston was preparing to conquer Texas as an independent filibuster. There was some evidence for this. Houston had been involved in the Nashville Company, which backed Sterling Robertson's empresario contract in Mexican Texas as early as 1822, and during his exile he was heard to boast, usually when drunk, that he meant to invade Texas at the head of an alliance of Cherokee and Creek Indian warriors. There was nothing to it, however, and Houston's actions in Cherokee councils invariably worked to dissuade young Indian hotheads from raiding south of the Red River. The filibustering stories that Jackson heard were mainly spread by Houston's enemies to discredit him with the president. Whether he believed the tales or not, Jackson could not afford to have Houston wreck his Mexican diplomacy, such as it was, and during the three years that he tried to purchase Texas, he had Houston watched and even had his mail opened, but discovered no conspiracy.

With Houston restored, though, Jackson put two and two together. He had tried and failed to acquire Texas with his checkbook, and he recognized

that in Sam Houston—if he sobered up—was a proven leader who could gal-
vanize the huge but amorphous desire, especially in the South, to incorporate Mexico's troubled province into the Union.

As Jackson and Houston weighed their options, the Anahuac Disturbances flared, and down in Texas two of Stephen F. Austin's biggest
headaches, the brothers William and John Wharton, wrote a letter of introduction for one of their confederates, Dr. Branch T. Archer. It was addressed
to Sam Houston, whom the Whartons knew well from earlier Tennessee
days, with the aim of convincing Houston to come to Texas, where "matters
are getting worse every day," and assume leadership of the war party. Dr.
Archer "is intimately acquainted with matters and things there, and is in the
confidence of all their leading men. He is of opinion that there will be some
fighting there . . . and that a fine country will be gained without much
bloodshed, he is very desirous that you should go there, and believes that
you can be of more service than any other man." The Whartons had every
confidence that Archer could "put you in the notion of going."

During at least one of the meetings between Houston and Jackson,
Houston's favorite Washington cousin, John Houston, was present. He later
confided to a diplomat that Jackson told Sam Houston that if the American
colonists in Texas started a revolution, he—Jackson—would "defend the
Neches." In other words, he would uphold by force of arms the old 1806
Neutral Ground as sovereign United States territory. The intention was that
if Houston could put himself at the head of a Texas revolution and draw a
Mexican army into the Neutral Ground, the United States would enter the
war and conquer the Texas they had been unable to purchase.

With Mexico's guard up, it was necessary to find a convincing and in-
nocuous pretext for sending Houston to Texas. Jackson had set a course
for removing the remainder of the Five Civilized Tribes—Cherokees, Chick-
asaws, Choctaws, Creeks, and Seminoles—from their homelands in the
American South and relocating them in the Indian Territory, just across the
Red River from Texas. Those who had already made the journey found
themselves in conflict with the natives already resident there. Houston was
therefore issued a passport to visit San Antonio, arrange a council with Comanche Indians, and invite them to visit the American post at Cantonment
Gibson near the Arkansas border, where they could discuss the situation
and make an amicable arrangement. The cover was plausible, but thin. Most
of the Cherokees' trouble in the Indian Territory was with Osages, not Comanches, and moreover, those Comanches around San Antonio were only
distantly related to, and indeed only dimly aware of, Comanche bands

whose hunting grounds were anywhere close to the Cherokee or other lands. Nevertheless, Houston was issued a passport soliciting "all lawful aid and protection" in his diplomatic mission. The issue closer to Houston's own mind, the opportunities for fame and wealth in an Americanized Texas, surfaced in a letter he wrote to a friend from his youth, a lighthearted West Point washout named Fent Noland of Arkansas. Houston desired Noland to accompany him to Texas: "If we should live, our wealth must be boundless."

By 1832, even Stephen F. Austin's exemptions from the Law of April 6, 1830, had expired, and all American immigration was now illegal. The stream of "leatherstockings," as Austin referred to the troublemaking American squatters, continued unabated. Most still came overland from Louisiana, some by coastal schooner, but the man who assumed an unparalleled place in Texas affairs for the next thirty years came by a back route. Sam Houston splashed across the Red River on a borrowed horse, riding into the squatter settlement of Jonesborough, near the present location of Clarksville, on December 2, 1832.

From the border, Houston rode south to Nacogdoches, where he reconnected with old friends from Tennessee days, including Adolphus Sterne. Then he had a streak of luck that was nothing short of phenomenal. He continued his journey to San Felipe, the capital of Austin's colony, 150 miles southwest of Nacogdoches. Austin himself was away on business, so Houston avoided a possible confrontation with the great empresario, who not only viewed the ruined Tennesseean with suspicion, but was so utterly different in his personal nature and habits that serious conflict between them would have been all but inevitable. Houston was able, however, to apply for a grant in Austin's colony from the empresario's assistant, Samuel May Williams, with whom he opened a friendship that subsequently proved useful on many different fronts.

Houston's official Comanche business required both the permission of the provincial government and help in finding the Comanches. By chance, Houston met and ate Christmas dinner with Jim Bowie, the legendary knife-fighter and late participant in the Battle of Nacogdoches. The two American icons knew each other by reputation, of course, but contrary to wide popular belief, they were not bosom chums from earlier days, and this was their first meeting. Bowie happened to be married to Doña María Ursula de Veramendi, the daughter of Texas' vice governor. Bowie was on his way to San Antonio and could gain Houston that influential support straightaway. By further luck, traveling with them was Bowie's Louisiana neighbor, Caiaphas Ham, who had lived with Comanches in the San Antonio environs for several months and could introduce him to the chiefs. Once in San Antonio, Houston quickly disposed of his official duties, hosting his council with the Comanche headmen and inviting them to a talk at Cantonment Gibson in the United States—a trip that both he and they knew was unlikely ever to take place.

Houston's unofficial business, of course, was to spy out the political situation in Texas for Jackson. After cleaning up his affairs in Béxar, Houston repaired east to Natchitoches, Louisiana, where he sent the president a shrewd assessment of what he had learned, saying that he was "in possession of some information, that . . . may be calculated to forward your views, if you should entertain any, touching the acquisition of Texas by the United States. . . .

"That such a measure is desired by nineteen-twentieths of the population of the province, I can not doubt . . . ," Houston advised him. "Mexico is involved in Civil War. . . . The people of Texas are determined to form a State Government, and to separate from Coahuila, and unless Mexico is soon restored to order . . . Texas will remain separate from the Confederacy of Mexico. She has already beaten and repelled all the troops of Mexico from her soil. . . . She can defend herself against the whole power of Mexico, for really Mexico is powerless and penniless. . . . Her want of money taken in connection with the course which Texas *must and will adopt,* will render a transfer of Texas inevitable to some power, and if the United States, does not press for it, England will most assuredly obtain it by some means. . . ."

If Jackson still entertained any timidity about intervening in Texas affairs, more of Houston's letter seemed calculated to edge him in the right direction: "I have traveled near five hundred miles across Texas, [and there] can be little doubt but the country East of the River Grand . . . would sustain a population of ten millions of souls. . . . I should censure myself if I were to conceal from you . . . any facts, which could enable you, during your administration, to acquire Texas.

"Now is a very important crisis," he insisted. "England is pressing her suit for it, but its citizens will resist if any transfer should be made of them to any power but the United States. . . . My opinion is that Texas, by her members in Convention, will, by 1st of April, declare all that country [north of the Rio Grande] as Texas proper, and form a state constitution. I expect to be present at that Convention, and will apprise you of the course adopted. . . . I may make Texas my abiding place! In adopting this course, I will *never forget* the country of my birth."

Houston did move quickly to establish himself in Texas. When in Nacogdoches Houston boarded at the ample home of the mayor, Adolphus Sterne, the German draft dodger condemned and reprieved for his earlier insurrectionism. Texas law required landowners to be Catholics, and Houston had applied for a grant. However, when he was baptized into the Catholic Church in the Sternes' parlor, the mayor's son recalled that it was not to make him eligible for land, but to make him eligible to represent Nacogdoches at the upcoming political convention of which Houston had tipped Jackson. All present, according to Sterne's son, regarded the religious restriction to be a joke. After independence, he wrote proudly, "men were permitted to hold office whether a member of the Roman Catholic Church, Holy Rollers, Baptists or whatnots."

And indeed it was politics, not religion, that was driving events in Texas at the opening of 1833.

TWENTY

THE QUIET BEFORE THE STORM

STEPHEN F. AUSTIN WOULD HAVE MUCH PREFERRED TO remain neutral in the Mexican civil wars, but now the die had been cast, and fortunately for Texas, Santa Anna emerged victorious from the coups and counter-coups of 1832. Texas, having declared for Santa Anna, could claim some sympathy from him, and after the commotion caused by the Anahuac Disturbances died away, a convention was called to plan further action. Summoned by Austin's own ayuntamiento at San Felipe, fifty-five delegates from sixteen districts, mostly separatists representing the "leatherstocking" element, met in that town on October 1, 1832. Austin, who was not entirely in favor of the convention, chaired it, believing it easier to control the beast by riding it than by standing in front of it. "I had an ignorant, whimsical, selfish and suspicious set of rulers over me," he griped in a letter, "a per-plexed, confused law to execute, and an unruly set of frontier North Ameri-can republicans to control who felt . . . that they were beyond the arm of government or of law."

Predictable resolutions were passed, petitioning the government to fur-ther extend the earlier tax relief, to repeal the most odious provisions of the Law of April 6, and to reconstitute Texas as a state within Mexico, instead of being a province attached to Coahuila. Some of their resolutions were re-markably forward-looking, such as one requesting donations of government land for bilingual primary education, and another protecting Cherokee lands in East Texas from encroachments by white squatters. With an eye back to Bradburn and the Anahuac troubles, they asked that tax collectors be appointed by local ayuntamientos, not sent by the state administration. None of the resolutions were ever presented to the government, probably because Austin pointed out that Santa Anna did not yet control the govern-ment, and also because the gathering was fatally flawed: the largely Tejano-populated San Antonio had refused to send delegates, which made it appear that only the ex-Americans were disaffected, which would call their loyalty into question again. (Predominantly Tejano La Bahía did send repre-sentatives, who approved the convention's actions, but they arrived too late to participate.) Moreover, the *jefe político* in San Antonio, Ramón Músquiz, declared the proceeding illegal, which cost the colonists some of the sympathy that Músquiz had demonstrated for them in his four years on the job.

Taking their pattern from the American Revolution, the 1832 Convention kept its issues alive by appointing a Central Committee of Safety and Correspondence. The following spring, while Austin was in the Hispanic settlements trying to win their cooperation, his leatherstockings called a new convention for April 1, 1833, which by chance was the same day that Santa Anna assumed power in Mexico City. This time they meant to go further. Sam Houston, who had arrived in Texas two months after the first convention, got himself elected to this one, and was made chairman of a committee that drafted a constitution for Texas as a Mexican state. The 1833 Convention ignored Austin and elected the independence-minded William Wharton to preside over the gathering. Nevertheless there was a subtle shift in Austin's own position, and when he addressed the delegates he gave them his cautious support. While extolling the Anglo settlers' progress and their "faithfully performing their duty as Mexican citizens," he argued that "the *right* of the people of Texas to represent their wants to the government, and to explain in a respectfull manner the remedies that will relieve them cannot . . . be doubted or questioned." In their efforts to obtain redress for very real problems in the judicial and administrative hierarchy, Texans, said Austin, "beheld the Mexican confederation torn and broken asunder by political parties each of which sustained its pretensions to the supreme . . . power by force of arms. Civil war raged in every part of the Mexican territory."

Thus there was a certain unanimity of purpose beginning to coalesce among the Anglo factions, even among those who couldn't otherwise stand each other. As Sam Houston guided the drafting of the state constitution, David G. Burnet drafted an able and deferential memorial to the Mexican congress on the legality and desirability of separating the province of Texas from Coahuila. Burnet was the New Jersey–born son of a Continental Congressman who had come west to try to live up to the family name. He was also a principal of the Galveston Bay and Texas Land Company. He had come to loathe Houston because of his drinking and their previous land dealings, but for the present, they worked well in tandem. The extreme distance to the state capitals (Saltillo and Monclova were feuding over which should be recognized), Burnet argued, left the mail in chaos and rendered the frontiers open to Indian attack. He pointed out further that trial verdicts appealed to the state courts deep in Mexico gave an unconscionable advantage to rich litigants who could afford representation far in distance and arcane in procedure. The differing interests and economies between the two regions made passage of mutually agreeable legislation improbable.

Thirteen days after convening, a constitution was approved and three delegates were selected to journey to Mexico City to present Texas' desires: Austin, Dr. James B. Miller, and Juan Erasmo Seguín, a leading citizen of San Antonio, who could testify that Tejanos as well as the Anglo settlers were suffering under the present system. Ultimately, Miller stayed behind to treat a cholera outbreak, and then there were only funds to finance one emissary, and Austin packed for one more mission to the capital. When he arrived there in mid-July, he found Mexico City to be in no less a state of intrigue than on his first visit more than a decade earlier. Santa Anna had been elected as a federalist, but the capital was a stronghold of centralist upper classes, and of the military and the clergy who habitually sided with them. Shrewdly, the new president took a leave of absence to "recover his health" at his estate near Vera Cruz, leaving his vice president, Valentín Gómez Farías, to undertake the new administration. Santa Anna could observe from afar, and if the federalist reforms were accepted, he could return and govern in safety. If they were not, he could reconcile with the centralists, blame the trouble on the vice president, and return and rule as an autocrat.

Ultimately the latter would take place, but Gómez Farías was acting president at the time of Austin's arrival, and their meeting, while friendly, was unproductive. The wobbly executive was unwilling to consider Texas matters while trying to trim the power of the Church and the army. Austin spent a fruitless summer in the capital, surviving an epidemic of cholera that nearly shut down the city. On October 1, two and a half months after his arrival, Austin and Gómez Farías exchanged heated words. Austin returned to his lodging and wrote an intemperate letter to the ayuntamiento of San Antonio, advising that they might as well proceed to organize a state government without waiting for approval from Mexico City. For a man of Austin's legendary tact and patience, it was a blunder of stupefying proportions.

Santa Anna returned to assume his office, and Austin met with him on November 5. The president, mindful of the Texans' declaration for him, received Austin cordially and agreed to all the Texan requests except separate statehood. The federal constitution, he argued, provided that Texas must have a population of 80,000 before taking that step. At this time in Texas a census might have found 30,000. But Santa Anna even agreed to lift the ban on further immigration from the United States—that hateful provision of the Law of April 6—and eventually issued the necessary decree. When Austin left Mexico City on December 10, he was hopeful that the concessions won would preserve some harmony between Mexico and his pro-American rustics.

He returned via Saltillo. On January 13, 1834, while he was visiting the military commander there, he was suddenly arrested and taken in irons back to the capital. Loyal centralists on the ayuntamiento in San Antonio had read his letter urging them to renegade statehood, and they sent it straight back to the government. Santa Anna was gone again, Gómez Farías was back, and it was he who ordered Austin's arrest.

In Mexico City, Austin was clapped into the Prison of the Inquisition and allowed to see no one, except for visits by the good Padre Muldoon, who arranged for an American businessman to post a bond to get Austin out of jail. When the bond was rejected, Muldoon interceded with Santa Anna himself, seeking out the president-general at his estate. On May 9 Austin was allowed books and writing paper, and described his situation to his brother-in-law. "I arrived here . . . on the 13 Feby—on that day I was locked up in one of the dungeons of this vast building *incomunicado,* that is I was not allowed to speak to, or communicate with any person whatever except the officer of the guard. I remained in this situation untill yesterday." He blamed himself for his predicament. "The truth is I lost patience and was imprudent and of course to blame." He counseled peace and tranquility at home. "I have no idea when I shall be at liberty. I think that all depends on the report of Almonte, who has been sent to Texas."

Austin was charged with sedition, but no court would take jurisdiction of such a trumped-up case, and Austin spent 1834 either in jail or under house arrest. News of Austin's seizure reached Sam Houston in New York, where he had gone to try a final time to wring his legal retainer out of some land investors whose agent had engaged him to represent their interests in Texas. The news about Austin sent him scurrying back. Over a long lifetime Houston gained a reputation as a seer of keen insight, and on this occasion he made a series of predictions to the New York land agent: "I do think within one year that [Texas] will be a Sovereign State and acting in all things as such. Within three years I think it will be separated from the Mexican Confederacy, and will remain so forever—Still, if Mexico had done right, we cou'd have travelled on smoothly enough. You need not hope for the acquisition . . . by this Government of Texas during the Administration of General Jackson—If it were acquired by a Treaty, that Treaty, would not be ratified, by the present Senate—!!! . . . Keep my predictions, and see how far they are *verified!*—The course that I may pursue, you must rely upon it, shall be for the true interests of Texas."

Houston returned via Washington, visiting relatives and signing an auto-graph book for a young cousin in Virginia. That cousin, Narcissa Hamilton, overheard enough of the adult conversation to write that Houston was "making plans for the liberation of Texas." After this, he virtually disap-peared for the rest of 1834. One report sighted him at the head of native warriors in the Indian Territory, recalling the rumors since 1829 that Hous-ton pictured himself filibustering Texas at the fore of an Indian horde. Late in the year he was spied having mysterious meetings at the Travelers Inn in Washington, Arkansas, seen there by a British travel writer, G. W. Feather-stonhaugh (pronounced "Fanshaw"), who described him as "seeing nobody by day and sitting up all night. The world gave him credit for passing these . . . hours in the study of [cards] . . . but this little place was the rendezvous where a much deeper game than faro or rouge et noir was playing . . . whose real object was . . . to throw off their allegiance to the Mexican govern-ment." In that day Washington, Arkansas, was an important road hub and staging area; doubtless Houston was clearing the pike for American aid and volunteers once fighting started. By spring of 1835, according to recently discovered documents in the Nacogdoches Archives, Houston was back in East Texas plying his law trade, waiting on events.

With Houston having labored so hard to prepare for war, however, the crisis in Texas suddenly seemed to ease. There might be no war at all. Austin's imprisonment kept his colonists quiet, lest the empresario should come to a filibuster's end. But to greater effect, the state legislature began enacting important changes that Texans had been clamoring for—adminis-trative and judicial reforms, including trials by jury and increasing Texas' representation in the Coahuila y Tejas state legislature. As Austin had al-luded, Colonel Juan Almonte arrived in Texas in the spring of 1834 and found renewed prosperity and peace. The economy did have its peculiari-ties—"Money is very scarce," he reported home, "not one in ten sales are made for cash. Purchases are made on credit, or by barter; which gives the country . . . the appearance of a continual fair." Still, the state legislature had recently allowed Anglo colonists to go into business as retail mer-chants, an enterprise theretofore limited to native Tejanos. Crops were bur-geoning; Almonte's only criticism was on the point of slavery, which he recommended be limited by closing the border to further slaves and limiting terms of servitude to ten or twelve years. Almonte's report might have caused the 1832 Nacogdoches and Anahuac bloodshed to recede into mem-ory and tranquility to prosper, but once again, events in Mexico spun a dif-ferent fate.

TWENTY-ONE

COME AND TAKE IT

SANTA ANNA RESUMED PRESIDENTIAL POWERS AGAIN, this time pronouncing the federalist reforms a national calamity. He made his peace with the centralist elements and in short order banished Gómez Farías, abrogated the constitution, suspended the state legislatures, and assumed dictatorial powers under the custom-drafted *Siete Leyes,* the Seven Laws. Rebellions against him broke out in four states; the governor of Zacatecas led an army of five thousand, which Santa Anna defeated in a prelude to a gothic slaughter of thousands that would have made even his old commander, Joaquín de Arredondo, blanch. When the legislature of Coahuila y Tejas censured Santa Anna for this butchery, he sent troops under his brother-in-law, General Martín Perfecto de Cos, to dissolve that body, and they arrested the governor, Agustín Viesca, as he attempted to flee to Texas.

One thing that the centralist troops uncovered in the state capital was a nest of Texas land speculation that has confused discussion of the causes of the Texas Revolution for generations. It was true that Anglos were making a fortune in improvident land disbursements won from the legislature, fueling the argument that Texas was "stolen" from Mexico by bribe-wielding, land-mad North Americans. It was also true that many prominent Mexicans and Tejanos were involved in the same trade, such as Lorenzo de Zavala and José María Carbajal, secretary to the ayuntamiento of San Antonio, fueling the negative argument. More to the point, it was the federalist legislature of Coahuila y Tejas that was using its land policy to finance its opposition to Santa Anna after he showed his true centralist colors. When Cos dispersed the legislature, the Texas elements returned home, spreading the alarm that Santa Anna was planning an invasion of the Anglo colonies. What they found instead was that in the calm and stabilizing Texas economy described by Almonte, most people either didn't believe them, or else felt that the speculators had gotten their just deserts in being broken up. Austin had been released from prison into house arrest, and Santa Anna's intentions did not seem, at that moment, hostile toward Texas. There was no shortage of Tories.

Almonte's report had estimated that among cotton, livestock, timber, and other products, Texas was now generating nearly one and a half million dollars in trade per year. Such figures weighed against Texas' perennial claim of poverty, and port duties were the principal income of the centralist government. In spring of 1835 Santa Anna sent customs officers, and troops to support them, back to Galveston and Anahuac to begin collecting taxes. The Anahuac Disturbances, instead of fading into memory, were instead set for a reenactment.

One of the Texans who took advantage of the new law allowing Anglos to go into business was twenty-four-year-old Andrew Briscoe, formerly of Mississippi, who opened a store at Anahuac. The customs official there, Captain Antonio Tenorio, made a practice of collecting all duties, but Briscoe learned that the receiver in Galveston, at the other end of the same bay, collected only tonnage. Briscoe refused to pay Tenorio's higher rate, and when he loaded his boat with ballast to make Tenorio think it was loaded with untaxed goods, he and his partner were arrested and jailed. Word of renewed trouble at Anahuac raced through the colonies. At San Felipe, Anglo warhawks stripped a Mexican courier of his dispatches on June 21, and read a letter from Cos to Tenorio that reinforcements would shortly be on their way to him. To the horror of most of the San Felipe community, the war party commissioned William B. Travis, who had been involved in the 1832 business, to round up volunteers. A couple dozen pounded down to the coast with a small cannon; they demanded and received the surrender of Tenorio and forty-four soldiers. Only one shot was fired, no one was hurt, and the captured Mexicans were paroled to go home. All across Texas, though, communities dissociated themselves from Travis and the war party, passing resolutions condemning the move against Anahuac and renewing their fealty to Mexico. Cos moved from the capital to Matamoros, at the mouth of the Rio Grande, where he received word that a deputation from San Felipe and other communities had been en route since July 21 with still more mollifying letters.

Cos might have preserved peace in Texas, at least for a while longer, by letting the new Anahuac disturbance pass, but with his brother-in-law now dictator of Mexico, he determined to teach Texas a lesson. He would not meet any peace delegation, he announced, until they delivered up several troublemakers for military trial. He wanted, among others, Travis and Samuel May Williams, Austin's longtime secretary, who was lately involved in the land speculating; longtime agitator Francis W. Johnson; and San Felipe lawyer and publisher Robert M. Williamson, who had used his newspaper to criticize Mexican authority. Cos' terms left the colonies in shock; all those named except Travis were widely respected leaders. Johnson was an irascible jack-of-all-trades who, at thirty-six, was identified with the war party, but he was also part of Austin's inner circle, had once done Austin's bidding in trying to forestall the Fredonian Rebellion, and had since served the Great Empresario as surveyor-general and alcalde of San Felipe. Williamson, a Georgian of about thirty, was popular for his irrepressible spirit. (A disease during his adolescence, probably polio, left one leg bent permanently back, and he used a prosthesis from the knee down, leading to his sobriquet of "Three-Legged Willie," which he didn't for a moment let stop him from being one of the most celebrated dancers in Texas.) Most Texans disapproved of Travis' actions, but almost none were prepared to give up him or any of the others to a military tribunal for summary execution in the midst of a merciless civil war.

Despite Austin's letters from Mexico urging quiet, it was apparent that the situation had progressed beyond diplomacy. Ever since early July, various ayuntamientos, acting through their Committees of Correspondence, had been calling for a new convention—this time they called it a Consultation—to decide what to do. Two of Texas' biggest advocates for independence and full separation from Mexico were still the brothers John and William Wharton, old Sam Houston friends from Tennessee. On August 18, the committee in Columbia, a new town on the Brazos near Brazoria, chaired by William Wharton, issued a call for each district to elect five delegates, to meet in San Felipe on October 15. But on the first of September Austin suddenly materialized at Brazoria, freed in a general amnesty, after an absence of two years and four months. Everyone expected that he would oppose the planned Consultation and resume his old policy of seeking accommodation with the Mexican government. A week after his arrival the citizens of Brazoria planned a welcoming dinner, where Austin would make an address.

What they discovered that night was a changed man, sick and wasted and angry. "I fully hoped to have found Texas at peace and in tranquility," he told them, "but regret to find it in commotion; all disorganized . . . and threatened with immediate hostilities." Austin had witnessed Santa Anna's transformation from posing liberal to sashed and bemedaled autocrat. "The revolution in Mexico is drawing to a close. The object is to change the form of government, destroy the federal constitution of 1824, and establish a central or consolidated government. The states are to be converted into provinces. Whether the people of Texas ought or ought not to agree to this change . . . is a question of the most vital importance; one that calls for the deliberate consideration of the people." He drew attention to his reputation as the last man in Texas to embrace revolution. "My friends, I can truly say, that no one has been, or is now, more anxious than myself to keep trouble away from this country. No one has been, or is now more faithful to his duty as a Mexican citizen, and no one has personally sacrificed or suffered more in the discharge of this duty. I have uniformly been opposed to have any thing to do with the family political quarrels of the Mexicans. Texas needs peace, and a local government. . . . But how can I, or anyone, remain indifferent, when our rights, our all, appear to be in jeopardy?" Austin called for the Consultation to be convened "as speedily as possible." The battle could then be fought whether to declare independence, or make still more representations to the central government. This night, however, was given over to celebrating Stephen Austin's return. So many attended that the dinner had to be eaten in three shifts. "The long room was filled to a Jam," Austin's cousin Henry wrote, and following the meal, there were "at least sixty or eighty ladies who danced the sun up, and the Oyster Creek girls would not have quit then had not the room been wanted for breakfast."

When wars approach, minor incidents can become major symbols. The commandant at San Antonio, Domingo de Ugartechea, sent out to the municipality of Gonzales to reclaim a small cannon that had been lent them for Indian defense some four years previous. By now Cos had moved from Matamoros, landed at Copano Bay below Refugio, and was marching an army to occupy San Antonio. The Gonzales ordnance, usually described as a brass six-pounder, would have availed little in a contest with Cos, but Gonzales' citizens bucked at the thought of being disarmed. Therefore their alcalde, thirty-one-year-old Virginian Andrew Ponton, six years resident in Texas, sent a wordy and semiliterate prevarication to the *jefe político* in San Antonio to buy time. He and the ayuntamiento had been absent when Ugartechea's dispatch arrived, and moreover they were unaware of the manner in which arms were usually appropriated in the country. "At least until I have an opportunity of consulting the chief of this department on the subject," Ponton wrote, he would have to keep the gun, but if he found it to be his duty, he would send it without delay. Meantime, he caused the cannon to be buried in a peach orchard and plowed over. Several letters were sent from Gonzales to other Anglo colonies, for volunteers to converge and resist.

In the traditional recitation of Texas history, the letters soliciting the aid of the other colonies were emphatic in their patriotism and their determination to hold out for democratic virtues in the face of tyranny. One recently discovered such letter, however, authored by Elijah Bailey of Robertson's Colony, cast a distinctly more urgent and practical complexion—that the coming soldiers would strip the settlement of cash and food:

I am requested to give some information relative to the situation and feelings of the people at Gonzales and that vicinity.

I left Gonzales on Wednesday last and the people of that place were then assembled to decide upon what answer to give to a file of Mexican soldiers who they expect in one or two days to demand a brass cannon which was in their possession. When I left there were but three names in favour of giving up the cannon, so that the retaining of it seemed to be almost unanimous with the people. Several individuals there named that they wanted assistance from this Colony as they expected in refusing the cannon Mexican troops would be sent immediately upon them to enforce the order and perhaps commit depredations upon their property, and if so nothing could save their provisions & stock but assistance from this Colony. The Alcalde said to me that he had in possession about $1000 Dols and was fearful that the military would also demand that. Several families were talking of moveing, and some have actually prepared their waggons to do so. They wish to move their families this side of the Colorado and to return themselves to the defence of their frontier. A number more said they should move their families as they expected their refusing to give up the cannon would bring foraging parties of soldiers as they (the military at Bexar) were short of provisions.

E. Bailey

When Ugartechea's first communication failed to produce the cannon, he sent a hundred dragoons, who arrived at the Guadalupe River opposite Gonzales on September 29. It was a show of force only; the dragoons' commander, Lieutenant Francisco de Castañeda, was ordered to take care not to precipitate general fighting, and to use violence only as a last resort. The townspeople had secreted the ferry, and Castañeda found that no boats remained in the river, which was running high and fast. In the absence of Ponton, Castañeda was met on the opposite bank by eighteen militia volunteers and Gonzales' second-ranking executive, the *regidor*, who claimed that Ponton would arrive in a few hours and speak to him.

Meanwhile, the gun was excavated from its peach orchard, mounted on heavy wooden trucks, and repaired by local blacksmith Noah Smithwick. He had an accurate take on the frame of mind of the assembling volunteers, who were giving little thought to legalities. "Some were for independence," he wrote, "some for the constitution of 1824, and some for anything, just so it was a row." No right-thinking Americans could go into battle without a flag, but fabric in that lonely place was a scarce commodity. The problem was solved when Naomi DeWitt, the daughter of the colony's founder, sacrificed her wedding dress. On the white banner was drawn the outline of a cannon, and beneath it, much to the point, was the legend: COME AND TAKE IT.

When Ponton failed to show, Castañeda returned to the riverbank in the morning, only to be met again by the *regidor,* who yelled across the river from a prepared text: "In the absence of the *alcalde* it has fallen to my lot to reply to the communication sent to him asking a second time for the cannon. . . . The right of consulting our political chief seems to be denied us. Therefore my reply reduces itself to this: I can not nor do I desire to deliver up the cannon. . . . Only through force will we yield. We are weak and few in number, nevertheless we are contending for what we believe to be just principles."

Their principles may have been just, but the angry men under the COME AND TAKE IT banner were dealing less than squarely with Castañeda. Not only had they never intended to hand over the insignificant little gun, they weren't that weak, either; volunteers had streamed into Gonzales to the number of perhaps 140. To their surprise, an American approached them from the Mexican camp, one Launcelot Smither, an unlicensed doctor who had been tending the San Antonio garrison. When he heard of the trouble, he had interceded for the Gonzales residents with Ugartechea, who sent him with an escort to Castañeda, who in turn sent him to the rebels to repeat his peaceable intentions. Smither encountered Mathew Caldwell, who informed him that if Castañeda and Smither came over together, the Mexican officer would be received like a gentleman, and Smither carried this word back to the Mexican camp.

Unable to get his hundred dragoons across the river, Castañeda withdrew, probing the swollen stream for a place to ford upstream. On the night of October 1 he went into camp about seven miles above the town. Fearing that he had pulled back to await reinforcements, the Texans crossed the river and were discovered as they approached the Mexican camp. There was an exchange of musketry, and the Texas Revolution began. The volunteers chose for their commander John Henry Moore, a Tennesseean of thirty-five, one of Austin's Old Three Hundred, and one of the ringleaders whom Cos had demanded for military justice. At the first firing, a furious Castañeda had Launcelot Smither arrested while impounding his stock, gear, and money. After getting his men under cover, however, he discovered that he needed an interpreter, released Smither, and sent him to Moore with a demand to know why they had been attacked.

Moore, equally suspicious of Smither's friendliness with the Mexicans, had him arrested again and taken to the rear. Such was the fate of a would-be peacemaker at the opening of the Texas Revolution. Castañeda and Moore themselves then met between their miniature armies, and exchanged sentiments and principles: the Texans maintained that they were fighting for the Constitution of 1824. Castañeda identified himself as a federalist, and against Santa Anna, but he was only obeying orders to ask for the cannon. He had no orders to seize it, and he didn't want any trouble. The volunteers had discussed Castañeda's peaceable intentions the night before, and decided that since they had come for a fight with "the enemy," to return home without a clash was not acceptable. When the parley between Moore and Castañeda faltered the Gonzales volunteers renewed the assault, and in the dawn fog of October 2 a brand was touched to the COME AND TAKE IT cannon. After a hot fight, Castañeda withdrew to San Antonio, leaving one dead.

In the report of the clash that the Gonzales Committee sent to Austin, the Guadalupe became the Rubicon, and the dragoons became two hundred instead of one hundred. But their blood was up, and "in as much as we expect a formidable attack from Ugartachie, should the forces long remain idle," the volunteers determined to carry the fight to him instead, and attack San Antonio itself.

Even after learning of the fracas at Gonzales, Ugartechea steered a moderate course. Addressing Austin in a letter of October 4 as "My Worthy Friend," he protested that he had done all he could to avoid hostilities, but that he was compelled to march the next day, "with a force of every description of arms, sufficient to prove that the Mexicans can never suffer themselves to be insulted." Nevertheless, he assured Austin, "if you make use of your influence . . . to have the gun delivered up to me," he would halt any punitive action. If the Gonzales cannon was not surrendered, "I will act militarily, and the consequence will be a war declared by the colonists. . . . I remain your attached friend, &c."

Ugartechea's letter was intercepted by the volunteers and read before being forwarded to Austin with a note of their own, pleading with him to come take command of their sort-of army. "You will see by Ugartachea's letter to you, he proposed a sort of compromise. That will give us an opportunity to entertain him a little while . . . until we can get in more men. We . . . request you *earnestly* to come on *immediately,* bringing all the aid you possibly can—we want *powder and lead.*"

The Texans had begun their revolution, but it was a tall question whether they could finish it.

TWENTY-TWO

WHO WILL GO
WITH OLD BEN MILAM?

IN HIS REPLY TO THE MASSING VOLUNTEERS AFTER THEIR fight on October 2, Austin cautiously endorsed resorting to a defensive war, cleverly reserving a bit of wiggle room—so he could argue to the leatherstockings who didn't quite trust him that he was with them, but also argue to the Supreme Government, if all became lost, that he had acted only in defensive *extremis*. Fifty miles south of Gonzales lay Goliad, as the old settlement of La Bahía was renamed in 1829, in an H-less anagram honoring Hidalgo. The Texans learned early that Cos meant to land an army at the Copano port, reinforce the Texas garrisons with Santanistas, establish his headquarters in San Antonio, and end up in San Felipe. Some Texan volunteers intended as early as mid-September to intercept Cos at Goliad and prevent his march, but they altered their course to Gonzales as word spread of the threat there.

The citizens of Goliad had already been given a taste of what to expect from a Mexican occupation. In preparing the town for Cos' arrival the garrison commander, Colonel Nicolás Condelle, had disarmed the citizens and forced them to do army labor, bivouacked troops in their houses, and placed the alcalde under arrest. Cos entered Goliad on the same morning that the COME AND TAKE IT cannon boomed on the Guadalupe. In an odd duplication of events in Gonzales, Cos sent a detachment to Victoria to impound a cannon there and arrest Carbajal, but volunteers from that town, led by their alcalde Plácido Benavides, prevented it. Unwilling to be distracted by what he considered a minor incident, Cos prepared for the march one hundred miles northwest to San Antonio. He left Goliad on October 5 with the Morelos Battalion, numbering about 400; with this and other units, he intended to ensconce himself in Béxar with about 1,400. There weren't enough wagons or pack animals to transport all his supplies, and he left them behind at Goliad. Cos reached San Antonio without incident, leaving at Goliad a garrison of a few dozen men under Lieutenant Colonel Francisco Sandoval to guard his supplies.

From Victoria, Benavides and John J. Linn of De León's Colony, a veteran of the New Orleans militia, rode to Gonzales to begin training the rapidly swelling ranks of volunteers. They urged the men to strike Cos before he reached the safety of San Antonio, but the idea of assaulting an entire battalion produced no enthusiasm in the ranks. More energetic recruits began gravitating about George M. Collinsworth of Brazoria, and on their own hook they swept southeast from Gonzales to Victoria. Collinsworth was a Mississippian and planter, another veteran of the 1832 Velasco trouble, who raised a company of men from the Brazoria vicinity as soon as the revolution commenced. Once he learned how lightly defended the garrison at Goliad was, he sortied the twenty-five miles west from Victoria with as many as 150 volunteers. At 11 P.M. on the night of October 9—as Cos was entering San Antonio—Texans broke into the Goliad church where the Mexican troops were bedded down. Sandoval surrendered after a thirty-minute fight, losing seven wounded and three dead, with twenty-one taken prisoner. As many as twenty Mexican soldiers escaped, however, spreading the alarm to the Refugio and Copano garrisons. Rather than fortify, however, they withdrew to join the garrison at Fort Lipantitlán near San Patricio, more than fifty miles southwest of Goliad on the Nueces River. Collinsworth had zero dead, but that was not the importance of the fight. He was in possession both of Cos' supplies, which the Texan volunteers badly needed, and his line of supply by sea. However, with the Texans unable to guard or feed so many prisoners, the captured Mexicans were released on verbal parole to cause no more trouble.

Cos, meanwhile, entrenched himself in San Antonio. Just east of the city he fortified the chapel of the old Mission San Antonio de Valero, now known as the Alamo, long since decommissioned and fallen to ruin. News of the capture of Goliad elated the volunteers back at Gonzales, and the cry was taken up to march to San Antonio and expunge the Mexican army from Texas soil. Squabbles among popular company commanders, however, soon increased the general call for Stephen Austin to join and lead the army. Already informed of this by letter, Austin was dubious, knowing first that he was no soldier himself, and second that his leatherstockings would follow him exactly as long as it pleased them to do so. Since returning to San Felipe he had been living with the Mexican liberal fugitive Lorenzo de Zavala, who seconded Austin's fears about the volunteers. "There is individual patriotism," he admitted, "but there is no unified patriotism . . . they do not realize the necessity for cooperation." But Austin also knew he was the only man who stood any chance of unifying the army. After a painful three-day ride he reached Gonzales on October 11, was acclaimed commander with the rank of general, and the next day the march began to San Antonio, and Cos.

Austin began trying to concentrate the disparate forces on San Antonio. He sent orders to fortify Goliad but reduce the garrison there to a hundred, sparing three companies to join the main army outside Béxar. Collinsworth had left Goliad to round up more recruits, and command passed to Philip Dimmitt, a hard Kentuckian of thirty-five, resident of De León's Colony, and husband of a Mexican woman. He agreed with Austin on the need to fortify Goliad and prevent Cos from recapturing it, and he sensed danger from the remaining Mexican garrison in South Texas, concentrated at Fort Lipantitlán. Dimmitt was right, for Cos had already decided on that base as a springboard from which to retake Goliad, and had ordered Lipantitlán's commanding officer, Captain Rodríguez, to attack. Dimmitt sent out a force of sixty under Ira Westover; they approached the fort in secret by staying off the roads. With Rodríguez absent, Westover easily took Lipantitlán and forced Rodríguez to abort his assault on Goliad. Rodríguez returned and engaged Westover's Texans at Lipantitlán and was defeated, leaving all of South Texas in volunteer hands. Yet again, the Mexican prisoners were freed on parole.

Texas volunteer citizens began congregating at a campground on Salado Creek, a short distance from San Antonio. Some arrived individually or in small groups, some were already organized into companies with elected officers; each man was clad and equipped with whatever he owned. According to Noah Smithwick, the smithy who had repaired the Gonzales cannon, "Words are inadequate to convey an impression of the appearance of the first Texas army. . . . Boots being an unknown quantity; some wore shoes and some moccasins. Here a broadbrimmed sombrero overshadowed the military cap at its side; there a tall 'beegum' rode familiarly beside a coonskin cap, with the tail hanging down behind. . . . There the shaggy brown buffalo robe contrasted with a gaily checkered counterpane. In lieu of a canteen, each man carried a Spanish gourd. Buckskin breeches were the nearest approach to uniform."

At one time Austin had perhaps six hundred men under him, but once they found out how boring a siege could be, desertions cut that number to four hundred. One night the entire camp guard, a whole company, melted away. Among his remainder, Austin was so mortified at the level of drunkenness that he began posting a night guard to keep the men in and the liquor out. He also wrote a letter to the temporary government beseeching them to make sure no more alcohol made its way to the front. "If there is any on the road, turn it back." Augmenting his numbers, however, were companies of native Tejanos led by Juan Seguín, to the number of 135, giving the lie to any notion of the Texas Revolution as a purely ethnic conflict. Austin was finding it difficult to get his officers to obey orders. He settled on two as his chief aides, James Walker Fannin, a thirty-one-year-old Georgia slave trader and captain of the self-styled Brazos Guards, and the charismatic Jim Bowie, to whom men seemed naturally to gravitate.

Events of the war had caused the date of the Consultation to be pushed back to November 1. Only 31 of 98 delegates presented themselves in San Felipe; most of the rest were with the army, leaving no quorum with which to organize a government. One delegate who did show up was Sam Houston, who took on the job of riding out to the army to compel the soldier-delegates to attend. He was shabbily mounted, having given his own fine horse to Bowie a few weeks earlier. Houston "rode into our camp alone," noted one observer, "mounted on a little yellow Spanish stallion so diminutive that Old Sam's long legs, incased in the traditional buckskin, almost touched the ground."

Sam Houston's reputation as a fallen Jacksonian, an Indian lover and a drunk, a man who had humiliated and abandoned his wife in Tennessee, offset his renown as a magnetic and charismatic leader. The volunteers were deeply conflicted about him: many adored him; just as many detested him. And Houston returned their mixed emotions in full measure. In the military and in politics he had proven himself as a leader of men; he loved leading men, but the emotions he felt when he beheld this motley volunteer spectacle were anything but good. When he had fought as a lieutenant in the 1814 Creek campaign, he had seen Andrew Jackson struggle to maintain discipline among such militia, even executing one for desertion. Such men fought when they pleased, obeyed whom they pleased, and left when they pleased, and Austin himself gave Houston an earful on the subject. They were not an army, and no army could be legitimately organized until there was a government to do it; nor could they expect help from foreign powers until there was an authoritative structure in place to give the color of legitimacy to their actions.

The whole mob was called together for a meeting; Houston warned them that Santa Anna would soon be on them with a real army, and in their present chaos they were candidates for slaughter. They must, he said, withdraw to a safe distance and organize, drill, and work themselves into a fighting force that would have some chance against the Mexican regiments. He also insisted that delegates who had been elected to the Consultation get themselves to San Felipe and organize a government. The yahoos before him were not inclined to accede to either point. Although they had their doubts about Austin's firmness for war, they wanted to hear his views. So sick that he was barely able to mount his horse, Austin, as he habitually did, fashioned a compromise. He agreed with Houston that government organization was essential, and elected delegates must go at once. He was disinclined, however, to give up any ground already won, and while the Consultation took place at San Felipe, they would maintain their siege of San Antonio.

Power, of course, lay in the ranks, and after deliberations of their own, the volunteers decided that delegates could leave for the Consultation—except William Wharton and Austin. They were afraid that Austin might try one more time to smooth things over with Santa Anna—the first thing Austin had done on arriving in San Antonio was send Cos an offer to negotiate, which Cos had spurned—and they wouldn't let him out of their sight. Thus the general became a captive of the men he was ostensibly leading. After Houston left, Austin sent a letter after him: "The country must have organization. . . . All depends on it." The Consultation finally convened on November 1, organizing itself as a provisional authority—exactly what kind was still to be determined, but at least giving Texas a nucleus around which to form a government.

On October 28 Austin sent his two ranking officers, Bowie and Fannin, on a reconnaissance to the Concepción mission, only two miles from the city, with orders to return by dark. Instead Bowie let his ninety men be seen by Cos' scouts and spent the night in a pecan bottom to await an attack. Austin was frantic when they failed to return. In the morning Ugartechea and nearly three hundred Mexicans, supported by two field guns, pounced on Bowie's detachment. The grapeshot crashing through the tops of the pecan trees rained ripe nuts down onto Bowie's men, who snacked on them without concern. The Mexican infantry surged forward three times, each time beaten back by Bowie's rifle fire. The Texans' guns had twice the range of the Mexican muskets, and the Mexicans quit the field leaving more than fifty on the ground. They were sent off by a shot from one of their own cannons, which the Texans had captured, and by the arrival of Austin and the main army, who had rushed to aid at the sound of the firing. Austin found not disaster but victory, and ordered an assault to capitalize on the gains. But disobedience was followed by more disobedience, and his officers rejected the order on the grounds that San Antonio was too well defended with artillery. Bowie had lost one killed, a fellow whom the other volunteers knew as Big Dick. He had exposed himself to enemy fire in order to get a clearer shot, and became the first fatality of the revolution.

On November 12 the Consultation named Sam Houston, a former major general of Tennessee militia, commanding general of the army, a deliberately disingenuous title, since the gaggle of volunteer companies had never been officially commissioned as an army. In that time, regular officers and volunteer officers were distinctly different species, and at least some in the Consultation who were counted among the Houston-haters were satisfied to have made him commander of whatever army he could raise. From a military standpoint, the situation was intolerable, but as Houston swung into action there were at least a few of the officers maintaining the siege at Béxar who began reporting to him. One was the leader of the Nacogdoches volunteers, Thomas Jefferson Rusk. "I marched a detachment of forty cavalry within 300 yards of the wall & remained there 20 minutes they were afraid to come out they fired their cannon but done us no damage all we want is two or three hundred reinforcements . . . & some thing like organization. Much depends on you & what you do must be done quickly." Even Fannin, who would not himself always obey orders from Austin, accepted Houston as commander. "If a 'Regular Army' be organized, I would be glad to receive some honorable appointment in it— . . . I have not time to give my views on the [present] 'modus operandi.' "

On November 18 Austin received word from the Consultation that he was being relieved of command—the newly forming government felt that he could be of better service as their commissioner in the United States to raise money and supplies. He kept the news to himself, but inwardly felt a wash of relief. Army command was "an office that I never sought, and tryed to avoid, and wish to be relieved from," and he welcomed the new posting to the U.S. "I have no ambition but to serve the country in a station where it is considered I can best serve. I believe that my worn out constitution is not adapted to a military command, neither have I ever pretended to be a military man." In his final order as general of the army on the 22nd, he ordered an assault on San Antonio for the following dawn. He was shocked again when the volunteer officers refused to obey. He canceled the order and prepared to leave, sharing Houston's doubts about the readiness of these drunken yahoos who were playing at war in the woods. "This army . . . is without proper organization," he wrote darkly to his sister's husband. "The volunteer system will not do for such a service." He reviewed the troops on the 24th, but rather than upbraid them for their mutinous conduct, he gave them in his farewell address his usual fatherly encouragement to discipline themselves and follow orders.

Elected to succeed Austin in command was Ed Burleson, a North Carolinian who had seen army and militia service in Missouri and Tennessee. Days short of turning thirty-seven, he was a member of the ayuntamiento of San Felipe; he had arrived in Texas within weeks of the passage of the Law of April 6, and stood to lose everything if the centralist enforcement trumped the more lenient state interpretation. Burleson barely had time to assume his duties when on November 26 a Mexican unit approached San Antonio to reinforce Cos, and Colonel Ugartechea went out with cavalry to escort them in. This was spied by one of the Texans' wiliest scouts, Erastus "Deaf" Smith, who reported the movements to Burleson.

What most interested the citizen soldiers was Smith's observation that the column included a loaded pack train, which fueled speculation that the Mexican army was about to enjoy a payday. Burleson sent out forty cavalry under Jim Bowie to engage the mounted Mexicans of about equal number, and a hundred infantry under Pat Jack to disperse the Mexican soldiers and seize the pack train. Ugartechea's cavalry fought back skillfully, and engaged Bowie in rough ravines along Alazan Creek. When reinforced by fifty men and a cannon sent out by Cos, Ugartechea pinned the Texans in a crossfire and counterattacked, four times. The arrival of Jim Swisher and Texas reinforcements finally turned the battle their way and the Mexicans retreated into the city. The Texans managed to return to their camp with forty captured animals, and when the packs were unloaded they proved to contain not pay, but hay, for the Mexican cavalry. Four volunteers had been wounded in what became known rather drolly as the Grass Fight. Ugartechea lost three dead and fourteen wounded.

Forage, of course, was not an unimportant issue when operating with horses, in winter, when there was no fresh grazing. December arrived, and many of the Texans camped outside the city were ill equipped for the cold. Some began to slip away for the warmth of home, while others began pressuring the new general to attack San Antonio and get it over with. Burleson was more inclined to heed Sam Houston's advice, fall back into a winter camp, and gird their loins for Santa Anna's certain advance. On December 4, one of Burleson's scouts, the quarrelsome, semiliterate Kentuckian named Ben Milam, rode into camp and learned that the majority of the volunteers had finally agreed to the retreat.

Benjamin Rush Milam was already something of a legend as an old Texas hand. He had been imprisoned with James Long and Félix Trespalacios for their filibustering, was released, became persuaded that Trespalacios had had Long killed, plotted to kill Trespalacios, and was imprisoned again, then released again after American intercession. He returned to Mexico in 1824, reconciled with Trespalacios, obtained an empresario contract, and became a colonel in the Mexican army. He was in Monclova on land business when Santa Anna nullified the constitution and suspended the state legislatures. He was imprisoned along with Governor Viesca, escaped, and reached Texas in time to help Collinsworth and his volunteers secure Goliad.

Milam had just turned a prickly forty-eight, and when he learned that Burleson intended to fall back, he stoked the volunteers with a fiery oration on their purpose. He also, according to tradition, reminded them of the urban pleasures, some of them feminine, to be had so close at hand, and concluded with an exhortation now famous: "Who will go with old Ben Milam into San Antonio?" The following dawn, December 5, three hundred followers divided into two divisions, one led by Milam and the other by Francis W. Johnson, and stormed into the city. Meanwhile, Burleson's artillery commander, James C. Neill, opened fire on the Alamo and the remainder of the volunteers kept most of Cos' army occupied there. The Texans rapidly took part of the city, including the Garza house and Veramendi palace, home of the vice governor, and fortified and connected them with trenches. On the sixth the volunteers made slow progress, while getting bogged down in house-to-house combat. Milam never enjoyed those urban pleasures he had alluded to, shot through the head by a sniper before the ten-foot portal of the Veramendi palace on the seventh. On the eighth Cos' garrison received more than six hundred reinforcements, but most of them were conscripts who wanted none of the fight, and Burleson committed a hundred more volunteers to the battle.

When Cos was unsuccessful at overrunning the Texans' camp he withdrew into the Alamo, but then four companies of his cavalry deserted. When volunteer Bailey Hardeman materialized with a captured eighteen-pounder that was trained on the fortress, Cos asked for terms early on the ninth. Burleson accepted his surrender, but unable to feed several hundred prisoners, he extended them parole—as had become the Texan habit—to return to Mexico, on their word not to reenter Texas under arms. After they departed, no hostile Mexican troops remained in the Anglo colonies.

South of the Rio Grande, however, Santa Anna—now calling himself the Napoleon of the West—positioned his armies of invasion and fastened more medals to his chest. Jubilant Texans were soon to learn about a vastly different kind of warfare.

TWENTY-THREE

PRETENDED GOVERNMENT

STEPHEN F. AUSTIN WAS DISMAYED BY THE CHOICE OF men who were to accompany him to the United States as his fellow commissioners. William Wharton had been his enemy for years, "a man I cannot act with," he wrote, "a man . . . destitute of political honesty, and whose attention is much more devoted to injure me than to serve the country." He had a slightly better opinion of Dr. Branch T. Archer, who had been the Whartons' messenger east to contact Sam Houston in 1832. He believed that Archer had good intentions, but "he is very wild." Austin knew, however, that if the people in the United States could see the three of them cooperating despite their differences, Texas would have a much better chance of success at negotiating the million dollars in loans that they needed so desperately.

The fact that men as disparate as Austin and William Wharton were yoked together in the cause was just one way in which the new sort-of government waffled and hedged its bets. They billed themselves as the "Consultation" because they knew that the word "convention" was a red flag to Mexican centralists. In debate, Austin's stated positions were hampered because the empresario himself was not allowed to attend, and his faction was led by Don Carlos Barrett, a Pennsylvania lawyer of forty-seven who had settled in Mina (later Bastrop). His position wasn't as weak as it could have been, because some of the most tainted land speculators were so unpopular with the average citizens that they were defeated and never attended. William Wharton's radical positions were argued by his brother John, who counted as allies perhaps a third of the delegates.

The Consultation finally gathered on November 1, but had no quorum for three days, after which Archer was elected president of the assembly, until he left to join Austin on the mission to the U.S. The delegates were, and felt themselves, only barely empowered to act on behalf of the province. Of 98 men who had been elected to serve, only 58 showed up even after Houston bullied the volunteer army into delivering up its delegates. None of the heavily Hispanic districts—Béxar, Goliad, Refugio, San Patricio, Victoria—were represented at all. Nor was there any agreement on the nature of the gathering: moderates asserted that, as their name suggested, they could merely discuss the situation and make recommendations. Those allied with the Whartons claimed sovereign power. In a compromise that presaged the confusion to follow, the delegates created and recognized governmental authority in the "Permanent Council"—for a period of two weeks.

While about a third of the delegates favored a declaration of independence, and the separatist John Wharton chaired the committee charged with drawing up a document, the moderates were strong enough to win passage instead of a "Declaration of Causes." In it the Texans acknowledged taking up arms, and alleged that Santa Anna's nullification of the Constitution of 1824 had dissolved the bond between Texas and Mexico. Nevertheless, they contended, they were fighting for the "principles" of that constitution, not for independence. They pledged support for "Armies now in the field," and promised land to volunteers in payment for service, but Mexico would find them loyal if the constitution was restored.

Worse confusion followed. In a bid to force the factions to cooperate, the "Organic Law" under which the council would govern Texas gave both the governor and the council the same powers. Elected governor was a tactless forty-seven-year-old Kentuckian named Henry Smith. Husband and widower of two sisters in succession, before marrying a third (who was the second's twin), he had come to Texas in 1827, and although he was seriously wounded in the Battle of Velasco, he later won enough Mexican confidence to be named a *jefe político*. Now he was an ardent independence man, and his selection as governor was largely a concession to that party for forgoing a declaration of independence. Moderates made up the majority of the council. From the outset Smith antagonized them and rebuffed attempts at compromise.

While the Consultation acted without clear direction, Sam Houston's own maneuvering took more turns than a corkscrew. Having agreed with Jackson in 1832 to win Texas for the United States if possible, and having spent much of 1834 lining up support for a revolution, he then on his own initiative had assembled volunteers in Nacogdoches under his own command. At the Consultation, however, he allied himself with Austin and Barrett, arguing that a declaration of independence would alienate Mexican liberals and unite the country against them. Let them now organize and prepare, and independence could be proclaimed at an appropriate time. Houston sometimes defended his stance in a bareknuckled way that lengthened his growing list of enemies. At one juncture a militia captain who had been talked in from the field, Mosely Baker, moved to disband the Consultation and get on with the fight. Houston, whose overriding concern was governmental organization, silenced him by reminding the members that Baker had originally come to Texas on the lam from an Alabama forgery. "I had rather be a slave," he bellowed, "than be a convicted felon!" The Consultation continued, but to the day he died Baker set bear traps in Houston's path. Houston made still more enemies when he moved that the new government nullify the specious land deals that the legislature of Coahuila y Tejas had made with shady empresarios to finance the state's opposition to the centralists. Santa Anna had announced that his forthcoming expedition into Texas was to root out the illegal speculators, and Houston wanted to defuse the dictator's justification for the coming war, while at the same time unifying the American colonies against him and also disempowering the land sharks, whose unpopularity in Texas fueled Tory sympathies. Many of those land dealers, however, were among the most influential leaders in Texas, both Anglo and Tejano.

All this left Houston in a very odd position when the council began debating military measures. The radicals called for creation of a regular army with a commanding general; the moderates felt that militia volunteers were a sufficient force, but should be well supported. In another ill-starred compromise, the council on November 13 created a regular army, but declined to incorporate the existing volunteer companies into it. The choice for commander in chief was Houston, but those present who believed that his famed drunkenness and moral reprobation disqualified him from command also believed they had won something: if Houston wanted troops, he would have to go out and recruit new ones. One person who saw through the smoke was Houston himself: "I very soon discovered that I was a General without an army, serving under . . . a pretended government, that had no head, and no loyal subjects."

And as if all this were not enough to cripple the infant revolution, a new wrench was then thrown into the works. Down in Goliad, Philip Dimmitt began pressing a case that a Texas force should be sent south to neutralize the port of Matamoros at the mouth of the Rio Grande, then held by centralists. There was strong federalist sentiment among the people there, and taking Matamoros could spread the insurrection on into the state of Tamaulipas. The idea began not with him but with Mexican federalists fleeing Santa Anna, whose number included De Zavala, Viesca, Mexía, and even the dictator's erstwhile vice president, Gómez Farías. As Dimmitt's own political stance hardened him from moderate into hawk, it brought him into increasing conflict with Austin, who removed him from command but was overridden by the council, which reinstated him. But surprisingly, Austin did at first endorse the planned action against Matamoros; all agreed that a Mexican should lead it to avoid ethnic overtones, and Mexía was chosen.

Mexía attacked Tampico and was quickly defeated, which prompted Austin to withdraw his support from the Matamoros scheme, but too late. The council had taken it up for reasons both public and private. In its view, to conquer Matamoros would disable Santa Anna from his intended Texas invasion. As much to the point but more quietly, leading Texans who had invested fortunes in the Monclova land speculation saw seizure of the port and its revenues as their last chance to recoup what they had risked. Among that number were Austin's own secretary, Samuel May Williams, and his partner, Thomas McKinney. Ben Milam had been in on it, too, as well as Green DeWitt, Austin's neighboring empresario, and that perennial gadfly Haden Edwards of the Fredonian Rebellion. Houston at first was open to any merits of reducing Matamoros, but after Mexía's defeat, and especially after Dimmitt himself conceded that federalist sentiment on the Rio Grande was not as strong as he once hoped, Houston saw its elevation on the council into an *idée fixe* as lunacy, which sharpened his conflict with the speculator class. Also by now the Matamoros scheme had one other impetus: after the fall of San Antonio, and with the fun over, many of the volunteers began returning to their homes. The prospect of adventure and plunder was needed to keep the men in camp.

With Texas' government, such as it was, distracting itself over Matamoros, Austin once again put his personal feelings aside and undertook his mission to the United States with the hated Wharton and mistrusted Archer. There was no doubt that he considered himself the leader of the three, and for use in the United States he had calling cards printed that identified him simply as "Stephen F. Austin, of Texas."

He spent Christmas at the mouth of the Brazos, upset that a town he wished to start there would have to be postponed because his secretary Sam Williams' Monclova land troubles had prompted him to flee for safety to the United States. Austin had heard dark rumors about Williams' doings in Mexico but refused to believe that his deeply loved right-hand man would deal behind his back. His mood improved considerably after he and Wharton and Archer linked up. In New Orleans on January 6, 1836, they addressed a huge gathering to enormous applause, and came away with loans and pledges for a quarter of a million dollars—a running start at the million they hoped to raise. From there, though, everything went wrong. They were stranded in Nashville in early February, with ice storms having rendered both river and roads impassable, and he and Wharton both were desperately ill with influenza. They also discovered that the farther they traveled away from Texas, the less passionate people felt about it. A general sentiment prevailed that unless Texas declared independence from Mexico, they had little business asking American aid. Up to now Austin had thought talk of independence premature, but now realized that without credentials from a provisional government, it would be "almost useless for us to appear in Washington."

Eventually able to continue north and east, Austin spent three frustrating weeks in New York City, meeting with any bankers who would see him, but he left empty-handed, dismayed that the United States financial establishment was more worried about protecting its profits than supporting a struggle by fellow Americans for freedom in Texas. "Had I known as much of these kind of people . . . as I do now," he wrote bitterly, "I should not have spent any time upon them." When Wharton joined him in New York, the two together finally managed a $100,000 loan for Texas, but only 10 percent of it was paid down. One thing that Austin did gain from the trip was an appreciation of Wharton, whom he had always regarded as a threat. Now in common cause, however, they were "on the best of terms, and I have no doubt will always continue to be—it is not any fault that we ever were otherwise . . . we [had] not known each other personally as we might and ought to have." He also grew quite fond of Branch Archer, whom he now described as "truly a noble fellow . . . and I am very much attached to him."

The more cruel was the irony, then, as Austin successfully made a show of unity with Wharton, that back home their rival factions tried their best to destroy each other. With disputes over state policy catalyzed by personal animosities, Governor Smith suspended the council, the council impeached Smith, and the would-be government paralyzed itself. Houston, witnessing the whole edifice crumble, took what little authority he had as commander in chief of a nonexistent army, repaired to the tiny village of Washington, on the Brazos River about thirty miles north of San Felipe, and began issuing orders, depending on his reputation and personal magnetism to begin collecting a fighting force about him. Houston intensified his argument that with Santa Anna's invasion imminent, Texas should forget about silly Matamoros and establish an interior line of defense from Copano through Refugio and Goliad to Gonzales, and he issued orders for volunteers to assemble in the latter two towns. This plan abandoned San Antonio to the centralists, but the fact that he could never muster enough men to hold the place, plus its lack of military value, and its mostly centralist population, made defending Béxar an untenable idea. He did have some confidence that as new companies arrived from the United States, as he had spent much of the previous year arranging, they would report to him personally. This was fortunate, because when in mid-January 1836 Houston arrived in Goliad to see what kind of force had assembled, he found the largest gaggle of volunteers clustered about none other than Mosely Baker, whom he had insulted at the Consultation.

He also found the Goliad force infected with Matamoros fever, and indeed Houston himself had orders from Governor Smith to forward the expedition. Houston had forged a working relationship with the cantankerous Smith, and those orders were half-hearted and worded with prevarication, giving Houston room to wiggle. Still, he was probably disobeying orders, and certainly defying the will of the council, when in a tour-de-force stump speech he argued most of the volunteers out of the idea. He praised their stand, but pointed out that it was a quartermaster's nightmare to supply them on a march of two hundred miles south through hostile territory, and even if successful, their absence would leave the interior of Texas open to Santa Anna's invasion, which would come from the west. Houston won himself enough of a breather to send Jim Bowie to San Antonio with orders either to retrieve the artillery from the Alamo, blow up the fortifications, and abandon the place, or else to use his own discretion in the matter—an ambiguity that would lead to passionate historical debates in subsequent generations.

After the Consultation adjourned in mid-November, the council became the ad hoc governing body and reassembled in Washington-on-the-Brazos. To the previous layers of intrigue another was added when the chairman of the Military Committee, Wyatt Hanks, saw in the Matamoros scheme a way to undercut Houston: he hadn't been able to prevent his elevation to commander in chief, but when the council reaffirmed the scheme, Hanks authorized them to siphon off the men Houston had assembled. Named to lead the re-endorsed Matamoros assault were two men: a no-show delegate to the Consultation named James Grant, who was a Scotsman and had been secretary to the legislature at the time Santa Anna broke them up, and Francis W. Johnson, Austin's surveyor and former alcalde of San Felipe, who had led a column in the storming of Béxar in early December. Both men were intimately connected with the Monclova land deals and had personal motives to seize the port and its revenues. When Grant and Johnson suddenly materialized at Houston's headquarters with new orders for Matamoros, the "commander in chief" was stunned, but powerless.

The council's shenanigans were already damaging efforts to enlist new soldiers; one of Houston's recruiters, Colonel Henry Millard, had already written of his own problems with them, "I had reason enough to curse the Dmd council before I left them but their late acts I believe justly brought down the curses of the country." With his soldiers reassigned from under him, Houston rode back to Washington to see for himself how things stood there, and was appalled at the chaos and infighting which, if not checked, would leave the country defenseless against Santa Anna. The only hope was to call a new convention to assume plenary powers and declare independence, and put the present operation out of business, as soon as humanly possible. Houston strengthened his alliance with Smith, declaring that he no longer regarded the council as a legitimate body, but instead of returning to the army to contest for authority, he headed east to negotiate a treaty with the Texas Cherokees to ensure that they stayed out of the fight. Houston had been planning this mission for weeks, and of course, the pacification of potentially troublesome Indians was a necessity noted elsewhere on the scene at this time. (Philip Dimmitt did the very same thing with Karankawas in South Texas before attacking Fort Lipantitlán.) But more important, Grant and Johnson now had legitimate command of the army, and Houston could only hope that the whole Matamoros craziness would sort itself out before Santa Anna arrived. Besides, detouring into heavily populated East Texas was the best way to drum up support for a new convention. Perhaps Houston's greatest political skill was his ability to recast bad situations into good results, and on this Cherokee mission he forged critical alliances with the men who accompanied him, including Millard; Irish immigrant John Forbes, who became an invaluable aide-de-camp and commissary general; and George Washington Hockley, whom Houston had known since his days as a Tennessee congressman, and who before long was serving Houston as chief of staff.

The headman of the Texas Cherokees was Duwali ("The Bowl," just as often known by the Anglicized "Bowles"). About eighty years old, he had abandoned the Hiwassie Island branch of the Tennessee Cherokees about seven years before Sam Houston as a young army lieutenant became the government agent to that band. With a couple hundred followers, The Bowl led a long odyssey that ended in East Texas, where they had tried at least twice to win secure land titles from the Mexican government, but failed.

Houston was the ideal emissary: he knew their language and customs, was sympathetic to their culture, and had a long reputation in Tennessee and in the Indian Territory for doing right by them even in the face of white opposition. However, though the Cherokees loved Houston more than any other Anglo leader, they were still annoyed with him for trying to sneak his Creek friends from the Indian Territory onto their Texas land a couple of years previously, which Houston had done in an early attempt to stock Texas with native allies to prepare for the eventual revolution. Complicating the picture further, the man who had acted for several years as Mexico's agent to them, Peter Ellis Bean, was an officer that Houston wasn't sure he could trust. While Bean had offered Houston his help a couple of years before, he had also shown disturbing instances of loyalty to Ugartechea in San Antonio. Houston also likely felt personal jealousy of Bean's considerable influence among the Cherokees.

In negotiating the treaty with The Bowl, it was probably to smooth over his misstep with the Creeks that the new document guaranteed that "no other tribes or Bands of Indians, whatsoever shall settle within the limits" of the Cherokee reservation. In their years in Texas, the Cherokees had also endured continual harassment from Anglo settlers, and their interests were repeatedly ignored by empresarios scrambling to control the land. Houston knew better than to ask the Cherokees to supply warriors for the coming battles; the most he could hope for now was that the Cherokees would just stay out of the fight entirely.

The treaty was concluded at The Bowl's village on February 23, 1836, and formalized at a reception at Adolphus Sterne's house in Nacogdoches soon thereafter. One incident from that meeting demonstrates that Houston was not by now taking anything for granted with The Bowl's Cherokees. Sterne's wife Eva was Houston's godmother, a woman of culture in a frontier town. Her prized possession was a marble-top center table, a recent gift, that stood in the middle of the parlor. When the Texas Cherokees trooped in to solemnify their agreement, the elderly Bowl strode to the middle of the room, and assuming that the marble table had been placed there for him as a kind of throne, grandly sat on it. Mrs. Sterne refrained from direct action, but drawing her husband into the adjoining chamber, hissed angrily, "Make that old Indian get off my table!" Sterne and Houston, wisely, refused to risk offending the Cherokees whose amity they needed.

TWENTY-FOUR

I AM DETERMINED TO DIE
LIKE A SOLDIER

WITH AUSTIN AND WHARTON IN THE UNITED STATES AND with Houston in the Redlands, the Texas Revolution fell for a time into the hands of self-interested military amateurs with delusions of grandeur. Volunteer companies of frontier yahoos that christened themselves with romantic names like the Invincibles were easy marks for the likes of Grant and Johnson. Before the council's dual Matamoros commanders arrived in Houston's camp and swept his command out from under him, they had done the same thing to Colonel James C. Neill, left in command at the Alamo in San Antonio with only a handful of men. They also cleaned out Dimmitt at Goliad.

There is no question that Houston preserved the revolution by talking most of the volunteers out of the Matamoros expedition. With Houston's blessing, some two hundred of them followed Fannin to the coast to regarrison the presidio at Goliad. Others held themselves in readiness while Houston went east to secure the Cherokee treaty. When Grant and Johnson finally headed toward Matamoros, they mustered between them only about sixty-five men, and then they divided their command roughly in half between them. Doubtless the volunteers expected to find adventure and pillage and conquest, and things began auspiciously enough, as Grant's group captured a mounted Mexican detachment. The prisoners escaped soon after, and then, amazingly, the command distracted itself in a mustanging expedition, capturing and corralling wild horses, ranging as far away as the present site of Raymondville to obtain them. It was a fatal dalliance, for what they found next was not mustangs but Santa Anna's ace general, José de Urrea, at the head of a southern invasion column already spearing its way into Texas.

A career military man of thirty-nine, born in Tucson, Urrea had been active in most of the insurrections since Iturbide, as prominent officers were expected to cast their lots and take their risks. Often he was allied with Santa Anna, under whom he had risen to become military governor of Durango, but his dossier lacks evidence of any thirst for personal power. He was a careful planner and mover; before departing Matamoros with a force of four hundred on January 18, he was fully apprised of the Texans' intentions toward that city, and he placed scouts throughout the brush country of South Texas. He had no trouble homing in on the rebels, and on February 27 Urrea pounced on Johnson's half of the expedition near San Patricio. After a series of small actions Johnson and about four others made good an escape; thirty of their companions were killed or captured in the worst bloodshed yet of the war. On March 2 at Agua Dulce, about twenty miles away, Urrea similarly accounted for Grant's half of the Matamoros expedition in a sharp ambush. Urrea's diary states that Grant was killed in the fighting, but a different story, credited by early Texas historians but since allowed to drop from the canon, was that Grant was captured. After Urrea left the area, the local commander tied Grant to one of his wild mustangs, which dragged him to death.

The effects of the Matamoros effort rippled wider than the death of Grant and flight of Johnson. Once the council realized the danger in which Neill and the Alamo had been left, they detailed the man only recently named their chief recruiting officer to round up a hundred men to reinforce Neill's nearly naked fort.

Of all the southern hotspurs who flooded into Texas in the late 1820s and early 1830s, William Barret Travis could stand as a metaphor for any of them. He was young, twenty-six, or only twenty-two at the time of the Anahuac Disturbances, in which he was a principal player. He was troubled, "G.T.T." in the wake of abandoning his infant son and pregnant wife in Alabama. There is a family tradition, variously affirmed and denied, that he dispatched his wife's lover and obtained the leave of a local magistrate before heading west. He arrived in Texas after the Law of April 6, 1830, making his entry illegal. His intention to start life anew was suggested by his applying for, and receiving, land as a single man, and by his courtship of Rebecca Cummings. He agitated for independence from the time of his arrival, which put him at odds with Austin and the peace party. Even some of the tough old Texas hands who otherwise thought separation from Mexico a good idea also thought that Travis was a conceited dandy and hothead who needn't be taken too seriously. When he was directed to the Alamo, Travis requested that five hundred men be assigned to him. With the council's sights set on Matamoros, they authorized Travis to recruit one hundred new men, with the stipulation that he pay for their equipment himself.

Travis tried to get out of it. "Sir," he wrote Governor Smith, "I must beg that [you] will recall the order for me to go to Bexar in command of so few men. I am willing, nay anxious, to go to the defence of Bexar, and I have done everything in my power to equip the enlisted men and get them off. But, sir . . . by going off into the enemy's country with such little means, so few men, and them so badly equipped—" Smith stuck by his order. Travis, to his further dismay, had trouble finding men willing to sign up. "The people are cold and indifferent . . . and, in consequence of dissensions between contending and rival chieftains, they have lost all confidence in their own government and officers." When Travis reported to Colonel Neill at the Alamo on February 3, he had only thirty men in tow. Once within the walls, however, his mood shifted to a strange kind of fatalism. He disagreed with Houston's view that San Antonio was expendable, and if glory in life or death was to be met here, so be it. "We will never give up the Post of honor," he now wrote. "We consider death preferable to disgrace which would be the result of giving up the Post which has been so dearly won."

At the Alamo Travis found Bowie and about thirty more volunteers who had arrived with Houston's suggestion to level the place and retreat. Bowie, however, joined Travis in a kind of thrall that the place must be defended at all costs. At the siege of Béxar in November, Bowie had exasperated Austin with his apparent inability to obey any order given him, and now he went against the commander in chief's wishes as well. Perhaps mindful of Houston's violent temper, Bowie wrote not to him, but to Governor Smith: "the salvation of Texas depends in great measure on keeping Bexar out of the hands of the enemy." If they lost it, "there is no stronghold from which to repel [Santa Anna] on his march toward the Sabine . . . we will rather die in these ditches than give it up to the enemy. These citizens deserve our protection, and the public safety demands our lives rather than evacuate this post."

It was probably in Bowie's group that another man whose name has become inextricably linked with the Alamo entered the fortress: James Butler Bonham, an Alabama lawyer who turned twenty-nine on February 20. He and Travis had been friends a long time, and he shared Travis' temperament: having been expelled from college, he became a lawyer anyway and once served time for contempt when he refused to apologize for caning an opposing lawyer. At the outbreak of the revolution he raised a company of volunteers calling themselves the Mobile Grays, brought them to Texas, and won Houston's endorsement as a cavalry lieutenant. Since he placed himself under Houston's command, Bonham was not part of the Matamoros scheme, and spent January waiting for orders; once at the Alamo he became Travis' most reliable courier.

Into this growing mix of resolve and defiance, both of the Mexicans and of their own command structure, there filed into the Alamo on February 8 a party of about a dozen men just lately arrived from Tennessee, with frontier legend David Crockett in the lead, more famous for his buckskin coat and coonskin cap than for his homespun failure as a congressman. Like Houston, Crockett at forty-nine was a disgraced refugee from Andrew Jackson's political entourage, but where Houston went into exile as a drunk and squaw man in the Indian Territory before coming to Texas to reinvent himself, Crockett after his defeat for reelection hunted bears, published memoirs, and promoted himself into a woodsy American Everyman. When a fresh attempt to take on the Jackson machine failed, they could, said Crockett, go to hell, and he would go to Texas. Even Travis was impressed and offered Crockett a share of command, but with appropriate modesty Crockett asked only to serve as a "high private" on some section of the wall with his Tennessee boys.

Just when it seemed the situation at the Alamo might jell into an adequate defense, if they could get in more men, it was riven by schisms similar to those that had crippled the government itself. When Colonel Neill was called away to tend to urgent family illness, he left Travis in command, but many of the volunteers, finding him a posturing young prig, shunned him in favor of the middle-aged and affable Bowie. Nothing had improved their inclination to take orders. Travis expected Santa Anna as soon as the prairie grass could feed the Mexican horses, and had he worked the men to the dropping point to prepare the ruined Alamo to receive an attack, it might or might not be ready in time. But the nonmilitary yahoos, still enjoying the freedom of the city, preferred to spend time in the cantinas listening to the legendary Bowie tell his stories. Travis was beside himself, protesting to Governor Smith, "Bowie was elected by two small companies, & since his election has been roaring drunk all the time; has assumed all command—& is proceeding in a most disorderly & irregular manner & turning everything topsy turvey."

On February 14 Travis worked out a power-sharing arrangement with his more famous rival, but Bowie's grand gesture at citizen soldiery was short-lived. Weakened by long and superhuman alcohol consumption, he fell into a lethal delirium of pneumonia and probably diphtheria, and was not a factor thereafter. Travis turned to the talents of Green Jameson as his engineer to prepare gun emplacements and shore up gaps in the wall surrounding the three-acre compound. Suddenly, on February 23, lookouts in the bell tower of San Fernando Cathedral raised an alarm that the Mexican army was approaching—weeks before Travis was expecting them. Santa

Anna was enough of a commander to know the value of surprise, and he moved with astonishing speed. Gathering battalions from different points, counting Urrea in the south and Joaquín Ramírez y Sesma on his flank, he would aggregate about six thousand troops to prosecute the campaign. He reviewed his own contingent in Saltillo on January 25, and crossed the Rio Grande on February 16 with more than two hundred carts and wagons, nearly two thousand pack mules, and more than twenty cannons. The dictator reached San Antonio a week later, driving his men through weather so foul that several animals and even a number of soldiers froze to death in a sleeting norther. It was cruel, but militarily it was a bold accomplishment.

In surprise that must have approached shock, Travis rounded up his men from the town and hustled them into the still unfinished fortress. Mustering only about one hundred fifty, he sent appeals for aid as fast as he could write them. One was to the alcalde at Gonzales: "The enemy in large force is in sight. We want men and provisions. Send them to us." Jointly with Bowie he sent to Fannin at Goliad: "We hope you will send all the men you can spare promptly. . . . We have but little provisions. . . . We deem it unnecessary to repeat to a brave officer, who knows his duty, that we call on him for assistance." As the Mexican army took possession of San Fernando Cathedral, they unfurled from its tower a banner of solid blood-red, a signal that no quarter would be given the American defenders. Travis ordered his largest gun, the eighteen-pounder on the southwest parapet, trained on the tower, and fired. Santa Anna placed four of his artillery pieces west and south of the fortress and himself opened fire. As the gravity of the situation enveloped them, Travis sent another appeal to the incipient Texas government on the following day—a document traditionally praised as one of the most heroic in American history, and sometimes debunked as an artifact of jingoistic stupidity. Travis feverishly scratched out at least three copies and sent them by different messengers to be sure that at least one got through:

> Commandancy of the Alamo—.
> Bejar, Feb'y 24th, 1836—

To the People of Texas and all Americans *in the World*—
Fellow Citizens and Compatriots—I am besieged, by a thousand or more of the Mexicans under Santa Anna—I have sustained a continual bombardment & cannonade for 24 hours & have not lost a man—The enemy has demanded surrender at discretion, otherwise, the garrison are to be put to the sword, if the fort is taken—I have answered the

demand with a cannon shot, and our flag still waves proudly from the walls—*I shall never surrender or retreat. Then,* I call on you in the name of Liberty, of patriotism & everything dear to the American character, to come to our aid with all dispatch—The enemy is receiving reinforcements daily & will no doubt increase to three or four thousand in four or five days. If this call is neglected, I am determined to sustain myself as long as possible & die like a soldier who never forgets what is due to his own honor & that of his country—VICTORY OR DEATH.

William Barret Travis
Lt. Col. Comdt.

P.S. The Lord is on our side—When the enemy appeared in sight we had not three bushels of corn—We have since found in deserted houses 80 or 90 bushels & got into the walls 20 or 30 head of beeves—

Travis

TWENTY-FIVE

THE NEW NATION

THE CALL FOR A NEW CONVENTION OF THE PEOPLE THAT Houston felt was indispensable to the survival of the revolution got caught up, like everything else, in the strife between the governing council and the governor. The council in San Felipe issued the call, Smith vetoed it, and it was passed over his veto. The delegates were to convene in Washington on the Brazos River on March 1.

The Consultation was baited into removing to Washington by a committee of eight local boosters, who on February 18 had rented an unfinished house from real estate developers Peter Mercer and Noah T. Byars, with a three-month lease for $170 and Mercer and Byars to finish out the building by the time the convention began. The committee then offered use of the premises for free if the convention would meet in their town. (Byars was also a gunsmith, which gave rise to the legend that Texas' independence was declared in an unfinished blacksmith shop furnished for free by the proprietor. As with much of Texas' traditional history, that was close but not entirely accurate.)

The town was less than a year old; only in subsequent years was the name amplified to Washington-on-the-Brazos to avoid confusion with that other, better known, capital. It was founded by one John Hall on land deeded to him by his father-in-law, Andrew Robinson, one of Austin's Old Three Hundred, in exchange for a promise of care in Robinson's old age. One of the first to arrive for the convention was William Fairfax Gray, a Virginian who hoped to obtain an appointment as secretary to the meeting. In the town's only boardinghouse he found "the host's wife and children, and about thirty lodgers, all slept in the same apartment, some in beds, some on cots, but the greater part on the floor. The supper consisted of fried pork and coarse corn bread, and miserable coffee. I was fortunately lodged on a good cot with a decent Tennesseean named Kimball, who is looking for land, but said that the state of anarchy is such that he is afraid to buy and is waiting to see the course of things after the meeting of the Convention."

"It is laid out in the woods," Gray wrote of the town, "with only one well defined street, which consists of an opening cut out of the woods. The stumps still standing. A rare place to hold a national convention in. They will have to leave it promptly to avoid starvation."

Early arrivals who reached Washington at the end of February had been bedding down in their shirtsleeves, but in the wee hours of the appointed day, March 1, they awoke to a norther that roared through during the night and dropped the thermometer to 33 degrees. The forty-four delegates who assembled that morning flapped and shivered in the Mercer-Byars house and discovered it still unfinished, and prey to the elements. Still, they set straight to work, appointing a committee to draft a declaration of independence. Seven more members arrived on the third, and stragglers coming in over the following week increased the eventual total to fifty-nine men. Only two were native Tejanos; by far the overwhelming majority of the remainder were Southerners. The plurality were Tennesseeans, of whom there were thirteen. Only one was from Illinois; two were from New York and two from Pennsylvania. It was a gathering largely of newcomers: of fifty-nine delegates, nine or ten were resident in Texas by 1830, and perhaps only three of them were legal immigrants before the Law of April 6 closed the border. Fifteen had arrived in 1835 alone. Strictly by the numbers, it was a convention of Southern squatters, but examination of the membership reveals a wealth of intellect and political experience.

Unanimously elected president of the convention was Richard Ellis of Alabama, fifty-five, who had served in his state's constitutional convention in 1819 and gone on to become an associate justice of their supreme court. He didn't settle in Texas until 1834, but was known in Texas from previous visits, during one of which he acted as Austin's emissary to Haden Edwards to attempt to reason him out of his Fredonian Republic fantasy. Ellis had a reputation for being brusque but reasonable, and on that first day he appointed a committee to draft the declaration of independence. That committee was chaired, either ironically or appropriately, by the one delegate who had spent less time in Texas than any other, George C. Childress of Tennessee, who had arrived only ten weeks earlier. Well educated and well connected, the thirty-two-year-old widower was the brother-in-law of Tennessee congressman, and later American president, James Knox Polk, and the nephew of Austin's rival empresario, Sterling Robertson.

Assisting Childress on the committee were James Gaines, Edward Conrad, Collin McKinney, and Bailey Hardeman, who mixed with an interesting chemistry. Childress' youthful brilliance was ballasted by age and practical experience. Collin McKinney of Red River was seventy, the oldest man present at the convention. A shrewd merchant and lay preacher, he had participated in Ben Milam's land speculations, but hedged his bet by maintaining his interests in the border counties of Arkansas, whose sovereignty was uncertain. He knew how to tread water. James Gaines of Sabine, born in 1776, had for many years run the ferry at Gaines' Crossing on the Sabine River, where the old Camino Real entered the United States. Most land immigration from the United States came by him, and he was an early drumbeater for the war party. His spelling and penmanship were crude, but he had no difficulty making himself understood. Forty-one-year-old Bailey Hardeman of Tennessee was a mountain man and Santa Fe trader who had just begun a new life. Together with his sister, two brothers, and their families, they located to Texas in the fall of 1835, and no sooner arrived than Bailey volunteered for the military. He arrived at San Antonio with a captured eighteen-pounder, after the city fell but before Cos capitulated, helping the besieged general make up his mind to surrender. Edward Conrad, a Philadelphia printer, was just short of twenty-five, and had arrived in Texas only three months before as a volunteer in the revolution. He arrived at the convention with Sam Houston, the latter having been elected to represent Refugio municipality. The army camped there, however, desired its own voice at the convention, and so elected and sent Conrad and David Thomas to Washington with their own petitions and the request that they be seated as delegates. Conrad's presence gave the army representation on the committee.

Childress' group retired to meet, and produced a document in one day—fueling the belief that Childress had come to the convention with a draft already prepared. The document was modeled closely on the United States' Declaration of Independence, with a preamble and a lengthy list of causes. Some charges were true, some were artfully stretched, and some contained more propaganda than fact.

- "It has denied us the right of worshipping the Almighty according to the dictates of our own consciences." That was true, and latecoming squatters who had no right to any land anyway may have found this offensive, but legitimate settlers were aware that Catholicism was a condition of landholding at the time they immigrated.
- "It has demanded us to deliver up our arms; which are essential to our defense." That was true in the specific instance of the Gonzales cannon, but no general effort—excepting Cos' march north—had been made to disarm the population. Still, persons now taken under arms were liable to summary execution.
- "It has sacrificed our welfare to the state of Coahuila." In truth the

concessions granted by Santa Anna the previous year went a long way
to improve Texas' footing as the junior partner in the dual state. Moreover, Coahuila's hostility to Santa Anna had cost the state government
its very existence, and that was a legislature by whom many leading
Texas Anglos had done very well indeed in the land-speculating business. There was a keen awareness on the part of convention members
of the role that the shady land dealing had played in matters coming to
the present pass. Delegate James Collinsworth of Brazoria, who when
a temporary government was formed became chairman of the military
affairs committee, wrote of his intense dislike of those men around
him who seemed motivated by their chances for personal wealth. He
named among them the convention president, Richard Ellis, and
Robert Potter of Nacogdoches.

- "It has made piratical attacks upon our commerce." The imposition of
  port duties both in 1832 and 1835 had in fact been done with legal authority, although clumsily and in some instances perhaps corruptly.

- "It has suffered the military commandants stationed among us to exercise arbitrary acts of oppression, thus . . . rendering the military superior to the civil power." That was true enough, but would have been
  true during any civil war.

- "It incarcerated in a dungeon, for a long time, one of our citizens, for
  no other cause but a zealous endeavor to procure the acceptance of
  our constitution." Stephen F. Austin was not mentioned by name, but
  Childress acknowledged to the empresario's nephew that he felt that
  the hardships that Austin bore and the respect that he deserved mer-
  ited special mention.

- "It has invaded our country, both by sea and land, with intent to lay
  waste our territory and drive us from our homes; and has now a large
  mercenary army advancing to carry on against us a war of extermination." Use of the term "our country" was specious since there was no
  country recognized by anyone else, and alleging the employment of
  a "mercenary army," with its vague allusion to the Hessians used
  against the American colonies, may have been calculated to gain sympathy from home. But Santa Anna had certainly invaded, and certainly
  he intended to sweep the Anglo colonies from the map in a campaign
  that, in a subsequent century would have been called by another
  name: ethnic cleansing.

- Last and most important, the Mexican government "hath been, during the whole time of our connection with it, the contemptible sport

and victim of successive military revolutions and hath continually exhibited every characteristic of a weak, corrupt, and tyrannical government." That was undeniable, and therein lies the salient issue of the Texas Revolution's legitimacy: whether Santa Anna's seizure of power and formal nullification of the Constitution of 1824 ended the obligation of fealty on the part of Mexico's federal components. Other states thought that it did and had been crushed for their impertinence. The Mexican Revolution had not taken place in a vacuum; the principles of free government espoused by Simón Bolivar and others had already shaken Latin America to the southern tip of the Andes as early as 1810—a context almost universally forgotten in discussing the Mexico-Texas conflict. Texas' parent government, the state legislature of Coahuila y Tejas, was broken up by troops of Santa Anna's reactionary regime, and prominent Mexican federalists were even then fleeing through Texas, angry and fearful and desperate to bring the dictator down. With the rest of Mexico prostrate, Texas stood alone against him. "We are, therefore, forced to the melancholy conclusion that the Mexican people have acquiesced in the destruction of their liberty, and the substitution therefor of a military government."

The convention approved the Declaration of Independence, and instructed that an official copy be presented for signing the following day. When that copy, "in a fair hand," was produced on March 2, it was found upon reading to be so full of mistakes that the ceremony was put off until a corrected version could be signed, on the third day. (The dearly loved myth that Sam Houston requested that the signing be delayed one day until March 2, his birthday, is not true—alas.) Although the date of March 2 remained on the document, the signing actually took place on the 3rd, and delegates who reached Washington after March 3 signed it as they arrived.

The next task to be undertaken was the drafting of a constitution, which continued until word came of the arrival of Santa Anna in San Antonio de Béxar. With the Alamo besieged, most members were ready to vote to ride to its relief. Sam Houston, who had exercised all his influence to get the convention together, insisted that the others stay put and get a government organized. As commander in chief of the army, he would lead the defense, and rode off. The convention continued until mid-March, until news arrived of disaster in San Antonio. "I shall never forget the alarm manifested by many honorable members of the Convention the night the news arrived of the fall of the Alimo," wrote delegate Collinsworth. "The *venerable* president of that body rose in his seat with much trepidation and pulling a small pistol from his pocket and proposed adjourning . . . as the enemy would upon us before morning. This was objected to & overruled. But the news of the fall of the alimo was unpleasing music to the ears of those aforesaid land speculators and they were now willing to lead the retreat." No sooner was the constitution signed than the convention packed up and the newly organized "Ad Interim Government" rumbled off to the coast in retreat.

With the Mercer-Byars house having never been finished, and only occupied for two weeks of the three-month lease, the committee of gentlemen stiffed Mercer and Byars for the rent on their rustic Independence Hall. The newborn government, cognizant that it had not been party to the rental contract, wasn't good for it, either. As late as 1850, Byars petitioned the Third Legislature for relief, seeking to "respectfully represent to your Honourable boddy that . . . he never had obtained one cent." The legislature referred the matter to a committee, which considered the plea, and then basing their decision on the lack of evidence submitted, stiffed him again.

TWENTY-SIX

BRILLIANT, POINTLESS, PYRRHIC

IT WAS TRUE, AS WILLIAM BARRET TRAVIS WROTE TO THE convention, that he answered the Mexican demand for surrender with shot from his eighteen-pounder, a single round from which required the expenditure of twelve pounds of precious powder. There was much more to the story, however.

Jim Bowie from his sickbed heard the boom of the big gun, but immediately sensed the wisdom of talking things out. Being the most prominent American in San Antonio and the son-in-law of the late Governor Veramendi, he took the lead. He sent Green Jameson with a message under a white flag disavowing the defiant shot. He explained that it was fired "at the time that a red flag was raised over the tower, and a little afterward they told me that a part of your army had sounded a parley, which, however, was not heard before the firing of said shot. I wish, Sir, to ascertain if it be true that a parley was called." Santa Anna's aide-de-camp, José Batres, replied that "the Mexican army cannot come to terms under any conditions with rebellious foreigners to whom there is no other recourse left, if they wish to save their lives, than to place themselves immediately at the disposal of the Supreme Government from whom alone they may expect clemency after some considerations are taken up."

Travis was royally incensed that, once again, Bowie dealt behind his back and undercut his authority. But seeing the full power of Mexico filing into San Antonio brought even the truculent Travis to his senses. He sent out his own emissary, this one to Colonel Almonte, who recorded in his journal that Travis' message was "that if I wished to speak with him, he would receive me with much pleasure." Almonte, whose sympathy for the Americans was well known in the colonies, replied now in the same manner as Batres.

The citizenry of San Antonio de Béxar, in general, welcomed the arrival of Santa Anna. Undoubtedly their overall hostility to the cause of independence was one reason that Houston saw no point to defending the city. The dictator's occupation of the town was rough, however, as it was wherever the Mexican army bivouacked. Supplies were seized, citizens were pressed into menial labor for the troops, and in later years more than one woman recalled staying mostly hidden during the siege, for Santa Anna was accustomed to his choice of girls with whom to reinforce his reputation as a lothario.

From the very beginning of the siege, a simple narrative history of the Alamo that is certain to be factually accurate becomes all but impossible. Indeed, the emergence of the record during the nineteenth century renders this inevitable. The valor of the Anglo defense became instant legend. Yet as the years went on, historical interest in the Texas Revolution reached such a low point that the Alamo chapel itself was very nearly demolished, and most of the outbuildings of the mission were in fact demolished. In the 1920s University of Texas scholar Amelia Williams began a years-long scholarly reconstruction of the siege and battle that stood, by default, for decades, although she herself probed the story only enough to realize that many questions lingered. In fact she discouraged publication of her famous doctoral dissertation on the Alamo until further work could be done. Only in the past couple of decades has the Alamo story been subject to a flood of new research—some illuminating, some awful, and some merely mischievous.

With that caveat in mind, it is certain that Santa Anna began a wary encirclement of the fortress with fortified breastworks, and Travis could feel the noose tighten day by day. "The enemy have been busily employed," he said in his last appeal for aid, dated March 3. There were now camps, "in Bejar, four hundred yards west; in Lavilleta, three hundred yards south; at the powder house, one thousand yards east by south; on the ditch, eight hundred yards northeast, and at the old mill, eight hundred yards north." Travis' accounting of Santa Anna's troop placements revealed a curious gap: there were camps northeast and southeast, but not due east. One leading Bexareño, José Antonio Navarro, was a friend of the Anglos and a special friend of Austin himself, but he maintained that Santa Anna deliberately left an eastern corridor open, hoping the Alamo defenders would make an escape and not force a costly battle. The dictator had announced as clearly as he could, in flying the red banner from San Fernando Cathedral, and with the occasional playing of the *Degüello*, the dolorous bugle fanfare of no quarter, that he intended to take no prisoners. Yet, the consistent success with which Travis sent and received dispatches, and with which reinforcements entered the compound, makes one wonder whether Navarro was right.

The dictator covered his entrenchments with a nonstop bombardment, first from the two six-pounders that arrived with him, and as his heavier guns arrived, from two long-range nine-pounders, and one eight-inch and one five-and-a-half-inch howitzer. Keeping the defenders' heads down was crucial, especially after the arrival of Crockett and his Tennesseeans. Travis assigned them the most vulnerable point on the perimeter, the makeshift south palisade, where they used their .58-caliber long rifles to lethal effect. It was probably Crockett who was observed by Don Rafael Saldaña of the Tampico Battalion, stalking the top of the wall. "He wore a buckskin suit and a cap all of a pattern entirely different from the suits worn by his comrades. This man would kneel or lie down behind the low parapet, rest his long gun and fire and we all learned to keep at a good distance when he was seen to make ready to shoot. He rarely missed his mark and when he fired he always rose to his feet and calmly reloaded his gun, seemingly indifferent to the shots fired at him by our men. He had a strong resonant voice and often railed at us, but as we did not understand English we could not comprehend the import of his words other than that they were defiant. This man I later learned was known as 'Kwockey.' "

With such bravado, and with his fiddle and his storytelling, Crockett did much to preserve morale in the doomed garrison. In fact, taunting from the walls, though not understood by most of the Mexican soldiers, did lead them to nickname the Texans the "Goddammyes." Travis reported that after more than two hundred rounds of ball and canister had been directed at the fort, he had not suffered any casualties. "The spirits of my men are still high," he maintained, "although they have had much to depress them. We have contended for ten days against an enemy whose numbers are variously estimated at from fifteen hundred to six thousand men. . . . A reinforcement of about one thousand men is now entering Bejar from the west. . . . The citizens of this municipality are all our enemies except those who have joined us heretofore; we have but three Mexicans now in the fort. . . . Col. Fannin is said to be on the march to this place with reinforcements, but I fear it is not true, as I have repeatedly sent to him for aid without receiving any." Travis entrusted the March 3 letter to James Bonham and sent him off.

Others in the garrison also had the chance to write letters home; none of them were under any illusion about their chances of survival. The defenders comprised a microcosm of Anglo hopes and dreams for Texas, from middle-aged men who had failed at business back east and wanted to start over, to restless teenagers who volunteered because they didn't know what else to do with themselves. One of them, lawyer Daniel Cloud, who had just turned twenty-two and had enlisted with four friends from the same county in Kentucky, summed up their thoughts: "If we succeed, the Country is ours, it is immense in extent and fertile in its soil. . . . If we fail, death in the cause of Liberty and humanity is not a cause for shuddering."

The most common response to Travis' appeals for help was silence. The largest force in Texas was with Fannin in Goliad; he made a half-hearted attempt on February 26 to march to San Antonio with over three hundred men, but hardly started before a broken-down wagon and strayed stock prompted him to return. Soon after he left with the latest dispatches, Bonham, disgusted at the country's inertia, returned to die with his mates. The only aid Travis received, in response to an earlier appeal, was thirty-two additional volunteers from Gonzales. Led by a New York hatter of twenty-six named George Kimbell, they threaded their way through the Mexican camps and into the compound at three o'clock on the morning of March 1. Recent research suggests that there could have been other reinforcements, but this evidence is inconclusive and the traditional figure of 183 defenders, with a handful of noncombatants, still serves. Sam Houston had long since advised San Antonio be abandoned and the Alamo blown up, and his strategy of falling back and preparing some kind of creditable army to meet Santa Anna was as well known as it was unpopular. Travis still contended that the showdown should be there and then. "The power of Santa Anna is to be met here, or in the colonies; we had better meet them here, than to suffer a war of desolation to rage in our settlements. . . . I look to the *colonies alone* for aid: unless it arrives soon, we shall have to fight the enemy on his own terms." That doomed contest, of course, was exactly what Houston hoped to avoid. "I will, however," Travis wrote, "do the best I can under the circumstances; and I feel confident that the determined valor, and desperate courage, heretofore evinced by my men, will not fail them in the last struggle: and although they may be sacrificed to the vengeance of a gothic enemy, the victory will cost the enemy so dear, that it will be worse for him than a defeat."

That this would genuinely prove to be the case was ensured by the highest card in Travis' hands, the arsenal of heavy guns sequestered within the fortress. His artillery commander, a former U.S. Army gunner from Pennsylvania named Almaron Dickinson, arranged his assets for maximum effect. To protect the fort from the east, Dickinson piled up earth inside the east wall of the roofless, ruined chapel, and mounted three twelve-pounders overlooking the approach. Supporting Crockett and his Tennessee boys along the wooden palisade just south of the chapel's entrance was a battery of four-pounders; a similar file of eight-pounders protected the north wall, with two more eight-pounders mounted on a redoubt in the middle of the plaza to repel any break into the area. Various other pieces of ordnance were strategically placed—the long-range eighteen-pounder on the southwest parapet facing the town, a small swivel gun atop the hospital, and other single guns covering entrances and weak points. Solid shot for all the calibres of guns was in short supply—it would have been of limited utility anyway—and Dickinson's assistant, Sam Blair of Tennessee, utilized his time chopping up horseshoes into charges of grapeshot.

Santa Anna realized the same thing that Bowie and Travis had known from the beginning. The whole mission complex encompassed between two and three acres; it would have taken a thousand men to have any chance of defending it successfully. He also knew that he did not have time to protract the siege indefinitely. With his latest influx of reinforcements, Santa Anna may have had as many as four thousand men at his disposal, although recent writers have begun theorizing a smaller figure. But it was enough to assault the Alamo from all sides at once, find a weak point, and break through; his artillery had already punched a hole in the eastern wall. On Friday, March 4, Santa Anna's guns began shelling the fort from 250 yards' distance, and the following morning from only 200 yards. Eventually Travis realized that no more help was coming, and assembled his men and presented their options: surrender, fight to the death, or try to escape. Only one man, a friend of Bowie's named Louis Rose, announced his preference for escape. Nicknamed Moses for his age, fifty-one, he had been a French lieutenant and was a rare survivor of Napoleon's invasion of Russia; he knew a losing proposition when he saw it. He was let out through a window that night and made good his escape; in later years it was he who began the legend that Travis had drawn a line on the ground with his sword. The tale was an unnecessary embellishment, for the decision of the rest of the band to stay to the end needed no amplification.

With the walls severely battered, Santa Anna began assembling his entire force to attack in the wee hours of the morning of Sunday, March 6. He intended to attack in four places: the makeshift palisade on the south near the church, the east wall, the northeast corner where a section of wall had come down, and the northwest corner where a postern gate could be opened once they were inside. Each infantryman had ten rounds of ammunition; each column was in position by 4 A.M. They attacked an hour later, with a cheer for the dictator. It was Travis' second in command, Captain John Baugh, who first saw them coming and spread the alarm. Travis, with his sword and double-barreled shotgun, took a position on the north wall. Rifle fire and grapeshot beat back the first assault, giving rise to a brief cheer from the defenders. First light was not yet full, however, before the columns regrouped and surged forward again, and were beaten back again.

In the third assault, the column that attacked from the east was bled by Dickinson's twelve-pounders from atop the chapel wall, and they shifted their attack to the northeast corner, where in company with the troops already engaged there as well as the northwest column that also merged, they finally made it over the wall. Most accounts agree that Travis was one of the first to fall, shot in the forehead while directing fire from the eight-pounders atop the north wall. Some of the Mexican soldiers then inside made their way to the west corner of the north wall and opened the postern gate, allowing a second tide of invaders to flood into the courtyard. The eight-pounders in the plaza redoubt raked into them, but there were just too many. The fate of the Anglos was sealed. At a signal from Baugh they retreated into the Long Barracks and sold their lives as dearly as possible, room by room, as the swivel gun on the roof boomed charge after charge of grapeshot into the Mexicans now swarming the plaza. Bowie was killed in his hospital sickbed; after the fight, his body was paraded around the plaza, held aloft on bayonets.

A separate furious assault led by General Juan Amador finally wrested control of the southeast palisade from Crockett and his boys, who retired to a secondary line at the nearby chapel entrance. The eighteen-pounder on the southwest parapet fell into Mexican hands, and it was wheeled around and used to batter the barricade before the chapel door. Captain Dickinson dashed into an anteroom of the church where his wife Susanna, his infant daughter, and a few other noncombatants were huddled; he told her that the battle was lost and she should try to save herself. He then disappeared into the fatal melee. The next time the door of the anteroom crashed open it was an Anglo defender, who was killed before their eyes. At the close of the fight a small knot of defenders, six or seven, were cornered in the church, attempted to surrender, and were summarily executed. Crockett may or may not have been among them.

A Mexican officer entered the anteroom and demanded that Mrs. Dickinson come away with him. The others in the room followed, mostly Tejana women and Travis' slave, Joe. The floor of the chapel was ankle-deep in gore; one recalled her shoes filling with blood as she made her way out. As she was led away another shot echoed, and Susanna Dickinson took a ball in the leg. She was taken to the house of Ramón Músquiz, a former *jefe político*, where she had lodged before the Mexican army appeared. She was only twenty-two, but had the presence of mind, according to one account, to show her husband's Masonic apron to an officer in hopes of humane treatment. When Santa Anna finally met with her, he gave her two dollars and a blanket, assigned her Almonte's servant as a guide, and sent her east toward Gonzales with a letter to Houston, warning him to give up the war or suffer the fate of the Alamo garrison.

Santa Anna ordered San Antonio's alcalde, Don Francisco Antonio Ruiz, to take charge of disposing of the hundreds of bodies, and assigned dragoons to assist him. The dead Texans, 182 by Ruiz' count, were arranged in layers of cordwood in two huge pyres, which were lit in late afternoon. The dictator ordered that dead Mexican soldiers be interred in the cemetery. "Not having sufficient room for them," Ruiz recalled, "I ordered some of them to be thrown in the river, which was done on the same day." Some recent research casts Ruiz' account into doubt, but other reminiscences confirm the demoralizing sight of rafts of dead soldiers snagging brush along the San Antonio River downstream from the city. Ruiz estimated Santa Anna's dead at 1,600 men, almost certainly too high, but perhaps close to the mark if used to describe both killed and wounded. The Alamo's defenders were nearly all frontier marksmen, armed to the teeth and backed by artillery primed with grapeshot. The Mexicans had assaulted the walls in Napoleonic formation, and for all their bravery, until they reached the base of the walls they were easy targets. For the Texans to have sold their lives at three to one, not an unreasonable guess when fighting from a fortification, an estimate of 500 to 600 Mexican dead is probably more accurate.

Whatever the exact figure, the Alamo remains a monument to supreme courage in the face of overwhelming odds. It is not, however, a monument to military intelligence. Houston was absolutely right in asserting that neither the Alamo nor San Antonio itself had any strategic or tactical importance. In the Mexican army, General Vicente Filisola made the same argument to Santa Anna. From a purely military standpoint, the only thing dumber than the decision to defend it at all costs was Santa Anna's decision to take it at all costs. But the Alamo siege, the sacrifice of hundreds of Mexican infantry in taking it, and the immolation of its defenders show it had become a symbol of something else: the degree to which the Texas Revolution had become a contest of wills between an iron-fisted autocrat determined to reduce the entire country to his subjection and a hard-bred race of frontier Americans who were just as determined to live under their notion of democracy, however imperfect it was. If by immigrating into Mexico and swearing allegiance to that country they bound themselves to submit to whatever form of government might be imposed, Anglo Texans can be faulted for doing so. If, however, tyranny must be overthrown, they were asserting inalienable human rights.

Santa Anna congratulated his officers on the brilliance of the triumph—it was said to have been the perspicacious Almonte who muttered that another such victory would ruin them. Overlooking such pyrrhic comments, Santa Anna sent a glowing report home: "The Fortress is now in our power, with its artillery, stores, etc. More than 600 corpses of foreigners were buried in the ditches and intrenchments, and a great many, who had escaped the bayonet of the infantry, fell in the vicinity under the sabres of the cavalry. . . . We lost about 70 men killed. . . ."

The dictator's majestic lying had the desired effect on the enrichment of his personal cult; when the report reached Mexico City it caused a swell of pride. "With pleasure do I sincerely congratulate Your Excellency for the brilliant triumph achieved over the perfidious colonists by the national arms under your command," answered his secretary of state. "It will teach the sympathizers among our evil-disposed neighbors not to contend against your military talents. . . . Glorious with these titles, and ever patriotic, Your Excellency has garnished your temples with laurels of unwithering fame."

He also sowed the seeds of a horrifying revenge.

TWENTY-SEVEN

HOW DID DAVY DIE?

FOR OVER A DECADE, THE QUESTION OF THE EXACT MAN-
ner of death of David Crockett has been the hottest battlefront in Texas history. Defenders of Texas' traditional heritage are outraged at the suggestion
that the Tennesseean's life ended in any less glorious blaze than the legend
enshrined in film and television until the end of the twentieth century. That
he and perhaps others actually surrendered and were executed, however,
has been accepted as a possibility by students of the documents virtually
since the end of the battle. Legend can overtake history, and no episode of
the Texas Revolution is more the stuff of legend than the Alamo, but documents must be considered carefully. It is worth a pause to detail this
dispute, not only for its currency, but also as an example of the larger arguments at play. The new controversy arose with the hotly debated discovery,
contested authentication, and lucrative sale of the diary of a Mexican officer,
Lieut. Col. José Enrique de la Peña. His is only one of many accounts of the
battle.

What gives the debate its particular rancor is that it has sharpened the
differences between two competing schools of thought on how Texas history should be approached. On one side are traditionalists, typically older
and more conservative, who, even their sympathizers have to admit, sometimes treat the subject like the proving ground for a cultural value system
and who become annoyed at any presentation of contradictory evidence. On
the other side stand revisionists, mostly academic, who, while they raise important new questions, often enrage traditionalists with an affirmative-
action scholarly agenda and with conclusions that sometimes leap beyond
the arguments constructed.

What both sides largely miss is that the first point on which one could
begin correcting the Crockett legend is the initial assumption that he came
to Texas for the purpose of fighting. In fact, he did not. He came to explore:
first, the geography, to see if it was a place where he would wish to relocate
his family, and second, the political waters. Like Sam Houston, Crockett was
washed up in Tennessee, and he was curious to assess whether he might be
able to duplicate Houston's feat of trading on his old fame for new luster,

and re-create himself as a great man. On the first point, he was as enchanted by Texas as Houston had been. It is, he wrote home on January 9, "the garden spot of the world. The best land and the best prospects for health I ever saw, and I do believe it is a fortune for any man to come here." On the second point, he had heard of the new convention, and "I have but little doubt of being elected a member to form a constitution. . . . I am rejoiced at my fate." When armed conflict arose, Crockett had no hesitation to sign up for the battle. Thus, while he did not come to Texas purposed "to fight for his rights," the political advantage to be gained by affecting that posture was far from lost on him. "I have taken the oath of government, and enrolled my name as a volunteer and will set out . . . in a few days." Crockett's character loses nothing in the stipulation, for his gallantry during the siege was universally attested from both sides.

Concerning his death, virtually no contemporary accounts survive free of later editing or exaggerating. Santa Anna himself was a shameless liar, and some of the accounts by other Mexican officers, given after their capture at San Jacinto, may have been colored with a motive to avoid the hangman. Many Texan accounts are equally distorted with either racism or the widespread impetus to relate their revolution as a kind of Norse hero-saga. And many individuals who were in some way connected to the Alamo story later gloried in the personal fame that resulted from puffing up their actual roles to the point of impossibility.

By way of example, Mexican army sergeant Felix Nuñez believed he saw a man fall who fit Crockett's description. "He had on a long buckskin coat, and a round cap without any bill, made out of fox skin with the long tail hanging down his back. . . . of the many soldiers who took deliberate aim at him and fired, not one ever hit him. On the contrary, he never missed a shot. He killed at least eight of our men, besides wounding several others. This being observed by a lieutenant who had just come in over the wall, he sprang at him and dealt him a deadly blow with his sword, just over the right eye, which felled him to the ground, and in an instant he was pierced by not less than twenty bayonets." This account survives only after two interpolations, first by the professor who recorded it (or claimed he did), and second by the reporter who rewrote it for newspaper publication. These edits make it difficult to corroborate with the details of other accounts; for instance, we don't know whether "over the wall" refers to the barricade before the chapel or the perimeter wall of the whole compound.

Nuñez' story is substantiated in pertinent part by the woman who had been acting as Bowie's nurse, Andrea Castañón de Villanueva, aka Madame

Candelaria: Crockett, stationed at the front of the chapel (presumably after the first retreat from the palisade), claimed that he could stop an entire regiment from coming over the barricade. "The words hardly died on his lips before a storm of bullets rained against the walls. Every man fell at the door but Crockett, I could see him struggling with the head of the column. . . . I saw Crockett fall backwards." Madame Candelaria basked for years in recounting her presence in the Alamo, and if all her versions are taken together as true, the physical requirements necessary to place her in all her claimed locations would have qualified her for lasting metaphysical glory. Susanna Dickinson, widow of Travis' artillery commander, also present during the slaughter within the chapel, was later escorted from the smoldering ruin, clutching her infant daughter. Near (but in her version, outside) the chapel door she saw Crockett "lying dead and mutilated. . . . I even remember seeing his peculiar cap by his side." She does not say whether he died fighting or after surrender, but her account would seem to cast doubt on the surrender version because Santa Anna did not enter the fortress until after it had been secured.

In his March 6 dispatch reporting the fall of the Alamo to the government, Santa Anna announced the deaths of Travis, Bowie, and "Crockett of equal rank and all the other leaders and officers," but he mentioned no surrenders and left the impression that all died in battle. If some defenders were executed, the less said about it, the better, for some of his junior officers averred that they were repelled by his conduct. In a manuscript memoir penned the year he died, Santa Anna, identifying the Alamo defenders as "filibusters," wrote that they "defended themselves relentlessly. Not one soldier showed signs of desiring to surrender, and with fierceness and valor, they died fighting. Their determined defense [made] it necessary to call in my reserve forces to defeat them." Santa Anna's memoir, while full of braggadocio and self-sanctification, does contain a higher quotient of truth than anything else he wrote about the campaign.

Santa Anna's fifer, sixteen-year-old Apolinario Saldigua, left an account declaring that Santa Anna ordered that once the fighting ceased, nothing should be disturbed and no bodies moved until he had inspected the scene; Santa Anna engaged three or four San Antonio civilians to point out the prominent Americans to him. Saldigua claimed to have accompanied Santa Anna into the fortress, where they saw that "the bodies of the Texians lay as they had fallen; & many of them were covered by those of Mexicans who had fallen upon them. The close of the struggle seemed to have been a hand to hand engagement. . . . Santa Anna . . . was then conducted to the body of

[Crockett]. This man lay with his face upward; & his body was covered by those of many Mexicans who had fallen upon him. His face was florid, like that of a living man. . . . Santa Anna viewed him for a few moments, thrust his sword through him turned away." Polin Saldigua, as a prisoner of the Texan army, had every reason to ingratiate himself to his captors by making inflammatory accusations against Santa Anna, and in fact he did so, also alleging that Bowie was captured and tortured before being cast still alive onto the funeral pyre.

It is even possible that the whole Saldigua account was a creative figment of the man who recorded it, William P. Zuber, whose other sanguine reminiscences of the revolution are notorious. But the important elements of Saldigua's account—that Santa Anna conducted an inspection of the fortress immediately after the battle, that he desired to be shown the bodies of the prominent Americans, and that none of the leaders are said to have surrendered—are seconded by the memoir of Don Francisco Antonio Ruiz, alcalde of San Antonio (and son of a signer of the Declaration of Independence). Santa Anna "directed me to call on some of the neighbors and come with carts to carry the [Mexican] dead to the cemetery, and to accompany him, as he desired to have Colonels Travis, Bowie, and Crockett shown to him." Ruiz' account does not eliminate the possibility that Santa Anna could have ordered survivors executed, and then ordered that he be shown the bodies, but that seems less likely than his desiring to be shown the bodies of the famous men whom he had never seen. Some evidence suggests, however, that Ruiz may not have even been in the city at the time of the battle.

In his 1849 memoir, General Filisola asserted that the later fury of Houston's army was one of "the consequences of the executions of the Alamo" and of similar killings after the other early battles. However, Filisola mentioned no names or number. Rather, he wrote of his continuing mortification that "after the first moments of the heat of the battle, there [were] atrocious authorized acts unworthy of the valor" of the victory. "There were deeds that we refrain from relating . . . acts [that] were denounced immediately by all who were disgusted upon witnessing them." It is possible, from other ambiguities in his memoir, that Filisola was referring not to hacking down a captive Crockett and others, but to the parading of Bowie's lifeless body around the plaza, hoisted on bayonets, or similar brutalities mentioned in other accounts.

All this leads to the celebrated diary of Lieut. Col. de la Peña. Recent detective work has pretty well established its authenticity, but veracity is another matter. It is also important to remember that the Peña account is not a "diary"; it was not written day by day as the events occurred. It is a *diario*, more accurately described as a memoir, written after the fact, and in the construction of which Peña refreshed his memory by consulting other sources, some of which he plagiarized rather heavily. According to Peña, "Some seven men had survived the general massacre and guided by General Castrillón, who sponsored them, were presented to Santa Anna. Among them was one of great stature, well formed and of regular features, in whose countenance there was imprinted the sentiment of adversity, but in which was noted certain resignation and nobility that commended him. He was the naturalist David Crocket, very well known in North America for his strange adventures, who had come to travel over the country and had been in Bejar in the moments of surprise had locked himself up in the Alamo, fearful that his quality as a foreigner would not be respected. Santa Anna answered the intervention of Castrillón with a gesture of indignation and immediately directing the sappers, who were the troops nearest to him, ordered them to shoot them. The chiefs and officers were irritated by this behavior and did not second the voice, hoping that the first moment of fury had passed, these men would be saved." Then, according to De la Peña, Santa Anna's junior staff officers who had not been in the battle, seeking to ingratiate themselves to the dictator, taunted the survivors with their swords before killing them.

The De la Peña diary contradicts both the specious Saldigua and the earnest Ruiz (if he was really there) saying that Santa Anna was himself conducted to the bodies of the prominent Americans whom he would not have known by sight. Moreover, if Castrillón conducted Crockett to Santa Anna, the dictator would have had to have been right outside the chapel when he ordered their execution, for Susanna Dickinson to see his body where she did. And one of the Mexican women who survived the battle in the chapel anteroom, Eulalia Yorba, recounted seeing Crockett's body in the same general location as Mrs. Dickinson and Madame Candelaria. Yet Santa Anna actually seems to have entered the fortress only a bit later.

Castrillón's intervention for Crockett and others is seconded in an account by Colonel Juan Almonte, which itself is corrupted. (It was supposedly translated from an interview, but Almonte, who was a veteran of a diplomatic mission to London, probably spoke better English than the Alamo's defenders.) Other contemporary versions of Crockett surrendering, one by General Cos as related by Zuber and one by Sergeant Francisco Becerra in the papers of later Texas Ranger Rip Ford, are almost certainly bogus. Yet some of the earliest accounts of the battle to appear in the American press allege that Crockett had surrendered and been executed. A letter from Sam Houston shortly after the battle indicates that he believed it as well. Still, Travis' slave, Joe, when interviewed by the Texas cabinet, recollected Crockett's dead body surrounded by twenty-one Mexican corpses that he and his Tennesseeans had dispatched before being overwhelmed.

A synoptic comparison of Alamo scriptures would take hundreds of pages. This sampling is given only as the short answer on the Crockett question, that the jury is and likely always will be hung. The dispute, ultimately, is an extraordinary signal of the passion of its participants. Crockett and his Tennesseeans—indeed, all the defenders of the Alamo—elected to stay and fight for their cause at a time when escape was still possible, and when they knew that the decision to stay on the walls would all but certainly cost them their lives. Whether Crockett or the others died in combat, or whether, out of ammunition and ringed by bayonets, they were cut down as prisoners of war, their heroism was of the same, imperishable, measure. It is also worth remembering that Crockett spent only a few weeks in Texas. He had invested neither time nor money; Texas to him was a symbol of what the future could be. But the fact that he risked his life for an idea, and for a future, seems at least as ennobling as the Texans who surrounded him fighting for their established homes and hearths.

TWENTY-EIGHT

THE ILL-FATED FANNIN

BACK IN WASHINGTON, THE CONVENTION THAT DE-clared Texas independent of Mexico continued, thrashing out a constitution for the new republic. News of the Alamo siege hit the members like a concussion, and Robert Potter put forward the motion that they suspend their proceedings, take up arms, and rush to the scene of the action. It was the very kind of thing he would do; he was thirty-six, violent, and stupid. He had been expelled from the North Carolina statehouse after castrating an elderly minister and a seventeen-year-old boy for having relations with his wife, which they did not, and he was jailed and fined. He had G.T.T. after further outrages, and once in Texas became a favorite of the land speculating class. Sam Houston strong-armed the convention into staying to finish their work. The evils of competitive army commands had finally become too plain for even the dimmest of them to ignore, and Houston was confirmed anew, over Potter's lone dissent, as commander in chief of all Texas forces, regular and volunteer.

If the question of Crockett's alleged surrender has bedeviled the Texas historical community, some have in more recent years been equally determined upon another question: why didn't Sam Houston ride to the aid of the Alamo? He left the government with the vow that he was headed to Gonzales to collect volunteers and then relieve the beleaguered forces in Béxar. Of course, the very morning he took to the road the Alamo fell, but Houston couldn't have known it. There was a story, perhaps apocryphal, that after leaving the convention, he listened every day with his ear to the ground, Indian-style, for the vibration of a signal gun to let him know the defenders were still in place. More pressing, however, was unifying the headstrong volunteer units to his command, and luring the Mexican army into the old Neutral Ground, where American forces could destroy it. The Texas government was—and in Houston's mind had to remain—unaware of the scheme.

James Walker Fannin was one man Houston felt he could rely on, and en route to Gonzales the commander in chief sent orders to him to withdraw from Goliad and hold in Victoria for further instructions. Bowie, however, was a man on whom no one could rely; Houston had adjured him weeks before to remove the artillery, destroy the Alamo fortress, and abandon San Antonio to the centralists. Bowie had disobeyed him as blithely as he had disobeyed Austin. If Fannin had arrived in Gonzales with his army it would have presented Houston with the stark decision whether to endanger—and possibly doom—the revolution by marching to San Antonio for a general engagement. Of course, the relief column would have learned of the Alamo's fall as they approached the town, and subsequent events would probably have transpired much as they did anyway. The whole question was obviated by Fannin's failure to respond to Houston's order.

Houston stopped two days at Burnam's Crossing on the Colorado, pondering how to lure Santa Anna into the Redlands of East Texas. Some later alleged that the commander in chief was in a drunken paralysis over what to do, citing the statement of a local named Thompson that Houston denied that Santa Anna could be in San Antonio. Actually, it was Houston who had been predicting Santa Anna's arrival since early winter and had been jeered by the yahoos for doing so. If he said it at all, it was probably more with the aim of preventing panic in the countryside, a worry that occupied much of his time. Judging from later events, Houston's two days at Burnam's was a time of furious activity—his network of scouts and spies had to be deployed to keep him informed of Mexican movements, the gates of supplies and volunteers from the United States had to be opened, more dispatches had to be sent out—for his operatives in the Redlands to engineer a pretext for moving the American forces in Louisiana right up to the border, and to the American commander there, General Edmund P. Gaines, to make sure his men were ready.

The defenders of the Alamo died without ever knowing that Texas had declared independence from Mexico. They believed they were still contending for restoration of the Mexican constitution of 1824. It was left to the living to know they were fighting for their freedom—but for a while it looked as if there would be no more fighting, only running. When Houston finally arrived in Gonzales on March 11, he took command of an assemblage of 374 volunteers, many without arms or ammunition, or any military training to speak of. He also arrived almost simultaneously with the first word of the fate of the Alamo—and of the deaths of virtually the entire able-bodied male population of Gonzales, who had ridden to their relief. At once Houston sequestered the bearers of the incendiary news, but not before about twenty deserters pounded out of the army to spread the panic and begin the "Runaway Scrape." He dispatched his most trusted scout, Erasmus "Deaf"

Smith, west to learn the truth of it, and Smith promptly returned with Susanna Dickinson and details of the battle.

Worse, it was learned that although Santa Anna was still in San Antonio, a force of 700 regulars under General Joaquín Ramírez y Sesma was even then advancing on Gonzales. With Mexican army units barely a day behind him, Houston had no choice but to retreat, but not before he sent out scouts to make sure all the families were rounded up. With flames of the burning town licking the sky behind them and with a train of wailing widows and orphans that streamed far to the rear, Houston retired eastward into the evening of March 13. He tried to offer encouragement, riding up and down the line, pretending to count soldiers and claiming that they were nearly eight hundred strong. Four days of hard walking brought them back to Burnam's on the Colorado, deep and swift, and once the stream was crossed there was time to breathe and think.

The night before Houston regained the Colorado, the convention that he had lately departed reached a momentous milestone. The Constitution of the Republic of Texas was adopted—but delegate Jesse Grimes, representing the local municipality of Washington, grieving for his son killed at the Alamo, recorded with disgust how it happened. A company of volunteers under Captain Henry Teal were passing through on their way to San Felipe in search of firearms with which to equip themselves when a rumor, the latest of many, raced through town that a Mexican army was approaching. Two riders named Miller and Alcorn were sent after Teal with orders for him and his men to arm themselves, return, and guard the convention. The two men "had gone but a few miles," wrote Grimes, "before they returned in full speed under whip and spur and all breathless, with the alarming tiding that Gouiana [General Antonio Gaona] was upon the city—The convention was then in session, late at night; and being seized with dreadful apprehensions, immediately adopted the Constitution, then lying upon the table, and passing a Resolution authorizing the Secretary to sign the names of the members of that body to the Instrument, adjourned in great confusion. The alarm proved to be false—Alcorn and Miller had overheard two Mexicans who were out on the prairie, guarding a cavayard of horses, in conversation, and they were lying on the grass and mistook them for the spies of Gouiana. The convention met the next day, and after appointing the officers of the Govt. ad interim then dissolved."

The constitution was an eclectic and pragmatic document. Most of its provisions were modeled on the U.S. Constitution, and some even looked ahead to an American annexation of Texas—slavery, for instance, was legal, but the African slave trade was not, which conformed to U.S. law on the subject. Other clauses aimed to prevent the kinds of abuses suffered under the Mexican government. The president, for example, was not to lead military forces unless the Congress consented, and clergy were not to hold public office. Other considerations, such as the granting of "headright" lands to heads of families, had the very practical aim of populating the vast country.

With the constitution came a new authoritative body, the Government Ad Interim, composed, easily enough, of members of the convention, intending to hold power until the constitution could be ratified and elections held. Mistrustful of handing executive authority to one of their own partisans—their late experience with Governor Smith and the council cured them of that notion—they almost elected as president ad interim a last latecomer to the convention, former four-term North Carolina congressman Samuel Price Carson. By six votes, however, he lost to a man who was not a delegate at all, New Jersey trader and adventurer David Gouverneur Burnet. Carson was then elected his secretary of state ad interim.

Burnet was just short of forty-eight and had never found a successful place. The fourteenth child of a prominent Continental Congressman, he was orphaned young and raised by older half brothers, one of whom was a U.S. senator and another the mayor of Cincinnati. Far from living up to the family name, when he was seventeen his guardians farmed him out to a commission house in New York, from which he escaped on a filibustering sortie to South America. That failed, and later he moved to Natchitoches, where he based himself as a trader to Comanche Indians in Spanish Texas. So wasted by lung disease that he fell from his horse, he was nursed back to health by the Comanches. After the failure of the Fredonian Rebellion, Burnet applied for and received an empresario contract for part of the forfeited lands, but back in the U.S. he was not able to raise enough settlers to fill his part of the bargain. He sold his interest in the grant to a group of New York–based investors known as the Galveston Bay and Texas Land Company. It was possibly through that sale that he conceived a lifelong spleenful hatred of one of the company's investors and its later legal counsel, Sam Houston. Burnet's settlement from the sale included four leagues of land, but it was the Law of April 6, 1830, not Houston, that barred Burnet from taking possession of his domain. When he finally reached Texas in spring of 1831, he opened a sawmill, which went broke; he applied for additional land grants, which were denied; so he turned his attention to agitating against Mexican rule. He did gain by the 1834 reforms, becoming a district judge in the new Texas court system. This led him to moderate his opinions about independence, and for this he failed to be elected to either the Consultation or the following convention. He attended the latter anyway to petition on behalf of legal clients, and by virtue of being in the right place at the right time, this lifelong hard-luck case was elected president ad interim of the Republic of Texas.

The members rethought their decision not to elect delegates to executive offices when it came to picking a vice president, and settled the office on the prominent Mexican federalist Lorenzo de Zavala. He was the same age as Burnet, but had succeeded in a useful career for his country, whereas Burnet had been frustrated. A native of Yucatan, De Zavala's youthful expressions of ardor for democracy had earned him a stretch in the San Juan de Ulloa prison, where he used his time studying English and medicine. After Mexican independence in 1821 he represented his home region as a deputy in the constituent assembly and then as a senator, and twice served as governor of Mexico state. He served the federalist Guerrero as treasury secretary, but was forced into exile by the centralist Bustamante—again using his time profitably, traveling to New York and Europe and writing two books. Santa Anna appointed him his minister in Paris, but after Santa Anna assumed dictatorial powers De Zavala broke from him and relocated his operations to Texas, where he had acquired a fortune as a colonial empresario. His selection as vice president ad interim had the happy effect of putting a more national face on the Texas rebellion, but also, significantly, it gave an influential voice to the class of land speculators who had otherwise earned such a hard name among the unlanded observers.

As Sam Houston led his dispirited army east from Gonzales, Fannin remained at Goliad—bravely renamed Fort Defiance. He did not receive Houston's order to retire eastward until March 14, and he delayed his departure even longer to await the return of two units who were out on operations. While Fannin was anxiously watching for the arrival of Urrea and his army, eighty-odd local Tejanos who resented Fannin's occupation enlisted under Carlos de la Garza as a kind of advance cavalry for Urrea. In company with Karankawa Indians, the De la Garza force began looting the ranches of Anglo settlers near Refugio, thirty miles south of Goliad. Fannin sent out Captain Amon B. King on March 11 to round up the Americans and escort them back to Goliad. King and his thirty or so men effected this by the following day, but rather than obey orders and return to Goliad, King learned that a force of Tory rancheros were camped on a ranch less than ten miles distant, and he moved to attack them. Instead, King was himself ambushed by De la Garza, in company with advance units of Urrea's army.

King sent back to Goliad for reinforcements. Fannin, his anxiety increasing, sent out the Georgia Battalion under Colonel William Ward, who managed to rescue King and his men. Astonishingly, King refused to return to Goliad—he still wanted to fight. Ward and King had a hot disagreement over who was in charge, and while Ward waited in Refugio's ruined mission, King took a mixed bag of men out on a sortie. On March 15 they killed eight encamped Mexicans, only to discover that Urrea had cut off their escape route. King's firefight with Mexican regulars lasted until dark, when the Texans attempted a getaway across the Mission River. During the crossing their gunpowder got wet, and De la Garza easily captured them the following day. On March 16, after some local ranchers and Germans were separated out, King and a couple dozen followers were marched about a mile north of the mission, lined up, and shot. Ward, meanwhile, had borne the brunt of Urrea's assault at the ruined mission, inflicting heavy casualties on the Mexican army—perhaps forty killed and over a hundred wounded. Ward and most of his men slipped away during the night of March 14, but by the time they made their way to Victoria, Urrea had already occupied the town and moved on to attack Fannin at Goliad. Ward surrendered his force at Dimmitt's Landing on March 22.

Amon King's fatal attempt at vainglory had cost Fannin two days' delay and about 20 percent of his force. Fannin now compounded the disaster with stupefying errors of his own. Indecisive and unsure of himself, Fannin refused to budge until he learned of King's defeat, and then he hesitated another day, calling a council of war, and preparing baggage wagons. Houston had ordered him to sink his cannons in the river; Fannin hitched them to oxen so underfed they could barely walk. When Fannin finally left Goliad on March 19, Urrea was entering the town with six hundred fresh reinforcements from Santa Anna. As Urrea overtook him, Fannin was within a mile of timber and water along Coleto Creek, from where he could have mounted a successful defense. As his officers remonstrated hotly with him to get to cover, Fannin ordered a defensive square formed on the prairie, with his cannons at the corners as Urrea, incredulous at Fannin's stupidity, himself took possession of the nearby cover.

Urrea decided to attack before Fannin could finish his barricades. "In order to obtain a quick victory," he wrote in his diary, "I ordered my troops to charge with their bayonets at the same time that Colonel Morales did likewise on the opposite flank, [while] the central column advanced in battle formation." Attacked from three sides, Fannin fought back skillfully; he "quickly placed three pieces of artillery on this side, pouring a deadly shower of shot upon my . . . column. A similar movement was executed on the left, while our front attack was met with the same courage and cool-ness." Repulsed once, Urrea determined to prevent Fannin from finishing his entrenchments and placed himself at the head of a second charge. Fan-nin, he wrote, "received me with a scorching fire from their cannons and ri-fles." Urrea began the battle with four rounds allowed per soldier, and was counting on his supply train to replenish ammunition shortly, but when it failed to appear Urrea was forced to break off the action. Fannin's men spent the night fortifying their position, but on the morning of March 20 the Mex-ican supply train, with artillery, arrived. Nine Texans had been killed and about fifty, including Fannin, wounded—perhaps a fourth as many casual-ties as they inflicted on Urrea's army. Urrea fired a few rounds of grape and canister—just enough to let Fannin know that his situation was hopeless, and Fannin, shot in the thigh, limped out under a white flag to inquire into surrender terms.

Negotiations were difficult at first, as there was little bilingualism on ei-ther side, but proceeded once it was discovered that one of Fannin's men, a German named Herman Ehrenberg, could speak with Urrea's engineer, Juan José Holzinger, who before he became a soldier of fortune had once been Jo-hann Joseph Holzinger of Mainz. The specifics of the surrender have long been controversial. The document that Fannin signed shows clearly that the Texans surrendered "at discretion," and Urrea's handwritten endorsement reinforces that "I must not, nor can I, grant anything else." But accounts state just as clearly that additional verbal inducements were made. Urrea as-sured him that Mexico did not execute prisoners of war. Holzinger assured them of parole. "Gentlemen," he said, "in ten days, liberty and home." Back inside Fannin's barricade, the men knew their position was hopeless, and for many of them, especially the new arrivals from the United States who labored under volunteers' lack of ardor for an adventure gone bad, the thought of being deported back home was a small price to pay for their ill-conceived lark. Fannin could not bring himself to actually tell them that they were surrendering at discretion.

Once the surrender was concluded, the Texans were taken under guard back to Goliad, joining the scattered remnants of Ward's command and other rebels rounded up in the area, making a total number of over four hun-dred. Urrea pondered how to navigate. He was already on Santa Anna's bad side over the order for no quarter, having sought to evade executing Texans taken around San Patricio and leaving their fate to others. Aside from his own generous nature, he was also influenced by Holzinger, who had saved more than two dozen of Ward's men with a claim that he needed them to transport artillery. Amon King's own bloodthirsty truculence eased Urrea's way to having him and his men shot, although Holzinger ferreted out two Germans among them and had them spared as well. Ironically, Holzinger was a favorite of Santa Anna's, having designed the dictator's mansion at Manga de Clavo some years before, but it is doubtful that even he could have interceded for Fannin. In his report to Santa Anna, Urrea praised the valor of arms of his own troops, and then put in a good word for Fannin. "Immediately upon the surrender of the enemy, their fury was changed to the most admirable indulgence. This show of generosity after a hotly contested engagement is worthy of the highest commendation, and I can do no less than to commend it to Your Excellency." Urrea then moved on, with his operations, to Victoria, hoping to look busy and avoid the dictator's fury that was sure to follow. Fannin was permitted to accompany Holzinger to Copano to book passage for his men on a ship back to the United States.

March 26 was a difficult day for the junior colonel whom Urrea left in command at Goliad. José Nicolás de la Portilla was twenty-eight, a native of Jalapa, and a mestizo so darkly complected that he was known by the sobriquet of "El Indio." He intended upon a military career, and the last place he wanted to be was between two feuding generals. During the day, Holzinger and Fannin returned from Copano, where they had discovered that the ship with which Urrea intended to repatriate the Americans had already sailed. When Santa Anna read Urrea's report that he had Fannin's men prisoner in Goliad, he was apoplectic. Ignoring Urrea, he wrote straight to Lieutenant Colonel Portilla. "The supreme government has ordered that all foreigners taken with arms in their hands, making war upon the nation, shall be treated as pirates. I have been surprised that the circular . . . has not been fully complied with in this particular." Fannin and his "detestable delinquents . . . having had the audacity to come and insult the republic," should be put to death, without delay. Santa Anna's courier clattered into Goliad at seven in the evening. An hour later, a messenger arrived from Urrea. "Treat the prisoners well," he ordered, "especially Fannin. Keep them busy rebuilding. . . . Feed them with the cattle you will receive from Refugio."

Portilla allowed the prisoners a ration of beef, and tortillas that they were permitted to barter from their guards in exchange for their personal effects.

It was virtually the first food they had had in days, which had led to speculation among the captives that the Mexicans were deliberately starving them into a riot as an excuse to kill them. Portilla let one man into his confidence, Colonel Francisco Garay, Urrea's second in command, and sadly made up his mind.

March 27 was Palm Sunday. Early in the morning Garay awakened some doctors and men who had acted as nurses among the American prisoners and ordered them to his camp about a quarter of a mile away. At about the same time Francisca Álvarez (one of several possible spellings), the wife of a Mexican officer and later known as the "Angel of Goliad," acting in concert with Garay, rounded up as many prisoners as she safely could and hid them in odd corners of the compound. When Portilla appeared with the bulk of the garrison, word spread among the prisoners that they were going to be marched to Matamoros. The wounded, including Fannin, were left at the chapel.

As the Americans were organized into three groups, it was noticed that the soldiers were wearing parade uniforms, and carried no gear to indicate a lengthy march. Upon departure it was also noticed that the units were being led in different directions. The group containing Ehrenberg, who had translated the surrender talks, was walked a short distance down the Victoria road, then told to halt near the line of a mesquite thicket bordering the San Antonio River. No sooner were they ordered to kneel than the firing began, almost simultaneously with the execution of the other two groups.

Back at Goliad, the distant volleys could have only one meaning, and the American medics at Garay's headquarters became alarmed. "Gentlemen, keep still," Garay told them. "You are safe. These are not my orders, nor do I execute them." His intention, if questioned, was to claim that they had been taken without arms. Among them were Jack Shackelford, who had led seventy volunteers calling themselves "Red Rovers" from Alabama to Texas, and J. H. Barnard, who lived to relate that Fannin was not so lucky as they— he and the other wounded men were lined up against the wall of a small courtyard just west of and fronting the chapel where they had been confined. Fannin had three requests: he entrusted his money and his watch to the officer in charge, asking that it be sent to his wife, and he asked that he be shot in the heart and given a Christian burial. He was instead shot in the face and cast onto the pyre with the rest.

Texan dead from the Goliad massacres numbered between 340 and 390. A total of 28 escaped the rural fusillades, either feigning death beneath the corpses of their comrades, or dashing into the thickets along the river and eluding pursuit. Ironically, if Urrea had had his way and the Americans had been repatriated, the effect would likely have dampened American enthusiasm for the Anglo cause in Mexican Texas. Instead, Santa Anna created a pantheon of martyrs, leaving enough survivors to pump the bellows of independence. When later confronted about the mass execution, Santa Anna blamed the entire affair on Portilla.

TWENTY-NINE

YOU MUST FIGHT THEM

SANTA ANNA'S EASTWARD SWEEP ACROSS TEXAS HAD two purposes: the first was to cleanse the province of American colonists; the second was to implant a military force on the Sabine River border to improve his position in ongoing negotiations with the United States over the boundary. He had long been annoyed, as he told the British ambassador in front of a dozen other diplomats in December, that "Jackson sets up a claim to pass the Sabine, and that in running the division line, hopes to acquire the country as far as the Naches. Sir," he added emphatically, "I mean to run that line at the Mouth of my Cannon." If war with the United States was the result, he vowed politely to the British minister, he would lay Washington, D.C., in ashes, as the English had done very well once before.

Even as Santa Anna's army creaked and rumbled across Texas in April, his foreign minister, Eduardo de Gorostiza, was in Washington trading politely venomous barbs with Jackson on the subject. The American president was candid in his claim that the Texas boundary was and would be the Neches. The land between the two streams had long been vacated as the "Neutral Ground," and Jackson told Gorostiza he meant to maintain it as such. He also criticized the brutality of Santa Anna's campaign, at which point Gorostiza defended Santa Anna's right to the usages of war. "Santa Anna, and all others," said Jackson flatly, "will find such immolations very unsavory and indigestible. . . . It is my duty to preserve neutrality; and, with that in view, I have ordered General Gaines to a position favorable to a speedy execution of the boundary treaty, and to prevent interference with the Indians." Jackson let Gorostiza know that he was aware that Mexican agents were among the Indians, working against the American interest, and he would have none of it.

In Louisiana, General Edmund Pendleton Gaines had his needed pretext, and he moved fourteen companies of infantry to the Sabine River crossing of the old Camino Real. "Should I find any disposition on the part of the Mexicans or their red allies to menace our frontier," he wrote the U.S. secretary of war, in a classic emphatic use of the preemptive-war doctrine, "I cannot but deem it to be my duty . . . to anticipate their lawless movements, by crossing our supposed or imaginary international boundary, and meeting [them] wherever they are to be found." His direction, he stated, came from Jackson himself. The ferry on the Sabine was run by General Gaines' cousin, James Gaines, who had signed the Texas Declaration of Independence, and who, after seventeen years in the Redlands, knew every path and trace through the woods.

Of these preparations Santa Anna had no hint. With the Alamo in flames and Fannin's army exterminated, the only thing that stood between the dictator and his enforcement of his intended boundary was Houston and his harebrained frontiersmen. They were retreating pell-mell before him, and taking with them thousands of terrified civilians. After several days' rest in San Antonio, Santa Anna set out eastward with confidence. The victorious Urrea was on his right flank in South Texas with two thousand men; before him to the east, General Joaquín Ramírez y Sesma was chasing Houston with about eight hundred men, and on his left, Gaona had already entered Bastrop with about a thousand more. The dictator left General Juan José Andrade behind in Béxar with a reserve of fifteen hundred. It was a broad sweep of ethnic cleansing that would undo all American settlement since Moses Austin came in 1820.

This effort promised to succeed even more completely than his military campaign. Houston's failure to stifle news of the fall of the Alamo, or to sequester deserters, and then the fact of Houston's retreat itself, spread precisely the kind of panic in the countryside that Santa Anna hoped for. In a pathetic exodus of refugees that became known as the Runaway Scrape, whole families quit their land grants, fighting panic and epidemics of measles and fevers, taking only what they could carry, and joining the eastward flight through mud and swollen rivers. The Trinity was more than a mile wide with the bottomlands flooded; at the mouth of the San Jacinto, five thousand people were waiting to cross at Lynch's Ferry by the second week in April. Planting families were unnerved at being forced to depend on the labor and loyalty of slaves, many of whom knew that Mexican victory meant liberation. Some of the settlers joined the army; most, to the surprise and disgust of Houston and Rusk, did not, including a number who had signed the Declaration of Independence. Noah Smithwick, who had repaired the Gonzales cannon, became part of Houston's network of scouts, detailed to round up stock to feed the army as it retreated. Of the depopulated countryside, he wrote that they found houses "standing open, the beds unmade, the breakfast things still on the tables, pans of milk moulding in the dairies. There were cribs full of corn, smokehouses full of bacon, yards full of chickens that ran after us for food. . . . Hungry cats ran mewing out to meet us, rubbing their sides on our legs." The countryside was emptied.

This was not the revolution that Sam Houston had envisioned. Leading both army and refugees eastward, his nerves were on a razor's edge. Only a few miles into the retreat from Gonzales, he became alarmed as the march ground to a halt; he discovered the impediment to be a Private Rhodes, who stopped to take a drink from a stream. "Knock him down, God damn him," he bellowed. "Knock him down—standing there and impeding the march of the whole army. God damn him, knock him down!" Many of Houston's walleyed yahoos, untrained and many unarmed but willing to fight the devil, raised the charge of cowardice against Houston from the first order to retreat. "Be it known to all future generations of Texans forth," wrote one of them, named Creed Taylor, that if anyone other than Houston had taken command, there would have been no lengthy retreat from Gonzales, and they would have done "as we had done before—whip ten-to-one the carrion eating convicts under Santa Anna." Houston knew better, of course, but revered or reviled, he was now the only locus for the concentration of volunteers, and when he reached the Colorado on March 17, his numbers had grown to about 600, just over 400 effective. (Houston did not share Creed Taylor's racist sentiments about the Mexicans, either. In fact, he entrusted the crucial task of protecting his rear to a company of native Tejanos, led by a prominent young Bexareño named Juan Seguín.)

Unlike the shallow streams of the San Antonio area, the Colorado was deep and swift, and rising from spring rains. The army crossed the river on Burnam's ferry and shepherded the refugees over. The ferry was then burned. Behind this barrier, Houston adjusted his position downstream some thirty miles, to Beason's Crossing near Columbus. Having already complained that his recruits "did not know the first principles of the drill," Houston stayed at Beason's a week, organizing the army and teaching them to march and maneuver and fire by companies. It was pathetically little training, but perhaps, he hoped, enough to see them through a battle with troops so disciplined they had marched unflinching into fire at the Alamo. The general also issued nonstop orders, trying to coordinate the larger war effort—supplies, more recruits, cover from the newly minted Texas navy of four small schooners to keep more Mexican reinforcements from landing. After sending orders to Fannin to be ready to link up with him, he learned that Fannin had surrendered. He kept this news to himself.

In the midst of all this, Sesma materialized on the west bank of the Colorado. The arrival of two hundred fresh Kentucky volunteers under Colonel Sidney Sherman meant that Houston's army probably outnumbered Sesma's, and the Texans clamored loudly for a fight. Partly they were inspired by the banner that the Kentuckians had brought with them, depicting a bare-teated Liberty, surging forward with her sword aloft, trailing a ribbon that read "Liberty or Death." Knowing that he must give the volunteers a taste of battle or risk a general mutiny, Houston reluctantly allowed a small force to cross the Colorado, expose themselves to Sesma, and attempt to draw him into an ambush. The trick failed to inveigle Sesma, and also failed to satisfy the Texan soldiers, who demanded a more manly contest. Certain that a general engagement here would be premature and probably disastrous (and also would not further the strategy of American intervention), Houston stunned his army with the news he had been saving, of Fannin's capture. Those present, he told them, were "the only army in Texas," and for that reason the fate of the country rested on the first battle. "There are but few of us," he told them, "and if we are beaten, the fate of Texas is sealed." Houston also judged it time to plant a little disinformation. "I am told that evilly disposed persons have told you I am going to march you to the Redlands. This is false," he lied. He announced his intent to retreat them to the Groce Plantation on the Brazos, where "you can whip the enemy ten to one, and we get an abundant supply of corn." The troops groaned, but Houston had let them vent just enough steam to get them to comply.

They arrived at San Felipe late on March 27, and upstream at Groce's soon after. This encampment provoked the most acute crisis to date over Houston's leadership. Two of his most belligerent captains refused to take another step to the east. One was Mosely Baker, the Alabama forger and former speaker of the statehouse whom Houston had insulted at the Consultation the previous winter. After taking such pains to get a government organized, Houston heard Baker move to adjourn so the delegates could return to the fight, and quickly cut the ground out from under him. Baker, however, had recruited the single largest company of volunteers in the army, and had formidable influence with the men. The other was Wiley Martin, a tough old bird of sixty, who under Andrew Jackson at the Battle of Horseshoe Bend had fought as a captain when Houston was a mere lieutenant. In response to their defiance, Houston assigned Baker's and Martin's companies to guard the Brazos River crossings—Baker here at San Felipe and Martin downstream at Fort Bend. With Santa Anna's multiple prongs all advancing, they could hardly refuse, and the order got the most seditious voices out of camp and away from men whom Houston might still control.

In front of the soldiers Houston was a portrait of confidence and self-possession, but "before my God," he wrote one of his few confidants, "I have found the darkest hours of my past life." Not all the troops vilified him; in fact there were probably as many who approved of his leadership as did not, but they filled much less newsprint in subsequent years. "A respectable number of our men reposed unlimited confidence in General Houston," wrote one of his supporters, citing "his inflexibility, his confidence of success, and courtesy to his soldiers. Also he kept no bodyguard. When we were encamped, the door to his tent generally stood open, and any soldier who wished could enter at liberty." Unlike Bowie, Houston did not affect to be their buddy, and while respectful, he was formal with them, although there were a couple of occasions when he played along with practical jokes.

Houston stayed at Groce's for two weeks, stalling to get stronger. His recruiters forwarded three new companies, and other men arrived from Georgia, all of whom had to be integrated into the routine. One of the Georgians, a dark-complected, classics-spouting, long-haired newspaper editor with the euphonious name of Mirabeau Buonaparte Lamar, was incredulous that the men were drilling when they could be fighting, and offered himself for command. Houston calmly had some graves dug, announcing that they would be filled by any men who tried to mutiny, and Lamar enlisted as a corporal of cavalry. The general was only barely in control of the troops.

On April 6 the ad interim secretary of war joined Houston and the army; it was Thomas Jefferson Rusk, who had led the Nacogdoches volunteers during the siege of Béxar, and who had been one of the first to accept Houston as the responsible commander of the Texas army. He entered camp with explicit instructions in his pocket from President Burnet, that he must without fail persuade Houston to arrest his retreat, and Rusk delivered a note from Burnet to Houston: "Sir: The enemy are laughing you to scorn. You must fight them. You must retreat no farther. The country expects you to fight. The salvation of the country depends on your doing so." If Houston did not obey, Rusk was in all probability authorized to relieve him and assume command himself—an act that undoubtedly would have been met by cheers from the disgusted soldiers.

Almost surely Houston's response was to bring Rusk into his confidence about the scheme to trap Santa Anna between the Sabine and the Neches. This cannot be certain, but there was no doubt that Rusk emerged from their meeting solidly on Houston's side against Burnet and the Houston-haters in his government. Rusk's defection dismayed the troops, who grumbled that Houston must have used some kind of Cherokee magic on him. Buoyed at having his authority confirmed, Houston even ventured a sarcastic reply to Burnet: "I am sorry that I am so wicked, for 'the prayers of the righteous shall prevail.' That you are so, I have no doubt, and hope that Heaven, as such, will . . . crown your efforts with success on behalf of Texas."

Scorn was not the only pressure that Burnet sought to bring on the detested Houston. The ad interim president had elevated the other principal Houston-hater in the government, Robert Potter, to secretary of the navy. In his youth Potter had served six years on American vessels as a midshipman, before resigning in a snit after his superiors saw no merit in promoting him. Burnet and Potter assigned a protégé of theirs, James Hazard Perry, as an aide to Houston's camp. Houston welcomed him, but Hazard Perry's real job was to spy on the general, and either catch him drinking or provide some other justification for relieving him. In truth, Houston had not touched a drop of alcohol since the beginning of the campaign, and Perry grew so frustrated that he started a rumor that he was using opiates instead. Houston intercepted his seditious report back to the government and had him disarmed and watched, but not before Perry joined Baker and Martin in spreading unrest over the endless retreat.

Inevitably, Sesma trailed Houston and his army, and on April 7, with Santa Anna in company, appeared at San Felipe, opposite Mosely Baker, who had burned the town to deny cover to the enemy. Baker's riflemen kept the Mexicans from crossing, forcing Santa Anna to probe downstream as far as Fort Bend. There the dictator employed Colonel Almonte, who spoke perfect English, to fool the ferryman into bringing his barge to the west bank. The vessel was seized and the first Mexican troops set foot east of the Brazos. The truculent but outnumbered Wiley Martin found Houston's order to abandon Fort Bend and rejoin the army one that he could obey without haggling.

With Santa Anna now across the Brazos, Houston was compelled to do the same, using the 130-foot steamboat *Yellow Stone*, which he had kept standing by, to effect the crossing in mid-April. On the east bank the army was greeted by a welcome addition, two six-pounder cannons, a gift from citizens of Cincinnati. Houston had been expecting their arrival for days, and had used them as an excuse to stand pat and not yet move south toward Santa Anna. In fact, Houston still intended to hew to his plan to lure Santa Anna into the Nacogdoches area. Collateral evidence for this was that during the stay at Groce's, he asked the loan of a pair of oxen from a local, Mrs. Pamelia Mann, a pioneer woman whose two years in the Texas wilds had left her as crusty as the roughest of the army yeomen. Draft animals were precious and Mrs. Mann was loath to let them go, but Houston assured her that the army would be following up the Nacogdoches road, and her oxen would be in no danger. Indeed, Houston's latest intelligence confirmed that the plan was working:

One of his Nacogdoches informants sent Houston a letter with word that Santa Anna meant to follow him: "Jose Elias has Told her that he conversed with St. Anna and that he Told him he meant to March his army To Sabine And Teach Old Jackson To keep his people at home And make them behave themselves." Further confirmation came, amazingly, from Santa Anna himself. After the dictator crossed the Brazos, he had Almonte write out a taunting note, which he sent out with the ferryman whose vessel he had commandeered: "Mr. Houston: I know you're up there hiding in the bushes. As soon as I catch the other land thieves, I'm coming up there to smoke you out." At least two couriers were now shuttling between Houston and General Gaines in Louisiana, who believed that the pivotal battle for Texas independence would take place directly across the Sabine from his position. In addition to his own infantry, he also sent for aid from militia units in New Orleans and elsewhere in the South. Among them were to be new volunteers from Tennessee under General Richard Dunlap, who had been one of Houston's steadiest friends during his days as major general of the state militia, and was now recruited into the new web.

Thus, while Sam Houston's army grumbled and threatened mutiny at the endless and seemingly shameful retreat, and while Ad Interim President Burnet sent Houston near-hysterical letters that he must stand his ground and fight, only the commanding general and his most trusted circle, including Burnet's own secretary of state, knew the specific goal: to lure Santa Anna into a disastrous American ambush on the Sabine. From the dictator's point of view, the destruction of the American colonies and their pretended government was only a step from completion. He had already chased Houston and his rabble across the breadth of Texas, depopulating it of Americans as he went. At this point, however, fate sent events spinning in a new direction entirely.

THIRTY

THE BATTLE OF SAN JACINTO

AMID ALL THE MISSTEPS OF TEXAS' NEAR-COMICAL GOVernment in opening a war against a considerable military power, one thing they did understand correctly was the need for a naval presence in the Gulf of Mexico. They granted letters of marque to a few ship owners, but more importantly arranged the purchase of four small schooners that were fitted for war service.

The first and smallest was the four-gun, sixty-ton privateer *William Robbins*, which the government purchased and renamed the *Liberty*. On the day the Alamo fell, the *Liberty* dueled and captured the Mexican schooner *Pelicano*, which was taken as a prize when her cargo of flour was discovered to be concealing munitions for Santa Anna. Largest and least useful was the 160-ton, ten-gun *Brutus;* sluggish, unmaneuverable, and constantly under repair, she spent time plugged up in Matagorda Bay by the Mexican *Vencedor del Alamo*. The 125-ton *Independence* was a former U.S. revenue cutter, mounting a long nine-pounder and half a dozen six-pounders. While Houston was waging his long and vexsome retreat, the *Independence* captured a number of small Mexican vessels loaded with supplies, before being forced into Galveston after an unequal duel with the Mexican warships *Bravo* and *Urrea*. Even more useful was the *Invincible*, 125 tons, which had been built in Baltimore as a slave carrier for the infamous Africa trade. On the morning of April 3 she engaged and ran aground the Mexican cruiser *Montezuma* near the mouth of the Rio Grande. That afternoon, she overhauled an American brig, the *Pocket*. *Invincible*'s captain, Jeremiah Brown, boarded her, and discovered Mexican naval officers bearing communiqués and escorting a concealed cargo of munitions. Brown took the *Pocket* as a prize to Galveston before continuing on to New Orleans for repairs. U.S. capital interests and insurers, who stood to profit from Mexico's war effort, were furious at the interference, and they had the *Invincible*'s crew arrested for piracy upon arrival, but couldn't make the charge stick.

Reverses suffered by the Mexican navy were an annoyance to Santa Anna, but once he crossed the Brazos at Fort Bend, he still had every reason to feel confident. He was now farther east than Houston, who was to his north and, according to Tories and scouts, fleeing cowardly to Nacogdoches and possibly even refuge in the United States. He could be dealt with in time. Ahead of him lay the heavily populated heartland of the Anglo Texas colonies, which now could be systematically vacated. He sent word to all commanders behind him, aggregating some 3,500 men, to rendezvous at Fort Bend for this irresistible sweep. Then came one of those blessings in disguise that make some people believe in destiny. The dictator received intelligence that the Texas government, having been spooked out of Washington, was removing to Harrisburg, near the coast at the present site of the city of Houston, and only thirty miles distant. Santa Anna quickly concluded that if he could overtake and execute them, he could end this war at a stroke and get on with his larger business on the U.S. border. Without waiting for his scattered forces to link up, the dictator sortied toward Harrisburg with only nine hundred lightly equipped troops.

Houston learned of Santa Anna's movement almost as soon as he started, and recognized it as a godsend. For weeks he had been hoping that Santa Anna would chase him into American hands near Nacogdoches, but the Neches was still a hundred miles to the northeast. The Texas army, surly and rebellious, might not follow him that far. But if throughout his career Sam Houston perfected any art, it was pragmatism, and he quickly realized that for the dictator to separate himself from his main force was an error. Waiting only until the quarrelsome Mosely Baker and Wiley Martin rejoined the army with their 350 men, Houston decamped and headed east on April 14. The quarry, suddenly, had become the hunter, but then incredibly there was more insubordination. Houston ordered an early start on the morning of April 17, but Wiley Martin would not order his men to move until they'd had breakfast. In a rage, Houston gave him the job of escorting the refugees to safety, which he could obey or go to hell, he said, but in any case he was to clear out. When Martin peeled off to escort the survivors of the Runaway Scrape, as many as 400 men went with him—as clear a measure as can be taken of Houston's unpopularity.

When Houston and the army entered the northern limits of Harris County, the road forked at the Abram Roberts farm, and by a traditional story, a tree grew at the fork whose principal limbs seemed to point two directions—northeast, to Nacogdoches, and south, to Harrisburg. The famous "Which-Way Tree" became a defining ebenezer for Houston's career. Just like the soldiers in the army, Texas historians have argued vociferously over whether Houston was the author of an order to take the Harrisburg fork, or whether he was merely swept along by the tide. "I never heard any talk as to Houston not designing to fight," wrote Private James Washington Winters, "or of officers or men insisting on his taking the road to Harrisburg; or of anyone doubting his intention to do so. We went as straight as we could go to Harrisburg." Captain R. J. Calder's company was in the lead, and he did not "recollect to have seen or heard of any altercation, nor do I think there was any mutinous conduct." Regimental surgeon Nicholas Labadie, on the other hand, wrote that he and others prevailed upon Roberts to stand on his gate and point out the south fork to Houston: "That right hand road will carry you to Harrisburg just as straight as a compass." The controversy is unlikely to be settled decisively.

One thing that is now known for certain is that some time around the passage of the Which-Way Tree, Houston opened a dispatch from one of his secret operatives, Sam Price Carson, Burnet's ad interim secretary of state. When Burnet sent him to the United States to raise money and aid, Carson, covered under the excuse of needing to visit his Red River lands before undertaking the journey, went instead to General Gaine's camp in western Louisiana, to make sure that the Piney Woods trap was ready to spring. "I am warranted in saying that volunteer troops will come on in numbers from the United States," he wrote. "You should fall back, if necessary, to the Sabine . . . You must fall back, and hold out, and let nothing goad or provoke you to a battle, unless you can, without doubt, whip them." Whether Houston ordered columns right or followed columns right, he could smile at his luck that he could now, without doubt, whip them.

One Texan who was not pleased with Sam Houston's new line of march was Pamelia Mann, whose oxen Houston had borrowed to haul his artillery. Not long after the Harrisburg turn she materialized, boiling up to Houston and demanding the return of her stock. The general pleaded that the guns could not get through the mud without them, but one of the soldiers remembered her reply: " 'I don't care a dam for your cannon, I want my oxen.' She had . . . a very large knife on her saddle. She turned a round to the oxen & jumpt down with the knife & cut the raw hide tug that the chane was tied with. . . . No body said a word. She jumpt on her horse with whip in hand & away she went in a lope with her oxen."

Soon after, Houston's wagon master, a Pennsylvania Dutchman named Conrad Rohrer, came up the line to fetch the oxen to pull the Twin Sisters out of mud. Enraged at finding them gone, he set up the Nacogdoches fork after Pamelia Mann, matching her oath for oath. "Rohrer," Houston warned him, "that woman will fight!" When Rohrer reentered camp that night he was livid, and there were no oxen to be seen. Houston, his right shoulder useless from his 1814 war wound, dismounted with his men and applied his left shoulder to the trucks to keep the artillery moving.

Santa Anna reached Harrisburg on April 15, only to discover that the Texas government had moved on, about ten miles farther east to New Washington, on Galveston Bay. The fastest Mexican units followed and clattered up to the shore, just in time to see Burnet and other officials in a rowboat, pulling toward Galveston Island. They were still within rifle range but Colonel Almonte, seeing Mrs. Burnet in the boat, deflected the first gun to aim and ordered them to hold their fire. Santa Anna then turned his attention to sacking New Washington.

Houston led his men into Harrisburg on April 18, having driven them fifty-five miles in only two and a half days, through appalling conditions. Santa Anna had burned the town, and Houston let his men get a long look at the charred remains. Deaf Smith, his most trusted scout, captured dispatches that revealed Santa Anna was still in New Washington, and planned to cross the San Jacinto River at Lynch's Ferry. With much labor and haste, Houston crossed his army and artillery to the south bank of Buffalo Bayou.

With a fight now inevitable, it was imperative that Houston know that his grousing troops were behind him, and he lined them up for an address. "The army will cross and we will meet the enemy," he said. "Some of us may be killed and must be killed; but, soldiers, remember the Alamo! the Alamo! the Alamo!" The effort had the desired effect. "After such a speech," one of them wrote prophetically, "but damned few prisoners will be taken—that I know." The ferry over Buffalo Bayou was so decrepit that flooring had to be ripped out of a nearby house to reinforce the hull before the Twin Sisters could be trusted to it, and the crossing took most of the day. Once on the south bank, they marched east five miles more to the mouth of the bayou and seized Lynch's Ferry. Santa Anna was just coming up from New Washington, three miles farther southeast, and had not reached it yet. A thick bottom of live oaks covered the shore of the bayou and Houston concealed his men in it, looking out across the San Jacinto plain, a marshy grassland about a mile broad, across which Santa Anna must come.

In charge of Houston's artillery was Colonel James C. Neill, onetime commander of the Alamo. With the men sheltered, Houston had Neill position the guns in the open just beyond the tree line, where the Mexicans could not help but see them. The Texas army had now increased to some

900. Recent research reveals that the source of much of this reinforcement was not local volunteers, but infantry from General Gaines. Once it was apparent that the great battle for Texas would not be fought in the Redlands, Gaines looked the other way as a number of his troops shucked their uniforms—it was important not to compromise American neutrality—and made their way south, singly and in small groups. Rusk was still with Houston, and now that battle was imminent, both were disgusted at how few local settlers were showing up for the fight. "Are you Americans?" Rusk demanded in a broadside to the public. "I look around, and see that many, very many, whom I anticipated would be first in the field, are not here. Rise up at once . . . a vigorous effort and the country is safe!"

"Be men, be freemen," Houston added. "Rally to the standard." In a private letter to his friend Henry Raguet in Nacogdoches, the general stated that Texas should have been able to field 4,000 soldiers, but after leaving a camp guard, he would only be able to attack with about 700. "It is the only chance of saving Texas. . . . Every consideration enforces it. No previous occasion would justify it." One reason, of course, that Texas did not field an army of 4,000 was that not all citizens supported the war, a fact that was brought home in the early morning of April 20, when a flatboat was discovered loaded with flour, with which local Tories meant to gift Santa Anna. It became instead the first bread that the Texas soldiers had tasted in several days.

Santa Anna arrived, saw Houston's exposed cannons, and took up a position on the opposite side of the San Jacinto plain. He had only one gun, a brass twelve-pounder dubbed the Golden Standard, and it was moved forward to a clump of trees and fired. He had thought that Houston was far to the north, but wasn't concerned by the sight of the guns. He ordered the bugler to sound the *Degüello*, the no-quarter fanfare that accompanied the annihilation at the Alamo. Shrapnel killed Houston's horse as he rode among his troops, and wounded Neill, but when the Twin Sisters opened up they proved accurate, and after a cavalry assault failed to capture the rebel guns, the Mexican artillery was forced to withdraw. Following the gunnery duel, Sidney Sherman, who had brought so many recruits into the service, approached Houston to press for action. The thirty-year-old Massachusetts native had been trying to throw his weight around ever since arriving in Texas, first disrupting Henry Millard's recruiting efforts, then pestering Houston to engage Sesma on the Colorado. After a heated exchange, the general permitted Sherman to make a reconnaissance-in-force only to scout out the enemy positions, but in no event to precipitate a general engagement. He led out a mounted force of sixty, immediately assaulted the Mexican cavalry, got cut off from safety by lancers, and had to send back to the Texan camp for reinforcements. When the irate general refused the request, first one company and then one of his two regiments marched out onto the plain to help Sherman, openly sneering as Houston bellowed impotently at them to countermarch. Sherman managed to disengage before a general imbroglio got started, and back under cover, Houston humiliated him with a savage dressing-down, removing him from cavalry command and giving it instead to Corporal Lamar of Georgia, who had distinguished himself in the skirmish by, among other things, saving the life of War Secretary Rusk. Sherman comforted himself with having made himself a hero to the disaffected men, and they now talked openly of installing him in command if Houston could not be brought to fight.

Believing that he had Houston trapped against Buffalo Bayou, Santa Anna established his camp for the night with stunning carelessness. With the San Jacinto River on his right and a sodden marsh around Peggy Lake at his rear, the only possible escape, if one became necessary, was on his left, to the southwest. His officers expressed their consternation, but the dictator dismissed them.

Sam Houston was a lifelong insomniac; he had been taking his naps on the ground, having given even his saddle blanket to the soldiers to rip up into wadding for the Twin Sisters. It struck the troops as exceedingly odd that on the night before the expected battle, Houston slept deeply and soundly. Everyone expected to attack in the early morning, but no order came, and then at nine the Texans were infuriated to see Santa Anna be reinforced by General Cos and over 500 more troops.

According to one tradition, Houston spent part of the midday in a tree, espying Santa Anna's tent with his telescope, finally descending with the comment, "I hope she keeps him in there all day." The reference introduces one of the most hotly debated aspects of the San Jacinto battle: the Yellow Rose of Texas. Long known as Emily Morgan, on the erroneous assumption that she was the slave of James Morgan of New Washington, Emily West, as established by her recently discovered indenture papers, was in fact a free woman of color from Connecticut, bonded to Morgan for a year of service in exchange for $100 and transportation to Texas. She was a light-skinned mulatto, hence the sobriquet of the Yellow Rose. When Santa Anna sacked New Washington, she was among the black women who were carried away to service the Mexican soldiers (a seldom-discussed aspect of the military establishment of a country that had outlawed slavery). It is highly probable that Emily West was in the Mexican camp at the time of the attack, and it is certain that Santa Anna was a philanderer who spread his charms as widely as possible. It is not certain that his pants were down at the time of the attack.

In any case, Houston called for a meeting of his officers, and put the question to them of whether to mount an assault, or receive an attack in their covering woods. Considering the open ground, and the fact that the Texans lacked bayonets, only two of them voted to attack. Houston moved calmly among the men, inquiring if they were ready to fight and receiving a barrage of profanity in the affirmative. "Well," he said, "get your suppers and I will lead you into the fight." At about three in the afternoon, Houston formed his army for attack, in a thin line a thousand yards across. Still with the army was Juan Seguín and his company of Tejanos. Houston initially assigned them to the camp guard, afraid that they might be mistakenly killed in the confusion of a battle. Seguín protested vigorously that no one in Texas had suffered more from Santa Anna than they, no one had a greater stake in the outcome, and indeed, they had no homes to go to unless the dictator was defeated. Houston heard him out and said, "Spoken like a man." The Tejanos took their place in the line, with scraps of cardboard in their headbands to identify them as Texans.

Now indeed was the time for reckless bravery, and Houston gave the obstreperous Sherman command of the Second Regiment on the far left; to Sherman's right Ed Burleson, prominent at the siege of Béxar, commanded the First Regiment. The general and the artillery took the center; to his right was Henry Millard and four companies of infantry, and beyond them Lamar's cavalry to cut off any Mexican escape. Knowing that General Vicente Filisola must be somewhere close by, Houston left a strong camp guard to retard any attempt by Filisola to reach Santa Anna, and also to keep an eye open for any more help from Gaines. Then on Deaf Smith's advice, a small bridge over Vince's Bayou, the only access to the field, was destroyed to impress on all that this was a fight to the death. "Trail arms," Houston ordered. "Forward."

They were screened from Mexican view by a rising swale of ground; two hundred yards from Santa Anna's barricades they knew the surprise was complete. Cos' men were exhausted by the night march and Santa Anna's men by the night labor of throwing up barricades. Houston attacked during their siesta. The Twin Sisters thundered to life, only to nearly kill Houston himself. After giving the order to fire, there was a hitch in getting the guns turned and aimed, and as Houston bellowed, "God damn it, aren't you going to fire at all?" his horse plunged in front of one of the guns. Ben McCulloch, an old Tennessee acquaintance who had been given command of the cannons after Neill was incapacitated, snatched a brand back from the touch hole just in time.

Three fifers had been found, but there was only one tune that all of them knew, a raunchy barroom tune called "Will You Come to the Bower?" which was not entirely inappropriate since their only flag was the busty Liberty who came with Sherman's Kentuckians. The six-pounders were reloaded and fired a couple more times and the men charged. Houston had drilled and drilled them to move and fire by companies, and this they remembered to do, once. Most didn't reload, just loped forward, drawing fearsome Bowie knives and turning their rifles to use as clubs. The rout was complete and immediate. One of Santa Anna's best field commanders, General Manuel Fernandez Castrillón, disgusted at his men, stood defiantly on a crate until he was blown off his feet.

The battle was over in a famous eighteen minutes; the killing, however, continued until dark. Wounded boys pleading for their lives had their brains blown out. Fleeing soldiers who made it as far as Peggy Lake were picked off in the bog by the score. With the day won, Houston tried repeatedly to get his men to regroup so as to repel Filisola if he came, and to take prisoners. "Boys," one officer relayed, "you know how to take prisoners, take them with the butt of yor guns, club guns & remember the Alamo . . . & club guns right & left & nock their God damn brains out." John Wharton tried to obey, only to hear one of his men respond, "Colonel Wharton, if Jesus Christ were to come down from heaven and order me to quit shooting Santanistas, I wouldn't do it, sir!" Moses Austin Bryan, the empresario's nephew, saw Wharton draw his sword, but the soldier cocked his rifle, and Wharton "very discreetly (I always thought)," left the field to the slaughter. When the horror ended, 630 Mexican soldiers were dead and some 730 under guard, in exchange for which the Texans lost eight killed and a couple dozen wounded.

The Alamo and Goliad were avenged—in fact the number of Mexican dead tallied almost exactly the Texans who fell with Travis and Fannin. But of Santa Anna there was no sign, and no one would be safe if he made it back to his army at Fort Bend. One of the first to hear news of the victory was General Gaines in Louisiana, who warned Houston, "be *vigilant*—be magnanimous—be just—and be generous, to the vanquished foe. But above all, *be vigilant.*"

Throughout the engagement, Houston had three horses shot from beneath him and had his left ankle shattered by a Mexican ball. It was late in the afternoon, after seeing columns of Mexican prisoners being filed into the Texas camp, when Houston told Wharton that he was wounded and was helped back to camp.

Clots of Anglo refugees huddled upriver heard the thunder of the artillery, and when they learned of the overwhelming victory, the departing tide of populace reversed itself. However, if Sam Houston had ever failed to comprehend the perennial ingratitude of Texas settlers that kept Stephen F. Austin in chronic melancholy, he got a remedial dose of it as he recuperated on his pallet under a live oak tree. Peggy McCormick, on whose land the battle had been fought (Peggy Lake was named for her), wanted the Mexican corpses removed. Even in his pain, Houston puffed himself up for the first of countless orations on the Battle of San Jacinto: "Madam, your land will be famed in history as the classic spot upon which the glorious victory . . . was gained! Here was born, in the throes of revolution, amid the strife of contending legions . . ."

"To the *devil* with your 'glorious history,' " she snapped. "Take off your stinking Mexicans!"

BOOK THREE

FROM NATION TO STATE

THIRTY-ONE

INDEPENDENCE AND THE SOUTHERN CONSPIRACY

MEASURED PURELY BY ITS SUBSEQUENT HISTORICAL IM-pact, the Battle of San Jacinto was one of the most pivotal in history. The freedom of Texas led to annexation to the United States and then the Mexican-American War, which transformed the U.S. into a continental power for the first time. In the shorter sight of the time, however, Texas had simply won its nationhood, and now had to begin acting like it. The first test was over the fate of the president-general of Mexico.

At the onset of the Texan assault, Santa Anna dashed out of his tent. One of his staff officers, Colonel Pedro Delgado, recalled seeing "His Excellency, running about in the most excited manner, wringing his hands and unable to give an order." Deaf Smith's suggestion to destroy the bridge over Vince's Bayou proved fortunate, as the dictator sought to flee over it to reach his army at Fort Bend. Finding it down, he hid in brush until dark, and changed into some clothes he found in an abandoned house. Early the next day, a Texan detail poked around the field looking for further prisoners and discovered him hiding in tall grass. (Other accounts had it that he was captured disguised in a Mexican private's blouse.) Upon entering the Texan camp, the first officer encountered happened to be Major John Forbes, one of Houston's most trusted supporters. Santa Anna stepped forward and produced a letter addressed to him, to indicate who he was. He made a gesture toward the camp and demanded, "Sam Houston!" Forbes was joined by another of Houston's most loyal, his chief of staff George Washington Hockley, and they escorted the dictator to where the wounded general was lying. As they passed by the Mexican prisoners they heard gasps of "El Presidente!"

According to Santa Anna's biographer, Houston uttered a stunning biological profanity at being roused. The two principals had never met, and a runner was sent to bring Colonel Almonte to verify his identification and translate. The oft-related details of their rather baroque exchange vary widely—whether the dictator was seated on a chair or a crate, whether he was composed or trembling. But there is a certain concordance. "The conqueror of the Napoleon of the West is born to no common destiny," said the dictator. "He can afford to be generous to the vanquished."

Houston was unimpressed. "You should have remembered that at the Alamo."

Santa Anna sought refuge in the decrees that Texas rebels were to be treated as pirates, which he was bound to obey, but Houston would have none of it. "You are the government yourself, sir," and not even those decrees could excuse the mass murder of Fannin and his command. By one account Santa Anna, believing that he was about to meet the execution that he would himself have undoubtedly meted out had he been the victor, asked for the box of opium in his captured camp kit. The volunteers' blood was still up, and without Houston's protection he would have been lynched. But the general realized that Santa Anna alive afforded them a measure of protection, and the dictator compliantly drafted orders to Filisola to withdraw to San Antonio and to order Urrea to pull back to Victoria. Excusing that his capture was the result of his operating only with a "small division" of his forces, he added a personal note that his and the other prisoners' safety depended on their obedience.

News of the Mexican catastrophe at San Jacinto, and Santa Anna's order to his army to withdraw eastward, reached Filisola two days later. Older and more experienced than either Santa Anna or Urrea, Vicente Filisola was a formidable officer. Italian by birth, he had fought as a royalist in the upheavals of New Spain, went over to the emperor Iturbide, and in fact conquered a large swath of Central America to add to the empire, territory that was lost when the would-be autocrat fell. Santa Anna had made him commander of the Eastern Interior and then second in command of the Texas expedition, and his every instinct was to fight on. He knew the numbers were still on his side, and Urrea backed him up. As Houston feared, they had no intention of abandoning the war. But with Santa Anna's coerced orders in hand, on April 25 Filisola, in agreement with Urrea and other senior commanders, decided to retire west of the Colorado River and send for instructions from their government.

Nature then intervened on the side of the rebels, as rain began to fall, and it fell harder, and harder, and still harder. At each step the Mexican infantry were sucked deeper into river-bottom gumbo; cannonballs and other materiel had to be cached and left behind; soldiers finally began discarding their firearms. With the rain came dysentery. By the time they completed their exhausting retreat through what they called the Mar del Lodo, the Sea of Mud, they had little left to fight with. Not until the end of May did the generals receive the instructions they asked for. The order was to hold all conquered territory, but by then the troops were south of the Nueces and had no alternative but to continue to Matamoros. It was not lack of nerve but logistical imperative that prompted the generals to abandon Texas. Charges were nonetheless brought against Filisola, and it took five years for him to clear his name.

Santa Anna, meanwhile, offered to negotiate the terms of independence with Houston, who was happy to point out that unlike him, he was not a dictator, and the formal cessation of hostilities would have to be worked out with the civilian government. Ad Interim President Burnet and his cabinet, no longer confined to Galveston Island, established a temporary capital at Velasco, at the mouth of the Brazos. Santa Anna had bypassed it and, thus, not put it to the torch. The dictator was spirited away from the vengeful Texas army to meet with Burnet, and on May 14 signed the Velasco Treaties, one of them public and one private. The public treaty provided for a cease-fire; repatriation of prisoners, including Santa Anna, who was not to resume hostilities thereafter; restoration of Texas property taken by Mexico; and safe conduct for the Mexican armies, who were to withdraw beyond the Rio Grande. The secret treaty gave Santa Anna freedom immediately, in exchange for his influence in securing the agreement of the rest of the Mexican government to recognize independent Texas, with the Rio Grande boundary, and ensure that Texan delegations would be received in safety. The boundary provision was significant, for while the Rio Grande was the more notable stream, the usual political demarcation had been the Nueces.

Burnet's treatment of Houston during these days was far less statesmanlike. The commanding general's shattered ankle became dangerously infected, and the surgeon general of the army, Alexander Ewing, recommended his removal to New Orleans for treatment by specialists. The steamboat *Yellow Stone* was standing by to take him, but Burnet, hoping to charge Houston with desertion, denied him permission to leave the army. When Ewing and the steamboat's captain took Houston to Galveston anyway, Ewing was stripped of his rank by Burnet's newly minted secretary of war and budding political ally, Mirabeau Lamar, the recent cavalry corporal. The provisional president then refused Houston passage to New Orleans on the Texas warship *Liberty*, forcing him to go on a tatty little American trading schooner, the *Flora*. Burnet was playing a losing game, however; what he was not able to prevent was the thunderous reception that the fainting Houston received on the New Orleans docks. News of the lopsided victory at San Jacinto had spread like a shock wave throughout the United States. Houston had won it, and the fact that he was destined to become a hero of the American pantheon poured like hot coals on the brows of Burnet, Potter, Sherman, and a host of lesser figures who vilified him to the end of their days.

Burnet had a much bigger problem than either Houston or Santa Anna, however, and that was his own army. He elevated Lamar to the war portfolio as a means of trying to control what was rapidly becoming an armed mob. The revolution had ended so abruptly that many companies of volunteers were still on the road to Texas when the fighting stopped, some of them led by would-be martinets who had more in common with the filibusters of thirty years earlier than with the Texans who had actually braved the war. One of them was Thomas Jefferson Green, a planter who had served in the statehouses of both North Carolina and Florida. On June 4 Burnet put Santa Anna, Almonte, and their secretary on board the *Invincible* to transport them home as specified in the treaty. Green and a couple hundred of his men, furious that Texas' archenemy was to be set free, boarded the vessel and demanded his execution. At one point Green even threatened Burnet to his face, but the provisional president, to his credit, maintained his authority defiantly, declared that Texas would not begin its nationhood with such an outrage, and spirited the dictator away; eventually he wound up at Lorenzo de Zavala's Orozimbo Plantation about twenty miles upriver, where he was kept in close confinement.

Filisola, meanwhile, had issued passports to three Texan emissaries to visit Matamoros and supervise the repatriation of prisoners held there. The Mexican senate immediately repudiated the Velasco Treaties as having been signed under duress, and called for a renewal of the war. The Texas delegation was arrested and jailed with the rest. Rusk, who had been supervising the withdrawal of Mexican forces to the Rio Grande, suddenly reported to the government that Urrea was about to assault Goliad. Despite such an alarm being raised, Urrea had no materiel left with which to attack anyone. Rusk also inflamed passions anew against the Mexicans by visiting the sites of the Goliad massacres, reporting that he finally buried the rotting bodies with honors. Portilla's men had made a halfhearted effort to cremate the remains shortly after the executions, with results more grisly than if he hadn't bothered.

The Mexican land forces were whipped, but hostilities continued at sea as though no treaties were ever signed. The *Invincible* continued to engage enemy ships until she was overmatched and run aground near Galveston on August 26; *Brutus* was lost in a storm the following year. Oddly, the biggest naval victories that took place after San Jacinto were the result not of broad-

sides beneath tall canvas but of the trickery of a company of mounted cavalry. With peace proving elusive, Rusk shrewdly ordered Major Isaac Burton,
a Georgian who had fought at San Jacinto, to take his cavalry company and
watch the lower coast for vessels trying to supply the Mexican army. Sure
enough, they discovered the *Watchman* in Copano Bay on June 2. They lured
the commander ashore and seized the ship, laden with supplies. This prize
was followed quickly by similar captures of the *Comanche* and the *Fanny Butler*, after which Burton's detachment was approvingly dubbed the "Horse
Marines." They suffered no casualties.

Burnet's desperation to control the army led him to once more hold out
the prospect, to keep them occupied, of an expedition south to pillage Matamoros. The idea was popular, but awaited Houston's return. Knowing that
his own appointment was only provisional, Burnet called national elections
for September 5, with the new president, vice president, and members of the
Texas Congress to take office the following December. On August 4 Stephen
F. Austin, who along with Wharton and Archer had scurried back to Texas
upon hearing news of San Jacinto, issued a statement. "I have been nominated by many persons," he wrote demurely, "whose opinions I am bound to
respect, as a candidate for the office of President of Texas, at the September
elections." In an era in which it was considered bad manners to appear to lust
for office, Austin announced he would serve if elected. The former provisional governor Henry Smith also entered his name, intent upon vindicating
his half of the fratricidal mayhem with the General Council.

Although back in Texas, Houston was laid up, recuperating at the home
of his friend Phil Sublett in San Augustine, as names began to be bandied
about for president. "Austin is the negociation candidate," he read in a huffy
letter from Texas brigadier Thomas Jefferson Green, who had threatened
Burnet's life if Santa Anna escaped with his. "Who is to be the fighting candidate? . . . some one in the name of God *firm & honest* who will fight us out
of this difficulty." Another unruly brigadier, Mississippian Felix Huston (no
relation to the commander in chief) also laid the responsibility on the
doorstep of Burnet and those around him. *"They had better beware,"* he threatened. This pugnacious truculence among Texas' new army officers was undoubtedly one reason that Houston did finally allow his name to be run for
president, on August 20; he was the one man in the country who might control them. As soon as he announced, Smith retired from the race and supported him.

When the votes were counted, Austin was buried in a landslide for Sam
Houston. Houston received 5,119, Austin only 586—about 150 fewer even

than Smith, whose name had remained on the ballot. Austin felt deeply and personally humiliated. He blamed his loss partly on Houston, who apparently at one time had told him that if he, Austin, ran for the presidency, he would not oppose him, but then changed his mind. It was a grudge that the Austin family bore against the Houston family for generations. Even more, Austin blamed his longtime secretary and dearest friend, Samuel May Williams. Before war broke out, Williams had traveled to Monclova to lobby the legislature, and using Austin's good name and reputation secured shady but lucrative land deals for himself. Rampant land speculation had been a prime mover in Santa Anna's decision to cleanse Texas of Anglos, and during the election campaign Williams' double-dealing became a hot topic, with Austin taking the brunt of the blame. To Williams' refuge in the United States, the betrayed Austin wrote: "Sam Williams you were wound around and rooted in my affections more than any man ever was or ever can be again. . . . You must have known that . . . those Monclova matters . . . were morally wrong and they have some very criminal and dreadful features." But what stung Austin more than anything was the realization that his fifteen years of hard service in the creation of Texas were so overwhelmingly thrown over in the celebration of a war hero. "A successful military chieftain is hailed with admiration and applause," he wrote with exquisite woe to his cousin Mary Holley, "but the bloodless pioneer of the wilderness, like the corn and cotton he causes to spring where it never grew before, attracts no notice. . . . No slaughtered thousands or smoking cities attest his devotion to the cause of human happiness, and he is regarded by the mass of the world as a humble instrument to pave the way for others." What Stephen Austin never could quite grasp was that his people lost faith in him when he held too long to peaceful conciliation toward Mexico. He was a man to whom loyalty was a paramount virtue, even to friends who didn't deserve it, or to a country that didn't reward it. That was his downfall.

The September 5 election also gave people the choice to ratify the Texas Constitution, which they did in a landslide; fewer than three hundred voted to allow the new congress to change it. It also contained a referendum on the question of annexation to the United States. Andrew Jackson had sprung his protégé Houston to Texas in 1832 with an eye—albeit a pragmatic one—toward union, and such a step would actualize the dreams of filibusters dating back to the turn of the century. Tied to the U.S. by kin and culture, more than three thousand Texans voted to pursue annexation; fewer than one hundred voted against it.

East of the old Neutral Ground, however, the question was more complicated. Houston had foreseen the pitfalls. "You need not hope for the acquisition (if ever) by this Government," he warned an investor in April 1834, "during the Administration of Genl Jackson—If it were acquired by a Treaty, that Treaty, would not be ratified, by the present Senate—!!!" And that was where the case still lay in Washington. The addition of Texas to the Union as a slave state would upset the delicately preserved Senate balance between slave states and free. Northerners and abolitionists, sensing in the grassroots movement to annex Texas an attempt by the South to gain an upper hand in the Senate, began throwing up every conceivable roadblock. With the Senate in certain deadlock, Texas' most dangerous enemy across the dome in the House of Representatives came to be the former president, John Quincy Adams. When he had moved into the White House in 1824 despite Andrew Jackson's plurality in the popular vote, as the alleged beneficiary of the "corrupt bargain" with Henry Clay, Adams had pursued a moderate and national-oriented policy, often even appointing Jackson's partisans when they were the best men to fill vacant posts. He grew increasingly frustrated, however, by the shrill and small-minded sectionalism that took over the national debate. He retired in 1828, but two years later consented to serve his Massachusetts district in Congress; now, at nearly seventy, he was the first and among the ablest foes of slavery in national service.

Much of Adams' antislavery and anti-Texas ammunition was funneled to him in the writings of his friend, none other than Benjamin Lundy, the Quaker abolitionist whose almost-realized Texas colony for free blacks had been derailed by the revolution. That experience left him convinced that a Texas in the hands of slaveholding ex-Americans must never be let into the Union. Among other polemics, Lundy wrote a pamphlet with copiously italicized passages called "The War in Texas," in which he asserted that he knew the real cause of the upheaval there, to which the North must be alerted:

> The prime cause, and the real objects of this war, are not distinctly understood by a large portion of the honest, disinterested, and well-meaning citizens of the United States. . . . They have been induced to believe that the inhabitants of Texas were engaged in a legitimate contest for the maintenance of the sacred principles of Liberty, and the natural, inalienable Rights of Man:—whereas, the motives of its instigators . . . have been, from the commencement, of a directly opposite character and tendency. *It is susceptible of the clearest demonstration, that the immediate cause and leading object of this contest originated in a settled design, among the slaveholders of this country (with land-speculators*

*and slave-traders,) to wrest the large and valuable territory of Texas from the
Mexican Republic, in order to re-establish the SYSTEM OF SLAVERY; to
open a vast and profitable SLAVE-MARKET therein; and, ultimately, to
annex it to the United States.* And further, it is evident—nay, it is very
generally acknowledged—that the insurrectionists are principally citizens of the United States, who have preceeded thither *for the purpose*
of revolutionizing the country. . . . Whether the national *Legislature*
will . . . lend its aid to this most unwarrantable, aggressive attempt,
will depend on the VOICE OF THE PEOPLE.

Lundy proceeded to a more detailed, if no more objective, history of
events leading up to the revolution, maintaining that the conspirators' ultimate object was to multiply the power of the South in Congress by breaking
Texas up into four or five slave states. The good Quaker Lundy's voice was
one of influence in the North, and his partisans took "The War in Texas" as
gospel. Lundy and Adams made sure that every member of the U.S. Congress received copies of this and his other publications, and the two were instrumental in moving the government away from annexing, or even
recognizing the independence of, Texas—at least for the time being.

Revisionist historians have made some trade in recent years resuscitat-
ing Lundy's argument about a "Southern Conspiracy." Astute men in the
South were indeed aware that Texas annexed could increase their power in
the U.S. Congress. Felix Huston, now a Texas martinet, was still a lawyer in
Natchez, Mississippi, when he first volunteered his services to Sam Houston, including in his letter that "we are alive to the importance of the contest
in relation to its immediate and prospective effect on the whole Southern
Portion of the United States."

However, the belief ran deep in the North as well as the South that
Americans in Texas had contended for, and many had died for, the kind of
political freedom that was the soul of the United States, and whose survival
was impossible under the despotism of Santa Anna. Some Americans who
removed to Texas even took it as their duty to announce themselves to their
new government, and pledge their willingness to volunteer, should hostilities flare again. Shortly after his inauguration, President Houston received
an unsolicited letter from one new arrival, S. B. Conley. "I have come as a
settler in Texas, and am willing to share her dangers, as I expect in future to
share her prosperity—my profession is the Law; studied, & licensed in New
York—I neither ask, nor desire, publick employment, and only now wish to
report myself as in the country, & ready to obey her calls at this unsettled

moment. . . . I shall be found at Bastrop, or near there . . . with me will be five able bodied men, with good rifles, & steady nerves."

The desire for personal freedom had also lured across the ocean others who had no notion of the Southern Conspiracy. A Westphalian lawyer, Robert Justus Kleberg Sr., and his wife Rosa von Röder came to Texas late in 1834 because, he said, "I wished to live under a Republican form of government with unbounded personal, religious and political liberty; free from the petty tyrannies, the many disadvantages and evils of old countries. Prussia . . . smarted at the time under military despotism. I was . . . an enthusiastic lover of republican institutions, and I expected to find in Texas, above all other Countries, the blessed land of my most fervent hopes." When he arrived and found instead another military dictatorship, he joined the army and fought at San Jacinto. The 320 acres of land he received for less than four months' service was a barnyard compared to the ranching empire he went on to establish. This democratic streak ran particularly deep in the German émigrés. Another one, Johann E. F. G. Bunsen, cousin of the chemist who devised the laboratory burner, took part in insurrections against Russian hegemony in Poland, and against the autocracy in his native Hesse, before fleeing to Texas. He was killed at San Patricio.

As much as Andrew Jackson ached to add a Texas star to the American flag, and as much as the Texans desired it, in his last year as president he simply lacked the political leverage to make it happen.

THIRTY-TWO

A NEW COUNTRY, A NEW CITY

AD INTERIM PRESIDENT BURNET ESTABLISHED THE NA-
tional capital in the village of Columbia, on the Brazos in Brazoria County; it
was another settlement bypassed and thus spared by Santa Anna. Columbia
had little more to recommend it for such distinction than had Washington,
where the Texas government was born. The few buildings were mostly commandeered for official use; there was at least a saloon and a hotel, but according to one early visitor, the most popular sleeping spot was the ground
beneath a spreading live oak tree. The town was laid out in 1824 by Josiah
Bell, Austin's good friend from Missouri days, who resettled from Nacogdoches as one of the Old Three Hundred. During Austin's first long sojourn
in Mexico City to salvage his contract, it was Bell who had run the colony. He
turned to planting sugar, developed an estate valued at well over a hundred
thousand dollars, and was responsible for much of the improvement in the
lower Brazos Valley.

In Columbia, abstract provisions of the March constitution began to take
concrete shape. Texas opened its congress on October 3 with representatives from twenty-two counties, a number that increased in the following
years to thirty-six as new areas were settled. No party tickets had yet developed, and the man elected vice president was a growing Houston nemesis
and Burnet ally, Mirabeau Lamar, who, as in the United States, would preside
over the senate. The law provided for judges over four judicial districts, who
when acting together would constitute the supreme court under the chief
justice, James Collinsworth, the former chairman of the ad interim government's military affairs committee and a Houston ally. Moving beyond the
Velasco Treaties, the Texas congress announced its boundary with Mexico to
be the Rio Grande from mouth to source, and then north to British Oregon,
a territorial claim that vaulted Texas sovereignty into the northern Rockies.

Of more practical reality, President Burnet still found himself unable to
stem insubordination and looming mutiny or even coup d'état from the
army, which as weeks rolled by changed its complexion dramatically. The
volunteers who defied the Mexican government, and with them the regulars
who prosecuted the revolution, were coming to the end of their enlistments,

taking their land bounties and retiring to civilian life. The army was now more than twice as large as it was at any time during the rebellion, but it was manned almost entirely by new arrivals from the United States who knew little of and had no real ties to Texas. Houston was almost as universally lionized by them for San Jacinto as he was vilified by the earlier generation of soldiers who believed ardently that the Runaway Scrape was unnecessary and shameful. Burnet maintained his authority fiercely over the military, but once the recuperating Houston was in Columbia, he resigned suddenly on October 22 and turned the reins of government over to their hero. The generalissimos like Green and Felix Huston rejoiced, and Burnet probably saved democratic government in Texas. He did, however, abandon his office so unexpectedly that the government was left in some confusion. Even worse, Sam Houston, who loved to make a good speech, did not have enough time to prepare an inaugural address.

It was just short of four years since he had crossed the Red River with a borrowed razor and a joke to its owner that with a little luck, it might one day shave the chin of a president. To another he had once chided that he might one day just go to Texas and start a little two-horse republic. Certainly, he had come with the fondest hopes of Jackson that he would succeed. But now the reality of it, that he was president of the Republic of Texas, took him aback. Sitting in the Texas congress were men who fervently admired him, and just as many who couldn't stand him. His speech was almost extemporaneous, but he had made a few notes. "I am perfectly aware of the difficulties that surround me," he told them, and if they could not find a way to work together, "wreck and ruin must be the inevitable consequences of my administration." No sooner had he mollified his opponents with an appeal that they correct and sustain him with their superior wisdom, than he exasperated them with a gesture mimicking George Washington's farewell, by surrendering to the people the sword of San Jacinto. In his youth, Houston had acted in amateur melodramas, and now he clung to his sword just long enough, his eyes just dewy enough, to remind all present that Texas' freedom, in his mind, was his doing.

Houston also vowed that he would appoint a unity cabinet from all factions, a promise that he delivered on four days later. The secretary of the treasury was to be Henry Smith, long of the war party, while he appeased Burnet by making his ad interim auditor, Asa Brigham, treasurer of the Republic, and Marshall Pease, the General Council's former secretary and Houston critic, comptroller. The naval secretariat went to Austin intimate S. Rhoads Fisher, while Rusk, who had proven himself reliable and moderate, was reappointed secretary of war. James Collinsworth, who as chairman of the military affairs committee of the general council had been the man to whom Houston reported at the beginning of the revolution, declined the attorney generalship to be chief justice, so that office went to one of the recent army generals, North Carolina lawyer J. Pinckney Henderson, who had only arrived in June and was given his billet by Burnet. However, he impressed Houston as less hotheaded than Green or Huston.

For secretary of state, Houston made the only sensible choice: Austin, the man who stood the best chance of making annexation happen. Physically as well as spiritually Austin was now all but spent, and he refused at first, but as always he proved susceptible to an appeal to his sense of duty. Annexation offered the safest future for Texas, and Houston agreed that he would allow Austin to retire if the office proved too much for him. William Wharton, with whom Austin had proved able to work in good concert, was accredited minister to the United States, and he brought the additional advantage of being a Jackson intimate from pre-Texas days. Columbia's resources were being overwhelmed by the gathering government, and the only lodging Austin could find was the loosely clapboarded shed room in the cabin of Judge George McKinstry, who as an ardent Wharton partisan and supporter of the war party had never been one of Austin's favorite people. From this drafty bedroom office, fitted with neither stove nor fireplace, Austin wrote out Wharton's instructions and began working through the Mexican consul in New Orleans, arranging the repatriation of prisoners of war. Working in concert with Houston, a plan was devised to get Santa Anna and Almonte out of the country—and danger—on a visit to Jackson in Washington, D.C., where the captive president-general would swear his amity to Texas and finally be allowed to go home. Riding through swamps and on back roads with a vigilant escort, the escape was effected. Santa Anna's release renewed the furor for his execution, which Houston, typically, dealt with by making light of it. Santa Anna free, he quipped, would keep Mexico in commotion for years, and thus keep Texas safe.

Austin also began attending to his personal affairs. During the war, feeling himself the head of a kind of Texas royal family, he had forbidden his relatives to flee the country, and the ordeal had been particularly hard on his much-loved sister, Emily, and her family. Austin's house at San Felipe was burned with the rest of the town, and his remaining land comprised less than twenty thousand acres, but he sold enough to raise $3,000 to send her back to the United States to rest and arrange an education for her children. In mid-December a powerful norther ripped through the town; Austin took a cold that soon deepened into the death grip of pneumonia. Closely tended, he was bedded on a fireside pallet in the main room of McKinstry's house. Two days after Christmas the doctors applied a chest poultice and he seemed to rally, and asked for tea. He sat up briefly and seemed to breathe easier. "Now," he said, "I will go to sleep." He napped fitfully, starting awake shortly before noon. "The independence of Texas is recognized!" he said in delirium. "Don't you see it in the papers? Dr. Archer told me so!" Half an hour later his spent spirit escaped his body after forty-three years.

Houston heard the news almost at once, and issued a melancholy proclamation: "The Father of Texas is no more! The first pioneer of the wilderness has departed." The Texans that grumbled and mistrusted and ignored him in life gave him all the pomp in death that their rude circumstances could muster. Government officials wore black armbands for a month, cannons boomed slow-interval twenty-three-gun salutes, and the *Yellow Stone,* which had stood by Texas during the revolution, conveyed his body, with Houston as part of the honor guard, for burial at the family compound at Peach Point.

Sam Houston found himself president of a country populated by, it was estimated, thirty thousand whites, five thousand slaves, and perhaps four thousand Mexicans, but that number started to dwindle as Tejanos began to feel the weight of racism and resentment, and so immigrated to a Mexico that many of them had never seen. There were also between ten and fifteen thousand native Indians, belonging to a patchquilt of different tribes whose experience with, and demeanor toward, the Anglos varied tremendously. One of the first tasks that Houston set himself was to win secure land titles for the Texas Cherokees and convince the senate to ratify the treaty he had made with them at the outset of the revolution. The president had lived six years of his life with Cherokees and sympathized with them deeply, but despite his best efforts he could not get the Texas senate to concur. They stalled him for nearly a year before scuttling the treaty, after Lamar mendaciously charged that they had secretly aided the Mexicans. The betrayal shook and angered the Cherokees, and they would not forget it.

Of still greater worry were the wilder Plains tribes, who as settlement expanded to the west and north found their hunting grounds encroached upon. The various tribes of the Brazos Valley—Wacoes, Keechis, and the like—often stole and sometimes murdered, but the real terror lay beyond, with the Comanches, who despite the most determined effort of the Spanish military, had never been subjugated by Western military technology. The full horror of a Comanche attack broke upon the new republic at a remote stockade of religious dissidents on the Navasota River in present Limestone County. Partly fueled by the so-called Second Great Awakening of unlettered evangelism, the Baptist denomination had been splitting into strident off-shoots who legalistically but fiercely contested points of doctrine. There were predestinarians, two-seeders, and antimissionaries, one of which sects was headed by Elder John Parker of Virginia. At his remote "Parker's Fort," he, his wife (known as Granny), and about thirty kin and followers farmed and worked out their salvation. On the morning of May 19, 1836, a large number of Comanches, with some Keechis in company, approached the fort under a white flag and asked for a cow. Upon being denied, they killed Benjamin Parker and Silas Parker before they could regain the stockade, and two more fell at the gate as the Indians stormed the fort. Inside, Elder John was overtaken, tortured, castrated, and killed, while Granny was pinned to the ground with a lance driven through her body and raped by as many warriors as wanted to defile her. The war party pounded away when the remaining men of the settlement came dashing in, armed, from distant fields. The Indians took with them two women, two boys, and a girl as captives. One of the women, Elizabeth Kellogg, was located by Houston's Delaware intermediaries and ransomed in December for $150. The other, Rachel Plummer, bore a child of her multiple rapes, which the Indians killed, and she was rescued by mountain men only after a year and a half of slavery. The boys were not ransomed for six years, and the girl, Cynthia Ann Parker, was traded to a distant band of Comanches, and while she was occasionally seen in following years, she acculturated and became a member of the tribe.

The danger posed by Indian attack had been present since the first outsiders stepped onto Texas soil, but Houston established and walked a unique tightrope of Indian policy. On the one hand he commissioned Ranger companies to protect frontier settlements from such hideous attacks, with limited success, while on the other hand he argued in defense of native rights, with even less success, to Texas' congress and people, whose revulsion at such customs combined with their innate ethnocentrism to encourage a policy of all-out war.

Most Indians, at least, remained at a distance. Burnet had resigned to give Houston a chance to bring the army to heel, and it was imperative that he begin at once. Typically for him, he began to play for time. He made Felix Huston commanding general of the army, and while writing him encouraging letters, quietly sabotaged any attempts to mount an expedition to Matamoros. Shortly after New Year's Day of 1837, Houston left Columbia on an extensive inspection tour of army posts that confirmed previous reports of drunkenness, low morale, mistreatment of citizens, and an appalling want of supplies. Many of his soldiers actually were, as he was warned by one loyal officer, "bear footed and hongry." It was also apparent that Huston had been actively cultivating his own popularity among them. Upon his return, the president directed a sweeping reorganization of the army, under a new commanding general. He was Albert Sidney Johnston, a thirty-three-year-old Kentucky widower and West Pointer, who had come to Texas and modestly enlisted as a private. Rusk spied his abilities and elevated him to adjutant general. Huston was to be retained as junior brigadier, but galled at the demotion, he challenged Johnston to a duel and on February 7 dangerously wounded him with a shot through the buttocks. Huston thus retained his command, and became even more blustery in his demands that Houston support the long-stalled invasion of Matamoros. Now aware of the kind of enemy he faced, the president awaited his chance. Eventually Huston was brazen enough to ride into the capital, without Houston's leave, to lobby key congressmen on the matter. Acting in the dead of night, while Huston lay sleeping as his guest, Houston sent out couriers with orders to furlough all army troops down to the number of six hundred, with such excess soldiers to collect at the various ports for free transportation back to the United States. Felix Huston did not discover until he returned to his headquarters that he had no more army; at once he wrote to Houston demanding an explanation, and the president responded innocently that he was unaware that any soldiers had been furloughed.

One flaw in the plan was the country had no means to pay passage for well over a thousand volunteers to sail home, but by collecting the men at the ports and making their furloughs subject to recall, Houston gave them incentive to find their own way. It was one of many creative ways he devised to finesse the Republic's finances, for he had assumed the presidency of an infant country whose debt totaled a very adult one and a quarter million dollars, against the meagerest of receipts. The question of credit was further complicated by reports reaching Columbia that the Republic's agents in New Orleans, Thomas and Samuel Toby, who as Houston's enemies gossiped belonged to "the . . . sect of Jews," had been manipulating Texas' standing to generate personal profit. Houston greeted the news with a squall of profanity; the cultured Henderson went to New Orleans to investigate, persuaded the president that there was nothing to it, and begged him to moderate his language. "However," he wrote, "a *dam* occasionally may do no harm." In point of fact, the firm of Toby and Brother did yeoman service for the Republic; they were entrusted to raise money by selling tracts of public domain for the best prices they could get, in exchange for supplies needed by the Texas government. By the end of their relationship with Texas, the Toby brothers had managed to dispense nearly a million acres, and shipped so much cargo to Texas that they had a balance of nearly eighty thousand dollars against the Republic—a debt that was finally settled for just over half that amount, nearly fifty years later.

Land, however depreciated, was virtually the only resource. There was no bullion for national coinage, nor would there be for the duration of the country. Houston did authorize a conservative issue of promissory notes as a kind of currency, which held their value surprisingly well as the hundred other chores of starting a country were tackled. By mid-spring of 1837 the administration was functioning in a roughly reliable way, but Columbia suited no one as a permanent seat of government. The previous autumn, two enterprising New York brothers, Augustus C. and John K. Allen, approached the Texas congress with a proposal to move the capital to a new town that they were developing on a half-league of land near Harrisburg on Buffalo Bayou. When they offered to throw in a free capitol and nominal rent for government offices, the deal was accepted. Construction ran late on the two-story, porticoed capitol, and when the government relocated, congress met under tree branches lashed to the rafters to serve as a roof. The president was enchanted to discover that the new metropolis was to be named Houston, at the suggestion of A. C. Allen's wife, Charlotte, and there would be a two-room dogtrot on the lot next to theirs to serve as the executive mansion.

The move would be completed in plenty of time to celebrate a ball in honor of the first anniversary of San Jacinto, so while Houston was being fitted with reinforced red-topped boots to allow him to dance on his San Jacinto ankle, he decided to make one more run at convincing the congress to grant the Cherokees secure land titles. They had not heeded his pleas up to this point, so the president used San Jacinto Day to make a small demonstration on the topic. Secretly he sent for several groups of natives to assemble around the city of Houston, and had a large new flagpole erected in the middle of town. On April 21, as the gold Lone Star on its azure field was hoisted aloft, the Indians marched into the city and performed an elaborate dance of homage to the Texas Republic. It still availed them nothing.

The San Jacinto ball, held that night in the unfinished capitol, was noted as the first occasion that Texas women had of unpacking their finest dresses, many of them not seen in years. The president decided to use this occasion for political double duty as well, as a way to annoy Mosely Baker, his onetime rebellious infantry captain, now a representative from Austin County and still a thorn in his side. Baker was away, and Mrs. Baker, who by accounts was one of the most beautiful women in the country, was desperate to attend, so the president took her as his escort. Gentlemen removed their boots in favor of dancing slippers, except the president, by orthopedic necessity, and in a nightlong fête of cotillions and reels, the greatest nimbleness was exhibited not in the dance steps, but in avoiding the sperm oil that dripped sizzling from the improvised chandeliers.

One of the youngest and most ambitious of the new Houston belles was Dilue Rose, an ingenue who had survived the Runaway Scrape and wrote about returning home over the "grewsome" battlefield of San Jacinto in her father's wagon, requiring him to pull the dead Mexicans out of the road. Dilue was nearly thirteen. Feeling herself becoming an old maid, she had set her sights high—on the president himself. She was nearly within reach of what she described as her greatest ambition, to dance with Houston, when she was politely bumped aside by an eligible widow. Benjamin Fort Smith, one of Houston's oldest friends and a veteran of Jackson's Creek Indian campaign, had established a hotel nearby, and he provided a midnight supper of chunks of venison, whole roast turkeys, wines, cake, and coffee. Dancing continued until sunrise.

Within four months of its establishment, Houston was home to more than 1,500 people. Galveston with its port remained the commercial key to the country, but Houston, by hosting the government and its collection of educated people, quickly challenged for cultural leadership. Masonic lodges and a new Philosophical Society of Texas took root. This was, however, largely social veneer; the reality of Houston beneath the cravats and fans and curtsies was that it was filthy. Street sanitation depended upon the appetite of feral hogs, drinking water came from the bayou, which was also the sewer, and typhoid and dysentery began to take their toll. When the first epidemic of yellow fever hit in 1839, one in eight died, and the visitation was repeated every three to five years. The ambient level of street drunkenness hardly has a modern counterpart, and violence was common.

Houston's principal hotel became the Mansion House, whose proprietress was none other than Pamelia Mann of the oxen and the Which-Way Tree. Having relocated to where the commerce was sure to be, Mrs. Mann's Mansion House was more famous as a saloon and brothel than as a hotel, known for its whiskey downstairs and "fawn-necked damsels" upstairs. (One of the working girls, for a time, was said to be Susanna Dickinson, widow of the Alamo's artillery commander, who had to support herself until she could make a marriage, of which there were eventually five.) Mrs. Mann still knew how to take care of herself, and was often prosecuted for larceny and assault—doubtless by patrons who didn't want to pay for services—but she and President Houston became fast friends. He stood as best man at the wedding of her son, whose given name was Flournoy but whom everybody just called Nimrod.

Like any frontier boomtown, Houston was populated mostly by single men, which made it a target-rich environment for capable women. Nimrod's wedding, in fact, was an important chance for one of them. Dilue Rose was to be the bridesmaid, which meant that the best man—the president— would escort her. She presented herself at her prettiest, only to be elbowed aside at the last moment by another widow, a Mrs. Holliday, who cooed that Dilue was too young and timid for such a public function. Dilue Rose could have murdered her. Houston city, she carped in her memoirs, "was at that time overrun with widows." (By way of consolation, her pouting was interrupted by a young strapper named Ira Harris. They were married within a year, and their three-decade union produced nine children, followed by a widowhood of forty-five years, during which she was honored as a bountiful font of tales of early Texas history.)

The capers of another managing woman followed a signal event in the cultural life of the city, the first performance by a professional theater troupe, on June 11, 1838. The playbill asked the patrons' indulgence, because the orchestra had not yet arrived from Mobile, but there would still be a performance of "A New National Texian Anthem," written for the occasion by one of the company. The scenery, damaged on the voyage, had been repaired, and they would present two comedies, *The Hunchback* and *The Dumb Belle, Or, I'm Perfection.* The stars of the company, Mr. and Mrs. Barker, had been having marital difficulties, which culminated in the former actually poisoning himself on stage. Ever chivalrous, the president vacated his house to lodge the grieving widow and her three children, and public subscriptions were collected for her benefit. In gratitude, she performed scenes from Shakespeare's *Romeo and Juliet,* which so moved bartender Tom Hoffman that he proposed marriage. Mrs. Barker accepted, he lent her a thousand dollars to visit her family in England, and she was never seen again.

Through such occasions the president seemed ubiquitous, as pickup fiddle ensembles played "Hail to the Chief." Even one of Lamar's partisans had to admit that he found Houston "extreamly courteaous when he out for general inspection, this seldom oftener than once in sunshine, between eleven

& two, he . . . dresses himself gaudily in self peculiar taste viz. black silk velvet gold lace crimson vest and silver spurs." By taking a stiff drink, Houston
"makes himself again *Hector* upon his feet and no longe the wounded
Achilise of San Jacinto . . . and with a tread of dominion in his aroganic step
strides . . . across his own nominated metropolis . . . to the barkeeper."

Both heroes having been wounded in the foot, the taunt was unkind, but
accurate, down to the fact that Houston's drinking had gone out of control.
He was without question the darling of the rabble, but he was paying a personal toll for it. He had been living without companionship since leaving
Diana Rogers at Ft. Gibson, and since 1833 he had courted the beautiful
Miss Anna, daughter of his friend Henry Raguet of Nacogdoches. She was
less than half his age, beautiful, accomplished and virtuous, and she had inspired Houston to finally file for divorce from Eliza. While she was flattered
to have the attention of the president, Anna Raguet was chilled by his reputation and made sure that their relationship stayed more chivalrous than
amorous. His frustration over her was at times agonizing; at the same time
his relationship with the Texas congress became often hostile, especially
over Indian and defense policy, and he was grieved over the deaths of various
intimates, including, most painfully, Deaf Smith. He bet Houston city
founder A. C. Allen a suit of clothes he could stay sober for a year; but his
reputation increased to the point that when twenty-four-year-old Kentucky
newspaper editor Hamilton Stuart, a teetotaler, arrived in Texas with letters
of introduction to Houston, he was terrified how the president would react
if he declined to drink with him. He needn't have worried, as Houston put
his arm around him. "Young man, I never insist upon any one drinking with
me. I sometimes think I drink too much myself."

For all his public parties and private trials, Sam Houston never had his eye
off the goal of annexation for long. After Austin's death the state portfolio
was taken up by Attorney General Henderson, who quickly proved himself
smart and capable, but opposition to Texas in the United States was simply
immovable. As early as November 1836, when he dispatched Santa Anna to
Washington, Houston sent at the same time a private and confidential letter
to Jackson, begging his intercession for Texas' admission to the Union. "It is
policy to hold out the idea . . . that we are very able to sustain ourselves
against any power . . . yet I am free to say *to you* that we cannot do it. . . . My
great desire is that our country Texas shall be annexed to the United States
on a footing of Justice and reciprocity to the parties. . . . This is a matter of

great distress. . . . I look to you as the friend and patron of my youth . . . to interpose on our behalf and save us."

Jackson wanted desperately to help, but he could not. Five days after San Jacinto, Burnet had sent Collinsworth to Washington to begin the annexation process, and Jackson had stalled him. Now he did the same with Houston's minister, William Wharton, with the additional backdrop of Santa Anna's soothing assurances that he had no more hostile designs on Texas. Under this pressure, Jackson stalled some more. Stymied, Houston withdrew the offer of annexation. His entire political career had been one of watchful pragmatism, and now with this issue, as with others before, he would monitor events for a favorable occasion to strike in other ways. It was a pale consolation, but Jackson as his last official act as president did recognize Texas independence. Texans had won what they fought for, a bump-and-rumble frontier republic, and for better or worse that's what they got. Now they had to look after themselves as best they could in the world's contentious family of nations.

THIRTY-THREE

POET AND PRESIDENT

ONCE THE WHIGS AND ABOLITIONISTS IN THE AMERICAN
Congress made it clear that they held the power to block Texas' admission to
the Union, President Houston set to work with resignation to bring Texas to
the notice of the European powers. He sent a new emissary to Washington,
Dr. Anson Jones of Brazoria, the chairman of the foreign relations committee of the Texas house of representatives. A Massachusetts native of forty,
Jones was a man of sour personal disposition acquired after multiple business failures in the U.S., and his newfound financial stability with medical
and apothecary practices in Texas did little to cheer him up. Jones went to
Washington with instructions to withdraw the offer of annexation, an act
that was accomplished with some show of injury and insult. Together—
although in what respective proportions cannot be determined—Houston
and Jones struck the course of angling toward annexation by making the
U.S. jealous of Texas' success at relations with Europe.

It would not be an easy game to play. British business was heavily invested in Mexico, and moreover the British frowned mightily on the institution of slavery. Houston noticed, however, that that disapproval did not
prevent them from buying American cotton. Moreover, Britain and the U.S.
were in a diplomatic chill over collateral issues, and Texas dangled before
them an alternative supply of cotton independent of American goodwill and
unencumbered by American tariffs. The president had already seen this
coming. When he addressed the Texas congress on May 5, 1837, he made
sure that the British consul at Tampico, Joseph Tucker Crawford, who had
also been assigned to watch over British interests in Texas, was seated on
the dais to hear him attack the slave trade. "This unholy and cruel traffic has
called down the reprobation of the humane and just of all civilized nations,"
Houston intoned, and he requested British naval assistance in overhauling
slaving vessels attempting to smuggle human cargo into Texas. This was
well received in England, and it also made them more receptive to
Houston's following argument that Texas' geography and economy made a
quick end to the institution unrealistic. Shrewdly, this stance also kept
Houston safe with the planters in his congress, because he attacked the

slave trade, not slavery itself, and the importation of new slaves had been illegal even in the United States for nearly thirty years. Houston then appointed J. P. Henderson, a man upon whom he was increasingly coming to
rely, as minister to the courts of England and France. His instructions on
how to respond to the British were equally simple, that "on the matter of
slavery you can speak with candor and truth, admitting that its institution
was cruel and impolitic [but] under existing circumstances . . . it *must*
continue."

Texas still had no political parties, only sentiments that echoed the political slogans in the United States. However, since the most potent political
force in the country was the president, and he was a man who aroused extravagant passions in both his friends and his enemies, issues came to be regarded in terms of his stance on them. Interested parties stood as either
pro-Houston or anti-Houston. Quite apart from the army volunteers who
thought him a coward for not fighting the Mexicans before San Jacinto,
Houston was an easy man to hate. In an era in which alcoholism was thought
to be a moral failure and not a disease, his drinking disqualified him from
much polite society. In a place in which most men would as soon shoot an Indian as let him live, Houston had sojourned six years of his life with them,
and loved and respected and defended them. And in a culture that revolved
around cotton and slavery, Houston's disapproval of the "peculiar institution," paired with his consistent stance against land speculation, made him
anathema to the richest citizens and a traitor to his class. He was in every
sense still a Jacksonian, a champion of the common people, but simple like
a fox.

Under the 1836 constitution, the term of the first president was limited
to two years, and he was ineligible to succeed himself as he might have in
the United States. Former provisional president Burnet had acted to save
the country in turning the government over to Houston in October 1836,
but his personal opinion of him, probably conceived long before either of
them had set foot in Texas, never wavered from disgust and vituperation.
The ablest and most intelligent of Houston's opponents, however, was undoubtedly the vice president, Mirabeau B. Lamar. He was a man in whom
the Old South met the larger Age of Romanticism. He was an equestrian, he
fenced, and he had an unshakable faith in the rectitude of slavery. He also
painted in oils and wrote poetry that was considered good enough to publish. He married a consumptive, and when she died he was cast into melancholy, finding solace only in mournful travel. Goethe would have loved him.

The long-haired, poetry-spouting Georgia cavalry corporal had distinguished himself in battle, too.

The two candidates Houston approved of to succeed him had both, ironically, been Burnet's ministers to the United States: James Collinsworth, the chief justice; and Peter W. Grayson, who had been a close aide to Austin and had served Texas ably in a variety of posts. Their candidacies were disastrous. Like Houston, Collinsworth was an alcoholic, but at only thirty he lacked the president's confidence in the future. During the campaign, after a binge of several days, he either fell or cast himself from a boat into Galveston Bay and drowned. Grayson was a fifty-year-old Virginian, bright, successful, and widely experienced but too sensitive for politics. He also believed himself to be possessed by a fiend. During a mission to the United States for Houston, he became overwhelmed by romantic rejection and the lies being spread about him by Lamar partisans, and shot himself to death in Kentucky.

At the last moment, Robert Wilson, a senator and an entrepreneur who had developed Harrisburg and lost all when Santa Anna burned the town, entered the race as the pro-Houston candidate. It is doubtful whether Lamar would have been elected over creditable opposition, but Wilson was a virtual nonentity. At the contest on November 16, 1838, Houston supporters saw little reason even to vote, handing the election almost unanimously to Lamar, and the vice presidency to Burnet. Houston's defeat would hardly have been more bitter had he been running himself. As the time for transition approached, Houston and Lamar traded civil notes on transferring the furnishings of the executive dogtrot, but the outgoing president and one-time melodramatist was saving up his own show of scorn for his replacement. At Lamar's inauguration on December 10, Houston was to be allowed a valedictory of his administration. He arrived dressed as George Washington and orated for three hours, leaving Lamar in such a fit that he had to have his secretary read his speech for him.

The new president was prepared to humiliate Houston in equal measure, though. One of his first acts was to redesign the Texas flag. Houston's beloved golden Lone Star on its deep blue field was transformed into the red, white, and blue tricolor familiar today. He also commissioned a team to scout the interior and locate a spot for a new capital far from the city named for Houston. They settled on a location where the Colorado River emerges from the Hill Country, some eighty miles northeast of San Antonio. Continuing a short distance upriver from the tiny settlement of Waterloo, they platted out a new city to be called Austin, with broad avenues, public squares, and a more suitable two-story executive mansion. Only nine months into Lamar's term, the Texas government picked up and moved to the Comanche-ridden interior, leaving Houston city to survive on its commercial prospects. President Lamar did agree with Houston on one subject: six weeks after taking office, he had the Texas congress ratify the withdrawal of the annexation offer. To Houston it had been a tactical retreat; to Lamar it was a statement of purpose. He was already dreaming of a great Texas empire rivaling the United States itself, and had no intention of ever raising the subject again.

With word out that American annexation was dead and with France newly at odds with Mexico, the Lamar government, represented in Europe by James Hamilton, an ex-governor of South Carolina, won commercial treaties with France in September 1839, and with the Netherlands a year later. The British were unwilling to leave the French with a free hand in Texas, but for reasons that Houston had learned all too well, they drove a stiffer bargain. Their price for a treaty was British freedom to interdict slave traders, and Texas had to guarantee Mexico's bonded indebtedness to British investors, in exchange for which the English would intercede with Mexico for the principle of Texas independence. That deal was finally signed in November 1840.

Lamar's efforts at dealing with Mexico, by contrast, were a function first of his own overweening dreams of empire, and second of Mexico's perennial internal strife. His secretary of state was Hamilton's brother-in-law, Barnard Bee Sr., whom Lamar sent on a mission to Mexico that was tugged by subtextual undertows. Bee had been one of the commissioners who escorted Santa Anna from Texas to Washington after San Jacinto; during that trip, Bee had lent the dictator three thousand dollars to meet his expenses, which Santa Anna, once safely home, refused to repay. Bee sailed to Vera Cruz (on a frigate belonging to France, with whom Mexico was at war) with authorization to offer Mexico a $5 million settlement for Texas independence and the Rio Grande boundary—although bankrupt Texas had no $5 million, except in the loan they were angling from France. In spring of 1839, Santa Anna was out and Bustamante was back in. Bee was aware that he could not be received as a Texas minister without Mexico extending backhanded recognition of Texas independence—in which case he was to try to work the deal as a purchase of those portions of Texas not in the "original boundaries"—which would constitute a backhanded admission that the Rio Grande boundary itself was a land grab justified only by conquest. Bee was received, but only locally and not formally, and the government rejected his offers. Bustamante was presently out again and Santa Anna was back in, but he also refused to meet with his former protector, and Bee sailed away empty-handed.

A second attempt to reach a settlement the following autumn was the project of a British subject named James Treat but was backed by the British minister to Mexico, Richard Pakenham. It also came to naught. "If peace can only be obtained by the sword," Lamar told the Texas congress, "let the sword do its work." He recommended a war to force Mexican recognition of Texas (a dumb notion, considering Mexico had already repudiated the Velasco Treaties as having been signed under duress), but the pro-Houston element in the congress was strong enough to block it. When a third diplomatic mission also returned without success, Lamar began casting about for ways to harass Mexico short of the declared war he couldn't get. His first enterprise was to make contact with a rebel state government in Yucatan, and he leased them the services of the Texas navy to prey on Mexican shipping. Houston during his term had taken steps to replace Texas' first fleet of four small schooners with much more substantial vessels, and by putting them in the service of Yucatan, Lamar got to annoy Mexico and also collect a very welcome eight thousand dollars per month. Three ships made the initial cruise across the Gulf under Commodore Edwin Moore, a former American naval lieutenant of barely thirty and still a Virginia hotspur at heart. He found that he enjoyed command, especially under this slightly piratical complexion, and he acquired a habit of independent action that ran him into serious trouble with the government in a later year. Moore took numerous prizes in short order, but at the end of the day, the relationship with Yucatan was neither lengthy nor productive.

The second enterprise involved enforcing by conquest Texas' boundary claim to New Mexico east of the Rio Grande. Houston's remaining partisans in the congress sensibly blocked Lamar from a military expedition, but the president, not to be outdone, recast the scheme as a peaceable "trading expedition" to Santa Fe. Once he conned the congress into approving it, he composed a far less innocent appeal directly to the citizens of Santa Fe. "You have doubtless heard," began Lamar's letter in his own hand, "of the glorious Revolution by which the late Province of Texas has been emancipated from the thraldom of Mexican domination." Blithely assuming that the Mexicans in New Mexico shared the Anglo Texans' political bent, and baiting his offer with the wagonloads of mercantile wares, Lamar went on to airily invite the Santa Fe Mexicans to treason: "The two Sections of Country, which being strongly assimilated in interest, we hope to see united in friendship and consolidated under a common Government." The oratory doubtless lost some of its flower in translation, but the intent was clear. The letter was entrusted to four commissioners, including prominent Bexareño José Antonio Navarro, along with Dr. Richard F. Brenham, George Van Ness, and William G. Cooke. They also took the president's blessing to set up a Texas government in Santa Fe, but they were to employ military force only if they were certain that the majority of the populace was behind them.

Investors assembled some two hundred thousand dollars in merchandise, an astronomical investment of the Texas economy, which was loaded into twenty-one wagons pulled by oxen, escorted by six companies of volunteers led by General Hugh McLeod, a New Yorker who had graduated last in his class at West Point but had served Texas well as adjutant and inspector general. The military escort, explained Lamar in his letter to Santa Fe, was only to defend the train against hostile Indians and explore a permanent route of communication. The whole assemblage of more than three hundred men set off on June 19, 1841, from a fort on Brushy Creek north of Austin, and disappeared into the hot summer wilds. While the Texas government and citizens waited for news, the column reached a forested area called the Crosstimbers, on the upper Brazos, a month later, after which the expedition became a tragedy of errors. First they mistook the Wichita for the Red River, and followed its diminishing trickle upstream for nearly another month before they were abandoned by their Mexican guide. They turned north, and when they finally did reach the Red River after fighting off repeated Indian raids, they were confronted with the dilemma of getting the unwieldy wagons up the precipice of the Cap Rock. McLeod divided his command, sending some men ahead to locate a route to Santa Fe. The governor of New Mexico, Manuel Armijo, had troops waiting for them, and piecemeal apprehended the entire Texan Santa Fe expedition without a fight. Suffering mightily after more than three months in the wilderness, the broken-down pioneers and businessmen hobbled into Santa Fe under arrest. Far from exhorting the citizens of the city to defect to Texas sovereignty, they were themselves marched, on foot and often with barbaric cruelty, including frequent roadside summary executions, all the way to Mexico City and on to the infamous dungeon at Perote Castle.

THIRTY-FOUR

THE SANGUINARY SAVAGE

MIRABEAU LAMAR WAS NOT SO BUSY AS PRESIDENT OF Texas that he had to leave off writing poetry. One of his favorite muses had become Sarah Ann Hoxey, daughter of large-scale planter Asa Hoxey, who was one of the founders of Texas' cradle of independence, Washington-on-the-Brazos. For her he composed quatrains on such subjects as the importance of friendship, and he devised this acrostic for her birthday:

> *May pleasures fill this happy day,*
> *In youth, in age, while life shall last;*
> *Succeeding years become more gay,*
> *Surpassing each the year that's past.*
>
> *Supremely blest with PARENTS kind,*
> *And FRIENDS, whose hearts do warmly beat;—*
> *Remember to preserve thy mind*
> *Against the WORLD'S unseen deceit.—*
> *Henceforth on this fond day review*
>
> *All of thy life that's gone, and say;—*
> *No folly past will I pursue,*
> *No virtue ever cast away.*
>
> *How happy then will be thy life—*
> *Of parents and of friends carrest;—*
> *Xempt from folly and from strife—*
> *Endeared as DAUGHTER, SISTER, WIFE,—*
> *Year after year shall find thee BLEST.*

Shakespeare, he was not. Hopefully such literary dalliances afforded relief from the more bloody-minded necessity of his position, for equally reckless with his dream to expand Texas to the west was Lamar's ruthless bearing toward Texas Indians. As careful as Houston had been to cultivate cordial relations with the Indian tribes, Lamar's policy was one of unremitting hostility.

Lamar saved up the height of his oratorical vituperation for the Texas Cherokees, whose friendship had been so carefully nurtured by Houston. "The white man and the red man cannot dwell in harmony together," he thundered to the congress. "Nature forbids it. As long as we continue to exhibit our mercy without showing our strength, so long will the Indian continue to bloody the edge of the tomahawk, and move onward in the work of rapacity and slaughter. . . . How long shall this cruel inhumanity, this murderous sensibility for the sanguinary savage be practiced? Until other oceans of blood, the blood of our wives and children, shall glut their voracious appetite?"

While the poet president had found a new outlet for his alliteration, and while such a speech might well have described the Comanches, the Cherokees were hardly fit subjects for his characterization of them as "impudent and hostile." It was true that they had not been happy since their trusted Houston failed to win them secure land title from the congress, many of whose members had a financial stake in old empresario grants that overlapped Cherokee lands. Late in Houston's term, Mexico had exploited their anger quite skillfully. Vicente Filisola had been left in command at Matamoros, a good position from which to meddle in Texas' affairs, in this case encouraging a once-prominent Nacogdoches Tejano named Vicente Córdova to foment a rebellion. With a few hundred mostly Tejano followers he raised a flag on an island in the Angelina River, but the Indians with him were mostly Kickapoos. The Cherokees saw no advantage in supporting him.

Houston dealt with the situation personally, packing the executive department into his saddlebags and taking up residence in Nacogdoches for several weeks. He corresponded earnestly with the elderly Bowl to keep the trouble tamped down, but also issued detailed orders to Rusk, warning him from his own experience of the style of Cherokee warfare, urging vigilance against ambush, but also cautioning him against the kinds of carelessness that could set off the Cherokees needlessly. As he always did in Indian affairs, Houston attempted to steer a middle course, balancing fair treatment for the natives against the imperative of frontier security. Rusk disobeyed Houston's order and crossed the Angelina River to cow the Cherokees with a show of force; knowing that Lamar was more of his own persuasion on the Indian question, Rusk also kept the vice president closely apprised of the situation. It was the beginning of a twenty-year rift in his friendship with Houston, but once he received word that Córdova and his mob had been defeated, Rusk disbanded his own militia and stood down.

Even after the failure of the Córdova Rebellion, Mexico still thought it worthwhile to make another run at the Texas Cherokees, this time in the person of Manuel Flores, formerly Mexican agent among the Caddo Indians. He was also a man who had tried to instigate a Fifth Column among Texas Indians during the revolution, and had escaped to Mexico before being caught. This time the communication importuning the Indians to rebel against the rebel state was accompanied by a stock of weapons. Flores' group attacked and killed four of a survey team east of San Antonio and fled north, pursued by a company of Rangers until they were overhauled near the North San Gabriel River, about twenty miles north of where streets were soon to be cleared for the new capital of Austin. On May 17, 1839, Flores and several others were killed and their materiel seized, including letters to the Cherokees that seemed to indicate that Bowl and his people were already invested in the plot. That conclusion was shaky—all Bowl had done was hear the Mexicans out—but the Cherokees' existence as a focal point for Mexican mischief was itself enough, in Texans' minds, to consider the Cherokee lands forfeit.

With Sam Houston now not just out of power but out of the country, a force of about 500 soldiers took the field; Rusk and Burleson were with them, but overall command went to Nacogdoches merchant Willis Landrum. They marched northwest toward the headwaters of the Neches, stopping a few miles south of the Cherokees' main village. Under such a show of force Bowl and his people assented on July 12 to leave Texas and join other Cherokee bands in the Arkansas Territory, and the Texans agreed to reimburse them the value of their lost property and crops, and pay the costs of the removal. The Cherokees, however, wished to leave on their own, while the Texas negotiators demanded that they submit to an armed escort. Bowl, who was in his mid-eighties, accepted his oncoming fate with equanimity. The land belonged to the Cherokees by right and by settlement; if he fought the whites, he said, they would kill him, but if he didn't fight, his own people would kill him. As the Cherokees departed the area—perhaps to leave the state and perhaps to join reinforcements of Delawares and Shawnees—the Texas forces attacked on July 15. In a running fight of several days on land west and north of the present site of Tyler, they inflicted more than a hundred casualties on the fleeing Indians, against eight of their own.

The Cherokees' aim was not up to the Anglos', but they came close. Present in the fight was Nacogdoches' former mayor and Sam Houston's close friend, Adolphus Sterne, with his son Charles, who recalled that "Col. Peter Tips was near my father & was making strikes at his left ear like he was brushing off flies. My father said, 'Tips, what is your trouble?' Reply: 'One of them damn bullets has taken off some of my locks & tipped the end of my ear.' Father replied, 'You can't stop them with your hand, they are coming too fast.' About that time my father slapped his hand to his vest & Tips asked, 'Captain, what is your trouble?' Father replied, 'One of them damn bullets has made two holes in my breeches & a mark across my chest.' Tips rejoined, 'You can't brush 'em off, they are coming too fast.' " Bowl was killed on the second day, in the Neches bottoms. Wounded in the thigh and back, he ordered a retreat and dragged himself to lean against a tree and await the end. He was dispatched by Captain Jesse Watkins, whose father-in-law had been executed by Cherokees some time before. Soon he was scalped, a razor strop cut from his back, and his tricorn hat was later sent to Sam Houston as a defiant insult.

With the Cherokees in flight, the militia began to disperse. Those who returned to Nacogdoches, according to Charles Sterne, "passed through the deserted homes of the Cherokee Indians & usually camped where they found a few chickens & occasionally a stray pig that had been left by the Indians. Also they found roasting ears, peaches, plums, pumpkins, watermelons & many places with bee gums & honey. At every camp they had almost a feast." Sterne justified the looting with a claim that the bounty relieved the sick and wounded, which failed to explain the necessity of burning the villages and more than two hundred acres of ripening corn.

Almost simultaneously with the move against the Cherokees in the east, Lamar opened a two-front war, attacking Comanches in the west. His initial sword was Colonel John Henry Moore, one of the Old Three Hundred who settled on the upper Colorado in 1831 and built a blockhouse around which grew the town of La Grange, and who had taken up Indian hunting as early as 1834 against the Brazos Valley tribes. In February 1839 Moore attacked a Comanche village in the San Saba Valley; he did little damage but sparked a spate of raiding and a revenge attack by about three hundred warriors near the later town site of Belton. The southernmost band of the Comanches, the Penatekas or "Honey Eaters," did not have the long history of contact with Europeans as did the Lipan Apaches, who had delivered Spanish missionaries into Comanche ambush on the San Saba in 1757. They were, however, the least warlike of the major Comanche bands, and they began sending in feelers to test the chance of a peace council. After negotiations, the Comanches agreed to come into San Antonio with all their white captives, of whom they were believed to possess about a dozen.

When they entered the town on March 19, 1840, the chiefs and warriors brought women and children with them—taken as a sign of peaceable intentions. They brought with them only a single captive, however, a fifteen-year-old girl named Matilda Lockhart, who was in appalling condition. She was given over to a group of ladies to be cared for, among them Mary Ann Maverick, wife of San Antonio's treasurer and former mayor. Matilda Lockhart's "head, arms and face were full of bruises," she recalled, "and sores, and her nose actually burnt off to the bone—all the fleshy end gone, and a great scab formed on the end of the bone. Both nostrils were wide open and denuded of flesh. She told . . . how dreadfully the Indians had beaten her, and how they would wake her from her sleep by sticking a chunk of fire to her flesh, especially her nose." She had also been, wrote Mary Ann Maverick with sympathetic discretion, "utterly degraded."

At least the suffering Matilda got a measure of revenge. In two years of forced labor, mostly as a horse herder, she learned enough Comanche to be able to tell the Texan commissioners that while she had seen fifteen other white prisoners at the Comanches' main camp several days previously, the Indians were going to bring them in one at a time, to see how high a price they could get. The Texan spokesman was Colonel William S. Fisher. Once the council was assembled with a dozen Comanche headmen, Fisher demanded of the ranking chief, Muk-war-ra, why they had not brought in all their captives. The chief responded that they brought in the only one they had; the others were with other bands beyond his control, but he was sure that their freedom could be purchased. The independence of the various Comanche bands, and the inability of one chief to force his will outside his own following, are well documented. However, Matilda Lockhart's evidence was at hand.

Muk-war-ra asked smugly, "How do you like this answer?"

"I do *not* like your answer," glowered Fisher. "I told you not to come here again without bringing in your prisoners." He then instructed the interpreter to inform the Comanche chiefs that their women and children were free to go, and their warriors could leave to fetch the rest of the white captives, but until they were returned, the chiefs would be held as hostages. At first the interpreter refused to translate, but when Fisher insisted, the interpreter edged toward the door as he spoke. Amid war whoops, knives flashed out and bows were quickly strung; a company of troops who had been concealed in an adjoining chamber filed into the room. The Indians were told they would not be harmed if they submitted quietly. One chief stabbed a sentry by the door in an attempt to escape. He was shot down, and once the firing started, it didn't stop. The fifty-three other Comanches in the court-yard began to take flight, in all directions, at the first whoop within the Council House. Those who sought escape to the river were met by another company of troops under Colonel Lysander Wells. Others fled down streets, between houses; some tried to hide in houses and kitchens. Only one escaped. Eighteen men, three women, and two children were killed, in addition to the dozen chiefs. They exacted a toll of three dead soldiers, three civilians, and one unidentified Mexican. Two old Comanche men and twenty-seven women and children were captured and jailed, and all their goods were captured and destroyed.

After considering the best course, the Texans decided to declare a twelve-day truce, and sent a Comanche woman, mounted and provisioned, out to the tribe with the offer to exchange all the jailed Comanches for all the Anglo captives. The Comanche custom of grief was self-mutilation, and when news of the Council House Fight spread among the bands, the mourning was frightful. As the truce expired, a Penateka chief named Piava came in to deal, and eventually was able to repatriate seven white captives. Two were Texans: a girl named Putnam who was captured at the same time as Matilda Lockhart, and a boy named Booker Webster, who was able to tell authorities that they were spared because they had been adopted into the tribe. The other thirteen Anglo prisoners, after news of the fight, were skinned and burned over slow fires. Matilda did not fare much better. Disgraced and disfigured, she survived about two years before succumbing, probably as much to despair as to infections from her wounds.

Oddly, Southern chivalry did what the Comanches were unable to do at the Council House Fight: kill the Anglo leaders. During the truce, another Penateka chief named Isananica clattered into San Antonio screaming for a fight, but was told that the soldiers and their prisoners had removed to the San José Mission. Isananica pounded off for San José, where Captain William D. Redd, who had commanded the company in the rear of the Council House, informed him that the truce was still good and he could not have a fight, unless he waited around three days for the truce to expire. Isananica galloped away. Colonel Lysander Wells, who had cut off the Comanche retreat at the river, was so incensed by Redd's conduct that he called him a coward. They duelled with pistols and killed each other.

The highest remaining chief of the Penateka Comanches was Po-chee-naw-quo-he-ep (Long Time Hard Penis, known to the whites by the more acceptable appellation of Buffalo Hump). After the Penatekas recovered from their grieving, he led the revenge raid, the most spectacular Comanche war party ever seen, plunging down the Guadalupe Valley far southeast of their usual territory, pillaging as they went, until they reached and attacked Victoria on August 6. The Indians decided to have some fun with one man whom they captured alive; they skinned the soles of his feet and forced him to run behind a horse for several miles before they put him out of his misery. There were perhaps five hundred warriors, and about an equal number of women to load and haul away booty. Victoria was too large and well defended to reduce, but they killed numerous settlers and slaves who couldn't reach the safety of the town, and they captured over 1,500 horses—a huge prize for the nomadic Comanches. But instead of heading for home, Buffalo Hump led them still farther southeast to the town of Linnville, on Lavaca Bay, which they attacked on August 8. As the residents jumped into boats and rowed away to save themselves, they witnessed the Indians' empty houses and stores alike. Three whites who were unable to reach the safety of the bay were cut down, and the wife of the customs officer, Juliet Watts, was taken captive. (Attempts to rape her were defeated by her whalebone corset.) The warehouse was piled with recently unloaded merchandise intended for shops in San Antonio, and from the water the townspeople watched in astonishment as the Comanches pranced around in gloves and top hats, popping open umbrellas and dragging feather mattresses behind their horses. Eventually the town was torched.

Help had been summoned from the first shooting in Victoria, and as they withdrew the Comanches were slowed by hauling more than a quarter of a million dollars in booty and herding more than three thousand horses. About 125 hastily assembled settlers lay in wait for the Comanches the day after Linnville was sacked, and the warriors engaged them while their women continued their retreat with the merchandise. The Comanches withdrew once they believed their families were at a safe distance. Such a raiding party was not difficult to track, but the fact that the Indians had fresh horses in huge supply made it impossible to gain ground. San Jacinto veteran Ben McCulloch, realizing the Comanches' intended route, made an end run to the town of Lockhart and hastily assembled enough volunteers, some two hundred, to ambush them on Plum Creek before they could reenter the relative safety of the Hill Country.

The Comanches were still laughing and celebrating as they reached the Big Prairie near Plum Creek, and were startled to see the volunteers lined up to block their crossing. In a running battle fought across a dozen miles on the blistering hot day of August 12, the Texans killed by most estimates about a hundred of the raiders in the Battle of Plum Creek, while suffering only one killed and a handful of wounded. Again, the warriors fought to cover the getaway of their families and plunder, and the Texans were treated to the remarkable sight of Comanche Indians fighting in evening dress; one prominent warrior sported a dress coat over his breechcloth (although he was wearing it backwards), firing his gun while shading himself with a parasol. As the Comanches killed their captives, Mrs. Watts was tied to a tree and shot with an arrow, but her life was saved by the arrow being deflected by her corset. A few of the Comanche women and children were captured and parceled out as forced labor to San Antonio families, but they eventually escaped. The bulk of the Linnville merchandise was not recaptured until J. H. Moore led an expedition, guided by Lipanes, to the upper Colorado the following October. He administered a severe defeat; the Penatekas lost at least another hundred killed, and their reputation as the least warlike of the Comanche bands was cemented.

The Tonkawas had arrived and fought on foot with McCulloch's men at Plum Creek, but were finely mounted and equipped with what was captured from their enemies. After the battle, the Tonkawa warriors ate one of the Comanche casualties. In recent years, politically correct writers have performed varying degrees of intellectual gymnastics to drop the Tonkawas, as well as many other Texas tribes, including the "friendly" Tejas, a mulligan on the issue of eating other people. They explain that it was part of their religion, or they only ate a little, or it may not have really happened at all—but the fact is they were cannibals. Early accounts make it clear that it was ritualistic, but it was a feast, not a communion wafer. Young Robert Hall, a twenty-six-year-old Tennesseean whose family had built the first house in Memphis, was wounded in the fight, and now lay resting in camp. "The Tonkawas brought in the dead body of a Comanche warrior," he related, "and they built a big fire not far from where I was lying. My wound had begun to pain me considerably, and I did not pay much attention to them for some time. After awhile they began to sing and dance, and I thought that I detected the odor of burning flesh. I raised up and looked around, and, sure enough, our allies were cooking the Comanche warrior. They cut him into slices and broiled him on sticks. Curiously enough the eating of the flesh acted upon them as liquor does upon other men. After a few mouthfuls they began to act as if they were very drunk, and I don't think there was much pretense or sham about it. They danced, raved, howled, and sang, and invited me to get up and eat a slice of Comanche. They said it would make me brave. I was very hungry, but not sufficiently so to become a cannibal. The Tonkawas were wild over the victory and they did not cease their celebration until sunrise." Young Hall recovered from his wound, later took a land grant at Seguín, about twenty miles southwest of the battle site, settled down, and fathered thirteen children.

Mirabeau Lamar's visionary quest at empire building very nearly bankrupted the Republic. His Indian wars alone cost some $2.5 million, and while they did have the effect of pushing the Comanche menace further back from the frontier, that tribe built up such a spleen against Texans that when Americans first contacted them from the east, the Indians accorded them safety once it was established that they had no connection with the hated "Tehannas." That was a fury to be vented at a later time. During the three years of Lamar's administration, government expenses outdistanced receipts by $4.85 million to only $1.08 million. Added to the obligations already existing at the time he took office, Texas by the end of 1841 had a public debt of about $7 million.

Lamar's greatest hope for financial relief lay in seeking a $5 million loan from France, but that came to naught after a brief fracas known as the "Pig War." After establishing formal relations, France sent to Texas as her chargé d'affaires a somewhat blustery journeyman diplomat, Alphonse du Bois, Comte de Saligny. He arrived at the distant outpost of Austin with his chef, Eugène, and took up lodging at Bullock's Hotel at Pecan Street (now 6th Street) and Congress Avenue while his comfortable Creole-style residence was a-building on a hill east of the town. Bullock was the nominal owner of several semiferal hogs that roamed the streets, some of whom broke into the chargé's study and ate some diplomatic dispatches. Through the good office of Eugène they wound up on Monsieur le Comte's dining table. Du Bois then refused to pay the entirety of his hotel bill, which he claimed was padded (leading local wags to begin referring to him as the no-account de Saligny), for which Bullock punched him in the nose. Du Bois puffed that the dignity of France had been offended, but the local authorities declined to prosecute the matter as anything grander than simple assault. Du Bois withdrew to New Orleans with frontier guffaws ringing in his ears, but in a sad way the joke was on them: Du Bois' brother-in-law was the finance minister, and Texas never got the $5 million from France.

The best that Texas did manage to obtain was a loan of nearly a half million from the Bank of the United States, arranged through the influence of James Hamilton with the bank's president, Nicholas Biddle. The money was welcome, but made little headway against the deficit. Lamar's answer was to print ever more paper money. A new series of "redbacks," each more prettily engraved than the last with scenes of agriculture, industry, and bare-breasted goddesses, was issued in each of the three years of his administration. Eventually over $3.5 million was launched into circulation, and traded at horrendous depreciation—sometimes at less than 10 percent of face value.

Not all aspects of Lamar's tenure resulted in costly boondoggles like the Santa Fe Expedition. Two laws, both enacted within weeks of his taking office, moderate judgment of his missteps. One provided for public education, setting aside fifty leagues of the public domain for the support of two universities, with each county allotted three leagues for the support of public elementary schools. At a later time, when history was taught as a succession of easily memorized labels, this was enough to award Lamar the sobriquet of Father of Texas Education. The other act was the Homestead Law, which exempted family homes from being seized for debt. Stephen F. Austin had promulgated a similar measure in his colony, knowing that many settlers came to Texas to escape adverse financial judgments in the United States. The law also made particular sense, by encouraging actual settlement in a land where absentee speculation had always been a problem. Texas' Homestead Law, and its subsequent modifications, established a protection never found before in Anglo-American legal history.

THIRTY-FIVE

RETRENCHMENT

WHEN SAM HOUSTON RETURNED FROM HIS SOJOURN IN the United States through spring and summer of 1839, having had a long visit with Jackson and now engaged to an Alabama beauty named Margaret Lea, his mortification over Lamar's handling of the government was almost beyond containment. In absentia he had been elected to the Texas congress, representing San Augustine, where he had maintained a law office. From this platform he scorched and plotted. He attacked the removal of the capital to Austin, "the most unfortunate site upon Earth for the Seat of Government," isolated from the rest of the population, vulnerable to attack from Mexico, and where killings by Indians on the outskirts were a regular occurrence. He attacked Lamar's irresponsible fiscal policy; it would take so long to repair the damage, he said, that Lamar could not be embarrassed by any sudden improvements on the part of whoever should succeed him. His harshest words were for the fate of the Cherokees, whose only fault, he maintained, was that they "received a pledge from the provisional government of Texas . . . and were *dupes enough to believe it!*" He vowed to keep bringing bills before the Congress for justice for the Cherokees until the issue "would stick like a blister!!!"

He had been constitutionally forbidden to succeed himself, but having suffered through three years of fuming over "the extent of Lamar's stupidity," he was champing at the bit for a second term, and a chance to lead Texas into the United States. Opposing him in the presidential election of 1841 was Lamar's vice president and Houston's truest and heartiest enemy, David G. Burnet, who ran somewhat by default because neither Thomas Jefferson Rusk nor General Albert Sidney Johnston would run against Houston. The campaign was breathtaking in its invective; the two men despised each other so much that the very genuine policy differences between the two camps were all but forgotten in a glorious orgy of name-calling. Newspaper columns, bylined "Publius" but authored by Burnet or his minions, accused Houston of cowardice at San Jacinto, the most degraded drunkenness, and incompetence such as to disqualify him from respectable notice. Houston took a vicious delight in writing the replies to Publius, signed

"Truth," indicting Burnet as a "political brawler and canting hypocrite, whom the waters of Jordan could never cleanse from your political and moral leprosy." He went on to enumerate occasions when Burnet had also humiliated himself drunk in public before various witnesses. "Oh, shame," he scolded, "where is thy blush?"

From Houston's side, much of this was for show. His private letters show that much of the high dudgeon of the Truth letters was high fun. He nicknamed Burnet "Wetumpka," which he said was an Indian word for hog thief, and allowed that in former days when he himself drank, he paid for the spirits himself, unlike Burnet, whose brandy came off the public tab. Burnet was so scalded by the exchange that he sent Branch T. Archer as his second to challenge Houston to a duel, but Houston refused to receive it. "I am compelled to believe," he told Archer, "that the people are equally disgusted with both of us." That turned out not quite to be true, for on September 6 the Texas electorate returned Houston to the presidency by nearly three to one: 7,508 to 2,574.

The rhetorical assaults on Houston's drunkenness would once have been true enough, but they were behind the times. He had left off drinking with his marriage in 1840 to Margaret Lea, whom he worshipped. While his closest friends predicted disaster for the Baptist Alabama belle's marriage to the most famous wildman in America, one was astonished to report of a barbecue held in honor of his victory: "Strange to say, it was a cold water *doins*. The old Chief did not *touch*, taste, or handle the smallest drop of *ardent*." The choice of words was not accidental, echoing the temperance pledge. At Houston's swearing in, he wore a pioneer outfit of pantaloons, hunting shirt, and broad-brimmed fur hat. Margaret had been left ill in the care of friends in Houston city, but from that distance she still cast her spell. At the inaugural ball that evening, Houston declined to dance, for the reason, he wrote her tamely, "that you wou'd prefer that I wou'd not." He didn't drink, either. The consensus was "that I wou'd get into a 'spree' before all was over, but they were wide of the mark. I 'touch not taste not, and handle not, the unhallowed thing!' "

Some of Lamar's moves to chisel Houston out of the national heritage, such as changing the flag, the victor of San Jacinto would have to live with. In his own mind, however, Houston did not accept Austin as the capital of the country, and while he could not move against it immediately, he laid that task aside for another day. One piece of Lamar's mischief that he was able to defuse was a heinous bill ordering Texas' free blacks to leave the country within two years or face enslavement; Houston waited for the Texas congress to adjourn and head for their homes, then issued a pardon for those who might violate the law. He also attempted to intern Lamar's adventurous navy, which was a budget breaker, but Commodore Moore wisely sailed for the southern Gulf the day Houston was sworn in and managed to evade orders to return to port for some months.

Houston's suddenly straitened personal morality quickly made itself felt in national affairs, as the sixth congress that assembled quickly gained the nickname of the Retrenchment Congress. Seeking to restrain Lamar's fiscal policy, they limited new currency to $200,000 in so-called exchequer bills, which were backed by making them receivable for debts to the government. The national budget was reduced drastically; salaries were slashed, positions eliminated, and so only about half a million public dollars were spent during the entire three years of Houston's second term. The new president talked personal friends into taking administration posts, and then cajoled them as long as he could to live without salaries. Thomas William Ward, who had lost his right leg to a Mexican cannonball at the siege of Béxar and his right arm in an accident the following year, became land commissioner and set up office in Austin. "Peg Leg" Ward was soon pleading with Houston that, while the citizens of Austin were hostile to the administration, "I am compelled to ask of them favors" to keep fed and housed. "I have no money and being here on the frontier have no opportunity of collecting any." Houston sent him his heartfelt thanks, and some tobacco, but there was no money. Texas envoys in Washington, D.C., fared no better than bureaucrats in Austin. James Reily, who had been Rusk's aide-de-camp and then law partner, was sent as chargé d'affaires to the United States to try to rekindle annexation talks. Sam Houston's bachelor days were still remembered there and Reily was reduced to threatening, perhaps only partly in jest, that if the Texas government did not support him in his post, Mrs. Houston would learn some interesting stories of his earlier days. After negotiating a treaty of amity with Daniel Webster, Reily abruptly resigned over being left to provide for himself. Houston treated the matter lightly. "His mind seems to have fallen into a queer snarl about money matters," he wrote his new secretary of state. "He does not understand them."

That secretary of state was one of the president's shrewder choices for office: Anson Jones, the Brazoria congressman who had withdrawn the annexation offer in the U.S. capital during Houston's first term. He was brilliant but foul-tempered and just entering the long decline of mental illness, and he complained of the lack of pay even more vociferously than Reily. "Houston promised when I took office that I would be paid in par funds," he complained to his diary. "This has not been done, and I *have been obliged* to do something for a support." What Jones and Reily and Ward and many others refused to understand was that *nobody* had any money; the retrenchment congress had cut the presidential salary in half, to $5,000, but even then Houston could not present his vouchers to the Treasury for pay because it was empty. One newcomer who was invited to dinner with Houston recalled that the meal consisted of a wild turkey, bread, and coffee, and had it not been for the kindness of a neighbor who had been hunting, there would have been no turkey. A deputation of impoverished veterans who appealed to Houston for aid were turned away. George Childress, presumptive author of the Texas Declaration of Independence, also joined the parade of financial ruin. After three separate failures to make a successful law practice, he committed a kind of Texas hara-kiri with a bowie knife in Galveston in 1841. He was only thirty-seven years old.

The chaotic poverty had a hand as well in a far greater domestic bloodletting known as the Regulator-Moderator War. In the rough-and-tumble Redlands of East Texas, and more particularly in the old Neutral Ground, where the law had always made at best a limited impression, the most prevalent token of wealth was land scrip. Most of it was fraudulent and everybody knew it, but disputes led to killings, which led to revenge killings, which led to the formation of organized mobs and the browbeating of honest neutral citizens into choosing sides. To investigate the extent of the mayhem Houston sent his trusted attorney general, George W. Terrell, a man whose many public services to Texas remain insufficiently examined. He had served as attorney general of Tennessee when Houston was governor of that state, and had played roles in all administrations since coming to Texas.

The center of the Regulator-Moderator trouble was Shelby County. "It really appears to me as if society were about to dissolve itself into its original elements," he reported to Houston. "At a called session of the district court in Sabine a few days ago . . . a man was shot down at the door of the court house. . . . I was sent for last week to try . . . twelve men in Nacogdoches who was charged with hanging a horse thief. It was represented to me that the *regulators* . . . were the strongest party, and they and their friends were determined that they should not be tried. . . . When I arrived there I found at least two hundred armed men in the courthouse."

(A more famous story from that time concerns one of Texas' leading jurists, Robert M. Williamson, who went to Shelby County to hear a case, only to have one of the ruffians thump a bowie knife into the judge's bench and proclaim, "This, sir, is the law in Shelby County." Unfazed, Williamson drew his gun, saying, "And this, sir, is the constitution that overrules your law.")

Unable to ignore a large swath of the country in pandemonium, Houston issued a call for five hundred militiamen, which quieted things for a time, but a second flare-up of trouble in the summer of 1844 caused the president to take to the saddle personally to mediate their differences. The deal he struck held good, albeit tensely, but still there was no money for the militia to back it up, and the troops had to live off the land and the private funds of their officers.

Nothing was clearer to Houston as he resumed office for his second term than that Texas' salvation lay in joining itself to the United States. And that was even before Mexico, or more specifically Santa Anna, who was in power again, cast a vengeful eye back across the Rio Grande. The British admitted that they were having little success in convincing Mexico to accept Texas independence, but said they would keep trying; Houston had been regularly discouraging hotheads and latter-day filibusters from making private fights or enlisting new companies of recruits to move against Mexico. Above all, Texas could not afford a war. Houston left his new private secretary, a brilliant young wit named Washington Miller, at his post in Austin to relay him any important developments, and left for Houston city. "The battalions of the *redoubtable* Santa Anna have not yet made their appearance," Miller wrote Houston on February 16, 1842. "Let them come."

In fact, five hundred Mexican soldiers under General Rafael Vásquez soon crossed the Rio Grande, and in lightning strikes they seized San Antonio, Refugio, and Goliad. The countryside was panic-stricken. On March 10 Houston issued orders to Brigadier Alexander Somervell to take the field and "defend our liberties to the knife." Instantly the call went to the United States for volunteers, and militia units began forming. Then, as sudden as it was amazing, the Mexican forces withdrew, all of them, back where they came from. The whole operation had been a feint, leaving Houston with the serious problem of quelling public demand for a reprisal against Mexico. "Fools only pursue phantoms," he soothed, "and children will chase butterflies," but he knew that if he recalled the Texas congress they would declare war. The Lamar faction had already passed, over his veto, an absurd bill claiming the northern two-thirds of Mexico west to the Pacific. "I cannot trust their wisdom," he confided to his treasury secretary, and he delayed assembling them until late June. He published thanks to the troops, "who have so spiritedly rallied," but directed them to return to their cornfields. On March 22 he sent a hot and insulting letter to Santa Anna and had it widely published, but he made certain that no irrevocable steps toward war were taken.

The Mexican attack and withdrawal gave Houston the excuse he needed to open a war of a different sort. At first news of the invasion, Hockley reported from Austin that he was burying the archives of the various government departments beneath their buildings, so that if the town was burned, the records would survive. Houston's response was to order the archives—and therefore the government—withdrawn from Austin back to Houston city. When word got around, five hundred Austin residents signed petitions asking the president to reconsider, making it equally clear that they were prepared to do much more than sign a petition to prevent it. Both Terrell and Miller, Houston's two most trusted advisers, warned him that the citizens of Austin were in earnest on the matter, and it would be unwise to insist on the removal of the government papers. Houston left the archives where they were, for the time being, but when he called congress to meet, it was back in his own preferred Houston city.

By fall it seemed as if the crisis had passed. War Secretary Hockley, enraged that full war with Mexico never materialized, broke his friendship with Houston and resigned on September 10. Britain and France both promised to press their efforts to convince Mexico to accept Texas as an independent nation, and on that understanding Houston on September 12 withdrew the naval blockade he had posted in March. On the preceding day, unknown to Houston, Santa Anna had sent across the Rio Grande an army of fourteen hundred under the French mercenary General Adrian Woll, to take San Antonio yet again. Woll occupied the city for nine days, during which time militia companies formed and began to organize much as they had at Gonzales in 1835. One company, led by Mathew "Old Paint" Caldwell, who had fought prominently in defeating the Comanches at Plum Creek, reached a forward position on Salado Creek and waited for other units to join up. Another company of volunteers from Fayette County under Nicholas Mosby Dawson had left home with fifteen men, but numbered fifty-three as they neared the scene of action. Believing Caldwell was under threat, Dawson forced the march to reach him, was surrounded by several hundred Mexicans, and in the following firefight thirty-six of the fifty-three were either killed or shot down while attempting to surrender. Only two escaped; the remaining fifteen were captured. (Caldwell, ironically, was holding his own quite well on the Salado.) Woll withdrew from Béxar, taking the Dawson prisoners with him, as well as numerous other hostages, including the judge, jury, and witnesses of a court he had bagged while in session.

This time Santa Anna had gone too far, and Houston was unable to avoid renewed war. He ordered Somervell to the Rio Grande with a force of about 750; that army occupied Laredo on December 8 and continued down the river for another week and a half. With no one to fight and with Woll's hostages beyond help in the interior, Somervell ordered his men home, but the volunteer insubordination that nearly brought the revolution to disaster made itself felt again. Colonel William S. Fisher, who had sparked the Council House Fight in 1840; General Thomas Jefferson Green, still smarting that he had not achieved the glory he once imagined for himself; and several other officers who were disgusted with Houston's temperate attitude toward Mexico led nearly 300 soldiers in defying Somervell. On their own they crossed the Rio Grande and seized the small town of Mier on December 23. Their own scouts, including Ben McCulloch, told them of large Mexican forces in the area, and quit the scheme when their warning was not heeded. Fisher's 260 men in the town were pounced on by General Pedro de Ampudia and a Mexican army of at least 2,500. The Texans fought savagely, killing perhaps a fifth of the Mexican force, but surrounded and out of powder, they surrendered.

Thirty of the Texans had been killed in the fighting, and Santa Anna ordered the remainder to be shot, but Ampudia got the order rescinded on December 27. They were marching toward prison in the interior on February 11, 1843, when Ewen Cameron led an escape at the town of Salado. Too far into Mexico to regain safety, 176 of them were recaptured. Santa Anna again ordered them shot, but Francisco Mexía, the onetime federalist now back in power as governor of Coahuila, ignored him, and foreign intervention reduced the sentence to decimation. On March 25, seventeen black beans were placed in a crockery jar along with 159 white ones, it was shaken lightly, and the Texas prisoners were forced to draw. William A. A. Wallace, who once wrote home that he would rather see his sister dead than in Texas, noticed that the black beans were larger, felt the difference, and drew a white one. Major James Decatur Cocke drew the first fatal black bean, and held it up. "Boys, I told you so; I never failed in my life to draw a prize." Others picked up on his gallows humor. The condemned men were blindfolded and seated on a log, their backs to the firing squad. The firing was from such a distance that the men were picked and maimed for a quarter of an hour;

Henry Whaley was hit fifteen times before he was finally given a coup de grâce. Ewen Cameron drew a white bean, but when Santa Anna learned of it he sent a courier with a death warrant; near Mexico City on April 26, Cameron refused both priest and blindfold, opened his shirt and himself ordered, "Fire!" The rest filed into Perote Castle with the Woll prisoners and the survivors of Lamar's Santa Fe folly.

Houston was horrified by news of the Salado execution. He sent for, read, and kept for several days the farewell letter that one of the condemned had written to his mother. But in this instance, Texas was as powerless to carry war into Mexico as Mexico was powerless to sustain an effort in Texas. Justice would have to wait.

The president resumed his retrenchment government. One great saving of money came when the town boosters of Washington, just as they had when they lured the Consultation out of San Felipe in 1835, offered to furnish government accommodations free of charge if the capital was removed to the middle Brazos. The government relocated, and Houston used the opportunity in the matter of the archives. He sent two rangers to Austin to hire wagons and transport the government papers back to Washington. Several days later they returned from Austin, with the manes and tails shaved from their horses. At the end of the year he tried again, laying much more detailed plans, and in the early morning of December 30, twenty men began loading the archives into three large wagons. They were spied by Angelina Eberly, proprietress of the boardinghouse where Houston lived when in Austin. She dashed to the town square, where a cannon was kept primed to repel Indian attacks, and fired it. A mob quickly gathered, reloaded the gun with shrapnel, and trained it on the land office; Peg Leg Ward had no intention of losing any more limbs for his country, and the wagons rumbled off with as many papers as they had already loaded. The angry posse followed, overhauled the wagons, and recaptured the archives with no further shooting. The papers were not returned to their respective offices but housed for safekeeping in Mrs. Eberly's boardinghouse, and Houston was compelled to admit defeat in the Archives War.

The government, however, continued to operate from Washington, which was now larger, with 300 to 400 residents, but only slightly less rude than it had been when hosting the Convention of 1836. The House met in the old building where the Declaration of Independence had been signed; the Senate was put up in a billiard hall above the "grocery" (read: saloon) owned by Major B. M. Hatfield. Lawyer W. Z. McFarlin turned over his one-room structure to serve as the presidential office—door on the west, fireplace on the east, windows on the north and south. The state department where the cantankerous Dr. Jones had to establish himself was a made-over carpenter shop, with rags stuffed in the log chinks to keep the wind out. The president had no residence of his own. He boarded with Judge J. W. and Eliza Lockhart, at least until he became overwhelmed by cares and (for a rare time) fell off the wagon, got loaded on a bottle of imported Madeira, and chopped down one pillar of Mrs. Lockhart's prized mahogany four-poster bed.

His attempts to conserve the public funds proved to be more constant than his temperance pledge. As indispensable as the navy had been in Texas' defense, it was still the largest item in the budget, and moreover Commodore Moore had become a powerful political enemy. Houston undertook to sell the vessels. He kept the plan a secret as long as he could, but once notice had to be posted, a Galveston mob (Moore retained great popularity there) forcibly prevented the ships from being auctioned.

On another front, knowing the amount of money that Lamar had wasted in trying to exterminate Indians, and knowing that peace was cheaper as well as more humane, Houston painstakingly labored to regain the trust of the various tribes. He hired a mixed-blood Cherokee with wide experience in trading horses to many tribes, and who spoke ten or twelve of their languages, to visit their camps and talk up Houston's Indian sympathies and trustworthiness. He was Jesse Chisholm, the nephew of Diana Rogers, Houston's late former Cherokee wife. An attempt to gather the Brazos tribes for a council in 1842 proved abortive, but on April 9, 1843, hundreds of Indians—Wacoes, Tawakonis, Keechis, and others—gathered in Washington for a ten-day sojourn and peace agreement.

The Indians played games, gave archery demonstrations, and mixed affably with the townspeople; even the dubious citizens had to admit that they were on their best behavior, except on the point of their personal grooming, which included picking, and snacking on, the lice pulled from each other's hair. Drawing on his years of living with Indians, Houston navigated jealousies among rival chiefs, and with great solemnity and ceremonial smoking, he signed a treaty of peace that reduced violence in the Brazos Valley for years. It was also a platform from which to launch an effort to reconcile with the Comanches. In 1844 Houston met and negotiated a treaty with Long Time Hard Penis (Buffalo Hump), the Penateka who had assumed the leadership after the chiefs who outranked him were killed at Lamar's Council House Fight. Of that event Houston had the satisfaction of saying that "the man who counseled to do this bad thing is no longer a chief in Texas. His voice," he added poetically, "is no longer heard among the people." Buffalo Hump, for a variety of reasons unrelated to Houston's imagery, put his mark to the Treaty of Tehuacana Creek on October 8.

After the capital was withdrawn from Austin, the European powers restocked their Texas offices with new emissaries, most notably the Briton Captain Charles Elliot, who was exiled to Texas to keep him out of trouble after his posting in Canton, where his objection to reducing innocent Chinese citizens to British-financed drug addiction led to the Opium War. France replaced the pouting Comte de Saligny with Jules Edouard Fontaine, Vicomte de Cramayel, and the United States sent the ill and elderly Joseph Tucker Eve. Other countries were beginning to notice Texas as well. Word came that King Leopold of the Belgians, who had a considerable personal fortune, was interested in investing in Texas if he could get favorable trade concessions. The empress of China sent as a goodwill gesture a dazzling painted porcelain tea service, which must have delighted Houston's wife, Margaret, but so unnerved Houston that he sent to Galveston for a coffee set of plain white stoneware. The finest gift of state came from the sultan of the Ottoman Empire: a suit of crimson silk for the president, complete from flat-topped fez down to curled-toe Arabian Nights booties of yellow leather sewn directly onto the legs of the pantaloons. Margaret, who took up residence in Washington-on-the-Brazos to ride herd on the president's sobriety, had suffered through pregnancy, asthma, depression, and sore nipples, but was reduced to helpless laughter by the Turkish outfit. Nothing could induce Houston to wear the red silk pantaloons, but he was enchanted by the blazing crimson silk robe that surrounded the suite. He wore it until he wore it out, meeting Indians in it, lounging in the one-room presidential office in it, pacing through sleepless nights in it. What occupied his thoughts was not the glory of international recognition, however, but the puzzle of how, finally, to squeeze Texas into the American Union.

THIRTY-SIX

THE ANNEXATION QUICKSTEP

IN JANUARY 1843, HOUSTON WROTE AN ARTFUL LETTER to Charles Elliot, the British chargé d'affaires in Texas. The two had become warmly familiar, with Elliot often closing his letters to the president, "Attachedly yours." In it, Houston asked the aid of British influence in repatriating the several score of Texan captives being held in Mexican dungeons. He took care to mention what good relations Texas enjoyed with England, and what a strategic link British influence in Texas was to the security of British Oregon. Houston was banking on two things: first, that the English would realize that losing their prestige in Texas would loosen their grip on Oregon, which along with Texas was being greedily eyed by American expansionists; and second, that news of British help to Texas in dealing with Mexico, when it reached the United States, would be regarded as a calamity. He was absolutely right, but just to make sure they got the message, Houston's private secretary, Washington Miller, wrote to U.S. President John Tyler expressing his "concern" over the growing British influence in Texas.

Houston also took care to maintain an active correspondence with his "Venerated Friend," Andrew Jackson, first out of genuine personal attachment, but also because he knew that the palsied old victor of the Battle of New Orleans was still influential, several years into retirement. The specter of a British Texas linking British Oregon with the British Indies created in Jackson's mind, if not in reality, "an Iron Hoop around the United States . . . that would cost oceans of blood and millions of money to Burst asunder." He was obsessed by the ease with which England could then march an army from "Canady" south all the way to the Gulf, recapture New Orleans, crush American ambitions in Oregon and California, foment Indian uprisings, and "excite the negroes to insurrection." The more Jackson allowed his mind to work on it, and the more Houston baited him with his willingness to accept British help, the more rabid Jackson became on the subject.

A second element of Houston's strategy, since the United States had proven so indifferent to Texas, was to assert Texas' claims to the very limit of her territory, which under the Velasco Treaties extended north all the way into present-day Wyoming. This meant that the lucrative trade between the

U.S. and Mexico via the Santa Fe Trail crossed Texas' sovereign territory. Houston authorized the creation of a force of land-cruising privateers, under command of the former army paymaster and, briefly, acting secretary of war, Jacob Snively. Acting not on behalf of the government but agreeing to split with the government any "prize" (i.e., Mexican commerce) they seized on the trail, Snively and about 150 recruits gathered at a ramshackle fort south of the Red River in present Grayson County. Calling themselves the Battalion of Invincibles, they headed northwest on April 24 to uphold the national dignity of Texas on its northern frontier. Yet again, volunteer yahoos proved incapable of the discipline needed to carry out a mission, but Texans would not learn of their fate for months.

Houston also reactivated a stratagem from more youthful days serving as Jackson's "Literary Bureau" in Tennessee politics. He planted "anonymous" letters hostile to annexation in cooperative Texas newspapers, to give the impression in both Washingtons that the idea of joining their destiny to America was regarded only indifferently by most of the populace. One that appeared in the *National Vindicator*, published in Washington-on-the-Brazos by Houston operative Thomas "Ramrod" Johnson, alleged that annexation was supported by few, with fewer reasons. "In the first place, the United States rejected us with scorn when he first made the overture. Her policy was not deep enough to foresee when she might have use for us." If war ever erupted between America and Britain, Texas as an American state "would be the weak point, and the most likely to suffer," but Texas independent would prosper. "England will give us a high price for our cotton, and induce thousands of planters to leave the United States and come to Texas to raise that cotton that she will not take from the U. States, and . . . we can then supply the United States and Mexico with European goods, and receive their gold and silver in return; and thus engross the business of three . . . nations." Judging by its unique literary style, the author of this shiny but specious argument was none other than Texas' scheming president.

(Public sentiments in Texas toward annexation were much more favorable than Houston let on. Not atypical was Judge Robert M. Williamson, who named a son born during this time "Annexus.")

Engaging in still another angle of attack, Houston began a long and delicate rapprochement with Santa Anna, with a view toward an eventual armistice. It was important to keep the dictator pacified and guessing until an annexation deal with the United States could be formalized. In this endeavor he fell heir to an amazing stroke of luck. Among the captives that General Woll rounded up in San Antonio was James W. Robinson, a firebrand for independence who had feuded with Henry Smith over executive authority during the days of the General Council. Of all the Perote prisoners, Robinson was the likeliest candidate to be faced against a wall and shot, but with unabashed nerve he began writing letters to Santa Anna, assuring him that most Texans would prefer to return to the Mexican fold if only reasonable terms were offered them. If Santa Anna would prepare such an offer he, Robinson, would volunteer to carry it back to Texas. The dictator fell for it, and sent Robinson home with an offer of amnesty, internal autonomy, and freedom from Mexican troops being stationed on Texas soil, in return for their acquiescence to Mexican sovereignty. Robinson materialized in Washington-on-the-Brazos on April 6 and presented himself to Houston. Blessing his good fortune, Houston composed a reply that was sent to Santa Anna in Robinson's name, representing that Texas was not as torn by factions as they had thought, and that Houston had pacified the Indians and was authorized "to accept the services of forty thousand volunteers" to defend against Mexico. Still, "Robinson" claimed, Houston wanted peace, and it would have a salutary effect if the Texan prisoners in Mexico were released in a gesture of good faith. Houston then nudged Elliot that this was a good time to mention the subject of the prisoners to the dictator once more.

The Robinson ruse bought time, and in June 1843, Houston followed up on it by declaring a unilateral armistice with Mexico as a pledge of Texas' good faith. He sweetened things further in September by releasing and repatriating all Mexican prisoners still held in Texas. Santa Anna was charmed, and Houston dispatched as special envoys to Mexico to negotiate a permanent armistice his former secretary of war, George Hockley, and one of Texas' most experienced operators, Samuel May Williams, who had issued land titles for Stephen F. Austin nearly a quarter century before. President Houston hardly needed to instruct them not to be in too great a hurry to make a deal.

Eventually word reached Texas of the fate of Jacob Snively and the Battalion of Invincibles. After weeks of prowling the Santa Fe Trail for prey, they became increasingly discouraged at how little trade actually moved on the route. In late June they did soundly whip a column of a hundred Mexican troops, killing seventeen and taking the rest prisoner, but later they were surrounded, forced to surrender, and disarmed by American dragoons under command of Philip St. George Cooke. Disputes over command of the volunteers actually did more to destroy the expedition than Cooke, but Houston elevated it to the level of a diplomatic incident. When he opened congress in December 1843, he made only a single frosty reference to the United States' incursion onto Texas' sovereign territory, and extravagantly praised Texas' excellent relations with the British and French.

Houston spent most of 1843 playing his British card, and it worked to the extent that the Tyler administration reopened talks with Texas aimed at annexation. When Tyler enlisted Jackson's aid to use his influence with Houston to remind him of his true and natural loyalties, Houston decided it was time to tip his hand to Jackson, to encourage the ailing Old Hickory in a renewed effort to redeem Texas for the Union. He also needed a man on the scene he could trust completely, and dispatched his treasured private secretary, Washington Miller. Jackson received the envoy at the Hermitage in early spring of 1844, and read a letter from Houston acknowledging that he was still willing to pursue annexation, but warning that time and patience were running short. "Now, my venerated friend, you will perceive that Texas is presented . . . as a bride adorned for her espousal. . . . She has been sought by the United States, and this is the third time she has consented. Were she now to be spurned, it would forever terminate expectation on her part, and . . . she would seek some other friend." Yet, "so far as I am concerned, or my hearty cooperation required, I am determined upon immediate annexation to the United States."

Houston's letter was all Jackson needed; he gave Wash Miller a letter of introduction to Senator Robert J. Walker of Mississippi, who was leading Jackson's annexation effort in the Senate. Jackson forwarded Houston's letter on to Walker with the advice that it be used to the best advantage. It was imperative to proceed in secrecy, not only because of the danger of Mexican outrage at being falsely dealt, but also because if John Quincy Adams and the abolitionists got wind of it, they could wreck everything for their own reasons.

By October 1843, Tyler's new secretary of state, Abel Upshur, was ready to negotiate a treaty of annexation. Houston's special minister to the United States was his ace J. Pinckney Henderson, who had previously served Texas as chargé to England and France, assisted by a young legislator, Isaac Van Zandt. Henderson saw the nature of Houston's strategy, and marveled. "All things really prove now the *very great* desire of the U.S. to annex us," he wrote to Thomas Jefferson Rusk. "You would be amused to see their jealousy of England. Houston has played it off well & that is the secret of success if we do succeed." The only item that the United States balked at was Houston's requirement to shield Texas from Mexico during talks, but again fate intervened. Upshur was accidentally killed in an explosion on a warship, and he was replaced with John C. Calhoun of South Carolina. Calhoun hated Houston perhaps even more than Burnet did, extending back to Houston's days as an army lieutenant when Calhoun was secretary of war. Fortunately, he hated the British even more, and he did guarantee Texas' safety in the event of a Mexican tantrum.

A treaty of annexation was finally signed in Washington on April 12, 1844. When it was submitted to the Senate ten days later, it could no longer be kept secret. The abolitionist former president, John Quincy Adams— "that arch fiend," Jackson boiled about him, "this wretched old man"— began laying traps and snares for it from his position in the House of Representatives. Adams' effort received unexpected (and unwitting) aid from a whole new cast of players, with whole new motives, who began to swing into action. Calhoun, while posturing his support for the treaty, wrote an incendiary and very public letter to the British minister in Washington, complaining of British attempts to meddle in slavery in Texas, and contending that the United States had actually concluded the treaty to protect slavery in the American South. The very idea was outrageous, but the letter instantly galvanized Northern opposition to the annexation treaty in the Senate. One of Jackson's operatives informed him that Calhoun's motive was to save the acquisition of Texas for a new Southern Confederacy that he intended to carve out of the United States.

If the acquisition of Texas could have been posited solely on the grounds of national security, Jackson's people reasoned, and the issue handled discreetly, they had some hope that the still-powerful Senator Henry Clay of Kentucky might be won over and would bring many influential Northern senators with him. Calhoun's machinations dashed that hope altogether, but then worse happened. Martin Van Buren, Jackson's one-term successor in the White House, was planning a political comeback, and before he was aware of the depth of Jackson's involvement in the Texas matter, made a Texas pronouncement. He did what he usually did, he straddled the fence. Annexing Texas might provoke a war with Mexico and would certainly heighten sectional tensions, for which reasons he opposed it, but if it were clear that acquiring Texas was the popular will, he would accede. As matters then stood, however, and Van Buren cited Calhoun's letter that Texas was being acquired for the protection of slavery, he must oppose it. Jackson was dismayed, but not yet defeated. His point man for annexation in the Senate was Walker of Mississippi, who at one point assured Jackson that he could command the thirty-five votes necessary for Senate ratification. Jackson's own operatives were far less sanguine, and they were right; against this confusing backdrop, the Texas annexation treaty failed in the U.S. Senate by a decisive 35 to 16 votes, which was no surprise to Houston; he merely re-sumed his European flirtation until it should do its work.

Old Hickory meanwhile developed an alternative plan, instructing one of his closest associates, William B. Lewis, to tell Walker to do everything he could for the treaty. If it failed, however, he should resubmit the matter in the form of a bill, or joint resolution, which would have the same force of law and need only a simple majority to pass. The drama dragged on until it became ensnared—indeed it was the central issue—in the U.S. presidential election of 1844. The Jacksonian candidate was James Knox Polk of Ten-nessee, an unapologetic expansionist and old friend who had served in Con-gress with Houston. He campaigned vigorously for the acquisition of both Texas and Oregon on the slogan of "Fifty-four Forty, or Fight," referring to the northern latitude of the Oregon country (while cleverly speaking of Texas in terms of its "reannexation"). It was a matter of intense public de-bate. Tracts were published and songs composed, among them a fast march entitled "The Annexation Quickstep." In the election Polk squeaked by the antiannexation Henry Clay with a majority of only 38,000, but with a com-fortable electoral margin. President Tyler, now a lame duck, considered Polk's win a mandate for expansion, and was prepared to cooperate more closely in the acquisition of Texas.

Texas also had a presidential election in 1844, in which, after the failure of the treaty, the annexation question was the elephant in the parlor that no one would discuss.

On December 9, 1844, Texas inaugurated her fourth president—or fifth, counting Provisional President Burnet. Houston's secretary of state, Anson Jones, was elevated to the office, which he believed he was the only one competent to fill (not excepting Houston). Jones had campaigned for the of-fice with only lukewarm support from Houston, and Jones never committed himself on the subject of annexation. Well into her ninth year of indepen-dence, the Republic was not just recognized but courted by the major world powers, because her cotton and her location on the map made her a crucial piece on the international chessboard. Yet a vignette of Anson Jones' inau-gural ball reveals something closer to how things really stood in Texas.

The event was held in the senate chamber, located above, and provided by, Major Hatfield's "grocery," as the saloons were delicately called. To spare government officials from having to pass by the bar on the way to work, Hatfield had boarded over the interior stairway, and constructed an outdoor stair. But with the senate not always in session, the planks over the interior stair were merely laid over the opening, not nailed down, and some of the seating for Jones' inaugural ball was inadvertently located on these loose planks. "During one of the intervals in the dancing," recalled J. K. Holland, "I was sitting beside a young lady, and we were waiting for the tap of the fiddle to take our places on the floor and join the dance. She was rather large. . . . When the signal came we sprang up to take our places, but I observed that she was pulling back; and on looking around I saw that she was sinking through the floor into the saloon below. I just had time to catch her by one arm. General Chambers lent his assistance, and together we drew her up and relieved her from her awkward position. . . . The delay occasioned by the accident was but momentary; we took our position at once, and the dance went merrily on." It is doubtful whether Henderson or Ashbel Smith ever witnessed a similar event at Buckingham Palace or the Tuileries.

With the annexation game now public knowledge, Texas' emissaries abroad had to face British and French displeasure at having been played like a couple of fiddles. George W. Terrell, in Britain, had been negotiating amiably with British Foreign Secretary the Earl of Aberdeen on adjustments to the mutual trade agreements. At a meeting on February 8, reported Terrell, "I had scarcely taken my seat in his office before I discovered, both from his looks and manner, that something had gone very wrong since I had seen him last."

"I have just been informed," said Lord Aberdeen frostily, "—I do not know that my information is correct, but the gentleman from whom it comes has good opportunities of knowing,—that your new President, Mr. Jones, is secretly in favor of annexation, and is doing all he can privately to forward the measure, while the Texas newspapers are holding out to the world that he is opposed to it. This is something I do not understand."

But then, he didn't need to. With Jackson, Tyler, Polk, and Walker all working together, the Texas question was resubmitted to the Congress in the form of a joint resolution, and on terms infinitely more favorable to Texas than the rejected treaty had been. Texas could join the Union directly as a state, with the option to split into four more at a later date if she wished. She had to keep her debt, but was allowed to keep her vast public domain as a means to pay it. The resolution passed the House comfortably, and after cliff-hanging debate in the Senate, passed by a vote of 27 to 25; Texas was required to accept the offer by the end of 1845. Once the terms of the joint resolution became public, England and France rushed to head off the deal and preserve their spheres of influence. Elliot and du Bois de Saligny, who had finally recovered from his bloody nose and resumed his duties, wrested from President Jones a promise not to pursue the deal for three months, to allow them time to persuade Mexico to recognize the independence of Texas, on condition that annexation be dropped forever.

President Jones played his role well, delaying his call of the Texas congress to allow Elliot's and du Bois' "umpires" time to prepare an offer from Mexico. When the Congress did gather, Jones was able to lay before them a clear choice between annexation to the United States and a treaty with Mexico recognizing Texas on the condition that she never join herself to the U.S. The Texas congress unanimously voted for annexation, and undertook the remaining formalities. A state constitutional convention assembled on July 4, appropriately enough, prepared a state instrument, and passed an ordinance approving annexation. On October 13 the question of statehood was submitted to Texas voters for ratification, which came in a tally of 4,254 in favor, only 257 opposed. In a solemn ceremony at the log capital in Austin, the national Lone Star was lowered on February 16, 1846. For all of Anson Jones' later complaining that he and not Sam Houston had been the brains behind annexation, the two cooperated on this last occasion. "The final act in this great drama is now performed," Jones closed his speech. "The republic of Texas is no more." He lowered the Lone Star from its pole, and Houston stepped forward and collected it in his arms. Few dry eyes witnessed it, but they became tears of pride and joy as the Stars and Stripes were hoisted.

Houston had kept the great powers on two continents guessing his true intentions for three years, but he revealed soon after he left office that his strategy had really been quite simple. "My friends," he told a cheering audience at the New Orleans Arcade, "I have been accused of lending myself to England and France; but, I assure you, I have only been *coquetting* with them. . . . Supposing a charming lady has two suitors. One of them she is inclined to believe would make the better husband, but is a little slow to make interesting propositions. Do you think if she was a skillful practitioner in Cupid's court she would pretend that she loved the other 'feller' the best and be sure that her favorite would know it? [Laughter and applause.]

"If ladies are justified in making use of coquetry in securing their annexation to good and agreeable husbands, you must excuse me for making use of the same means to annex Texas to Uncle Sam. [Laughter and cheers.]"

Captain Elliot was too good a sport to take his defeat badly. The British chargé was possessed of perhaps the most elegant writing kit in Texas—dove gray paper with laid watermarks, and a small pot of brilliant blue ink. "My Lord," he wrote home to the foreign secretary with appropriate British disinterest, "the Government of this Republic will be dissolved this day, and suffering from a recent attack of indisposition I take the liberty to proceed to New Orleans for a change of air."

THIRTY-SEVEN

NOTHING WANTING,
NOTHING TOO MUCH

THE NORTHERNERS AND ABOLITIONISTS IN CONGRESS did not easily give up the fight against Texas. Their leader in the House, John Quincy Adams, drafted in his crabbed elderly hand a last-minute challenge to the action, claiming that since the U.S. Constitution did not specifically provide for the expansion of the nation in this fashion, such a step must be illegal. It was a thin straw to grasp at, because those governing clauses of the Constitution provide only that the country might not take in new territory to the detriment of the rights of existing states. (That same empty argument, interestingly, was resurrected 150 years later by antigovernment fringe groups in Texas as a justification to resist paying federal taxes.)

Adams' and the abolitionists' fears of the so-called Southern Conspiracy, however, and its intended enhancement of slaveholding power in the Congress, soon appeared to be substantially borne out. Texas entered the United States at the midpoint of the regular decennial American census, but an incomplete tally in 1847 enumerated just over 100,000 whites in the new state—more than triple the number there were at the time of the Texas Revolution. During the same period, the number of slaves leaped from 5,000 to nearly 40,000, an eightfold increase. (The same census counted 295 free persons of color living in Texas.) There had been an almost tidal wash of immigration from the U.S. during the decade of independence, but there was much more to Texas' demographic story than that.

One exception to the burgeoning growth, not acknowledged until recent years, was that the Hispanic population actually declined. While the Texas Revolution is most accurately seen as just one theater of the larger Mexican civil war, and while many Tejanos were committed heart and soul to Texas independence and fought valiantly, after it was over American Texans began to recall it as a clash of cultures or even a race war, white against brown. Some of the most prominent Tejano families, including the Seguíns of San Antonio and the De Leóns of Victoria, were forced to seek refuge in Mexico. Ranching families in South Texas were driven off land that had been in their families since it was granted by the kings of Spain. The 1838 Córdova Rebellion in the Nacogdoches area was in some measure a reaction to such abuses, but it resulted in Hispanics in that area also being forced out of the country. The reduction of Tejanos to second-class citizenry was abhorrent, but by the time of the 1847 census, the largest ethnic minority in Texas was not them but, of all people, some 8,000 Germans.

The Republic of Texas, like Mexico before it, seized upon the empresario system to attract newcomers from beyond its shores, using the possibility of free land and new lives to populate its frontier. The Republic's first real attempt to sponsor an interior colony was inept and ended badly. Early in 1841 Lamar approved a 16,000-square-mile grant to a petitioner from Louisville, an English-born musician named William S. Peters, to settle families between the upper Trinity and Red rivers. Peters represented a consortium of ten English and ten American investors, intending his grant to give a fresh start to hard-laboring English industrial workers. His motive was also financial, as the bounty land granted to him for introducing settlers was almost as generous as what was allowed under the old Mexican empresario deals. That was the downfall of the company; new investors plotted to gain control, immigrants settled by one director had their titles challenged by another, and the Republic realized it had promised more land than was actually contained in the grant and had to expand it twice, and extend the duration of the contract twice. Moreover, many established Texans desired to claim their headrights on that tract, a number of squatters moved in with no leave from anybody, and many of the settlers in the Peters Colony, to local horror, turned out to be Free-Soilers who had little sympathy for slavery. Texas finally canceled the contract and the colony disassembled into lawsuits, confusion, and repeated legislation, but the net result was 2,205 families located in the prairies and oak forests of North Texas. One of the litigants in the courthouse fray was John Neely Bryan, a Tennesseean in his early thirties who established a trading post at a ford on the Trinity a full two hundred miles north of Austin. He first visited the place in 1839 and was subsequently unaware that the land had been reserved for the Peters group. Good lawyering established his title (he was not without political influence, having served a stint as postmaster of the Republic), and good politicking attracted surrounding neighbors to his settlement, whose streets were platted in 1844. Whether the town was named for local pioneer Joseph Dallas, or for Polk's vice president, George Mifflin Dallas, it took, and a few years later Dallas became the permanent county seat.

In February 1842 the Texas Congress attempted to better organize immigration with a general colonization law, under which vacant lands in a grant were closed to any settlers but those brought by the empresario, who was granted ten sections of land for every hundred families he introduced. The 1842 law gave rise to three colonies, the first of which caused an enormous shift in Texas' cultural balance.

German immigration might have taken a much different, and slower, path had it not been for the proselytizing of the first one to bring his family to settle, Johann Friedrich Ernst. In circumstances recalling his more famous predecessor the "Baron" de Bastrop, he arrived in 1831 after a change of name, and on the lam from an embezzling charge. He was born Christian Friedrich Dirks at Gödens Castle, where his father was in service to the Duke of Oldenburg. He became a soldier and was decorated for duty against Napoleon, after which the Duke appointed him a postal clerk, a job he held for ten years before absconding with his skimmings in 1829. With his wife and five children he escaped via Brussels to New York. After a brief stint managing a boardinghouse, he resolved to move his family to Missouri, along with a fellow German business partner, Charles Fordtran. At sea bound for New Orleans, they chanced across literature praising Austin's colony in Texas, changed their plans, and arrived at Harrisburg in the early spring of 1831. Both Fordtran and Ernst, as he now called himself, took grants in Austin's colony a few weeks later, and Ernst wrote a long account of his travels to a friend back home in Germany, praising Texas as a new Eden.

Ernst's letter was published in a newspaper and widely read, and it struck a responsive chord among the German working class, for the labor market there was depressed. Some few actually embarked for Texas themselves and sought Ernst out. He became a kind of godfather for German immigrants—housed them until they were settled, lent them money. He parceled off part of his league into lots that he sold to them, forming a settlement that became the town of Industry, about thirty miles northwest of San Felipe and the first German town in Texas. Some of the required cultural adjustments were easy; Oldenburg lay in the Lutheran portion of Germany, and before Ernst could receive his land, recalled his daughter Caroline, "my father had to kiss the bible and promise, as soon as the priest should arrive, to become a Catholic." As it happened, Padre Muldoon was shortly expected on one of his circuit visits, but when he arrived, "the people of San Felipe made him drunk and sent him back home . . . no one ever became Catholic."

Other adjustments were much harder. Industry was well named, for the immigrants worked hard, but they were woefully unprepared for life in the wilderness. They came better supplied with tools, but with only two houses between San Felipe and Ernst's grant, they were on their own in terms of survival skills. Lacking know-how to build a cabin, the Ernst family erected a hexagonal shelter in which the family lived for three years, holding umbrellas over their heads on rainy nights. "At first we had very little to eat," wrote Caroline. "We ate nothing but corn bread." Then they grew cowpeas, and once they got some seeds, vegetables were plenty. They had no cookstove and no spinning wheel, discovering to their consternation that commercial calico cost fifty cents per yard. Ernst's salvation proved to be the raising of tobacco, which everyone considered indispensable but which no one else grew. By the time of the revolution, the Germans had established a thriving community, and some individuality began to assert itself. Some who had come to escape the Prussian autocracy volunteered for the Texas army and fought with distinction; others, such as Ernst, were apolitical and either herded their families through the Runaway Scrape or sat out the war on their farms. Ernst hid his family camp in the Brazos River bottoms and let the storm pass; his farm escaped Santa Anna's scorched earth only because German Catholic neighbors fleeing eastward had left holy relics in the house. They buried their few family valuables before they departed and left the spot unmarked; when they returned they discovered that Mexican soldiers had excavated around two decoy markers but failed to obtain any booty.

While the Duke of Oldenburg charged Ernst with embezzlement, other German nobles saw possibilities in the notion of settlements in Texas, especially after independence and diplomatic recognition by the Rhine Palatinate. Partly their motive was altruistic, a way to help the overpopulated working class start new lives for themselves overseas. But partly it was nationalistic and self-interested. Establishing and maintaining settlements was a prime way to stimulate German maritime shipping. The German-Texan communities could be counted on as sources for raw materials, and as markets for the industrial products of the fatherland—functioning much like a colony, without sovereignty. And finally, if managed properly, the business of colony building, just as Austin had been an empresario, might even be profitable. Accordingly, twenty-one interested noblemen founded the Society for the Protection of German Immigrants, later known as the Adelsverein, in April 1842. They sent two of their titled members, the counts of Alt-Leiningen and Boos-Waldeck, to Texas to investigate the possibilities. The two went to see President Houston to discuss the project, and happened to arrive when the new colonization law was still fresh on the

books. Texas' eastern lands were already too thickly parceled out in head-
rights and veterans grants to locate there. Houston suggested a plot in the
Hill Country, west of Austin. A look at the map, and the reputation of the
Comanches, was enough to discourage them.

Boos-Waldeck purchased a league of land, naming it Nassau Farm, near
that of Friedrich Ernst, to serve as a staging area for the German influx, and
Alt-Leiningen returned to Germany to start organizing emigration. The society meant well, but they were gullible and not prepared for dealing with
speculators who had spent years sharpening their tricks. First they were
swindled by a French speculator named d'Orvanne, who sold them his settlement rights to a colony west of San Antonio, where in fact his contract
had expired and he had nothing to sell. Then they were approached by an
even sharper character, Henry Francis Fisher. Himself German-born, he
came to the Texas Republic as consul for the Hanseatic League, became a
Texan, and returned to Germany as Texas' consul in Bremen. He was also a
colonial entrepreneur, and with Burchard Miller as his partner, sold an interest in their tract to the Adelsverein. That society formally organized, staked
with eighty thousand dollars from the founding noblemen; its president was
Queen Victoria's half brother, the Prince of Leiningen, and its general commissioner was Carl, Prince of Solms-Braunfels. With prospective emigrants
signing up by the hundreds, he was dispatched to Texas to prepare the way.
Upon arriving he discovered that their Fisher-Miller grant was in the same
Comanche-infested Hill Country west of Austin that Alt-Leiningen and
Boos-Waldeck had refused two years before.

Making the best of it, Solms-Braunfels purchased two leagues of land at
Comal Springs, northeast of San Antonio, for the Germans to live on until
they were prepared to move onto the Fisher-Miller grant. He founded the
town of New Braunfels, and the first of the Adelsverein immigrants stepped
off the boat in December 1844 to make their way inland. They lived well
until their line of credit was exhausted, at which point they found themselves in a predicament similar to that of Friedrich Ernst a decade before.
Nonetheless, they labored hard, and prospered. Some Germans came to
Texas thrilled with the idea of living under American-style democracy; others were quite satisfied with the old ways. Progressives and free thinkers
were annoyed with the Prince of Solms-Braunfels' Texas hunting parties,
clattering through the forests in their uniforms and medals. At one point the
prince's party stopped at a house and was provided watermelons for refresh-
ment. Ernst's son, Fritz, who was in the party as guide and interpreter,
lopped off a piece of melon and went outside to eat it. He was soundly

dressed down by the prince's retainers. "How could he dare to eat," they demanded, "when His Highness had not yet tasted?"

His Highness soon tired of roughing it and retired to his castle. His successor as general commissioner of the Adelsverein could not have been more different. He was Ottfried Hans, Freiherr (Baron) von Meusebach, thirty-three, red-bearded, optimistic, and full of gusto. He became so enthused by democracy that he renounced his title and changed his name to John O. Meusebach, common man. He was a lawyer, linguist, forester, mining engineer, financier, and to the Germans in Texas, a godsend. Through repeated hardships he took possession of the wild Fisher-Miller grant and founded the town of Fredericksburg (named after Prince Frederick of Prussia) on the Pedernales River some eighty miles west of Austin in May 1846, which quickly grew to a thousand residents. Other settlements founded under Meusebach's leadership in the Hill Country included Comfort, Boerne, and Sisterdale. The settlements gained a distinctive look, as the Germans eschewed the American-style dogtrot cabin in favor of sturdy houses of *fachwerk*, a stout timber frame chocked in with cut limestone.

With equal determination (the motto on the Meusebach crest was TENAX PROPOSITI: Steadfast Purpose) he undertook to reach a comprehensive agreement with the Penateka Comanches. Texas officials warned him of the dangers of contacting the Indians, but Meusebach was between a rock and a hard place, for he had to actually settle families on his western grant by the end of 1847 or he would lose his rights to it. A treaty was concluded on March 2, 1847, near the San Saba River. The Comanches, led by Buffalo Hump, Old Owl, and Santana, were impressed by the frankness of El Sol Colorado, as the natives called Meusebach for his flaming red beard. For a consideration of three thousand dollars in presents, they agreed to let the Germans live in safety. The Indians would be welcome in the towns, and they entered Fredericksburg on May 8 to receive the payment. The Meusebach-Comanche Treaty was a signal achievement because it held good; the key to its success was undoubtedly that the Indians retained the freedom to the lands, where American and Texan treaties almost always required surrender and removal.

Old Texas hands, especially those who had fought as Texas Rangers against the Comanches, viewed the treaty with disgust, and indeed they did have some ground for complaint. For years the Comanches held the balance of power in weaponry, for a warrior could advance and loose several arrows in the time it took an Anglo to reload his firearm. The advent of the Colt repeating revolver altered the situation dramatically. Manufactured beginning in 1837 and purchased by the Texas navy two years later, many of the revolutionary five-shot, .36-caliber handguns made their way into the hands of Rangers in the companies of John Coffee "Jack" Hays and Samuel Walker. These Rangers entered the Penateka haunts on the Fisher-Miller grant repeatedly to punish Comanche raiders. The turning point came in June 1844, when Hays led fourteen of his men in a hunt for a raiding party under a chief named Yellow Wolf. They scouted as far north as the Pedernales before heading back. On June 9, having made camp and engaged in cutting a bee tree, one of the Rangers saw a large war party following their trail. "Jerusalem, Cap'n!" he called out, "yonder comes a thousand Indians," although the actual number was closer to a hundred. Twice Yellow Wolf's warriors tried to taunt and bait the Rangers into an attack, but Hays slipped behind them under cover. The Comanches, accustomed to waiting until a white man fired his gun and rushing him with bow and arrow, discovered to their horror that, as one said, each white had as many shots as he had fingers. In the course of a running fight, sometimes hand-to-hand, the Rangers lost one killed to a couple dozen Comanches. Walker was lanced through the body by a warrior but survived, and based on this and later experience, he advised the Colt company in manufacture of a new model featuring a six-shot cylinder with automated loading lever, and an increase to .44 caliber that was said to equal the stopping power of the standard-issue army rifle. The engraving on the cylinder of the so-called Walker Colts depicted what became known as "Hays' Big Fight" on the Pedernales. When Meusebach and the Germans entered the Hill Country shortly after, they found the Comanches ready to make peace, although it was Hays and Walker who had bloodied them into such malleability.

The Indian issue was only one count on which many of the more established Texans viewed the German influx with disapproval. Another point was the Peculiar Institution. Some Germans who settled in the plantation country came to accept the notion of slavery; others, especially free thinkers who settled with Meusebach in the west, would not countenance it. What really wound up being expressed was the Americans' jealousy of the Germans' hard work and resourcefulness; they had moved in long after the Americans, outstripped them economically within a couple of years, and did very well for themselves without benefit of slaves. When the Germans began in numbers to exercise their coveted franchise, they read American commentary that lumped them together with Mexicans in ethnic epithets. "On election day," complained a conservative newspaper after the defeat of some American candidates on a city ballot, "a horde of political lepers crawled to the ballot-box and there nullified the vote of thousands of your countrymen. . . . The unanimity with which the German and Mexican vote was cast *against* the American candidates [cannot mean] that the thousands and tens of thousands of these ignorant, vicious, besotted *greasers* who swarm the land, are more capable of self-government than [we are]. . . . Great God! Shall these things always exist?"

In the decade and a half before the Civil War, it was common for new-comers entering Texas from the East to hear vicious stories about lazy, venal Germans from cotton-planting hosts who housed travelers two or three to a bed and fed them fried pork for every meal. One such traveler, when he finally encountered the German towns, was shocked by what he found. "I never in my life, except, perhaps, in awakening from a dream, met with such a sudden and complete transfer of associations. In short, we were in Germany. There was nothing wanting; there was nothing too much. The land-lady enters; she does not readily understand us, but we shall have dinner immediately. In two minutes' time, by which we have got off our coats and warmed our hands at the stove, we are asked to sit down. An excellent soup is set before us, and in succession there follow two courses of meat, neither of them pork and neither of them fried, two dishes of vegetables, salad, a compote of peaches, coffee with milk, wheat bread from the loaf, and beautiful, sweet butter. . . ." There was a guest room, "with blue walls, and oak furniture. Two beds, one of them would be for each of us, the first time we had been offered the luxury of sleeping alone in Texas." The American Texans' annoyance at being shown up by the Germans would last for generations.

Meusebach resigned as commissioner of the Adelsverein in the summer of 1847 and removed to a bountiful farm at Loyal Valley, some twenty miles north of Fredericksburg. He married an Austrian countess, fathered eleven children, and lived to eighty-five. The Adelsverein faced irreversible financial troubles by 1847 but struggled on, and by the time it disbanded and assigned its remaining assets to its creditors in 1853, all had to recognize that it had not been a profitable venture. It had been cheated opportunistically by Texas land shills and perennially wrong-footed by optimistic mismanagement, but the fact that it brought to Texas more than 7,000 German settlers—thus for decades supplanting Hispanics as the state's largest ethnic minority—was a remarkable achievement. It also provided Texas with a new and unique national presence, from food to the arts and sciences, quickening its cultural diversification.

The second colony licensed by the 1842 law went to Henri Castro, a wealthy Alsatian who rounded up colonists from the Rhine provinces of France and relocated them on the Medina River west of San Antonio. His colony took root mainly on the strength of his personal fortune, but the isolation of the town he founded, Castroville, was such that their unique cultural identity was preserved to a degree even greater than the Germans'. Of particular note was a comfortable two-story inn whose bathhouse, with fire and laundry facilities on the ground floor and hot water piped to a communal lead-lined tub above, was the only place for a hot bath between San Antonio and the Rio Grande. From an initial settlement of 300 in 1844, Castroville increased to over 2,000 three years later.

In 1844 the Texas congress decided that the empresario system no longer served the country's interest, and so passed legislation ending it. President Houston vetoed the bill on January 29 and granted a final colonial contract to Charles F. Mercer, a man whose stature as a former Virginia congressman could not overcome his reception as a pariah in Texas because he was a Southern abolitionist. Congress overrode Houston's veto the following day, and that dubious beginning, plus the location of the Mercer Colony between the Peters and Robertson tracts, resulted in a blizzard of conflicting land claims and competing surveys. The Mercer Colony sank in a legal whirlpool, title to some tracts not being settled for nearly a century—not a dignified ending to a colonial system that did much not only to populate Texas' empty reaches, but also to enrich its cultural milieu.

THIRTY-EIGHT

THE STATE OF TEXAS

ANSON JONES HAD COVETED THE TEXAS PRESIDENCY. The annexation treaty failed in the U.S. Senate before the 1844 Texas presidential campaign, allowing Jones to be elected without having to declare himself on the issue. After the joint resolution was introduced, his cooperation with the French and the British gave them three months to extract a Texas treaty from Santa Anna, time that he gained for them by delaying the call of the 1845 Convention. All of this caused several Texas leaders to suspect that Jones was quite happy being president, and would sabotage annexation if he got the chance. They were wrong, but when the names were bandied about for the first team of state leaders, Jones was not on the short list.

Elected to Congress was David Kaufman from Nacogdoches, a former two-term house speaker in the Texas congress. Philadelphia-born and Jewish, he became a lawyer in Mississippi before removing to Texas and gained some reputation as an Indian fighter, wounded by the Cherokees in the Battle of the Neches. He remained the only Texan of Jewish heritage elected to Congress from Texas for 130 years.

When the legislature convened, they chose Sam Houston and Thomas Jefferson Rusk to go to Washington as Texas' first two U.S. senators, the former drawing a two-year term and the latter a full six-year term to preserve the Senate's mandate of staggered tenures. President Jones was mortified that one of those Senate seats did not go to him, and the snub finished deranging him. He retired to private life on his plantation, combing through his voluminous papers and writing disrespectful memos on them about his erstwhile colleagues. Based on those notes he composed an argumentative history of the Republic, which was not published until the year after he mounted the steps of the former capitol in Houston, ranted for a bit, put a pistol to his head, and pulled the trigger.

The overwhelming choice as first governor was J. Pinckney Henderson, whose diplomatic representation to all three powers that had competed for Texas' favor played an important role in annexation. He had built up a law practice in San Augustine, trying to repair the personal financial damage he had incurred as a seldom-paid Texas diplomat. Henderson had two opponents, Jones' vice president, Kenneth Anderson, who died, and Dr. James B. Miller, who had been active in Texas' political affairs since the Convention of 1833, most recently as secretary of the treasury in Houston's second term. Unable to compete with Henderson either in elegance or breadth of experience, he picked up only 1,725 votes to Henderson's 7,853. As able a governor as Texans gained in J. P. Henderson, they got an even more amazing first lady, although she never came to Austin to undertake the duties of official hostess. Twelve years younger than the governor, Frances Cox Henderson was Philadelphia-born and Paris-educated. They had met when Henderson represented Texas at the Tuileries, and they married at St. George's Chapel in London. She was a mathematician, a musician, and an effective organizer of new congregations of the Episcopal Church. When Henderson was out of town, she ran his law office. Just as a sideline, she spoke twenty-five languages (eighteen of them fluently) and published translations of foreign-language short stories—all of which leaves one to wonder how high she might have risen had women in that era enjoyed opportunities anywhere nearly equal to those of men.

The whole progress of Texas annexation went down hard in Mexico, and one of the principal Whig objections to admitting Texas, that it would mean war with Mexico, began to appear imminent. After seizing hostages from San Antonio in the invasion of September 1842, and with the accumulation of Santa Fe and Mier hostages, Santa Anna believed he had enough chips to bargain with. He let himself believe in the authenticity of the Robinson letters, because Houston backed them up with an armistice and repatriation of Mexican prisoners in Texas. When the commodore of the Texas navy sailed to maintain hostilities, Houston branded him a pirate and publicly sought international help to apprehend him on the high seas, and the British and French ministers in Mexico were incessantly busy on his behalf. The man who defeated him at San Jacinto also sent commissioners to Mexico and they signed a treaty agreeing to continue Texas as a Mexican department. Santa Anna responded—and Houston gained one of his objectives—when all of the remaining Texas prisoners were freed in September 1844. Only with submission of the annexation treaty did the dictator learn just how thoroughly he had been played, but he had no opportunity to act on his chagrin as he was toppled in an internal coup in 1845 and exiled to Cuba.

When the joint resolution passed and the clock began running for Texas to accept its terms, Mexico ended diplomatic contact with the United States on March 6, 1845. The U.S. acted to honor its obligation to protect Texas while annexation was pending; Polk dispatched General Zachary Taylor with an army to a position just south of Corpus Christi, infringing on the Nueces Strip, but not far south enough to trigger a response from Ampudia's army in Matamoros. Taylor, for his part, requisitioned Texas volunteers to help with the job: two infantry regiments and two of cavalry. For Texas' militaristic huns and yahoos, this was a dream come true. Sam Houston had tricked them out of their intended Matamoros pillaging during his first term, and those expeditions that did later enter Mexico, either with Lamar's blessing in 1841 or in defiance of Houston in 1842, met grievous ends. Service with Taylor was seen as a chance to even those accounts, and the recruiters were all but overrun; as many as 7,000 volunteers eventually signed up for duty. The feeling for war in Texas was so one-sided that even the Regulators and Moderators, the East Texas feudists who had made it their business to shoot, burn, and hang each other for five years, fought together—although they enlisted in separate companies. When Taylor, popularly known as "Old Rough and Ready," got an eyeful of the Texas volunteers, his reaction was much like Sam Houston's in 1835, pronouncing them the damnedest excuse for soldiers he had ever seen. Governor Henderson, himself a former officer in the North Carolina militia, asked for and received the legislature's leave of absence to command the Texas troops.

By June, however, it appeared that Mexico might not give them the excuse to start shooting, and Polk was anxious to avoid a war if he could gain Texas without one. Mexico's new federalist president, José Herrera, could not be considered friendly to the American stake in the contest, but it was Herrera who asked for talks, and Polk believed he could be bargained with. In November he sent a special minister with plenary powers, John Slidell of Louisiana, to try to reach a settlement. Emphasizing that the U.S. and Mexico were, "I trust, destined in future to be always friends," Polk empowered Slidell to assuage their feelings with up to $5 million to accept the Rio Grande boundary, and up to $25 million to purchase California. Reverting to Jacksonian rhetoric about Texas having been included in the Louisiana Purchase, though, he specifically instructed Slidell that the Rio Grande boundary itself was not open to question.

Slidell got nowhere. Once Herrera learned that Texas' reversion to Mexico, or even a Nueces boundary, was not on the table, he declined to receive the American. Nevertheless, Herrera was soon overthrown by a still more anti-American centralist, Mariano Paredes, who ordered Slidell to leave the country. In truth, the identity of the Mexican president was beside the point; the national mood was so angry that no president could have accommodated Polk and remained in power.

With Slidell's failure, Polk ordered Taylor to a new position near the Rio Grande, which was accomplished by late March 1846. Once the main army was camped by the Laguna Madre, Taylor sent Major Jacob Brown to erect a makeshift fortification on the river directly opposite Matamoros. Paredes reinforced Ampudia, and on April 24 a Mexican force under Mariano Arista crossed the river; an entire brigade trapped and engaged a sixty-man cavalry patrol, resulting in sixteen American dead or wounded and the remainder taken prisoner. Taylor marched west with 2,200 men toward "Fort Brown" to face Arista's 3,500. They met on a rise called Palo Alto on May 8 and boomed through an artillery duel that delivered no knockout but left the Americans in possession of the field. Arista took up a new position at an oxbow lake, Resaca de la Palma, from which Taylor routed him on May 9, and Arista withdrew beyond the Rio Grande. Knowing of the small cavalry defeat but not yet aware of Taylor's victories in the Nueces Strip, Congress declared war on Mexico on May 13. Subsequent reliance on Polk's famous message to the Congress that Mexico had "spilled American blood upon American soil," quoted either in the affirmative that it justified the war, or in the negative that it was a shameful hypocrisy, was really moot, because Mexico had already declared war upon the United States on April 23.

Texans had fought in these first two engagements only in small numbers, as scouts and couriers under Samuel Walker, although their effectiveness, and Walker's élan particularly, raised Taylor's shaggy eyebrows. As the war moved into the Mexican interior, the Texas troops proved themselves invaluable. At the battle for Monterrey, it was six companies of Rangers who stormed Federation Hill, took the Mexican artillery position, and turned the guns around on the fleeing enemy. At the following Battle of Buena Vista, the steeply outnumbered Americans again owed their victory largely to Texas troops, but their lack of discipline and disdain for authority exasperated Taylor. "We can't do without them in a fight," he griped, "and can't do anything with them out of a fight." Sam Houston could have nodded sagely, but instead used his powerful new position on the Senate Military Affairs Committee to defend Polk and the war from the attacks of thoroughly incensed Whigs. To adherents of Manifest Destiny the war was about conquest and national expansion; to Houston it was simply about security for Texas, which it could never have as long as it could be affected by Mexico's endless cycle of coups and counter-coups.

Indeed, as war continued to go badly for Mexico, Santa Anna demonstrated that even he was not out of the duplicity game quite yet. From Havana, he contacted the Americans, hinting that if he were back in power an amicable deal might still be reached. The tightening U.S. naval blockade was relaxed just enough to let him return, but once back on his home turf he turned all his energies to organizing resistance, and was given overall command of Mexican forces.

A southern front of the war opened when General Winfield Scott landed at Vera Cruz and began a drive toward Mexico City. It was a calculated act to select Texas Rangers to keep the lines of supply and communication open behind him. They did so effectively, but with a ruthlessness to the local inhabitants that cemented their reputations as *los tejanos diablos*. "Should Captain Walker come across guerrillas," wrote one journalist, "God help them, for he seldom brings in prisoners." Of lasting import to Texas from the Mexican War was the death of Samuel Walker, killed in a firefight at the town of Huamantla on October 9, 1847. While Rangers took out their vengeance on the townspeople, far more Texans in the war were felled by tropical diseases, either in Mexico or back home after years of debilitation, than were killed in action—by which measure the Rio Grande boundary was even more hard-won than independence itself.

In the meantime, Paredes had been overthrown by former vice president Valentín Gómez Farías, who was soon pushed aside by Santa Anna, who had done the same thing to him in 1833. The war effectively ended with the fall of Mexico City in September, resulting in Santa Anna's expulsion back into exile while the new executive, Pedro María Anaya, opened peace negotiations. By the Treaty of Guadalupe-Hidalgo, signed in February 1848, Mexico ceded virtually all its territory north of the Rio Grande and the 32nd parallel, land that eventually became the states of California, Nevada, Utah, Arizona, and New Mexico; land that without Texas independence and annexation might never have become part of the United States. Texas' statehood was now finally secure, and she brought with her an enormous if bloody and dubiously gotten dowry.

Back in Texas, Henderson resumed gubernatorial authority for the remaining year of his term, and did not run for reelection. Oddly, the choice of his successor revolved around one of those verbal tiffs that frequently engulf jealous officers after a conflict. In one report, Henderson had omitted mention of the gallant performance of Colonel George T. Wood in the Battle of Monterrey; Wood took umbrage and wrote a piece minimizing Henderson's role in the fight. Wood was a popular officer, and on the strength of the ex-soldier vote became Texas' second governor. Wood, a veteran of Andrew Jackson's Creek campaign of 1814, was known as mirthful and hospitable, but eccentric, a trait expressed most visibly in his steadfast refusal to wear socks.

With the Mexican War concluded, yet another of the evils that the Whigs had correctly forecast had to be dealt with: what to do with a slave state whose territory extended north of the Missouri Compromise line. Since 1820 it had been illegal to introduce slaves north of the 36°30' parallel, and Texas, which the United States had admitted to the extent of her territorial claims, extended north into the Medicine Bow mountains of present Wyoming. Early in the war, Santa Fe was occupied by an army under General Stephen Watts Kearny, who was no friend to the South or slavery, and he organized a civilian government there without regard to the Texas claims. Six months after he returned to office, Governor Henderson quizzed Polk's secretary of state, James Buchanan, as to what this portended. Buchanan, as was his political wont, hedged, assuring Henderson that Texas' claims were still valid but the matter would have to be decided in Congress. Abolitionists had already opened an intrigue, however, in the Wilmot Proviso, a rider to appropriations bills in both 1846 and 1847 that forbade the introduction of slavery into any territory conquered from Mexico. It passed in the House, and only Southern parity in the Senate prevented its becoming law.

Soon after Wood became governor and five days after the signing of the Treaty of Guadalupe-Hidalgo, the Texas legislature acted preemptively, proclaiming most of New Mexico east of the Rio Grande as Santa Fe County and the 11th Judicial District of Texas, and dispatched Spruce Baird as commissioner to organize a new civil administration. Quite apart from Kearny's hostility, the people of Santa Fe did not wish to be part of Texas in 1848 any more than they had in 1841. Mass protests and a grassroots convention there gave rise to a petition to make New Mexico a territory of the United States. Opposed by both the army and the local populace, Baird accomplished nothing. Wood espoused the use of force in maintaining Texas' claim, but he failed in his reelection bid and was replaced with Peter Hansborough Bell, a Virginia private at San Jacinto who had also served under Wood in Mexico. With the hawkish encouragement of Congressman Kaufman, Bell also took an aggressive stance on the New Mexico question, but the legislature decided to attack the problem piecemeal. They split the Santa Fe County into four smaller ones and sent another commissioner, Robert S. Neighbors, to organize the environs of El Paso del Norte as a Texas county, intending to work northward from there. The sheer distance from Texas settlements to El Paso argued the impracticability of claiming or organizing them as part of Texas. On his first mission to El Paso, Neighbors and his escort, a tough Ranger named John Salmon Ford (who during the late war wrote so many condolence letters that he began abbreviating "rest in peace" to R.I.P., leaving him known to history as Rip Ford), got lost repeatedly and nearly starved to death.

Undeterred, Governor Bell echoed the Texas sentiments by convening a special session of the legislature, in which he insisted that "Texas will maintain the integrity of her Territory at all hazards and to the last extremity." Beyond the sight of most Texans, however, the federal wheels had been turning to reach a solution. Henry Clay, the elder statesman of the Senate, proved that he had one last great compromise left in him. During 1850 he steered a series of bills into passage, including one that truncated Texas' northern boundary at the 36°30' parallel—the old Missouri Compromise line—and paid Texas ten million dollars to cede New Mexico, defined as land west of the 103rd meridian, to the United States. Texas was allowed to keep El Paso as its own, giving the state the distinctive shape familiar today. Clay had been supported by Kaufman and Houston, who allowed that he was less than enthusiastic, but as a political reality it was the best deal that could be obtained. Texas entered the Union with its public debt as well as its public domain; ten million dollars was a powerful incentive, and another special session of the legislature approved it in November.

Hansborough Bell won reelection in 1851, but a month before the end of his term he resigned to take a seat in Congress. He was replaced during those weeks as governor by the lieutenant governor and former congressman of the Republic, James Wilson "Smoky" Henderson, who was ever doomed to be confused with the more illustrious James Pinckney Henderson. In 1853 Texas elected its fifth governor, Elisha Marshall Pease, a Connecticut lawyer of forty-two with a long Texas history. He had fought for the COME AND TAKE IT cannon in 1835, and served as secretary first to the General Council and then to the committee that created the Constitution of the Republic. He ran for governor as a Democrat; the political party affiliations and structures of the mother country had begun to make themselves felt in Texas, and the Whig candidate for governor, William B. Ochiltree, ran strongly enough that another prominent Democrat, Regulator and Ranger Captain Middleton Johnson, withdrew from the race and supported Pease. (Johnson had re-

cently been improving his land grant in Tarrant County, and starting a settlement at the forks of the Trinity he named Fort Worth to honor the commandant of the U.S. military's new Department of Texas, William J. Worth.)

In addition to the $10 million received in compensation for her claims to
the upper Rio Grande, the new state was far from shy about presenting receipts for expenses that were now federal responsibility, such as revenue
bonds and frontier Indian protection. In 1854 the Congress wearied of the
snowfall of Texas bills and passed an appropriation of $7.5 million to cover
all miscellaneous federal debts. This was nearly double the amount actually
owed, which allowed Texas to take a few years of state-tax holiday and commence a building campaign for an infrastructure suitable to the new largest
state in the Union.

Texas already had a new three-story Greek Revival capitol in cut limestone; Austin was finally made the permanent capital in 1850, and the capitol was built on the square originally platted for the purpose in 1839. Still
needed was a base from which to administer the vast public domain, and
construction began on a new Land Office Building, a three-story crenellated
Bavarian castle built in the Rundbogenstil on the southeast corner of the
capitol grounds. No state more than Texas depended upon the safety of her
deed records, and this was a structure against which Angelina Eberly's 1842
cannon shot in the Archives War would have made little impression. Construction was as close to fireproof as the technology of the day could manage: flues were buried in two-foot-thick stone walls, shutters were metal,
the dizzying spiral staircase was of set limestone (a second one followed
later of cast iron). The building opened in 1857 after an expenditure of fifty
thousand dollars.

When Austin was first settled, Mirabeau Lamar had been in such a hurry
to have a suitably luxurious manse in which to ensconce himself that the
President's House—a two-story dogtrot with exterior stairways—was built
of green lumber and began to pull apart at the seams within a couple of
years. Houston in his second term declined to live there, and by 1845 it
leaked and creaked and stood open to whoever had the curiosity to pilfer
through it, tenanted only, according to one explorer, by a colony of bats.
Henderson and his successors lived in boardinghouses, but construction
started in 1854 on a Governor's Mansion, with a legislative appropriation of
$17,000. The architect was North Carolinian Abner Cook, a brilliant master
builder who came to newly settled Austin at twenty-five, thinking that the
new capital would have much profitable construction. Shrewdly, he acquired interests in a sawmill and brickyard, assuring himself of supplies at

the cheapest possible rate. He became a practitioner of the Greek Revival style, espoused in his copy of the *American Builder's Companion* and reinforced in *The Beauties of Modern Architecture*. The Texas Governor's Mansion that he composed was massive but simple, four rooms downstairs with seventeen-foot ceilings, and four upstairs with thirteen-foot ceilings, arranged two on either side of a central stair hall. The house was set behind an impressive Ionic portico, with a servants' wing and stairs attached to the rear. Adapting the style to the climate, the house faced east, with floor-length windows in the parlor and library for maximum coolness. He also intended it to have the most modern conveniences, and began construction of a privy at a rear corner of the lot.

Before the mansion was completed, a neighbor living on the street behind complained of the construction of the gubernatorial outhouse directly across from his front gate, and offered to pay to rebuild it if it was moved. The commissioners who oversaw the construction met and approved his request. (The neighbor was not alone in his objection to having a privy located where it could be seen. Most people thought it more discreet to use a chamber pot, or at least quietly disappear into a clump of bushes. To let the whole world know your intended purpose by closing yourself in a structure dedicated to it was considered obscene, and in fact the first outhouses built in Austin were torn down by nocturnal vigilantes who believed they were protecting family values.)

Of the appropriation, $2,500 was set aside to furnish the new residence, a task given over to Swante Swenson, the first Swedish immigrant to Texas. He divided his time between his Austin mercantile and his avocation—at the encouragement of Sam Houston—of beckoning other residents of his native Småland to follow him. (He sold his Fort Bend plantation and established a small but thriving Swedish colony on a tract east of Austin, near the site of present Decker Lake.) Swenson spent $2,495.67 of the money and barely softened the echoes in the cavernous house. "Furniture is most extravagantly dear here," first lady Lucadia Pease wrote her sister; a small marble-topped bureau cost fifty dollars, "and everything in proportion." They finished out the rooms with their own possessions. Mrs. Pease eschewed the Texas summer heat, using that season to visit Connecticut relations, and thus she was absent when the Governor's Mansion was opened to the public for the first time. The invitations went out on August 20, 1856, boldly announcing the GOVERNOR'S LEVEE, with a lace-cuffed hand pointing to the announcement that "THE EXECUTIVE presents his respects to his friends and the public, and will be pleased to meet them on that occasion."

"Last night my great party came off," Pease wrote triumphantly to Lucadia on the 24th, "and Mr. Purvis says that it is the talk about town that it was the best one ever got up in Austin. The ladies turned out well, there was a perfect jam. It is estimated that there were present at different times during the evening at least five hundred persons, and that over three hundred staid to supper. . . . It was the first Public party ever given by a Governor of Texas, and I felt anxious that it should be a creditable one, as it will be the standard by which my successors will be measured." It was a lofty standard; he spent $121.80 for the foodstuffs, the cakes alone costing $35. Cleverly, Pease delayed laying the mansion's carpets and floor mats until the public finished its housewarming trample. Otherwise, "that party would have given the matting a polish from which it would never have recovered."

The new Governor's Mansion gave Austin society a locus for the polite custom of "calling." In the hot summer of 1856, Marshall Pease was surprised late one Sunday afternoon by the doorbell ringing in the mansion. "Knowing that the servants were all away," he wrote Lucadia, "I went down to the door, with only my pantaloons & shirt, and who should I find there but a lady. She inquired if Gov. Pease was at home. I replied that he was and asked her to walk into the library. I then went and put on my vest and coat, and came back and introduced myself as the Gov. She then introduced herself as Mrs. Hamilton from Minnesota. Passing the house she thought she would call and see the Gov. She had no business with me, and trusted I would excuse her freedom. She sat and talked about an hour."

Cooler weather brought the return of Lucadia Pease, who discovered that there was much more to running the First Household than entertaining callers. The gubernatorial salary was meager compared to the social responsibilities that came with the office, there was no expense allowance, and the two-acre lot on which the mighty house sat had to produce. The preserves and brandied fruit served at the governor's great levee had been put up by her. "We are now in the midst of gardening," she wrote a Connecticut friend one February. "Have planted Irish Potatoes and most of the early vegetables. . . . We have just killed six hogs and I am deep in the business of lard making and curing of hams. We shall put up twelve hogs this winter and hope to have enough—last year they had to buy pork while I was away."

Lucadia Pease's experience in a way encapsulated much of antebellum Texas life, caught between the gentility of the Old South and the necessity of hard labor to do for oneself on the frontier. It was an economic, emotional, and political schizophrenia that produced contradictory tensions in the character of the new state, tensions that would last for a long time.

COURTESY TEXAS STATE LIBRARY AND ARCHIVES COMMISSION

San José Mission was established in 1721 to serve the Indians in the San Antonio area. This 1877 photo shows the ruins of the assembly hall and friary. Restoration of the chapel began in 1928 after the bell tower collapsed.

COURTESY CENTER FOR AMERICAN HISTORY, UNIVERSITY OF TEXAS

Jane H. W. Long, often celebrated as the "Mother of Texas," was the first in a line of tough Texas viragoes who endured brutal frontier conditions.

COURTESY TEXAS STATE LIBRARY AND ARCHIVES COMMISSION

Stephen F. Austin labored for over a decade to reconcile his colonists with Mexican authority, but as revolution approached, he lost favor with his people for remaining loyal for too long. This portrait is attributed to Catlin.

While many Tejanos remained loyal to Mexico, José Antonio Navarro (*top left*), who had been one of Stephen Austin's best friends, was prominent among those who joined the revolution. Officers within the Mexican Army were similarly conflicted over obedience to Santa Anna. In command of the Goliad fortress, Lt. Col. José Nicolás de la Portilla (*top right*) received orders from General Urrea to treat his four hundred prisoners humanely, but was forced to obey Santa Anna's order to execute them. The dictator's insistence on besieging and storming the Alamo (*bottom*) in San Antonio gave Texas rebels a potent rallying cry.

While the ruin of the Texas Capitol at Columbia testifies to the rudeness of frontier conditions, the Republic's currency, with its symbols of commerce and mythological figures, showed great ambitions.

Bitter rivals: The vast policy differences between Texas President Sam Houston (*top*) and his successor, Mirabeau Lamar (*bottom*), were escalated by their intense personal dislike of each other.

Texas was where the South met the West. Construction of an elegant Governor's Mansion in 1856 heralded Texas' emergence as an antebellum power, but life on the frontier still had its risks. Cynthia Ann Parker was captured by Comanches at the age of nine and was completely assimilated. She was the mother of future chief Quanah Parker by the time of her recapture a quarter century later.

The Civil War in Texas began with the seizure of U.S. Army stores in San Antonio, a scene believed to have been captured in this 1861 ambrotype. Hugh Cook (*left*) of Waller County was a late-blooming seventeen when he enlisted. When older men in his company kept him away from the front, he complained to his captain, "I didn't come here to hold horses, I am here to shoot Yankees." Union attempts to invade Texas failed repeatedly, including this effort by gunboats in the Red River, which were sent back downstream on a floodcrest in a spectacular defeat.

General Gordon Granger had been a minor figure in the war before he arrived in Texas to begin the occupation. His proclamation of freedom for slaves on June 19, 1865, is still celebrated, but reality for hundreds of thousands of liberated slaves changed little over the next half century. Here, cotton pickers' sacks are weighed.

Not all Native Americans advocated war to oppose the spread of white civilization over their plains. Striking-Eagle's-Talons, whose name was deflated by sign language into Kicking Bird, was killed by one of his own medicine men for pursuing the peace policy. The Indian's place on the Texas prairies was taken by the Anglo cowboy, epitomized by Charles Siringo, trail driver and later hired gun and Pinkerton detective.

Far-flung ranches had to be supplied, leading to the rise of small-town general stores such as this one in isolated El Dorado, forty miles south of San Angelo. Urbanization in the larger supply centers became inevitable. In Lubbock's town square, covered wagon met horseless carriage and even bicycle.

COURTESY TEXAS STATE LIBRARY AND ARCHIVES COMMISSION

In Texas the century turned with momentous changes. Six to eight thousand people perished in the Galveston hurricane of September 8, 1900, still the deadliest natural disaster in American history. Several weeks later the discovery of oil at Spindletop led to the tall forest of the Big Thicket being replaced with a tall forest of a different kind.

Texans followed news of the Great War with interest in their naval namesake, the USS *Texas* (here in New York, 1916) whose fourteen-inch rifles were the largest guns ever mounted up to that time, and with news of largely Texas-recruited regiments. The 90th Division suffered nearly 10,000 casualties, and the stress was released by staging plays featuring both drag and blackface. Back home, Texas schoolchildren by state law underwent ten minutes per day of instruction in "intelligent patriotism," in addition to playing doughboy and nurse.

Further oil strikes after the war made Texas even richer. Between Fort Worth and Abilene, Desdemona increased from 340 inhabitants to more than 16,000, and shares in one oil company went from $100 to more than $10,000. When the wells went dry, the town all but disappeared.

Expanding the franchise to women was an uphill fight in Texas, thanks in part to editorial photos such as this. Nevertheless, Texas was one of the first states to allow women to vote.

COURTESY TEXAS STATE LIBRARY AND ARCHIVES COMMISSION

In the Texas Panhandle, the Great Depression became synonymous with the Dust Bowl, whose effects were ubiquitous by 1937. This abandoned farm is from Dallam County.

COURTESY THE FAYETTE COUNTY HERITAGE MUSEUM, LA GRANGE

Some had fonder memories of the "Chicken Ranch," a brothel near La Grange where, in the scarcity of cash, a man could donate a laying hen and forget his troubles with a basic "four-get": get up, get on, get off, get out.

Texas' wartime muscle was exemplified by the construction of Liberty Ships at the Irish Bend shipyard in Houston. As one vessel is about to be launched, the keel is already down for the next one.

The U.S. Army tried its best to force unwelcome female aviators to wash out, compelling them to pay their own way to desolate Avenger Field near Sweetwater and squeezing them into scorpion-infested barracks, but the women became indispensable to the war effort.

First elected to Congress during the Depression, Lyndon Johnson became a master of balancing his progressive instincts against the staunch conservative atmosphere in Texas. He became known as Landslide Lyndon after "amended" returns handed him the Senate election in 1948, but he and House Speaker Sam Rayburn gave Texas powerful advocacy in Congress.

When the NAACP won a federal court order to integrate the high school in Mansfield, near Fort Worth, in 1956, Governor Allan Shivers sent Texas Rangers to enforce the status quo. Ranger E. J. Banks is surrounded by adoring bobby-soxers who take no notice of the effigy hung from the building.

Before the Sharpstown financial scandal shook Texas government to its roots, powerful figures pose with former President Johnson: State House Speaker Gus Mutscher, who pled out; Governor Preston Smith, who was implicated but not indicted, and humiliated in his reelection effort; and Lieutenant Governor Ben Barnes, golden baby of Texas politics, innocent of any wrongdoing but thrown out with the Sharpstown bathwater.

As president pro tempore of the Texas senate, Barbara Jordan was accorded the traditional honor of serving as governor for a day. She went on to serve three terms in Congress and as a much-loved teacher at the University of Texas before her untimely death.

THIRTY-NINE

LIFE IN THE LONE STAR STATE

THE DECADE OF ANTEBELLUM TEXAS, FROM THE NOR-
malization of Texas within the Union to its secession in 1861, was in many
ways a halcyon period. With statehood came unhindered transit; the doors
of immigration were thrown wide open, and the population exploded. The
first U.S. census in which Texas participated was that of 1850, enumerating
154,034 whites, 58,161 slaves; ten years later there were 421,294 whites
and 182,921 slaves. The largest foreign population was the Germans, of
whom there were now more than 20,000, but they proved to be only the
forerunner of various European communities that settled in Texas. In addition to the Swedes who followed Swante Swenson and his relatives, Poles
distressed by continuous political turmoil at home also began to look to
Texas as a haven. A Polish priest, Leopold Moczygemba, was well established in the San Antonio area, and sponsored a hundred families who
founded the town of Panna Maria ("Virgin Mary") about fifty miles southeast of there on Christmas Eve, 1854. Within a few years seven hundred
more followed, firmly establishing that town and branching out to found
new ones, such as Cestochowa. Czechs and Bohemians, whose history of
having their nationality run over by powerful empires was similar to that of
the Poles, began arriving in numbers in 1851, settling mostly on the central
Texas plains, centered around Fayette County, southeast of Austin. By the
time of the Civil War there were about 700 of them. Norwegians came in
smaller numbers and settled generally southeast of Dallas; there were just
over a hundred of them by the 1850 census; one of them, Ole Ringness, later
contributed to farming development with his invention of the disc plow. (He
himself, however, was robbed and murdered on his way to Washington to
secure the patent.) Many European communities maintained their own customs of dress and conduct and diet—which in the case of the Czechs and
Germans included slow-smoking meat in a tenderizing sauce, from which
modern barbecue derived.

One of the last colonial ventures was also one of the most complete failures, and oddly enough it was the project of the world's premier colonizers,
the English. After his days of exploring the frontier and painting American

Indians were behind him, George Catlin took his art and his artifacts on a
tour of Britain, where they made quite an impression. Believing that Catlin's
idyllic canvases must reflect reality, a group of persons coalesced, imbued
with the possibilities of founding a great center of English civilization on the
frontier. Bravely incorporated as the Universal Emigration and Colonization
Company of London, financiers in 1850 sent naval officer Sir Edward
Belcher to arrange things on the frontier. He made a down payment on
27,000 acres in present Bosque County, in the very heart of the state, which
he paid to land agent Jacob de Cordova, who had been one of the founders of
Waco two years earlier. Far less organized than the German Adelsverein,
however, Belcher dispatched two shiploads of "broken down English clerks,
Superanuated Scotch officers [and] dissipated Irish boys," who found themselves stranded in central Texas with no dwellings, no implements, no supplies, and no idea how to actually farm. After a cold, wet month living in
dugouts, and moved to a savage sense of humor, they named the settlement
Kent, after the balmy resort county southeast of London. Those who did not
die of exposure and disease that first year either drifted home or into more
settled areas of Texas. Catlin, who had gone deep into debt to promote the
scheme, lost his paintings and trinkets to creditors (later recovered by the
Smithsonian Institution), while Sir Edward Belcher went on to become an
admiral in the queen's navy.

Economically, cotton was still king: 40,000 bales were shipped in 1848,
62,000 bales in 1852, 110,000 bales in 1854, and 420,000 bales in 1860.
This dramatic advent of Texas as a powerhouse of the cotton economy
heightened sectional tensions in proportion, and left Texas' more famous
senator, Sam Houston, in a thankless position. His perspective on the issue
was much longer than the typical Texas planter's. He had known and joined
political combat decades ago with the early principals of nullification and
sectionalism, such as South Carolina's John C. Calhoun, and he was in a better position to see that Southern extremism was more about their economics and egos than it was about the constitutional issue of states' rights. In
1854 Stephen A. Douglas of Illinois, hoping to pander to the powerful
Southern senators in a bid for the presidency, introduced a bill to allow
"popular sovereignty" to decide the issue of slavery in the new territories of
Kansas and Nebraska. Every Southern senator except Houston and Tennessee's Bell gulped the bait of extending slave territory. Houston argued
against it on the Senate floor for two days, pointing out that slavery made no
sense in a climate where cotton wouldn't grow, anyway, and adding that
those lands had already been granted in perpetuity by treaty to various In-

dian tribes. Houston's passionate plea made him a hero in the North, but in the South, including his own Texas, he was vilified in unprecedented vocabulary. As the old Whig Party disintegrated and the Democratic Party became radicalized by Southern separatists, Houston found himself increasingly unwelcome under any political banner. He began a flirtation with the so-called American or Know-Nothing Party in the mid-fifties, but he was troubled by their nativism and never made a firm commitment to them. The Know-Nothings did win a number of local elections in Texas, mostly because there was no alternative for Texans who harbored any hope for the Union.

The 1850s also saw the beginnings of a new and important segment of the Texas economy: cattle ranching. The early Spanish explorers had brought extensive herds with them, and by the mid-nineteenth century Texas was roamed by at least three million hardy, raw-boned, leggy wild longhorns. The first great ranching dynasty began with a chance meeting in Florida between two sailing captains, a dour-looking New York calculator named Richard King and a pudgy Pennsylvania Quaker named Mifflin Kenedy. Both were headed for service on the Rio Grande during the Mexican-American War, and after peace was restored they went into partnership, creating a virtual shipping monopoly on that stream, and using their profits to buy vast acreages in the Nueces Strip.

But whether cotton or cattle, the economy remained agrarian in its base. Over half of the heads of families registered their occupation as "farmer," appropriately for a state that had been giving away its public domain by the thousands of square miles. Cities were still quite small; San Antonio in 1860, with 8,200 people, just passed Galveston's 7,300 as Texas' largest. Austin, the capital, had finally put its Indian problems to rest and had 3,500 residents, five times its size in 1850. Marshall had 4,000, New Braunfels 3,500, and Dallas 2,000.

Manufacturing, what there was of it, was done by small proprietors. The first real harbinger of industrialization was the coming of the railroads, the first one of which, the Buffalo Bayou, Brazos, & Colorado Railway Company, was chartered on February 11, 1850. One of its principal investors was revolutionary figure Sidney Sherman, for whom the company's locomotive was named. Other entrepreneurs followed suit, until on the eve of the Civil War Texas had 470 miles of track belonging to nine companies. There could be no question that times were changing, as one traveler marveled that a 35-mile trip that once took a day and a half required only an hour and a half by train. Hard on the heels of this progress, though, came the realization that communities could be gouged for support to run the rail line to them. In

1858, in one of the earliest cases of a railroad's monopolistic abuse, the Houston & Texas Central demanded an $11,000 bonus from the town of Washington-on-the-Brazos to run their line through the onetime capital of the Republic of Texas. Washington, which had a thriving population of 750, refused, and city leaders, believing that their future lay instead with the river commerce with which they were familiar, purchased part interest in two steamboats instead. The railroad bypassed Washington and wound its way to Brenham and Navasota, and Washington-on-the-Brazos, clipped from the vine, went into a long decline. By the end of the 1800s the population was less than 200, and most of the original buildings were wrecked, burned, or plowed under, including Independence Hall, whose overgrown site was marked by a plaque in 1899.

The social life of the state was in flux during the antebellum period. Any kind of dance was called a ball; the great fêtes that had been so popular during the Republic began to lose favor as churches became more influential in the older, more settled areas. National holidays were still an occasion for patriotic speeches—the more perfervid the oratory, the better—and for parades and barbecues, and horse racing was still avidly followed. Virginia immigrants brought blooded hounds, and ladies were allowed to take part in fox hunts—properly escorted, of course. Favorite card games (presumably when the minister was away) were euchre and whist. Any kind of music other than fiddling was something of a rarity; the guitar was very much a Spanish instrument and thought exotic, but with time came more pianos.

Visual art in Texas generally meant portraiture and landscape. Anything more sophisticated was ahead of its time. One of the most cultured gentlemen in Texas was Dr. Ashbel Smith, formerly surgeon general of the army and lately minister to France and Great Britain. When he returned from Europe and reestablished his medical practice in Galveston, he hung on his office walls certain paintings he had acquired. Unfortunately, they were female nudes. When he proudly displayed his collection to some ladies of the town, they blushed and turned away. Being too well bred to actually criticize Dr. Smith, they instead found some other objects in his office to speak well of, and then hastily retreated. "Art," according to one observer, "had not yet been cultivated to such an extent in Texas at that time as to warrant the ladies in bringing to bear a full gaze at the pictures." The ladies did afterward cluck that Dr. Smith, "being an old bachelor," should have known better. Few in Texas had yet learned to distinguish between female nudes and naked women, and art that in Europe adorned the finest museums and most sumptuous palaces was, for the time being, in Texas relegated to bar-backs and bordellos.

Sophistication in any of the arts generally fell to the German immigrants, who established singvereins and the first orchestras, and whose community produced several painters of remarkable gifts and training, most notably Hermann Lungkwitz and his landscapes of the Hill Country, and his kinsman Richard Petri, known for his Indian portraiture. The Alsatian Theodore Gentilz also gained fame for his renderings of native people.

From the earliest days of Austin's colony, Texas had been a haven for professionals, and in the antebellum period the services of a doctor or lawyer were generally close at hand. An office call to Dr. Joseph Wood of Gonzales, who didn't like being bothered after hours, cost a dollar by day and two dollars by night. House calls into the country were fifty cents a mile by day and a dollar a mile by night; delivering a baby cost ten dollars by day and fifteen by night. Some frontier doctors were alert to the new environment in which they found themselves, and were vigilant in their observations of how the frontier impacted their practice, and how they could improve medical care. Ashbel Smith wrote a widely read tract on the treatment of yellow fever. The French doctor Theodore Léger, who had ministered to the dying Stephen F. Austin, produced a remarkable work, *Essay on the Particular Influence of Prejudice in Medicine on the Treatment of the Disease Most Common in Texas, Intermittent Fever,* which was at least a century ahead of its time.

The farther west one went in Texas, the more self-reliant a doctor had to become. When Meusebach's Germans moved into the Comanche wilderness in 1847, one of his settlers to receive a town lot in Fredericksburg was Christian Althaus, a former Prussian army doctor. As adaptable as most of the other Germans, he learned a number of Indian languages, served for a time as government agent to them, and was a signatory of the Meusebach-Comanche Treaty. He also became a saddler, merchant, and rancher, and aided by his wife Elizabeth, ran a small-scale hospital and orphanage. When he relocated his household to the even more isolated Cave Creek several miles northeast of town, he built his house directly over a spring to have cool water in which to preserve the medicines that he prepared himself from local plant life. When the government sent him to the little town of Bandera to treat an outbreak of diphtheria, he lost only one patient out of three dozen, treating them with a preparation of blackjack-oak bark, honey, and almond squeezings. Once when confronted with a patient with a mangled arm, he had to design an instrument with which to amputate it, and commission a local blacksmith to forge it before he could operate. The remarkable Dr. Althaus was rewarded with seven children and a life of ninety-four years.

Reading materials were often scarce in early Texas, but with statehood came a proliferation of newspapers and even bookstores. From the time of the first Anglo settlements in Texas it was axiomatic that a vigorous free press was indispensable to the establishment of democracy. The leaders of both the Gutiérrez-Magee Rebellion and the James Long filibuster published newspapers to record and justify (and propagandize) their insurrections. But fire begun with such heat can burn out quickly; at least seven newspapers flopped in Galveston between 1838 and 1842. Once the capital was established in Austin in 1839, some ten newspapers sprang up there during the years of independence.

Papers did not just report the news; they were for many people the only reading obtainable, and so contained poems, stories, recipes, and pieces of general interest, inspiration, or practical utility. One reported the discovery of a true unicorn in the wilds of Araby; another the discovery that insertion of lightning rods into the garden fertilized the soil with electricity, and eliminated the need for composting manure. A subscription to a typical weekly, of which there were sixty-five in Texas in 1860, was five dollars per year. A square of advertising generally cost a dollar for the first insertion and fifty cents thereafter, announcements for political candidates were ten dollars—but at least in the case of the *La Grange Intelligencer,* "no personal advertisements of an abusive nature [would be] inserted upon any terms." Advertising could become quite creative; one tailor in La Grange even waxed a little biblical in a six-verse advertisement announcing his services:

> John W. Kelly, the chiefest of ten thousand tailors speaks unto the people of the land. Hearken unto me!
>
> Bring unto me your cloth of wool and cotton and flax, and I will make you garments of strength and beauty
>
> So you may go forth from my door and hold up your heads on high, and verily you may shine with the great and mighty men of the land.
>
> And the men will praise your garments and by the ladies you will be exceedingly admired.
>
> Come ye therefore unto Kelly, all ye men, and he will make you beautiful garments,
>
> And as a reward for his labor, verily verily thou mayest feed the hungry.

A disproportionate amount of advertising space was taken, typically, with notices of runaway slaves, and one might read appeals from the high and mighty as well as the common people. "50 DOLLARS REWARD" one ad began in the *National Vindicator*. "Ran away from the subscriber on the Trinity River, Liberty County, a negro man named Frank, very black, 26 years old, 5 feet 8 or 9 inches high—the property of Mrs. Lea. Also a mulatto, named Warner, about 23 years old, 5 feet 8 or 9 inches high. The above reward will be given for apprehending and securing both, so that the owners can procure them, or 25 dollars for either." Nancy Lea was Sam Houston's mother-in-law. In time, crude woodcut illustrations began to appear in the papers, relieving the monotony of the typesetting. Runaway-slave notices typically featured either of two slugs, one of a furtive slave slinking away with his worldly goods tied in a handkerchief, hung on a stick over his shoulder; the other of a fleeing slave in a pose unnervingly similar to the modern Heisman Trophy. The first illustrated ad in an Austin newspaper featured the Capitol Hotel, the same building that still stands at Seventh and Congress.

With the defeat of Mexico came the end of state religion in Texas, and missionaries from the East began hustling to Texas to convert the heathen. Almost at once a close competition sprang up between the Methodists, who were considered much more ardent and evangelical and the great shouters, and the Baptists, whose persuasions were more gentle. That is rather the opposite of their reputations as they stand today. Revealing of the difference then was the recollection of one observer at the baptism of Sam Houston in Rocky Creek, near Independence, in the fall of 1854. His wife Margaret, a lifelong Baptist, finding herself unable to restrain her triumph after fourteen years of labor to strong-arm her husband into submission, "turned Methodist and shouted a little." Texas' senior senator, a famous roué in his wilder days, could only assimilate so much piety. When asked later if it was true that his sins had been washed away, he replied with a twinkle, "I hope so. But if they were all washed away, the Lord help the fish down below."

The Methodists' church building program dated back to January 17, 1838, when early missionary Littleton Fowler recorded in his journal, "San Augustine, Republic of Texas. To-day the cornerstone of a Methodist Episcopal Church was laid at this place, according to the usages of the Masonic Order. Between forty and fifty Masons were present, and from five to eight hundred people, about one hundred of whom were ladies. Two speeches were delivered, the first by myself, and the second by Gen. T. J. Rusk, in his clear and convincing style. The event was one of moral grandeur. This corner-stone is the first one of a Protestant Church west of the Sabine River. . . . This is only the beginning." Later that year, Fowler preached in Washington-on-the-Brazos to a large gathering, and a Mr. Gay gave a double lot for the construction of a Methodist church, but as Fowler noted darkly in his journal, "the Baptists have the frame of a church already up here." He needn't have worried; by 1860 the Methodists preached from 410 Texas churches, the Baptists from only 280.

If Littleton Fowler was the Methodists' St. Paul in Texas, Robert Alexander was his Timothy, younger, burlier, always ready to take on a challenge, especially a rowdy one like frontier Washington-on-the-Brazos. There, "a large body of gamblers and like characters had gathered in the town and held complete sway," according to resident James K. Holland. Reverend Alexander

> once engaged the room over Hatfield's saloon and announced that he would preach there on the following Sunday. The gamblers sent him word that he could not use that hall, that it was employed for other purposes, and that they would not allow him to preach in it. Mr. Alexander was a man of gigantic frame, being nearly seven feet in height, and had courage in proportion to his size. He repeated his announcement and was there on time. He walked leisurely into the hall and spoke courteously to the men there assembled. Assuming that they were there to hear him, though he knew that it was not so . . . he affected not to notice the cards that he saw them slipping into their seats behind them. He arose, and some of the more determined men in the crowd made demonstrations as if to rise also, but did not. He opened his Bible and laid it on the billiard table, then remarked that if there were those present who did not wish to hear him they could leave. None left. He then proceeded with a fire and brimstone sermon. . . . When he got through the men came forward, shook his hand and thanked him heartily, made up a purse for him, told him if he ever needed more money to call on them, and sent him on his way rejoicing.

From the beginning, the Baptist churches in Texas, to a degree even greater than the other denominations, assumed that their pastoral responsibilities included supervision over the private lives of their members, and they blended their rather crude notion of pastoring with the forms of frontier democracy. Early church records are thick with committee meetings to determine who was "in" and who was "out." Church meetings typically took place the day before Sunday worship, and parliamentary procedure was followed:

> The Church met in Conferance on Saturday before the third Lords day in June . . . and in order preceed to business. Refrence Cauld for and taken up. the cometee Report that Brother Stoe Had nothing against the Church that His non attendance was oing to His Dometic afairs the Church Received Brother Stoe excuse and the Cometee discharged The Church prefer a charge against Brother Sherwood for living in disorder Brother Sherwood taken up and tride by fellowship and Excluded from us. . . .
>
> Saturday before the third sunday in Decr . . . the Church met and in order proceeded to business. Brother Garrett came forward and acknowledged to the gilt of killing a man, being his own accuser, and [the Committee] posponed it untill our next meeting amendment to the above minute Brother Garrett acknowledges that he is sorry he had to do such a thing. . . .
>
> Saturday before the 3rd sunday in February . . . the church met and in order proceeded to business. . . . Took up the case of our two colored sisters for fighting and contradicting each other and recieved the report. The case of sister Charlotte was taken up for trial and [she] is Declared no more a member with us.

The frosty certainty with which early church leaders viewed their right to schoolmarm over the lives of followers and others was rooted more in the unlettered Second Great Awakening than it was in any biblical warrant. Nevertheless, it was the cornerstone upon which the evangelical church in Texas was built, and it influenced—and sometimes actuated—every subsequent moral debate in the state, from slavery and temperance in the nineteenth century to Prohibition, woman suffrage, and civil rights in the twentieth century to gay rights and control of public education in the twenty-first century. Early Texas Baptists did recognize something of their own disputatious nature, and one congregation's "Rules of Decorum" provided that "But one Person Shall Speek at a time, who Shall arise from his Seat, and address the moderator in order and no one Shall Speek more than three times to one Subject without Leave from the Church. No whispering,

Reeding, etc., in the time of public Speaking, and each Speaker Shall attend Strictly to the Subject in hand, without any unchristianlike Remarks on a former Speaker."

While missionary societies in the North had an important hand in encouraging the development of religion in Texas, the responsibility for the actual establishment of religious institutions was shouldered by many. Some persons who gained notice in other fields founded churches almost without credit. Abner Cook, the architect of many of Austin's Greek Revival buildings, in 1839 built its first church with his own hands, a Presbyterian one, of logs. Noah Turner Byars, whom Sam Houston had appointed as armorer to the Texas army during the revolution, was ordained as a Baptist minister in 1841 at that first church in Washington-on-the-Brazos. By the time he died at the age of eighty, he had founded no fewer than sixty churches, including the First Baptist in Waco. Frances Cox Henderson, when she declined to remove to Austin and play official hostess to her husband the governor, stayed behind in San Augustine and was singularly influential in the establishment of the Episcopal church there. She was also ahead of her times as a supporter of woman suffrage, so when the Episcopal Committee on Domestic Missions proved tardy in dispatching a minister to Texas, the San Augustine vestry conferred their authority on her to call a minister. She journeyed to Philadelphia, confronted the Episcopal hierarchy, produced her credentials, and got her minister, a shocking piece of behavior from the first lady of Texas.

The Catholic Church continued to dominate among Tejanos, and the arrival in the 1840s and '50s of Central European Catholics strengthened its presence. However, the nativist movement of the 1850s, with its anti-Catholic bent, increased animosity toward immigrants. Dissenting offshoots of the main Protestant denominations could also feel the sting of discrimination. The so-called Restoration Movement that began in Appalachia and became known as the Campbellite Church and later the Church of Christ, had only two well-known converts in early Texas, Collin McKinney, who signed the Declaration of Independence, and José María Carbajal, who had lived with the family of the sect's founder for a number of years. Lacking any organizational framework, they spread their vision as Baptist dissenters through part-time preachers, with little success at first. As one Nacogdoches resident remembered, "In 1851, a Mr. Pollock, a young lawyer from Kentucky, living in Nacogdoches, had a college mate, a minister of the Camolite [sic] (Christian) church, who came to visit him. Mr. Pollock in an effort to have his friend preach a sermon in Nacogdoches made application to the several churches of the town to use their church & was promptly refused." District Judge and former mayor Adolphus Sterne, who as a German Jew and nominal Catholic had a passing familiarity with the locals' religious prejudices, allowed Pollock's friend to preach a sermon in the courthouse one evening after the court had adjourned. (History is not without some sense of ironic justice: the courthouse where the Campbellite sermon was preached had been erected as the Methodist church, but they defaulted on the loan and sold the structure to the county. The itinerant preacher later found other fellow Campbellites in the village of Palestine— the precursors of what became the Church of Christ in Texas.)

Religion in frontier Texas was intricately bound up in the notion of temperance. Nacogdoches boasted more than a hundred members of the Sons of Temperance, but according to one of them, only "a minority remained entirely faithful to their pledge." The wily Sam Houston, whose spectacular alcoholism had scandalized refined Texans almost as much as it had Tennesseeans, addressed the first meeting of the Temperance Union in the new town of Houston, but himself declined to take the pledge. "Do as I say," he intoned, "not as I have done."

FORTY

STILL MORE FIGHTING

BOTH AS A NATION AND AS A STATE, TEXAS' HISTORY OF treachery and violence toward natives on the frontier, and the vast distances between settlements, invited opportunistic mayhem by Indians. The army activated a chain of new posts from 1848, beginning at Fort Worth and moving south and west through Forts Graham, Gates, Croghan, Martin Scott, Lincoln, Inge, and Duncan, with McIntosh and Ringgold on the Rio Grande. After 1851 they placed a second picket line of forts deeper into the Indian frontier at Forts Belknap, Cooper, Phantom Hill, Chadbourne, McKavett, Terrett, Lancaster, and Clark, in addition to four more in the trans-Pecos.

Duty in these isolated posts was rough, and stock thefts were costly and regular. Whether one was pursuing Comanche raiders or trying to contain banditry on the Rio Grande, the frequent droughts and dry brush of the Southwest proved expensive in keeping the cavalry regiments supplied with mounts. In 1855 the U.S. secretary of war, the former Mississippi senator Jefferson Davis, facing a tightened budget owing to the costs of the Mexican War and subsequent settlement payments, undertook an experiment in cavalry support. On May 13, 1856, the stores ship USS *Supply* offloaded at the Texas port of Indianola a cargo of thirty-three bawling camels, acquired for $12,000 from various North African markets and casbahs, plus five handlers, almost as exotic as the camels to local eyes: two Turks and three Arabs. Under the oversight of Major H. C. Wayne, the extraordinary caravan marched through Victoria on their way west to establish a new post named Camp Verde, about fifty miles northwest of San Antonio. After months of experiments with the beasts that took them deep into the trans-Pecos, Major Wayne issued a favorable report on their utility. They ate almost anything, drank little, and could carry over a quarter of a ton of supplies each. Of course, they stank and could be difficult to handle, but their positive attributes were so considerable that a second shipload of forty-one camels was also stationed at Camp Verde, receiving assignments such as the survey of a wagon road to New Mexico.

In addition to the army, Texas Ranger units were beefed up, and the companies took some pride in their ability to travel light and live off the land.

Captain Jesse Billingsley, despite the fact that one of his hands was permanently crippled at the battle of San Jacinto, "supported eighty men on the frontier with the wild game of the forest, and clothed them with the skins of the wild animals slaughtered, and we were only chargeable to the government for one sack of coffee and one sack of salt."

As Anglo ranchers moved into the Brush Country of the Nueces Strip, many of them acculturated or, like Mifflin Kenedy, married into the Hispanic culture. That did not end Hispanic resentment of the previous forty years of history, however, most recently including the loss of legitimate rights under Spanish land grants. One measure of revenge was to steal cattle from the prospering Anglo ranches, which became a sizable source of cross-border traffic. One of the boldest operators was Juan Nepomuceno Cortina, who had a special spleen against King and Kenedy. Cheno Cortina's legend began in 1847, in an incident which may or may not have actually happened, when he was hired to drive a string of mules. He murdered the owner and sold the animals to the American army. It is known that he fought with Arista in the early American-blood-on-American-soil engagements in 1846, but left the army to make a career in rustling cattle north of the river, driving them across and selling them. Because of his prominence in the valley community—his mother owned a huge estate outside Brownsville—he was able to sneer at both of the American grand juries that indicted him.

On July 13, 1859, Cortina saw the Anglo sheriff of Brownsville arrest and browbeat a former employee of his for drunkenness. Outraged, he shot the sheriff in the shoulder and left with the man. On September 28 he returned at the head of a group of about sixty mounted men, thundering through the streets, shouting, "Viva, México!" and "Death to Americans!" He took the city, shooting five white men, one of them the jailer. In a couple of days calmer heads prevailed, as José María Carbajal, long a presence in Texas-Mexican relations, talked him into withdrawing to his mother's hacienda. He did so defiantly, publishing an angry manifesto vowing vengeance to those who abused his people. Once he was out of town the local Anglos regained some courage, and in that very Texan way, formed a posse that called themselves the Brownsville Tigers, snagged one of Cortina's men, found a couple of small cannons, and set out for his hideout. Cortina's men scattered them, and before long a small army of disaffected Hispanics, both Mexican and Tejano, gathered at the hacienda, which sported a Mexican flag. In early November a Texas Ranger company arrived, hanged the prisoner, and attacked Cortina again, but was driven off. With Texas now the sovereign soil of the United States, the army had to act, and Major Samuel P.

Heintzelman, with 165 troops, in company with another Ranger company under Rip Ford, was sent to the area.

Cortina's ranks had swelled to perhaps four hundred as he moved upstream, spreading terror as he approached Rio Grande City. There Heintzelman administered a severe licking, killing about sixty Mexicans and forcing Cortina across the river. He soon reappeared, attempting to capture the King and Kenedy riverboat *Ranchero,* but was prevented from doing so when Ford's Rangers crossed into Mexico and drove him off. The Texas Military District now had a new commander, Colonel Robert E. Lee of Virginia, who arrived on the scene with a threat to invade in force if Mexico did not bring Cortina to heel. Such an action proved unnecessary, as Cortina holed up in the Burgos Mountains for several months.

The situation on the northwest Indian frontier was no better, though it was often not the Indians who were culpable. While Sam Houston stood in the Senate and thundered against the federal government's treachery toward Native Americans, his own Texans behind his back gave their approval to the expulsion of the Brazos Valley tribes, many of the same that Houston had concluded treaties with in 1843, and whom all their neighbors credited with being peaceable. The real issues were the land they lived on, and the fact that they were Indians. At least, unlike with the case of the Cherokees in 1839, the state of Texas intended to house and feed them. As concurred between the army and the legislature, General Randolph B. Marcy and the Texas Indian superintendent Robert S. Neighbors selected four leagues of land (18,576 acres) between Forts Graham and Belknap.

Neighbors was as tough and experienced as one could be for such a task. As a onetime quartermaster for the Republic of Texas army, he knew how to provision a large group of people; he knew about hard living, having been one of Adrian Woll's hostages snatched from San Antonio and imprisoned in Mexico. He had Indian experience, having formerly been a U.S. special Indian agent, taking part in treaty councils with Comanches, and was present at the Meusebach treaty. In 1854 Neighbors and a small staff supervised the relocation of some 2,000 members of miscellaneous Indian tribes, from the Caddoes on the east to the Tonkawas on the west, including Wacos and Anadarkos, to the new reservation. A second reservation was opened nearby to house the Penateka Comanches of the Hill Country. Some six hundred acres was planted in crops, and the Brazos Valley Indians were enlisted as scouts for the army to track hostiles.

It was peaceful only at first. The army's inescapable antipathy toward any Indians led to troops inciting local ranchers against the natives. Minor depredations in the area were always ascribed to the Brazos tribes, although it is possible that some were really committed by the Penatekas, who were jealous of their better standing with the military. The catalyst for a conflagration took the form of thirty-three-year-old John Robert Baylor, an implacable Indian hater who had grown up partly in Fort Gibson, Indian Territory. He secured a position as agent to the Penateka Comanches, but Neighbors fired him for his belligerent attitude. Baylor then made getting rid of Neighbors and the Indians his special project, organizing mass meetings and collecting an Indian-hunting militia of several hundred, and further disseminating his views by editing a Jacksboro newspaper he called the *White Man*. The attitude became so threatening that by 1858 even Sam Houston, who had consistently defended the Indians' rights, was petitioning for their removal to a safer place.

In December the situation began to collapse. Nineteen Indians who had been given a pass to hunt in Palo Pinto County were attacked in their sleep; seven were killed and four wounded. Troops from Fort Belknap occupied the reservation, while Neighbors summoned a Ranger company. He also learned the identity of the attackers, but the local ranchers would not indict them. On May 23, 1859, Baylor materialized at the reservation with a posse of two to three hundred, demanding to take away certain Indians and claiming that if the soldiers opened fire to prevent him, his men would fight. When the staff and soldiers prepared for battle, Baylor pulled back to reconsider, killing an old Indian man and a woman who was working her garden as he left the area. The infuriated natives stormed out after Baylor and his mob as the army, who had no jurisdiction outside the agency, watched. The Indians overhauled Baylor at a nearby ranch and attacked, killing two before withdrawing. Neighbors hastily made arrangements to house them and the Comanches with the Wichita Indians on a reserve in the Indian Territory. In a tense and vigilant march that began on July 31, Neighbors delivered them safely beyond the Red River, writing to his wife of his relief that they were safely "out of the land of the Philistines." Neighbors, however, was himself gunned down by an Indian-hating fanatic when he returned to Fort Belknap.

The delicate balance between providing justice for the native inhabitants and keeping the frontier safe for settlement was one that Sam Houston tried hard to maintain. That had been his very first job as a twenty-five-year-old Cherokee Indian agent in Tennessee, and had guided his Indian relations while president of Texas. In the U.S. Senate he was removed from the action, but when he became governor of Texas in 1859 he refused to pay Ranger companies for Indian-hunting excursions, and was wise to the game that white outlaws often played, of staining their skin and donning buckskins and feathers before committing crimes. This was a well-known tactic. One editor of a central Texas newspaper reported the facts of a so-called Indian raid, but allowed that he did not believe it was Indians. If the perpetrators were not white when they did it, he wrote, they could be made so by taking them to a creek and using a little soap on them.

Houston was a realist, however, and knew that Indians could be pitiless when their fury was aroused. Late in 1860 he directed Texas Ranger Captain Lawrence Sullivan Ross to raise a new company of men in the Waco area to move out to the edge of the frontier and attempt to quell a spate of legitimate depredations. Sul Ross had lately been under command of another Ranger officer on a similar mission, whose lack of success had caused considerable public censure. Houston believed that Ross would show more initiative, and he was correct. After hostile Comanches raided through Jack, Parker, and Palo Pinto counties, north of the former Texas reserve, Ross and forty of his men gave chase and overran a large village of about 150 warriors and perhaps three times that many dependents on the Pease River, surprising them as they were loading up their winter supply of buffalo meat. The bulk of the Comanches bolted when Ross attacked and captured 370 horses and mules, nineteen of which were branded as U.S. Cavalry mounts. Their retreat was covered by a number of warriors who stuck and fought. About a dozen of this rear guard were killed, and after the fleeing Comanches opened up some distance, the chief ordered the survivors to mount and ride after them. As he did so he pulled a woman up onto his horse behind him. Sul Ross himself gave chase, firing after them, but saw no effect until the mortally wounded woman fell from the horse five hundred yards later, pulling the chief off with her. The bullet had passed through her body and wounded the chief as well. Dismounted, the chief loosed a stream of arrows, one of which hit Ross' horse, and Ross returned fire until he struck the chief in the arm.

Ross sent for his Mexican cook-interpreter, Anton, asked who the man was, and learned that it was the chief of the band, Peta Nocona. "Tell him then that if he will surrender he will not be shot anymore."

After a brief exchange, Anton relayed, "You tell the white captain that when I am dead, I will surrender, but not before, and not to him." Nocona then fastened a rope to the tree and to a lance, hurling it at Ross, and began singing his death song.

"That is the bravest man I ever saw," said Ross. "I can't shoot as brave a man as that."

Unknown to Ross, his cook, Antonio Martínez, in his youth had been Nocona's personal slave, and had witnessed the chief kill his mother as she pled for their lives. What Ross could not do, Martínez quickly did. Ross ran up to where the chief fell, "and he looked up at him and breathed about three times, and between breaths gritted his teeth . . . and died."

Ross joined the pursuit of the other Indians, and when he returned saw one of his lieutenants, Tom Kelliher, trying to subdue one of the Comanche women. Ross rode over swiftly. "Tom, this is a white woman." Anton identified her as the wife of the dead chief, and as one witness described it, she "paraded around over Nocona a bit," and was later taken to Camp Cooper for identification.

An elderly Isaac Parker, survivor of the Parker's Fort raid a quarter century before, called, thinking it might be one of his relatives. He told the wild-eyed captive, "My niece's name was Cynthia Ann," at which the woman became excited and slapped her chest. "Cynthia Ann! Cynthia Ann!" It was all the English she remembered.

FORTY-ONE

SLAVERY AND SECESSION

TREATMENT OF INDIANS WAS NOT THE GREATEST ISSUE
that divided Sam Houston from the people he represented in the federal Senate. As the 1850s wore on, the cotton-belt South clamored with increasing
fervor to secede from the Union, and Houston fought with every weapon and
guile he could muster to foil them, until at the last he was the only Southern
senator (he considered Bell's Tennessee a border state) who publicly proclaimed himself a Unionist. His message, oft repeated, was that the powerful
planters in the South, by continuously agitating for expansion of slave territory and wrongly accusing the federal government of plotting against it, were
as guilty of creating a dangerous environment as were the radical abolitionists in the North. The difficult and painful issue of slavery could be worked
out, he insisted, if the troublemakers of both extremes could be muzzled.

Exponents of the Texas slavocracy, however, were past listening, and
many were longing for the reopening of the African slave trade. The importation of new slaves from Africa had been illegal since 1808, but opposition
to the ban was so widespread that some remarkably clever schemes were
hatched to circumvent it. One Mrs. M. J. Watson, for instance, aware of the
army's ongoing experimentation with transport camels, attempted to enter
Galveston Harbor in October 1858, declaring her cargo to be camels, which
was at best a partial truth. Alert port authorities, suspicious that Mrs. Watson was trying to use the camels to mask the reeking odor of a slave ship, refused her permission to unload. Her ship sat in Galveston Harbor for two
months before she dumped several dozen camels on the beach and departed
for Cuba—the Caribbean clearinghouse for the slave trade.

Passage of the Kansas-Nebraska Act, and Houston's opposition to it,
sharpened proslavery and pro-Union positions in Texas, and the move toward secession gained momentum. Texas' senior senator found himself in
the thankless position of attacking slavery in the South even as he defended
it in the North. In 1855 Sam Houston entered the high stronghold of the
abolitionist movement, Boston, and on George Washington's birthday delivered a window-rattling speech to a jammed Tremont Hall. Interspersing
jokes and homilies to keep the audience laughing, he pointed out that it was

only their lucky flood of immigrant labor to exploit that made it possible for them to free the capital formerly tied up in slaves, and build their industrial economy. Without foreign labor, "you would have had Negroes at work . . . to this day, just as sure as the world." Slavery, he said, was not nearly so profitable as Southern planters believed, and if the South had an influx of cheap labor such as they had enjoyed in the North, the Peculiar Institution would topple of its own dead weight. He then cut his argument the opposite way, that if suddenly abolition became law, the slave "would be cast into the streets. No one would take care of him. . . . You might call him free, but he would be an object of want and wretchedness." He would, in short, be in a similar condition to the Negro in the North.

Whatever solution they found to the admittedly thorny problem, dis-union must remain unthinkable. "Our country is too glorious," he con-cluded, "too magnificent, too sublime in its future prospects, to permit domestic jars . . . to produce a wreck of this mighty vessel of State. Let us hold onto it, and guide it; let us give it in charge to men who will care for the whole people, who will . . . reconcile conflicting interests. This can be done, and let us not despair and break up the Union." The applause was thunder-ous, and back in Texas, while the effort was not enough to forgive his Kansas-Nebraska treason, he received favorable notices in the newspapers.

If anything, Houston's campaign to keep the Union intact became lone-lier, and Texas secessionists struck to remove him from national notice. His Senate term did not expire until 1859, but in 1857 the Texas legislature ex-pressed its disapproval and announced that he would not be returned to that body when his term ended. It was an unprecedented insult, which Houston answered defiantly by running for governor in 1857—without resigning his Senate seat. "So now the whip cracks," he wrote a friend, "& the longest pole will bring down the persimmon. The people want excitement, and I had as well give it as any one." He campaigned furiously on borrowed money and accepted free transportation from the purveyor of a patent plow. From May 27 until August 1, he traveled over 1,500 miles, often camping at night by the roadside, delivering two- to four-hour speeches in forty-two cities and towns. Shaken, the secessionists were spurred to assemble what today would be called a rapid response team, appointing two of their sharpest stump speakers to shadow the old lion and address competing rallies every-where he stopped. They were Williamson Oldham, the editor of the fiery proslavery *Austin State Gazette,* and their biggest gun, state senator Louis T. Wigfall, a South Carolina native who had been attacking Houston and the Union ever since he arrived in Texas in 1848.

On the stump Houston taunted Oldham for coming to Texas after fleeing a bank fraud scandal in Arkansas, where he had risen to political prominence. And he capitalized on Wigfall's record of having killed two men in his native South Carolina—one in a duel and one in a fight—by referring to him as "a murderer named Wiggletail." Houston's actual opponent in the race, Lieutenant Governor Hiram Runnels, was all but forgotten. He was a poor speaker and made few appearances, but on election day he handed Houston the only defeat he ever suffered in a one-on-one contest, 38,000 to 23,000. Houston returned to the Senate for the 1858 session, with the Texas delegation in flux. Rejected by both the voters and the legislature, he was heckled by proslavery senators who demanded whether, at last, he was not ready to represent the wishes of his people. Houston's response was to sport a jaguar-skin waistcoat, and admonish that according to the Bible, the leopard cannot change his spots.

Luckily for Houston he did not have to suffer the murderer Wiggletail's presence in the Senate when the legislature elected him in 1858; Houston left Washington, D.C., in March 1859, for the last time. Almost at once he began receiving a flurry of letters urging him to run again for governor, some of them from people who had voted against him two years before and wanted a chance to repent. Kansas Territory was in bloody chaos, as he had predicted, and there seemed to be an uptick in Unionist prospects in Texas—even the state Democratic Party, in their 1859 convention, turned back a proposal to advocate reopening the African slave trade. Governor Runnels was vulnerable, and although he was a passionate exponent of the slaveocracy, he had shown himself unable to quell violence either along the Rio Grande or on the Indian frontier. Three months after his Senate term ended Houston announced his candidacy, but this time he meant to run a smarter campaign. He gave exactly one speech, in Nacogdoches, and he joked about the Kansas-Nebraska Act, quoting prominent Southern politicians who admitted that it was a fraud and a snare, and the South stepped right into it. Houston identified himself as the only Southern senator who had opposed it, "and for that you whipped me like a cur dog" in the previous election. "If I was wrong," he wagged, "I own it and take it all back, and if you were wrong I forgive you. So we will start even again." When the votes were counted, Houston defeated Runnels by a margin almost equal to his previous defeat, and became the only Unionist elected governor of a Southern state on the eve of the Civil War—a post of unprecedented challenge.

Six times in his last two years in the Senate, he had sought to unite North and South by proposing military imposition of a protectorate over

Mexico, whose two dozen coups and revolutions in as many years left the border in constant turmoil. Failing in that, he intended now to use his governorship to consolidate state power in his own hands, and when the rest of the South seceded, to lead Texas back into separate nationhood. Federal troops had been stationed on the frontier as Indian protection, he said at his inaugural, "but they are Infantry. . . . When depredations are committed by the Indians, they escape." Houston sought from the legislature a large increase in the force of Texas Rangers, and when he received that authority, he appointed as recruiters strong Union supporters, such as Jacob Kuechler, a farmer, forester, and founder of the experimental socialist utopia of Bettina near the Llano River, who knew to enlist appropriately sympathetic men into their companies. If secession occurred, Houston counted on having a well-armed and loyal cavalry under his command. He also turned to his trusted friend Swante Swenson, the Swedish immigrant merchant who had furnished the Governor's Mansion. Swenson had expanded his business into land and railroad investments and become enormously wealthy, perhaps the largest landowner in Texas at that time. He was also a committed Unionist, and he agreed to use his freighting operation, with which he had been supplying U.S. Army posts on the frontier, to provision Houston's loyalist militia.

The Republican nomination of Abraham Lincoln aroused a storm of indignation across the South. A shady organization known as the Knights of the Golden Circle began to appear in Texas; ultimately they organized thirty-two chapters, known as "castles." They had as their aim the extension of slavery by means of filibuster and conquest over Mexico and the Caribbean, and thus to corner the production of such tropical produce as cotton, rice, sugar, and coffee. They tried to curry favor with Houston, knowing of his previous proposals to impose an American protectorate over Mexico, but he refused their overtures and they accomplished little.

Lincoln's election was rendered inevitable when the Democratic Party fractured and fielded two opponents, and the Constitutional Union Party (for whose nomination Houston finished second) fielded still another. Knowing that secession must follow if Lincoln became president, Houston rose from a sickbed to deliver one more impassioned appeal for reason: "What is there that is free that we have not? Are our rights invaded and no Government ready to protect them? No! Are our institutions [slavery] wrested from us and others foreign to our taste forced upon us? No! Has our property been taken from us . . . ? No, none of these. . . . I ask not the defeat of sectionalism by sectionalism, but by nationality. The Union is worth more than Mr. Lincoln, and if the battle is to be fought for the Constitution, let us fight it in the Union and for the sake of the Union." The irony, as he was painfully aware, was that Lincoln's position on slavery was virtually identical to his own. He then undertook a hastily conceived speaking tour and delivered similar pleas in seven different towns in twelve days, to no avail. Lincoln was elected on November 6, and a few weeks later South Carolina withdrew from the Union, followed by six other states of the Deep South. On December 3, 1860, Texas newspapers printed notices of a special election to be held on January 8 to elect delegates to a convention to decide the secession of Texas, to meet in Austin on January 28. The entire proceeding was extralegal. State supreme court justice James H. Bell gave Houston cover, registering the opinion that only the legislature could call such a convention, and the governor resisted a barrage of insistence that he call a special session of the legislature to do so.

The battle over secession also affected the social life of the capital. Theretofore the Governor's Mansion, in a custom begun by Marshall and Lucadia Pease, had been regularly opened to receive callers. But as mobs paraded by torchlight and at least one attempt on Houston's life was foiled, Margaret Lea Houston suspended the practice. It was true that she had six rowdy children to supervise (the eldest, Sam Jr., was away at military boarding school) and she was just entering her eighth and final pregnancy when they moved in. Her nerves were delicate and she was often unwell, but for the mansion door to be closed to callers went down ill in Austin and contributed to her—and his—unpopularity.

The election of delegates took place without Houston's sanction; many Unionists boycotted the balloting for the Secession Convention, which therefore was dominated, seven out of ten, by slave owners, although they constituted a small minority of the overall population. Houston delayed calling the legislature until January 21, only a week before the convention was to meet, but most of the legislators were already in Austin because they were also delegates. They disappointed Houston, who hoped that they would disavow the gathering, but instead they offered the facilities of the capitol to host it.

The Secession Convention was organized by the state's leading fire-eaters, including Oldham and Stephen F. Austin's nephew, Guy Bryan, but none took a back seat to a state supreme court justice, Oran M. Roberts, a South Carolinian and open devotee of Houston's early archenemy, John C. Calhoun. Despite the fact that it was Houston who had appointed Roberts to his first district judgeship in 1844, the governor's antipathy toward him was revealed in one striking incident that took place after the convention was called to order and Roberts was elected to preside. One day as they met in the House chamber on the second floor of the capitol, Houston sat working and fuming in his first-floor office. A caller knocked on the door, which proved to be James Wilson "Smoky" Henderson, who had been governor-for-a-month after Hansborough Bell resigned and went to Congress. He had since entered private law practice, and he asked Houston to issue a pardon to one Mary Monroe, who had served three years of a six-year term for murder. Houston recalled the case and asked if she had not been fairly tried and convicted, and her appeal denied.

"Yes," replied Henderson, "it was the ablest opinion ever written by Justice Roberts."

"Oran Milo Roberts? That man who is leading that mob upstairs?" Houston paused darkly. "Well, then, I'll pardon her. No citizen shall be deprived of liberty by such a fellow." And he proved as good as his word.

Some peacemakers within the convention, notably moderate Unionist but Southern sympathizer John Henninger Reagan, who had resigned his seat in Congress and returned to Texas to attend, opened private talks with Houston to narrow the gulf between them. The old governor formulated yet another fallback position: he wished only that the forms of law be followed. If the people of Texas ratified secession, he would accede to their will. On February 1, 1861, it was Houston who presided over the final vote of the Convention, 166 in favor of secession, 7 opposed. The vote was oral and alphabetical; when James W. Throckmorton, a three-term state representative whose district included the largely pro-Union towns of Denton and McKinney, gave his précis of reasons for voting no, it elicited an audible hiss from the gallery. "Mr. President," he intoned defiantly, "when the rabble hiss, well may patriots tremble." The convention set the date of February 23 for the popular referendum, but they then surprised Houston. Before adjourning four days later, they created a Committee of Public Safety, which dispatched a Texas delegation to the forming Confederate government in Montgomery, Alabama, and authorized the seizure of United States property in Texas, including forts and supplies.

Bridling at this, Houston swung into action, hoping that the state troops he had been recruiting could get control of the federal stores before they were impounded by the rebels. He sent a confidential messenger to the U.S. Army commander General David E. Twiggs, in San Antonio, warning him of the impending action and asking whether he would be willing to accept a receipt for his supplies from state Rangers first. Before anything could come of it Ben McCulloch, Houston's old artillerist from San Jacinto who had gone over to the secessionists, rode into San Antonio at the head of several hundred militia and compelled Twiggs to surrender all federal forces in Texas—about a tenth of the entire U.S. Army, along with supplies worth some $3 million, on February 15—a week before the referendum. Twiggs was the second-ranking officer in the service, decorated for action in Mexico; he had written asking for instructions, but upon receiving none asked to be relieved of command, orders that arrived, ironically, the day after he surrendered. Twiggs was also from Georgia, sympathetic to secession, and he soon accepted a billet in the Confederate Army as he was stripped of his former honors.

The secession ordinance sailed through the referendum by three to one: 46,000 to 14,000. By the time the Secession Convention reconvened on March 2—the twenty-fifth anniversary of the Texas Declaration of Independence—the Confederate government had already accepted Texas. The referendum vote was accepted on March 5 and on their own authority the convention passed a requirement that all state officers—including, and especially, Houston—swear an oath of loyalty to the new regime. He received their ultimatum at the mansion on the night of March 15 and was informed that he was required to swear his allegiance at noon the next day. He spent the sleepless night stalking the upstairs hall in his stocking feet, stopping to write notes or kneeling to pray. In the morning he met his wife downstairs and said, "Margaret, I will never do it." In consequence, the convention declared the office of governor vacant, and swore in the lieutenant governor, Ed Clark of Marshall, as his successor. Houston made no speech but published a response, declaring the acts of the convention null and void, but vowing that he would maintain himself in office only as long as he could peaceably do so. The Civil War would not begin in Texas, by his hand.

In Washington, the newly inaugurated Lincoln followed Sam Houston's plight with keen interest. He had long been aware of his dedication to the Union; indeed, Lincoln's famous "House Divided" speech that brought him to national attention was in pertinent part a reworking of a "Nation Divided" speech that Houston delivered to the U.S. Senate at the time Lincoln was departing from his one term in the House. Acting command of U.S. forces in Texas had passed to Colonel Carlos Waite, a New Yorker with forty years in the army. He received orders to fortify himself at the port of Indianola and "communicate as freely as practical with General Houston." The governor's reply was firm. "Allow me most respectfully to decline any such assistance of the United States Government, and to most earnestly protest against the concentration of troops in fortifications in Texas, and request that you remove all such troops out of the State." Undeterred, Lincoln pressed into service one George Giddings, a Texas postmaster who was in Washington to lobby for continuation in office. Lincoln gave him a letter to deliver to Houston, which he did, banging on the door of the Governor's Mansion at one o'clock in the morning in mid-March. Finally Lincoln had his secretary of state, William Seward, bring him William Lander, a Californian ready to depart for home. The deposed governor was on the road to give a speech in Belton when he was overtaken by this letter, and had his driver turn for home.

That night Houston assembled four close friends in the mansion library, both loyalists such as James Throckmorton, and secessionist William Rogers, for whom Houston had named his third son but who became infected with the southern fever. He read them Lincoln's offer: a major generalcy and fifty thousand troops to maintain himself in office and hold Texas in the Union. Only Ben Epperson, who had supported a Houston presidency at the convention of the Constitution Union Party, advised him to accept. "Gentlemen," said Houston, "I had resolved to act in this matter on your advice, but if I was ten years younger I would not." He burned the letter in the fireplace.

"Our people are going to war to perpetuate slavery," Houston had recently told John Reagan, "and the first gun fired will be the knell of slavery." That gun was fired on Fort Sumter, South Carolina, on April 12, 1861. In Texas, while slaves had increased both in numbers and as a percentage of the population, more than two-thirds of Texas households owned no slaves whatsoever in 1850, and that figure increased to nearly three-quarters by 1860. And of those slave owners, only 10 percent, or about 2,100 planters, owned twenty or more. Yet it was the large-scale planters who produced 90 percent of the cotton and gave rise to the cultural stereotype of the Southern plantation. By the demographics, the Civil War can be seen as similar to most wars: it was the project of an economic elite undertaken for the enhancement of their own power and wealth, who sold the war to a well-meaning but gullible populace by appealing to their patriotism and conservative instincts.

FORTY-TWO

A LITTLE TERROR

UNIONIST SYMPATHY IN TEXAS WAS STRONG ENOUGH TO have elected Sam Houston governor in 1859, but over the following year that sentiment was increasingly cowed by the violence and illogic of the most ardent secessionists. Although the referendum on leaving the Union passed by a wide margin, that was not true in all parts of the state. In North Texas, in a tier of counties along the Red River, it did not gain a majority in seven counties, and barely passed in six others. In central Texas it failed to pass in Austin, Bastrop, and Georgetown, and barely passed in San Antonio. The referendum also failed in most of the western counties with large German populations. It was no coincidence that those areas were among the first to feel the weight of vigilantes.

Proslavery mob intimidation actually began long before the South left the Union. In 1860, mercantiles in North Texas began selling unstable new phosphor-tipped "prairie matches," which in the 110-degree July heat began to spontaneously combust in their packets. The result was serious fires in several towns, including Waxahachie, Kaufman, and Denton; the largest conflagration destroyed much of the central business district in Dallas. The ardently secessionist young editor of the *Dallas Herald*, Charles Pryor, attributed the fires to arson by abolitionists who, he charged in a letter to a fellow separatist editor in Austin, were united in a plot "to devastate, with fire and assassination, the whole of Northern Texas, and when it was reduced to a helpless condition, a general revolt of slaves . . . was to come off." Pryor's letter proved more incendiary than the prairie matches, as it was reprinted prominently throughout the state, and vigilante groups were organized to deal with the so-called Texas Troubles. Slavery was not widely supported in Lamar County next to the Red River, and young Pryor wrote the newspaper editor in the county seat of Bonham, "You are in as much danger as we are. Be on your guard, and make these facts known by issuing extras." In the mass hysteria that followed, hapless slaves were whipped into confessing before they were lynched, as the regular authorities looked the other way in the interest, they thought, of public safety. Exact figures are impossible to compile; at least thirty and possibly one hundred blacks and suspected white sympathizers were strung up.

Pryor was only twenty-eight when he began publishing the *Dallas Herald*. At the other end of the political spectrum was the *San Antonio Express*, whose editor, James P. Newcomb, was only twenty-four, born in Canada but a Texan from the age of two. His career in journalism began with a printing apprenticeship and work on five different newspapers in the San Antonio area. Newcomb was a vociferous Unionist. Secessionist vigilantes destroyed his press in May 1861. He escaped to Mexico and then California, returning to Texas with the California Column a year later. Pryor was rewarded for his alarmist publishing with an appointment as Texas secretary of state during the Confederacy; after Newcomb resettled in San Antonio in 1867 he held the same post during the Reconstruction regime, but bitterness against him and the pro-Republican newspapers he either founded or edited (including the forerunner of the *San Antonio Light*) prevented his election to any of the offices he ran for.

Also in North Texas, the border mixing of Unionist sentiment and slave state became a quagmire for different religious denominations. William Mumford Baker's Presbyterians were not the only ones thrown into schism by war. The Baptists in Texas were already in some disarray over the disagreements between the regular church and the antimissionary, primitive congregations such as that at Parker's Fort, devastated by Indians. Slavery complicated the rift, as the mainstream church declared that slaveholders could not be missionaries. Baptists in the South, who among other interpretations extrapolated St. Paul's instructions on the care of slaves into biblical sanction for the institution, split and formed the Southern Baptist Convention as early as 1845. By 1860 there was little dissension among Texas Baptists in support of slavery. Other denominations, especially from the border regions, found themselves in a hard contest. When the Missouri Conference of the Methodist Episcopal Church divided over slavery, it left one of its Texas circuit-riding missionaries, Anthony Bewley, in a hard spot. He refused to recognize the authority of the new Southern Methodists with their allegiance to slavery. He was well known as an abolitionist about his church, several miles south of Fort Worth.

As melodramatic and overwrought as the "Texas Troubles" were, local extremists produced a letter, which may well have been a forgery, implicating Bewley in a John Brown–like scheme to liberate Texas slaves. Bewley, a fifty-four-year-old father of eight, fled the area, but was overhauled by a Texas posse in Missouri and returned to Fort Worth. There he was lynched and left to hang for a day, was buried until he decomposed, and then his bones were displayed on the roof of a local storehouse as toys for children. The Northern Methodists, believing that Texas at least for the time being was beyond reach, withdrew from further missionary effort.

Violence in North Texas reached its zenith in Cooke County on the Red River, and in its seat, Gainesville. Security there was entrusted to militia brigadier William Hudson, who in a surrealistic extension of the logic that those who were not for him were against him, issued a call for volunteers to round up evildoers—and then ordered the arrest of every able-bodied man who did not volunteer. On the morning of October 1, 1862, Hudson's right-hand man, Colonel James G. Bourland, who was one of the largest slave-holders in a county in which 90 percent of the people held no slaves, arrested 150 luckless souls who were accused of insurrection or treason. Bourland handpicked slaveholding juries and mandated that conviction need not be unanimous, only by majority vote. Seven were sentenced to hang before patience with legal procedure gave out and fourteen more were lynched. The following week the officer who assisted Bourland in the trial, Colonel William C. Young of the 11th Texas Cavalry, was assassinated. Several of the previous defendants were tried again, and nineteen more were condemned and executed by Young's son, Captain Jim Young, making a death toll of forty in Gainesville. William Young's killer was not among them, however. Jim Young tracked that party down and supervised some of his slaves in hanging him, and then for good measure he killed the editor of the *Sherman Patriot*, E. Junius Foster, who had expressed his approbation of William Young's murder. Before the madness subsided five more suspected traitors were strung up in Decatur and five more in Sherman, where many more would have died but for the vocal intervention of James Throckmorton, one of the few legislators who had voted against secession.

The mass executions that became known collectively as the Great Hanging at Gainesville were acts of barbarity breathtaking even by the standard of rebel ardor. Confederate President Jefferson Davis was chagrined enough to dismiss General Paul Hébert, Texas' military commander, and he abruptly ceased calling for Northern authorities to investigate a similar incident, in which suspected rebel sympathizers were judicially murdered in Missouri. Most Texans cheered, however. The legislature reimbursed Bourland's troops, and Governor Francis Lubbock spoke in favor of Hudson's actions against the draft opponents.

Most committees of public safety contented themselves with burning out the homes and businesses of suspected Unionists and forcing them to flee. Noah Smithwick, the smithy who repaired the cannon at Gonzales, was turned out of his sawmill and sold his only remaining asset, a slave, to Houston for half price to get traveling money for California. Not atypical was the case of Reese Hughes, an old hand in northeast Texas and a onetime participant in the Regulator-Moderator War of the 1840s. Once his anti-secession views became known, Confederate authorities seized his Cass County iron furnace and used it for war production. Hughes lived nearly thirty years after the Confederate defeat but never recovered financially.

Sometimes the authorities found ways to compel unwilling service, quite apart from Bourland's volunteer-or-hang administration of border security. David Owen Dodd was born and raised in Victoria, before moving to Arkansas with his family shortly before war broke out. During the Union army's move across that state, Dodd's father got his family safely behind rebel lines, but the only way Dodd could obtain a pass back into Union-held territory to help his father tie up his business was to agree to report back on Union troop strength and disposition. Caught with a Morse-coded message in the sole of his shoe, Dodd manfully refused to name his co-conspirators and was hanged on January 8, 1864—at seventeen one of the youngest, perhaps the youngest, spy executed in the war.

The fervor for secession also ended or altered the careers of several moderate politicians. In Austin, for instance, Unionist Congressman Andrew Jackson Hamilton was said to have fled the city to his brother's ranch west of town, and when a mob followed, he took refuge in a limestone sinkhole on the property, which is still known as Hamilton's Pool. His day also came during Reconstruction.

The advent of war divided the large German community. Many of those who settled in the cotton country had come to accept slavery, and either volunteered for the rebel army or accepted conscription. Other community leaders, such as the eminent botanist and editor of the *Neu Braunfelser Zeitung*, Ferdinand Lindheimer, espoused loyalty to Texas, which had given them a home, but the tone of their loyalty suggested a practical eye toward their people's personal safety in a land where they were not particularly popular anyway. Those Germans who went west and settled on the Fisher-Miller grant, however, came to have largely a different opinion. Many of them were "freethinkers" who had fled Germany to be able to live out their progressive philosophy in a kind of utopia of labor and educated enlightenment. Only five families in and around Fredericksburg owned slaves, and secessionist vigilantes began to observe the western counties with a particularly narrow squint. Similarly to the extravagant rumors of a slave re-

bellion in the "Texas Troubles," secessionist newspapers—now the only
newspapers as Unionist presses were wrecked or burned—spread an alarm
that those counties were imminently to secede and set up a free state in
Texas' undefended west. The freethinkers' response was to establish the
Union Loyal League, a local militia to protect their farms and settlements
from molestation by either Indians or Confederate patrols. In the summer of
1862, attempts to enforce conscription in the Hill Country led between sixty
and seventy Germans to leave for Mexico. On the morning of August 10 they
were surprised in their undefended camp on the Nueces River by nearly a
hundred rebels, who killed nineteen Germans and then, Santanista style,
put nine wounded to death. (The massacre of prisoners was not usual for
Confederate regulars. In this instance the killings were probably the work of
James Duff, a Scottish-born freighter who, backed by his militia of "Partisan
Rangers" who were part of the attacking force, had declared a kind of personal martial law in the Hill Country and had been roughing up Germans for
some time.) The Unionists were able to kill only two of their attackers and
wound eighteen. Eight more Germans were killed closer to Mexico a few
weeks later, and the survivors either went into hiding or eventually found
their way into Union regiments. Among those who escaped was Jacob
Kuechler, Governor Houston's pro-Union recruiter.

While given color of purpose by the war, brutalizing the German population was at least in part an expression of an older hatred. The Germans
mostly had arrived many years after the Americans, hugely outperformed
them economically in only a couple of years, and did so largely without benefit of slaves—an offense that the Confederate extremists were now thrilled
to be able to avenge. The Germans' plight was shared by other Europeans of
principle who came to Texas for political liberty. One of the more prominent
was László Ujházi, a Hungarian aristocrat exiled to America for his anti-
Hapsburg involvement in the failed Kossuth rebellion. After touring the
United States he settled down to ranch near San Antonio, became an American citizen, but packed up again when war started, escaping to the North
and taking an American consular post in Italy.

The Tejano population greeted the war with even deeper ambivalence.
Their fate since the revolution—increasing racism and abuse from the
Anglo government, increasing social marginalization, and resentment toward Anglo landowners, a number of whom had illegally seized Tejano
ranches and been sustained by courts and backed by Rangers—led many to
see the Civil War as an opportunity to settle old scores. Those who enlisted
in federal service in the Rio Grande Valley became the backbone of the 2nd

Texas Cavalry (U.S.), and others made themselves useful as pro-Union guerrillas in the Nueces Strip. Many other Tejanos felt the same sympathies, but were cowed into silence, which only exacerbated their reputation for skulking and treachery. Of the roughly 2,500 Tejanos who did fight in gray, probably a majority were intimidated into doing so. Their desertion rate was high, although at least a few Mexican Texans saw action in almost every theater of the war. Probably no man exemplified their no-win situation better than Adrián Vidal of Brownsville, who enlisted at twenty-one in San Antonio, and became a militia captain cited for bravery in capturing a Union gunboat on the Rio Grande. Once he discovered, however, that his company would not be fed or clothed commensurate with Anglo rebels, he and most of his men mutinied in October 1863 and raided south Texas ranches as pro-Union irregulars. When federals occupied Brownsville a month later Vidal and his men joined federal service only to suffer similar discrimination. Again he deserted, crossed the river, and fought as a supporter of Benito Juarez until he was captured by Imperialist forces and executed in 1865. He was only twenty-five.

As casualty lists lengthened, discontent was no longer limited to ethnic communities or political allegiances. Taxes were doubled in 1863, and the ages of men liable to conscription were broadened, twice. Draft dodging and desertion began to increase alarmingly; one district commander estimated that there were perhaps a thousand dodgers in his part of the state. From mid-October 1863 in North Texas, a year after the Great Hanging, the job of rounding up draft dodgers and deserters became the responsibility of a horde of renegade irregulars led by a twenty-six-year-old psychopath named William Clarke Quantrill. Originally crossing into Texas to flee justice for the murders of hundreds in Kansas, Missouri, and the Indian Territory, they were widely loathed by the chivalrous Confederate officer corps. General E. Kirby Smith, however, the Confederate commander in Texas, ordered their incorporation into the effort to enforce loyalty. Over the following six months, so many of Quantrill's quarry were killed in cold blood that the brigadier in charge of the northern subdistrict, Henry McCulloch, younger brother of Ben, had the whole mob chased back across the Red River and into further infamy. (After the war McCulloch, who lived in Seguín, required an armed escort to return home, as so many Unionists threatened his life for having inflicted Quantrill on the country.)

Confederate provost marshals proved themselves no respecters of persons when it came to rooting out disloyalty. Governor Houston spoke at rallies, drilled cadets, and allowed Sam Houston Jr. to enlist, over Margaret's violent protest. Her fears were prescient; the Houstons' treasured eldest son was gone only a matter of weeks before he was listed as missing at Shiloh and his name dropped from the roll. Nevertheless, Confederate gumshoes monitored the deposed governor's movements and questioned his friends and neighbors, activities that wounded and angered him. Early in 1863, however, Houston visited his friends Eber Cave and Judge Alexander Terrell and asked their opinion, "as to how our people would feel in Texas about unfurling the Lone Star flag and calling the boys home," resuming the former status as an independent nation. Cave and Terrell "agreed that the conversation should be kept secret for obvious reasons." Even Sam Houston's iconic status might not be enough to save his life, if the proposal were made public.

FORTY-THREE

THE WAR IN TEXAS

SAM HOUSTON OFTEN PREDICTED A BLOODBATH FOR THE South, which came all too true, but it was not so for Texas at first. In fact, Texas' first action in the war was as successful as it was sensible, when Colonel William C. Young, who would soon have a role to play in the Great Hanging, led volunteers across the Red River and seized three federal forts in the Indian Territory, neutralizing any threat from that quarter for the time being. The former Texas Ranger Rip Ford was given a regiment with which to patrol the Rio Grande, and was kept busy by an almost constant harassment, either from Union troops who landed at the mouth of the Rio Grande early in the war, or by the dissident Tejanos and Mexicans whom the federals encouraged.

Texas' other defense, from hostile Indians, was confused and ineffectual from the beginning. Settlers on the Indian frontier were left to their own devices for nearly a year, until the Frontier Regiment was created to man sixteen camps along the fringe of settlement. Suffering from frequent reorganization and changes of command, they were largely helpless as the Comanches and Kiowas, quite aware that their enemies were now fighting among themselves, heaved the line of settlement a full hundred miles back to the southeast.

Notwithstanding this chaos, Texas opened a new theater in the war, which proved much more quixotic and costly. John Robert Baylor, the walleyed bombast who had brought about the destruction of the Brazos Valley Indian reservation, occupied Fort Bliss at El Paso with four companies of Rip Ford's border regiment. Gaining reinforcement from local volunteers, Baylor on July 24 led about three hundred men forty miles up the Rio Grande to Mesilla, New Mexico, to take its protective post, Fort Fillmore. Finding the town sympathetic to the Southern cause, Baylor waited for the nearly four hundred federals to attack—an assault that the Texans repulsed without loss. Cutting the Union soldiers off from their water supply, Baylor forced them to withdraw to nearby mountains, where he took their surrender. On August 1 Baylor proclaimed the existence of Arizona Territory, consisting of all of New Mexico south of the 34th parallel, with himself as governor, and Texas occupation reached as far west as Tucson.

The Confederate government ensconced at Richmond, Virginia, showed willingness to follow up on Baylor's initiative. Colonel H. H. Sibley, whose observations of Comanche teepees during five years' duty on the Texas frontier gave him the idea for the famous Sibley tent, persuaded Jefferson Davis to enlarge the western theater. Tempted by the prospect of adding more Confederate territory and capturing the rich mines of the continental divide, Davis sent Sibley to San Antonio, where he raised three regiments of troops and marched to take control of the New Mexico operation. The "Army of New Mexico" reached El Paso on December 14. Moving up from Mesilla, he defeated 3,800 federals under General E. R. S. Canby at the Battle of Val Verde on February 2, 1862, but unable to dislodge them from their fort, bypassed them and occupied Santa Fe and Albuquerque. Sibley's key objective was Fort Union, a hundred miles northeast of Santa Fe. He sent his main force out under Lieutenant Colonel William Read Scurry, an old Texas hand and former ally of Houston's who had become his enemy over secession. (Early in Houston's gubernatorial term, he said that he retained a man as state geologist when he discovered "six distinct strata of filth" on Scurry's neck.) On March 28, battle was joined at Glorieta Pass; Scurry lost nearly fifty dead before he forced the federals to retreat with about the same loss. Disaster struck, however, when Union troops and Colorado militia captured and burned the entire supply train of eighty wagons.

As an administrator, Baylor treated New Mexico natives as he had the Comanches. When Jefferson Davis saw a copy of Baylor's directive that his people "use all means to persuade the Apaches . . . to come in for the purpose of making peace, and when you get them together kill all the grown Indians and take the children prisoners and sell them to defray the expense," he had Baylor deposed. Sibley's loss of his entire provender made New Mexico untenable anyway, even before the California Column marched eastward and swept away the last of the rebel grand design for Arizona Territory. When Sibley returned to San Antonio in the summer of 1862, the army of New Mexico had lost about a third of its manpower; the men blamed Sibley bitterly and he was recalled to face charges.

Texas' location far from the scenes of the bloodiest battles preserved much of her wherewithal for the future, and politics proceeded with little disruption. Oldham and Wigfall became Texas senators in the rebel Congress. John

Reagan, who had brokered a sort of peace between Houston and the Secession Convention, left to become postmaster general of the Confederacy. Ed Clark, who became governor when Houston was deposed, failed in his bid by only 124 votes to be elected in his own right. He was defeated by Frank Lubbock, who had brought a boatload of merchandise to Texas when the capital was at Columbia in 1836, and had been a force in business and politics ever since. Although he had done very well in his mercantile business, he was inaugurated in a suit of homespun. During most of the war, the commander of the Texas Military District (which included Southern pretensions to New Mexico and Arizona) was John Bankhead Magruder, a fifty-five-year-old Virginia artillerist cited for bravery serving with Scott in the Mexican War. Named to replace Hébert after the Great Hanging, he was handsome and witty. He married a wealthy woman whom he only had to visit every few years, and his fellow officers accorded him the honorific "Prince John" for his lavish entertainments. Early in the war he had lured Union General George B. McClellan into excessive caution in the Peninsular Campaign, but Robert E. Lee was dissatisfied with Magruder's performance in the Seven Days' Battle and booted him to Texas. His superior as lieutenant general of the Trans-Mississippi Department was the much younger Edmund Kirby Smith, Florida scion of a military family that had served under George Washington. Also brevetted for valor in Mexico, Kirby Smith began the Civil War by being wounded at First Manassas, then won some notable if not decisive victories before receiving the Trans-Mississippi command with the rank of lieutenant general.

Far removed, for the moment, from the fighting, Texas' most precious contribution to the cause was men. No attempt at a definitive tally of Texans who served in the Civil War has succeeded, but the best estimate is that they numbered roughly 65,000, which was over two-thirds of the state's total male population between the ages of eighteen and forty-five. To their credit, the young men of the planter class volunteered for service in numbers at least equal to those less well off. Many of them were exempt from the Confederate draft by being responsible for the oversight of at least twenty slaves, or could have hired substitutes. But anxious for glory and the prestige that came with military titles, they made it clear that the increasing Armageddon was not just a rich man's war and a poor man's fight, but a struggle for the survival of a cultural identity. By one reckoning, Texas through the duration of the Civil War contributed ninety-seven colonels, thirty-four brigadiers, one major general in John A. Wharton (the son of Texas independence radical William Wharton), and two general officers, Albert Sidney Johnston (killed at Shiloh), who had previously commanded the army of the Republic of Texas, and John Bell Hood, who was maimed repeatedly but kept coming back fighting. His Texas Brigade left a legacy of valor—when a British journalist commented on their ragged uniforms, Robert E. Lee said, "Never mind the raggedness. The enemy never sees the backs of my Texans." Hood's Texas Brigade was shattered at Antietam, leaving Hood to say, when asked its status, that it lay dead on the field.

In an era in which whole companies might be composed of men from the same locale, numerous Texas units gained individual fame. Terry's Texas Rangers, the sobriquet of the 8th Texas Cavalry, were recruited by Benjamin Franklin Terry, who was killed in their first engagement near Woodsonville, Kentucky, in December 1861. His regiment of nearly 1,200 men fought through Shiloh, Murfreesboro, Chickamauga, and Chattanooga. After Atlanta they became raiders under Nathan Bedford Forrest, and then were attached to Joseph Johnston's army to the end of the war. Walker's Texas Division was the largest unit in the war to be composed of men from a single state, and were instrumental in frustrating the attempted Union invasion of Texas via the Red River; they were also known as the Greyhound Division for their capacity to fight after long forced marches. Even Granbury's Texas Brigade of eight regiments, which was not recruited until late in 1863, saved the Confederate Army from disaster with savage rear-guard fighting after Missionary Ridge; they fought with Hood in Tennessee, and after only a year of existence, were nearly wiped out at the Battle of Franklin, where both their generals, Pat Cleburne and Hiram Granbury, were killed. Ross' Brigade, named for its most famous commander, General Lawrence Sullivan "Sul" Ross, spent 112 days under fire during the Atlanta campaign. The roster seemed inexhaustible—until the casualty lists began to arrive.

The first recruits were often clad by their womenfolk, who spun and wove and sewed their uniforms, and the companies were outfitted with locally subscribed funds. However, the Confederate government quickly realized that Texas was one of the few places in the South where materiel could be manufactured safely. Before a year passed, uniforms were the responsibility of the Quartermaster's Clothing Bureau, which found a more efficient source of supply in the Huntsville Penitentiary, whose convicts by the end of 1863 churned out nearly 1.5 million yards of cotton garments and nearly 300,000 yards of woolen products. Similarly, the quartermaster established depots in several Texas cities for the production of shoes, but again the prison convicts were the most important source. Profits from the penitentiary accounted for more than a third of the state's wartime income.

War production became a burgeoning industry. The Field Transportation Bureau, also under the quartermaster's authority, opened works in seven different cities with a monthly production capacity of nearly two hundred wagons, a thousand harness sets, and over 350 saddles. The Confederacy, which famously sallied into the Civil War without a single cannon foundry, gained two with Texas, one by converting the state foundry in Austin, and the other run by Galveston merchant Ebenezar Nichols, a New Yorker who although at first opposed to secession, became captain of the Galveston Rifles, donated his home for use as Magruder's headquarters, and served the Confederacy in a variety of useful ways. Lesser foundries produced kitchenware and camp kettles. As the war opened the shortage of firearms was critical; during his one year as governor, Ed Clark dispatched agents abroad to purchase guns (without notable success), while at the same time making sure that the stocks in state armories stayed in Texas. As production ramped up, some 800 guns a month were produced in four factories, in Bastrop, Rusk, Tyler, and in the hopefully named town of Plenitude north of Palestine. The Colt revolver had proven its efficacy repeatedly on the frontier, and under contracts let by the state, Colt sidearms of all the various models were crafted in Columbia at the Dance Brothers factory, which may have been the oldest machine shop in Texas, and in Lancaster, south of Dallas. Tyler evolved into a nerve center of the war effort; it became Kirby Smith's headquarters, and after the factory there was expanded, two hundred employees assembled both Austrian and Enfield rifles. Late in 1863 the Little Rock, Arkansas, arsenal was transferred to Tyler to keep it from falling into Union hands.

Supporting the production of ordnance and firearms, gunpowder was manufactured in Marshall and Waxahachie. In Austin, the virtually fireproof new Land Office building was converted to the production of cartridges, and caps were made in that city as well as in Fredericksburg and Houston. The Texas legislature tried to foster still more production, offering half-section land bounties to proprietors who established machine shops, but there were few takers. With Twiggs' surrender of federal supplies in 1861, Confederate Texas did gain one asset that no one seemed quite sure what to do with: when Camp Verde passed into Southern hands they found themselves with about sixty camels and two Egyptian handlers, plus another fourteen camels captured from Union troops elsewhere in the Southwest. Some of the anachronistic ships of the desert were used to circumvent the ships of the blockade and haul cotton bales to Mexico; Captain Sterling Price used one to haul his company's baggage, but most were just turned loose into the brush country.

The emphasis on war production meant that domestic needs went un-filled. Basic food was never in short supply; in Texas one could always resort to the early standard of cornbread and fried pork. Salt, however, became al-most unobtainable, and coffee became so expensive that those families with no outside connections began roasting substitutes, using everything from acorns to okra pods. Candles became as dear as they had been on the early frontier; inks were concocted from roots and berries, and paper became so scarce that letters survive on every description of waste scrap.

Lincoln felt keenly his failure to pressure Houston to hold Texas in the Union, and from the federal army, Texas' position as a growing engine of Confederate war production made it, in some eyes, a priority target. With even the national capital under threat, other campaigns were more impor-tant, but just as during the Texas republic the idea of pillaging Matamoros drove some officers beyond reason, even so in important quarters of the fed-eral army the chimera of reducing Texas became an almost equally irrational *idée fixe*.

The first effective strike at Texas appeared to be the capture of Galveston on October 4, 1862, while people were still smarting over Sibley's eviction from New Mexico. (The loss of Galveston was a material blow to the Hous-tons, who had been reduced to raising money by selling wagonloads of fire-wood cut from their Cedar Point summer place across the bay.) The federal commander gave his rebel counterpart several days to evacuate civilians, and even then did not occupy the city until Christmas Day. Prince John Ma-gruder, however, newly installed in command of the Texas Department, moved with energy. Loading 300 of Sibley's survivors onto "cotton clad" gunboats as marines and assembling a land assault force on the mainland side of the railroad causeway, Magruder himself led the assault before dawn on January 1, 1863. Disaster threatened, as Magruder's artillery was over-matched by the heavy cannons on Union gunboats, who then turned their fire on rebel marines whose scaling ladders proved too short to reach the wharf. The two plucky little cotton clads—river steamers lined with cotton bales to absorb enemy shot in default of real armor—rescued the situation. The *Neptune* and the *Bayou City* rammed and captured the USS *Harriet Lane*, while the Yankee flagship, the USS *Westfield*, ran aground and was blown up to prevent her capture. Three more large gunboats withdrew, stranding the federal troops and forcing their capitulation. Galveston was redeemed with the capture of 600 federal troops, the destruction of the *Westfield*, and capture of the fast and rakish new *Harriet Lane*, which was something of a Union icon, being the first ship ordered to sea after Fort Sumter and a key to the federal capture of New Orleans. The Confederacy rechristened her the *Lavinia* and turned her into a blockade runner. Magruder's loss was 26 dead and 117 wounded, and the *Neptune*, which sank from damage sustained in ramming the *Harriet Lane*.

Another insult was heaped on the federal blockade when two more puffing little cotton clads, the *Uncle Ben* and the *Josiah A. Bell*, sortied out from Sabine Pass, mounting two guns each, and surprised and defeated the blockade schooner *Fairy* and the thousand-ton, nine-gun sailing ship *Morning Light*. The former also became a blockade runner; the latter was burned when she proved too heavy to get over the bar.

The Union commander of the Department of the Gulf was General Nathaniel P. Banks, a former Speaker of the House of Representatives and a warm friend of Sam Houston. Banks had been pressing to attack Mobile, Alabama, but political forces overbore him and he was ordered to assault Texas. Given the choice of landing, Banks chose Sabine Pass, at the eastern extremity of the state, which offered the shortest line of supply and the best opportunity to disrupt rail traffic and cotton production. The Texas-Louisiana border at the Gulf was also lightly defended—in fact laughably so. He had no idea he was setting himself up for one of the most humiliating Union defeats of the Civil War. Fort Griffin, on the Texas shore opposite an oyster reef that split the channel, mounted only six guns, manned by F Company, 3rd Texas Heavy Artillery, recruited from the Irish community in Houston. On September 6, 1863, their captain Frederick Odlum was in Sabine City; the fort was under command of his niece's husband, Lieutenant Richard Dowling. They were alert, following word from Magruder's headquarters that a Union invasion fleet was heading west to an unknown destination.

Dawn of September 7 revealed a dozen federal ships off the six-foot-deep bar; during the day several reconnoitered into the pass, then exited again. By the morning of September 8, twenty-two warships rode at anchor off the bar, where General William B. Franklin, flying his flag on the transport USS *Suffolk*, considered his options. He had four gunboats mounting twenty-six guns, and transports carrying five thousand soldiers with supplies, including mounts for four companies of Union Texas cavalry. Still Franklin was wary; Fort Griffin was more dangerous than it looked. The Louisiana channel was too far away to bombard it accurately; the Texas channel passed right under its earthworks, where his gunboats would be blown apart by its

32-pounders. At three-thirty that afternoon he opened his attack, with the gunboats *Sachem* and *Arizona* starting up the Louisiana channel to draw fire. Once the fort's guns were trained on them, the gunboats *Clifton* and *Granite City* were to steam up the near channel and cover the troop landings a thousand yards south of the fort. At least one of the boats would flank the fort by reaching Sabine Lake behind it and silence the rebel batteries.

Inside the fort, Dick Dowling received his orders: in the face of such firepower, it was left to his discretion whether to fight, or spike his guns and get out. His two 24-pounders pointed north, toward the lake, and were useless. His four 32-pounders, two smoothbores and two howitzers, were in disrepair. But what Franklin didn't know was that Dowling's company had staked range finders down both channels, and could shoot with hideous accuracy. As the first two boats turned up the Louisiana channel, the 1,000-ton *Arizona* grounded on a mud bank and had to muscle herself free. On just the third salvo, Dowling's guns splintered her superstructure and then silenced three of her guns. Just as she reached Sabine Lake, a shot from a 24-pounder pierced her steam drum, and she veered to starboard and stuck fast in the muck. In return, a nine-inch ball from the *Clifton* carried away the top of the sighting screw of one howitzer—nearly taking Dowling's head with it—as her commander, Acting Lieutenant Frederick Crocker, zigzagged up the channel. Only 300 yards from the fort, a lucky ball snapped her steering rope and she plunged fast to port into the Texas mud and was quickly pounded to pieces. As federal snipers tried to pick off Dowling's crews, he changed his solid shot for grape and canister. On the Union transports, the rumor spread that Franklin had stepped into a rebel trap of overwhelming strength, and the federal fleet weighed anchor and sailed, abandoning for capture the crews of the *Clifton* and *Sachem*, defeated by forty-seven celebrating Irishmen. Union bonds sank to their lowest premium of the war, the gunboats were repaired for Confederate service, Dowling was withdrawn from harm's way and used as a recruiting celebrity, and Jefferson Davis had special medals struck and cited the whole unit for bravery.

The humiliation of the Battle of Sabine Pass only increased Union determination to make Texas suffer. Her undamaged production was prolonging the war, and geopoliticians in Washington knew that the French were getting proprietary about Mexico again; Washington wanted to establish a Union presence in Texas to keep them realistic. Moreover, news of the atrocities committed against Texas Unionists in the northern tier of counties, and the concentration of Texas' war production in the northeast quadrant of the state, made an invasion by way of the Red River seem a likely stroke. While the Union probably should have been taking advantage of the fall of Vicksburg, about 27,000 troops were sluiced off for Banks to invade Texas via Shreveport, Louisiana. Screening him would be a flotilla of heavy gunboats under the Union's ace admiral, David Dixon Porter. On April 8, 1864, Kirby Smith himself attacked and defeated Banks' van of 8,000, making off with 22 cannons and 150 supply wagons and taking 2,500 prisoners. The next day at the Battle of Pleasant Hill, Banks inflicted rather more casualties than he received, about 1,500, but it was apparent that the Texas invasion could not be sustained and he withdrew. Stranded behind him was Admiral Porter on the Red River, his fleet stuck in low water. In one of the most spectacular retreats of the war, Porter built rock crib dams, waited for the water to back up, and rode the flooding crest through what he called "the heaviest fire I ever witnessed." Five of his gunboats were sunk or captured.

Frank Lubbock did not seek reelection as governor in 1863, instead joining both the Confederate Army as a lieutenant colonel and the staff of Jefferson Davis. He was succeeded by Pendleton Murrah, a lawyer from the town of Marshall who had once lost a campaign for the legislature to a member of the Know-Nothing Party. He was not well known but his opponent, Texas revolutionary tory T. J. Chambers, was no more popular than he had ever been, and Murrah, with the endorsement of secessionist editors, defeated him easily. Raised in an Alabama orphanage, he was of uncertain age but less than forty; he was a frail and pretty consumptive who came to Texas in 1850 to benefit his health. He was revealed as a true Southerner in his bizarre and unconsummated marriage to the former Sue Ellen Taylor of Marshall, whom he wed when she was only fifteen. After the nuptials, he waited for her to come downstairs to him; she waited for him to come upstairs to her, and neither one budged. The wounds to their respective egos never healed, and by the time they moved into the Governor's Mansion, they had lived in courteous frost for thirteen years.

Murrah's slender shoulders had to bear much work, however, for as the war began to go badly conflicts arose between Texas and the Confederate authorities. When Texas planters who had so warmly espoused the cause were faced with an army order to sell their cotton to Kirby Smith's own broker for rapidly failing Confederate notes, Murrah tried to help. He began a program of purchasing domestic cotton with state land warrants, but the Richmond regime beat him down. When the rebel army began pressing more aggressively for Texas conscripts, Murrah tried to exempt men on the frontier who were needed for Indian defense. If anyone understood Murrah's Indian problem it should have been Kirby Smith, who before the war had chased Texas Indians with the 2nd U.S. Cavalry, but he insisted that the Confederacy's need for men superseded Texas' domestic dangers. (Murrah's rearguard action against Magruder and Kirby Smith on the issue of conscription did have some effect, however, as perhaps two-thirds of Texas soldiers were not sent east of the Mississippi.) Under further pressure, Murrah relented and suggested to the legislature that the Frontier Regiment, which had been maintained at state expense for Indian and border protection, be transferred to the Confederate army. The legislature complied, with the stipulation that it remain under Texas command, which prompted Jefferson Davis to veto accepting the unit. It was instead reformulated as the "Frontier Organization," a militia in which every man liable for service living in a frontier county—as many as 4,000 men—was compelled to serve, but only a fourth of them at any one time, by rotation. While the patrols arrested Confederate army deserters and enforced conscription, it was a purely Texas force serving Texas interests. The fringes of settlement were organized into three districts, and from March 1864 until well after the end of the war, patrols of the Frontier Organization were the principal protection from outlaws and hostile Indians.

East Texas natives were so reduced that they no longer presented any threat, but the Apaches in the trans-Pecos and Kiowas and Comanches on the northwest fringe of settlement were acutely aware of the nature of the Civil War and the opportunity it presented them. The line of settlement, which had moved steadily out onto the Plains during the last years of the cotton era, suddenly reversed its progress and receded under the pressure of increased raids. One of the boldest forays took place in October 1864, when several hundred Kiowas and Comanches raided through the Elm Creek Valley northwest of Fort Belknap, killing several men and taking a number of women and children prisoner. The Indians fought a fierce battle with settlers who collected in a cabin, but the Indians were chased off by the timely arrival of troops; the raiders took their revenge, luring the soldiers into an ambush and killing five before escaping with their captives and stolen cattle. The hostages were later recovered through the intercession of a more peaceable chief named Isa-Havey (Wolf Road, which was the Comanche name for the Milky Way).

A few hardy souls elected to defend their new land, and as they could be protected only sporadically by the thinly spread Frontier Organization, they held their ground by moving into stockaded compounds known as "family forts." Mostly their protection lay in numbers, as the "forts" were merely shelters connected by picket barriers driven into the ground. A few were much more substantial. One of the largest was Fort Davis (not to be confused with the later, real, Fort Davis in West Texas), located on the Clear Fork of the Brazos about twenty miles northeast of the later town site of Albany. Behind its walls, over a hundred settlers spent the last year of the Civil War, watching for hostiles from a blockhouse, manufacturing household staples such as soap and candles, and cobbling together a social life of candy pulls, dances, and a sermon now and then. There was even a school, with the county clerk, Sam Newcomb, as teacher. "I have only nineteen schollars at present," he wrote, "and most of them very rude and wild." He was not certain he could discipline them for the fourteen weeks' course he planned, but word that the war was over reached the outpost in May and the settlers dispersed.

Galled by repeated frustration in attempting to punish Indian raiders, Texas' frontier defense force finally saw a major action in January 1865, in the desolate Concho River Valley. Nearly four hundred soldiers and militia attacked a much larger group of Kickapoo Indians, who had not been at war with anybody and were relocating from Indian Territory to Mexico. The Kickapoos whipped the Texans with heavy losses and never forgave them. They went on their way to Mexico, where they remained a thorn to Texans for years.

In spring of 1865, word was slow reaching remote areas of Texas that the war was over, but because of Brownsville's access to sea traffic, New Orleans papers had arrived with news, if people chose to believe it, of Lee's surrender on April 9 and Lincoln's assassination five days later. Rip Ford, who had tended to his duties along the Rio Grande for the duration of the war, had been offered generous surrender terms by the local Union commander, but no word had reached Texas' home units concerning when or how to stand down. On May 12 the Union garrison on Brazos Island, off the mouth of the Rio Grande, sent a force of three hundred mostly black infantry under Lieutenant Colonel David Branson, to establish federal rule in Brownsville, twenty-five miles inland. Halfway there, they encountered resistance, and routed 150 rebel cavalry led by Captain George Roberson. Branson took up a defensive position until he was reinforced by the 34th Indiana from Brazos Island, increasing his strength to 500. He resumed the fight on May 13, and was winning until Rip Ford arrived to help Roberson with seventy men and a battery of six 12-pounders. With the aid of artillery, Ford's men slowly pushed the federals back to the coast.

Union forces lost thirty killed or wounded, and Ford took 115 prisoners. As fate had it, that was also the day that the Texas government authorized Kirby Smith to stand down his army. "Boys," said Rip Ford to his soldiers, "we have done finely. We will let well enough alone, and retire."

FORTY-FOUR

FORTY ACRES AND A MULE

THE END, WHEN IT CAME, CAME QUICKLY AND IN CHAOS. With Robert E. Lee's surrender and the collapse of rebel government, the federals offered Kirby Smith the same terms granted to Lee at Appomattox. Smith, perhaps by the clock the last four-star general left in the South, believed that the western Confederacy could fight on, but he needed that region's governors to back him up or else be branded a renegade. Those state executives laid down unrealistic terms that the Union Army felt no compulsion to entertain. Smith stalled, but he and Magruder finally capitulated to General E. R. S. Canby on a warship in Galveston Harbor on June 2, 1865. Both rebel generals escaped to Mexico, where Prince John took a new commission, fighting for the Hapsburg emperor Maximilian; Smith within a few months was an insurance executive in Kentucky. The dying Murrah, seeing rebel governors clamped into prison across the South, donned a gray uniform and rode out of Austin on June 12 for the border as well; he reached Monterrey, where he expired on August 4. The night before he left Austin, the state treasury was looted by a band of forty thieves, but with Confederate money and bonds now worthless, the only thing worth taking from the vault was about $5,000 in coins. Left in charge in Texas after Murrah's departure was Fletcher Stockdale, the lieutenant governor, a lawyer and farmer from Calhoun County on Lavaca Bay, who had helped draft the secession ordinance in 1861.

Many of those Texas fire-eaters who swore to defend slavery with their lives, did so. Ben McCulloch, who distinguished himself first in the revolution, then as an Indian fighter and in the Mexican War, and who thwarted Sam Houston's design to place the Union Army supplies under his own command, ensured rebel control of the Indian Territory early in the conflict by making crucial alliances with the Civilized Tribes. Then, impressed into a campaign he protested (a harebrained scheme to capture St. Louis), he was killed at the Battle of Pea Ridge in March 1862. William P. Rogers, who once told Houston that he would wade in blood up to his neck before he would see his wife do a slave woman's labor, almost got his wish. He was blown off his feet by multiple bullets as he led an assault, brandishing the colors of the

2nd Texas Infantry inside a federal fort at Corinth, Mississippi. Rogers had kept Houston's friendship even after he turned secessionist when Lincoln was elected; William Read Scurry did not. "Dirty Neck Bill" rose to command the 3rd Brigade of Walker's Texas Division, and was killed in the Battle of Jenkins Ferry, Arkansas, at the end of April 1864. "Have we whipped them?" he asked as he lay dying. Upon learning the affirmative he said, "Now take me to a house where I can . . . die easy."

Texas' postrevolutionary generalissimos who never got the fight out of their systems mostly died unfulfilled. Felix Huston was an energetic supporter of secession, but he died in Mississippi in 1857. Thomas Jefferson Green, who never forgave Houston for not engaging in a general war against Mexico, was too old to fight, and died in grief and frustration over rebel failures in December 1863. A lesser Tom Green, a San Jacinto veteran and Rusk's aide-de-camp, survived Texas' fruitless invasion of New Mexico in 1861, and rose to the rank of brigadier with significant victories in Louisiana and Mississippi. He was one of the few to die actually defending Texas, assaulting Admiral Porter's Red River gunboats in April 1864. The highest-ranking veteran Texan to fall was Albert Sidney Johnston, former commanding general of the Texas Army during the Republic. After annexation he had taken a billet in the U.S. Army, but with secession refused a Union command and formed the Army of the Mississippi. He fell at Shiloh, along with much of the 2nd Texas Infantry.

Indeed, for some Texas regiments, losses were counted not in famous officers but in whole swaths of the rank and file. After Shiloh and Corinth, the splintered 2nd Texas, when it was repatriated after capture, could muster no more than a brigade. One of its survivors proved to be Sam Houston Jr., rescued from the field at Shiloh by a Yankee chaplain who had admired Senator Houston's defiant defeat in the Kansas-Nebraska vote. Like his famous father, Sam Jr. was wounded in the groin and left for dead on the field. A second ball that would have ended his life buried itself instead in the thick pocket Bible that his mother gave him when he enlisted. Hood's Texas Brigade, which at Second Manassas inflicted on New York Zouaves the highest casualty rate suffered by the Union in the entire war, was in turn mowed down in the cornfield at Antietam. Later attached to the Army of Northern Virginia, they suffered more than 60 percent casualties by the time Lee surrendered. The 8th Texas Cavalry, "Terry's Texas Rangers," were eventually attached to General Joseph E. Johnston in North Carolina; when he capitulated two weeks after Lee, some 248 men of the 8th Texas survived; 158

slipped away and made their own ways home, with the satisfaction at least of having never surrendered to anybody.

Many of the antebellum elite paid not with their lives, but with everything they owned. The mightiest to be brought low were the Mills brothers of Brazoria, David and Robert. Between them before the war they were worth about $4 million, owning eight hundred slaves to work four plantations, and then baling, warehousing, and shipping their own cotton on their own steamboats. They lost it all, both finally going bankrupt in 1873; two of the plantations, fittingly, were in time incorporated into the system of state prison farms.

Texans who did not share Kirby Smith's and Magruder's dreams of defiant grandeur (or their mobility to flee the country) had no choice but to await the arrival of the federal occupation. Eighteen hundred bluecoats landed at Galveston on June 19, under command of General Gordon Granger, a New Yorker, West Point class of 1845, a competent but little-known officer whose one moment of distinction in the war had come during the Union defeat at Chickamauga twenty months before. There, Granger's valiant reinforcement of George Thomas without waiting on orders to do so helped prevent a defeat from degenerating into disaster. Upon arrival in Galveston, Granger published several General Orders, outlawing all acts of the Texas legislature since secession, paroling most Confederate soldiers, decreeing that the cotton crop could be sold but only to Northern factors, and most importantly: "The people are informed that, in accordance with a proclamation from the Executive of the United States, all slaves are free." Since Lincoln's Emancipation Proclamation of January 1863 had had no practical effect in most of the South, African-Americans in Texas traditionally count June 19, "Juneteenth," as the day they were actually freed, and celebrate it as a major holiday.

The rest of Granger's order, however, has been largely forgotten: "The Freedmen are advised to remain at their present homes, and work for wages. They are informed that they will not be allowed to collect at military posts; and that they will not be supported in idleness either there or elsewhere." The full text of the order reflected the Union Army's experience throughout the South, that the emancipated slaves believed that freedom would include jobs or some other material benefit. Texas slaves had been very isolated both from the fighting and from the possibility of escape on the Underground Railroad. Unlike slaves farther east, very few, less than fifty, Texas slaves fought in black Union regiments. Many did run to Mexico, but they had little idea what life in freedom would be like. The "forty acres and a mule" that many believed would accompany their liberty was a dream and an aspiration, but nobody ever promised it to them. When they discovered that freedom meant freedom to look after themselves after generations of being fed and clothed and told what to do, the result was as grim as Lafayette had predicted to Sam Houston forty years earlier.

Houston had freed his dozen slaves in October 1862, doubtless taking a perverse satisfaction in defying a law against voluntary manumission. Exhausted by anxiety over the fate of his eldest son, Houston's health entered a steady decline shortly after Sam Jr.'s safe return. Serene on his deathbed in June 1863, he answered a caller's inquiry into what would become of his teenaged valet and driver, Jeff Hamilton. He had already been granted his freedom, Houston said, but he had charged Sam Jr. to look after his welfare. Jeff stayed with the family for some years after his emancipation, and when he did go out on his own, his experience was not uplifting. "The first two men I worked for were the worst hypocrites and the meanest men I ever knew," he wrote in his memoir. "The first man . . . was named Ross, a Baptist preacher, who was always praying and shouting and claimed to be so holy that he always carried a Bible in his pocket, but if his flock could have seen how mean and stingy he was at home, they wouldn't have listened to him preach. . . . He had three hands and he got us up before daylight and made us go to the muddy cow-lot in our bare feet, when it was raining and sleeting. We didn't have enough clothes to keep us warm, and he wouldn't advance us enough money to buy shoes or clothing. Many a day we had to drive four miles in the woods . . . and cut cordwood when a Texas norther was blowing."

Jeff Hamilton's second employer was even worse, stiffing him for five months' labor with no pay whatever. Hamilton at least had his connection with the Houston name. He walked ten miles to Independence, where the Houstons had lived much of the time, and white sympathizers ushered him in to see a judge whose father had been a friend of Sam Houston's back in Tennessee. The judge climbed into his buggy with Hamilton, drove out to the offending employer's establishment, and collected Hamilton's wage under threat of a horse whipping. Most Texas blacks, of course, had no such advantage.

While like abuse was all too common among Texas' quarter of a million or more freed slaves, it could have been still worse. Many people of means had followed Houston's lead in freeing their slaves before the presence of troops compelled them to do so. "A lot of slaves was turned loose long before we was," according to Mary Ann Gibson of Williamson County, who was interviewed by the WPA writers' project in the 1930s. Her owner, a planter named Rutherford, gave his freed people a choice to stay or go. As recorded in dialect, "Massa Rutherford was hitchin' his hoss, and he said, 'Yo'all is as free as I am, by God.' " Some planters—not many—gave their former slaves a start in free life with clothes, stores, sometimes some money or even small allotments of land, or retained them as sharecroppers.

Jeff Hamilton's hardship was not duplicated by the Houstons' senior servant, Joshua, who had belonged to Margaret at the time of her marriage. He was a skilled farrier, and Houston had always—unlike most masters—allowed him to keep the money he earned at outside employment. After Houston's death, his widow moved to Independence to be near her mother. After Nancy Lea's death the following year, Margaret Houston lived in such poverty that she once waylaid a freight wagon belonging to her merchant son-in-law and removed two sides of bacon. She didn't pay for it, she apologized, "for the simple reason that I had not the money." Hearing of her plight, Joshua rode from Huntsville to Independence and offered her his saddlebag weighted with his savings—$2,000 in prewar coins. Moved, she said that the general would have preferred he use the money to procure a Christian education for his children. This he did, and Joshua Houston and his descendants became leaders in Huntsville's early black community.

The experience of most Texas freedmen was doubtless closer to that of Jeff Hamilton. Even before the Civil War ended, the federal government created the Bureau of Refugees, Freedmen, and Abandoned Lands, to oversee the more humane aspects of Reconstruction: provide relief to white refugees from the South, and administer lands confiscated or abandoned during the war. By far the agency's largest job, for which it became known in short as the Freedmen's Bureau, was to monitor the assimilation of former slaves into the larger society. The principal administrator in each state was an army officer—in the case of Texas it was General Edgar M. Gregory, abolitionist colonel of the 91st Pennsylvania. He was succeeded by four others within five years, which turnover alone limited the effectiveness of the bureau in Texas. There were other problems as well. Not all officers in the Union Army were particularly sympathetic to the Negro cause; it was difficult to hire a full complement of traveling inspectors to implement the program, and then the vast distances in Texas made oversight and reporting lax. Funding was inadequate, because a vengeful Congress intended the bureau to maintain itself with income from seized rebel land. President Andrew Johnson frustrated this plan by returning most property to its owners, forcing Congress to pass an appropriation for the bureau. Since the directors and many of the traveling inspectors were military officers, whites in Texas viewed the Freedmen's Bureau as an extension of the Reconstruction occupation, and resistance to it was formidable. Their anger increased once it became clear that local inspectors and subcommissioners, of whom there were anywhere from forty to sixty in Texas at any given time, began feeding information to the Reconstruction regime on suspected disloyalty by white citizens. And when bureau officers did commit crimes, as some did, they were tried not locally but court-martialed by the sympathetic Union military. In Texas, whose economy was wrecked by the war but which had not suffered the physical devastation of the Deep South, swallowing the bitter pill of defeat came slower. The bureau's national commissioner, the famed "praying general" Oliver O. Howard, pronounced Texas his hardest case. Three officers of the Freedmen's Bureau were murdered and a similar number wounded or run off before former Confederates in Texas knuckled under to a grumbling compliance.

On balance the Freedmen's Bureau did good work. They audited court cases in which former slaves were involved, and had power to seize jurisdiction if it appeared that they might not receive justice—indeed, some inspectors may have gone too far on that count. They encouraged and supervised a system of contract labor for black sharecroppers, with power to nullify contracts that took unfair advantage of them, and later gave them a lien on the crop until they were fairly paid. Local officers tried to reassemble families that in former days had been sold piecemeal, and cohabitation during slavery was recognized as legal marriage. (State law did not legalize black marriage until 1869.) Their most important activity was the establishment of schools for freedmen, whose education had been illegal under slavery, and the program began in late 1865 with fifteen schools. Some of them were burned out by angry whites, but the schools thrived nevertheless, until by the time the program was discontinued in 1870 there were 150 freedmen's schools with nearly ten thousand students. Perhaps the most successful of the freedmen's school organizers was George T. Ruby, who also personified many of the elements that whites held against it. He was both black and a Yankee, a free man of color born in New York; he was perceived as a carpetbagger, having arrived in Galveston to play his role in the occupation. Further, he used his travels while organizing black schools to also organize Union League chapters; still worse, he married a mulatto who required a second look to determine that she wasn't white, and yet worse he worked his way into the black wing of Texas Republican politics, winning a seat in the state senate. What probably kept him alive was his tact and friendliness.

All in all, the early phase of Reconstruction, carried out by the Johnson administration, was effected with a light hand. In the spring of 1867, however, Radical Republicans gained a majority in Congress, seized control of the process, and undertook a far more punitive program. While it was intended to advance the position of blacks in Texas, their fiats were far more incendiary, in good measure because they also aimed to consolidate Republican power by disenfranchising ex-Confederate Democrats, and by grooming freedmen to support Republican candidates. After most white former Confederates were stripped of the right to vote, a former Unionist judge named E. J. Davis was elected governor in 1869. One of the elements of his administration was the formation of a state police force that became the single hardest aspect of Reconstruction for Texans to bear. Many of its officers were freedmen, and advantage was undoubtedly sometimes taken over the disenfranchised whites, who were left seething. Written histories of the state police have been colored to a high degree by the sentiments of their authors, with excesses being unduly emphasized in former years and now soft-peddled by more politically correct scholars.

With emancipation and the threat that blacks would make strides toward legal and social equality, and especially in response to the establishment of federal programs like the Freedmen's Bureau, Texas, like most states in the South, passed the so-called Black Codes, to define and regulate exactly who blacks were and what rights they possessed. Any person of one-eighth Negro blood or more was liable to the provisions of the statute. At first glance, many of its provisions were beneficial, confirming most rights enjoyed by white citizens, including legal competency, the right to make contracts and real estate transactions and have them enforced in courts, to which access was guaranteed. However, the Black Codes also strictly limited other rights: blacks could not vote or serve on juries, and could not testify except against other blacks, which negated much of what they gained in access to the courts. Even more dubiously, the code made one provision for "apprenticeship" labor contracts, and another allowed anyone arrested for vagrancy to be forcibly apprenticed into a trade. The employers in such cases were guaranteed performance of labor, under sanction of docking wages and administering physical beatings. The effect was one much more of intimidation than of economic advancement.

The imposition of congressional Reconstruction hardened white opposition to the Union occupation. And once the former rebels were deprived of the vote, their backlash against official oppression was driven underground and took the form of secret societies, from within the anonymity of which the white majority began to wreak their vengeance on former slaves. There was a grab bag of unlikely named organizations that came with a variety of mysterious rites and customs. Prominent in Texas were the Knights of the White Camellia, so named for the purity of the white race, and the Knights of the Rising Sun, which pledged itself to "maintain and defend the social and political superiority of the White race."

When the actual Ku Klux Klan was organized (in Tennessee in 1866) it did not have intimidation of freedmen as its goal; rather it was a spoof of a popular prewar college fraternity called the Kuklos Adelphon—hence its outlandish costumes, midnight meetings in cemeteries, secret handshakes and rituals, and its bizarre-sounding office holders, such as the presiding officer, the Grand Cyclops. The KKK reached Texas in early spring of 1868, and angry white Southerners quickly realized the group's potential for striking back at the occupation regime. Hiding behind the anonymity of the costumes and secret proceedings, the Klan undertook a program of terrorism, including arson and murder. The very fact that they were acting on their anger attracted disaffected members from the other secret societies, such as the Knights of the White Camellia, whose membership included the more respectable social element and which had shied away from overt violence. The chief organizer of the KKK in Texas was Roger Q. Mills, a Corsicana lawyer and former state legislator who had fought through several campaigns of the Civil War, and was wounded twice while rising to the rank of colonel in command of a regiment. He was not particularly effective at providing either organization or program, because the rapidly multiplying local chapters often had particular targets for their wrath in mind even as they organized, and went very much their own way.

Klan activities in Texas were largely centered in, although not confined to, East Texas, and especially such northeast towns as Quitman, Gilmer, Jefferson, and Marshall. Northern Unionists who moved to Texas to take advantage of the forcibly pro-Republican political climate, and who became known as "carpetbaggers" after a popular form of cheap luggage, were a special target, along with freedmen who presumed to social equality. As Union military authorities obtained nearly thirty convictions for Klan crimes by the end of 1868, the movement began to peter into dormancy, although the KKK managed a last hurrah the following year in Jefferson, killing a New York carpetbagger and merchant named George Washington Smith. After addressing a Republican rally on the evening of October 3, Smith and a black friend were shot at; Smith shot back and wounded two of his assailants. Anticipating his end, Smith sought refuge from the commander of the local occupation garrison, Major James Curtis; he was followed by a deputation of local officials, whose leader, Richard Crump, had been one of Smith's assailants. They demanded that Smith be handed over for trial for assault. Curtis was dubious, but upon being assured that Smith would be safely held and tried promptly, surrendered him, but detailed a military guard to protect him. The following night as many as a hundred hooded men overpowered the guard detail and shot Smith to death through his cell window. They also apprehended four of Smith's freedmen retainers and herded them into the woods; two were killed and two escaped.

The Smith killing was so brazen in its defiance of military authority that the army decided to make an example of the Jefferson mob, and incarcerated three dozen suspects in what became known as the "Stockade Case." In a convoluted investigation and trial lasting nearly a year, the citizen protests of which reached President Johnson (who was briefed and approved of the trial), three were convicted of murder and three on lesser charges, although the principal ringleaders, including Crump and the head of the local Knights of the Rising Sun, fled the jurisdiction. The Stockade Case, along with statistics showing that nearly half of Texas' 939 murders committed since the end of the war involved black victims of white killers, hardened the army's determination to put down secret organizations. Aided by a new federal law suspending habeas corpus for members of secret societies, they largely managed to do so. They failed, however, to rein in the most savage of the anti-Reconstruction outlaws, Cullen Baker of Cass County in the northeast corner of the state. Himself responsible for killing at least two agents of the Freedmen's Bureau, as well as numerous freedmen and even some whites who he felt were too friendly with their sharecroppers, Baker and his gang consistently eluded the army's best efforts to catch him; rather it was his own neighbors who eventually recognized his excesses and poisoned him.

The atmosphere of intimidation lingered, however, for several years. Blacks in Texas depended almost entirely on the army for protection, although there were isolated instances where they took their safety into their own hands. The most prominent occasion was in Millican, southeast of Bryan in Brazos County, which until recently had been one of the largest towns in Texas with a population of 3,000, but had started its decline after being bypassed by the railroad and suffering through an epidemic of yellow fever. In June 1868 a meeting of the Union League with a largely black attendance was broken up by an invasion of Klansmen, but for once, the freed-men armed themselves and fought back. They seemed to have succeeded, but after an uneasy month the Klan returned in force, burning and looting and killing their way through the black sector of town. Against such odds, meaningful progress seemed impossible.

Texas blacks grew weary of the endless abuse and controversy, and when they learned that a homestead act passed in Kansas offered them a chance at land, free for the labor of improving it, many began loading up their wagons. This was especially understandable since the Texas legislature passed a law disqualifying freedmen from participating in the state's famous largesse with land grants. Beginning with only a trickle in 1875, migration increased every year until it became known as the "Kansas Fever," thanks in part to the proselytizing of a former slave named Pap Singleton. It was known else-where in the South as the "Exoduster Movement." Another important booster was the erstwhile Union League and freedmen's school organizer and Texas state senator, George T. Ruby. Sensing that the end of Reconstruc-tion would allow the return of racial oppression in Texas, he removed to New Orleans, where he edited a black newspaper that espoused the reloca-tion of Negroes in the North. By 1880 well over ten thousand former slaves had turned their backs on Texas and left to follow opportunity. Inevitably, some unscrupulous hucksters took advantage of the freedmen's gullibility and sold them fake train tickets, but other white leaders, seeing in the black migration an answer to their own very different prayers, offered a measure of protection to those wishing to leave. Ironically, the "Exodus of 1879" also improved life for freedmen remaining behind, because so many Texas fields were left fallow for want of sharecroppers to work them that landowners were forced to grant better terms to tenants, with rents reduced by as much as 40 percent, on three-year leases instead of the former one-year terms. And—an irony even richer than the soil—the Kansas that twenty years be-fore had been viewed by the South as the first target of expanding slave ter-ritory into the North became a haven of improved conditions for Texas blacks, all the hardships of a prairie homestead notwithstanding.

FORTY-FIVE

SCALAWAGS AND CARPETBAGGERS

DESPITE THE OPPOSITION THEY FACED DURING RECON-
struction, African-Americans in Texas did make measurable progress during
that era. Fifteen years after the fall of the Confederacy, one-fifth of blacks
listed on the census as farmers owned their own land. And while most
urban blacks in Texas labored at menial jobs, others began finding success at
business and in the professions. But the racial story is only one facet of a
larger and more complicated history.

Two days before General Granger landed in Galveston, President Andrew
Johnson issued a proclamation undertaking the reconstruction of civilian
government in Texas. Lincoln had favored the reentry of former Confederate
states on the most generous terms, and had already begun the process with
Tennessee, Arkansas, and Louisiana. Lincoln's reasoning had been that
since secession was illegal, the Southern states had never actually left the
Union, and their rehabilitation was therefore purely a matter for the executive department—hence the general reference to the subsequent couple of
years as "presidential Reconstruction." This set him up, however, for conflict with the Congress, which contained a powerful but not yet dominant
bloc of Radical Republicans who desired to see the South much more severely punished. They maintained that the Confederate states had in fact
left the Union, and therefore only the Congress could readmit them—after
they should be sufficiently scourged and humiliated. Lincoln's assassination
on April 14, 1865, passed the presidency to Johnson, a much weaker executive and easier prey for the congressional radicals. Johnson favored Lincoln's
policy, and he appointed as provisional governor of Texas Andrew Jackson
Hamilton, the former Unionist congressman who was once chased from
Austin by a secessionist mob. He had accepted an appointment as brigadier
of volunteers from Lincoln, and spent the latter part of the war in New Orleans as Texas' designated governor-in-waiting.

Gordon Granger's 1,800 soldiers were the first wave of an occupation
army that soon numbered some 50,000, which were, however, concentrated somewhat disproportionately along the Rio Grande to intimidate the
French, who were fighting to control Mexico through the proxy of Maxi-

milian von Hapsburg. (The wholesale mustering out of federal troops that took place after the war, especially after it was realized that there was no threat to restart the conflict, reduced that number by more than 90 percent over the following months, making the Union occupation far less efficient— or alternatively, less brutal—than it might otherwise have been.) The first military force to be ensconced in Austin after the collapse of the state government was commanded by a brevetted major general of volunteers, just twenty-six years old, George Armstrong Custer. He was at first despised, naturally, but during his half year of duty his energy in the prevention of looting, and his care that white citizens not be abused by the army, won him a good measure of respect in Austin. Many of its residents had only reluctantly embraced secession to begin with.

Required to cooperate not just with Custer but with a larger hierarchy of department and division occupation generals, Governor Hamilton set to work methodically on August 9 to create a civilian state government. He had to appoint the entire slate of precinct, county, district, and state offices, which he filled almost entirely with former Unionists. Johnson's Reconstruction plan required Texas to fill four conditions: withdraw the ordinance of secession, cancel state debts incurred on behalf of the rebellion, abolish slavery, and codify the rights of freedmen. To accomplish this, Hamilton called a constitutional convention, and set the election of delegates for January 8, 1866, with the convocation to open a month later. The process began smoothly enough, but when the gathering convened it was apparent that many of the same old adversaries, Unionists and secessionists, faced each other once again and that bad blood still flowed—with the addition now of a contingent of Radical Republicans both native and newly arrived with their cheap luggage. Homegrown Republicans became lumped under the derisive term "scalawags," to distinguish them from the immigrant carpetbaggers. The history of the Reconstruction era as told by still-partisan Texas writers tended to lay all blame for the ills of the time on the carpetbaggers, but in truth the homegrown scalawags were more numerous—a fact that might have been anticipated by the strength of Unionism in Texas before the war, which was robust enough to have elected Sam Houston as governor, and which required mass hangings and massacres by Confederate goon squads to suppress.

Winning seats in the Convention of 1866 were such old-guard fire-eaters as former governor Hiram Runnels, and Oran Roberts, who had been instrumental in calling the Secession Convention. Set squarely among the contending parties was the man chosen president of the convention, the most influential moderate, James W. Throckmorton, who had voted against secession but then served the Confederacy as a brigadier. The gathering opened with three days of vociferous pettifogging on such issues as convention organization and whether an oath need be taken, before Governor Hamilton stepped in with a dark warning that the federal government meant to have its way, and doing less than was required would not be conducive to the goal of readmission as a state. Turning their attention to Johnson's demands of them, they elected to frame their work not as a new state constitution, but as a series of amendments to the original state constitution of 1845. The opening skirmish was over the so-called *ab initio* question, whether secession had been void from the beginning, or whether it was rendered void by the war. At stake was the fate of all Texas laws put into force during the Confederate era, which would be dead letter if that government had been illegal from the start. This was the stance of the radicals, and fierce debate produced duelling committee reports; the issue was finally sidestepped by nullifying secession without mentioning from when. Little controversy was occasioned over the issue of debt repudiation, as the convention exceeded the federal requirement and repudiated all state debts incurred during the war, whether related to the conflict or not. This seemed reasonable because few of those securities were still held by the original creditors, but had passed to speculators, and such indebtedness was contrary to the Constitution of 1845, anyway.

The majority of the body dug in their heels on the issue of race, however. They pointedly refused to ratify the Thirteenth Amendment to the U.S. Constitution, which outlawed slavery, and covered their defiance with the fig leaf that they had already acknowledged the supremacy of the federal document, to which the Thirteenth Amendment was already appended. Their claim that ratification now would be redundant was technically true, but the larger truth was they simply did not want their noses rubbed in it. The convention also passed the first framework of the Black Code granting freedmen only limited rights of citizenship. Again, technically, they stayed within the bounds of the requirements of presidential Reconstruction, as Johnson had not actually demanded that freedmen be allowed to vote and hold office. They all knew his personal preference, however, that suffrage be extended to former slaves of competent literacy, and ignored it. John Reagan, who was a moderate states-righter before the war but whose service in the Confederate Cabinet, capture with Jefferson Davis, and incarceration in Fort Warren near Boston outranked all others present, cautioned the convention that their foot-dragging would not be well received in Washington.

They ignored him, too, largely because he had written an open letter to his fellow Texans from prison, urging them as a matter of reason and necessity to accept the Northern victory. That letter was regarded as unmanly and disgraceful, and sensing the mood of the convention, Reagan retired for the time being to his farm. Governor Hamilton intervened again, this time on the race issue. "The Congress of the United States . . . will look at your action in reference to the education of the black man. He shall not vote, but he shall be taxed to educate your children." If they thought such a provision would stand scrutiny in Washington, "you have done nothing but deceive yourselves."

Heedless, there was much sentiment in the convention to simply declare their amendments to be law, but a majority relented and permitted them to be submitted to the people's ratification. This was done on June 25, 1866, in a general election that also embraced candidates for state offices. Throckmorton stood for governor, opposed by Marshall Pease. The former had a long reputation as a moderate, but spoke against any voting by freedmen; Pease was a highly popular and effective former governor of the antebellum era, but when he endorsed partial black suffrage, Throckmorton walloped him by fifty thousand votes to barely twelve thousand. Six weeks after the election the Eleventh Legislature convened, Throckmorton took over the reins of civil government from Hamilton, and on August 20, President Johnson declared the rebellion in Texas to be over. It was all too good to be true, as the legislature was dominated by former colonels and slave drivers with plenty of impudence still to show. Of the two senators they elected to represent Texas in Washington, one was Oran Roberts, and the other was David G. Burnet, formerly provisional president of the Republic. Neither one was eligible to serve, being unable to swear a test oath required of federal office holders that they had always been loyal. Neither was seated in Congress, nor likewise the three representatives elected to the House. When presented with the Fourteenth Amendment protecting the civil rights of all (including black) citizens, the lawmakers solidly rejected it, and instead refined the Black Code begun during the convention, excluding freedmen from land grants and subjecting them to forced labor apprenticeship.

From the acts of the Eleventh Legislature one would have thought they actually won the Civil War, but in fact, as they were soon to discover, Texas was still an occupied territory. Throckmorton argued that Johnson's Proclamation of August 20 placed Texas on an equal footing with any other state, with the civil government superior to federal troops stationed within it. He labored mightily to remove troops from the towns and get them onto the frontier where they were needed for protection from Indians, and to get the army to cede jurisdiction of court cases involving the Freedmen's Bureau. The military, he discovered, had a vastly different view of things. Cognizant that reports of agents of the bureau being assaulted or threatened came in, on average, once a day, the army lent its full weight to the black cause, sometimes even to excess. Some of the worst trouble came in Brenham, where the editor of the local newspaper published an unflattering barrage on the subject of the Freedmen's Bureau. A bureau agent arrested and fined him, and was backed up by occupation troops who torched the commercial district of the town.

Actuated by motives both altruistic (black freedom gained in the Civil War was being frittered away by Johnson's easy reentry plan) and selfish (renewed Southern representation in Congress would threaten the radicals' grip on power), the radicals fought for and won control of the Congress in the 1866 elections. Almost as soon as they assembled they passed over Johnson's veto the First Reconstruction Act on March 2, 1867 (which in a previous era had been Texas Independence Day), dismantling the state governments as put together thus far, and imposing military rule over the South. It further demanded that new constitutional conventions be held in Southern states, that the legislatures elected under them be compelled to ratify the Fourteenth Amendment, and otherwise render themselves obedient to the congressional will. General Charles Griffin, an Ohio artillerist, West Point class of 1847, strict and quick to anger but guided by duty more than by personal animosity, was given command of the Department of Texas. He was a suitably ardent radical, and reported to the division commander, Philip Sheridan, in New Orleans. Governor Throckmorton, unwilling to yield any of the dignities of his office, found them much tougher masters. A Second Reconstruction Act imposed an "Ironclad Oath," barring from public office or voting or even serving on juries any men who had supported the rebellion, and Griffin began cleansing state offices of virtually all white Democrats. ("A dog, mangy and full of fleas," is how Throckmorton once referred to Griffin, "and as mean as the meanest radical in Texas, and that is saying as mean a thing of a man as can be said.") The governor protested Griffin's actions with such vigor that Sheridan, at Griffin's urging, dismissed Throckmorton from the governor's chair as an "impediment" to Reconstruction. He replaced him with the more tractable Pease.

Griffin, for his efforts, was promoted to Sheridan's post, but died of yellow fever before taking the larger command. The job of governing Texas passed to General Joseph J. Reynolds, a former colonel of Indiana volunteers and onetime instructor of history and geography at West Point. Reynolds finished a project begun by Griffin, of cleansing public offices in Texas of former rebels—his record sweep seems to have been removing four hundred officials in fifty-seven counties in one order. He also finished a Texas voter registration begun by Griffin, which purged ex-Confederates from the rolls. Sheridan's successor at the division level, Winfield Scott Hancock, quietly relaxed such a tight grip on the registration, and by the time it was completed, perhaps only 10,000 former rebels were shut out of the polls, while just under 60,000 whites and 50,000 blacks were registered. Their competing sentiments, however, stood out in stark relief. In the vote to call the new constitutional convention, some 10,600 of the 11,400 votes against it were cast by whites; some 37,000 of the 45,000 votes in favor were cast by freedmen.

When the Convention of 1868 gathered in Austin, seventy-eight of the ninety delegates were Republicans; ten of those were freedmen, including the ubiquitous George Ruby. With so much power in the air, the Republican bloc fractured along regional and economic interests. The dozen or so otherwise irrelevant Democrats found themselves holding some balance of power, and lined up behind the moderate Republicans, led by A. J. Hamilton in alliance with Governor Pease. The Radical Republicans coalesced behind a new figure, whom they elected president of the convention, Edmund J. Davis, a Florida native who had immigrated to Texas to become a merchant and lawyer in Corpus Christi and Brownsville. Like Sam Houston he refused to take the oath of allegiance to the Confederacy, which cost him his judgeship, but then unlike Houston, and the darkest mark against him, he defected to the Union, met with Abraham Lincoln—which to Texans was the equivalent of sitting down with Satan—and emerged as the colonel of a regiment of Unionist Texas cavalry. He participated in the Yankee seizure of Galveston in 1862, from which he barely escaped when Magruder retook the city. The rebels finally captured him in Brownsville, but to their gall had to let him go in a diplomatic gesture to the governor of Tamaulipas.

Although they had gathered to write a constitution, the 1868 convention dissolved into a fracas of irrelevant issues in pursuit of personal ambitions and group agendas. The radicals raised the *ab initio* question all over again— *ab initio*, as it were—but once again had to give it up in compromise language. The biggest distraction was their move to declare East Texas unreconstructed, and split West Texas off into a separate state. This came alarmingly close to reality, but having convened on June 1 and run out of money by the end of August, they adjourned until December. With a special tax passed for their continued support, they met into the new year and finally produced a partial constitution that satisfied the demands of congressional Reconstruction. In some ways it was an enlightened document, making, for instance, several provisions for the financing of public education for all races. There was even a suggestion, reported out of committee but crushed on the floor, to extend suffrage to women. E. J. Davis opposed the overall document as insufficiently radical and slated adjournment for February 6, 1869, but General Reynolds, who as if the show were not already confused enough began nursing political ambitions of his own, took the convention records, lassoed a committee to prepare a sort-of-final constitution, got forty-six signatures on it, and undertook a new voter registration drive for a public referendum on it.

That referendum would also embrace a new election of civilian officials, and with conservative Democrats left out, the contest for governor was between the moderate Hamilton and the radical Davis. Reynolds, on the side, was trying to advance his own political prospects by telling President Ulysses S. Grant that Hamilton, if elected, might start the war again. Governor Pease, under attack as a collaborator and dismayed by the whole circus, resigned on September 20 and left General Reynolds to rule by decree, which he rather felt Reynolds was doing anyway. After the election, which occurred over four days beginning on November 30, it was announced that Davis had beaten Hamilton by eight hundred votes out of eighty thousand cast, although beneath the cloud of fraud, intimidation, and subterfuge, no honest tally was really possible. But army rule came to an end rather quickly thereafter. Those who won the balloting received their offices by appointment from General Reynolds, who gave up his own ambitions as he realized the depth to which he had alienated virtually everybody. The legislature met in special session on February 8, and in the following days knuckled under and ratified the Fourteenth and Fifteenth Amendments. Grant accepted the Texas congressional delegation at the end of March, and on April 16, 1870, Reynolds gave up his authority. But if average Texans thought that Reconstruction was over, they were in for a bitter disappointment.

Within the state it was once again safe, if not less despised, to have been for the Union. The bodies of the twenty-eight German Unionists killed at the Battle of the Nueces were reinterred with honors near Comfort in 1866 under a granite monument reading TREUE DER UNION. In North Texas a few listless trials took place of those responsible for the horrific hangings in Gainesville and elsewhere, but netted only one conviction, and a would-be Union League march on Decatur drew no turnout. Some prominent Unionist exiles returned. László Ujházi, the Hungarian freedom fighter and Texas émigré who had served Lincoln in a diplomatic post in Italy, returned to San Antonio, where he helped found the local Republican Party. Although offered amnesty by Austria-Hungary's imperial government, he farmed his Texas estate until his death in 1870. Merchant kingpin and land baron Swante Swenson, on the contrary, who had once fled for his life, returned only long enough to arrange his vast affairs before returning to New York for his remaining thirty years. He often visited his Texas holdings, but never lived there again.

E. J. Davis became governor of Texas with a majority of Radical Republicans in the legislature to support him, and while seething Democrats regarded his term as the nadir of Reconstruction, the legislature wasted no time in helping him solidify his hold on power. They passed an Enabling Act, allowing Davis to fill by appointment—and that meant patronage—thousands of administrative jobs at all levels, from clerks and surveyors to mayors and district attorneys, vacated by Texas' readmission. They made provision for publication of a state newspaper in each judicial district, ostensibly for the printing of official notices but in reality so he could have an organ of propaganda. The legislature also postponed the next regular election until November 1872, handing Davis an extra year on his term. Impotent Democrats referred to these and other bills in a lump as the Obnoxious Acts, but none of them was as incendiary or had such evil effect as the creation of a state police force. Early in his term Davis attempted, to his credit, to provide better protection to the Indian frontier with new companies of Texas Rangers, but the army opposed the idea and there was no state money to pay for it. Small companies of "minutemen" were created instead, but with little effect. There was one unit, the "Special Force" of state police under Captain Leander McNelly, that did yeoman service in establishing law and order in the state, with nearly thirty-five hundred arrests, but the state police as commonly perceived were another matter.

Numbering between 170 and 200 officers, the most controversial acts of the state police in effect filled the vacuum left by federal troops in the protection of freedmen. Nearly half the force consisted of freed slaves, some with an eye to give former masters a bit of their own; some of their commanders had an eye more to the main chance than to law and order. There were cases where the exercise of state muscle was clearly called for in protecting the lives of freedmen and compelling white obedience to the new order of things. Late in 1870, James J. Gathings, one of the wealthiest and most prominent citizens of Hill County, bullied officials into arresting black state policemen who were in pursuit of Gathings' son, who was wanted for murder. Davis declared martial law on January 11, sending fifty state police under their adjutant general, James Davidson, to restore order and free the captive officers. While required by statute to levy penalties on the county itself, Davidson arrested the remaining Gathings menfolk and fined them three thousand dollars, resulting in an embarrassing investigation by the state senate, although the Republican majority in that body sustained the governor's handling of the "Hill County Rebellion." Similar unrest broke out in Walker County at the same time, where a freedman who had testified against a number of white men in an assault case was found dead on a road near Huntsville. Investigation of this incident fell to Captain McNelly, and led to the conviction of three white men in the murder. A courthouse gunfight resulted in the escape of two of the culprits, but criticism of the way trouble was handled in Hill County led Davis to delay imposing martial law on Huntsville. When the boom was finally lowered, state military justice gave the freedman's murderer, with the appropriate name of Nathaniel Outlaw, a sentence of five years, and a number of other men were convicted of lesser offenses relating to the courtroom gunfight and escape. Among them was the Walker County sheriff, fined $250 for negligence, and the county itself was assessed over $7,500 for the cost of the occupation.

Rightly or wrongly, the impression gained purchase that Governor Davis was too quick and too political in his determinations of when to impose the extremity of martial law. Moreover, the escapades of rogue officers sometimes contributed to their general unpopularity. The longest and most lethal blood feud in Texas history, between the Suttons and the Taylors in south-central Texas, while it began as the murder of two black soldiers, reached its height with plottings and bushwhackings by Jack Helm, a Sutton partisan and state police captain. Much of the Texas coastal plain southeast of San Antonio was gripped by a reign of terror which got only worse when Helm himself was gunned down by Jack Taylor and a Taylor partisan, a young gunslinger named John Wesley Hardin, in the summer of 1873.

Even Governor Davis was compelled to recognize that some of his fellow sojourners were conducting their offices with dubious propriety, once it became known that Davidson had embezzled nearly $35,000 and slipped away to Belgium. The irregularities of the Davis administration were discovered to be larger than the state police, however; the governor also had to recommend the removal of the state treasurer, one George W. Honey, onetime chaplain of the 4th Wisconsin Cavalry, who was just then on trial for misappropriation. The Texas Supreme Court later exonerated him, but by then Honey had packed his carpetbags and decamped to the North.

Probably a fair portion of the mayhem in Texas that took place during the Davis administration can be laid not to his policies, but to a general shaking out and settling of old scores at the local level. In East Texas this might take place as the redistribution of wealth away from the former planter class, or elsewhere as a final expression of prewar animosities. One of the most vengeful rebel chickens that came home to roost after the war landed in El Paso. While the German counties in middle-west Texas harbored Unionist sympathies, in El Paso the referendum on secession netted only a handful of votes for the Union, two of which were widely known to have been cast by the brothers William W. and Anson Mills, immigrants from Indiana, the latter of whom gave the name El Paso to the former village of Franklin. Escaping the excesses of the Confederate "Committees of Safety," Anson escaped to become a Union brigadier, and William joined the Union forces in New Mexico. (A third brother, Emmett, also fled El Paso, on the last outbound stage, but was killed when the coach was set upon by warring Apaches.) After the rebels occupied Fort Bliss, William was captured on Mexican soil, shanghaied home, and jailed briefly as a spy, before escaping to rejoin the federal army in New Mexico. For his brutish treatment, Mills blamed El Paso county judge Simeon Hart, an ardent secessionist whose flour milling and army contracting had netted him a fortune of over a third of a million dollars. Returning in the triumph of radical rule, Mills was instrumental in getting the federal district court in Mesilla, New Mexico, to seize and sell all of Hart's assets for less than a penny on the dollar. Hart received a presidential pardon and won repeated court decisions restoring his properties, but was unable to collect. W. W. Mills, meanwhile, was appointed customs collector for El Paso, became the local Republican leader, and as such waded hip deep into the local graft and corruption of the so-called Customhouse Ring. Such carrion attracted buzzards even nastier than he, however, and by backing A. J. Hamilton over E. J. Davis in the 1869 election, Mills lost his customs post to the radical faction and was forced from the political scene. He was still able to keep his old enemy Simeon Hart tied up in legal wrangles until 1873, when the federal Supreme Court finally restored Hart's properties to him, but he died soon after. Mills' battles with his rivals wrecked the Republican Party in El Paso, but he was able to salvage an appointment as U.S. consul in Chihuahua before entering a lengthy retirement.

Eventually the dark energy of the era had to exhaust itself. As early as September 1871, a coalition of Democrats and moderate Republicans met in a kind of rump convention in Austin to attack the Davis administration. Among them were A. J. Hamilton, Pease, Throckmorton, and one of Texas' new senators, A. J. Hamilton's brother, Morgan Hamilton. With the demise of the Ironclad Oath in an amnesty, the Democrats swept all four Texas congressional seats in a special election the following month, and in 1872 they seized control of the 13th Legislature, which immediately began dismantling Davis' program. Absent the Ironclad Oath, and with his own standing with the national Republican Party eroded, and even under attack by some black politicians, Davis never stood a chance at reelection in December 1873 against Richard Coke, the Democrat. The latter was an abolitionist's nightmare, an enormous, barrel-chested, bearded lawyer from Waco with a foghorn voice, who had sat in the Secession Convention, served as a Confederate captain, been elected to the state supreme court, and been removed by General Sheridan as an impediment. In the polling Coke triumphed 100,000 to 52,000.

In a legal challenge, Davis' supporters succeeded in invalidating the election on the reediest of technicalities: the polls in the election were only open for one day, and the constitution specified that they had to be open for four days. Democratic legislators claimed that they had power to change the provision because the preceding clause in the constitution did allow them to change the polling locations. The Texas supreme court, consisting of Davis appointees, ruled that since the clauses were separated by a semicolon and not a comma, the legislature did not have power to change the voting duration, and therefore the election was unconstitutional, with Davis to continue in office. Technically, the court's ruling was correct, but the fact that their decision seized upon a punctuation mark to overturn such a lopsided majority allowed Democrats to hoot the justices down as the "Semicolon Court." The decision was ignored as Democrats proceeded to organize the legislature anyway and inaugurate Coke as governor.

Davis refused to concede, and for a time it appeared that the Civil War might begin anew, in Texas. Militia companies gathered and stood their arms on the capitol grounds; most of them, like the company under veteran Rip Ford, were for Coke. While Coke's forces held the first floor of the capitol, Davis locked himself in his office on the second floor and telegraphed an appeal to President Grant to be sustained in office. It was nearly ten years since Grant had won the war, and although he had lost his reelection effort in Texas by 20,000 votes, it was time to make peace. Grant declined to intervene, and Davis was forced to resign, on January 6, 1874—although it was said that he refused to surrender the key to his office. Coke's installation signaled the end of Reconstruction in Texas, a period of violence and vengeful excesses from all quarters. Much of it was perhaps inevitable, but had Texas—and indeed the South—accepted their defeat in the war and not attempted, by noose and hood on the one hand and by legislative truculence and subterfuge on the other, to preserve the most odious racial elements of the antebellum system, much fuel would have been removed from the fire.

BOOK FOUR

CATTLE EMPIRE

FORTY-SIX

CLEARING THE PLAINS

THE DEBILITATING EFFECT THAT THE CIVIL WAR, AND then Reconstruction, had on Texas was not lost on the South Plains tribes of the Indian Territory and Texas Panhandle. Having seen the white soldiers march toward the east to fight each other, they found the frontier ranches and settlers left for the taking.

War parties did not sortie with one horse per rider; especially on a long raid, each man had several horses to choose from on a given day. A war party of several dozen men would be driving hundreds of horses. (One brave visitor to the Quahadi Comanches in 1867 estimated that they ran a herd of perhaps fifteen thousand head.) Thus the traditional raiding season was considered to be from that time in spring when the grass was high enough to graze the ponies during the raid, until the autumn.

Increasingly with Comanches on their raids were warriors of another tribe that was newer to the South Plains, the Kiowas. Their earliest traditions placed them in the valley of the Belle Fourche River, which skirts the northern flank of the Black Hills on the North Plains. There, according to their mythology, the Son of the Sun knocked on a hollow log embedded in the ground, and in answer the Kiowas emerged from within the earth. Not many of them appeared, however, before a fat woman got stuck in the log; thus they had always been a small tribe. During the late nineteenth century they counted no more than 1,300 to 1,500 individuals, but despite their low numbers they boasted a complex, caste-divided social structure, no fewer than six warrior societies, and a skill in battle virtually equal to the Comanches'. The Sioux had forced them south even as they had driven out the Comanches, and the two tribes fought for control of the South Plains until they recognized the stupidity of it and formed an alliance about 1795. The Kiowas had fewer historical reasons for hating Texans than did the Comanches, but their economy was based on raiding no less than the Comanches', and they happily joined in the commerce of rape and pillage.

The Comanches in the preceding few generations had become fearsome experts in the art of Plains warfare. Their skill at breeding and riding horses was peerless; by braiding a loop through a mount's mane, a warrior in a charge could sling himself over to the side, protected from enemy fire, and shoot arrows from beneath its throat. Yet they had also become the prisoners of that culture. They were now dependent upon their white enemies for its essentials—horses and guns—and weakened by what many warriors saw as a third essential, whiskey. When they first arrived on the South Plains in perhaps the mid-seventeenth century, they roamed in a number of distinct bands, but after two hundred years they had coalesced into five principal groups.

By now the most peaceful, understandably, were the Penatekas, who had occupied the southernmost of the Comanche range. Their leadership had been decimated at the Council House Fight in San Antonio in 1840 and they had suffered a calamitous defeat at the Battle of Plum Creek the following year. The treaty that they made with John Meusebach at Fredericksburg in 1847 was largely motivated by whippings that they sustained from Texas Rangers with Colt repeating revolvers. Incarceration on their Texas reservation a decade later reduced them further; after they were escorted north to the Indian Territory and the Kiowas and other Comanches got a look at them, they became objects of derision. When the Kiowa chief Set-tain-te (Satanta, or White Bear) was admonished to settle down into a white lifestyle, he retorted, "This building of homes for us is all nonsense. We don't want you to build any for us. . . . Look at the Penatekas! Formerly they were powerful, but now they are weak and poor. I want all my land. . . ."

With a reputation even among other Comanches for their ferocity, the Quahadi ("antelope") band roamed the Staked Plains of the Texas Panhandle. Their leading chief was Parra-o-coom (Bull Bear, or He Bear), whose name the whites bastardized into Perry Corn, a puny distortion of his reputation among his own people. "He was a real big man with curly hair," remembered one Comanche informant. "He was a bad fellow, always wanted to kill people . . . always wanted to have hand-to-hand fights with the whites. Parra-o-coom made a talk: 'When I was a young man I met things straight ahead. I fight. I want you men to do the same.' No one would listen to commands until Parra-o-coom gave the word." And all that could be said of He Bear could be said equally of the Quahadis' second chief, Wild Horse. They had never been reduced by white contact, and even other Comanches took care not to provoke them.

The one band that associated most with them was the Kotsoteka, the "buffalo eaters," whose leading chief, Mow-way (Shaking Hand), was a granite-faced monument of a man who wore in his scalp lock the claw of a Plains grizzly he killed with a knife as it mauled one of his men. Generally southeast of them was the Yapparika ("root eater") band, whose two most influential chiefs were aging brothers-in-law, Isa Rosa (White Wolf) and Tabananica (Hears the Sunrise), who was characterized by officers who knew him as "a chief of fine physique, unmistakeable talents, and great power." Even in his old age he still stood straight as a rod, famed for his stentorian bellow of a voice. The last of the major bands, the Nokonis, seem to have entered something of a decline since the death of their founding chief, Peta Nocona. His son by Cynthia Ann Parker, Quanah (Odor or Fragrance), had departed for the Staked Plains to live with the Quahadis, and the largest remaining segment followed the lead of Chief Horseback, once a respected fighter, though age and tuberculosis had turned him into a peace Indian.

During the Civil War, the nation was shocked by hideous and unjustified butchery of Indians by rampaging militias, the Sand Creek Massacre in Colorado most prominently. Such outrages gave strength to an Indian reform movement back east, which had as its goal the pacification of native tribes as an alternative to their extinction. In 1865 federal representatives met delegations from all the South Plains tribes—Comanche, Kiowa, Southern Cheyenne, and Southern Arapaho—and concluded a treaty on the banks of the Little Arkansas River. The Kiowas and Comanches, for their part, were awarded a reservation in the Texas Panhandle, which amounted to nothing because Texas had retained its public domain when it became a state, and the federal government owned not an acre of land there to give to them. The Comanches and Kiowas, who had grown accustomed to thinking of Texans as of a separate nationality from Americans, accepted their presents and raided in Texas as before.

When William Tecumseh Sherman took over as commander of the Division of the Missouri, which embraced Texas, forts were placed back on line to protect the western frontier, starting with Fort Clark near the Rio Grande, then running north and bending east: McKavett at the northwestern edge of the Hill Country, Concho on the southern extremity of the Plains, Griffin on the upper Brazos, and Richardson near the headwaters of the Trinity. On a map they appeared to be an imposing bulwark; in reality they were a sieve, merely inconvenient points for raiding parties to avoid. In July 1867 the embattled Reconstruction governor, James Throckmorton, as part of his ongoing effort to get the army to improve frontier protection, tallied up 162 Texans killed in Indian raids since the end of the Civil War, in addition to 43 women and children carried off into captivity.

Recognizing the failures of the Little Arkansas Treaty, Congress authorized a new round of negotiations with the South Plains Indians, this time held at Medicine Lodge Creek in Kansas. The council itself seemed success-ful. The Indians agreed to live on reservations and forgo raiding in exchange for rations and supplies, but then the treaty misfired as badly as the Little Arkansas had. Congress was far more concerned with humiliating the South and President Johnson, a conference committee failed to resolve differences between the House and Senate, and it was not ratified—a technicality lost on the natives. The Comanches and Kiowas shrugged—what else can you expect from white people?—and resumed filling their needs from Texas settlers.

One unintended effect of moving the Penatekas among the other Co-manche bands was to give their young men a look at what they had been missing. In the war-based Comanche social system, success depended on taking scalps to impress fellow warriors, and returning home with booty to impress sweethearts and win wives. The Penatekas' old chiefs had seen enough of the white men's power to be resigned to their lot, but they were not always successful at controlling their young men, who went raiding with warriors from the other bands. In fact, one of the Penatekas' senior leaders, Tosawi (Silver Brooch), who was always helpful to the government agents as a peaceful influence, was unable to stop a raid into Texas in July 1868 that was led by his son-in-law and the son of the Nokoni peace chief, Horseback. Thirteen warriors came across an isolated ranch near Spanish Fort, in Mon-tague County just across from the reservation. As an informant later told the agent, one of them "saw a woman through the window, sitting in a rock-ing chair. He signalled to his comrades that all was right, and [they] entered the house with a whoop—some through the windows and some through the doors. The woman was afraid and fell on the floor. The thirteen ravished her, Tosawi's son being the first, and Horseback's son the last, who killed her by sticking his tomahawk into her head. Tosawi's son-in-law then scalped her, and killed three or four of her children. The party then started up the river. . . ."

The election of U.S. Grant as president changed Indian policy radically. In a bold reform known as the Peace Policy, military officers were removed as Indian agents, and reservations across the West were entrusted to repre-sentatives of various religious denominations to pacify and civilize the na-tives. The agencies of the Indian Territory fell to the Society of Friends. In Texas, the thought of Quakers trying to convert Comanches and Kiowas with gentle persuasion elicited hoots of derision. At their agency at Fort Sill, just a short distance north of the Red River, Friend Lawrie Tatum found him-self soon overwhelmed with the defiance of lifelong raiders. Texans soon complained, with considerable justification, that Indians were pillaging at will and then retreating to their "City of Refuge" at Fort Sill to rest, draw rations, and wrap themselves in the Quakers' skirts. The situation was in fact more complex than that—white outlaws from Texas made just as much business preying upon Indian horse herds north of the Red River—but their impression was not altogether inaccurate.

On one raid early in September 1870, just one but so typical it can stand for many, a war party of Quahadi Comanches, usual inhabitants of the Staked Plains, struck southeast all the way to Montague County, far off their usual war trail, southeast almost as far as Gainesville. They fell upon the homestead of one Jesse Maxey. He was absent, but as his wife clutched her baby to her breast an arrow skewered its skull to her chest. The Quahadis scalped her but she survived, and they killed her father-in-law before taking two other small children, a boy and a girl, captive. The girl wept and sniveled so much during the night that the irritated Comanches stripped off her clothes—no sense wasting perfectly good clothes—and brained her. Knowing that soldiers would be hot on their trail, they left her where she could be easily found, and the following day a column of 6th Cavalry discovered her impaled in the thorns of a mesquite tree. The little boy fared better, surviving three years of captivity, during which he forgot both English and his name, but he was ultimately ransomed and returned to his family.

Throughout all this mayhem there was one native chief who came to disapprove of it all, who perceived the approaching end of the Indians' freewheeling life and began influencing his people to accommodate the whites and adapt. He was a Kiowa named Té-né-angopte (Striking Eagle's Talons), whose name was quickly and thoroughly bastardized, by the inadequacy of the sign language, into Kicking Bird. His preaching of peace acquired such a following that he became a threat to the war chiefs, who had been making a fine living from pillaging along the roads, ransoming captives, and then bullying the Quaker agents into giving them rations as well. They went so far as to start rumors that Kicking Bird had lost his nerve and become a coward. It was a lie and they knew it, but they left Kicking Bird no choice but to recruit a war party to prove his mettle.

In one of the most spectacular Kiowa raids ever mounted, a sad and angry Kicking Bird led a hundred warriors. It was not a foray for plunder, only for fighting. The men took only their fastest horses and finest regalia, which meant too that they would have been painted in their family colors, as the Kiowas had a system of heraldry not too dissimilar from medieval knights. Despite the injunction not to pillage, some of the warriors split off and robbed a stagecoach in Jack County, which instantly set a troop of 6th Cavalry from Fort Richardson on their trail. Fifty-four men under Captain Curwen McClellan overtook the Kiowas in Baylor County, some miles east of the site where the town of Seymour was later established, in the morning of July 12, 1870. He attacked smartly, but was thrown into disarray when he discovered that the Kiowa chief had divided his warriors, flanked him, and was threatening to cut off any retreat. Kicking Bird kept the troopers in a running retreat all day, feinting, flanking, attacking, wounding a dozen and killing three, one of whom the chief personally lanced from his horse. The cavalry was so undone that McClellan ordered them to dismount and lead their horses to prevent a rout. Kicking Bird broke off the attack in the evening, after which McClellan rounded up twenty local cowboys for reinforcement, but by then found no Indians anywhere. Back on the reservation, Kicking Bird disavowed any more fighting, embraced the agency and the peace road, shamed the chest-thumping war chiefs, and earned from them, not respect, but a depth of hatred that later cost him his life.

During that year and the year following, Indian depredations, and outrage in the newspapers, reached such a pitch that General Sherman, now commanding general of the U.S. Army, decided to tour the Texas frontier posts and determine for himself whether greater troop strength was needed in the area. Accompanied by General Randolph Marcy, who had surveyed much of this very frontier nearly two decades before, plus two aides and an escort of fifteen troopers, Sherman went from fort to fort, riding in a military carriage then known as an ambulance toward the eventual destination of Fort Sill, Indian Territory. Sherman was no champion of the Indian, but in his travels he had seen more evidence of settlers' histrionics than he had of real Indian danger. After a short visit to Fort Griffin he arrived at Fort Richardson on May 17, 1871.

Meanwhile, unknown to Sherman, one of Kicking Bird's most dangerous rivals for influence, a medicine man and prophet named Walks in the Sky, led a war party onto Salt Prairie near Jacksboro. Also prominent in the party were the chiefs Set-ankia (Satank or Sitting Bear), a venerated old member of the most influential warrior society; Satanta, whose braggadocio at Medicine Lodge had led reporters to call him the Orator of the Plains; and a rising young war leader named Big Tree. According to Kiowa informants, in night camp on the 17th, Walks in the Sky inflated his owl skin for a seance, and emerged with a prediction: "Tomorrow two parties of Tehannas will pass this way. The first will be a small party. Perhaps we could overcome it easily. Many of you will be eager to do so. But it must not be attacked. The medicine forbids. Later in the day another party will come. This one may be attacked. The attack will be successful."

By dawn the Kiowas concealed themselves on a low hill that commanded a three-mile view of the stage road as it crossed the Salt Prairie. After several hours of waiting, a small carriage appeared at the western end of the road, preceded by a platoon of cavalry. Several young warriors gestured angrily to attack the easy prey as they clattered beneath the hill, but Walks in the Sky grimly forbade it, and the fifty Kiowas stayed in concealment. From within his rocking military ambulance, William T. Sherman glanced outside at the thin mesquite scrub rolling by and wondered what all this Indian alarm business was about. It was country he hated, anyway. If he owned hell and West Texas, he once said, he'd live in hell and rent out West Texas. Sherman continued on to Fort Richardson, which was newly manned by the 4th Cavalry under Colonel Ranald Slidell Mackenzie—West Point class of 1862, graduating first in his class, whose six wounds and seven brevet promotions in the Civil War had left him an officer of proven mettle, and whom U. S. Grant considered the most promising officer in the army. The next night a wounded teamster arrived with word of a new Indian attack, on the Salt Prairie that Sherman had just traversed.

The column that departed to inspect the scene included the 4th Cavalry's regimental surgeon, J. H. Patzki. Sherman resumed his journey, and upon arriving at Fort Sill was besieged by citizens, including women who threw themselves to their knees and begged mercy from the Indian attacks. He was embarrassed and disgusted by the melodrama, and still unconvinced. Then Patzki's report caught up with him, of what he had discovered on the Salt Prairie near Jacksboro:

Sir: I have the honor to report that in compliance with your instructions I examined on May 19, 1871, the bodies of five citizens killed near Salt Creek by Indians on the previous day. All the bodies were riddled with bullets, covered with gashes, and the skulls crushed, evidently with an axe found bloody on the place; some of the bodies exhibited also signs of having been stabbed with arrows. One of the bodies was even more mutilated than the others, it having been found fastened with a chain to the pole of a wagon lying over a fire with the face to the ground, the tongue being cut out. Owing to the charred condition of the soft parts it was impossible to determine whether the man was burned before or after his death. The scalps of all but one were taken.

The bodies of two other men killed while attempting to flee the massacre were discovered some hours later, and the troopers buried all seven by the road, utilizing a wagon bed as communal coffin.

In an important way, the beginning of the end for the South Plains Indians came the moment General Sherman realized just how close his graying red Caesar-curls had come to decorating a Kiowa lodgepole. Agent Tatum made his own inquiries among the Indians on the next issue day, and the attack on the Salt Prairie was not just admitted, but bragged about. "If any other Indian comes here and claims the honor," said Satanta, "he will be lying to you, for I did it myself." Calmly Tatum penciled a note to the post commander to arrest the ringleaders. Before being transported to Texas for trial, Satank chanted his death song, slipped his manacles, and rushed his guard until he was killed. Satanta and Big Tree were taken to Jacksboro, the nearest town to the site of the attack, and put on trial. The prosecuting attorney was a twenty-five-year-old schoolteacher, Samuel W. T. Lanham, newly admitted to the bar and appointed district attorney by E. J. Davis. In his summation, Lanham cut loose with all the misappropriated alliteration of the frontier orator, characterizing Satanta as "the cunning Catiline" and using other comparisons lost on the pistol-toting cowboy jury. They were happy to convict, though, and Satanta and Big Tree were sentenced to hang, although Eastern reformers prevailed on Davis to commute the sentence to life in prison.

The Kiowas were genuinely chastened by this visitation of justice, and under Kicking Bird's insistence returned the forty-one mules stolen from the wagon train. The Comanches, however, were unaffected. Seeking to finally get matters in hand, Sherman ordered Mackenzie out to their real refuge, the breaks and canyons at the edge of the Staked Plains. Operating where no column had ventured before, it was Mackenzie who was found by the Quahadis, who stole seventy of his horses, killed a couple of troopers, and wounded the colonel himself with an arrow in the thigh. It was not an auspicious beginning to army activity in the Quahadi range, but at least he proved it could be done.

With Satanta and Big Tree in prison, and with Kicking Bird working tirelessly for peace, the Kiowas left the Texas frontier alone, for the most part, during the winter of 1871–72. But by the rise of the spring grass the lure of the old life proved irresistible. One of the fiercest of their war chiefs was Big

Bow, a barrel-chested playboy in the prime of life, who had been recognized for bravery (and who had stolen his first wife) when he was only eighteen. In April 1872 he led a large war party deep into Texas—all the way to the El Paso–San Antonio road in present-day Crockett County. They intended to stay at Howard's Wells, a spring-fed oasis surrounded by dense brush country. In preceding years it had been a favored Kiowa campground, and they still resented being forced away from it by encroaching settlement. They discovered the camp occupied by a large army supply train, heavily laden with small arms and ammunition, with no soldiers in sight. In a lightning attack, seventeen Mexican teamsters were killed (one woman was left alive), and all the stock and materiel taken. That night a patrol of 9th Cavalry from Fort Concho pursued the raiders and recovered the stock, but the Kiowas killed two soldiers without loss to themselves and made good their escape.

The second in command of the Howard's Wells raid was the chief White Horse, short and stocky and one of the fiercest fighters in the tribe. As they returned to their base camp south of the Red River, White Horse learned that his young brother, Kom-pai-te, who had been left to help guard the spare horses, had disobeyed, gone raiding with Comanches, and gotten killed. The grief-stricken White Horse responded with another massacre, ransacking the ranch of Abel Lee only sixteen miles from Fort Griffin. Lee was shot from his rocking chair on the front porch, his wife cut down as she tried to flee through the back door, a daughter killed in the garden. Three other children, aged six, nine, and seventeen, were herded back into the house and discovered their mother still alive, scalped, her ears and one arm cut off. They were apportioned to the warriors as slaves. Description of similar episodes would become repetitive, but there were many—so many that the government determined upon a new round of peace talks, these entrusted to Captain Henry Alvord of the 10th Cavalry, a capable officer with extensive Indian experience.

The Kiowas, armed with guns and ammunition taken from the army supply train at Howard's Wells, were feeling very confident. And the Comanches, having humiliated Mackenzie in his first venture up onto the Staked Plains, saw little need to give ground, but Alvord was finally able to convene a conference of chiefs on September 6, 1872. One of the most important of them was Tabananica, who allowed that he wasn't particularly interested in raiding or fighting soldiers, but he insisted on maintaining the free life he had always known. "I have kept out on the Plains because the whites were bad," he growled. "Now you come here to do good, you say, and the first thing you want to do is pen us up in a narrow territory." He knew the buffalo were disappearing, but "I would rather stay out on the Plains, even if I have to eat shit, than come in on such conditions!" Tabananica was known for his booming voice, and according to one Comanche confidant, after his speech, Alvord, "and every one else within a radius of a quarter of a mile, knew that he meant what he said." Mow-way, the leading chief of the Kotsotekas, was less vituperative, but equally unmoved. He was as aware as anyone of the government's record of failure in living up to its treaty obligations. To convince him to come into the reservation, he said, "I was promised lots of things, but I don't see them. When the Indians in here are better treated than we are outside, it will be time enough to come in."

Alvord's intention was to sign up Comanche and Kiowa chiefs to visit Washington, D.C., in hopes that they would be so impressed with the white men's power and numbers that they would yield to reservation life. Several of the Kiowas made the trip, including their principal chief, Lone Wolf, but the Comanches who undertook the journey were mostly minor headmen. The real powers, the Quahadis and Kotsotekas, went back up to the Staked Plains to resume their life of hunting and raiding. And even as the train bearing the peace chiefs puffed eastward on September 20, Sherman had already sent Mackenzie back on the trail of the recalcitrants to have it out with them.

The formidable officer whom the Indians knew as Three Fingers led three troops of his 4th Cavalry out of Fort Richardson on June 14. He paused at his old supply base on Catfish Creek and sent out patrols, which encountered no Comanches. The whole command then traversed the Staked Plains all the way into New Mexico and back, without result. Not one to give up, Mackenzie went out again with six companies in September. Utilizing Tonkawa scouts, on September 29 he located in the maze of breaks and canyons a large encampment of at least five separate Comanche villages on a tributary of the North Fork of the Red River. The 4th Cavalry completely routed the startled Indians, killing twenty-three and probably more, against losing three dead. They captured over 1,200 Comanche horses, and most tellingly of all, took 120 prisoners, mostly women and children. Ironically, the village that Mackenzie overran was that of Mow-way, the Kotsoteka chief who had told Alvord that he would come into the reservation when the Indians there had it better than those on the Plains. In the fall the Staked Plains Comanches interned themselves at their Fort Sill reservation for the first time. He Bear, the Quahadis' powerful first chief, told Agent Tatum that they knew they were whipped, and would do whatever was required of them if they could have their families back.

Meanwhile, the Comanche-Kiowa delegation to Washington took an unexpected turn when the commissioner of Indian Affairs promised them that in exchange for their peaceful conduct, their chiefs Satanta and Big Tree would be paroled from the prison in Huntsville. The Office of Indian Affairs had no jurisdiction over them, and their release was sure to raise a firestorm of protest in Texas. As the Peace Policy now seemed to have a chance at success, however, Grant exerted pressure on the besieged Governor E. J. Davis to grant them parole. Davis was reluctant to do it, but with his state regime crumbling under the multiple woes of Reconstruction, he needed the support of the Grant administration. He caved in, and with Davis in attendance to emphasize that they would go straight back to Huntsville if there were any more raiding, the chiefs were returned to the Kiowa tribe for the duration of their good behavior. At the emotional repatriation, Satanta's elderly father, Red Tipi, ran his fingers gratefully through Davis' hair.

General Sherman was wroth. "If they are to take scalps," he wrote Davis, "I hope yours is the first." But now for the first time, all the bands of South Plains raiders were, at least nominally, enrolled with their agencies and at peace.

FORTY-SEVEN

BUFFALO DAYS

RANALD MACKENZIE'S CAPTURE OF MOW-WAY'S VILLAGE, and the subsequent agreement of the Kiowas and Comanches—even the elusive Quahadis—to live at and draw rations from the Fort Sill agency, was only a temporary breather in the violence on the South Plains. Mow-way and his fellow chiefs conceded that Three-Fingers Kinzie had outmaneuvered them in Texas, but despite He Bear's mollifying remarks to Tatum, they were certainly not whipped. They still cherished a wide wild streak, and Fort Sill's post photographer, William Soulé, put his life in the balance every time he trekked out to their camps to take pictures. The Quaker agent also sensed the continuing danger. Lawrie Tatum had incurred the displeasure of the Society of Friends for his too-frequent willingness to apply to the army for help in controlling the Indians, and they replaced him with James M. Haworth. He was a Kansas farmer of forty-three who was himself not all that successful a pacifist, having raised a regiment of Union volunteers and attained the rank of major. That gained him no credit with the army command at Fort Sill, however, for their quarrel was with the Peace Policy itself, and they vilified and obstructed Haworth from the day he set foot on the agency grounds.

The post–Civil War campaigns against the Plains Indians gave the army needed experience, but it could be equally argued that they were a waste of time. The powerful and elusive Comanches and Kiowas, and north of them the Cheyennes and Arapahos, could not finally be reduced until their means of subsistence was removed. That meant that the buffalo had to go. During the early 1870s a series of events took place that rendered inevitable the end of the Indians' free life of hunting and raiding in Texas. The first was the completion of the transcontinental railroad, which divided the great American stock of buffalo into two distinct herds, one north of the line and one to the south. The second was the development of the hide industry. The third was the U.S. military's realization that the end of the buffalo meant the end of the Indian, and they gave their open support to the hunters.

The Medicine Lodge Treaty of 1867 gave the South Plains tribes the right to continue to hunt buffalo in that large chunk of Kansas south of the

Arkansas River. For a few years that "deadline" held, first because there were still plenty of buffalo north of that stream, and second because the grisly fates suffered by outfits caught by Indians in the hunting reserve provided a powerful disincentive. The bulk of the buffalo market was for meat and to supply the demand for winter lap robes, but no process had been developed to render the thick, tough hides into useful leather. Thus the bison herds, while wastefully hunted, still appeared to be limitless.

That changed in 1870 when a hale, nineteen-year-old Vermont Yankee named Wright Mooar came west to seek his fortune. Employed as the woodcutter for Fort Hays, he received part of a contract from an English tannery interested in experimenting on buffalo hides. Mooar, equally enterprising, overshot his quota and shipped the excess skins to his older brother in New York to try to develop an American market for buffalo leather. Successful experiments netted the brothers a contract for two thousand buffalo skins at $3.50 apiece, and the infamous buffalo slaughter was on. The brother, John Wesley Mooar, dispensed with his New York jewelry business, and headed west to join Wright as a professional "hider."

Seemingly overnight, other tanneries joined in the market for buffalo skins, and entrepreneurs in Dodge City, Kansas, provided a clearinghouse to ship the hides east by railroad. Most prominent among them was Charlie Rath; photographs of his hide yard depict up to forty thousand hides stacked for shipment. The easy money attracted a swarm of young men on the make. One who became a close friend of the Mooars was Billy Dixon, a semiliterate muleskinner from West Virginia who had perfected his marksmanship guiding buffalo-hunting parties for Eastern tourists. The carnage was breathtaking; Dixon recalled for a memoir that in the months following the fall of 1872, "there were more hunters in the country than ever before. . . . I feel safe in saying that 75,000 buffaloes were killed within sixty or seventy-five miles of Dodge. . . . We had to make hay while the sun shone." The commander of the local military post, Major Richard Irving Dodge, kept a kind of tally, showing that in 1873 alone, trains pulled out of town carrying over three-quarters of a million hides. In that year, the hunters looked jealously across the Arkansas River—what they had been calling the "deadline"—and crossed in such force that the Indians retreated across the border into their reservation. By 1874, the number of hides shipped out of Dodge approached four and a half million.

In the cold months of early 1874, with most of the buffalo hunters taking their leisure in Dodge and the Indians in their winter camps, Wright Mooar and a companion ventured down into the Panhandle of Texas, to investigate rumors of an undisturbed buffalo herd there. They were delighted to discover that the Eden was real: "All day long," wrote Mooar, the herds "opened up before us and came together behind us." Nervous about venturing so far from safety, however, the hiders decided to sound out the army as to whether they could expect help if they got into trouble. Mooar and another leading hunter, Steele Frazier, were delegated to meet with Major Dodge. They were concerned enough about Dodge's reaction to the Texas proposal that they actually took a bath before meeting him, and wore new suits of clothes to make a good impression. They needn't have worried. "Boys," Dodge winked, "if I were a buffalo hunter, I would hunt where the buffaloes are."

The Mooars and Billy Dixon were among the first buffalo hunters on the Texas Plains. Living mostly off what they hunted, they still required a month's staples of "a sack of flour, five pounds of coffee, ten pounds of sugar, a little salt, a side of bacon, and a few pounds of beans." Most of the space in their wagons was taken up with caps, shells, gunpowder—four hundred pounds—and perhaps sixteen hundred pounds of lead for casting bullets. The Texas Panhandle around the Canadian River became a vast shooting camp. "Each outfit," wrote Mooar, "would take a wagon, a keg of water, a roll of bedding, a little grub and, with a four-mule team would drive out . . . to intercept the herds. . . . We stayed out there on the divide until we loaded out the wagon with hides and meat. We could haul 10,000 pounds when the ground was frozen. We would load, come back to camp, unload, and go back out again."

Where natives would run with a herd, chasing buffalo on horseback, the white hiders developed the far more efficient technique of shooting from a "stand." Knowing that buffalo have a keen sense of smell, but would not stampede if there were no leader to follow, they would approach a herd from downwind, and pick out and shoot the leader from two or three hundred yards away. The confused herd would then mill, losing several dozen head until it finally bolted. Mooar once killed 96 buffaloes from one stand, Billy Dixon 120. Each hunter employed one or more teams of skinners, and would not kill more than they could process in a day. "Killing more than we could use would waste buff, which wasn't important," wrote one of them. "It would also waste ammunition, which was." The favorite weapon of the buffalo hunters was the Sharps buffalo rifle, which came in both .44- and .50-calibre models. The largest kind weighed sixteen pounds, with a massive octagonal barrel that developed some 2,000 foot-pounds of muzzle energy. Fired from crossed rest sticks and equipped with the commercially available 10x or 20x scopes, they could drop a buffalo from five or six hundred yards. Adding to the "Big Fifty's" power was the eccentricity of the hunters, who regularly disassembled the cartridges and supplemented the ninety grains of powder with an extra ten or twenty grains. This altered the guns' reports considerably, and on the Texas range the hunters kept track of who was hunting where by the unique boom of the buffalo rifles rolling over the Staked Plains.

By the height of spring the number of hiders working the Texas range probably exceeded two hundred. It was a long, dangerous trek back to Kansas for supplies, so Charlie Rath, ever in the van of commerce, organized a thirty-wagon train to set up business in the center of the action. With fellow merchants Fred Leonard and Charlie Myers, he established a trading post on the north bank of the Canadian in present Hutchinson County. They called it Adobe Walls, after the nearby ruins of a fort where Kit Carson had fought Kiowas a decade before. There were two mercantiles, one with a restaurant run by Mr. and Mrs. William Olds, a blacksmith shop, and a saloon run by an Irishman named Hanrahan. Rath was said to have put his foot down against the prospect of bringing along a contingent of Dodge City's whores, but the clientele was nonetheless a motley rabble. Many were of the mass of young drifters who followed the edge of the frontier looking for easy work and the main chance. Mostly they were young; often they went by dime-novel sobriquets like Prairie Dog Dave, Shoot-'em-up Mike, or Light-fingered Jack, affable young poseurs who, when they arrived, often had no idea what life on the buffalo range was really like. They were easy marks for the older and tougher frontiersmen who looked on them sometimes as prey (Wright Mooar fled his first outfit when he overheard his partners plotting his murder) and sometimes as a butt of their peculiarly savage brand of practical jokes.

Coming south with Fred Leonard was a young adventurer of twenty: a Canadian raised in upstate New York, William Barclay Masterson, who went by "Bat" and was a favorite companion of Billy Dixon. Also in the caravan was an obnoxious greenhorn from Illinois named Fairchild, whose knowledge of the West had come from dime novels. Old hands were appalled by his "shiny broadcloth suit, plug hat, flowered vest," and cravat that one compared to a Rocky Mountain sunset. He also sported an enormous bowie knife with which he incessantly vowed to scalp a red Indian. By the time they approached the Canadian River breaks, the other fifty men had had about all they could stand, and conspired to arrange an elaborate "Indian" ambush with whoops and gunfire while stalking turkeys in the gallery forest of willow and cottonwood along the river. Believing himself the only sur-

vivor, Fairchild raced back to camp in near hysteria, where other conspirators, exclaiming that he had been shot, ripped the shirt off his back and
splattered it with scalding coffee. Believing that he had been injured,
Fairchild allowed the other hiders to dress the "wound"—but then they
shuffled the undone greenhorn back to the dark woods to stand "guard."
When he finally wandered back into camp he found the entire company in
rolling mirth.

Such dark humor had its use on the Staked Plains; it was their way
of whistling through the graveyard, for in addition to everything else in
his kit, each hunter was sure to carry his "bite," a Big Fifty cartridge emptied
of powder and filled with cyanide. After the Kansas hiders invaded the
Texas buffalo range, the Indians provided several object lessons on the preference of taking one's own life to being captured. By the end of May the Indians were picking off hunting outfits within twenty or thirty miles of
Adobe Walls; two killed on Chicken Creek were apparently taken alive.
Staked out on the ground, one with a wooden spike driven through his
body, their heads had been propped up to watch themselves die—scalped,
castrated, genitals shoved into their mouths, their ears cut off, and disem-
boweled. Attacks became more frequent in June, prompting the hunting
outfits either to retreat back to Kansas or to stay within fleeing distance of
Adobe Walls.

Elsewhere on the frontier, the failure of Grant's Peace Policy was often attributable to the ineffectiveness or even corruption of the Indian agents supplied by the churches. That was not the case with the Quaker agents in the
Indian Territory, who labored heroically to keep the warlike Comanches and
Kiowas out of Texas. (Their superintendent, however, later was busted for
corruption.) The failure was in the supply system, which relied on private
contractors, and in the army, which winked at the extermination of the buffalo herds on which those tribes subsisted. For the natives, the end was the
same: starvation.

Kicking Bird, the Kiowa peace chief whom the war leaders had heckled
into leading the Texas raid in 1870, visited the agent at Fort Sill to impress
on him that it was imperative to keep the Kansas buffalo hunters out of
Texas. "The buffalo is our money," he said. "It is our only resource with
which to buy what we need and do not receive from the government. The
robes we can prepare and trade. We love them just as the white man does his
money. Just as it makes a white man feel to have his money carried away, so

it makes us feel to see others killing and stealing our buffaloes." Even several of the war chiefs were willing to give the peace road a chance, but the government broke its promises repeatedly.

As Agent Haworth wrote angrily to his superiors, "to tell them in the face of an empty Commissary, if you go away I won't feed you, would only have made them laugh." Indian rage finally coalesced behind Quanah Parker, the Quahadi war leader. A companion-in-war of his was killed by Tonkawa Indians in Texas. Many years later he gave an account in sign language to the commandant at Fort Sill, who recorded, "A long time ago I had a friend who was killed by the Tonkaway in Texas, Double Mountain Fork Brazos in Texas—that made me feel bad—we grew up together, went to war together. We very sorry that man. Tonkaway kill him, make my heart hot. I want to make it even.

"I hear somebody call, 'Quanah, Old Men want to see you over here!' I see Old Man Otter Belt and White Wolf, lots old men. They say, 'You pretty good fighter Quanah, but you not know everything. We think you take pipe first against white buffalo killers—you kill white buffalo hunters, make your heart good—after that you come back, take all the young men, go to war Texas.' "

In the entire history of native-white conflict on the frontier, the Plains Indians' most mortal enemy was not the settlers or even the army, but the organized teams of buffalo hunters. Yet this was the only time in that bloody history when tribal leaders, sitting in sage conference, figured out who the enemy really was, and directed against them that tribal anger which up to this time had been wasted, as Quanah was about to do, in pointless revenge raids.

All young Quanah wanted at this point, however, was his vengeance against the Tonkawas, and to the old men he retorted, "You take pipe yourself after I take young men and go to war Texas." To this the chiefs quickly agreed, pleased to have succeeded in sluicing Quanah's anger into a useful channel. The enormous war party was organized at a time when all the talk among the Comanches was of a powerful young medicine man named Isatai (Wolf Shit). As Quanah remembered, "Isatai make big talk that time: 'God tell me we going kill lots white men—I stop bullets in gun—bullets not pierce shirts. We kill them all just like old women. God told me the truth.' " It needed no magic for the Indians to know of the establishment of Adobe Walls, and that was where they headed, picking off hunting outfits as they went. The assault was to take place, as was often the case on the Comanche range, on the dawn after a full moon, Saturday, June 27, 1874. Wright

Mooar, after surviving two Indian attacks in two days thanks to his marksmanship with a Big Fifty, crossed the flooding Canadian, unloaded his hides with Rath, and headed his outfit back to Dodge City on Thursday, June 25.

The war party was one of the largest ever assembled on the South Plains, perhaps five hundred or more warriors. As dawn on Saturday neared, they used the gallery forest along the Canadian as cover, walking their horses because a trot would have been audible to the hunters. "Enemy hear trot a long way off," remembered Quanah. Isatai provided the magic, ochre-colored war paint, but leadership was assumed by He Bear of the Quahadis and Tabananica of the Yapparikas. "All chiefs try to hold young men back," said Quanah, "say, 'You go too fast. No good to go too fast.' Pretty soon they call out, 'All right, go ahead!' "

What the warriors could not know was that the men inside Adobe Walls were almost all wide awake already. Either there had been a providential stroke of luck when the ridgepole in Hanrahan's saloon snapped during the wee hours or—what's more likely and was admitted by Wright Mooar nearly sixty years later—Hanrahan had been warned by Charlie Rath that an attack was imminent, and fired his revolver, shouting to the men sleeping in his saloon that the ridgepole was breaking. In either event, most of the men had spent the night repairing the roof (only upon subsequent inspection was it noticed that the original ridgepole was perfectly sound). But the element of surprise was lost, and by the time the whooping Indians reached the corrals, the hunters were barricaded inside the four buildings, except for two brothers, freighters named Ike and Shorty Shadler, who had arrived late in the night previous. The northbound Mooar had crossed them on the trail. "Ike," he said, "you better hurry back or the Indians will get your scalp." The Shadlers paid good heed, arriving at Adobe Walls on Friday evening, unloading their merchandise and reloading with buffalo hides before turning in. Exhausted, they bedded down in their wagon. By the time they awakened during the attack, they were already cut off from the buildings, and lay quietly concealed. Eventually a Comanche named Mihesuah lifted a corner of the canvas to see if there was anything worth taking and was shot pointblank, but the brothers had given themselves away and were quickly swarmed and scalped. They were savagely defended by their big black Labrador, which the Indians also killed, and they recognized its bravery by slicing a fur "scalp" from its side.

It was a classic Indian attack; all morning and into the afternoon the Indians circled the buildings at a gallop, firing at the buildings from beneath their horses' throats. Individual braves sought to establish their rank by charging up to the windows and emptying their guns. One warrior killed doing this was trying to expunge the shame he felt because his father, the Cheyenne chief Stone Calf, had refused to sanction the war. A third hunter, a young companion of Bat Masterson's named Billy Tyler, was shot through the lungs and mortally wounded by such a charge. The contest, however, was unequal, as the two dozen professional hunters unlimbered their Sharps buffalo rifles and began to exact a fearful toll. In the first rush, Quanah Parker reached the door of one of the buildings and beat at it with his rifle butt, and was shot through the side as he retreated.

Isatai had provided the warriors with ochre paint that he said would render them invulnerable, but the assault sputtered as their casualties mounted into the dozens. Atop a butte and out of sight of the settlement, the leaders met to decide what to do. The question was settled by a genuine stroke of providence on the part of the hunters. During the council, Isatai's horse, which was solidly doused in the magic paint, was struck in the head and killed by a stray bullet fired from the buildings. "All Cheyennes pretty mad Isatai," remembered the wounded Quanah Parker. "Tell him, whats matter your medicine? You got polecat medicine!" One Cheyenne warrior named Fat Buttocks produced a quirt to administer a whipping, but the older chiefs intervened, saying that Isatai's disgrace was sufficient punishment. An equally demoralizing demonstration of the hunters' guns came the next day, when men inside the compound noticed a group of Indians observing them from a distant bluff. They prompted Billy Dixon to show off his famous marksmanship. Dixon braced himself and fired, and several seconds later, a Comanche named To-hah-kah slumped from his horse. The legendary "long shot" was later paced off at 1,538 yards, over three-quarters of a mile; Dixon admitted it was a scratch shot—pure luck—but it had its effect. Confronted with such overwhelming firepower, even Isatai lost faith in his magic. "The whites," he admitted, "have a very strong medicine. Shoot today, maybe so kill you tomorrow." Their attack instead became a siege, which they loosened by degrees until they left the area entirely. The measure of their defeat is unknown; up to fifteen men were later named among the killed, but later army scouts found more than thirty burials in the buttes surrounding Adobe Walls. Minninewah (Whirlwind), the Cheyenne chief, later said there were 115 killed, but it is hard to imagine the hostiles continuing any resistance if that were true. But whatever the actual number, Quanah Parker had kept his bargain with Tabananica and White Wolf: he had attacked the white buffalo killers first; now he took the young men and led them to war in Texas.

After the battle, the hunters sent a courier to Kansas, whose governor appealed to the army's commander of the Department of the Missouri, General John Pope. Pope, who was one of the few officers who had some conscience where the natives were concerned, refused to send any help, pointing out that Texas was beyond his jurisdiction, and the buffalo hunters had brought the trouble on themselves. If he sent troops, he snorted, it would be "to break up the grog shops and trading establishments rather than protect them." The frontier commercial establishment was outraged. As one journalist claimed rather self-righteously, the hiders "are shrewd, go-ahead business men, [and] are in no manner responsible for the [Indian] outbreak." Joining the criticism was Pope's superior, Division Commander Philip Sheridan, who didn't like Pope anyway, and used the Texas attack to reprimand him that "regardless of the character of these men," Pope should have sent a relief column. (Sheridan, the following year, made pointed remarks on the topic to the Texas legislature, by way of opposing bills intended to protect the remaining buffalo. The hiders, he said, "have done more in the last two years . . . to settle the vexed Indian question than the entire regular army has done in the last thirty years. They are destroying the Indians' commissary. . . . Send them powder and lead, if you will, but for the sake of lasting peace, let them kill, skin, and sell until they have exterminated the buffalo.")

Back at Adobe Walls, scouts sent out from the buildings found less and less Indian sign. The hunters lost a fourth and final casualty four days after the fight, when the restaurateur, William Olds, spied some distant Indians from a makeshift watchtower and accidentally shot himself through the head while descending to spread the alarm. A decision was made to evacuate the place, which took about six weeks to arrange. Although Rath had sworn Mooar and Hanrahan to secrecy, somewhere amid the comings and goings the story gained credence that Charlie Rath, "shrewd, go-ahead business man" that he was, had pulled out of Adobe Walls on Friday night because he had been warned of the attack by a contact from the Cheyenne Agency trading post. He did not warn the others, it was said, because he didn't want to leave his merchandise undefended.

FORTY-EIGHT

THE RED RIVER WAR

AFTER THE BATTLE OF ADOBE WALLS, THE LARGE WAR party split. A couple dozen young Arapahos made their way back to the reservation, and the Cheyennes, who had more rage to vent, while basing themselves along the Cap Rock, turned their attention to raiding mostly in Kansas and Colorado. The Comanches, however, headed as usual into Texas.

Although some Kiowas fought at Adobe Walls, most of the tribe sat out that affair, preferring to make a decision on peace or war at their annual Sun Dance, held on the reservation the first week in July. The Comanches and Cheyennes, returning from their failure against the buffalo hunters, camped nearby and lobbied hard in support of Walks in the Sky, the Owl Prophet who had nearly relieved General Sherman of his hair in 1871, and the Kiowas' principal chief, Lone Wolf, who was recruiting a revenge raid for his son, Tau-ankia (Sitting in the Saddle), who had been killed on a Texas raid the previous December. Kicking Bird, however, succeeded in getting three-quarters of the tribe to follow him when he interned at the agency. The fifty or so Kiowas who did head south with Lone Wolf established a base camp near the later town site of Quanah. That night the prophet predicted success, especially for a novice who was participating in his first raid, named Tsen-tonkee (Hunting Horse). The next day they rode out to the Salt Prairie, near the site of the Warren Wagon Train Massacre of three years before, where they spied four local ranchers and gave chase. The cowboys escaped, cleverly, by galloping through a section of country whose jagged rocks cut the feet of the Kiowas' unshod mounts. The Indians stopped and shot several calves to make rawhide bandages for their horses' feet, when they discovered that they were being trailed by about two dozen mounted whites, all wearing white hats. The Indians concealed themselves in a rugged draw known locally as the Lost Valley and prepared an ambush.

These white hats were Rangers. One of the first acts of the legislature under Richard Coke, passed on April 10, 1874, with an appropriation of $300,000, was the reorganization of the Texas Rangers into two divisions: a Special Force, to control banditry along the Rio Grande, and the Frontier Battalion, six companies of seventy-five men spaced along the edge of settlement. The latter were just newly on station, and their commandant, Major John B. Jones of Corsicana, was making his first tour to inspect and organize. Jones was handsome and of average build, with jet hair and a beetling moustache; he was nearly forty, genteel, educated, and during the Civil War had gained a reputation for cool leadership and bravery, first in Terry's Texas Rangers and later with other regiments. His continuing Southern sympathies after defeat were evidenced by his trip to Mexico to scout locations for a proposed colony of former rebels (an idea he abandoned). He was elected to the legislature in 1868 but the Radical Republicans refused to seat him. By July 1874 all six companies of the Frontier Battalion were on station; Jones arrived at the camp of Captain G. W. Stevens, on Salt Creek near the site of Graham, late on the night of July 11. Having been apprised of an Indian outbreak, scouts were sent out the next morning who found the Kiowas' trail, and about twenty-five Rangers, including Jones and Stevens, took up the pursuit.

Jones' bravery was unquestioned, but his lack of experience at Indian fighting was a glaring drawback—and he was the only one of the Rangers that day who had ever seen battle of any kind. He entered the Lost Valley without considering the possibility of ambush; in fact two of the Kiowas, including Walks in the Sky, dashed out into the open so the Rangers would follow them; they were not even seen, but Jones came on obligingly. As the Indian trail split up into the forested cover of the high ground, Jones divided his little band to try to discover a main trail. Jones had only a half-dozen or so men around him when the Kiowas sprang the trap and swept down from cover. "Major," said Stevens coolly, "we will have to get to cover or all be killed." Jones managed to collect most of them in a firing line in a dry wash; some were already wounded, others were unaccounted for, cut off from the rest and quietly hiding. One of the Rangers, William Glass, was shot down trying to make it to the ravine, and a tense drama ensued as the wounded Glass, seeing two Indians ducking and weaving their way toward him, began screaming, "Don't let them get me! My God, don't let them get me!" The Rangers in the ravine laid down a covering fire.

One of the two Kiowas was young Hunting Horse, who thought this was his chance to fulfill Walks in the Sky's prophecy. "It was my chance," he recalled later. "We could see the man lying there in plain sight. The heads of the other Rangers could be seen sticking up from a dry streambed. Nobody dared go close enough to make coup." Following the lead of Lone Wolf's nephew, a chief named Red Otter, Hunting Horse made a determined effort to reach Glass. "Red Otter ran forward and took position behind a large tree.

He signalled for me to join him. . . . The bullets were throwing bark in our faces. Then we ran to another tree. But the bullets came thicker." Under heavy covering fire, two Rangers dashed out of the ravine and carried Glass to cover, but he died soon after.

"There is nothing to equal the thirst created by inhaling the explosions of fresh gunpowder," wrote one of Jones' Rangers later. Before Jones could stop them, two men rounded up canteens and tried to reach a waterhole on Cameron Creek about a half mile away. One was speared from his horse and the other escaped by diving into the pool and surfacing, luckily, near where two other Rangers were hiding after having been separated from the column. Their combined fire turned the Kiowas away. The Ranger who was killed trying to reach water was named David Bailey; it was over his body that Lone Wolf made his vengeance speech for his lost son, and attacked Bailey's head with his hatchet pipe until he was no longer recognizable. Revenge attained, the Kiowas headed back to the reservation, not intent on pursuing a general war. And Hunting Horse, in recognition of his bravery, was awarded Bailey's bay horse, which had been captured from the Rangers. During the night Jones and his men made their way, on foot as most of the horses had been killed, to the safety of the Loving ranch a few miles away.

While this first clash of the Red River War did not involve federal troops, the attack at Adobe Walls spurred the government to develop a final solution to the Indian problem on the South Plains. It was not hard to decide upon a strategy. The overall design was Sheridan's, and it was efficient. The Office of Indian Affairs was given a limited time to enroll peaceful natives at their agencies, after which the gates of the City of Refuge were to be barred to the hostiles. Five separate expeditions would then converge on the Texas Panhandle: 10th Cavalry would ride west from Fort Sill under John W. Davidson; 11th Cavalry would ride northwest from Fort Richardson, Texas, under George P. Buell; 4th Cavalry under Ranald Mackenzie would move north from Fort Concho and have another crack at his recent nemesis; 8th Cavalry under William Redwood Price would strike east from Fort Bascom, New Mexico; and the largest column, 6th Cavalry and 5th Infantry under Nelson Miles, would move southwest from Kansas. It was an aggregate of some 2,500 men, the largest force that had ever been thrown against Indians up to that time.

Miles' large force—five companies of 5th Infantry, eight troops of 6th Cavalry, scouts, two Gatling guns and a Parrot 10-pounder—began rolling out of Dodge City as early as August 11, first south to Camp Supply, Indian Territory, then west into the Texas Panhandle, leaving his supply train to catch up with him as best it could. With Miles, not surprisingly, were a number of the buffalo hunters who, after Adobe Walls, had drifted back to Kansas. With the bison all but gone, they now obtained good employment as scouts who knew the country—Billy Dixon and Bat Masterson among them. Miles was a martinet and regarded the hunters with disdain. "I find no trouble in getting all that class of men I want," he wrote to his wife, "and though they are a rough set . . . they will be valuable for what I want them for." Also with him were some favored newspaper correspondents, whom Miles figured to use to keep the world informed of his brilliance.

The reporters had plenty to write about, for as Sheridan had predicted, hostile Cheyennes who had been locked out of their agency enrollment were already there, on the Staked Plains and in the canyons cut into the Cap Rock, waiting for him. Even more dangerous than the renegade Indians, Miles also rode into the teeth of a blistering drought. Temperatures ran as high as 110 degrees, streams and even branches of the major rivers were dry, waterholes were foul, and troops desperate enough to drink from alkali springs at the base of the Cap Rock were immobilized as they vomited their guts out. Still, he pushed his men twenty-five and even thirty miles a day in hot pursuit of the Cheyennes, who managed to stay just out of reach, abandoning their villages and igniting prairie fires to cover their flight.

Near the end of August, Miles reached the Main Fork of the Red River— dry sand—his men nearly delirious, some opening veins to drink their own blood. The Cheyennes finally eluded him, and with Miles unable to go forward and unwilling to retreat, he sent back to find his supply train, while composing victorious-sounding reports of his actions. The Cheyennes "kept up a running fight for several days, the Indians steadily falling back until they reached the hills, where they made a bold stand, but were promptly routed . . . losing heavily in men, animals and baggage."

Thanks in large part to the admiring reporters in his entourage who were willing to shill for him, Miles became a hero in newspaper columns. One of the Cheyenne chiefs whom Miles was pursuing, Whirlwind, had his own opinion of Miles' performance, given in an interview with Wright Mooar more than fifty years later. Of his habit of saluting the raising and lowering of the flag with the Parrot gun, Whirlwind smiled, "Sundown, Miles shoot him big gun—*boom*—tell every Indian for fifty miles where he camp. Sunup, Miles shoot him big gun—*boom*—tell every Indian for fifty miles he still there." Miles, he then said, was full of bull. Of the victories Miles had been reporting through his correspondents, Whirlwind chuckled, "Me lead him on big trail, round and round. Braves make big trail for him to follow, then slip back behind, scalp stragglers and shoot up rear. Got him down in breaks on gyp water. Soldiers got sick. Braves get on bluffs and throw rocks at 'em. Too sick to move." A jot in the army records notes that two hundred hostiles had been seen in his rear, and one of the colonel's own news corps reported "a straggler killed and scalped within a half mile of camp." Whirlwind's account seems the truer one.

As Miles sat pinned around the upper Red River, his need for supplies became so acute that he sent British-born Captain Wyllys Lyman with a hundred men and three dozen empty wagons back up his trail to find the train that he knew must be en route. Lyman eventually found them in present Hemphill County, a good two hundred miles back up the trail and almost at the Indian Territory border. Transferring the supplies to his own wagons and turning south again, Lyman reached the upper Washita on September 9, where he was suddenly pounced on by an estimated three or four hundred Comanches who were fleeing punishment for looting the Anadarko Agency, and Kiowas who had been locked out of their agency until they could be punished. Lyman managed to keep the train moving for twelve miles while fighting, but upon encountering impassable ground had to halt and fortify with rifle pits. The properly English Lyman wrote an understated note to the commander at Camp Supply: "Sir: I have the honor to report that I am corralled by Comanches, two miles north of the Washita, on Gen'l. Miles' trail." He outlined the condition of his wounded, and "considering the importance of my train . . . I deem it injudicious to attempt to proceed further. . . . I think I may properly ask quick aid." He trusted the note to a small scout on a fast horse, who threw off Indian pursuit by ducking into a buffalo herd and stampeding them; relief arrived two days later and the Indians vanished.

The behavior of hostile natives at the Battle of Lyman's Wagon Train illustrates an important but little remarked aspect of Plains Indian warfare. In spite of the privation and provocation suffered by the Comanches and Kiowas, the purpose of war was not necessarily to wipe out one's enemies. The purpose was to prove one's bravery and establish one's status in the tribe, to win the respect of one's peers and the romantic interest of young women. For a warrior in a society of warriors, war was simply their business; the justification or lack of it was to some extent a white judgment. With an earnest effort the Kiowas could have overrun Lyman's supply train and caused the government a major disaster in lives and property lost, and forced Miles' withdrawal from the campaign. As it was, however, when the alerted war party arrived on the scene, they engaged in individual antics to prove their bravery to one another.

One lightly regarded young man named Botalye had particular incentive. Some time previously he had been engaged in roughhousing with Tsa-lau-te (Cry of the Wild Goose), Satanta's son, inside the chief's prized red tipi. Cry of the Wild Goose inadvertently knocked some coals against the dyed buffalo hides, which began to burn. Satanta arrived in time to extinguish the fire, but his son failed to take responsibility for the mishap and allowed Satanta to blame Botalye, whom he branded a coward, and told if he ever proved himself one, he would whip him. Now in his first battle, Botalye realized that if he could make it through Lyman's line, the soldiers could not shoot at him without endangering one another. Against the warnings of the chiefs he made the charge, then a second and a third, as bullets clipped the feathers from his hair, cut one of his stirrups, and creased his horse's neck. Walks in the Sky himself acknowledged his bravery but told him to cut it out, but Botalye made a fourth charge, and emerged from the opposite side of Lyman's rifle pits. He galloped to a nearby rise where he tried to give a masculine war whoop. In derision of Satanta's son, "I wanted to make it sound like the cry of a wild goose," he later said with amusement, "but only a frightened squawk came out. I had no experience." He returned to the main gathering of Kiowas, dismounted, and upon seeing Satanta said, "Whip me now."

The chief roared with laughter and embraced him, as Botalye's chief, Poor Buffalo, rewarded him with a new name: Eadle-tau-hain (He Would Not Listen). Inside his stalled wagon train, Wyllys Lyman observed the macho exhibitions of Botalye, and others, with wonder: "The Indian practice of circling [continued] until it became a wonderful display of horsemanship. Savages erect on their ponies, with shining spears, flaming blankets and lofty fluttering headgear, dashed along the ridges with yells . . . appearing and swiftly disappearing." Lyman himself was not too caught up in the romance of the adventure to miss that the "wild entertainment" had a purpose, which was to divert attention from dismounted firing parties trying to creep closer to the wagons.

As Lyman was treated to the native pageantry, Miles sat in his hot camp fretting where his supplies could be. On September 10 he dispatched two of his best scouts, Billy Dixon and a half-breed Cheyenne interpreter named Amos Chapman, with four troopers, to retrace his route all the way back to Camp Supply, if necessary, to locate Lyman and/or the supply train. They moved swiftly, already near the Washita on the morning of the 12th, when they found themselves surrounded by more than a hundred Comanches and Kiowas who were retiring from the wagon train fight. Previous fires had burned off any semblance of cover, and with the six whites crouching on bare dirt the Kiowas decided to have some fun with them. Distantly circling at a gallop, they used them for target practice, wounding three or four before Dixon spied a buffalo wallow some distance away that might offer some protection. Four of the six made it there, the exceptions being Chapman, who was shot through one knee, and Private George Smith, who had been given charge of the horses, mortally wounded through the lungs. The men deepened the wallow with knives and piled the dirt around the sides, and then beheld a violent squall line approaching, with rain pouring in sheets. The horses had bolted when Smith fell, carrying with them coats and blankets. Chapman, who lived at Camp Supply and was married to a Cheyenne woman, was well known to the hostiles, who as they edged closer took to taunting him, "We got you now, Amos!" After several attempts, though, Dixon finally managed to carry Chapman into the relative safety of the buffalo wallow.

The Indians tired of the game during the night and departed. Dixon managed to find and crush some tumbleweeds on which to bed down the wounded, which made the night only slightly less miserable, for the rain had brought with it an early-season norther that dropped the temperature drastically. Dixon was the least hurt of the five survivors; he set out in the morning to find the main trail, and luckily encountered Major Price and the New Mexico column on their way east. As relief neared, however, the jumpy men in the buffalo wallow opened fire, shooting the horse from beneath a surgeon's assistant and so angering Price that he left them where they were as he moved on to join up with Miles. It was an act of pique that the ambitious Miles was more than happy to answer by relieving Price and absorbing the 8th Cavalry into his own command. The five survivors recovered from their wounds, although Chapman lost his leg, and all received Congressional Medals of Honor. (Dixon's and Chapman's were later rescinded when it was realized that they were only civilian scouts, but Dixon refused to surrender his.)

Between the chronic supply problems and the activity of hostiles in his rear, it was increasingly evident that Miles had overextended himself, which he covered by opening quarrels with other officers and whining to his reporters that he was not being adequately supported. When General Pope ordered him to withdraw from the Red River back to the Washita, he obeyed, but fumed because that left the remaining real action for Mackenzie and the 4th Cavalry, now on their way up from central Texas.

Marching up from Fort Concho, Mackenzie was all too aware of Miles' early entry into the war, of his coterie of news reporters, and of his reputation for playing dirty politics. "I am not in the slightest degree jealous of him," Mackenzie wrote of Miles. "I regard him not as my Superior in any way and in some particulars I am sure he is not my equal." And considering the pickle that Miles got himself into by outrunning his supply train, Sheridan was disposed to agree. The hostiles too had much higher regard for Three Fingers than they did for Miles. It took some weeks to decimate the garrisons along the Rio Grande that were the 4th Cavalry's duty stations and collect them at Fort Concho. When Mackenzie marched he had over six hundred men: eight companies of 4th Cavalry, five companies of 10th and 11th infantry, Tonkawa, Seminole-Negro and Lipan Apache scouts, and an ace in the hole, a half-breed Comanchero named Johnson who had illicitly traded with the hostiles in their deepest haunts for years.

He would not make Miles' mistake of allowing hostiles to slip behind him; in fact the Texas Department had a new commanding general, Christopher Columbus Augur, a raptorish old man whose flaring sideburns scraped his epaulettes. He had fought Red Cloud in the Dakotas, and his final advice to Mackenzie before the campaign was that "a commander against hostile Indians is never in such imminent danger as when fully satisfied that no Indians can possibly be near him." Where Miles had nearly brought his column to ruin by outdistancing his supplies, Mackenzie had his ace quartermaster, Captain Henry Lawton, reopen his old Catfish Creek supply base, 150 miles west of Fort Griffin, before the main force ever got there. Thus when Mackenzie reached the camp on September 19, it took less than a day for his scouts to discover three different Indian trails, and he was out after them.

The summer drought was now not merely broken, but Mackenzie sometimes covered as little as three miles a day through mud that buried wagon wheels up to the hubs. When the weather cleared on the twenty-fifth he pushed a final twenty miles to Tulé Canyon. Word of his presence electrified the hostiles, who began collecting about him for a fight. Mackenzie had lost horses to them twice before, and on the night of the twenty-sixth every mount in camp was hobbled and cross-sidelined, with skirmishers placed every fifteen feet around the herd. When some 250 Indians attacked at ten that night, they failed to snatch a single animal. An extensive skirmish was fought the next day, but when the hostiles retired at speed, Mackenzie knew they were leading him away from their camp. He pretended to follow, and then after dark altered his march northward to the Palo Duro Canyon. Peering over its lip at dawn, the soldiers saw, twelve hundred feet below, a vast spread of hostile villages extending out of sight upstream on the Red River. The irritable Mackenzie believed he was losing the element of surprise in the time needed for the Indian scouts to find a steep trail down into the depths. "Mr. Thompson," he said to the chief of scouts once the path was found, "take your men down and open the fight."

One hundred and fifty yards down the trail they were discovered by a Kiowa sentry, a minor chief named Red Warbonnet, who fired his gun and whooped a warning before being killed. By the time the troopers led their mounts down the dizzying trail and formed up on the canyon floor, the Indian villages were in pandemonium. Fleeing up the canyon and taking cover on the rocky slopes, the Indians found organized resistance was impossible. One detachment of cavalry raced straight up the canyon to capture the hostiles' horse herd. The day was not a battle but a rout; only one soldier fell, and only three Indians were known to have been killed in the action, but Mackenzie was satisfied to know that their surrender was now inevitable. He was in possession of the renegade villages, and he burned them to cinders, depriving them of winter food and shelter. He was also in possession of their horse herd. Recalling his lesson from two years before that a large remuda simply cannot be secured from hostile capture, Mackenzie cut out a few hundred head as a reward for his Tonkawa scouts, then had the rest—over a thousand—led to the rim of the canyon and shot down.

Mackenzie's victory at Palo Duro Canyon, plus the loss of foodstores and hundreds of tipis that Miles had managed to destroy in his running Battle of Red River, left the Kiowas, Comanches, and Cheyennes hungry and afoot. Then the rain came down in sheets, day after day. At one point a miserable band of Kiowas were huddling from a storm in a creek bottom when it began suddenly to flood, and a swarm of tarantulas boiled from the undergrowth into their camp, causing the superstitious natives to bolt in terror. It just wasn't worth it anymore. About five hundred Comanches and Kiowas surrendered at Fort Sill around the first of October. Satanta, hoping for better treatment elsewhere, surrendered his following of 145 people at the Cheyenne Agency. He claimed, as usual, that he had been quietly camping with them and had taken no part in the fight. He was in chains and on his way back to the Huntsville penitentiary within a day.

Black Jack Davidson mounted two campaigns from Fort Sill, and on October 24 snared under a white flag a large Comanche camp under White

Wolf and Tabananica, the brothers-in-law whose sagacity had opened the war against the buffalo hunters. As he turned his attention to rounding up Kiowa stragglers, some of the Cheyenne Dog Soldiers—members of that tribe's most militant warrior society—surrendered at the Cheyenne Agency on October 20. A far more dangerous group of them, under the chief Gray Beard, routed a detachment of 8th Cavalry on November 6; but their camp was overrun and captured two days later in a daring raid by Lieutenant Frank D. Baldwin of the 5th Infantry. Having only a single company of cavalry at his command, he placed them in two dozen empty supply wagons and stormed the village with these "tanks."

There was a four-day ice storm from the fifteenth to the nineteenth, costing Davidson ninety horses frozen to death and nearly thirty men frostbitten. It was just as hard on the remaining hostiles, who continued to surrender mostly in small groups, and the Red River War was effectively over by the end of November. Some held out longer than others and patrols were kept up during the winter, but the level of fighting declined sharply. All the remaining Cheyennes, 820 of them who had placed themselves under the protection of the peace chief Stone Calf, surrendered at their agency on March 6, 1875, giving up two white captive girls, Catherine and Sophia German. There was wide outrage at the girls' treatment; their original captor, Medicine Water, had taken Sophia to wife and then traded her to Wolf Robe—a fate less brutal than Kate's. She was owned by a chief named Long Back, who shared her with anyone who wanted her. The Cheyenne women also would send her out to gather wood, knowing she would be raped anywhere from one to a half dozen times before she got back.

A government decision came down that the chiefs and principal warriors were to be rounded up and jailed, and Fort Marion in St. Augustine, Florida, was prepared as a suitable prison. At Fort Sill, Kicking Bird was coerced into selecting who would go to prison, which he desperately wanted not to do because he knew it would cost him his influence with his people. But, once forced to comply, he managed to save Big Bow, who had surrendered early and helped coax in other hostiles. There was no sparing Lone Wolf or Walks in the Sky, but for the remaining two dozen he selected unpopular men, adopted Mexicans and delinquents, not men of influence. As they were loaded onto wagons Kicking Bird consoled them and promised that he would work for their release. "You think you are a big man with the whites," sneered Walks in the Sky from his prison wagon. "But you will not live long. I will see to that." One week later the Kiowas' greatest and bravest peace chief dropped dead after drinking a cup of coffee—witched, as the Kiowas believed, or the victim of strychnine, according to the Fort Sill surgeon. His last words were "I have taken the white man's road, and am not sorry. Tell my people to take the good path." By Kiowa custom the penalty for hex murder was itself death, and Walks in the Sky pitched over and died before reaching Florida.

The toughest group remaining, the Quahadi Comanches, with Quanah Parker, stayed on the Staked Plains until summer. Mackenzie was placed in command at Fort Sill, and he wisely sent out negotiators to talk them in. The prison wagons were long gone by the time they surrendered on June 2, so only one Quahadi chief, Black Horse, who capitulated early, was jailed. In all only nine Comanches served time, which the Kiowas remembered with bitterness. Mackenzie was the most successful of the army officers to fight Indians in Texas, but after he took command at Fort Sill and got a firsthand look at the history and circumstance of the agency, he blasted the Office of Indian Affairs for having starved the Indians onto the warpath. Even he had to admit that the Peace Policy might have worked, had the government lived up to its promises to the natives and allowed the agents to do their jobs. Feeling "a heavy responsibility resting on me to try and act rightly for these Indians," he exonerated Agent Haworth and supplemented the pathetic Indian Office food issue with rations from the post commissary.

A different, and far more symbolic, end to the Native American presence on the South Plains was written a couple of years later. The buffalo hunters who had cleared the vast herds from the Staked Plains in 1874 turned farther south after the conclusion of the Red River War. They still managed another couple of years hunting on the rolling plains in the strip between the line of military forts and the Cap Rock, before turning to the far less romantic income of gathering buffalo bones, thousands of carloads of which were crushed into fertilizer. Wright Mooar, who as a youth had started the buffalo hide business, settled on a ranch in Scurry County, near the later town of Snyder. On October 7, 1876, while hunting along Deep Creek, he was stunned to find himself staring at a white buffalo, the most powerful medicine emblem of the Plains tribes. She was a cow, surrounded by three black bulls. Without pause, he aimed his Sharps and killed her, as well as the bulls who charged in defense, and hung the albino skin in his house. Had they known of it, none of the former buffalo Indians would have imagined that their old life could return after that.

FORTY-NINE

CATTLE EMPIRE

WHEN GENERAL SHERIDAN ADMONISHED THE TEXAS
legislature not to pass any laws to protect the bison, he promised that once
the buffalo were gone, "your prairies can be covered with speckled cattle and
the festive cowboy, who follows the hunter as a second forerunner of an advanced civilization." Sheridan's oratory may have been turgid, but it was accurate, for hardly had the bison and the noble savage vacated the plains than
the prairie was filled by cattle ranches.

In the days of the Anglo Texas colonies and the Republic, ranching was
not considered skilled labor. The South Texas longhorns were wild and so
plentiful that the army of the Republic was provisioned by driving herds of
the "public cattle" along their line of march. In peacetime, animals were
often slaughtered for hides and precious tallow; beef in the towns might
cost only three cents per pound. Pork cost twice as much; cured bacon or
ham five times as much. A few enterprising operators drove herds east
through the swamps to New Orleans, where the market price was double
what they could get at home.

At about the time of the Mexican War, Texas cattle ranching began to
evolve robustly in two directions, one in the size of the operations, and the
other in marketing. Mifflin Kenedy was a Pennsylvania Quaker and budding
businessman in his mid-twenties, engaged as a riverboat captain in Alabama. There he met and befriended river pilot Richard King, six years
younger, the son of impoverished New York Irish immigrants, who was on
the lam from breaking his apprenticeship to a jeweler. They enlisted for service in the war and made themselves nearly indispensable in ferrying troops
and supplies along the Rio Grande. After the war they remained in the area,
formed a steamboat partnership, and began buying land. Kenedy's first venture in sheep ranching ended with the loss of three-quarters of his stock and
he turned his attention to cattle. King purchased his first ranch, the 15,500-
acre Rincón de Santa Gertrudis, in 1853, followed the next year by the
53,000-acre Santa Gertrudis de la Garza. King and Kenedy became full partners in 1860; when they split in 1868, Kenedy bought another ranch, the
vast Los Laureles, closer to Corpus Christi. That later became the Texas

Land and Cattle Company, and King held more than a million and a quarter acres. In later years, while the ranches in North Texas were importing improved breeds of cattle, the King Ranch was busy creating its own, crossing shorthorns with big hardy Brahmas to give the distinctive, roan-colored Santa Gertrudis.

This advent of cattle as big business was also made possible by the development of a market for Texas beef, which came with the cattle drives northward out of the state. They began shortly after statehood, as small herds were walked up the so-called Shawnee Trail, through the eastern Indian Territory, across Missouri to St. Louis and then to points beyond. Local farmers there bought and fattened the cattle before slaughter. The successful transport of a 1,000-head herd up the Shawnee Trail in 1846 solidly established the route, but disaster struck only a few years later. The Texas longhorns were famous for their hardiness, but one disease to which they had developed an immunity, which they carried north with them, proved vastly fatal to Northern cattle. It was a parasite-borne blood disease called Texas Fever. Although its etiology was not understood at the time, the cause and effect were readily observed, and Missouri farmers began banding together, Texas-style, into committees of vigilance to keep Texas cattle out of their counties.

In 1855 that state passed a quarantine act banning diseased Texas cattle, but that did little good because it wasn't the Texas cattle that got sick, and the farmers were still left to their own devices. Violence flared, herds were stopped and cattle shot. Texas drovers sought to evade the law by taking their cattle through Kansas, but with the same effect, and when Kansas followed Missouri with a quarantine act in 1859, Texas cattle seemed barred from Northern markets. The California Gold Rush created a secondary market, and the reward was rich, for a steer bought in Texas for $14 would fetch $100 in a camp full of hungry prospectors. However, the challenge of driving a herd through some 1,500 miles of baking desert, lurking Apaches, and snowy mountain passes was too daunting for a great trade to develop.

The Civil War finally delivered the coup de grâce to drives up the Shawnee trail, and Texas turned its attention to supplying beef to the Confederacy. Cattle drives were resumed to New Orleans, but then the business took another unexpected turn. The fall of Vicksburg in 1863, which gave the Union control of the entire length of the Mississippi River, prevented Texas cattle from being shipped to sale in the Confederacy. Bad times, however, could prove to be ultimately good. With no market, there was no slaughter, so by the time the post–Civil War ranching era was ready to begin, there was a surfeit of cattle with which to resume. (A similar though smaller cycle repeated itself after the financial panic in 1873.) Despite Northern quarantines and the vigilance of Missouri farmers, about a quarter of a million Texas cattle found their way to market in 1866, but that was only a leak in the dike. What was needed after the war was new routes to the North. That problem was solved by an Illinois entrepreneur named Joseph McCoy, who constructed feedlots and shipping facilities in Abilene, Kansas, 150 miles west of Missouri and at that time virtually the edge of settlement. He got the isolated place exempted from enforcement of the quarantine and publicized his business. The link with Texas was made when Jesse Chisholm, the Indian-trading nephew of Sam Houston's Cherokee wife, quit Texas and began tending a trot-line of trading posts from the Canadian River, in the heart of the Indian Territory, north into Kansas. Herds coming up from Texas struck the trace he had made, and the "Chisholm Trail," which was called by a number of other names until this one stuck in 1870, became the main thoroughfare for the Texas cattle drives. Some 35,000 head first made the trip in 1867, and despite the Indian dangers, the traffic burgeoned; by 1873 more than 1.5 million head had made the journey. As the railroad moved west, Abilene was given competition by other Kansas towns, such as Ellsworth and later Dodge City, vying for the Texas business.

Other trails reached still different markets. Oliver Loving was a Kentuckian who came to Texas in 1843, farmed, and then moved west to ranch in the Crosstimbers of what became Palo Pinto County. In 1857 he risked sending a herd up the Shawnee Trail to Illinois, which returned the fabulous profit of $36 per head. In 1866 he was fifty-four, and blazed a new trail to Western markets. The army had interned some 8,000 Navajo Indians at Fort Sumner, New Mexico, and Colorado towns such as Denver now formed a new mining frontier. Combining his herd with that of a young partner named Charles Goodnight, Loving skirted the Staked Plains with its Quahadi Comanches, heading southwest to Fort Concho before turning north up the Pecos River. The army bought $12,000 worth of cattle for cash money at Fort Sumner before the two continued to Colorado. A second drive on their Goodnight-Loving Trail was also successful; on the third drive Loving was mortally wounded by Indians, but their trail continued to see heavy use.

Goodnight himself abandoned the dangers of the trail and settled in Colorado, contracting with a prominent Fort Concho–area rancher, John Chisum (no relation to Jesse Chisholm), to supply him with ten thousand head a year, for which he would pay a dollar each over their Texas cost. After Chisum assumed the risk, he lost about $150,000 in cattle to Indian raids between 1868 and the end of the Red River War, prompting him to quit Texas, unload his business and his problems on a St. Louis beef factoring company, and concentrate on accumulating stock for them on commission.

With the development of the well-defined trails, it became more profitable to walk animals to Northern markets and sell them on the hoof than to process them at home. Meatpacking, which had once been an important Texas industry—it was Gail Borden, onetime printing contractor to the Republic of Texas, who held the patent on tinned meat biscuits—dwindled away from fifteen packing plants in 1870 to only three a decade later. Another change wrought by the efficient drives was that the job of herding cattle to market became a specialized task that nearly all ranchers were happy to contract out to professional drovers, who received from $1 to $1.50 per head to deliver the stock safely to the railheads; about half of the money he paid in wages to the trail hands who did the actual work. This ushered in the heyday of the cattle drive and of the cowboy as a romantically remembered American cultural icon—though much of their equipage and lexicon were derived from the heritage of the Hispanic vaquero, from the chaps that protected his legs riding through thick brush, to the lariat with which he roped the cattle, to the remuda from which he selected his horse.

The reality of life on the trail was considerably less rapturous than the national mythology later made it out to be. The work was hard. A trail drive consisted of a herd of 2,500 to 3,000 head and it took about six weeks to make the trip. The trail boss might earn $100 and perhaps a share of the profit, the cook about $75, and the horse wrangler $50. The lowest wage, in the area of $35, was paid to the ten or twelve "waddies," who were usually just teenagers, whose job was to keep the cattle together. Two rode point at the head of the herd, several along the flanks. The worst job, often meted out as punishment by the trail boss, was to ride drag, following the herd, rounding up stragglers, and breathing the dust of the whole operation. The work was dangerous—the elements were brutal and torture by Indians was an ever-present threat, but most inexperienced waddies weren't even allowed to carry sidearms, because the far greater danger was a stampede, which could be set off by a gunshot.

Many of the cowboys couldn't swim and prayed they wouldn't slip from their horses while crossing the rivers; even when they were dry, quicksand blotched the beds that appeared dry and safe. The life was lonely—mortality both natural and violent always lurked, and what survives of contemporary cowboy poetry reveals an almost painful pathos usually lacking in the later odes to the range. But this also meant that bonding was strong, that reliance upon partners was essential; therefore a deep emotional connection was created.

The cattle drive era lasted less than twenty years—from 1867 to 1885, finally ended by a combination of hard circumstances, including brutal weather that forced many ranchers to sell their cattle at a loss, which caused a steep fall in prices, the reimposition of ironclad quarantines against Texas Fever by Northern states, and the arrival of the railroads in West Texas, which made shipping cattle from there possible. But those two decades were long enough to brand the cowboy phenomenon into the national psyche as a quintessentially and meaningfully American pursuit. And although the labor was less romantic than it was later depicted, the hard cash that the cowboys brought home was instrumental in Texas' economic recovery from the Civil War.

The herd of ranchers, like a herd of cattle, eventually needed to find a way of thinning itself. While the foolish ones were living from day to day, luxuriating in the simplicity of the open range, the shrewd ones could look ahead and know the flush times would not last, and they bought land while it was cheap as, well, dirt. Especially in West Texas, the range was only as good as the water on it, and those with capital soon understood that if they bought just the land encompassing water, they controlled the range around it, for the land was useless without access to the water.

Nowhere was this more true than in the Panhandle. After the Comanches were evicted, the first large operator to move in was Charles Goodnight. He was born the day before the Alamo fell, in Illinois, and came to Texas in the year of statehood, circumstances in which he took considerable pride. In his youth he worked as a freighter and overseer, but spent equal time learning frontier skills; as a scout for the Texas Rangers he led Sul Ross to Peta Nocona's camp and Cynthia Ann Parker. In 1857 he and a brother-in-law started a ranch in Palo Pinto County, where he fell into the productive friendship with Oliver Loving. After the latter's death he sojourned in Colorado, but sensing opportunity with the opening of the Panhandle he drove 1,600 longhorns down from Pueblo and set up an operation in and around the lower Palo Duro Canyon.

His famous JA Ranch began with 12,000 acres purchased from land patenter Jot Gunter and grew, piecemeal but steadily, for several years with tracts acquired with a shrewd eye to water and grazing. Goodnight moved his wife Mary Ann (universally known as Molly) into a cedar pole dugout, seventy-five miles from her nearest neighbor, Molly Bugbee, whom she only got to see a couple of times a year. Molly Goodnight, a former schoolteacher, nearly went mad from loneliness. One of the hands once brought her three chickens in a gunny sack: "No one will ever know how much company they were to me. . . . They knew me, and tried to talk to me in their own language." The Goodnights' first real home had rafters salvaged, symbolically enough, from derelict Comanche tipis, and eventually she became ensconced in a comfortable nineteen-room ranch house.

(Texas, of course, had produced far too many independent viragoes for all ranching wives to be content with playing supporting roles. The most celebrated of Texas' cattle queens was Lizzie Johnson Williams, a pretty brunette schoolmarm with a college degree who settled on a ranch near San Marcos. Freelancing as a bookkeeper for various well-off ranchers fired her interest in the business; she acquired a herd, registered a brand, drove her own cattle up the Chisholm Trail, kept her own money under a prenuptial agreement, and invested it in spreads in the Hill Country and Trans-Pecos.)

Few areas of ranch improvement escaped Goodnight's attention. It was Goodnight who devised the chuck wagon, an efficient mobile kitchen, from which to feed his hands. On cattle drives he fitted a bell on the neck of a lead steer named Old Blue, which made the herds easier to guide. (With this training Old Blue became rather spoiled, however, bedding down with the horses and eating at the chuck wagon, but he performed faithfully until his death in 1890.) Goodnight was particularly interested in breeding experiments, maintaining a small herd of buffalo that he crossed with longhorns to create what he called a "cattalo," and more practically importing Angus and Herefords to improve his stock. He realized that much of the Staked Plains was of little use without water, and drilled through the hardpan to tap the vast Ogallala Aquifer; continuously pumped by windmills, it threw open the whole Panhandle to development.

Among his employees he gained an impressive reputation for fairness; he once stopped a herd from crossing the JA because he suspected they carried Texas Fever, but he supplied a guide to escort them around his range. Three years after the end of the Red River War, when the discovery of Comanches off their reservation trying to make a buffalo hunt apprised him of their continuing destitution, he made a "treaty" with Quanah Parker to supply the latter's people with beef. It was generous but also smart, insuring against any possibility of another hostile breakout. (In a scene that has become Panhandle legend, Goodnight did once let them cut an old bison out of his herd for a last hunt. The former warriors whipped and whooped the animal into a trot, then rode it down and killed it. Rather than butchering it, they stared at it sadly for a long time, seeing the corpse of their whole former life, and filed back to the reservation.)

Another of the innovative early ranchers was Christopher Columbus Slaughter, located south and west of Goodnight's JA, on the Long S and Lazy S ranches, although there was nothing lazy about his knack for making money. Not to be outdone by Goodnight's Texas connection, Slaughter took pride in claiming to have been the first boy born to a Republic of Texas marriage, born in February 1837. He helped drive a small herd to the family homestead at twelve, and bought out an uncle's interest in the family cattle at seventeen. He had been interested in breeding improvements for even longer than Goodnight, and at one point sold out his ranching interests to concentrate on that. His experiments at blending shorthorns and Herefords into longhorn stock resulted in cattle that were hardy as well as meaty, and he became a founder of the Texas and Southwest Cattle Raisers Association. The sedulousness with which such ranchers as Goodnight and Slaughter applied themselves to improved breeding resulted in such visible changes to the herds that the traditional longhorn came to be associated with ranches in South Texas, and the stockier, more barrel-chested "Texas cattle" with the frontier range.

Ranching in the eastern Panhandle flourished to such a degree that the development of a marketing and supply center was inevitable. After hostile Indians sacked Adobe Walls in 1874, Charlie Rath, the "go-ahead" hide dealer, established a new trading post on Sweetwater Creek about fifty miles southeast of there, near the army's supply trail and a new post, Fort Elliott, established during that summer. With the proliferation of new ranches and nearby soldiers to supply, this settlement took root. At first it was called, rather unromantically, Hidetown, after the green buffalo hides laid over the "soddies" to keep out the weather, but in 1878 residents applied to the U.S. Post Office to change the name to Sweetwater. This was denied, because of a preexisting town of that name in Nolan County. Not to be denied, the locals requested Billy Dixon, the former buffalo hunter, to ask one of the native scouts what was the Indian name for "sweet water." After a moment's thought the former warrior replied, "Mobeetie." New application was made, it was approved by the Post Office, and the name became official. Only later, it was said, after a cowboy breaking broncs in a corral was thrown and landed in a fresh paddy of manure, and some Indian children watching from the fence laughed and pointed and shouted out, "Mobeetie! Mobeetie!" did some begin to grasp that they had been duped.

Nevertheless it became the locus of the Panhandle Stock Association, with Goodnight as the first president, and the town took off. Soon it became recognized as the cowboy capital of the Panhandle. Almost immediately there were three saloons, at least fifteen dance hall girls of enterprising employ, several lawyers, and a Chinese laundry. When order was finally called for and twenty-six counties of the Panhandle were organized as the 35th Judicial District, a dead-shot D.A. was imported in the person of Temple Lea Houston, youngest son of the Texas icon—born in the Governor's Mansion in 1860—who for a time bid fair to rival his famous father. He was the youngest lawyer licensed to practice in Texas. His courtroom histrionics won him cases, and he inherited enough of his father's eccentricities to strike the populace as colorful but not frightening. His oratorical flourish soon led to his election to the state legislature.

The heyday of ranching as a regional culture was too good to last. The miracle of the Texas cattle industry owed its birth first to the energetic free enterprise of hardworking entrepreneurs, but second to the ready availability of two important natural resources: vast free lands and vast millions of unclaimed cattle. The close of the frontier brought competition and serious, often violent disputes between the small cowmen, crowded out or strangled off from water by the big players. This was a process sharpened by the arrival of the barbed-wire fence. In 1875 a thirty-year-old salesman named Henry B. Sanborn arrived in Texas, hawking a new invention to which his wife's uncle held the patent. It was called barbed wire, spools of wire with sharpened links twisted at regular intervals down its length. He came with four carloads that he unloaded in Sherman, Dallas, Austin, and San Antonio. He racked up a million dollars in sales the following year, and then used his money to establish himself in the Panhandle cattle business. He prospered mightily and founded the city of Amarillo. As successful as Sanborn was, skepticism remained on the part of many cowmen until another agent, "Bet-A-Million" Gates, staged a legendary demonstration, fencing a herd of longhorns in Military Plaza in San Antonio. The advantages of the product were so apparent—restricting competitors' access to water, controlling breeding—that sales skyrocketed, and the fencing of the South Plains began.

The cowboy era had its birth and owed its existence to the free range, and small operators who lacked the capital of the big ranchers depended on the open range to keep going. They were quick to recognize barbed wire as the lethal threat it was, and for the next several years the Fence Wars were on. Those who favored fencing stretched barbed wire across public roads and sometimes cut off whole towns, and some free rangers sought to best the system by fencing in public domain to which they had no claim. (Rustlers found stealing cattle more difficult on the fenced range, and sided with the free-range faction.) Vandals took to donning masks at night, moving in gangs with names like the Owls or the Javelinas, cutting fences, burning pastures, resorting to the occasional murder, and posting bombastic notices in the towns. By 1883, fence cutting was reported from half of Texas' counties, and some $20 million worth of fencing had been ruined. Farmers, who saw in barbed wire a salvation for their fields from trampling, were balking at settling west. The following year a special session of the legislature stepped in with a stern but reasonable statute: fence cutting was made a felony, but fencing public domain a misdemeanor. Fences across public roads had to have a well-maintained gate at least every three miles. This law ended the worst of the conflict, but after its passage everyone knew that life in Texas had changed profoundly. The frontier was now gone.

The cowboy culture may have been a recent development, but with it came a decided sense of identity. Cowboys who lived and breathed cattle were virtually united in their hatred for sheep ranchers. During the Spanish entradas, the conquistadores had brought both sheep and cattle, but feral sheep fell to predators and the elements, where the longhorns had thrived. In the centuries since, sheep raising was thought of as a Mexican occupation, although herds of improved breeds came with the influx of Germans, who were scarcely more popular than the Mexicans, and Scots. It was true that sheep cropped the grass down to the roots, often ruining the range for later grazing by cattle, and sometimes infected their pastures with sheep scab, but it was also true that the antipathy was fueled largely by simple prejudice.

Practical men like Goodnight, and ranches financed by foreigners who did not share the disdain for sheep, incorporated them into their operation, and in the decade from 1870 to 1880, the number of sheep in Texas increased fivefold, from 1.25 million to more than 6 million. (A lot of that capital came from Scotland, famous for its sheep husbandry. In fact it was a cabal of Dundee investors that grew the legendary Matador Land and Cattle Company in the Pease River forks from 50,000 acres to nearly twenty times that size, managed by the naturalized Scot Murdo Mackenzie, whom Theodore Roosevelt once called the most influential cowman in America.) Ironically, it was the hated fences, and the fencing law of 1884, that brought an end to the sheep wars, because most of the conflict had been generated by nomadic flocks competing for grazing on the open range.

That other great innovation on the prairies, irrigation, brought conflict with another class of user, the farmer. Sodbusters, as the cowmen derisively called them, or nesters, complained of having their crops trod underfoot by passing herds of cattle. Cowmen's assertion that the range was only suited to pastoral use fell flat because the soil, once watered, proved quite fertile. Again it was fencing that ultimately settled the conflict.

But of all the disputes that accompanied this settling out of who would control the range, the most profound and most lasting was the huge influx of foreign capital to develop the big spreads. Cowboys who in former days could rise as high as their ambition and energy could take them suddenly found themselves low-wage employees with no say and little chance for advancement. In those earlier times cowboys were commonly paid in part with the cattle they ran, sometimes even including the privilege of cutting in their animals with the boss's herd on the same range. A cowboy who worked hard and got his own start could do very well indeed for himself. "Of the hands I employed," wrote one early ranch owner with satisfaction, "there are now at least three millionaires."

It was a system that functioned on diligent labor and mutual respect, and a system that even made it possible for African-Americans to move up the economic ladder. Perhaps a third of all cowboys on the range were black or Hispanic, operating in a setting where success depended more on skill than on ethnic background, and the vast new cattle country lacked the heavy baggage of slavery and Reconstruction. Successful black cowboy Daniel Webster Wallace was a case in point. He was born a slave and raised by a white family after the death of his mother, whom they had purchased to wet-nurse their children. Avoiding the trap of the mass of black sharecroppers, he went west in 1877 to learn the cowboy trade, and worked for such leading ranchers as C. C. Slaughter. His principal mentor was rancher Clay Mann, from whose "80" brand Wallace took his sobriquet of "80 John" Wallace. Mann withheld part of his wages in trust, as Wallace attended two years of college before buying land and cattle of his own in Mitchell County, about halfway between Abilene and Midland. By the time he died he owned 8,000 acres with 600 cattle, and he had ten tenant families working for him.

This custom of allowing hardworking cowboys to advance themselves changed with the advent of corporate managers. Financial syndicates were not interested in their employees' individual ambitions, and their power was hard to resist. Mifflin Kenedy sold his 242,000-acre Los Laureles Ranch in South Texas (all fenced) to a Scottish syndicate that became the Texas Land and Cattle Company. Even the independent-minded Goodnight had to knuckle under to a foreign boss who underwrote him with cash. John George Adair was an English aristocrat with a cold, though unerring, eye for the calculation of interest. Despite his ownership of huge estates in Britain, Adair came to America to open a brokerage house in New York, where he could lend money for a higher return than he could get at home. Once in America, he realized that the farther west he went, the higher the interest he could collect, and he relocated to Denver. Adair took a notion to the cattle business, and Goodnight needed a stake to get going. They became partners, with Goodnight borrowing his one-third of the venture from Adair, at 10 percent. To everyone's relief, Adair gave Goodnight a free hand to run the "JA" (John Adair) Ranch in the most profitable way, and seldom visited. He was arrogant and unsympathetic, traits that went down ill among the affable cowboys, and which left Goodnight in the middle trying to buffer the bad blood created. "He would have been beaten up several times if it hadn't been for me," he said once, and Goodnight himself was strict enough. He allowed no gambling, no drinking, and no fighting, which would have made for a very dull cowboy movie. Nevertheless, between Goodnight's know-how and Adair's pounds sterling, the JA ranch eventually embraced some 1.3 million acres, running over 100,000 head of bred cattle.

Corporatizing the Texas range gained still more momentum when the state sold a bloc of over three million acres—an area the size of Connecticut—in the Panhandle to pay for the building of a new capitol. The massive bloc of land was bought by a financial consortium of ten Chicago investors, and became the XIT, an acronym for Ten in Texas. One of the principal investors, Colonel Amos Babcock, came to Texas, obtained supplies from Fort Elliott with a letter from General Sheridan, and set off to have a look at the place. Stretching over two hundred miles along the New Mexico border, his inspection took over a month and covered over nine hundred miles. Originally, their intent was to ranch the land only until it could be broken up and sold profitably, but as this was likely to take time, another of the investors, John Farwell, went to Britain, organized the Capitol Freehold Land and Investment Company, and returned with another $5 million in development capital raised from such moneybags as the Earl of Aberdeen.

Not unusually for the capitalism of the day, some of the operation began to smell funny. The original purchaser of the contract who organized the XIT syndicate, Mathias Schnell of Illinois, excused himself from the venture amid charges of bribery. The XIT's first manager, B. H. Campbell of Wichita (known as Barbecue Campbell for his onetime Bar-B-Q brand), resigned after a state senate investigation of harboring fugitives and purchasing inferior cattle. But considering the size and complexity of the project, it took off running, and by 1886 the XIT ranch ran over 110,000 cattle within 780 miles of fencing.

A new general manager, Albert Boyce, took over and governed his 150 cowboys in a manner similar to Goodnight: no drinking, no gambling, no abusing the animals. At its height, the ranch boasted a hundred waterholes created by dams, and with three hundred windmills pumping water to improved breeds of cattle, production reached 35,000 calves per year. On the XIT, cowboys were almost restored to their halcyon days, but better organized and without the dangers of Indian attack. But even in its best years, profit was marginal considering losses to predators, rustlers, disasters of weather, and fluctuations in the market. The British investors, who wanted to see a return on their money, forced the XIT to begin selling off its land by the turn of the century.

Those aspects of the changing range that made cowboying less fun than it used to be—depressed wages, authoritarian managers, the lack of possibility for advancement—reached a head on the LS Ranch, a 70,000-acre spread in the northwest corner of the Panhandle, in early spring of 1883. It was owned by a land company headed by Lucien Scott (hence the "LS" Ranch), a banker in Leavenworth, Kansas, who also owned interests in ranches in New Mexico and Montana. A hand named Tom Harris drafted a demand for better pay on pain of a work stoppage and got a couple dozen others to sign it. If ignored, they intended to strike on March 31. Harris set up a small strike fund and attempted to organize cowboys on nearby ranches such as the T-Anchor, a 240,000-acre concern that had been started on the open range by a brother-in-law of Charles Goodnight but then was taken over and fenced by land traders Jule and Jot Gunter of Sherman, acting with financing from Illinois. Cowboys there and on the LX, LE, and LIT ranches signed on in a desultory way, perhaps to the number of three hundred, but not all at once or in concert. Newspapers reported the development with hysteria; Harris found himself demonized amid reports of threatened violence and mass slaughter of stock, none of which was true. The most sympathetic assessment came from the *Texas Livestock Journal*, which allowed that the cowboys deserved better pay, but added that if the ranch managers said they couldn't afford it, they could be taken at their word.

Strikers were summarily fired, but the action did have some backhanded success, as the managers raised the wages (a little) of the hands they didn't sack, some of whom were actually former strikers who returned and showed a little contrition. But between the number of cowboys who needed work at any wage, the lack of support in the press, and the fact that the Cowboy Strike of 1883 was ahead of its time, the phenomenon passed within a couple of months, and the May roundup was not affected. Because the strike was contemporaneous with other beginning signs of a national labor movement, some scholars have drawn perhaps more of a connection between them than actually existed, for the Cowboy Strike was a homegrown expression. What can be said is that the disadvantageous and often exploitative labor conditions that were one facet of the Gilded Age nationally made themselves felt even on the local range, and the Texas cowboys, or at least these Texas cowboys, reacted in a way that would have been well understood by coal miners in Kentucky or meatpackers in Chicago. In Texas no less than in the rest of the country, capital and labor had gotten badly out of balance, and it was a system ripe for reform.

FIFTY

THE POPULIST MOVEMENT

WITH THE END OF THE FRONTIER, TEXANS FOUND THEM-
selves set squarely within the gaudiness and excesses of the Gilded Age.
Nothing could have announced their arrival better than the behemoth capitol that was built with the cash raised from selling the lands that became the
XIT Ranch. Ground was broken for it on February 1, 1882, less than three
months after the colonial capitol burned down. The building was planned as
a vast Romanesque palace and it eventually cost $3,750,000, all but half a
million of which was covered by the land deal. The excavation alone took
over three years, during which time a special railroad was built to the quarry
near Llano from which its grayish-rose colored granite was extracted, by
(mostly black) convict labor. The cornerstone was laid on Independence
Day, March 2, 1885, and after three years of construction it was dedicated in
May of 1888.

Designed by Elijah Myers of Chicago in the popular Victorian Romanesque style, it was colossal—built to reflect the stature and aspirations
of the people who were governed from it. The building was 566 feet across
and 289 feet through, its 392 rooms lit by 924 windows in addition to sky-
lights over the house and senate chambers. Its cast-iron outer dome,
painted to match the pink stone, made a subtle point of states' rights, rising
308 feet—just taller than the dome of the federal Capitol in Washington. Its
front door, whether intended to make a point or not, faced south. Standing
atop the dome was a hatchet-faced Goddess of Liberty, cast in zinc, her features exaggerated to make them discernible from the ground a hundred
yards below; she held aloft a gilded Lone Star. Inside was seven miles of
wainscoting carved in a variety of woods that cost $115,600; the elaborate
plaster cornices around the 22-foot ceilings cost another $65,000. The brass
door hinges, knobs, and locksets were all specially cast in Texas motifs, and
the door transoms, which arrived from England in 114 cases, had the name
of each government office or department etched in acid. The 26-acre
grounds were girdled with a black wrought-iron fence from Ohio, topped
with a numberless enfilade of gilt Lone Stars.

A commemorative engraving depicts pedestrians and passing carriages dwarfed by the impossibly pharaonic structure. Nothing could have been more appropriate for a state that was supremely confident of its size and self-assertion. And indeed, Texans had every reason to feel that way, for just as on the frontier plains the buffalo and Indians had been replaced by cattle and ranchers, in that great bulk of Texas that lay safely removed from the frontier, tremendous changes had also been taking place.

The population had exploded. Between 1860 and 1870 it had risen only from 604,000 to 818,000, much of that increase accounted for by the arrival of refugees from the devastation of the Deep South. But during the seventies it doubled to nearly 1.6 million, which was more than triple the national rate of growth. Natural increase and immigration both contributed, but it was a resumption of homesteading largesse that brought about the boom. Although they still comprised a minority of the overall population, the urban population also grew at near-fantastical rates. The major cities at least tripled their populations between 1870 and 1890: San Antonio grew from 12,000 to 37,000, finally eclipsing Galveston as the state's largest; Houston from 9,000 to 27,000, and Austin from 4,000 to 14,000. Galveston lagged only slightly behind, but still doubled from 14,000 to 29,000. Newer cities that would later take leading roles burst on the scene. Dallas grew more than twelvefold, from 3,000 to 38,000; Fort Worth grew even more stunningly, from a village of 500 in 1870 to 23,000 in 1890. In the 200 miles of farms and hamlets between Austin and Dallas, the town of Waco emerged as the marketing and supply center, with only a hundred fewer residents than Austin in 1890.

Changes on the political scene had been no less dramatic. After the Reconstructionists fell from power in 1874, state government fell to a faction that called themselves, fittingly, Redeemers, who wished to cleanse Texas in an almost baptismal way of the detested postwar era. They required more basic reform than a legislature could accomplish, and in August 1875 voters approved a slate of delegates for yet another state constitutional convention. There were three representatives from each of the state's thirty senatorial districts, and they included some celebrated old faces, such as Rip Ford, and some newer-minted heroes, such as Sul Ross, the Indian fighter who had already "redeemed" Cynthia Ann Parker for her white relatives (although it was less widely reported that she tried repeatedly to escape back to the Comanches). John H. Reagan was restored to favor with a seat. There were fifteen Republicans, including six freedmen, and seventy-five Democrats, who expected no difficulty enforcing their slate of proposals.

The convention, and the document they produced, stood for severe retrenchment, not even voting money to record their own proceedings. State salaries were to be cut, the legislature was limited to meeting only every other year, and the ability of the state to incur debt was curtailed. They also drafted a brutal trimming of the powers of the governor, which the majority felt had been abused under E. J. Davis. The public school system, which once appeared to be the only accomplishment of his administration that was likely to last, was weakened. They were not entirely anti-education; they provided for an endowment, the Permanent University Fund, to finance an institution of higher learning. Having suffered many years under an occupation for which there was little redress, the delegates opened the new document with an extensive Bill of Rights, with more, and more closely defined, individual rights than were enumerated in the federal constitution. Finally, as the gathering took place in the wake of the Panic of 1873, it contained signal safeguards for common people from economic slumps: imprisonment for debt was outlawed, and a homestead exemption was created to prevent family domiciles from being seized and sold for debt. Ratified the following year, the Constitution of 1876's major fault was that in addressing so many specific grievances, the delegates created a document so detailed that ordinary legislation was precluded in many important areas. Hundreds of amendments have been necessary to what remains Texas' fundamental law.

The new constitution was not the only political upheaval, however. Some forty of the convention's ninety delegates were members of a new organization making itself felt on the political scene, the Patrons of Husbandry, better known as the Grange. In concept they were a multifaceted benefit society aiming to improve the lives of rural families with fellowship and educational opportunities, but after the Panic of 1873 they took a decidedly political slant, representing the cause of the farmer in a political environment increasingly dominated by big ranchers and business interests. Many of the protections embraced in the Constitution of 1876 were championed by Granger delegates.

Cowboy life and lore may have captured the national imagination, but simple farming remained the backbone of the economy, and late in the century people turned to the soil as never before. Between 1880 and 1900 the acreage of Texas land being farmed more than tripled, from 36.2 million acres to nearly 126 million. Much of that acreage had come to produce cereal grains, but there was no question that cotton still anchored the economy, a production that ballooned with a new influx of sharecroppers. The freedmen who deserted Texas for Kansas in the Exoduster Movement were more than replaced by poor white farmers coming west from the former Confederacy, and still more were turned out of the cities with each financial panic. And cotton lands, once limited to the well-watered eastern plains, extended steadily west with barbed wire, plus irrigation and the availability of commercial fertilizer. The increase in cotton was prodigious. From an 1869 crop of 350,000 quarter-ton bales (about 80 percent of the prewar level), a decade later it was 805,000 bales, then 1.5 million bales in 1889 and 3.5 million bales by the turn of the century. Such production, of course, glutted the market, and profitability fell with the price, finally depressed to less than six cents per pound; by one reckoning, farmers were making a quarter less money for harvesting a quarter more cotton.

The Grange certainly had its hands full in championing the cause of the farmer, but they were not the only organization that took increasing exception to the demands of big business. Another was the Southern Farmers' Alliance, chartered in 1877 in Lampasas County. It grew rapidly, thanks to its more overtly political tone, objecting to an economy in which "the capitalist holds your confidence in one hand, while with the other he rifles your pocket," according to their full-time paid lecturer and recruiter. The Farmers' Alliance quickly became a national force, claiming at its height some three million members, far more effective than the Grange, in part because they took concrete steps to help their constituency, such as opening cooperative stores where members could purchase merchandise at healthy discounts. It became increasingly apparent that these grassroots organizations, which often spread by means of revival-style stump speaking, had tapped into a seething discontent with the economic direction of the country, and that a broad desire for reform was finding expression.

Still another step was taken with the formation of Greenback Clubs, which were more overtly political and enunciated a fiscal program in sympathy with reformist aims. They began in Texas in 1876, and within a couple of years there were nearly five hundred of them. Their delegates organized a convention in Austin to field a slate of candidates as the Greenback Party. Amazingly, in 1878 they elected twelve candidates to the state legislature, supplanting the Republicans as Texas' second-largest party, and sent one of their number, George Washington Jones of Bastrop, to Congress, although it took a coalition of Republicans and progressives to overcome the Democratic contender. In office, they pressed for monetary reforms, such as making the federal greenback full legal tender redeemable for specie and receivable for federal bonds. They also of course favored regulating big business, especially railroads, which they believed were oppressing their agrarian constituency.

Railroading in Texas came to a powerful and controversial prominence. Texas was late coming to this mode of transport, laying no track at all until 1853, when there were over 9,000 miles of track nationally. In that year Sidney Sherman, the cavalry officer who nearly precipitated the Battle of San Jacinto prematurely, founded the Buffalo Bayou, Brazos, & Colorado Railroad. The following year the legislature realized the benefits to the state of encouraging rail construction, and offered sixteen sections of land for every mile of track laid, but the time wasn't right, and by the time of the Civil War, Texas had only 400 miles of track, all concentrated in the southeast. At the end of Reconstruction there were still fewer than 600 miles.

Although Grangers and reformers planted a provision in the Constitution of 1876 defining railroads as public carriers subject to regulation, it was deemed more important to get track laid, and a Land Grant Law passed that year offered a generous sixteen sections of land (10,240 acres) per track mile to companies who would just get on with it. Now the time was right; forty railroads took advantage of the program, and by the time the law was repealed in 1883 as too much of a good thing, nearly 3,000 miles of track were down and running, and the railroads had snatched up more than 32 million acres of Texas land—more than 5 million acres to the Texas & Pacific alone. There was a recognition, however, that even this largesse barely covered the costs, and numerous cities and towns began offering their own deals to the railroads. This was an engraved invitation to bribery and corruption, though there was plenty of honest incentive as well. In their course westward, for instance, the railroad reached Palo Pinto County, where rich seams of coal broke the surface and needed only to be loaded onto cars. The cheap availability of coal stimulated power-intensive industry such as the manufacture of bricks, which encouraged construction, which in turn kept the sawmills in East Texas humming.

But shenanigans there were, in plenty, and those who learned to play the system could do very well for themselves. Taylor County, in the southern swath of Comanche raiding country, was given administrative autonomy in 1873 and organized after the Indian danger had passed in 1878. At that time its only town was Buffalo Gap, which had maintained a feisty little existence for some twenty years, most recently as a center of buffalo hunting and then bone gathering. It was made the county seat, and by the early eighties boasted twelve hundred people, thriving businesses, a Baptist church, the beginnings of a Presbyterian college, and rosy prospects. Boosters touted Buffalo Gap as "The Athens of the West." Fifteen miles to the north, however, local ranchers who preferred that future development take place on their lands instead learned that the Texas & Pacific Railroad was coming west. A deputation met with the railroad's town-site locator, and apparently for alleged cash consideration convinced him to bypass Buffalo Gap and run the line over their property, where they would start a completely new city. Beginning on March 15, 1881, some three hundred lots, platted by Texas & Pacific surveyors, were auctioned in "Abilene," named for the Kansas cowtown. Aided by rail-borne commerce, Abilene thrived, replacing Buffalo Gap as the county seat two years later. Buffalo Gap competed gamely, opening the Presbyterian college and starting a weekly newspaper, but by 1884 the population had been cut in half, and by 1890 halved again, as Abilene swelled to over three thousand. A similar fate up in the Panhandle befell the cowboy capital and self-styled Queen City of the Plains, Mobeetie, when it was bypassed by several lines, and once cut from the vine it began to shrivel—from a height of 400 people to fewer than 200—a decline reinforced by the closure of Fort Elliott in 1890, and a tornado that destroyed virtually all the buildings a few years later.

Worse than the power that they held over communities, the railroads adopted business practices that, while not always illegal, infuriated the agrarian reformers. There were instances of a line charging lower rates to preferred customers, handing out free passes to advantage, conspiring amongst each other to not compete in given areas, and charging ruinous freight rates for small farmers on noncompetitive lines.

It was inevitable that the railroads would be the first and largest target of the Populist Movement. And while the charges of avarice and gouging largely rang true, to an extent it may have been something of a bum rap. While it was true that the legislature bestowed vast acreages of public domain on the rail lines, the land was worth little both then and for decades thereafter, compared to the cost of construction, but the lines were required to divest themselves of the lands within five years. The lifestyles of principal rail executives did not help. The most spectacular example of them, although it would have been better for the movement if he had come to Texas earlier than 1892, was Edward "Ned" Howland Robinson Green, a corpulent, emotionally damaged voluptuary who stumped around on one leg, having lost the other in his youth because his mother, the notorious Witch of Wall Street Hetty Green, was too cheap to take him to a doctor when the leg might have been saved. He took up residence in Terrell to run his Texas-Midland Railroad, roger any female within grabbing distance—a disposition not altered by his marriage to a former prostitute—and amass a fortune of some $40 million. Ned Green had a good side—he was an amiable "black and tan" Republican who cultivated respectful relations with black politicians, but knowing that Republicans were unelectable, also forged friendly alliances with winning Democrats. Most of his wealth was financed by family money more than by gouging poor sodbusters, but the ostentation and lurid private life of Green and barons like him made them easy targets.

Ironically, it was the railroads' attempts to survey and dispose of the lands they were required to survey and dispose of that revealed the shocking extent to which cattlemen had been fencing in public domain for their own use. This led to the Grass Lease Fight of 1884. With legal action looming, some ranchers took the easy way out by buying up the railroads' land certificates at admirable discounts—sometimes only a hundred dollars per 640-acre section. Others did not even bother with that, but just fenced open range with abandon. The then governor was John Ireland, who had called the special session of the legislature that made fence cutting a felony. With Texas school lands being materially affected by the illegal fencing, he had some reason to feel betrayed; the attorney general, John Templeton, got indictments for illegal fencing against some fifty leading ranchers, including Charles Goodnight.

In a fatal error, the trials were held in the town of Clarendon, smack in the middle of the dispute. If ever defendants enjoyed trials by juries of their peers, it was here, for the population was so thin that jury pools were comprised of sympathetic ranchers, and their acquittals were swift. It was also apparent that the presiding judge, Frank Willis, who was the first district judge to sit in the region, was partial to the ranching interests. First Templeton and then his successor as attorney general, a prominent lawyer from Tyler named James Stephen Hogg, pursued impeachment charges against Willis. His trial in Austin was a spectacle; grateful cattlemen hired Temple Houston to defend him, which he did with considerable drama, and his acquittal sparked jubilation in the Panhandle. Ironically, by the time of Willis' trial in February 1887, the whole issue had cooled. Goodnight had been among the first to realize that it was the arrival of the railroad in the Panhandle that saved their ranches and fortunes from disaster when the northern cattle drives imploded in 1885, and a series of settlements had been made to the satisfaction of all. And there was a final communal realization that the frontier and open range were now consigned to history.

Although the railroads were probably not (quite) as culpable a villain as progressives made them out to be, increasing corporate power and its frequent abuse led to popular indignation and a demand that regulations be instituted. Throughout the 1880s, the Grange, the Farmers' Alliance, and the

Greenback Party, which had become a more potent force than the Republicans, needed only a spark to become a major threat to the Democratic regime. That came in 1890, when a group of sympathetic Democrats split from their party and joined the progressives. This prompted the formation in Dallas on August 18, 1891, of the Texas People's Party. An increasing number of Texas newspapers began publishing their sympathy with their goals, but what promised to be a signal turn in Texas politics was averted when the Democrats nominated Jim Hogg for governor in 1890. Hogg was a Democrat, and while he shared many progressive beliefs with those further out on the left, he would never have deserted the party. He could also perceive, however, the grassroots strength of the Populists, and in a way commandeered their message for his own, both because it resulted in good policy and because it strengthened the Democratic Party.

During his two terms as state attorney general, Hogg had prosecuted the illegal range fencing case, and he recovered about a million and a half acres of Texas school lands, actions that the reformers approved, and moreover, Hogg campaigned for governor on the promise to bring the railroads to heel. His candidacy put the progressives considerably off their balance, as the issue of "fusion," whether to insist on running their own slate of candidates or tie their fortunes to a sympathetic Democrat, baffled the membership. In the end Hogg won, despite a respectable polling by the People's Party candidate, and aided by the presence on the ballot of a constitutional amendment to allow the creation of a regulatory Railroad Commission, which also passed.

Easily the most popular and powerful chief executive elected up to that time, Hogg was the first Texas governor to have been native-born. Physically enormous, his early career as a district attorney was almost cut short by the bullet of a would-be assassin, but he recovered. He married a belle named Sallie Stinson and fathered four rambunctious and sometimes incorrigible children, most famously, in later history, a daughter whom he named Ima, for a character in a novel written by a relative. (He claimed not to have realized at the time the gaffe he was making with her name, but Ima Hogg bore a lifetime of teasing, and later legends persisted that she had a brother named Ura.)

To head his new Texas Railroad Commission, Hogg selected John H. Reagan, who had been sent to the federal Senate in 1887. It took some heavy persuasion to talk him back, but no one in Texas had a greater reputation for moderation and impartiality. Reformers assumed that the commission would curb such abuses as preferential rates and noncompetitive pooling, but as clever, pro-business Democrats, Hogg and Reagan used the commission much more subtly.

One limitation on the zeal of Texans' progressive sentiments revealed itself in the touchy subject of organized labor, in the Great Southwest Strike. The year before the abortive—and unrelated—Cowboy Strike of 1883, organizers for the Knights of Labor moved into Texas, unionizing longshoremen, railroad workers, mechanics, stonemasons, and various others. They enjoyed considerable success within the state, and within three years set up 300 local assemblies with 30,000 members. Their reputation increased when they successfully struck Jay Gould's Wabash rail line in 1885, winning concessions from one of the nation's most ruthless commercial barons. In March 1886 a union foreman for the Texas & Pacific, another Gould line, was fired in Marshall; a strike was called and spread quickly. Gould cars were uncoupled from trains, switching stations were occupied. This time Gould fought back, hiring Pinkertons and "scab" replacement workers. Violence, probably in Texas as elsewhere provoked by the detectives, erupted, prompting Governor Ireland to dispatch Texas Rangers and state militia to maintain order. The rioting and the involvement of state forces turned public opinion, which initially looked unfavorably on Gould and the railroad, against the union. The strike was broken, the first major defeat of the Knights of Labor.

Nonetheless, common Texans maintained a strong commitment to the reform cause, partly thanks to the unemployment engendered by the Panic of 1893. The scorn with which large business interests reacted to the idea of relief for the working class was stunningly demonstrated in Texas in the spring of 1894. An organization calling itself the Commonweal of Christ was organized in Ohio by Jacob Coxey, who set off for Washington with a hundred jobless followers to demonstrate for employment on public works projects. Their number grew to five hundred and they became known as Coxey's Army. A second contingent of seven hundred left Los Angeles to join him there; as their train approached El Paso the mayor appealed to Hogg to place soldiers at Fort Bliss under state authority to break them up, but Hogg declined. Railroads refused to make cars available to them, and they camped for two days in El Paso, until the Southern Pacific agreed to take them across the state. Seventy miles into the desert, company trainmen uncoupled their cars and left them at a remote switch without food or water, where they were kept alive by nearby ranchers and resident Tejanos. In a drama lasting several days, Hogg reaped bountiful publicity and goodwill from Texas progressives by jawboning the Southern Pacific into completing their journey—after the cost was paid by sympathetic citizens of El Paso.

The Southern contingent of the Commonweal of Christ missed their date in Washington, however, helping to ensure the failure of Coxey's Army to generate any reform.

Jim Hogg's wisdom in assimilating the Populist Movement into the mainstream of the Democratic Party bore other fruit for many years. One case in point was the career of Joe Henry Eagle, a schoolteacher in the dusty little village of Vernon. After a stint as city attorney in nearby Wichita Falls, he moved to Houston, where as a Populist he was defeated for Congress in 1896. But he later served two separate tenures in Congress, as a Democrat. In 1916 he pushed hard and successfully for internal improvements and the Federal Farm Loan Act. He returned for the New Deal in the 1930s, winning important WPA contracts for his district and backing the creation of the Social Security Administration.

FIFTY-ONE

LIFE BY MAIL ORDER

MUCH OF THE PROSPERITY OF TEXAS FROM THE GILDED Age to the turn of the century owed to the hard work of a new influx of immigrants, many from countries not previously represented on the Texas landscape. From the 1880s until World War I, this second wave of immigration into Texas did much to enrich the existing mix of Anglo, Hispanic, and German cultures. European nationalities that had been present in small numbers earlier in Texas history began making a significant appearance, such as Swedes, who continued to settle north and east of Austin. An itinerant photographer who visited their Decker Colony in 1900 filled two huge privately subscribed albums with family portraits of Texas Swedes, well-dressed and confident. In 1870 Texas hosted fewer than 200 Italians, but in the subsequent decades they arrived by thousands, many maintaining their old regional identities. Sicilians stayed mostly around Galveston and Brazoria; those from the Piedmont gravitated to the Red River Valley north of Fort Worth. So many from Lombardy settled on the Gulf prairie and worked on the New York, Texas, & Mexican Railway that it came to be called the Macaroni Line.

Other groups that were regarded as exotic came later, by invitation. A Japanese consular envoy visited the southeast Texas rice country in 1902, where agricultural boosters told him that Japanese expertise in rice growing would be a valuable addition to the local economy. During the next eight years more than three hundred Japanese arrived, settling mostly between Houston and Beaumont. One of the largest colonies, of about forty immigrants, was started by Kichimatsu Kishi ten miles east of Beaumont. Their success was only mixed, complicated by the dredging of the Sabine-Neches Waterway, which ruined their rice paddies with an influx of salt water, and they offset their rice losses by hiring Cajun and Hispanic laborers to work mechanized truck farms, which led to ethnic tensions. Many Japanese borrowed heavily to start their enterprises, and most of those who survived the collapse of the rice market in 1920 went under in the financial collapse of 1929. While the Japanese Texans made steps at assimilation—many joined

Christian churches, and Kishi's son played football at Texas A&M—they continued to live in ethnic communities when possible.

Jews of the diaspora knew they needn't wait on an invitation, but murderous pogroms in Eastern Europe around the turn of the century set off a wave of departures. The North German Lloyd's Line happened to serve both Bremen and Galveston, and the presence of a hardworking rabbi named Henry Cohen at the receiving end gave organization and some security to their arrival and settlement, in such numbers that it became known as the "Galveston Movement."

Of all the new immigrant populations, probably none made more of a success of their opportunities, both as individuals and as a group, than did the Lebanese-Syrians. Mostly they were Maronites who had been driven from the Middle East by anti-Christian discrimination. Two of the most prominent became clothiers and succeeded with shrewd business sense. The brothers Abihider and Mansour Farah located in El Paso, utilizing the cheap labor of the area, and Joseph Haggar started a similar concern in Dallas, but farmed out piecework to women in need of extra cash. Unlike the European immigrants, who tended to settle together in ethnic communities, the Lebanese by and large assimilated quickly. They made their mark all over the state, even in the tiny Panhandle hamlet of Canadian, where Nahim Abraham settled in 1913. For over forty years he operated a celebrated mercantile, The Fair Store, that drew business from all the surrounding counties. Sensing that their success came at the cost of dispersal and the loss of heritage, these communities later organized the Southern Federation of Syrian Lebanese American Clubs to preserve their culture—and presumably enjoy some belly dancing without the gawking of Bible Belt prudes.

Although the population gains since 1870 had been impressive and some cities had undergone truly exponential growth, Texans were still overwhelmingly a rural people. Eighty-three out of a hundred still did not live in a town, and supplying them with life's wants was a challenge. While Nahim Abraham's Fair Store supplied the needs of settlers around Canadian, and county seats across the state maintained well-stocked mercantiles to supply everyday requirements, Texans who lived in the vast rural stretches put a unique spin on shopping for the home: reliance upon the mail order catalog. The exhaustive inventories of Marshall Field, Montgomery Ward, and Sears Roebuck, aided by the growing web of railroads, brought convenience to the nearest post office or train station. Even though the average working wage was only 22¢ per hour, the cost of relative merchandise had never been lower.

To Texans setting up a farm or ranch in the middle of nowhere, the mail order catalogs were a lifeline. A good Acme windmill with ten-foot blade span cost $23; the fifty-foot steel tower to mount it on cost $37. Hardware was extra. A light-duty one-horse gardening plow could be had for as little as $2.12, but heavy field plows ran more in the $8 to $12 range; a seated, horse-drawn hay rake averaged $14. Two-bushel grain sacks averaged only 16¢. For the subsistence farmer, a Boss Charcoal Peanut Roaster for a half-bushel load cost $12.25 with a cheap tin warming pan; one with a copper warmer ran $17.50. Gasoline-powered ones were about $4 more. A belt-driven grinding mill for grain or shelled corn was $12. For carting family and supplies around, a simple buckboard cost $37.50, a fancy four-seat topped buggy $118; a ten-pound pail of axle grease to keep them rolling cost 35¢. (Bicycles, by contrast, ran from $14 to $16.) A boxed set of everyday tools cost $2.55; a fully stocked mechanic's toolbox was $11.72.

Hunting and fishing were still important supplements to the family larder, and one catalog devoted thirty full pages to guns and ammunition. A cheap shotgun cost $18, a good Remington $20 hammer-fired or $35 hammerless. Small revolvers cost as little as $2; a simple bamboo fishing pole, when not crafted for oneself, cost a quarter, but fancy fly rods went up to $4.

In setting up her household, the Texas housewife could stock her kitchen with a simple, three-foot-tall icebox for $6, or a large high-quality one for $15. Her Acme Union cookstove cost $17.70, plus stovepipe; for cooking, enameled steel saucepans ran 39¢ small to 49¢ large, a twelve-quart steel stockpot, 43¢. In the dining room, the 100-piece set of everyday china cost $5.25; patterned, gold-rimmed china was twice to thrice as much. Cheap stoneware was sold by the piece—63¢ per dozen dinner plates, with other items in proportion. For what could not be grown or canned at home, staple foods could be ordered from large houses. Tea was 34¢ per pound for Young Hyson, nearly double that for choice Ceylon, coffee from 13¢ a pound. A 25-pound sack of Japanese rice was $1.10, 50¢ less than Louisiana rice. A ten-pound pail of salted fish ran 48¢ for herring, 77¢ for trout, $1.20 for mackerel; salmon could be had in one-pound cans for 12¢. Soda crackers could be ordered at 19¢ for a three-pound box; oyster crackers were popular at only a penny more. Fruit in 2½-pound cans ran 13¢ for pears, 14¢ for plums, 18¢ for apricots, 20¢ for peaches, and 23¢ for white cherries. A three-pound can of tomatoes cost 9¢.

For houses that had plumbing, the Acme Instantaneous Water Heater cost $15, with an admonition not to heat more than one gallon per minute. For those without the luxury of running water, a tin sitz bath cost $4.25; the enameled steel chamberpot, 54¢.

In the bedroom, an adequate oak suite of double bed, dresser with swivel mirror, and night table could be had for $13.75. The bed was fitted with 37¢ sheets, the four-pound blanket cost $1.35, more for the heavier ones. The bedroom might also be the location for the treadle-powered sewing machine, for as low as $12.75. For those who could afford them, store-bought ladies' suits started at $12.50, and for formal dress-up, plush capes cost $9 and up, and hats from $1.50 to $3. Men's store-bought suits ran from $13.50 to $20, shirts from 50¢ to $2. A good pair of suspenders cost a quarter.

For what little leisure time there was, one could order a wide variety of books—*Uncle Tom's Cabin* was still popular, as was Buffalo Bill Cody's *Story of the Wild West*, an era that was no less sensationally recalled in *Indian Horrors, Or, Massacres by the Redmen*. Self-made-men stories were popular, and humorous anthologies had a large audience: *Hot Stuff by Famous Funny Men* cost a dollar for eight hundred pages of "political wit, children's blunders, railroad jokes, riddles, puzzles," and a selection of prose by Mark Twain, Artemus Ward, and others. The more serious-minded could read of Stanley's travels in Africa, histories of the Boer and Spanish-American wars, and enormous illustrated travelogues such as the eight-pound, $5 *Glimpses of the World*.

For the more actively inclined, baseball bats started at 35¢ to 75¢ for quality, mitts $2 to $4.50. Social roles were learned early: many boys owned a 20¢ popgun, or they might be treated to a rocking horse for about $1.50, or a steel wagon or sled for about the same price. For the girls, a set of toy dishes started at 15¢, a toy laundry set for 75¢, and an eighteen-piece tin toy kitchen for a quarter.

Aside from supplying the necessities and pleasures, the mail order firms also took shrewd cognizance of taste and trends, including the growing temperance movement. In its 1900 catalog, Sears Roebuck credited the American conquest of the Philippines with its acquisition of a theretofore unknown native brew, Kava Kava, "a great non-alcoholic temperance wine." At a time when decent wine cost a dollar a quart, they offered Kava Kava extract sufficient to produce a gallon for $1.25; those who ordered enough extract to make five gallons received a pressed-glass wine set—tray, decanter, and six glasses—a $1.50 value, gratis. If such a substitution didn't end the craving for the real thing, the Stop Drinking German Liquor Cure was available at 50¢ for two dozen doses. Harder addictions were also treatable: the Reliable Cure for the Opium and Morphine Habit was 75¢ a bottle.

Mail order firms were also aware of the railroad freight games, and the ruinous rates charged to serve rural areas. "To equalize or reduce the cost of transportation," advised one catalog, "we advise the sending of club orders. . . . Simply have your neighbors or friends send their orders with yours and advise us to ship all to one person by freight. . . . The freight charges will be next to nothing when shared by several persons."

Commercial abuses by the railroads and other large corporations led to their regulation, but for the other sectors of business, caveat emptor still reigned. Pure Food and Drug laws still lay in the future, and home medicine shelves remained stocked with patent cures of dubious provenance. An entire home medicine cabinet of a dozen various curatives—customer's choice—could be mail-ordered for $1.50. Private complaints relating to intimate functions gave rise to the most bizarre treatments: timid men who suffered from "nervous weakness" had recourse to a variety of electric belts, including adjustable "suspensories," with the penis inserted into either a wire loop (cheap model) or short tube (deluxe) to be continuously invigorated.

Considering the jungle of patent medicines, it is not surprising that a few people experimented on their own, and some Texans parlayed kitchen chemistry into fortunes. One William Radam, a German immigrant supporting himself very modestly as an Austin gardener, was convinced that he had cured himself of a siege of diseases with a rosy concoction of water (99 percent), red wine, and sulfuric and hydrochloric acids. Marketed as the Microbe Killer, it cost Radam a nickel to produce a gallon that he sold for three dollars. Advertised nationwide with newspaper testimonials, the Microbe Killer became a sensation, eventually bottled in seventeen plants all over the United States, as Radam vacated Austin for a Central Park manse in New York. "I treated all my patients alike," he recalled triumphantly, "just as in my garden I would treat all weeds alike." He died in 1902.

Others brought their patent medicine fortunes to Texas. William Franklin Simmons, heir to the famous Dr. Simmons Vegetable Liver Restorer, parlayed his fortune into a land empire totaling 155,000 acres south of San Antonio. While he left off active management of the drug business, he never lost faith in the Liver Restorer, and required all his hands and employees to ingest it regularly. The brew vouchsafed him a spunky life—town building, dabbling in railroading, divorcing his first wife to marry her younger sister, and taking ever more Liver Restorer, until he died—kidney failure—in 1910.

Still others had more modest ambitions but were overtaken by events. One J. A. Lynch and his wife in 1877 sought relief from their multiple ailments by moving from the malarial Red River bottoms near Denison to dry and rocky Palo Pinto County, fifty miles west of Fort Worth. After a few months of drinking their rancid well water, they noticed their health improving. Word spread, and before long visitors flocked to the Lynch place seeking cures. Lynch laid out the town of Mineral Wells, but lacking a true proprietary eye, charged people only a nickel a quart for the magic water. Other entrepreneurs moved in on him, the railroad arrived, and soon there were hundreds of wells, supporting spas and hotels. Fame spread rapidly after two women reputedly driven mad by "feminine complaints" were cured after drinking from one well, and "Crazy Water," both bottled and in packets of crystals, became a minor rage. The fad eventually passed, but not before Mineral Wells was solidly established on the map.

Town drugstores also got into the healing act, and Texas consumers did just as well to down the potion of Waco druggist Charles Alderton, who began selling a home mixture of carbonated fruit syrups in 1885 at Morrison's Old Corner Drug Store where he worked. His patrons loved it, and when they insisted that the pharmacy's owner, Wade Morrison, give the brew a name, he honored the Virginia pharmacist he formerly worked for, a certain Dr. Pepper. Commercial manufacture of the soft drink began in 1891, begetting a series of business deals and buyouts that resulted in the formation of the Dr Pepper Company in 1902.

FIFTY-TWO

FINAL RAIDS

WHILE THE BLOODY MAYHEM WROUGHT BY THE CO-
manches and Kiowas had hogged the newspaper headlines until the end of
the Red River War, a few other actions had been necessary as well to pacify
the frontier. One was waged by Ranald Mackenzie in 1873, the year between
his two expeditions against the Quahadis.

Kickapoo Indians, linguistic relatives of the Cheyennes who had mi-
grated down from the Great Lakes as a result of population pressures
brought by both Anglo settlers and other native groups, were established in
Texas by the mid-1830s. They came at the invitation of the Mexican government, as part of an abortive plan to buffer Mexico from further American incursion. When that scheme fell through the Texas Kickapoos settled in
proximity to Bowl's Cherokees; both groups were thwarted in gaining secure land titles by the governments of both Mexico and the Republic of
Texas. When the surviving Cherokees fled to join relatives in the Indian Territory after Mirabeau Lamar's 1839 campaign, the Kickapoos, instead of
joining other bands of their tribe there or in Kansas, crossed the Rio Grande
into Mexico. There over the succeeding decades the Kickapoos made themselves so useful to the Mexican military by taking part in cross-border raids
that the government granted them the reservation they had been denied
when they actually lived in Texas. Their hostility toward Texas increased
after January 1865, when a band of nearly a thousand Indian Territory Kickapoos in transit to join those in Mexico was attacked by a force of nearly five
hundred Confederate soldiers and frontier militia at Dove Springs, about
twenty miles southwest of present San Angelo. After a desperate fight the
natives routed the whites, killing twenty-two and wounding nineteen—
about twice the number of their own casualties—and leaving them to make
their painful way to safety through the sleet and snow of a howling norther.
The Kickapoos considered the attack unjustified, and once they joined the
Mexican band they partook of the border raids with gusto.

These forays became so noisome that by 1872, claims filed by Texans
against the Mexican government dating back to 1859 demanded payment
for nearly 150,000 head of stolen stock. (Of course, Texas ranchers gave as

good as they got, and "wet stock"—cattle stolen in Mexico and driven north across the river—was a common enough sight on the range.) Still, by 1873 the U.S. Army determined to act against the Kickapoos, who had become a focus of the complaints. On May 18 Mackenzie, acting on Sheridan's orders but without Mexican permission, struck across the border near Remolino west of Eagle Pass with 400 of his 4th Cavalry. Seeking a tactical victory more than a bloodbath, Mackenzie waited until most of the Kickapoo warriors were gone hunting before taking the village, capturing the women, children, and old people, and removing them to the Indian Territory, where they were eventually joined by more than 300 deflated warriors. That was not the entirety of the Mexican Kickapoos, by any means, but the border quieted considerably.

Quanah Parker's surrender ended the South Plains tribes' organized resistance to Anglo settlement, although reports of isolated Indian depredations spiced local newspapers for a few years longer. How many of the incidents were actually perpetrated by natives, however, and how many were committed by white or other non-Indian outlaws done up in beads and feathers, could no more be determined now than it ever could. It is certain that Indians did leave the reservation for Texas on at least a few occasions.

Although it was starvation that forced the Kiowas and Comanches off the reservation in 1874, government food issues to the Indians after their surrender still often failed. Even irate letters from Ranald Mackenzie, who had defeated them in the 1874 Panhandle campaign, failed to improve their situation. Black Horse, the Second Chief of the Quahadi Comanches, who was partly disabled by a stroke while in Florida, had been allowed to return home. Faced with winter hunger, he led his band on a foraging expedition deep into Texas. Charlie Rath, who in 1874 had stolen away to Dodge City and let the buffalo hunters defend his store at Adobe Walls, had now opened a new operation called Rath City on the Double Mountain Fork of the Brazos, some one hundred miles south of the Red River in present Stonewall County. Near there, Black Horse's Comanches killed a buffalo hunter named Marshall Sewell. Nearly four dozen of the hiders lit out after the Indians and pursued them northwest all the way to Yellowhouse Draw, in present Lubbock, from where the Comanches escaped after a brief firefight on February 22, 1877.

Reservation hunger continued into the following year, and early in 1878 a party of Kiowas left the Fort Sill vicinity to hunt, this time escorted by a company of 10th Cavalry buffalo soldiers. It was winter and the Indians had been suffering greatly, but no game could be found. At one point two of them, trailing two deer, crossed the Red River into Texas but were immediately attacked by Rangers, who killed one of them and prepared to attack the whole party, only to be prevented from doing so by the cavalry. The Rangers withdrew, after an ugly verbal exchange with the black cavalry, and the hungry Indians returned to the reservation. The dead man was Ahto-tain-te (White Cowbird), who was one of the tribe's most important warriors, a member of the elite Kaitsenko warrior society who had been selected for the honor by Satanta himself when he retired from the post in 1874. Reservation Kiowas were shaken by the news. They had remained at peace for four years and knew that future antagonism was futile, but in the minds of many the death of such a man could not go unanswered. White Cowbird's brother, Pägo-to-goodl (Lone Youth), who was himself a member of the Kaitsenko, led a revenge raid into Texas the following April.

They did not ride far across the border, but lurked about a road near the site where the town of Quanah was established six years later. Shortly before noon a local rancher named Joe Earle rode by, leading by some distance a wagon loaded with supplies, driven by two teamsters. As leader, Lone Youth decreed this to be purely an eye for an eye, with no indiscriminate slaughter. Joe Earle was quickly surrounded and shot in the forehead; after coup was counted a fire was kindled on his belly. He was the last Kiowa victim in Texas. The terrified teamsters were allowed to unhitch their horses and ride away, although Satanta's son, Cry of the Wild Goose, had to be restrained from firing after them. The teamsters alerted local cowboys, who thundered onto the scene as the Indians finished loading badly needed supplies onto their ponies. They gave hot chase but lost the raiders in a dust storm. A complaint was lodged with the Indian Office, but the agent could learn nothing, and none of the Kiowas would discuss the affair until well after the turn of the century.

The famous Satanta himself had not been packed off to Fort Marion with the other Red River War prisoners; as soon as he surrendered in the fall of 1874, he was returned to the state penitentiary in Huntsville. On October 11, 1878, the Orator of the Plains sang his death song and hurled himself from an upper-story window. His body was not returned to the Kiowas until 1963.

Two months after Joe Earle was killed, the final Comanche foray into Texas took place, and it too was motivated by the usual cause: hunger. Experienced officers like Mackenzie knew they could not be expected to starve quietly. By 1878 all the leaders who had been sent to prison in Florida were returned, but it was the unreconstructed Quahadi chief Black Horse who bolted from Fort Sill. At first he stayed close by, leading a hunting party that found not a single bison on the reservation. Knowing that the approaches to his old haunts on the Staked Plains were blocked by cavalry patrols, Black Horse led a couple dozen men on a lightning raid deep into Texas, southwest all the way to the vicinity of Big Spring, where settlement had just begun. The hungry Comanches descended upon an isolated ranch on June 28 and killed and butchered a number of colts. They were still eating when they were pounced upon by Captain June Peak and six men of B Company, Frontier Battalion of the Texas Rangers. It was an even fight. Black Horse's men outnumbered Peak's, but the Rangers, while suffering two wounded, were better shots. The Rangers made off with the Comanches' horses, and the Comanches captured the Rangers' pack mules with supplies and ammunition. Black Horse fought a running retreat for several miles across hot red mesquite plains, until he concealed his men in a buffalo wallow and prepared an ambush. In the ensuing firefight Peak lost another man wounded and one dead, W. G. Anglin, the last casualty of Plains hostiles in Texas. Troops from Fort Concho who arrived on the scene on the thirtieth found the Indians had fled back to the foodless reservation, where they kept quiet about their adventure, and no repercussions followed.

The South Plains Indians were gradually and sometimes forcibly assimilated into Anglo culture; their children were sent to white schools and their reservations held in severalty were broken up into individual parcels. Some, such as Quanah Parker, adapted and prospered; most squeaked by. One aspect of their life continued unchanged, however: white stock thieves from Texas preyed on their herds as relentlessly as ever, especially now that they couldn't retaliate. By 1886 the once-feared Big Bow was well into a stiff middle age, when his son introduced him to a Texas gambler from whom he had won some money the previous night. Big Bow and some friends also won a little money from him that evening, and only after dawn did the onetime war chief discover that his horse herd was missing, and that the gambler had been letting the Kiowas fleece him of small change while he was casing their herds. The trail led west into the Texas Panhandle.

Big Bow was outraged but determined to go by the book. He rode out of his camp and returned in twenty-four hours, having ridden seventy-five miles to the agency, which had been moved to Anadarko, and then back. He had in hand a written pass to leave the reservation to recover his horses, but permission to fire a weapon only in self-defense. That was a moot point, anyway, as his old carbine had only one cartridge. He left in the company of a young man named Paykee, the son of a companion from the raiding days; Paykee had a Winchester and six bullets. With only a handful of food they covered 130 miles, following the trail of the stolen herd, which passed near the town of Mobeetie before turning north into the Canadian River breaks. They stopped at a house and asked for information. As the startled rancher fed them a meal and gave them biscuits to take with them, they learned that the stock had been driven by there the day before, and that the "gambler" was really a well-known horse thief with a lengthy record.

Big Bow and Paykee found the stock the next morning, with the gambler and an accomplice quietly breakfasting. The experienced chief took care to keep a gulch between them, and then approached with his agency pass in hand to demand the return of his horses. The thieves began shooting. The Kiowas sought cover in the gulch, as Big Bow admonished Paykee not to waste bullets. Paykee missed once before wounding one of the rustlers in the arm. At Big Bow's direction, Paykee stripped and slinked away through the grass to drive off the horses, as the old chief whooped and kept their attention on the gulch. The strategy worked, and once Big Bow saw Paykee driving off the horses, he mounted and rode to meet him—forgetting, in the excitement, to pick up Paykee's clothes. In the ensuing chase it was apparent that the thieves would overtake them, and the Kiowas dismounted, keeping their horses between them and the approaching whites. With his knife in one hand and pass in the other, Big Bow called out that he had a "safety paper," but as the thieves rode them down with guns drawn, the chief gave Paykee permission to drop the "gambler." Paykee shot him from his horse as the second rustler fled, and Big Bow advanced and put him out of his pain with his one bullet. Paykee was so mad at having to ride away naked he didn't speak to the chief for two days, even though he was able to bum some clothes from Cheyennes on the way home. His spirits were restored when he and Big Bow were greeted with the last Kiowa victory celebration. Big Bow was cleared of wrongdoing by an inquest, and he tied one final knot in the scalp-fringe of his leggings.

Throughout the South Plains, organized Indian resistance ceased with the 1874 Red River War, but Big Bow's recovery of his horse herd gave the Texas Panhandle's new ranchers a sobering reminder that the Plains Indians still remembered how to take care of themselves. Living isolated on the vast ranches, and now with the advent of women and children, the mere thought of being killed and butchered—or butchered and then killed—by lurking natives was still so unnerving that the mind could play tricks.

One case became quite famous. In late January 1891, while the Comanches and Kiowas were quietly ranching on their reservation, a foreman of the Rocking Chair Ranch in Collingsworth County told some of his men to shoot a steer for dinner. The cookfire got away from them and incinerated the whole animal, to their great and vocal annoyance. A rise or two away, one Mrs. Will Johnson heard shooting and what she described as "bloodthirsty yells," and saw the column of smoke rising. She quickly hustled her children to a neighboring farm, whose owner raced to the telegraph station in Salisbury in neighboring Hall County, and an Indian panic seized the countryside from Amarillo down to Plainview and over to Clarendon. Towns were fortified, militias organized, and officers elected—including Temple Houston, son of the revolutionary hero, who happened to be in the town of Panhandle at the time. Hardware stores were swept bare of arms and ammunition, and settlers gathered and huddled behind shutters in their isolated houses. Not until a Texas Ranger company arrived—by train—under command of the great Captain William J. McDonald was the cause of the terror finally rooted out. The many "victims" of what became known as the Great Panhandle Indian Scare were a laughingstock for almost as many years as it took for them to see any humor in it whatsoever.

FIFTY-THREE

FORT DAVIS: WESTERN ANCHOR

WHILE COMANCHE AND KIOWA FORAYS INTO TEXAS BE-
came a rarity after 1875, and the increasing population of ranchers plied
their trade in relative safety, this was not true on the frontier west of the
Pecos, which remained an active theater of the Apache wars for some years
longer. Of the various eastern Apache bands, the Lipanes were run out of
most of Texas by Comanches before Anglo settlement, but they continued to
raid into the country from their Mexican haunts. The Comanches were not
interested in adding the Trans-Pecos to their hunting grounds, and it became the domain of the Mescalero Apaches, a band based in southern and
central New Mexico, east of the more famous Chiricahuas. The Mescaleros
took such a beating during the Civil War that it became forgotten that just a
decade before, they were as feared in war and raiding as any other Apaches.

When Fort Davis, in the Davis Mountains and the heart of Texas
Apachería, was put on line in 1854 to try to control them, the Army discovered they were as bright and impatient as they were dangerous. When one
lieutenant opened a council with the imagery-laden blarney that they had
been foisting on the Plains tribes, "one old Indian jumped up. . . . 'What
does your chief talk to us in this way for? We an't babies, we are fighting
men; if he has got anything to tell us we will hear it, but we didn't come here
to be amused, we came here to be made drunk, and get some blankets and
tobacco.' " One powerful chief named Nicolás learned the game, though. He
came into Fort Davis, made a treaty, and was taken to El Paso and given royal
treatment. As the stagecoach passed back through his territory, he gushed,
"My heart is full of love for my white brothers. They have not spoken with
forked tongues. . . . When I lie down at night the treaty will be in my heart."
Then in a flash he jerked a colonel's pistol from its holster and tumbled from
the stage; the next day Nicolás raided Fort Davis, killing two herd guards
and making off with nearly all the stock. A platoon of fourteen who galloped
out in pursuit were wiped out to a man.

During the Civil War the Mescaleros suffered bad defeats and worse
treatment in New Mexico, and Texans turned their attention to the more immediate dangers of the Comanches and Kiowas. The Quaker Indian agents

who administered Grant's peace policy in the Indian Territory were honest and conscientious (although their superintendent was later busted for corruption), but the same could not be said for the Dutch Reformed Church, which bore responsibility for the Apache agencies. After the death of Mangas Coloradas in June 1874, leadership of most of the eastern Chiricahuas passed to a chief named Beduiat, known to the whites as Victorio. His lands bordered the Mescalero on the west, and there had been considerable intermarriage. Probably no Apache Indian of comparable status tried harder to accommodate what Apaches called the "white-eyes," or won equal respect and admiration from white administrators who were attuned to his situation. He had pressed for and received a reservation in his tribe's home territory near Ojo Caliente, New Mexico, and lived not just peaceably but harmoniously with Anglo neighbors. Then the government reneged and attempted to force all the Apache tribes into the unspeakable squalor of the San Carlos Reservation in the Arizona desert. As one of the honest agents wrote angrily to his superior, "There are no Indians in his Department *more faithful* than the Mimbres band of Apaches, when at peace. . . . They were driven by the *treachery of our own people* into their present hostile condition." But once those hostilities were opened, Victorio proved to be a raider of relentless effectiveness. After various outbreaks and reconciliations, he agreed to reside on the Mescalero Agency near Tularosa, about eighty miles north of El Paso. The agent there was helpful and cooperative, but when Victorio heard that he had been indicted for murder and saw the sheriff and district attorney riding into the agency, he did not wait to find out if their errand was innocent (it was, actually) before bolting for the final time. It was midsummer of 1879, and although he left with fewer than a hundred warriors, such was his reputation as a chief and leader that within a short time he led about three times that many, and with the Trans-Pecos located between him and his customary raiding grounds in Chihuahua, West Texas became terrorized by Apache depredations.

Colonel Benjamin Grierson, who had arrested the Kiowa ringleaders of the Warren Wagon Train Massacre, and his 10th Cavalry had already been transferred from Fort Sill down to Fort Concho. Now they were moved into Fort Davis to restore peace. Davis, in that desolate purgatory west of the Pecos River, itself was reduced during the Civil War—abandoned by federals at the outbreak of hostilities, occupied by rebels until the collapse of their New Mexico scheme, and then deserted entirely but for Indians who broke up buildings for firewood, before it was reactivated and rebuilt. Grierson was a remarkable officer, an Illinois music teacher who overcame his paralyzing fear of horses—he was almost killed by one when he was eight—to become a Civil War cavalry legend. His lightning raid through Mississippi in 1863 created such a sensation that, after the failure of the Union's two attempts to invade Texas, thought was given to assigning him to a similar raid through the rebellious Lone Star. Yet Ben Grierson was one of the least popular officers in the army. His willingness to take charge of a Negro regiment made him the subject of much chuckling into glasses of whiskey; while in command of the "City of Refuge" at Fort Sill his support of President Grant's peace policy led North Texas ranchers to demonize him. Grierson was not a West Pointer, he enjoyed the hearty dislike of General Philip Sheridan, and when the 10th Cavalry distinguished itself in the Red River War, the success of the buffalo soldiers turned other officers' amusement into loathing.

In three years of desultory raiding, Victorio had repeatedly bested or eluded troops from the black 9th Cavalry and white 6th Cavalry while savaging the countryside. The only thing that the army managed to do was limit his westward range. When Grierson was brought up to help in the campaign, his job usually meant responding to summonses from New Mexico to come join another ineffectual chase. Grierson was aware of his place in the officers' pecking order, but in 1880 he saw the futility of the existing operation; after an exhausting, 1,500-mile goose chase, he proposed a new strategy: what was necessary was to turn the Apaches' natural advantage—the desert environment—against them. Instead of continuing to respond to a new raid with another fruitless pursuit, Grierson suggested anticipating Victorio's next move and seizing the waterholes in front of him, and even the officers who had been mocking him were forced to agree.

In July 1880, Grierson received word that Victorio had been in a sharp fight in Mexico; Grierson believed that he would try to make his way back to Tularosa for fresh supplies and recruits. Grierson sent units of his buffalo soldiers to occupy the West Texas waterholes in his path, himself taking a position at Tinaja de las Palmas in Quitman Canyon, with two dozen soldiers and his teenaged son, Robert Grierson. Once his scouts were certain he had guessed correctly, Grierson just had time to send for reinforcements and fling up rifle cover by the time Victorio and his warriors came pounding up the canyon, chasing a platoon of buffalo soldiers in front of them. "We let fly from our fortifications at the Indians about 300 yds. off," wrote young Robert in his diary, "& golly!! you ought to've seen 'em turn tail & strike for the hills." The thirsty Apaches failed to dislodge Grierson and his men, and fled back to Mexico, leaving seven dead after the expected reinforcements crashed into them from both sides.

Desperate to resupply at Tularosa, Victorio crossed back into Texas on August 2. He almost succeeded in giving Grierson's scouts the slip, but the colonel learned of their presence just in time and guessed their route. Masterfully keeping the Sierra Diablo Mountains between himself and the thirsty hostiles, Grierson relived his earlier days as a cavalry raider, driving two companies of his 10th sixty-five miles in less than a day to seize Rattlesnake Springs before Victorio could get there. By the time the Apaches arrived Grierson had been reinforced with two more companies; there was a furious exchange of fire on August 6, 1880, in which no one was killed, but the strategic object was secured: the hostiles were denied water.

Victorio pounded away in the August heat and fell upon an army wagon train, but was jarred to discover that Grierson had kept up with him, charging into the fight and chasing them off again. Confused at confronting a white officer with guile equal to his own, Victorio crossed into Mexico to rest and recoup in his Mexican strongholds. With the chief's luck broken, some of his followers began deserting him to drift back to their different reservations. Unknown to Victorio, the American army had begun sharing information with the Mexican military, and several weeks later the remnants of Victorio's renegades were surrounded and exterminated by a force under Joaquín Terrazas. A consummate soldier-politician, Terrazas invited American columns into the country to help bottle the chief up, then won face with the local inhabitants by ordering the hated gringo soldiers out of the country before attacking Victorio on October 14. They killed seventy-eight hostile Apaches, including the chief. The fact that the attacking Mexicans lost only three dead was a strong indication that Victorio was out of ammunition.

With the end of the Apache threat came the end of Fort Davis' usefulness. While the desert surrounding the Davis Mountains is of unforgiving aridity, the mountain meadows offered lush grazing, and stockmen soon had the land divided. Military life at the fort continued pointlessly until it was decommissioned in 1891.

The success of a colonel like Grierson, who was so unpopular throughout the rest of the officer corps, and even worse, the success of the black buffalo soldiers in bringing order to the Trans-Pecos, was almost more than the white man's army could stand. Grierson had a reputation for treating his Negro cavalry with respect and fairness, including one remarkable man, 2nd Lieutenant Henry Ossian Flipper, the first African-American to graduate from the U.S. Military Academy.

Flipper was in the perfect time and circumstance to be a demonstration project. Born a slave in Georgia in 1856, he was schooled at the American Missionary Association and admitted to Atlanta University before accepting an appointment to the Academy. At West Point he studied engineering, graduating in the lower middle of his class—fiftieth out of seventy-six. That he graduated at all was a testament to his courage and fortitude in the face of galling treatment he received from fellow cadets and instructors. The previous four black students had all washed out rather than endure not just the brutal hazing that all new cadets were subjected to, but the additional humiliation of "silencing," being walled off from any social life and not even being spoken to by any other cadet. Flipper too might not have lasted without West Point's black janitors and porters, who slipped him gifts and encouragement. He took his commission and joined the 10th Cavalry in January 1878, employing his engineering skills in draining malaria-infested ponds around Fort Sill, where "Flipper's Ditch" is still a National Historic Landmark. In the brutal draws and canyons of the Cap Rock that nearly destroyed Nelson Miles' command in the Red River War, he ran a telegraph line from Fort Elliott nearly a hundred miles to Camp Supply. He also sited and built a road from Gainesville, Texas, to Fort Sill when a troop of the vaunted 4th Cavalry got drunk and shirked the job. Assigned to Fort Davis in 1880, he took part in the defeats of Victorio and settled in as Fort Davis' quartermaster and acting commissary of subsistence. Little did he realize that his success was leading to a trap.

Command of Fort Davis passed to Colonel William Shafter in 1881. Like Grierson he had commanded all-Negro regiments, beginning with the 17th Infantry during the Civil War. Obese and bad-tempered, he lacked Grierson's sympathy for the duty, and upon arriving at the post moved immediately to get the black officer out of his way. He relieved Flipper of his quartermaster duties, but continued him as commissary since there was no one to replace him. Civilians around the fort warned Flipper that the white officers were going to find a way to get him, and shortly thereafter, he found money missing from the commissary till. Unable to find it, he attempted to conceal the loss, but was discovered and court-martialed. He was found not guilty of embezzlement, but convicted and removed from the service under the second charge, the convenient catch-all of conduct unbecoming an officer and gentleman. He appealed, but the fix was in and he was dishonorably discharged from the army.

If the army had no use for Henry Flipper, surveying and mining companies were eager to utilize his skills after he settled in El Paso—including his employment ironically by a consortium of former Confederate officers. His race was less an issue in the Hispanic culture, and over the years he gained note as an author, editor, translator, and expert consultant on Mexican mining and land law—a knowledge that led him to the position of special assistant to the secretary of the interior. After five years' work in Venezuela he retired and lived out his remaining years with a brother in Atlanta; he died at eighty-four in 1940 having never, despite constant effort, been able to get his conviction reversed. Not until 1976, when an integrated army needed black heroes, did he receive his honorable discharge, dated back to June 30, 1882. The occasion was the dedication of a bust of Henry Flipper at West Point, and the establishment of an annual award for the cadet who best bears up under "unusual difficulties."

FIFTY-FOUR

LAW VS. OUTLAW

CATTLE RUSTLERS WERE NOT THE ONLY LAWBREAKERS adversely affected by the fencing of the frontier. The disappearance of unoccupied public domain, the squeezing of travel onto marked roads, and the increasing inaccessibility of traditional hideouts made it harder to be an outlaw of any kind.

One of the last of the free-range badmen was Sam Bass, an Indiana orphan who ran away from the uncle who was raising him, and lived in Mississippi for a year before arriving in Denton in 1870 at the age of nineteen. He first worked at wrangling, freighting, woodcutting, and other unskilled labor. Disappointed that the reality of the Wild West was not what the dime novels pictured, Bass acquired a fast mare and supported himself for a couple of years by racing her. In 1876, he and a partner held themselves out as drovers, contracted with several ranchers, and took a herd north. Bypassing Abilene, Kansas, they made $8,000 on the herd farther north, but before returning to Texas to pay off the ranchers they blew the money on vices in moral sinks such as Deadwood. To recover the funds they took to robbing stagecoaches; the haul was anemic at first, but they accumulated a gang and struck it rich—$60,000 in Black Hills gold—holding up a train. Half the gang were killed by lawmen soon after, but Bass slipped back to Texas and gathered a new gang about him. Starting in the spring of 1878 they menaced the roads and rail lines around Dallas; after six heists Texas Rangers and citizen posses made that territory too hot, and Bass headed south, intending to hold up the bank in Round Rock, a small town north of Austin. Unknown to Bass, Ranger Major John B. Jones had gotten one of the robbers to turn informant, and Rangers of the Frontier Battalion were waiting for Bass in Round Rock. The end of his career came, symbolically enough, when he was asked his authority for carrying a concealed weapon and was mortally wounded in the ensuing gunfight. He was found concealed *in extremis* in brush the next day and brought back into town, where he died on July 21, 1878, his twenty-seventh birthday.

Sam Bass was in it purely for the money; outranking him as a sociopath, both in blood spilled and in his habitually feeling justified in his murders, was his contemporary John Wesley Hardin. A native of Bonham, Hardin started killing when he was fifteen, one victim a schoolmate and another a black man. He claimed to have killed three Union soldiers as a fugitive before getting out of the state on a cattle drive. Back in Texas, in Gonzales in September 1871, Hardin killed two of E. J. Davis' state policemen who were trying to arrest him, which made him something of a local hero and embroiled him for a time in the Sutton-Taylor Feud. He cemented his reputation by killing Jack Helm, a hated state police captain, but became a marked man by subsequently killing a deputy sheriff in Comanche, far northwest of the Sutton-Taylor conflict. He removed to the Deep South with his family and several accomplices, trailed by Texas Ranger John B. Armstrong, who had long since earned his reputation as "McNelly's Bulldog."

In a train station in Pensacola, Armstrong burst into their car, shot dead one of Hardin's men, pistol-whipped Hardin senseless before he could draw his gun, and arrested the other three. Another Ranger legend was born, and Armstrong's bravery was unquestioned, but had it not been for the hammer of Hardin's revolver getting hung on his suspenders as he tried to draw it, the famous lawman's career would have come to an untimely end. Sentenced to twenty-five years, inmate Hardin studied religion, tried to escape, studied law, tried to escape, and upon his pardon in 1894 settled in El Paso to open a law practice. His release, and the faith in his rehabilitation, was owed in some measure to his having become superintendent of the prison Sunday school, but being a sociopath he found it impossible to go straight. He was gunned down on August 19, 1895, by a crooked constable named Selman, apparently in anger at not being paid for his service in killing the husband of Hardin's mistress. He was buried without mourners, having killed over thirty men, but because of his Confederate sympathies, the sanctimonious memoir he left behind, and the fact that some of his victims may have, in popular estimation, actually needed killing, his reputation became more quixotic than condemned.

One of the few men to perhaps outdo Hardin's body count was Bill Longley, but of his purported total of thirty-two victims, most were self-proclaimed and unproven. Like Hardin, Longley enjoyed some measure of public approbation because the majority of his victims had been blacks or sympathizers; whether out of sympathy or a desire to witness justice, his 1878 execution in Giddings was attended by thousands. As Texas became increasingly unsuitable for a career as a dime-novel outlaw, some, such as the Ketchum boys of San Saba, decamped for points west. But Texas' reputation for vastness attracted others; after the notorious Dalton gang was finished in Kansas, the last four survivors sought refuge in Texas, where they were hunted down and killed in 1897.

Lawlessness in Texas as a private enterprise was one facet of frontier violence; another was its common association with organized factions, as seen in the Regulator-Moderator War during the Republic, or the Sutton-Taylor Feud of Reconstruction. The last manifestation of the latter was the Jay Bird–Woodpecker War in the town of Richmond, in history-laden Fort Bend County near Houston. By 1888, the federal occupation and its regime had been relegated to the status of warmly nursed grudge throughout the state. Only in Fort Bend, where freedmen and Republican sympathizers constituted a large majority, did they retain political power. About two hundred regular Democrats organized in July with a parade and demonstration, with the goal of regaining power for white conservatives. They adopted a paramilitary organization, including loud uniforms, for which they were called Jay Birds—an easier handle than the Young Men's Democratic Club—also fitting because they intended to drive the black "Woodpeckers" from their nest in the county courthouse. After intimidation that included one shooting on each side, and five prominent blacks being given ten hours to get out of town, the Republicans fielded no slate of candidates in the election that year. There were, however, more jubilant Jay Birds than there were offices to fill, and the disappointed Democrats began forging alliances with blacks and Republicans to win offices back. After several more shootings, including a pitched street battle before the courthouse in which the sheriff, a Woodpecker, was killed, Governor Sul Ross sent Texas Rangers under another capable leader, Ira Aten, to restore order. Aten, who as a teenager in Round Rock saw the end of Sam Bass, and as a young Ranger had killed one of Butch Cassidy's men hiding in Texas, ended the violence. Power, however, was eventually left in the hands of the Jay Birds, and despite the black majority in the county, the local government made no room for blacks until the Jay Birds were forced to desegregate in 1953.

Most prominently it was the Texas Rangers, still deployed as the Frontier Battalion and the Special Force, that tamed the frontier when it was beyond the reach of local authorities. But of those local lawmen, it was not always easy in late-nineteenth-century Texas to know just who the bad guys were. There were instances where those who were clothed with official authority used their station to so oppress people that violence flashed. The racist enormities of that first incarnation of the Ku Klux Klan were largely suppressed by Union troops before 1870, but the white racial superiority they espoused became so deeply interwoven with the "Jim Crow" system which followed that the KKK may as arguably have won their contest as lost it.

Those two principal features on the Texas scene of the 1870s, ethnic prejudice and the privatization of formerly public domain, came together in a particularly ugly way in the Trans-Pecos. During the Civil War, Hispanic residents around El Paso and San Elizario feared that their usual source of salt in Tularosa, New Mexico, was about to be cut off, and began mining salt deposits at the foot of the Guadalupe Mountains, about a hundred miles east of the towns. With profit to be made by selling the salt back home, quarrels arose over who would control it. The dispute became caught up in El Paso's corrupt Reconstruction politics, although the Guadalupe salt deposits remained a public resource. Emerging more or less victorious in the political fray was Louis Cardis, an Italian who had soldiered for Garibaldi, and a Republican who managed to posture himself as a friend of the Mexican community. After the Republicans broke into bitter factions, Cardis allied himself with a Democrat from Missouri, Charles Howard. The two supported each other in their subsequent elevations, Cardis to the state legislature and Howard to a district judgeship. When Cardis tried to resurrect the idea of turning the salt beds into a moneymaker, Howard responded by himself filing a claim on the land, and attempting to collect fees from the Mexicans who came to load up their bullock carts with the salt. As their former friendship disintegrated, Cardis inflamed the Hispanic community against Howard, and Howard assaulted Cardis on at least three occasions. After the third time, Howard was captured by a mob and taken to San Elizario, where he saved his life by signing away his claim to the salt, agreeing to leave the area, and posting a bond. As traffic flowed freely across the Rio Grande, it was impossible to determine who in the mob were Tejanos and who were Mexican nationals, but from the safety of Mesilla, Judge Howard wired to Austin that an invasion was imminent, and Texas Rangers from the Frontier Battalion quickly arrived.

Feeling himself somewhat buttressed, Howard returned, despite his pledge and bond, and shotgunned Cardis to death on October 10, 1877. After being arraigned and freed again on bond, and learning that a cart train had gone to gather salt, Howard entered the Rangers' station to press trespassing charges against them. The San Elizario community finally boiled over, and with help from across the river, laid siege to the Rangers for five days. Proving that there can sometimes be honor among thieves, Howard purchased the lives of the Rangers by giving himself up to a local firing squad. As the Rangers were disarmed and allowed to leave, Howard, his agent, and one of his bondsmen were shot, mutilated, and dumped in a well.

Noting the involvement of foreign nationals, the army reestablished Fort Bliss near El Paso to keep a lid on things. Subsequent inquiries uncovered few of the convoluted facts, but as Howard had been the principal stressor in the situation, the salt deposits were quietly commercialized and fees paid without further incident. The Tejano and blended Tejano-Mexican communities, however, continued to pay a price in violence. San Elizario, already looted once by alien nationals involved in killing Howard, was pillaged again by an amalgam of Rangers, U.S. Cavalry, and citizen volunteers. This and later suppression of Hispanic protest in Alpine, Laredo, and Rio Grande City left no doubt in the minds of valley Tejanos that, similar to the resubjugated freedmen in the cotton lands, they were now the second-class citizens in West Texas.

Not all law enforcement along the Rio Grande was so vivid in its class warfare. One large chapter of the Law West of the Pecos—in fact that's what he called himself—was the one written by Judge Roy Bean, lord and master of the lonely train stop of Langtry, two hundred miles west of San Antonio and three hundred miles east of El Paso. As the rail line approached the Rio Grande on its way to El Paso, the nearest settlement was Fort Stockton, well over a hundred miles to the north. Texas Rangers needed the appointment of a justice of the peace somewhere in that vast stretch to avoid the arduous journeys otherwise required to deliver culprits to the law. To undertake this office the Pecos County commissioners appointed Bean, a white-bearded personality of about sixty who had come west to sell whiskey to railroad construction crews.

In his youth Bean had roamed widely across the West, mostly in tow of two older brothers, Joshua and Samuel, each of whom held offices of public trust but were unable to keep the younger Roy from having to flee scrapes with the law. He eventually settled down in San Antonio with a Mexican wife with whom he had more children than happiness, and from a bailiwick on South Flores Street—still known as Beanville—he operated a string of dubious retail operations, including a dairy, one of whose customers found a minnow in his milk. In 1882 Bean acquired a stock of liquor and skipped town, intending to supply the rail crews.

Just west of the Pecos River and the tiny hellhole of Vinegarroon, named for an enormous species of scorpion, Bean accepted the commission as justice of the peace and established the settlement of Langtry. For sixteen of the next twenty years he held court in, or often on the front porch of, his sa-

loon and pool hall, the Jersey Lilly, named if not correctly spelled for Lillie
Langtry, the celebrated British actress, native of Jersey, and mistress of the
Prince of Wales. Bean looked to her as a beacon of courtly, unattainable love,
and the two did actually correspond; while Langtry regretted that her sched-
ule did not permit a visit soon, she offered the donation of a public drinking
fountain. Bean had to decline, on the grounds that water was the one liquid
that no one in Langtry drank.

The larceny of Bean's court became legendary. Jurors who didn't buy
drinks were dropped from the roll; train passengers who demanded change
when it was due were fined that amount in contempt as their train was
pulling out. Perhaps his most famous disposition came when a body was
found at the foot of the high bridge over the Pecos. When the dead man's
pockets were found to contain a pistol and forty dollars, Bean confiscated
the revolver and fined him the forty dollars for carrying a concealed weapon.
His rulings were also celebrated for their impromptu practicality. Once
when a threatening crowd gathered in support of a railroad worker who had
killed a Chinese laborer, Bean scoured his sources and pronounced himself
unable to find a law against killing a Chinaman. And when it was pointed
out that in Texas, justices of the peace had no power to grant divorces, which
he regularly did, Bean insisted that since he had the authority to marry
them, he must necessarily have the authority to fix the mistakes. But while
it was true that in his celebrated "Statoot Book," cheating at cards was
logged as a hanging offense, "if ketched," Bean himself had almost been
hanged at least twice in his youth, and he never actually executed anyone.

His greatest notoriety came in 1896, when boxing promoters were attempting to find a location near El Paso to stage a bout between Bob
Fitzsimmons and Peter Maher. Prizefighting was illegal in Texas, New Mexico, and Chihuahua, but Bean entrained the principals and spectators from
El Paso to Langtry. Leaving police and Texas Rangers stranded in El Paso, he
staged the fight on a sandbar in the Rio Grande reached by a pontoon bridge.
Bean himself, of course, operated the concession stand, but as Maher went
down almost immediately, the venture was less profitable than a real contest
would have been. After the Fitzsimmons fight Bean failed in his reelection
bid (as he had only once before, in 1886) but he continued blithely to carry
on, with the explanation that "once a justice, always a justice." He resumed
the job officially two years later and held it until he retired in 1902. The fabulous Lillie Langtry finally arranged to visit the Rio Grande, but Bean died in
March of 1903, ten months before she alighted from the train. Greeted by a
swarm of hooting and pistol-shooting cowboys, the legendary beauty was

swept away to a ceremony at which she was presented with Bean's gun as a keepsake. The celebration dissolved into pandemonium, however, when the late Judge Bean's pet bear broke loose and charged.

The failure of Texas society to universally condemn outlaws such as Hardin and Longley calls attention to a uniquely Western ethic, a recognition that law did not always render justice, and that one could keep a measure of honor by answering to a personal code. This was soon to be given literary exposition in the first Western novel, Owen Wister's *The Virginian*, but it had long been a reality in Texas. In fact, there were times when citizens recognized the shortcomings of the legal system, and voted into office gunslingers who could count on their violent reputations to forge order out of fear. This was a plan tried elsewhere on the frontier, with such lawmen as Wyatt Earp.

In Texas the most notable exponent was Ben Thompson, elected city marshal in Austin in 1881. English by birth but brought as a child to Austin by his parents, he trained as a printer but turned to gambling instead. He was an affable and polished dandy and acquired devoted friends, but when he drank he became violent, and he drank a lot. He went to prison at twenty-five for killing his brother-in-law, who was at least the fifth man Thompson had slain. He served only two years, on evidence that the brother-in-law was abusing Thompson's sister, after which he located in Abilene, Kansas, opened a bar, earned money as a railroad enforcer, and became friends with Bat Masterson.

Back in Austin in 1876, Thompson opened a gaming parlor over the Iron Front Saloon at Congress and Pecan streets, and it became a highly popular venue. On Christmas Eve of that year, however, Thompson engaged in a shootout with the owner of a rival establishment and was later indicted for murder. Thompson was acquitted on the grounds of self-defense, after which he found himself something of a celebrity, and while his many friends knew to avoid him when he had been drinking—he once swaggered down Congress Avenue shooting out streetlights, for example—they also noted that he always apologized for his sprees in a courtly manner, and paid for the damage. In 1879 Thompson attempted to parlay his standing into public office and ran for city marshal, but was defeated. Given time to reflect on the advantages of hiring the meanest gun in town to protect them, the public elected him two years later.

He had to resign in less than a year when he was indicted for murdering Pegleg Harris, owner of San Antonio's Vaudeville Theater. Thompson's acquittal, again for self-defense, restored his popularity, but in March 1884 he returned to San Antonio in company with another famous gunfighter, King Fisher. The word was that Fisher had offered to mediate the dispute between Thompson and Harris' friends and partners. Once in the theater, they were conducted to an upstairs table; an argument eventually broke out, then shooting. Thompson and King managed to kill one and wound one before being dispatched by at least twenty-two shots, most of them fired from a curtained theater box overlooking their table. The inquest's finding that they had been killed in self-defense did not go down well in Austin. His brief tenure as city marshal touched off an energetic debate on the wisdom of hiring violent gunslingers as law enforcement officers, but it was undeniable that during Ben Thompson's ten months in office, Austin recorded no burglary, no assault, and no murder.

FIFTY-FIVE

POLITICAL EVOLUTION

THE CONSTITUTION OF 1876, IN REACTION TO THE EXCESSES OF E. J. Davis, gutted the powers of the governor's office, but Texans still managed to fill it with men who were culturally authentic, if not great statesmen.

Bald, burly, bearded, 250-pound Richard Coke was reelected in 1876, but resigned soon after when the legislature elevated him to the Senate. He served three terms in Washington, slowly adjusting to genteel society. When he finally found dress gloves that fit his enormous hands, he regarded them and said they looked like canvassed hams. And once, at a White House reception, an elegant matron engaged his attention as though she wished to speak to him. She was "bowing to me, and I bowed, and she bowed, and I bowed again." They bobbed at each other like birds greeting until Coke realized he was standing on the train of her dress, although, he protested, "I weren't within fifteen feet of her."

When Coke left for Washington he was succeeded by his lieutenant governor, the even burlier Richard Hubbard, who stood five feet nine inches and sometimes tipped the scales at 400 pounds. An attorney from Tyler, he had a voice as stentorian as Coke's, with oratorical flourishes that led to his being called the Demosthenes of Texas. The legislature did not meet during his term, and Hubbard was criticized, probably unfairly, for not doing more to quell outlaw depredations and for his (unproven) abuse of finances and patronage. He failed of renomination, the necessary two-thirds majority being blocked by William W. Lang, the progressive candidate supported by the Greenbackers, and former Unionist James Throckmorton, who commanded a tightly loyal bloc at the convention. More interesting than his gubernatorial term, Hubbard was later appointed U.S. minister to Japan as a reward for his oratorical fireworks in support of Grover Cleveland. If the half-frontiersman Coke had found himself socially at sea in Washington, Hubbard, a Georgia native and graduate of Harvard Law School, adjusted well to life abroad and wrote a perceptive book, *The United States in the Far East*, about the experience. He particularly voiced his approval, presumably outside of Mrs. Hubbard's hearing, that in Tokyo a man was required to house his mistress in a different quarter of the city from his family, "a first-class, sensible kind of arrangement," he affirmed to a friend, "sure as you are born."

After a week's deadlock at the State Democratic Convention in 1878, all parties united in acclamation behind a surprising dark horse, sixty-four-year-old Oran Milo Roberts, onetime bane of Sam Houston and the man who called the Secession Convention in 1861. He had thought he was done with politics, retired to his farm and Gilmer law office with his ubiquitous, well-worn Prince Albert coat and corncob pipe, and he had to borrow fifty cents to telegraph his acceptance of the nomination. Once recalled to the public arena, though, he had to campaign hard to run by the Greenbackers, who had spurned the Democratic Party and for the first time ran their own slate of candidates. Their man was William Harrison Hamman, a popular Civil War general of Texas state troops. Hamman had industrialist tendencies—he chartered companies or took interests in railroading and bridge-building, and, believing that commercial markets could be found for natural petroleum, he was Texas' first wildcatter. (In fact, he owned oil leases at two unlikely-looking places called Spindletop and Sour Lake, but sadly for him never sank a well at either location.)

He became converted to the idea of monetary reform and attracted much public sympathy for the new party. Roberts of course was a Texas legend and Hamman never seriously imperiled his chances, but from the Greenback Party's initial slate of candidates they elected ten members of the legislature. Hamman himself polled nearly 60,000 votes and put the Democrats on notice that they had some fences to mend with their grassroots constituency.

Oran Roberts' election as governor marked the end of the Reconstruction era. At his inauguration he proclaimed his clear conscience for his past actions and declared Texas fully reconstructed—although when President James A. Garfield was mortally wounded, Roberts was the only governor in the United States not to proclaim a day of prayer for his recovery. "Church and state," he intoned, "are and ought to be, kept separate." Roberts described his fiscal policy as "pay as you go." He called attention to the fact that the debts from the Davis era had never been retired, and that receipts since then had never matched disbursements. Faced with the unpopular prospect of raising revenue, Roberts opened the Texas government's long love affair with "sin taxes," levying a two-cent surcharge per drink served in each saloon, and one-half cent per beer drawn. Every establishment had to acquire a hand-cranked counter that rang a bell to register that the tax had been paid. The Bell Punch Tax became a state joke; Texans continued their own long love affair with scoffing at taxes, and ignored it. But thanks to those who did fork over the extra pennies, and with Roberts' parsimony elsewhere, he retired a half million dollars of state debt and built up a cash balance of about $300,000.

With some fiscal restraint in place, Roberts then began restoring a commitment to education shirked in previous years. One state teachers college was founded in Huntsville, and another for the higher education of freedmen in Prairie View, near Houston. Construction also began in 1882 on a flagship state university in Austin, on forty acres set aside by the Republic for the purpose. After two terms in the Governor's Mansion Roberts joined the law faculty at his new university. The man who came to public prominence as a fire-eater for slavery and secession ended his career as a professorial wisp, gentle, white-bearded, introspective, soft-spoken, and so fixated upon precise speech that he once interrupted himself in a reminiscence about his days as a Confederate officer. Having said, "I threw my regiment across the creek," he paused and interjected, "Now you understand I didn't take each man up myself and pitch him across the creek. . . ." According to one listener, he was not trying to be humorous. He died in 1898, the university's beloved "Old Alcalde."

In January 1883 Roberts was succeeded by John Ireland of Seguin, yet another former Confederate colonel, yet another veteran of General Sheridan's hit list of "impediments to reconstruction." The election was a high-water mark for progressives, whose candidate polled more than 100,000 votes. Although most noted for his dour first lady Anne Maria, who snubbed the inaugural ball to register her disapproval of dancing, Ireland began restricting the state's open-handed land giveaways, and even vetoed a railroad bill whose $10,000 per mile cash award he thought too extravagant. Ireland's scrutiny of the railroads was so stern that the corporate interests began circulating the unflattering nickname of Ox-Cart John, after the only mode of transport Texas would have left, as they alleged, if he got his way. It was an appellation of which Ireland was not in the least ashamed.

Sul Ross, who had recaptured Cynthia Ann Parker from Comanches in 1860, was elected governor in 1886, and it was as though Texas saved up its mightiest warrior for last before turning to a younger generation; in addition to his Comanche battles, he rose from private to brigadier in the Civil War and fought in some 135 actions. Such was his reputation, despite a poor voice for public speaking, that in the poll for governor he garnered 73 percent of the vote, against the Republican's 6 percent, and 21 percent for the candidate of an emerging Prohibition Party. He reversed Ireland's policy, selling or granting another 3.5 million acres of public domain. A legislative minimalist, his largest legacy to the state, after he left office, was undertaking the presidency of Texas A&M University. Before Ross' arrival it was a languishing institution whose enrollment had plummeted to eighty students after it began hewing to its mandated core classes of agriculture and mechanics. Ross' Civil War renown prompted people to consider that a college devoted to producing farmers and engineers and soldiers was not such a bad idea.

With Hogg's election in 1890, progressives had hope that their programs would finally be written into law. Hogg made good on his promise to create a regulatory Railroad Commission, and persuaded the veteran John H. Reagan to return from Washington to chair it. As actually administered, however, the Railroad Commission acted less to protect small farmers from abusive railroads, and more to shelter Texas-based businesses from competition by foreign corporations (that is, "foreign" in its legal definition of businesses headquartered outside of Texas). To be sure, other measures were enacted that the progressives approved: cities and counties were limited in their ability to incur further bond debt; and to get more land into the hands of Texans, further land grants to foreign corporations were curtailed and the great land-holding companies formed to manage the huge railroad grants were given a time limit to start divesting. But in fact the so-called Hogg Laws were just enough to bleed steam out of the progressive boiler while nurturing homegrown business.

However tentative were the Hogg administration's baby steps toward reform, the corporate interests, especially the railroads, turned on him like wolves. To run against him the banks and railroads put up one of their own attorneys, an old-style Confederate veteran and former friend and ally of Richard Coke named George Clark, most recently prominent for his thwarting of Prohibition campaigns. To save his career, Hogg turned to his politically suave friend, Edward M. House, a scion of a Texas sugar fortune whose obsession with politics dated from his years in a Connecticut boarding school, when he grew fascinated with the 1876 presidential election crisis. When not managing the family empire, House had become a political junkie, cultivating powerful friends and mastering the arts of compromise. Hogg took care of himself on the stump, debating Clark before raucous crowds, demonstrating his mastery of the progressive persona. Before a heckling mob of 20,000 in Cleburne, Hogg noted Clark pausing in his speech for a sip of water. When he took the podium, Hogg seized the whole pitcher and quaffed a far manlier portion. Meanwhile, House worked quietly backstage on Hogg's behalf, reaching out to the black and Hispanic vote, and corralling into the center just enough support from both the progressive and pro-business extremes to give Hogg, narrowly, a second term.

This was fortunate, as movers probably would have found it impossible to evict Hogg's wild children from the Governor's Mansion, where they enjoyed a kaleidoscopic menagerie that included four dogs—one for each child—plus assorted cats, squirrels, raccoons, a shrieking flock of cockatoos, and two gawking ostriches that Hogg purchased from a disbanding carnival. The oldest boy, Will, was sixteen and knew some decorum, but Ima was eight, and Mike and Tom were six and four, respectively, and Hogg indulged them. When not stampeding through the house like baby elephants, their favorite activity was sliding down Abner Cook's high curving stair banister, at least until Tom once fell off halfway down, cracked his chin on a step, and fell like a rag doll into the entrance hall. Angry and frightened, Hogg studded the banister with tacks to prevent any repeat performances.

As Hogg's attorney general, Charles Culberson used his own considerable legal skills to defend the constitutionality of the Railroad Commission. When he ran to succeed Hogg as governor in 1894, Culberson, managed as Hogg had been by E. M. House, continued the balancing act. Once the nomination was secured, Culberson cut into progressive strength by endorsing unlimited silver coinage. The conservative wing of the party was furious but was by then bound to him. As governor, Culberson continued treading water, blocking overly abusive corporate practices and strengthening the Railroad Commission, but not taking any steps that would genuinely damage business in Texas. He was also deafeningly silent when Texas labor was condemning the violent breakup of the Pullman Strike in Illinois. By the time he sought reelection in 1896, progressives had begun to descry that the Hogg and Culberson reforms had been to some extent a bait-and-switch, and they mounted their own effective campaign for the governorship behind Palestine lawyer Jerome Kearby, who polled a respectable 238,000 votes to Culberson's 298,000.

Throughout these years the Republican Party continued to decline in numbers and influence. After his ouster from the Governor's Mansion, E. J. Davis continued to lead the state party until his death in 1883. Thereafter, increasing prominence fell to a mixed-race (slave mother, white father, and in Texas that meant he was counted as black) stevedore and labor organizer named Norris Wright Cuney, of Galveston. Starting as a protégé of George T. Ruby, Cuney rose through a succession of patronage appointments, rising so high as to become Texas' national committeeman to the Republican Party. This split the Texas party, however, for many Republicans, while they talked a good game for freedmen during Reconstruction, could not actually make themselves knuckle under to the leadership of one. Progressives who had placed their faith in the Grange and in the Greenback Party and finally in the People's Party had difficulty putting a finger on exactly who was responsible for ills and injustice; it seemed to be all the big corporations: the railroads, the mills, the banks, the merchants. But while progressives remained committed to their cause, much of society had moved on, and the political limelight was stolen by the movement to enact Prohibition. The tolerance of personal vices common to the Old West was brushed aside in a march toward straitlaced morality.

FIFTY-SIX

GOD GOES PRIMITIVE

IT IS IMPOSSIBLE TO UNDERSTAND THE MESMERIZING fervor for Prohibition that gripped so many Texans without first considering how religious worship evolved its unique local identity. Anglo Texas had begun as a land of scoffers; the required conversion to Catholicism was observed only to obtain land, and most people simply couldn't be bothered with worship. Almost every town begun in Texas had at least one saloon before thought was given to a church. As religion finally began to take root, the single greatest influence as far as the common people were concerned was the phenomenon known as the Second Great Awakening. This mighty flood-crest of evangelical fervor that rolled down the Ohio and Mississippi rivers began around 1800 and reached Texas just about the time that independence ended the Catholic monopoly.

Unsophisticated in theology, with little frame of reference to ancient history or biblical context, some of its practitioners seemed to equate education with worldliness, and ignorance with true motivation by the Holy Spirit. When the Cumberland Presbyterian missionary Sumner Bacon, one of the first Texas evangelists, sought a license from the Arkansas Presbytery, they refused him with the suggestion that he should learn to read first. (The Cumberland Church itself was an offshoot of the Presbyterians, which separated in a quarrel over the need for education among clergy.) Equally important, many followers of the Great Awakening placed a huge premium on physical manifestations of possession by the Holy Spirit—shouting, jerking, rolling. Some camp meetings degenerated into mass hysteria, as the depth of one's faith was expected, at least implicitly, to show itself by outdoing one's neighbors. One preacher became so enraptured by "the jerks" during his sermon that he cast himself from his pulpit and rolled completely down the hill on which the meeting was held. "No pen or tongue," wrote one observer, "could give adequate description of these . . . mad extravagancies & I fancy most will distrust the evidence of their senses. They call it a revival."

In the latter third of the nineteenth century, the Baptists became the largest denomination in Texas, a feat accomplished despite their continuing intramural fratricide. The State Convention had been operating the denomination's flagship educational institution, Baylor University, in Independence since 1846. Rufus Burleson headed the school for ten contentious years, from 1851 to 1861, when he and the entire faculty of the "male department" resigned in a feud with the trustees. He was succeeded briefly by George Washington Baines, great-grandfather of Lyndon Baines Johnson; the president who followed Baines, William Carey Crane, got the "female department" weeded out of the school and set up separately as Baylor Female College, which later became the University of Mary Hardin–Baylor.

Another topic of argument in the Baptist Church was the extension of membership to African-Americans. In antebellum Texas, slaves were commonly allowed to sit in on services, and with determination might become recognized as a brother or sister. The Southern Baptist Convention had split from the Northern church largely over the rectitude of slavery, and after the war most Texas churches, which still adhered to that affiliation, refused to brook full acceptance of black members. Others felt it to be their duty, however—not from a desire to extend communion to freedmen, but because without the "superior intelligence" of the white churches, as one conference concluded, the black believers would fall into error. It was the African-American Baptists themselves who answered the question, though. Reconstruction had given them a taste of freedom and dignity. No longer willing to be patronized in such a way, they simply withdrew from the white congregations and started their own in such numbers that it ceased to be an issue. In general they remained staunchly loyal to the denomination, forming their own convention as early as 1866, and through the rest of the century, about seven of every ten blacks who registered a religious preference listed themselves as Baptists.

In 1886, the year after Crane's death and the year that females were allowed back into Baylor, the State Convention united with the Baptist General Convention of Texas to form the Baptist General Convention. Under their direction the Baylor campus was moved from Independence to Waco in 1887, where it has been ensconced ever since. This show of harmony, however, was soon disrupted elsewhere. A new denominational journal, the *Baptist News*, began publication in Fannin County late in 1888, and in less than a year moved to Dallas to siphon readership and influence away from the existing Baptist newspaper, the *Texas Baptist and Herald*. The latter journal was embroiled in a feud with the pastor of the First Baptist Church of Dallas, with whom the *Baptist News* allied itself. When the pastor, R. T. Hanks, was cleared of a charge of immorality brought by the editor of the *Texas Baptist and Herald* (although he was convicted of "indiscretions"), he bought part interest in the *Baptist News*. After further name changes it emerged as the *Baptist Standard*, and in 1914 was transferred to the General Convention, which made the newspaper its permanent official weekly journal.

The Great Awakening, while expressing itself in almost all denominations in Texas at some time, never quite carried all before it. Naysayers could be found not just among the heathens, but also among educated believers who found its excesses either troubling or ridiculous. "We have little faith in them," the *Fort Worth Democrat* criticized such camp meetings. Shouting and getting the jerks "are not potent agents for conversion of the heart." Nor did everyone endorse the ascendancy of evangelical Baptists as the faith of choice. Some were vocal in their opposition, even downright mean. William Cowper Brann, a newspaper editor who had worked in Galveston, Houston, San Antonio, and Austin, took up residence in Waco as chief editorial writer for the *Waco Daily News*. He was also the publisher of a protest journal called *Iconoclast*, which at its height circulated 100,000 copies. In it Brann railed against various groups—he had little use for blacks, women, Episcopalians, or the British—but his favorite targets were Baptists in general, whom he considered to be pompous blowhards, and Baylor University in particular, which he called the "great storm-center of misinformation." Cowper Brann was no coward, bearding the Baptist lion in its own den for two and a half years, but he was living dangerously. On October 2, 1897, Brann was shanghaied to the Baylor campus by a group of students and warned to retract his writings or leave town. Four days later he was beaten on the street by three men, one of them a Baptist judge. Still he stayed, and prominent citizens began choosing sides. The following month, the editor of the *Daily News'* competitor, the *Waco Daily Herald,* and his brother, who were Baylor supporters, shot it out with a Brann partisan, who happened to be the county judge. The judge's arm had to be amputated, but he killed the other two. Brann continued his anti-Baptist rebukes until April 1, 1898, when he was shot in the back on a Waco street. He died, but not before he managed to turn and kill his killer.

Not all assaults on the Baptists came from the left. After 1888 they began to be challenged by a denomination even more conservative, known as the Church of Christ, a sect of dissenters from the more progressive Disciples of Christ. They were as often referred to at the time as Campbellites, after their founder Alexander Campbell. Like the Baptists they believed that only a full-immersion baptism could achieve salvation, but they were even more legalistic, eschewing instrumental music as being unbiblical and engaging in horrific, congregation-splitting debates on such issues as whether communion should be served in one large cup or numerous tiny ones. (There was no argument on what should be served at communion. In the lead of the temperance movement, biblical references to wine were interpreted as unfermented grape juice.) The Churches of Christ were each autonomous of the others and developed no denominational hierarchy, but the fervor of their preaching and their adroitness at prooftexting verses to defend doctrinal positions won large numbers of converts, especially in rural areas. Alternately prayed for and disdained by other churches for their stance that they were the elect and the only ones going to heaven, there were in 1906 more than 30,000 Campbellite adherents in Texas, worshipping in more than 600 testy congregations.

The Church of Christ, in its turn, was too liberal for some. In a complicated fusion of like-minded congregations, the Church of the Nazarene was founded by compacts agreed to in Rising Star in 1904 and Pilot Point in 1908. Vividly Pentecostal and antipredestinarian, the Nazarenes emphasized sanctification by the Holy Spirit as a separate necessity, apart from baptism, to achieve salvation. Other literalist groups emerged—one splinter of Baptists, noting that God rested on the seventh day after Creation, worshipped on Saturdays. Known at first as the Seventh-Day Baptists, they took their own name from their watchfulness for the Second Coming, as Seventh-Day Adventists. A colony of them started the town of Keene, in Johnson County southwest of Fort Worth, in 1893, but despite their self-evident ability to count to seven, the idea of not worshipping on Sunday was too radical for mainstream acceptance, and the Adventist doctrine, aided by their rather Campbellite penchant for quarreling and splitting, never gained wide acceptance.

If the Nazarene movement had a taproot it was Methodist, which was consonant with that heritage, for in the early days of Protestant evangelizing in Texas, the Methodist Church was in the forefront of demonstrative worship, and they were known as even greater "shouters" than the Baptists. By the close of the nineteenth century, however, Methodists had mellowed into one of the tamer denominations. Apart from the Nazarenes, this did not sit well with other revivalist-oriented members; calling themselves Free Methodists, they broke off and established the Metropolitan Church Association, more often known as the Society of the Burning Bush. Headquartered in Wisconsin, they established what could only be called religious communes in three other states before a favorable land trade made available a 1,520-acre former plantation at Bullard, south of Tyler on the Cherokee County border. Early in 1913 a special train brought 375 Burning Bush

Methodists down from the north. Bankrolled by two wealthy patrons, they planted fruit and pecan orchards, and expanded their living space from the former plantation manse into male and female dormitories for unmarried believers and small houses for families. Most important, they built a capacious church, sixty feet by eighty, in which they worshipped with abandon. The tabernacle had a sawdust floor for comfortable thrashing about, and they turned back flips, which led to their nickname of the Holy Jumpers. Following the biblical tenet of hospitality, visitors were received with kindness, but members of the sect were discouraged from mingling with outsiders.

Taking their cue from the early communities of St. Paul, possessions were held in common and dispensed according to need, meals were taken in a large refectory, and wages earned outside the farm were turned over to a common fund. Those who broke the rules were not punished or exiled; they were hauled into the church and wailed over. The failure of the Burning Bush Colony was their financial overreach. They purchased advanced farm machinery that was the envy of their neighbors and built a cannery, in addition to a water and sewer system, a power plant, a school, and a hostel for visitors. With little understanding of Southern agriculture, however, the Burning Bushers were not successful farmers. Receipts never equaled the ambitious expenditures, and a financial downturn dried up contributions from the two patrons on whom they had come to depend. A local grocer allowed them to run up a tab of $12,000 before suing, and the Metropolitan Church Association property was auctioned off on the courthouse steps in Tyler in April 1919. Some of the members settled locally, but most returned whence they came.

As the western stretches of the state began to settle and organize, Texas began to approach its final tally of 254 counties, and ironically it was in one of the last areas to be populated that religious expression was the least charismatic. Circuit-riding preachers regarded the vast stretches of empty country in West Texas with dutiful foreboding. The Methodist W. B. McKeown was sent in 1900 to a Panhandle parish covering six counties in which there was no existing Methodist roof over church or parsonage. He was consoled by a friend, "The bishop has given you a bunghole for a circuit and he expects you to build a barrel around it." That isolation reached its extreme in the deserts of the Trans-Pecos, where in 1888 there arrived in Fort Davis a Presbyterian missionary of forty-one named William B. Bloys.

Short, skinny, and sallow-chested, but aided by a dynamic wife, Isabelle, with whom he had seven children, he was the scion of a family of Tennessee Unionists and educated at Lane Theological Seminary. Bloys was to his grief disqualified from foreign mission service by lung disease, and was posted to Texas instead. After forming numerous churches around Coleman, he was sent to Fort Davis for the dry climate, and there he volunteered his services to the army post as chaplain. After starting a church, he was moved by requests from the isolated ranches and cow camps to conduct services for them all, regardless of their own denominations. In October 1890 he began the Cowboy Camp Meeting, a two-day sort of religious rendezvous held under a brush arbor at Skillman's Grove, sixteen miles southwest of Fort Davis. Forty-three people attended the first one; eventually he was joined in sponsorship by the Baptists, Methodists, and Disciples of Christ, and the event was expanded into a five-day annual event in midsummer. Unusually nondenominational, lonely ranch families seized upon it and began several traditions: all food is free and cooked over open fires, no buying or selling is permitted, even for fundraising—contributions must be not just voluntary but self-motivated, for no collection was ever taken—and all decisions by the governing board had to be unanimous. The arbor was replaced by a tent and finally by a permanent tabernacle, but even after electricity was provided, the meetings were timed for the full moon. As much a social as religious gathering, the Cowboy Camp Meeting became cemented into local tradition, and attendance first topped one thousand in 1912. The frail Bloys sought to retire, but learned how indispensable he had become. The unanimous decision of the board was, "Sit down, Bloys, there'll be time enough to elect your successor when you're gone!" The beloved Little Shepherd of the Hills died in 1917, and the annual event was renamed the Bloys Camp Meeting.

Considering the ease with which disciples could be won to seemingly any new sect, it isn't surprising that one arose of practical value almost equal, in its own way, to what Bloys had accomplished. Martha White McWhirter was a Belton housewife, the mother of twelve children, six of whom died, and who believed that her merchant husband was unfaithful. An interdenominational-minded Methodist and anchor of a women's prayer group, she questioned the value of the way she was living her life, and was rewarded with a vision in which she was convinced that she received the Holy Spirit. Others in her prayer group—equally unhappy in their domestic circumstances—received similar enlightenment, and followed McWhirter's lead in conjugally withdrawing from their husbands, refusing to have sex, but continuing to manage their households. Eventually the "Sanctified Sisters" organized as the Belton Woman's Commonwealth; some members left their families entirely, and moved into a home that McWhirter built for them on her husband's lot, an unprecedented act of independence that placed Belton in something of a gossipy uproar. Apart from that property, McWhirter did not ask her husband for contributions; at first she maintained the group with her butter and egg money, but with time and her deft management the sisters became not just a self-supporting commune, but were so intertwined in the commerce of the city that McWhirter was elected to the Board of Trade. The women cashed in their Belton assets at the turn of the century and moved into a three-story Italianate villa in Washington, D.C., where a full-page feature story in the newspaper marveled at the success of "A Happy Home Without Husbands." Martha McWhirter died there in 1904, just short of her seventy-seventh birthday.

Most Texas women were willing to settle for simple sobriety on the part of their husbands. In its earlier years Texas had been a land of two-fisted drinkers, and by the twentieth century there was widespread recognition that Texas had a serious problem with alcohol. The truth was that after years of frontier carousing, Texas was ripe for both religion and temperance. In the bingeing Panhandle town of Mobeetie, the saloons had to close after a revival netted some three hundred converts.

Signal in the movement toward Prohibition in Texas was the coming of the Woman's Christian Temperance Union, whose president, Frances Willard, made her first mission to Texas in 1881. She did not venture deep into the state, speaking at Denison and Sherman before journeying east to Paris, where she organized Texas' first WCTU chapter. She had been invited by Paris lawyer Ebenezer Dohoney, who was both one of the state's most prominent Prohibitionists, having authored the local option clause of the 1876 Constitution, and most prominent progressives, publisher of the *Greenback Advocate* and a founder of the People's Party. As a legislator and state senator he was a civilizing influence; supporting a ban on carrying guns in public places and making an unsuccessful run to approve female suffrage. Willard returned twice more, speaking and organizing in sixteen cities, but it was after the election of fifty-year-old Jenny Bland Beauchamp, wife of a Denton Baptist minister, as president, in 1883, that the Texas WCTU flourished. In five years, as Beauchamp traveled thousands of miles and spoke incessantly, the organization grew to some one hundred local cells with about 1,600 members.

The principal selling point of the campaign against alcohol was the abuse and suffering that drunkenness caused in families, and Beauchamp was compelled to pursue other avenues of reform as well. She was successful in prodding the legislature to start state orphanages and to mandate the separation of juveniles from hardened criminals in the penitentiary. The WCTU became a leading voice in the Prohibition chorus, and it received a jolt of new energy in 1900 with the return of Nannie Austin (distant kin to the empresarios) Curtis as state organizer. As Nannie Webb she had been elected secretary at the 1881 organizational gathering, but it was a false start for her, as she was compelled to resign and leave the state to care for a sick husband and "numerous and persistent babies." Widowed, returned, and remarried, she studied oratory for two years at the Texas Female College in Sherman and took to the Chautauqua circuit. She realized early that Prohibition would likely not happen without woman suffrage (a point of view shared by Jenny Beauchamp), and from a succession of stages Curtis linked the two with intelligence and ferocity, gaining celebrity as the "Queen of the Southern Platform." Her skill and effectiveness on the lecture circuit drew the notice of the WCTU's national leadership, and in 1909 Nannie Curtis became president of the Texas WCTU, in addition to assuming duties with the national organization.

Prohibition as a political goal had a long history in Texas, but not a very successful one. Local option—the authority of a city or even a neighborhood to ban the sale or consumption of alcohol—was passed by the Republic in 1843, and saloons were outlawed in 1845, but the statute was never enforced and it was repealed a decade later. Sam Houston, himself a reformed alcoholic, refused to support it, saying that if he could not drink in moderation that was his bad luck, but to enforce Prohibition on the whole people was "a species of legislation that will not be tolerated . . . in a free land."

Heartened by the support of fundamentalist churches, Prohibitionists formed their own political party in 1886, but were frustrated in their statewide efforts. Their candidates were not successful, and the statewide referendum that they managed to get on the ballot in 1887 was crushed at the polls by a majority of 90,000 votes. What they did excel at was intensive local organization. One county after another was chalked into the "dry" column. By 1895, when Texas had 239 counties, only 102 of them were "wet," with unrestricted access to alcohol. Seventy-nine had at least one dry community, and 53 counties were totally dry. Fifteen years later, with the exception of the Rio Grande Valley and Trans-Pecos with its Hispanic majority, and of those counties with heavy immigrant populations, no county in Texas above the latitude of Austin was completely wet. Prohibition as a state law, however, was still only a dream, even though the evangelical churches were near-unanimous now in hawking God as a teetotaler.

FIFTY-SEVEN

GAINING CULTURE

THE ESTABLISHMENTS OF TEXAS A&M AND THE UNIVER-sity of Texas, and the numerous reforms in financing education, reflected a greater commitment to learning which bore fruit by the end of the century, when literacy surpassed 85 percent of the population and there were more than a half million pupils in the public schools. This was progress hard won, for although the Congresses of the Republic and the early legislatures had passed various bills providing for public education, most acts amounted to rather little because they were not funded.

This acceptance of illiteracy was even more pronounced when it came to the arts. Not surprisingly, it was the German communities, who had sometimes financed their own education, that placed a greater premium on aesthetics than did Anglo plowmen and cowpunchers. While the Americans were struggling to write bad poetry and cowboy ballads, the Europeans were providing the Texans with their first symphony orchestras, the first choral societies, the finest painters—and there might have been even more, but for Texas' high cost in mortality of the immigrants. One of their finest artists, Conrad Caspar Rohrdorf of Switzerland, was shot dead in Round Top almost as soon as he arrived; Richard Petri drowned in the Pedernales in 1857 after only five years painting the Hill Country landscape and Indians. Petri's brother-in-law, Hermann Lungkwitz, garnered the greatest reputation partly because he lived until 1891.

For Texans of American descent, interest in art might have miscarried entirely in June 1882, as the result of an impromptu lecture tour by a foppish young Irishman named Oscar Wilde. His glory days and homosexual notoriety still lay in his future, but in Europe he was already the foremost spokesman of the so-called Aesthetic Movement. An early tour of the United States concluded in the states of the Old South, with stops in Galveston and San Antonio. He was already quite famous, or infamous, for his high-toned mannerisms as well as his velvet knee breeches, scarlet silk stockings, and bow-toed pumps. His welcome, in fact his safety, in Texas was uncertain. Old-time news editors were quick to register their consternation for the morals of Texas' youth by exposure to this "apostle of sublimated frippery," but also published the admonition that he be allowed to conduct his business in peace. "We expect he will have a splendid reception," one San Antonio paper wrote hopefully, "even though it may be mixed with a considerable amount of . . . abuse." The *Galveston Daily News* conceded the young fop's oddities, but declared that "one thing's certain, if the visit of Oscar Wilde to these shores shall tend in any measure . . . to smooth down [our own] artistic crudities and enormities in our architecture, in our furniture, or even apparel . . . he will have done us a good deed." As elsewhere in the American West, Wilde won over most of his thoughtful critics with his lethal combination of wit, sincerity, and articulate genius, but the mass of rubes merely left shaking their heads.

History, which for the better part of a generation had meant little more than honoring Confederate veterans, had a reawakening as the pangs of Civil War subsided and people remembered that there was a robust frontier and Republic heritage to preserve and cultivate. The state papers had long been administered by the Department of Insurance, Statistics, and History, suffering a woeful litany of neglect, pilfering, and damp storage. Almost as soon as he became governor in 1891, Jim Hogg put his considerable weight behind financing a Texas state library, whose staff included an archivist as well as a Spanish translator to make accessible thousands of pages of early documents in the Béxar and Nacogdoches archives. Interest soon reached critical mass sufficient to establish a Texas State Historical Association, whose organizational meeting in 1897 was lent credibility by the presence of such historic figures as Reagan, who was instrumental to the gathering; Stephen Austin's nephew Guy M. Bryan; and former governors Lubbock and Roberts. Legendary Ranger and shootist Rip Ford also attended, but left in a huff over the decision to extend full membership to women. Ladies, he protested, by definition could not be "fellows" of anything. Almost immediately the new Historical Association undertook publication of a quarterly journal of memoirs and articles; within a few years their *Quarterly of the Texas State Historical Association* metamorphosed into the *Southwestern Historical Quarterly* and became a leader of its genre.

This rediscovery of Texas history jump-started Texans' efforts in the letters and arts. Predictably, the first notable Texas books were memoirs and reminiscences of frontier days, such as Lubbock's *Six Decades in Texas* and *The Evolution of a State* by Noah Smithwick, the now superannuated smithy who repaired the Gonzales cannon that opened the revolution in 1835. Charles Siringo's cowboy memoir, *A Texas Cowboy*, gained great popularity.

Novels were by and large not thought of as serious literature, but one writer gained national attention. Mollie Evelyn Moore Davis grew up in Texas and wrote for the paper in Tyler before marrying and moving to New Orleans. Two of her novels in particular depicted the Texas experience: *Under the Man-Fig* (1895), about the great changes in Brazoria County from the antebellum through the progressive era, and *The Wire Cutters* (1899), about the fence-cutting war.

When Americans in Texas finally got up the nerve to paint pictures, they also began predictably with historic scenes. Robert Onderdonk was born and trained in New York and didn't arrive in Texas until 1879, and that was only with the intention to make enough money painting portraits of celebrated Texans to allow him to study in Europe. He stayed, however, and became an important force in the cementing of an arts community. One commission of his, a 1901 panorama entitled *The Fall of the Alamo*, came to hang in the Governor's Mansion and forever linked his name to Texas arts, almost as much as that of his son, Julian, whose landscapes featuring meadows of bluebonnets became wildly popular and probably had much to do with its being named the state flower. Following in Robert Onderdonk's historical genre was Henry McArdle, whose monumental *Dawn at the Alamo* and *The Battle of San Jacinto* could only be properly housed in the vast new capitol, as were William Henry Huddle's equally huge *The Surrender of Santa Anna* and his portrait of David Crockett. Huddle became fascinated with historical panoramas while studying in Munich, and painted the surrender in sections before assembling the entire canvas. Oddly, the painting was so detailed and became so accepted that it virtually became a reference work on San Jacinto itself, leading several of its small errors to be repeated in written works.

In literature and in painting, the life of the Texas range and the cowboy completed its transition into American legend, but back on the actual plains there was a lot of uncertainty. No longer able to avenge the murders of their people south of the Red River, but still able to recover their stolen cattle in the Panhandle, the South Plains Indians were running out of reasons to take to their ponies. Their old ways had passed; even their religious ceremonies were now frowned on by the missionaries who ran the agencies. About the only occasion they had at the end of the century for appearing picturesque was to perform in Buffalo Bill Cody's Wild West Show, or when they trekked to Charles Goodnight's ranch near Amarillo to bum a buffalo from his carefully husbanded herd. The buffalo was nearly as extinct as the former life-style of the Indians.

But as the frontier closed, the cowboys and drifters and army scouts did find a venue to mount up and relive their glory days of riding and whooping and shooting one more time: the Spanish-American War. Many faces in the army had changed, but much remained the same. Sherman and Sheridan were gone, and higher command was in the hands of former Civil War boy wonders now grown old. Nelson Miles never achieved his principal ambition, the presidency of the United States, but the rank of General of the Army was not a bad way to end his career. In the years since his Red River battle in that blistering summer of 1874, he garnered the reputation of being a shrewd, opportunistic grabber, who had the knack for riding into a theater of operations with his bevy of news reporters and accepting the laurels of Indian surrenders out from under the more capable officers who had actually done the fighting. He did it in the Nez Perce campaign against Chief Joseph; he did it again in 1886 at the end of the Apache wars in Arizona. The frontier military racism that succeeded in getting rid of Lieutenant Henry Flipper also found its warmest advocate in Miles. A proponent of the matchless ability of rugged white men against any ethnic adversary, his final victory over the Apaches was effected with the aid of friendly native scouts, whom he then shackled and exiled along with the hostiles.

Americans' attention had increasingly been drawn toward Cuba, partly in horror at Spain's treatment of the colonial Cubans, and partly in jealousy that the United States was being left out of Europe's race to amass colonial empires. When the American battleship USS *Maine* was sunk (probably an accidental munitions combustion) in Havana harbor, President William McKinley was forced not for the first time into a course he would have preferred to avoid, and declared war on Spain. A recruiting station was rigged on the San Antonio fairgrounds before the gaudy, neo-Moorish pavilion. It was presided over by a Miles favorite, Leonard Wood, a national hero, Medal of Honor winner, body builder, and exponent of the white ideal. Twelve hundred cowboys and yahoos were recruited into the 1st United States Volunteer Cavalry, whose direct command fell to another self-made, self-imaged he-man named Theodore Roosevelt.

It was a choice spectacularly strange. From a prominent New York family, he had been a sickly and pampered boy, and had endured the deaths of his wife and mother and birth of a daughter, all on the same day. Overwhelmed, he went west to remake himself, riding, hunting, and cowboying in the Dakotas. The West bronzed him physically and psychologically; he was not just a product of the West, but also its student, and he corresponded with artists who sought the meaning of the West—with Frederic Remington and with Owen Wister, author of *The Virginian*.

Wood began signing up Texas volunteers in late April; Roosevelt arrived about three weeks later and was enchanted. "They were splendid shots, horsemen and trailers," he wrote. "They were accustomed to living in the open, to enduring great fatigue and hardship, and to encountering all kinds of danger." But what he also found was that his Texas volunteers were as independent and grumpy as Sam Houston had discovered in the 1836 revolution. They despised the butt-bumping McClellan army saddles they were issued, preferring the stouter Western saddle; and they found in Roosevelt a sympathetic ear for their preference for the Winchester over the standard issue Krag-Jörgenson carbines. At various times calling themselves the Rocky Mountain Rustlers or Teddy's Terrors, the nickname that has lasted, the Rough Riders, was settled on gradually. Their service began jauntily enough, decked out in slouch hats and blue bandannas, with one of the men recalling that they were as "distinct, grotesque, and peculiar types of men as perhaps were ever assembled . . . and one—possibly two—Democrats." On May 30 Miles ordered the regiment to Florida, where the lark began to fall apart. Transportation foul-ups resulted in most of the horses never being loaded onto ships, and the Texas cowboys found themselves fighting as infantry, on foot, including on their famous charge up San Juan Hill. Spending most of their time in jungle trenches, suffering significant casualties when they engaged the Spanish and increasingly falling victim to yellow fever and malaria, the Texas cowboys were withdrawn, with thanks, on August 7 after the fall of Santiago.

Their involvement in the Spanish-American War was better reminisced about than lived, and most of the Rough Riders were happy to be going home, but the Caribbean tropics soon had an even nastier surprise in store. At the close of the nineteenth century, citizens of Galveston had long since reconciled to the fact that their position as Texas' leading and most influential city was behind them. In the glory days of the Republic and state, San Antonio had been the center of Hispanic life in Texas, and Galveston the center of American life. For a time after statehood, Galveston was actually larger than San Antonio. But by the century's turn, her commerce had been eclipsed as the state's economy had grown and diversified. Regular and inexorable hurricanes struck, including storms in 1867 and 1875. Galveston could not get ahead because it was forever rebuilding—an exercise in optimism that really required the fortunate influx of new people unfamiliar with the history, the danger of living there, and the futility of investing a fortune there.

By century's end, though, it had been a generation since the last hurricane. Galveston luxuriated in her reputation as the "Queen City of the Gulf." Broadway was lined with magnificent houses of the latest and most fashionable architecture—sturdy brick and granite Romanesque fantasies, weird variants like a kind of Danish Tivoli house, and most of them solid frame Queen Anne, packed so tightly into the grid of numbered streets and alphabet avenues that their bargeboards nearly touched over the lot lines. Few stopped to consider that the houses were so new and fashionable because storms had destroyed most of the older ones. The Gilded Age in Galveston was about optimism. The population had grown to 37,000; the cotton industry had recovered, and wharves were piled high with burlapped bales; the port was a hive of arrivals and departures. The United States was now a major power, with far-flung colonies just like the European powers, colonies that now had to be guarded with a world-class navy, and in September 1900 the harbor played host to a special guest, the USS *Texas,* a powerful battleship of the growing "Great White Fleet."

The tourist industry was thriving; the clean beige beaches were lined with merchants and bath houses and fishing piers. September was a peak month for visitors; autumn had not yet arrived, and the days could still be blistering hot. September, however, is also the peak month for hurricanes, because three months of intense summer heat warms the Gulf water to exceedingly un-oceanlike temperatures, creating a colossal idling engine of energy, just needing the pass of a low-pressure system to begin spinning around it. Such a storm was first observed 125 miles northwest of Martinique on August 30; Texans first heard of it on September 4 as it passed over Cuba and appeared headed for Florida or the eastern Gulf. Unexpectedly the hurricane swung to the west and dealt a glancing, but damaging, blow to the Mississippi Delta, and the weather service expected landfall now in the Louisiana bayous. At 4 A.M. on Saturday, August 8, Isaac Cline, the director of Galveston's weather office, was roused from his bed by his brother, who confessed to a premonition of disaster. Cline, who had eighteen years on the job, berated his brother for his alarm, but as the wind increased he made his way to the beach, where he saw a storm tide overflowing low areas of the city up to four blocks away, despite a heavy northwest wind. "Such high water with opposing winds never observed previously," he telegraphed. The eye of the storm was still two hundred miles away.

Cline later probably overstated his energy in alerting the neighborhoods near the Gulf shore to seek shelter to mask his own error in judgment. Saturday was a workday, and Galvestonians on their way to jobs paused by the beach to see giant waves shattering bath houses and fishing piers. No one took particular alarm. From midmorning, however, the storm's fury increased exponentially. When the last train arrived from Houston at eleven, the tracks on the trestle were only two feet above the water, which was rising at one foot per hour. Between eleven and noon the wind increased from 30 to 75 miles per hour. No one knew exactly how hard the wind eventually blew, for the anemometer flew away after it registered 96 miles per hour. The barometer, however, recorded a low of 28.44 inches, the hallmark of a tightly wound, powerful hurricane.

It only made sense that hundreds gathered in St. Mary's Cathedral, seeking protection either from the divine, or in the most solid-looking structure in the city. Safety under the vast roof span was illusory, and they perished, either crushed when it collapsed, or pinned in the wreckage to drown in the rising water. By midafternoon the entire island was under water; houses ripped free of their foundations, floating out to sea and carrying their terrified residents with them. The railroad trestle floated free, some sections of it two hundred feet long, flattening whole blocks of houses before it. As the wind approached perhaps 120 miles per hour, roofing slates whirled through the air, hacking down and sometimes decapitating those still seeking shelter. The storm tide rose to fifteen feet, and only the most substantial homes, such as the castle-like "Bishop's Palace," built by a local tycoon and congressman and later given to the church, rode out the hurricane, with survivors huddled on the upper floors. As the eye passed, a sudden wind shift released the pent-up storm tide, sending a five-foot wall of water surging through the devastation. The eye came ashore, west of the city, that night and the weather reduced to windy squalls; dawn lightened almost calmly upon the deadliest natural disaster in American history, a record that still stands. As far as the eye could range there was a flat tangle of lumber, furniture, clothing, toys, mud-encrusted photographs, bodies, and parts of bodies. Every several blocks a house lay askew, not quite completely torn from its foundation. Between 6,000 and 8,000 people were dead, and a recovery effort of stupefying proportions lay ahead. It was symbolic of the decline of old Texas and it, too, would be memorialized in myth and history.

BOOK FIVE

OIL EMPIRE

FIFTY-EIGHT

EARLY GUSHERS

JUST AS THE NINETEENTH CENTURY IN TEXAS ENDED with scenes of unparalleled destruction, the twentieth century opened with an even bigger surprise, and what nature took away with staggering violence in the Great Storm of 1900, nature remitted a few months later with a bounty that was even more staggering.

The presence of petroleum in Texas had been known ever since Spanish conquistadores pulled into coastal bays and caulked their vessels with natural tar seeps. Commercial production, however, was hardly conceived of, and it frequently happened that water wells that struck oil first were capped in disgust. That was the case in Corsicana, where city fathers in 1894 contracted the drilling of wells to supplement the municipal water supply. They capped the wells when oil was discovered, but noticed that oil continued to flow out around the sealed head. Sensing a commercial possibility, they invited successful Pennsylvania drillers John Galey and James Guffey to develop an oil industry. Two wells failed before a third produced only 22 barrels per day, and Galey and Guffey pulled out. By then, however, local interest had caused more than four hundred wells to be drilled, which produced a total of 66,000 barrels of oil in 1897—an amount that collapsed the infant industry. Without any refining capacity or ability to transport the crude, it was virtually worthless. (The dumping of unusable crude on the ground, poisoning the land and fouling the groundwater, led the legislature to pass its first-ever antipollution bills.) Locals then recruited another Pennsylvania oilman, Joseph S. Cullinan, to advise a course of action. He saved the day by building a refinery and producing kerosene, gasoline, and lamp oil, for which there were paying markets; the price of crude oil recovered to over a dollar per barrel, and by 1900 the Corsicana field was producing over 800,000 barrels per year—a tiny fraction of the total American production, but plenty to whet the appetite for the new industry.

In deep southeast Texas, meanwhile, God could be said to have taken a hand in further oil exploration, in the person of Pattillo Higgins. He was born in the midst of the Civil War, a former brawler and bully who lost an arm in a shootout with a deputy sheriff before finding Jesus at a Baptist revival when he was twenty-two. He settled down to become a real estate broker, girls' Sunday school teacher, and brick manufacturer. He also became an amateur geologist, convinced, contrary to prevailing wisdom, that petroleum would be found beneath the features known as salt domes. Interested in finding a cheap, even-burning fuel for the making of bricks, he was blessed with a vision of an industrial utopia centered around his brick and glass works, which would come to pass atop Spindletop Hill, a fifteen-foot rise (which in Southeast Texas counts as a hill) near Beaumont. Higgins named the prospective paradise Gladys City after a favorite in his Sunday school class. No knowledgeable oilmen would invest in the project, so funded by a fellow Baptist he started the Gladys City Oil, Gas & Manufacturing Company, obtained a lease on Spindletop, and began drilling in 1893, a year before the big oil strike at Corsicana. Funds gave out after three attempts to penetrate the salt dome were defeated by subterranean quicksands.

The prickly Higgins broke with the company in a dispute over drilling contractors. Unable to raise funds to proceed on his own, and becoming a laughingstock, Higgins was reduced to advertising for a mining engineer willing to tackle the salt dome. He received one response, from a Dalmatian-born salt miner named Anthony Lucas, then employed in Louisiana. An authority on salt dome geology, he came to Beaumont and found himself agreeing with the persuasive Higgins that oil lay just beyond their reach. Lucas and Higgins formed their own company, and Lucas drilled to 575 feet before the money ran out again. Lucas, unlike Higgins, had the clout to interest Guffey and Galey into backing further efforts; egotistical, unpleasant heathens often convert into egotistical, unpleasant Christians, and in the deal that Guffey and Galey struck with Lucas, they wanted Higgins cut out. Lucas, who had tried to work with him for a year, quietly agreed. Higgins was bitter, but shrewdly kept his hand in with other leases.

Lucas went back to work, now armed with a revolutionary rotary drill bit and the services of Al and Curt Hamill, drillers from Corsicana who were uncanny in their ability to extemporize modifications in the drilling as underground conditions warranted. The treacherous underground quicksands were finally passed and left behind, and when the new rotary drill bit reached 1,139 feet it pierced the prehistoric pressure of the salt dome. It was 10:30 A.M., January 10, 1901, the tenth day of the new century. The ground shook, and roughnecks working the rig fled for their lives as six tons of four-inch pipe began shooting like javelins out of the well, shattering the crossties of the rig. There was an explosive eruption of mud and rocks and natural gas, and after a few moments of pregnant silence, a geyser of green-ish-black crude oil shot out of the hole, topping the derrick by more than a hundred feet and falling back to earth like rain. Texas tea had arrived.

Barely able to speak, Lucas laughed and hooted and pointed, finally telling reporters that nothing like this had ever happened in the history of the world. The gusher roared unabated day after day, and Lucas realized that, having found a fortune in oil, he was in danger of losing it all at the staggering rate of 100,000 barrels per day. He quickly had dams constructed near the railroad tracks to capture as much as he could, and nine days after the strike he managed to design, build, and force into the place the first "Christmas tree," a series of valves that finally shut off the flow. New and different hazards quickly materialized; sparks from a passing train ignited some of the captured oil, alerting all to the need for fire precautions; the polluting smoke drifted over Beaumont, and when it rained the tidy white houses were suddenly a greasy yellow-brown.

The shallow oil found at Spindletop didn't last long—1902 yielded a stunning 17,500,000 barrels but quickly played down after that. Further strikes, though, each seeming more splendid than the previous, kept the industry going. The year 1901 saw further gushers explode in Saratoga, Batson, and Sour Lake, followed by strikes near the Corsicana field. A whole new area joined the industry in the former Comanche-Kiowa haunts in the Pease River breaks, with discoveries at Henrietta in 1902 and Electra and Petrolia in 1904.

As technology improved, old fields were kept in production by reaching new oil at ever deeper levels. The state also began to reap a windfall from the gushers, first collecting $101,403 from a tax on oil production in 1905, and the amount grew quickly thereafter. Beaumont became Texas' first oil boomtown; its population quintupled to 50,000 as special trains unloaded a stream of investors, speculators, and independent drillers who became known as wildcatters. Two-hour waits to eat in a restaurant were common; those who cut in line were beaten up. Telephone operators collected bribes to place calls and land values soared beyond comprehension; leases were traded on tracts of land so small they became known as doormats, just large enough to contain a single well. One lease bought for $20,000 sold again a quarter of an hour later for $50,000. Whores and lawyers were everywhere. The ladies of pleasure were not the tenderest of pickings, either. As one patron opined, "There was some young girls mixed up in there, but most of them were old cats who had been kicked out of the higher class. . . . They was just as tough as a boot . . . has-beens, drunkards, dope fiends and what have you."

Pattillo Higgins, whose vision began the whole Spindletop venture, returned to sue Lucas and his former partners for royalties on the discovery, and won an out-of-court settlement. He formed new companies, drilled on new leases but usually pulled out before the big money came in, and made and lost fortunes. A dour Prohibitionist who lived with his mother until she died, he was scornful of public merriment, the theater, dancing, and swimming. He adopted orphaned girls and caused a scandal by marrying one (Annie, not Gladys, for whom the town was named) the year after his mother died; he was forty-five, she was eighteen. But his flinty existence agreed with him; he died in 1955, aged ninety-one. Also prominent on the new Beaumont scene was former governor Jim Hogg, whose years of honest public service had left his family short of cash. With his public trust acquitted, Hogg now purveyed his clout and influence openly, and companies who knew that he could, for instance, smooth pipeline rights-of-way with county commissioners, were happy to retain him. Hogg also acquired oil leases of his own, which he parlayed into a fortune. He continued to lobby for progressive principles, more vociferously than he could when he was under the management of E. M. House. He died in March 1906, just short of his fifty-fifth birthday, having indoctrinated his children in the virtues of philanthropy, and Texas benefitted for generations from bequests of Hogg money.

The Spindletop and subsequent oil discoveries remade the economy of both Texas and the nation in ways that were revolutionary. The Texas coal industry, which despite labor strikes had come to be worth some $5 million per year, went into a decline in the face of such abundant and cheap energy. Locomotives and eventually ships were converted from burning coal to oil. Texas' electric streetcars and interurban rail lines began going out of business, unable to compete with increasingly popular automobiles that ran on cheap gasoline. Whole industries had to be ramped up to handle petroleum—drilling equipment and supplies, storage tanks to hold the product, rail cars and tanker ships and pipelines to transport it, and refineries to crack the crude oil into its component products.

Within a year of Spindletop, more than five hundred oil companies had been chartered in Texas, and well over a billion dollars invested. As many companies went broke as struck it rich, either victimized by sharp dealing (some people started calling it "Swindletop") or by locking themselves into long-term contracts before market conditions had stabilized. But there was plenty of new money to obscure the bankruptcies of the improvident. Despite this flood of cash, the greatest significance of Spindletop and the other oil strikes was not the obscene wealth they generated for a lucky few Texans.

They were important because they finally broke the chokehold in which the Standard Oil monopoly had held the national economy. Companies that were formed to exploit the Texas oil market included the Texas Company (later Texaco), the Humble Oil Company (later Exxon), the Magnolia Petroleum Company (later Mobil), as well as Gulf, Sun, and other energy conglomerates that reshaped the American corporate landscape.

FIFTY-NINE

A NEW CENTURY

AS THE TURN OF THE TWENTIETH CENTURY AP-
proached, all the governors of the Redeemer Era, those who had pulled
Texas out of Reconstruction, lined up at the pearly gates to claim their rewards: Ox-Cart John Ireland died in 1896, Richard Coke in 1897, Oran
Roberts and Sul Ross in 1898, and Richard Hubbard ended the parade in
1901. During their flirtation with progressive principles Texans had turned
to the younger generation with Hogg and Culberson, but with that dalliance
ended, they reached back into the thinning ranks of Confederate officers
again in 1898 and elected seven-term Congressman Joseph Draper Sayers of
Bastrop as governor. Or rather, he was selected by the kingmaker of growing
influence who had managed Hogg and Culberson, Colonel E. M. House.
Both Hogg and Culberson had been attorneys general before succeeding to
the Governor's Mansion, but House decided to break the pattern with Sayers, who was a longtime political insider, a former state representative, and
lieutenant governor before going to Congress.

Recovery from the Galveston storm occupied much of Sayers' attention,
but it was only one of the disasters to afflict his administration. Soon after
he took office the Brazos River flooded from heavy rains, inundating 12,000
square miles, killing some 284 people, and leaving thousands homeless.
Sayers coordinated the relief effort, siphoning his attention away from rebuilding the state penitentiary, which had been devastated by a fire. After
the Galveston hurricane Sayers lent his prestige to the effort to raise Eastern
capital to rebuild the city, but on the ground in the devastated city, recovery
was for a time an extemporaneous effort. Two of the town's spiritual leaders, Rabbi Henry Cohen and Monsignor James Kirwin, joined forces to get
streets cleared and the thousands of bodies buried or cremated. Cohen, who
had done so much to settle Jews throughout Texas, marshaled the resources
of that community for the benefit of the whole. "There is no such thing as
Episcopalian scarlet fever," he said. Citizens who were reluctant to be conscripted to dispose of bodies and forestall pestilence were persuaded by
Cohen's shotgun. Sayers appealed to the army for 50,000 rations and 10,000
tents, but only a small portion of that was available. Thus Sayers' receipt of

a telegram from the legendary Clara Barton was doubly welcome: "Do you need the Red Cross in Texas? We are ready." Barton was seventy-eight, and she had directed disaster relief from Russia and Armenia to Johnstown, Pennsylvania. She arrived in Galveston to perform her last public service, working herself literally until she dropped, before retiring to write her memoirs.

Galveston's port had always been its lifeblood, and with an expenditure of over a third of a million dollars, the wharves opened again to shipping only two weeks after the Great Storm passed. With the concept of government disaster aid still far in the future, the city's business leaders realized that for Galveston to default on its sizable bonded indebtedness would make it impossible to raise the capital needed to rebuild. Instead they acted quickly to refinance the city debt and preserve its credit rating, and undertook numerous fund-raising trips to New York, sometimes accompanied by Governor Sayers. With even greater publicity, they reorganized the city government in a radical way to streamline the rebuilding. Instead of electing a mayor and councilmen from various wards of competing constituencies, the "Galveston Plan," as it came to be called, provided for government by a city commission, partly elected and partly appointed by the governor, with each commissioner responsible for one aspect of city government, such as safety or public works. The Galveston Plan was seen across the country as an important progressive reform, embodying as it did the ideal of efficient government with minimal opportunity for corruption by bosses and ward heelers. Within twenty years some seventy-five Texas cities, including Houston and Dallas, adopted the Galveston form of government; endorsed by such reformers as Theodore Roosevelt and later Woodrow Wilson, over four hundred cities around the country embraced the "Texas Idea." The commission form of government was not perfect, however. Electing all at-large seats, for instance, diminished the effect of minority voting, and the lack of mayoral leadership sometimes led to stalemates among competing departments. Eventually the Galveston Plan was abandoned, but left a legacy in a new council–city manager form of government that proved more satisfactory.

In Galveston, construction began of a granite seawall along the Gulf shore, seven miles long and seventeen feet high, after which some 30 million cubic yards of sand were pumped from the sea floor to raise the grade of most of the city; surviving structures were elevated on new foundations. It was a herculean effort in which the new form of city government proved indispensable. The seawall was a success, and subsequent hurricanes in 1909 and 1915 claimed only a minimal loss of life in Galveston.

Recovery of their economic leadership faced a new challenger, however. Fifty miles up Buffalo Bayou the city of Houston, long languishing in the shade of Galveston's brilliance, began dredging a ship channel to capture the port trade for themselves, bringing the ships to the railroads in the safety of an inland harbor. It could have happened no other way, that the biggest survivor of the Galveston storm was the spirit of boosterism and competition that has always marked relations between Texas cities. No sooner had Houston snatched economic hegemony from Galveston than they both began to be challenged by the growing business power of Dallas. There the word was that if the business interests touting Houston could suck as hard as they could blow, they wouldn't need to hire contractors to dredge a ship channel. Interestingly, when an 18½-foot-deep ship channel finally opened in 1908, Houston residents found an unexpected bonus: their long association with what was delicately known as the bowel complaint ended. For generations they had used Buffalo Bayou both as sewer and source of drinking water. At the insistence of the Army Corps of Engineers, wells were finally drilled for fresh water, ending generations of cramps.

On the national scene, Texas politics opened the new century on an unexpected note: a final attempt to assuage the bitterness left by the Civil War and Reconstruction. Many Texans remembered those days while still seething just beneath the surface. Regimental reunions were avidly attended, the Confederate widows' home in Austin was generously supported, and the mere mention of the word "Yankee" was likely as not to be greeted with a spit of tobacco juice. In May 1901 President and First Lady William and Ida McKinley passed through on a national excursion. McKinley, who had been a Union staff major, was going to have dinner with Texas' governor, Joe Sayers, who had been a Confederate staff major, and having once been wounded, returned to the battle on crutches.

In Houston, McKinley shook hands with Mary Jones, the widow of the last president of the Republic of Texas, and continued his pilgrimage to San Antonio, where he addressed a throng from a review stand before the Alamo. Everywhere he spoke, the president was careful to praise Texans' valor, their spirit, and their great contribution to the country as a whole, peppered with humorous sentiments that he was grateful that the South lost the war, so the nation might not be deprived of the glory of Texas. Whether he succeeded was a close question to call; no yellow-dog Democrats were converted, but McKinley's gracious gestures were noted and approved.

In Austin, Texas first lady Orline Sayers redecorated the Governor's

Mansion in anticipation of McKinley's stop for dinner, the overstuffed furniture almost hidden, in the high fashion of the day, behind pots and baskets and buckets and ropes and garlands of flowers and greenery. The dining table was so smothered with it that the Sayerses' blocky, plain white gubernatorial china could barely fit. So much decoration to leave so little room for substance—it was a metaphor for McKinley's visit itself. And also, in a way, a metaphor for Sayers' two terms as governor. Business was good, populism had receded into a mild backlash of conservatism, and it was Sayers' fortune to preside over a kind of internal era of good feeling. He was succeeded after two terms by another frontier figure, Samuel W. T. Lanham, who had come to Texas in a covered wagon in 1866, and taught school with his wife in Weatherford in a log cabin school, concealing from the students the fact that he was only semiliterate, and that his wife primed him at night for the next day's lessons. After becoming a lawyer, it was Lanham who as a young district attorney had prosecuted and won capital convictions of the Kiowa raiders Satanta and Big Tree for the Warren Wagon Train Massacre of 1871.

Lanham, like Sayers, was managed by E. M. House, who took cognizance that the Democratic Party was increasingly riven by factions, and so settled on Lanham as a candidate who would not create any disturbances. During the campaign, one wag noted, Lanham "managed to say nothing in a convincing and masterly way." Lanham's tenure was in policy virtually indistiguishable from Sayers'; in fact, probably the most notable event in the change of administrations was that the Sayerses' dog refused to leave the mansion, and the Lanhams had to adopt him.

While the excesses of the Spindletop boom produced early legislation for conservation of that resource, no such fetter hobbled Texas' other kingpin industry, lumber. Fueled by Galveston rebuilding, logging in the East Texas piney woods grew unabated, topping out at 2.25 billion board feet in 1907, netting fortunes for lumbermen such as John Henry Kirby and Thomas L. L. Temple, and consigning workers to long hours of dangerous labor for low pay, as often as not living in a company town and buying their goods from a company store. Kirby had ingeniously financed his empire by buying cheap forest land, selling oil leases to drooling investors, and using the money to buy more cheap forest land, until he owned some eight *billion* board feet of timber. Rapacious overcutting, however, doomed the industry to an early decline, with the slump lasting until replanted areas could finally be harvested. Conditions on the farms were even more difficult. The Mexican boll weevil arrived in 1904 and began claiming some share of the cotton crop every year, and the exhaustion of public domain made it more difficult for those who failed to start over. By 1900 about half of all Texas farms were worked by tenants, a dramatic increase over the preceding two decades, but with attention focused on oil riches and business opportunities, fewer farmers won seats in the legislature to argue their cause.

One accomplishment of the Sayers-Lanham years was the overhauling of the piecemeal and vulnerable electoral system. To regularize voter registration and prevent the stuffing of ballot boxes, a poll tax was instituted in 1903, accompanied with a requirement that county conventions be held on the same day, and in 1905 primary elections were mandated for major political parties. The guiding force behind the electoral reform was a colorful state representative of seventy-five, Alexander Watkins Terrell. During his first run for office, a district judgeship in 1857, he incurred the ire of Sam Houston, but the two later became close friends. Terrell fought with distinction against the Red River invasion of 1874, served four terms in the state senate, and did a stint as U.S. minister to the Ottoman Empire before returning to the state legislature in 1903. Terrell denied a racist motivation for the poll tax and primary, declaring it his intention to make it more difficult for "the thriftless, idle and semi-vagrant element of *both races*" to vote. While the so-called Terrell Election Laws were usually assessed as progressive reforms, and while they did erode the power of behind-the-scenes operators like House, it was a dubious reform that caused voter participation to drop from nearly 80 percent to barely 25 percent, and solidified power in the hands of a single party.

Another probusiness act of this time was a constitutional amendment in 1904 to allow the chartering of state banks, which allowed much of that lovely inflowing oil capital to be put to work within Texas. There were also fair-minded progressive laws enacted; one banned the issuance of company scrip for spending in company stores, another exempted labor unions from antitrust regulations, still another limited working hours of railroad workers.

Although easily reelected in 1904 with a campaign expenditure claimed of only twenty dollars, Lanham did not enjoy his gubernatorial term. New colleges opened in Denton and San Marcos, but the bulk of his attention was diverted to the "office-seekers, pardon-seekers and concession-seekers" who, he said, overwhelmed him. Unlike Sayers, who continued a career of public service on various state boards for a quarter century after re-entering private life, Lanham died only a year and a half after leaving office.

The declining fortunes of farmers and workers after eight years of probusiness government led to an increase in pressure for reforms that had greater effect than those of the Hogg-Culberson years. A popular candidate for governor appeared in the person of Thomas Campbell, a childhood neighbor and best friend of Jim Hogg. He had never run for office before, although Hogg had appointed him to a couple, and he had a reputation as a more insistent populist than Hogg was able to be. He demanded, for instance, an end to child labor in machine shops. Campbell was indeed able to deliver greater substance. Insurance companies were required to invest 75 percent of the premiums collected in Texas in in-state securities or land, again a melding of progressive goals with a benefit to state business. (Some twenty-one foreign insurers left the state rather than comply, but Texas companies raked up the business, and the law survived for over fifty years.) An antinepotism law was passed, railroad regulation was increased, including the banning of wholesale railroad passes, insolvent corporations were barred from doing business in the state, and corporate political contributions were outlawed. Taxable corporate value was doubled by including intangible assets, and while he was unable to get an income tax through the legislature, he did win an inheritance tax and a franchise tax on liquor sales. Telegraph workers were granted eight-hour workdays, and a system of deposit insurance was put in place in state-chartered banks. Prison reforms were enacted, among them ending the system of leasing convicts to private businesses. A prototype of a pure food and drug law was also passed; its enforcement powers were puny, but it was a start down a new road of government responsibility. Campbell was also a believer in local autonomy, and under his administration Texas cities of more than 2,000 residents obtained power to regulate utilities. While Campbell was unable to get statewide referendum and recall provisions out of the legislature, he had the satisfaction of seeing them written into numerous city charters.

The greatest triumph of the Campbell administration came with sensational revelations of a corporate shenanigan on which the state collected handsomely. The Waters-Pierce Oil Company, which had once been barred from Texas for its ties to the Standard Oil monopoly, obtained a new state charter on the representation that it no longer had any ties to the corporate giant. Discoveries in a Missouri lawsuit in 1905 revealed that this was a lie. Standard Oil, anxious to get in on the Texas boom, had merely buried its ties a little deeper. The Texas attorney general, Robert Davidson, went after them and obtained a judgment, eventually upheld by the U.S. Supreme Court. To show their scorn of the Texas suit, Waters-Pierce representatives pushed their remittance up Congress Avenue in a wheelbarrow—$1,808,483.30 in small bills, but all they managed to do was publicize their own shame.

Campbell was reelected in 1908, but the legislature elected that year was markedly more conservative, and the governor's second term was one of frustration. State politics were increasingly dominated by the issue of Prohibition, which he attempted to straddle, staking out the position (which cost him popularity) that while he believed in it in principle, it was a matter of personal conscience, not legislative fiat. In 1910, a statewide Prohibition amendment appeared on the ballot. Where a similar amendment had been decisively defeated only a few years before, this one failed by only the narrowest of margins, 237,000 to 231,000. Partly this defeat rode the coattails of the new governor-elect, Oscar Branch Colquitt, a largely self-educated newspaper editor from Northeast Texas. He was a decided "wet," which caused his opponents to tease that his middle initial stood for Budweiser.

Where Hogg and Culberson had campaigned more progressively than they intended to govern, Colquitt reversed that polarity, running as more of a conservative than he intended to govern. He advocated further penal reform such as the outlawing of whippings; he drew crowds to his speeches by demonstrating the "bat," a vicious, five-foot cowhide whip used to punish inmates. Colquitt's wetness and his push for prison reform were seen as appeals to the German, Mexican, and (largely overlapping) Catholic vote, which caused old-time Southern Democrats considerable consternation. Yet while the legislature was paralyzed with the Prohibition fight, Colquitt euchred them into passing significant educational, eleemosynary, and labor reforms. Aside from Prohibition, two other issues cost Colquitt popularity. The first was his openly pro-German sympathies in the growing European conflict, and the second was the deteriorating situation along the Rio Grande, where the Mexican Revolution of 1910 caused sporadic mayhem in South Texas and cast a spotlight on a thorny situation of very long history and very new complications.

SIXTY

VALLEY OF THE SHADOW

EVER SINCE THE TEXAS REVOLUTION, ATTEMPTS HAD been made in the legislature and the courts to disenfranchise Tejanos of their citizenship. In 1896 one Ricardo Rodriguez, pointing out that Texans of Mexican descent could not vote unless naturalized, petitioned the federal district court in San Antonio for citizenship. He was opposed by Anglo San Antonio politicians, who cited an 1872 federal law that only Caucasians and Negroes qualified for citizenship, and Mexicans, many of whom were partially of native descent, were neither. They also raised an issue of educational preparedness for exercising the franchise, and the best that Rodriguez' character witnesses could say was that he would be a good citizen if he knew what the laws were. Judge Thomas Maxey, a Confederate veteran, handed down his decision in the hotly contested *In re Ricardo Rodriguez* in May 1897. He found unequivocally for Rodriguez, citing citizenship granted to resident Mexicans in the Republic of Texas Constitution, the citizenship allowed for the same class in the Treaty of Guadalupe-Hidalgo ending the Mexican War, and in the Fourteenth Amendment to the U.S. Constitution, which placed no racial test for citizenship. From that time, the right of Tejanos to vote was protected, but that hardly defined the extent of their difficulties. A state census in 1887 enumerated some 83,000 Hispanics, a figure that doubled by 1900, with half of them new immigrants from within Mexico. At least another 100,000 arrived in Texas by 1910, mostly seeking to escape the economic stagnation and political oppression that resulted from the dictatorship of Porfirio Díaz, a career revolutionist who had seized power in 1877 and governed Mexico for the benefit of the wealthy class and foreign investors.

As most of Texas left its frontier days behind and began its process of modernizing and urbanizing, the still largely Hispanic strip along the Rio Grande, a hundred and sometimes two hundred miles wide, was in great part left behind. The large ranchos were usually still run on the ancient Spanish system of the benevolent *patrón* watching over the interests of the *peóns* who worked the spread. Moreover, the massive influx of immigration in the 1890s brought a heavy reinforcement of interior Hispanic culture,

455

largely free of Anglo influence. It was a region, for instance, largely bereft of professional services; there was only one medical doctor between Laredo and Corpus Christi, and the population relied on curanderos, often-unlettered faith healers who won the loyalty of their patients more for their sincerity and generosity than for their herbs and rituals. Perhaps the most celebrated was Don Pedrito Jaramillo of the Los Olmos Ranch near Falfur-rias, who as his fame spread, received large amounts of money in mostly small donations. He donated much to churches, and bought food in bulk to give to the poor, many of whom he treated for free. Don Pedrito's grave is still a shrine, and his career makes it understandable why modern medicine was resisted in the Valley. But Hispanic reliance on curanderismo was more than a vignette of cultural quaintness. It materially exacerbated the cultural tensions between Anglos and Hispanics that were becoming increasingly serious. When Laredo was stricken with an epidemic of smallpox in the spring of 1899, the Anglo response was, of course, removal of patients to a quarantine, and mass inoculation of the public. Both aspects of this regimen ran counter to the rituals of curanderismo and violence broke out, in the news accounts of which the Hispanic population inevitably appeared unfa-vorably for attacking police who were trying to protect the public health. "The smallpox situation in Laredo has turned riotous," reported the *Austin Statesman* on March 20, "as health officials tried removing smallpox patients to the pest house. The Mexican population, which is superstitious, is op-posed to vaccination and isolation. A mob of several hundred Mexicans as-saulted city officers by throwing rocks and firing shots."

When the twentieth century arrived in the Valley with the railroad, mechanized irrigation, and the development of large-scale commercial farms, a tremendous social displacement occurred. Urban development ac-celerated; next door to Brownsville the wild hamlet of Six-Shooter Junction incorporated under the name of Harlingen, and farther upriver the town of McAllen was started. An increasingly Anglo-dominated political hierarchy developed, which took its cue from the patrón-peón tradition, and which be-came known, accurately, as "boss rule." This occasioned little disruption be-cause it was a form of domination with which the peóns had long been familiar. And it was a political system in which Tejanos did enjoy some ad-vantages—a Hispanic sheriff, while serving an Anglo political boss, could dispense a far milder form of justice than could be expected from Rangers. Economically, however, with the arrival of large investment capital, Tejanos whose families had owned land for generations suddenly found themselves performing stoop labor for minimal wages on the land that had been bought by outside investors with no knowledge of or sympathy for the long-standing way of life, and whose interests were vindicated by a law enforcement apparatus—usually in the person of Texas Rangers—whose historic antipathy toward Mexicans resulted in summary justice that could only be described as draconian. Of Tejanos who earned their way as tenant farmers, most of them had to give over half their crop to the landowners, whereas among Anglo sharecroppers who were able to furnish their own implements, one-third was the more common figure.

The federal government failed to recognize any danger in the situation, and in 1903 proposed to close down Fort Brown and withdraw its garrison. It was left to South Texas' freshman congressman, and future vice president, thirty-five-year-old John Nance Garner of Uvalde, to importune the secretary of war and future president William Howard Taft to head off the calamity. "Mr. Secretary," he cajoled, "it's this way. We raise a lot of hay in my district. We have a lot of stores and we have the prettiest girls in the United States. The cavalry buys the hay for its horses, spends its pay in the stores, marries our girls, gets out of the army and helps us develop the country, and then more replacements come and do this same thing. It *is* economics, sir. It *is* economics." With such wheedling to keep federal troops and spending in the Valley, Cactus Jack Garner opened his fifteen terms in Congress which eventually led him to the speakership.

As Indians and peóns sought new lives on the northern side of the Rio Grande, and as Mexican editors and intellectuals who found it too dangerous to criticize Díaz in Mexico also relocated to Texas to print their tracts, they entered a volatile realm. Once across the border they were equally appalled at the treatment of Tejanos and found themselves compelled to publish a two-front war, attacking both the Díaz regime and seeking to obtain justice for the Valley Tejanos. One of the first to get caught in this web was the journalist Catarino Garza, who began publishing the liberationist *El Comercio Mexicano* in Eagle Pass in 1886. He soon found himself caught between Díaz agents who seized his press and intimidated Tejanos found with copies of his literature, and Texas Rangers, who arrested and jailed him on libel charges for criticizing the conduct of Starr County sheriff W. W. Sheley, who was responsible for the deaths of numerous Mexicans who perished while in his custody. Finally moved to violence when Díaz operatives murdered a colleague, Garza organized a small force and struck south of the river three times in 1891, with enough success that at his height he commanded the movements of some 1,200 irregulars in the so-called Garza War. The Díaz regime struck back brutally, causing the U.S. to station troops on the border, who were not as effective as specially commissioned Texas Rangers, who were less hesitant to shoot. Knowing his life to be forfeit if he was captured by either side, Garza left Texas in 1892, and was probably killed pursuing further revolutionary activity in Colombia three years later.

Garza's cause was soon taken up, however, by other exiles, most prominently by Ricardo Flores Magón, a highly educated Oaxacan Indian. Repeatedly jailed and banned from publishing in Mexico, he and his brother Enrique relocated to Laredo and resumed publishing the subversive *Regeneración* from San Antonio in 1904. Hounded from there to St. Louis to Los Angeles, he was finally apprehended in Tombstone, Arizona, and imprisoned, first for violation of the neutrality laws and subsequently for libel that interfered with American military policy. He eventually died in prison in 1922, but he was successful in founding the "floresmagonista" movement, whose most incendiary legacy in Texas was Aniceto Pizaña. Pizaña was born in Cameron County in 1870, and beginning in 1904 agitated for improving conditions for the Valley Tejanos.

This sad litany of cultural misunderstanding and indifference makes it hardly surprising that when a nondescript laborer named Gregorio Cortez Lira was abused by a South Texas sheriff and responded by trying to shoot his way to Mexico, he became a revered folk figure. Mexican-born but long a resident of the village of Manor, near Austin, Cortez had a wife and four small children when he resettled as a tenant farmer, along with his brother Romaldo and sister-in-law, in Karnes County, about halfway between San Antonio and Corpus Christi. In June 1901 the county sheriff, a popular three-termer named Brack Morris, arrived at the Cortez place investigating a horse theft in neighboring Atascosa County. In an escalating tragedy of mistranslation, a deputy named Boone Choate first told Morris that Romaldo Cortez had informed his brother that he was a wanted man, when he had actually told him only that the lawmen wanted to talk to him. Choate and Morris believed that they caught Cortez in a lie when he denied that he traded a horse in Atascosa County—he hadn't, he had traded a mare, a sharp distinction in Spanish but not in English. When Boone moved to arrest him, Cortez protested in Spanish, "You can't arrest me for doing nothing," which Choate garbled as, "No white man can arrest me." Gunfire was exchanged; Morris shot Romaldo Cortez in the face, and Gregorio Cortez killed Morris as the deputy ran for help. Secreting his family with a friend in the town of Kenedy and carrying his brother to a doctor that night, Cortez fled, knowing if he was caught there was only one end for a Mexican who killed a sheriff. Reasoning that the authorities would expect him to run for Mexico, he headed in the opposite direction, only to discover as he reached the nearby town of Runge that Morris was being buried there. It took him a day and a half to walk to the house of a friend near Gonzales, but there he was ambushed by a posse.

Back in Kenedy, Cortez' wife had been discovered, and "pressured" into divulging his plan. There was another gunfight in which a second sheriff and a deputy were killed, after which Cortez lay concealed in a thorn thicket as the lawmen tortured a thirteen-year-old boy in the belief that he knew the fugitive's whereabouts. Over the next week Gregorio Cortez, with a thousand-dollar price on his head and mounted on an indefatigable little mare, led hundreds of newly sworn deputies on a harrowing chase, covered day by day in sensational news stories. Only thirty miles from Mexico he was captured in Cotulla; once the circumstances of his flight came out at trial he was spared the death penalty and pardoned in 1913. The Valley Tejanos, with little to celebrate in their own lives, lionized him.

After years of such ambient tension, relations between Texas and Mexico reached a crisis in February 1914. A Laredo rancher, Clemente Vergara, suffered the theft of eleven horses that he had grazed on an island in the Rio Grande. He suspected the local Mexican federalist commander of the crime, and reported it to the Webb County sheriff. Against the advice of Texas Rangers, Vergara crossed the river for a meeting about compensation for his lost stock, and was savagely beaten and lynched. Governor Colquitt sought federal assistance, but with the Wilson administration still trying to pacify Mexico without choosing sides in their insurrection, Colquitt got the runaround from Wilson's secretary of state, William Jennings Bryan (whom Texas thrice supported for the presidency), and the governor of Nuevo León. Colquitt publicly lambasted the Wilson government and posted a thousand-dollar reward for Vergara's killers, and with the threat of increased violence in the Valley, Wilson was compelled to shift more troops to the border area, which served Texas' interest anyway.

Tempers had barely cooled over the Vergara murder when a far more sinister scheme was uncovered the following year. Authorities in South Texas took into custody one Basilio Ramos Jr., a Duval County beer distributor and sympathizer of Victoriano Huerta, a warlord who had helped Francisco Madero finally bring down Díaz but then turned on Madero and had him killed. Found on Ramos' person was an irredentist manifesto dated January 15, 1915, at the town of San Diego, forty miles west of Corpus Christi. It announced the beginning of a new revolution to begin on February 20. All persons of color in Texas—Mexicans, blacks, Indians, even Japanese—were to rise up and reclaim the territory lost by Mexico in 1848. All white males over the age of sixteen were to be summarily executed, and Texas and the Southwest would form an independent country which would later seek annexation by Mexico. This "Plan de San Diego" struck Texas like a bombshell, but February 20 brought no revolution, only another windy publication, and authorities relaxed their guard. Violent raids did commence the following July—sabotage of communications and transportation facilities, with the deaths of about twenty Texas Anglos. Also implicated in the Plan de San Diego was the border activist Aniceto Pizaña, who at first opposed such an incendiary scheme and advocated peaceful reform. (This was a tack espoused by a sizable segment of the Hispanic community, most prominently by Laredo leader Nicasio Idar and his family, publishers of the long-running *La Crónica,* a journal advancing both Tejano political rights and cultural advancement.)

An attack by Texas Rangers on his Los Tulitos ranch, eighteen miles north of Brownsville, on August 3, 1915, during which Pizaña's son was wounded and his wife and brother captured, so embittered him that he became a commandant of the Plan de San Diego movement, crossing the border freely and leading attacks on such installations as the Dodds pumping station in Hidalgo County. The most dramatic incident occurred on August 8 when a Mexican force of about sixty, fighting under a red banner proclaiming "Igualdad e Independencia," assaulted an outpost of the King Ranch.

The United States entrained troops for the border, and even employed its infant air wing of eight Wright Brothers aeroplanes for surveillance. (The rugged duty broke down six of the flimsy pushers, prompting the commander, Captain Benjamin Foulois, to burn the last two, which were so decrepit that he wrote, "I didn't want to take the chance that somebody would order us to keep flying them.") Despite the presence of U.S. troops, most of the actual fighting was undertaken by Texas Rangers, who prosecuted a race war that depended upon sheer terror to crush any irredentist ambitions. Warlord justice south of the border could hardly have been more summary; cementing a reputation first earned during the Mexican-American War, the *rinches,* as Tejanos referred to the Rangers, killed raiders and innocent residents alike. The most commonly cited figure was that some 300 Mexicans and Tejanos were killed in the Valley, but the total probably ran much higher, as the reprisal for the raid on the King Ranch alone may have accounted for a hundred Mexican dead.

The most tragically ironic thing about the Plan de San Diego was that the border Tejanos who suffered so grievously for it were not, in fact, responsible for it. It was, rather, one of the more byzantine machinations of the Carranza regime, which intended to blame the plan on their rivals, whether Villistas or Huertistas, and spook the United States into action against them. Most of the raiders who crossed the border into Texas were actually Carrancista regulars, out of uniform. Eventually Americans noticed that attacks under the aegis of the Plan de San Diego increased when there was tension between Carranza and the American government, but ceased once Carranza got his way. And after the Wilson government recognized Carranza as president of Mexico and demanded an end to the raids by Aniceto Pizaña, the border raider was arrested (later, he was quietly released and allowed to live out his long life near Matamoros). Carranza had less success in corralling one of his rebellious former confederates, Francisco "Pancho" Villa, who broke with him and pillaged the town of Columbus, New Mexico, to register his displeasure with American recognition of Carranza. In response, Wilson authorized a limited invasion of Mexico to capture Villa, with American troops commanded by General John J. Pershing. When Carranza's protest against violating Mexican sovereignty went unheeded, attacks heralding the Plan de San Diego resumed, but that game was now finished, and Texas Rangers cleansed the Valley with a brutal finality.

SIXTY-ONE

INTELLIGENT PATRIOTISM AND
FLYING MACHINES

THE CHRONIC COMMOTIONS IN THE RIO GRANDE VALLEY eroded the popularity of Governor Colquitt, at least in part because his most prominent antagonists, conservative evangelical Prohibitionists, were increasingly able to portray consumption of alcohol as a vice practiced principally by Mexicans and Germans. And he made himself even less popular when he lambasted the state board that approved school texts for rejecting a history book because it contained a photograph of Abraham Lincoln. Identifying himself proudly as the son of a Confederate veteran, he proclaimed nevertheless, "I want the truth of history taught." As he ran for a second term in 1912, he was opposed by William Ramsay, a justice of the state supreme court, who capitalized on the flap by extolling Southern valor and having bands play "Dixie." The majority of newspapers endorsed him, but Colquitt ran a modern campaign, being the first gubernatorial candidate to stump by automobile, and when all was said and done, he prevailed comfortably in the primary.

In the general election the Prohibitionists, who had supported Ramsay, ran their own candidate, Andrew Jackson Houston, second son of Big Sam and a former wild child. Colquitt ran over him; in fact his most dangerous opponent proved to be sixty-four-year-old Reddin Andrews Jr., perhaps Texas' most prominent Baptist. Andrews was a former president of Baylor University who had overseen the school's move from Independence to Waco, and was once contributing editor of the *Texas Baptist Herald* and president of the unification committee that consolidated the warring conventions into a single entity. He was a native of La Grange, but had held pulpits in more than a dozen Texas cities and towns and was most recently associated with Tyler, where he edited *Sword and Shield*. What set him vastly apart from other evangelicals was his fiercely held conviction that belief in Christianity mandated a loyalty to socialism. It was as a socialist that he opposed Colquitt for governor, and he finished second, ahead of both A. J. Houston and the Republican.

Colquitt's reelection occurred simultaneously with the election of the first Democratic president in years, Woodrow Wilson of Virginia. When E. M. House disappeared from Texas politics, he went into Wilson's service, was instrumental in his success, and was rewarded by being given freedom to plant Texans in the national cabinet. Texas had never enjoyed such broad influence, but their effect was mixed, as for instance when the new postmaster general, Albert Sidney Burleson, segregated postal employees while Wilson looked the other way.

As conditions on the Rio Grande continued in turmoil, Colquitt quickly became exasperated with the Wilson administration's recognition of the Carranza regime and their policy of "watchful waiting" to avoid antagonizing Mexico. The fact that the state was still struggling under an inadequate tax structure left from the Campbell administration, compelling Colquitt to raise taxes, might have been more of an issue, but by 1914 all other matters were shelved for what was intended to be a final bloodletting on the issue of alcohol. The "drys" had been quietly gaining strength for years, honing their organization in local option elections, and they finally felt ready to strike for good and all, for statewide Prohibition. What they didn't count on was the sudden emergence of a political juggernaut in the person of James E. Ferguson, a banker from Temple who, although he had never held political office, marshaled the support of the Texas business community into a nomination for governor. The product of a hardscrabble background, he had spent much of his youth roaming the country in search of odd jobs before settling back in Bell County, getting educated enough to become a lawyer and entering the banking business, with sidelines in insurance and real estate. He had long been interested in politics, but limited his activity to behind-the-scenes dealing, rather like E. M. House had done in Austin, only in local and down-ballot races.

As a candidate, Ferguson proclaimed that Prohibition was a stupid distraction that diverted the state's attention from solving real problems, and he vowed that, as governor, if any bill relating to alcohol, pro or con, reached his desk, he would strike it "where the chicken got the ax." He was attacked as a countrified demagogue, but Ferguson ran a campaign that was nothing if not shrewd. As a lawyer and banker he announced himself as the business candidate, but the central plank of his platform was relief for tenant farmers, limiting the amount of crops that a landlord could claim as rent. He stood for the improvement of country schools, and he agreed with Colquitt that the federal government should do more to contain the Mexican Revolution south of the river—thus picking up support from each constituency. Oppos-

ing Ferguson in the primary was Tom Ball, once a three-term mayor of
Huntsville before going to Congress, then settling in Houston and becoming a levering influence behind construction of the ship channel. He was
also, significantly, chairman of the Prohibition Statewide Executive Committee and the hand-picked standard bearer of the dry zealots. For all his
country crudity, Ferguson proved to be possessed of a gift for the demolition
of hypocrisies. Why, he demanded, if Tom Ball was such a Prohibitionist,
did he belong to the Houston Club? When Ball responded lamely that he
enjoyed their literary pursuits, it was easy for Ferguson to produce the
Houston Club's financials, showing $112 in recent purchases of reading ma-
terials, and $10,483.15 for liquor. Humiliated, as well as tarred by his asso-
ciation with Texas' increasingly apostate Senator Joe Bailey, Ball faded and
Ferguson won easily.

For a time after his election Ferguson seemed to have a golden touch.
The legislature passed his limitations on sharecropper rents (although it
was declared unconstitutional some years later), textbooks authorized by
local school boards were made available for free, and after the Villista raid in
New Mexico, Wilson called up the Texas National Guard and posted army
troops on the border. The state prison system was put on a self-sustaining
basis, and Texas institutions for the disabled were vastly improved. What
was harder for the public to see was Ferguson's darker side—he was corrupt, derisive of the woman suffrage movement, and deeply, hatefully racist.
His opponent in the 1916 primary, a Winnsboro banker (and Prohibitionist,
of course) named Charles Morris, raised the spectre of Ferguson's financial
shenanigans, including the deposit of $100,000 of state funds in his own
bank without paying interest. No one seemed interested, however, and Ferguson was easily reelected.

After a U-boat torpedoed the British liner *Lusitania* on May 7, 1915, resulting
in the drowning of 128 Americans among the 1,198 total dead, Texans
joined in the national outrage, and a resolution was introduced into the
state senate calling for the severing of diplomatic relations with Germany. It
is often forgotten that right up until America entered the war on the side of
the English and French, Anglophobia was a viable sentiment in Texas; it was
quite respectable to voice the German point of view, and many did, especially the Germans in the Texas Hill Country. Public opinion overall, however, drifted steadily against them. In March 1917 the argument virtually
ceased with publication of the so-called Zimmermann Telegram, a secret

message sent by the German foreign minister, Arthur Zimmermann, to the German ambassador to Mexico. Intercepted and decoded by British intelligence and turned over to the Americans, the note proposed, in the event of war between Germany and the U.S., an alliance between Germany and Mexico, with the latter's reward to be restoration of Arizona, New Mexico, and Texas. Following only weeks after Germany resumed unrestricted submarine warfare, the pressure became irresistible and the U.S. declared war on Germany on April 3, 1917.

Some 989,600 young Texans registered for the draft, and either through conscription or by volunteering, 198,000 Texans served, in addition to 450 female nurses. Texas A&M University, which almost failed before Sul Ross' presidency gave it military respectability in 1891, had been churning out officers ever since and contributed some 2,200 of them to the war. It long remained a subject of pride that A&M's entire class of 1917 volunteered. In all, some thirty-two military training camps were located in Texas, in addition to an officers' training school at Leon Springs near San Antonio.

Two fighting units comprised primarily of Texans gained particular notice. The 90th Infantry Division was mobilized at Camp Travis just northeast of San Antonio. Composed of recent conscripts from Texas and Oklahoma, they adopted the divisional T-O insignia, optionally for Texas-Oklahoma, Texas' Own, or after they arrived in France, Tough 'Ombres. It was a mixed-race division, with Hispanics and Native Americans interspersed among white servicemen, and African-Americans assigned to cooking and custodial drudgery. The 90th reached a divisional strength of 31,000 at the time they shipped overseas in June 1918. Fighting in Lorraine, St. Mihiel, and the Meuse-Argonne, they suffered 9,710 casualties, and after armistice performed occupation duty inside Germany. The Texas National Guard was incorporated into the U.S. Army as the 36th Infantry Division, mobilized at Camp Bowie near Fort Worth. Augmented by additional manpower from Oklahoma, their insignia was an arrowhead in recognition of the latter, enclosing a block T, for which they were nicknamed "T-Patchers." After nearly a year of training, their overseas deployment was completed on August 12, 1918, and they sustained 2,601 casualties in the Meuse-Argonne offensive. They stood down in June 1919.

By the close of the conflict, four Texans had been awarded Congressional Medals of Honor. The first Texas officer killed in the war had also been the University of Texas' first All-American football player, Louis Jordan of Fredericksburg. Known for his fearlessness on the field—he disdained wearing a helmet—he volunteered, became a lieutenant in the 149th Field Artillery, and went to France in August 1917. "This is the real thing now," he wrote in one of his last diary entries the following March. "It is very exciting, but most enjoyable. . . . Somehow or other I feel safe." Jordan felt safe in his bunker right up to the instant it was shattered by a German artillery shell. He was one of 5,170 Texans who died during the war, about a third of them stateside, many of influenza.

In addition to the home regiments, Texans felt connected to the war effort through another close tie: the aging USS *Texas* of Teddy Roosevelt's Great White Fleet had been retired and sunk as a gunnery target, and replaced with a wondrous new vessel to carry the state's name. A second-generation dreadnought displacing 35,000 tons and mounting ten .45-caliber 14-inch rifles in five turrets, the new *Texas* when she was commissioned was the most powerful warship on earth. During a courtesy call in Galveston, a state delegation presented her officers with an elaborately chaised baroque silver service for the wardroom. With a new range-finding clock mounted on the forward cage mast and a bearing compass striped around the circumference of B-turret, she and four other American battlewagons served throughout the war detached to the British Grand Fleet in Scapa Flow. Despite repeated Atlantic patrols, the *Texas'* only action came on January 30, 1918, firing 5-inch shells at the periscope of a German U-boat and heeling hard over to avoid a torpedo. The 14-inch main battery was never fired in anger.

At the outbreak of war, President Wilson sought out a mining engineer turned humanitarian, Herbert Hoover, to increase the nation's food production and conserve consumption. Texans willingly "Hooverized," planting war gardens and eschewing meat on Tuesdays, pork on Thursdays and Saturdays, and wheat on Mondays and Wednesdays. At home, citizens also promoted the war effort with the purchase of Liberty Bonds and Victory Bonds. Those too poor to purchase bonds still coughed up coinage for War Savings Stamps. Separate donation campaigns supported the Salvation Army and Red Cross, and "Do Your Bit" and "Give Till It Hurts" were the order of the day. The legislature passed bills for the benefit of soldiers, exempting them from the poll tax and protecting them from having property seized in judgments until a year after their discharge.

Some of Texas' response to the war footing, however, was downright silly, such as banning teaching the German language at the University of Texas. It was worse for the descendants of German Texas colonists. They had never been popular with the Davy Crockett crowd, in antebellum days because most of them did not and would not own slaves, then during the Civil

War because most of them were Unionists, and now because they did not support Prohibition. Once Germany was declared to be the enemy, the German Texas community was scrutinized for its proportion of volunteers, houses were casually visited to make sure no pictures of the Kaiser were displayed, bank accounts were examined to ensure they were buying as many bonds as they could afford, and cultural expression was generally suppressed. These excesses were often committed by officers of local defense councils, some fifteen thousand of which operated under the coordination of the Texas State Council of Defense, created by the legislature to enforce patriotic fervor among the populace and to coordinate the "volunteer" giving.

It was an attitude that fit comfortably with the legislative mandate that all Texas schoolchildren receive ten minutes a day of "Intelligent Patriotism." No slackers or protesters were tolerated. Georgia O'Keeffe, a thirty-year-old instructor of art, fashion design, and interior decoration at West Texas Normal College in Canyon, nearly lost her job for demanding, "What does patriotism have to do with seeing a thing as green when it is green and red when it is red?" Although she was revered by her students, other faculty regarded her with suspicion because her abstract expressionist paintings did not appear to actually represent anything. Her landlord, a physics professor, once asked her what the subject was of one of her paintings. She replied that it was Palo Duro Canyon. "It doesn't look like the canyon to me." "It's how I *feel* about the canyon." "Well, you must have had a stomachache when you painted it." Even worse, O'Keeffe encouraged her senior students to finish their degrees before enlisting in the military. Finally touched by personal scandal for taking unescorted walks on the plains with one or another of her students, she judiciously took a medical leave to recover from the influenza, resigned her position the next year, and abandoned Canyon to the habitation of oafs. (Georgia O'Keeffe went on to become an artistic legend, but always treasured the inspiration she found on the Staked Plains. The town of Canyon made its own penance in later years, with its Panhandle-Plains Museum becoming a widely respected arts center.)

Anti-intellectualism did not hold sway everywhere; the small educated class fought back, striking at the state's foremost Luddite, Governor Farmer Jim Ferguson. The acting president of the University of Texas was William J. Battle, a spindly professor of Greek and dean of the College of Arts. His handling of the university budget ran him afoul of Ferguson, who was attempting to make faculty positions subject to his own patronage. Ferguson demanded the firing of six professors, and when asked why replied, "I don't have to give any reasons, I am the governor of the State of Texas." The Board of Regents turned for leadership to one of their own members, forty-three-year-old philanthropist Will Hogg, eldest son of the late former governor, who began collecting political dirt on Ferguson. If the university had been his only enemy Ferguson might have overcome them, but during his three years in office he had amassed a powerful coalition against him—including Prohibitionists who hated his unabashed wetness, and a growing army of suffragists mortified by his stance against women's rights. (Once pressed about woman suffrage, Ferguson replied, "If those women want to suffer, I say let 'em suffer.")

Ferguson knew that he was vulnerable for various financial irregularities, but he summoned the UT Board of Regents to his office and announced his intention to veto the entire appropriation for the university. Late in July 1917, however, a grand jury in Austin indicted Ferguson for embezzlement. Speaker of the State House Francis Fuller summoned a special session of the legislature, which was illegal, but in a tactical blunder, Ferguson called one himself to consider the university appropriation. Instead, it impeached him on twenty-one charges, and despite his vigorous defense, convicted him of ten, removed him from office, and banned him from holding any office in the future. Ferguson resigned before the measure was official, allowing him to claim, albeit speciously, that he had not been impeached and was still eligible to run for office.

The lieutenant governor suddenly elevated was William Pettus Hobby, a newspaper editor from Houston and at thirty-nine the youngest man to assume the office up to that time. He was a supporter of both Prohibition and woman suffrage, but any such reforms would have to await the end of the war. One of his first measures was the so-called Hobby Loyalty Law, under which he appointed a thousand Special Rangers to crack down on dissent or lack of patriotism. A socialist newspaper published in Hallettsville with a circulation of 23,000, *The Rebel*, which had been in publication for six years under the banner "The Great Appear Great to Us Only Because We Are on Our Knees," was forcibly closed.

In Huntsville, a white mob killed a black man and six members of his family for his allegedly having dodged the draft. A far bloodier incident occurred in Houston, where soldiers of the long-segregated 24th Infantry were stationed to guard two new military camps along the ship channel. The soldiers had been entrained from New Mexico, and while they did not expect equal treatment, they believed that they deserved some consideration for their service to the country. Yet on August 23, 1917, a black soldier was arrested for interfering when police arrested a black woman. A group of other black soldiers were chased away with gunfire. At their camp, rumors (ultimately false) flew that a white mob was approaching, at which about a hundred of the infantry mutinied and surged toward downtown and the 4th Ward police station, where the captured soldier was being held. Five white policemen and ten white civilians were killed, along with four of the rampaging soldiers, two of whom were mistakenly shot by their own men. Order was restored after Sergeant Vida Henry, who had led the assault, counseled the soldiers to make their way back to camp, and then committed suicide. The Army quickly spirited the 24th Infantry back to New Mexico, but returned those charged with mutiny to San Antonio for trial at Fort Sam Houston. Sixty-three were assessed life sentences, nineteen were hanged. No whites connected with the incident were punished in any way.

Aside from contributing nearly 200,000 of her men and 500 women, Texas' greatest contribution to the war effort was probably in the advancement of aviation. At the outbreak of World War I, the European powers were far ahead of the United States in the development of air forces. The hidebound old horse soldiers of the American army could not conceive of any use for flying machines beyond reconnaissance, even after the engaged countries were dropping bombs from them. Once this prejudice began to break down, the army realized Texas' advantage of vast space and generally sunny climate for pilot training. Various Texans had been interested in flying for much longer—in fact it is possible, but not provable, that the first powered flight was not carried out by the Wright brothers in 1903, but by Jacob Friedrich Brodbeck, a German immigrant and early resident of Fredericksburg, whose spring-powered "airship" may have lifted off the ground in 1868. It crashed upon landing, which would seem to imply that it got off the ground, but Brodbeck's plans were stolen in Michigan during a fund-raising mission to finance a second machine, and he abandoned the venture. Similarly, one William Browning Custead, a cousin of Buffalo Bill Cody who lived in Elm Mott, near Waco, was sworn by a witness to have attained a tethered flight in his machine around the turn of the century. Like Brodbeck's, it featured movable wings, like a bird, but with slats that opened on the upstroke so as not to negate the power of the downstroke. Custead's flying machine had a 60-foot wingspan, powering up and down at three strokes per second, but before it could be perfected the Wright brothers' fixed-wing design proved obviously superior. Custead was so galled that he sailed off to Hawaii and became a nudist.

The first airborne plane to be seen in Texas appeared in 1910, although where and flown by whom is debatable. One likely candidate was Captain Foulois of the Army Signal Corps, who was subsequently put in charge of border reconnaissance during the Valley disturbances. He was stationed at Fort Sam Houston in San Antonio with three Wright and two Curtis aeroplanes and instructed to teach himself to fly. That was no mean feat considering that he himself had had only fifty-four minutes of instruction from the Wright brothers. His rough-and-tumble education resulted in his suggesting various improvements, such as the replacement of landing skids with wheels, which were adopted.

During World War I, when France and Germany had in their arsenals about five hundred airplanes each, the United States had exactly twenty-one, but once this folly was recognized the turnaround was swift. Foulois, who had been banished from Fort Sam Houston along with his planes after a training crash killed Lieutenant George E. M. Kelly, was sent back to San Antonio to the newly purchased Kelly Field, on 627 acres southwest of the city. The military's previous inattention to airplanes made instructors hard to come by. Foulois was self-taught, as was Floyd "Slats" Rodgers, who grew up on a farm near Waco and taught himself to fly in 1912 with a plane that he built himself, which he christened "Old Soggy" because one wing sagged. He was a maverick, but the army hired aviation talent wherever they could find it. By the end of the war, 27 air cadets were killed in training crashes, but Kelly Field turned out 1,562 pilots for the war effort. When it came on line, Kelly Field joined Hicks Field near Fort Worth, where the Canadian Royal Flying Corps was already training, along with their American volunteers, and Call Field near Wichita Falls, which turned out 500 more pilots.

A few months after the war ended, the USS *Texas* made a small mark in aviation history when a Sopwith Camel biplane was slung aloft from a catapult mounted atop B-turret. It was the first plane ever launched from an American battleship, and a symbolic preview of air power's replacement of the big gun as master of the sea. Texas made one other signal contribution to war aviation, in the first-ever manufacture of helium from natural gas. From the beginning of the war in Europe, dirigibles and barrage balloons were floated aloft with bags of hydrogen. They suffered a high rate of destruction because hydrogen is extremely flammable. The existence of helium gas had been long theorized, but was successfully isolated only a few years previous. It is twice the weight of hydrogen but has 93 percent of its lifting power, and although it is the second-most-abundant element in the universe, it is present on earth only in trace amounts, and is prohibitively expensive to cull from the atmosphere. However, when natural gas discoveries on the Staked Plains near Amarillo proved to contain as much as 1.5 percent helium, the embattled British lobbied hard for the American government to find a way to extract it. Operating in strictest secrecy (lest the Germans learn what was going on, the product was referred to as "X-Gas"), the U.S. Navy and Bureau of Mines began producing helium in a plant in Fort Worth, guarded by troops from Camp Bowie. The presence of helium in Panhandle gas remains a freak of nature, and the high plains hold a near monopoly of the world's proven reserves. It was such a highly guarded secret of national security that helium was not made commercially available until 1937.

SIXTY-TWO

FLAPPERS AND FERGUSONISM

ARMISTICE IN 1918—ON THE ELEVENTH MONTH, eleventh day, eleventh hour—left Texas with a long ledger of old business to have to sort through. The most acute was the aftermath of the Texas Rangers' brutal occupation of the Rio Grande Valley during the previous decade. It was a situation finally brought under control by the determination and sand of the state representative from Brownsville, José Tomás "J.T." Canales. Born in 1877, in many ways he typified the Valley Tejano—his family still held lands acquired by royal grant, he was fluidly cross-border, with relatives and interests on both sides of the river, and he was a great-nephew of the mid-nineteenth-century bandito/folk hero Cheno Cortina. He also stood apart from his community—he left the Catholic Church to become a Presbyterian—but he was professionally trained to take up their cause, being a graduate of the University of Michigan Law School.

The path to public service for a Tejano in South Texas meant conforming himself to the somewhat servile position of working within the Anglo-dominated "boss rule" system, in his case attaching himself to Jim Wells, the patrón of Cameron County. As a landed, educated conservative he was made welcome in the machine, and he represented Brownsville in the legislature for three terms before breaking with Wells in 1909. Seeking wider Anglo support he backed Prohibition and woman suffrage (Wells' wife, Pauline, was a leader of the state women's antisuffrage constituency). This bid for independence was a failure, and Canales returned to the Jim Wells organization as superintendent of schools in Brownsville, where he reestablished his credentials by pushing English-only education and American patriotism. As relations between Anglos and Hispanics in the Valley deteriorated, however, he proved equally insistent upon social justice for the Tejano people. When he resumed his seat in the legislature in 1919, he called for hearings to investigate the Texas Rangers' bloody excesses there.

Canales' ties to the South Texas political bosses and his targeting of the Rangers put him on the bad side of Governor William P. Hobby, who had used the Rangers in 1918 to suppress voting for Democratic primary rival James E. Ferguson in the Valley and Brush Country. Despite the impeach-

472

ment verdict barring him from holding public office again, Ferguson won a court order to put his name on the ballot, and he waged a vociferous campaign to unseat Hobby, whom he termed a "political accident." Ferguson mocked Hobby's sail-eared appearance; Hobby answered that he might look funny, but at least he knew the difference between his own money and the state treasury. Farmer Jim was clobbered in the primary, but in state senate elections in South Texas, Hobby's Rangers proved unable to outfraud the masters, bosses such as Jim Wells, who was a Ferguson ally.

Canales' inquiries also inflamed some prominent Rangers, particularly six foot three inch, 230-pound Frank Hamer, whose exploits in the Valley had led to locals calling him the Angel of Death. Hamer cornered the slightly built Canales in Brownsville, threatening, "You are hot-footing it . . . between here and Austin complaining to the Governor and the Adjutant General about the Rangers, and I am going to tell you if you don't stop that you are going to get hurt." Canales turned for advice to Cameron County Sheriff W. T. Vann, who had himself looked the other way when Rangers summarily executed Tejano and Mexican suspects. Vann in response hinted that after such a threat, no jury would convict Canales if he killed Hamer. Unwilling to become what he was trying to fight, Canales appealed to the governor, without effect, for protection. Before the hearings began Hamer continued to shadow Canales in Austin, prompting Canales' legislative allies such as Samuel Ealy Johnson (father of Lyndon) to surround him closely as he walked to forestall an assassination.

Canales got his hearings, but Hamer (and an openly hostile committee chairman) had so rattled him that he backed off from exposing the worst aspects of their reign in the Valley. Still, what the committee found smelled bad enough that the record was sealed for some fifty years. The resulting reform law, while not what Canales had envisioned, radically truncated the Ranger force from hundreds of privately enlisted vigilantes down to seventy-six professionalized state police (still later pared down to sixty investigators).

Disillusioned by the personal cost of obtaining justice for the Tejanos, Canales did not seek further terms in the statehouse, but he remained very active in their affairs. He also remained controversial for his lack of radicalism in that community. When a convention met in Harlingen in 1927 to consider the issue of ethnic discrimination, Canales was savagely criticized for insisting that it be considered as a Mexican-American problem, and he influenced the convention to deny membership to Mexican citizens. Two years later, however, he was a founder of the League of United Latin American Citizens (LULAC) when it organized in Corpus Christi, and was the author of its constitution. He served in many other civic capacities until his death at the age of eighty-nine. There is no doubt that J. T. Canales had justice on his side in pursuing his bill to reform the Texas Rangers, but doing right by the Tejanos was not what got the act through the legislature. What did it was the fact that the Rangers began making themselves widely unpopular with their energetic enforcement of Prohibition, which at last became state law in 1920, after a long, uphill battle. Where local law enforcement could often be bought off, the Rangers drew upon their legend of incorruptibility and began wrecking stills and smashing bottles of homemade hooch left, right, and center. The wet vote was happy to see the Rangers' numbers trimmed.

Prohibitionism in Texas had been gaining momentum ever since 1915, when the Anti-Saloon League in Texas reorganized and assumed leadership of the effort. They built upon momentum achieved two years earlier, when the very dry five-term Congressman Morris Sheppard of Texarkana took the Senate seat of Joe Bailey, of whom Texans finally managed to divest themselves. In 1917 a dozen more counties voted themselves dry under the local option law. Senator Sheppard gained the distinction of introducing a national Prohibition amendment and steered it through the Congress. Once turned out to the states for ratification, Texas embraced it in 1918. The only way Prohibition passed in Texas, as well as nationally, was to attach it to patriotism and the war effort: drinking beer was something Germans did, in addition to the fact that American soldiers, virtuous but vulnerable in their training camps, had to be protected from demon rum. (In Texas, reaction against Farmer Jim Ferguson's ties to the brewing industry also helped.) National abstinence did not take effect until 1920, so the state dry forces got their state law in 1919 to empty the saloons and cupboards at the earliest possible moment. What the legislature gave with one hand, though, they took away with the other, starting a pattern of underfunding anything in the way of enforcement. This opened the door to monumental hypocrisy.

Where there was a will to imbibe, resourceful Texans usually found a way. In the little town of Hurst, on the northeast side of Fort Worth, stills hidden in the thick woods along the Trinity River became an important mainstay of the local economy. Drinkers in Austin even came to rely on a kind of booze fairy: those in the know would drive up a dirt road near Barton Springs and leave a dollar beneath a rock, where a return trip later in the day would reveal a bottle of whiskey. These operations represented mere pocket change, however. The real money, in Texas as in the nation, came to be in racketeering. Galveston became the center for liquor smuggling, and was famous for its "Rum Row," a picket line of foreign vessels that slowed down well beyond U.S. territorial waters, with holds full of liquor to sell to anyone with a speedboat fast enough to elude the Coast Guard. Some of this alcohol was intended for local consumption; the larger part was distributed into the interior of the country. Canadian brewers and distillers who tired of the cat-and-mouse on the Detroit River hit on the scheme of sending the product to British Honduras, where it was loaded onto freighters for Rum Row. Control of Galveston's local market was contested by two rival mobs, the "beach gang" and the "downtown gang." After negotiations, partly settled by a shootout on Tremont Street, leadership passed to the latter, and to the barbering Sicilian brothers Rose and Sam Maceo. Their celebrated speakeasy, the Balinese Room, sat on pilings over the Gulf, at the end of a long, covered pier. A lookout on the beach signaled the proprietors whenever a police raid arrived, giving them time to unload liquor and gambling paraphernalia into the water through trap doors. It was said that on one raid spearheaded by Rangers, they stormed down the pier and crashed into the club to find the band playing "The Eyes of Texas" and the emcee announcing, "And now, ladies and gentlemen, we give you, in person, the Texas Rangers!"

Such mockery was not unexpected in Galveston, whose open lifestyle had long been a thorn in the side of the rock-ribbed, but opposition to Prohibition ran much deeper than that. Not all the illegal hooch came into Texas from Rum Row. "Slats" Rodgers, the former Army flight instructor, bought a new plane to ferry alcohol over deserted stretches of the Rio Grande. He was quite good at it, but then he took up moonshining for himself, got caught, and served six months.

The most notorious center for homegrown vice came to be the desert-dry community of Mexia, forty miles east of Waco. After an oil strike increased the population more than tenfold, the boomtown arrivals needed a place of recreation and settled on the Winter Garden, a club outside of town protected by armed guards on the premises and crooked cops on the payroll. In January 1922, Ranger (and now Captain) Frank Hamer, fresh from his harassment of J. T. Canales, took over the Winter Garden with guns blazing and made it his headquarters while cleaning up the county. Once a declaration of martial law freed him from the necessity of obtaining search warrants, he destroyed 9,000 quarts of whiskey and 27 stills, seized a huge store of gambling equipment and narcotics, recovered fifty stolen cars and turned the Winter Garden into a POW camp to temporarily house many of the 600 people he arrested. Some 3,000 others were run out of town. It was just the beginning of Texas' Prohibition woes.

Another issue held over from World War I was that of woman suffrage. In a way it is not surprising that Texas, which was politically reactionary on such issues as race and alcohol, nevertheless took a leading role in the assumption of political rights by women. The state's Spanish and more matriarchal heritage, later inculcated into the laws of the Republic and the state, had long given women legal status not enjoyed in other states. (In 1851, Sam Houston outlined Texas women's property and homestead rights to an audience in Philadelphia, concluding, "If you can beat that, I will give up.") In 1893 the only suffrage agitation taking place in the South was in Texas, although it was by no means universally popular even among women. When the Texas Woman's Christian Temperance Union endorsed the vote for women, their membership took a nosedive. When the Equal Suffrage League of Houston was formed in 1903, it was the project of three sisters named Finnegan, but when they left the state the enterprise collapsed. One of them, Annette Finnegan, later returned to the state and with socialite Eleanor Brackenridge organized the Texas Woman Suffrage Association. Things gained momentum in 1915, when that group, by now boasting 2,500 members in twenty-one chapters, elected the immensely capable Minnie Fisher Cunningham as president. Three years later there were ninety-eight chapters, and for good reason national suffrage leader Carrie Catt was referring to "Minnie Fish" and her aides as the Texas Heavy Artillery. One reason for the growing support was that the TWSA (now renamed the TESA: Texas Equal Suffrage Association) began cleverly tying the issue of the vote for women to the issue of Prohibition, letting the otherwise conservative dries assess how much closer their cherished goal would be if the preponderance of females could vote for it.

Lobbying the legislature on the subject proved hardly less daunting than working around Ferguson. In 1915 a resolution supporting a constitutional suffrage amendment fell only three votes short of the two-thirds needed for passage. But equally telling was the reception that suffragist Jane Yelvington McCallum received from one state senator. She was the university-educated daughter of a frontier sheriff from Wilson County, southeast of San Antonio; president of the Austin Women's Suffrage Association; and an able lieutenant of the redoubtable Minnie Fish. She had raised $700,000 in Liberty Bonds during the war. She had also been to finishing school in Mississippi and knew how, ladylike, to hold her gorge.

Calling on the senator to encourage his support, he answered her sourly, "You ought to get married and tend to a woman's business."

"But I am married."

"Then you ought to be having children."

"I have five. How many would you suggest I have?"

"Then you should be home taking care of them."

"They are in school, and their grandmother is there in case they get home early."

"Then you should be home darning socks!"

Another impediment was Joe Bailey, who explained more articulately, "It would be useless to talk to a woman about the great and fundamental principles of government. . . . To her way of thinking, no man should be permitted to do anything which she thinks a good man ought not to do." But Joe Bailey was toppled from office in 1913, and one of the women who helped defeat Ferguson in 1918 was the orator (known as the Queen of the Southern Platform) and president of the Texas Woman's Christian Temperance Union, Minnie Curtis. She early backed William P. Hobby in his primary campaign, and they and the TESA provided Hobby a godsend of volunteer labor. With Hobby's support, the legislature passed a bill in March 1918 giving Texas women the right to vote in primary elections. Hobby, facing a counterattack by Ferguson in the 1918 primary, did well by doing good, as in just over two weeks 386,000 Texas women registered to vote, and were advised on how to vote in classes supervised by Nell H. "The Ramrod" Doom. They were largely responsible for Hobby's victory.

Not content with vicarious wins by Democratic allies, the suffrage organizations ran their own choice that year for their first statewide office, state superintendent of schools. The candidate was Annie Webb Blanton, president of the Texas State Teachers Association. She was opposed in the primary by a Fergusonite named W. F. Doughty, who called her an atheist. It was a fatal mistake. Blanton, who hadn't even wanted to run, responded that if he had "carried his candidacy to the Creator in prayer as earnestly as I have, he would not have been endorsed by the breweries." The withering broadside carried her into office, after which she thanked the editor of her hometown newspaper, the *Denton Chronicle*, for his endorsement by packing him a box of homemade fudge.

In June 1919 Texas became the first state in the South to ratify the federal equal suffrage amendment, and again, far from resting on its laurels, the TESA organized six statewide suffrage groups into a Women's Joint Legislative Council and opened an office in the Austin capitol. With Jane McCallum as their executive secretary, they won grudging admiration as the "Petticoat Lobby" as they argued aggressively, and often successfully, for laws on what were seen as women's issues, including education, prison reform, and of course Prohibition. The first woman elected to the Texas house, Edith E. T. Williams, served only one term in 1923–25 before overreaching, campaigning for governor and being edged out of politics. The first woman state senator proved to be smarter. She was Margie Neal, editor and publisher of the *East Texas Register* in Carthage, and was elected in 1926; during her four terms she introduced important legislation in the areas of education and the handicapped.

For Texas women to gain the right to vote in state primaries even before the ratification of the Nineteenth Amendment was an important advance for civil rights in the state. But it was only a step; a long journey still stretched ahead, as was discovered by one Christia Adair, a crusading suffragist in the South Texas town of Kingsville, near Corpus Christi. When she tried to exercise her new franchise, she was turned away from the polls. Christia Adair was black, and African-Americans were one constituency to which no ruling cabal owed any favor or consideration. Mortified to discover she had been fighting the wrong battle, Adair threw herself into the struggle for racial equality. A Sunday-school teacher, she realized the scope of her task when in 1920 the Republican candidate for president, Warren G. Harding, campaigned in Kingsville and she lined up several children to meet him. The Republican Party was the traditional refuge of Texas blacks, but he reached right over them to greet white people standing behind them, which ended any thought she had of ever being a Republican. Five years later she and her husband, Elbert, a railroad brakeman, relocated to Houston, where Christia Adair joined the local chapter of the National Association for the Advancement of Colored People.

This was an act of bravery, for the Texas NAACP, the first chapter of which was formed in El Paso in 1915, was undergoing dangerous times. Shrewdly, the national organization tied membership drives during the war with the promotion of Liberty Bonds, and by war's end Texas had thirty-one chapters with over seven thousand members—one of the largest state NAACP networks in the country. However, the hostility felt by the majority of whites to black organizing was powerful and always just a step away from violence. This was brutally demonstrated in the summer of 1919, following the killing of a local black youth, Lemuel Walters, in the Northeast Texas town of Longview, which had a population of about 7,500, one-third of them black. Walters had been in a relationship with a white woman, who was apparently his willing partner. A leader of the local black community, Samuel L. Jones, reported on the murder to the *Chicago Defender*, an African-American newspaper of national circulation, for which Jones was beaten, allegedly by brothers of the white woman. Local temper found this an insufficient lesson, but when about fifteen armed white men advanced on Jones' house they were met by shotgun blasts. This set a mob in action, ringing the alarm in the fire station and breaking into a hardware store for more arms and ammunition. They advanced on the black section of town, burning houses—Jones' first—and killing another black leader, Marion Bush, as he fled from the sheriff. The mayor called Governor Hobby, who sent the National Guard and Texas Rangers. They disarmed everyone, including the local police, and arrested seventeen whites and twenty-one blacks, but no one ever came to trial.

Among the few allies that Texas blacks found were the white suffragists who had just won the vote themselves. Prominent among them, for instance, was Jessie Daniel Ames of Georgetown, who in 1918 had been treasurer of the Texas Equal Suffrage Association, and the following year became the first president of the Texas League of Women Voters, among many other civic positions. She later moved to Atlanta, Georgia, and founded the Association of Southern Women for the Prevention of Lynching, an informally organized but effective organization that protested the "false chivalry" of the lynching culture. They knew that the defense of white women's virtue was merely a pretext for the grisly racial intimidation that lynching was meant to achieve, and they were determined not to allow bigots to depict them as damsels in distress. (Curiously, though, the association did not itself accept blacks as members, believing this would damage their cause.)

Theirs was a small voice, however, against the wall of hostility toward civil rights for blacks, opposition that was both official and social. Officially it took the form of the state attorney general's mounting a legal challenge to the right of the NAACP to organize in Texas, news that brought the organization's national secretary, John Shillady, to Austin. There he was taunted and beaten, and heard Hobby's advice that things would go easier if the NAACP simply stayed out of Texas. Of the thirty-one local branches organized during war bond drives, only five survived by 1923. Informally the opposition took the form of a frightening resurgence of the Ku Klux Klan, an issue that became a near crisis during the administration of Hobby's successor, Pat Morris Neff of Waco.

The candidate to beat in the gubernatorial contest of 1920 was Joe Bailey, bent on vindication from the voters despite his unsavory Senate record. He ran against Prohibition, Woodrow Wilson, and woman suffrage—too late on all counts. Against him, Pat Neff's candidacy was almost too good to be true. He was a former boy-wonder speaker of the state house from two decades before, who had settled down in his native Waco as a feared prosecutor. Of 422 cases he tried, he won 406, a record he achieved by going for certain conviction rather than maximum sentences. He was a pious Baptist and spotless, able to claim that his virtue had never fallen to alcohol or tobacco—or coffee or tea, for that matter—and he took pride in the fact that he was the first Texas prosecutor to imprison bootleggers. Taking on a wet old sinner like Joe Bailey was a task that Neff undertook not just with vigor, but with joy. History, he declared, had produced three supreme egotists, "one was Napoleon, and Senator Bailey the other two." His tornadic campaign earned him the sobriquet the Wildman of Waco: he gave 850 speeches—up to seven per day—in 152 counties, 37 of which had never before been visited by a candidate for governor. He drove his own Ford, he flew in aeroplanes, he rode mules, and covered over 6,000 miles. When the votes in the primary were counted, Bailey eked out a tiny plurality, but Neff had forced a runoff, which he won.

There was no inaugural ball, of course, since dancing was a sin, but Neff set to work on an extensive program of reforms. Believing that prison was a place to punish and reform people, not torture them, he rooted out corruption on the Prison Commission and at the reformatory, and ended the practice of hanging inmates by their wrists. When a railroad strike in North Texas threatened violence, he traveled incognito to Denison to investigate firsthand. He thought that a few Rangers would set things right, but he was strong-armed by the Harding administration into sending the National Guard. He founded Texas Tech and Texas A&I universities, increased funding for rural schools, and revamped the Highway Commission. Unfortunately, in his zeal he neglected relations with the legislature, which allowed many more of his ideas to die quietly.

One program important to Neff did take root, which was the inauguration of a state park system. With a heritage of exploiting land for whatever gain could be made, the idea of conservation came slowly to Texas. The Texas Forestry Association had been created during the Ferguson administration, but that sounds more creditable to Farmer Jim than it really was. In reality it was the project of a fellow Temple banker, W. Goodrich Jones, whose earnest espousal of silviculture was acquired as a youth in walks in the Black Forest of Bavaria. Slightly built and bespectacled, Jones' publicity campaign that every tree cut should be replaced with a seedling planted led him to smother Temple with hackberry trees—fast growing but almost universally considered a nuisance—and he was chuckled over as the town eccentric. When "Hackberry" Jones approached Ferguson for a $10,000 appropriation to begin a state forestry program, Ferguson was flabbergasted. "Why do you need ten thousand dollars?" he demanded. "Why, for five hundred dollars I can get you a good man to cut all the trees you want!"

Neff was more sympathetic to issues of nature, and was often seen feeding or petting tame deer kept in a pen on the mansion grounds. Neff's mother, Isabella, had willed six acres of the family farm to the state in 1916 to develop into a park, but with no legislative basis for a state park system, Neff made that a goal of his administration, successfully realized in 1923 with the creation of the State Parks Board. The legislature, however, was too stingy to appropriate any money to purchase land, instead authorizing the state only to accept donations. Within a couple of years, public-spirited Texans contributed some sixty tracts of land—the largest was seven thousand acres—for parks, but even then an appropriation for their development was years in the future. Governor Neff himself stepped up to the plate, donating the rest of the family farm in Coryell County as the 259-acre Mother Neff State Park, the first in Texas.

After his term, Neff went on to chair the Railroad Commission, and then served as president of Baylor University for fifteen years, from 1932 to 1947. He doubled the size of the campus and more than tripled the student body, but his reputation as a disciplinarian and his lack of empathy for students who saw nothing intrinsically evil with makeup or nylons caused some hard feelings and a good deal of ridicule.

While Neff was reelected handily in 1922, one aspect of the Texas political landscape marred his tenure—the growing influence of the Ku Klux Klan. In a way it was a regeneration of the secret society of the post–Civil War era, and white racial superiority was still their keystone, but to broaden their appeal they also proclaimed their antipathy toward Jews and Catholics, and their allegiance to Prohibition and traditional family values. They also deliberately reined in the level of overt murder and assault, in order to portray themselves as a civic organization. The tactics worked, and at their high point between 1922 and 1924, they had between 100,000 and 150,000 duespaying members in Texas. Crosses were burned brazenly, and parades of robed and hooded men took to the streets without fear of reprisal. They controlled the councils of most of the large cities, and had such influence in the legislature that in 1923 they passed the "White Primary" law, barring

African-Americans from voting in primaries. With their tacit support, Earle B. Mayfield won election to the Senate to replace the now-doddering Charles Culberson, who failed in his attempt for a sixth term.

The KKK did not flourish completely unopposed, however. Civic leaders of any conscience sought to undermine them, such as the McLennan County sheriff who touched off a riot when he attempted to stop a Klan march in the town of Lorena, near Waco. Klan organization in Galveston actually backfired. When Klansmen sought a permit from the city to mount a recruiting parade, they were opposed by two heroes of the 1900 hurricane, Rabbi Henry Cohen and Monsignor James Kirwin. With a large segment of the city behind them, they managed to get the Klan's permit denied. At their height, though, the Klan even ran their own candidate for governor in 1924, Judge Felix Robertson of Dallas.

He might have won, too, had it not been for the resurgence of what was called "Fergusonism." Most political observers had Farmer Jim pegged as a corrupt demagogue, but he still enjoyed a large body of support among tenant farmers and the rurals whom he claimed to champion. His own comeback was thwarted when he lost the Senate primary to Mayfield, but Ferguson's motto was, "Never say die. Say *damn!*" In a brilliant maneuver, he entered his wife, the former socialite Miriam Amanda Wallace, in the gubernatorial primary in 1924. Borrowing a sunbonnet and posing for photographs beside a mule, she became "Ma" (from her initials) Ferguson, and Farmer Jim became "Pa." "Put On Your Old Gray Bonnet" became her campaign song, and indeed it was all a put-on; few if any ever dared call Miriam Ferguson "Ma" to her face.

The campaign became an open referendum on Ferguson's term as governor; in fact their slogan was "Me for Ma—and I ain't got a durn thing against Pa." Promising "two governors for the price of one," Ma opened the rallies and then turned the oratory over to Pa. Although Jim Ferguson's term had been colored by his deep personal racism, they now attacked the KKK savagely and effectively. Felix Robertson led the fractionated ballot in the primary, but in the runoff Ma beat him by nearly 100,000 votes. In the general election the Republicans pointedly nominated a former dean of the law school at Pa Ferguson's deadly nemesis, the University of Texas, and Ma defeated him. It was, however, the closest election in years, as thousands of Texas Democrats found it more palatable to vote for a Republican than for a woman.

The Fergusons' daughter Ouida recalled her mother driving the family

Packard into the mansion's porte cochere. "We departed in disgrace," she said with satisfaction. "We now return in glory." Ironically for a woman who had opposed suffrage for her sex, Ma was the first woman elected governor of an American state (although by two weeks she was the second to actually be sworn in). Her term was mostly ineffectual. The legislature presented her a bill to sign rescinding Jim Ferguson's ineligibility, and she procured an act to outlaw the wearing of masks in public—aimed at the Klan. It was struck down by the courts. Once Ma Ferguson was ensconced in the gubernatorial office, the prophecy of getting "two governors for the price of one" became reality, as Pa's desk was moved in to abut hers. This coziness led to some spiky humor about the often-sniffed Ferguson corruption, especially the widely accepted sale of pardons from the state penitentiary. One story had a man accidentally treading on Ma's foot in a capitol elevator. "Oh, pardon me," he said, to which she replied matter-of-factly, "You'll have to see Pa." In reality their graft was usually less naked than that; a real aspirant to get a relative out of prison might, for instance, offer to buy one of Farmer Jim's calves—for a sum exorbitant enough to get the paper signed. Or, hopeful bidders for highway construction contracts knew to take out expensive advertising in the *Ferguson Forum* if they wanted to be noticed. Pa also took to sitting in on meetings of the Highway Commission to oversee his interests, but an increasing number of those contracts came to be nullified by a troublesome young attorney general named Dan Moody.

Only thirty-one when elected, Moody was a crusading redheaded prosecutor who had come to national notice for winning convictions of three Klansmen who savagely whipped a black man in Moody's hometown of Taylor. He was a reformer and a protégé of the squeaky-clean Pat Neff; war with the Fergusons broke out almost immediately. Moody won a $600,000 judgment for the state against one of Pa's preferred highway contractors; Ma pardoned the most culpable of Moody's Taylor Klansmen, who had gotten a five-year term; Moody issued a ruling that declared Pa's restoration of electoral eligibility unconstitutional. The Fergusons were outraged at the interference by "that young spud," and Moody found them so odious that he entered the 1926 primary to unseat her. Shortly before the canvass began he married Mildred Paxton of Abilene, combining honeymoon with campaign, leading the Fergusons to charge that he had no qualifications for office, except "a lipstick, a new wife, and a big head." At a rally in Sulphur Springs, Ma issued a famous challenge: if Moody won the primary by a single vote she would resign, providing that if she won the primary by 25,000 votes, he would resign. Moody accepted and won by a small plurality, but the prospect of a runoff prompted Ma to renege on the wager, despite widespread catcalls for her resignation. It was only one reason she lost the runoff by 125,000.

One of Moody's first appointments as governor was for the office of secretary of state, which went to Jane McCallum, who had led the former suffrage coalition in support of his campaign. While that appointment secured her place in Texas history, she is also remembered for an important discovery. While assaying long-neglected papers of her office in a capitol vault, she came upon the Declaration of Independence of the Republic of Texas. The priceless document had been sent to Washington, D.C., in 1837 to buttress Texas' case for annexation, and it lay there discarded for the next sixty years. Found and returned to Texas in 1896, it was deposited in the vault and quietly forgotten for the next thirty years. McCallum had a special niche carved into the granite wall of the rotunda, where the glassed-in leaves of the Declaration could be read by turning a wrought-iron crank. She considered it one of her proudest achievements.

The appointment of a woman to statewide office was only one product of Dan Moody's progressive sympathies, but as with most reformers, the legislature was cool to most of his ambitions. The graft of the Ferguson years, however, did prompt the lawmakers to endorse his call to create an office of state auditor. One result of this was that the cost of highway construction was practically halved. Moody was unable to procure a state civil service act, though, or centralization of the prison system, or the calling of a constitutional convention to enact reforms that required more fundamental changes. He won reelection in a landslide in 1928, the same year that Texas Democrats had to choose for president between their own candidate, Governor Al Smith of New York, a Catholic who drank, and Herbert Hoover, the Republican humanitarian. After much agony, they went for Hoover.

One of the great rows of Moody's tenure was occasioned over redecorating the Governor's Mansion. The cavernous old house had received scant attention since it was expanded under Colquitt to include a conservatory and an upstairs private family apartment. Its condition was acute enough that soon after moving in, the new governor shot a huge rat in the basement, which crawled into a wall space to die, two days before an official entertainment. "You can imagine," Mildred told a reporter, "how bad that party was." A suitable appropriation was passed for repairs and renovation, $500 of which was to replace the old "brown oatmeal" wallpaper in the house. The job was entrusted to the first lady, and Mildred, a newlywed who had never kept her own house, blew every dime of it on historic-scene Zuber paper for the state dining room. Moody's reaction was vivid, but he went on personal credit to paper—economically—the remaining rooms. Peace was restored with the recommendation that a Board of Mansion Supervisors be created to furnish the house in a dignity befitting the office and the state. The legislature complied, and Mildred was placed on the board, exercising her good taste without further ruining the family budget. Moody could have sought a third term had he chosen to, but his $4,000 salary, his rapidly growing family, and his need to support Mildred in her style militated toward his returning to private law practice.

Texas had changed dramatically during the 1920s. The population had increased to more than 5.8 million, and was urbanizing so rapidly that the cities were growing more than six times faster than the rural population. The number of automobiles quintupled during the decade. Texas had now produced more than two billion barrels of oil; in 1929, in fact, oil surpassed cotton as the largest segment of the state's economy, and more jaw-dropping oil discoveries in the Panhandle had turned the former Comanche hunting ground into a wild maze of smelly boomtowns. The village of Borger, fifty miles northeast of Amarillo, exploded to a population of 45,000 "oilmen, prospectors, roughnecks, panhandlers, fortune seekers, card-sharks, bootleggers, whores, and dope peddlers." The local district attorney, after writing to Governor Moody for help in getting the lawlessness under control, was shot down in his backyard after he began arresting corrupt local officials. Frank Hamer had quit the Texas Rangers in disgust under Ma Ferguson's tenure, but he reentered the service and Moody sent him to Borger, where he reprised the collar-grabbing, butt-kicking success he had scored in Mexia. Martial law lasted almost a year in Borger, and when Hamer ran out of space in the jail, wanted men were chained in the street in a "trot-line" until officers from other jurisdictions could come and nab those wanted elsewhere.

The power of the KKK was on the wane, but still strong enough to precipitate the occasional race riot, such as one in Sherman in May 1930. Not even Frank Hamer was able to save the life of a black man named George Hughes, accused of raping a white woman. Once thinking him safe in the jail, Hamer saw the mob advance, wounded three with his shotgun, fired tear gas, and still the crowd managed to set the courthouse on fire. Hoses were mysteriously slit; women carrying babies walked in front of fire trucks.

Defeated for the only time in his career, Hamer departed and cursed Sherman to the end of his days.

There was now leisure time, and luxury goods, which elicited a shrill counterattack by fundamentalist preachers who railed against Darwin and motion pictures and bobbed hair and rumble seats, and who baptized masses of the fearing faithful in public swimming pools. Southern-fried religion and the KKK intersected in the life and career of J. Frank Norris, a showboat evangelist and pastor of the First Baptist Church in Fort Worth from 1909 until his death forty-four years later. Acquitted of arson in the burning of the inadequate old church facilities, Norris replaced them with an auditorium for five thousand, with a swimming pool and gymnasium, proclaimed by a spotlight and revolving electric marquee. He broadcast a radio show, making him a pioneering televangelist, and he gained further attention for his implacable hostility toward civil rights for blacks. He attacked his alma mater, Baylor, for secularism, accusing them even of teaching evolution, and maintained that the Southern Baptist denomination had been captured by liberals and socialists. For such antics as these, First Baptist in Fort Worth was frozen out of the meetings of the General Convention in the early twenties, but Norris was undeterred. He accepted a second pastorate, in Detroit, to which he commuted by airplane, and shot dead a friend of Fort Worth's mayor, with whom he disagreed on points of religion (but was acquitted on the grounds of self-defense). After the election of Herbert Hoover, Norris was honored by the Republican Party for his efforts against Al Smith, the wet Catholic Democrat.

Norris was not alone; modernization did not come easily to many Texans, and some entrepreneurs who promoted new products and services found it tough going. Jordan Lawler acquired the old grist mill on the Medina River in Castroville and converted it to produce hydroelectric power, but discovered that not everyone was in a hurry to become electrified. One potential customer turned him down with a remark that she saw no need to alter her routine of getting up when it was light and going to bed when it was dark, as God intended. One old man finally allowed Lawler to wire his house, but he had to agree not to bill him until he actually used the service; one night he got sick and his wife couldn't find matches to light the lantern. "Dammit," he said, "turn on the electric light and tell Lawler we are customers."

SIXTY-THREE

SO LONG, IT'S BEEN GOOD
TO KNOW YOU

THE MAN THAT GOVERNOR MOODY TAPPED TO CLEAN UP the Fergusons' road-building graft was his highway commissioner, Ross Sterling, a big, self-made businessman and president of the Humble Oil and Refining Company. The firm's name was not meant to describe anyone's demeanor. The town of Humble, twenty miles north of Houston, founded around 1870 by a man with the wry name of Pleasant Humble (with a silent *H*), became a boomtown following oil strikes in 1904. Sterling was running the feed store, and it was noted that weighing over 250 pounds, he could heft a 200-pound sack under each arm. He entered the oil business, got wealthy and then wealthier with investments in lumber, pipelines, banks, railroads, and finally newspapers. Sterling's *Houston Post-Dispatch* had supported Moody against Ma Ferguson, and at the time he entered public service he was worth maybe fifty million dollars—the polar opposite of the farm-posing Fergusons. As highway commissioner Sterling had proposed a massive overhaul of the state road system, including a bond issue financed by a gasoline tax. Incensed that the legislature let the proposal die, he announced for governor in the 1930 election.

Ma Ferguson was one of eleven candidates who entered the 1930 primary, which was enough to put Moody on the stump in support of Sterling. Although the full weight of the Depression was not yet felt in Texas, the economy was faltering enough that having a self-made multimillionaire in charge had a certain appeal. Weighing against that was a sentiment that the mass of poor Texans would not vote for someone so obscenely wealthy, and that view almost proved correct. Ma Ferguson led the initial primary with a plurality, but with hard campaigning Ross Sterling became governor in January 1931.

The free-borrowing and free-spending twenties had been good to the Texas business establishment, but that did not prevent some in the financial community from trying to make the times even better by some pretty nefarious means. The Texas Bankers Association famously published a reward of $5,000 for dead bank robbers, but "not one cent" for live ones. It was Ranger

Captain Hamer who noticed that they were really contracting hits on luckless drifters and paying the "rewards" to fellow embezzlers. When the New York Stock Exchange crashed on October 29, 1929, Texans not tied directly to the financial industry did not feel immediately threatened. It was estimated that only 2 percent of the people owned significant stock. Instead, in the wake of such behavior, many poor people who read of financial misdeeds believed that the speculators and margin borrowers had gotten what they deserved.

The larger story in Texas in 1930 was not the troubles on distant Wall Street, but in the oil patch. Virtually coinciding with the election was the most colossal oil strike yet made, the East Texas field, centered around Kilgore but spreading across all or part of five counties. The field came to light as the result of the determination of the dean of independent wildcatters, Columbus Marion Joiner, who at sixty-six had already made and lost two fortunes in Oklahoma oil. As with Spindletop, conventional wisdom disallowed the possibility of oil in Northeast Texas but Joiner, touting a largely doctored geological assessment of the area's potential, sold enough shares of a syndicate to assemble a shoestring drilling operation in Rusk County on a tract belonging to a woman named Daisy Bradford. Inferior equipment wrecked the attempt when the pipe reached a depth of just over a thousand feet. Joiner sold more shares, often utilizing his personal charm to barter for equipment and services, and sank a new well. This one passed 2,500 feet before suffering the same fate. Joiner renewed his effort, often selling the same shares to different people—and tried again. The Daisy Bradford No. 3 struck crude at 3,592 feet and flowed three hundred barrels per day.

It was enough to set off a boom of exploration, with a huge number of small-time operators trying to take advantage of it. Oil leases were often sold in square feet instead of acres; one acre of a producing area might contain forty or more rigs. Only with the sinking of thousands of wells into the pool of 5 billion barrels plus did the 140,000-acre extent of the field become apparent. Spurred by the exigency of the Depression, the small independents were making the same mistake that Texas farmers had been making for decades, producing more and more for less and less, for the sake of generating even a little cash flow. When the East Texas field opened up, the Depression had been on for a year and a half, but crude still brought a dollar a barrel; once the production panic set in, the price fell to a dime. The Texas Railroad Commission, which had the authority to limit production in order to prevent waste, issued an order to cut production in the field by 75 percent. The Texas Supreme Court quickly ruled that order invalid, but Sterling viewed the situation as being so dire that he declared martial law and sent in the National Guard to shut down all pumping until the market stabilized and production could be "prorationed," by which all wells would be allowed to produce only a certain percentage of their capacity.

The response of the small producers to this attempt to limit production was twofold. The first was simply to start selling "hot oil" on the black market, which found a way to thrive despite the scrambling of inspectors. The second was to open a game of legal tag, and eventually all nineteen of the Railroad Commission's prorationing orders were struck down by the federal courts; in February 1932, martial law itself in the East Texas field was declared illegal. That autumn Sterling called a special session of the legislature, which made selling hot oil a felony, and he was backed up by President Franklin D. Roosevelt, who issued an executive order mandating prorationing. This tangled the legal thicket even more, and when paired with continuing low market prices caused a shakeout of the players. C. M. Joiner was recognized as the father of the East Texas field and was given the honorific of "Dad," but his many years of fast dealing began to catch up with him, and he sold all his interest in the field for a million dollars to another independent who was gaining in power, H. L. Hunt of Dallas. Because Hunt became fabulously wealthy and Joiner eventually died with nothing, some historians have sympathized with Joiner's hard times and imputed carnivorous dealing on Hunt's part. In fact, Hunt was tolerant of Joiner's endearingly larcenous nature and gave him every consideration in making the buyout.

While the Great Depression ruined the dreams of many Texans, others found opportunity. One Elmer Doolin purchased a corn chip recipe and small distributorship in San Antonio, and using a kitchen potato ricer and the labor of family members, began marketing a snack food called Fritos. They quickly went national, and their acquisition of the Lay potato chip factory in Atlanta paved the way for Frito-Lay to eventually become the United States' largest vendor of salted snacks. Another company that reached a national profile began with a Texas entrepreneur of this era, James Field Smathers from the Hill Country. A secretary in an era when that field was dominated by men, he grew impatient with the clunky mechanisms of the typewriters of the day, and he patented an electric model as early as 1912, when he was only twenty-four. With attention focused on European troubles, however, he had difficulty getting anyone interested in developing it. Eventually he sold the patent to a company that in 1933 was acquired by International Business Machines, a concern that later went by its initials, IBM. They hired Smathers as one of their principal idea men and became an American business giant.

Early in the Depression, the Texas press shared the Hoover administration's denial of the seriousness of the event, and regularly printed the sunny releases handed out by the Commerce Department. When they could no longer ignore it, they put a good face on it. The times, said the hopeful, will teach us thrift. We will be prompted to turn back to God, said the religious. Relief was handled by charities. As the Depression deepened, however, private resources became overwhelmed, and different Texas cities staged fundraising. Then the cities became overwhelmed; unemployment skyrocketed and thousands of people had no money, no food, and no place to stay. As more and more Texans felt the need for a drink and Prohibition became less of a concern, Texas Democrats rued the day they were preached and exhorted into voting for Herbert Hoover. Many rural Texans were reduced to hunting feral pigs for protein, derisively naming them "Hoover hogs." (That was in East Texas; in the West the same name was given to armadillos.) Any given hobo encampment became "Hooverville." "Depression is my shepherd," the newspapers mocked, "I am in want. He maketh me to lie down on park benches; he leadeth me beside the still factories." By New Year's of 1932 San Antonio had 20,000 unemployed, Dallas 18,000. As economic reality settled over the state like a pall, about 400,000 Texans lost their jobs, and perhaps a quarter of those had nowhere to turn.

No matter how dreary one's real life was, for those who had the chance to get into a movie theater life was all about tuxedos and pillared drawing rooms and splashy production numbers. And when not transported to a life of ease, they could guffaw at the hapless mischances of the obese "Fatty" Arbuckle. Born in San Antonio with the given name of Maclyn, he proved himself a failure at various professions, most notably as a lawyer, at which he made so little money that he was unable to afford a room and slept in his office. His campaign for Bowie County judge consisted mostly of reciting Shakespeare in barrooms. In 1888 he appeared in his first play at the age of twenty-two, in Texarkana, and slowly worked his way up through the ranks of actors until he appeared for four years in London. With the advent of motion pictures he returned to San Antonio to help start, and act in, a film company. He then started a shuttle between Hollywood and New York, where he appeared in such plays as *Daddy Dumplins*, and he directed and acted in films with such legends as Buster Keaton. Arbuckle's career came to a crashing halt with a sensational rape trial; although the charge against him was shown to be not just untrue but a setup, he became the scapegoat sent into the wilderness bearing the sins of the hedonistic acting community.

Aside from having its own small movie business, San Antonio also played host to Hollywood. The same climatic advantages that led the army to establish its aviation training center in San Antonio also led to the city's selection as the filming location for *Wings*, a breathtaking flight epic, which in 1927 won the first Academy Award for Best Picture. The costume designer for *Wings* was Travis Banton, working very early in a 160-film career that revolutionized his craft. During the "flapper" era, the desired look for actresses was so stylized that any one looked very much like another. It was Banton, born in Waco in 1894, who sculpted the highly individualistic looks that made many actresses of the Golden Era so unforgettable. Mae West and Marlene Dietrich were his most distinctive creations, but he also worked extensively with Carole Lombard, Claudette Colbert, Merle Oberon, and other stars who revered him. Difficult and sensitive, an alcoholic often absent from the set, he was sustained by the devotion of his clients, some of whom, like Lombard, sought him out to work with him on picture after picture. As a final legacy to the industry before his death in 1958, Travis Banton discovered, employed, and trained eight-time Oscar winner Edith Head.

What Banton did to create looks for Dietrich and Mae West, his greatest rival, the legendary Adrian, did for Greta Garbo and another Texan, Joan Crawford. Born Lucille Fay LeSueur in San Antonio in 1906, the longevity of her career spanned the flat-chested platinum androgyny of the twenties and the penciled eyebrows of the thirties. After being remade by Adrian, her padded shoulders and caterpillar eyebrows made Joan Crawford an icon. Moviegoers who saw her wrenching portrayals of a woman alone against the world—and at less than five feet tall she always appeared to be fighting uphill—had little idea how closely the roles shadowed her own life. A girl of modest circumstances and menial jobs, she opened her career by performing in her stepfather's dance hall in Lawton, Oklahoma. She entered real show business after winning a Charleston contest, and embarked on a career of tempestuous rivalries, rocky marriages, and alienated children.

A host of other Texans, either by birth or long residence, were prominent in the entertainment industry. Sharing Broadway fame with Fatty Arbuckle was "That Two-Gun Texas Gal," Mary Louise Cecilia "Tex" Guinan, who

convulsed audiences with her trademark "Hello, suckers," and her practice
of whacking tennis balls at them during her act. She was also a queen of the
Western two-reelers, of which she made some two hundred. Notorious for
her easy liaisons and disdain for Prohibition, Guinan was disowned by her
native Waco, to which she responded by moving her parents to New York
and ramping up the questionable content of her act until she was banned in
Europe and much of New England.

Probably Texas' greatest film artist was the director King Vidor, son of a
lumber baron for whom the town of Vidor, next to Beaumont, was named.
Born in Galveston in 1894, he survived the great storm, which was the subject of his first attempt at filmmaking in his teens. After launching a small
studio in Houston in 1915 he headed for Hollywood. At a time when D. W.
Griffith and others were lionizing the white race, Vidor, a Christian Scien-
tist, attacked racism in his films, culminating in *Hallelujah!*, the industry's
first musical featuring an all African-American cast. He was equally outspo-
ken on the subject of war and militarism in 1925's *The Big Parade*, and won a
humanitarian award from the League of Nations for *Our Daily Bread*. Far
from just empty preaching, however, Vidor possessed a keen commercial
eye, directing such hits as *Northwest Passage* before teaming with David O.
Selznick for *Duel in the Sun*. Unlike other Hollywood personalities who tried
to put humble roots as far behind them as they could, King Vidor incorporated them into his artistic vision and relished his role of championing
thoughtful content within entertaining movies. After his retirement he
taught filmmaking at both USC and UCLA; nominated five times for an
Oscar as best director without winning, he received an honorary Academy
Award in 1978, four years before his death.

Texans of the Depression era could also listen to music that reflected
their own roots, most popularly the songs of Jimmie Rodgers, a Mississippi
railroad brakeman who couldn't read music. Forced from his job by virulent
tuberculosis, he took up performing as "The Singing Brakeman," cut his
first record in 1927, and responded to questions of how he was doing with a
famous gesture of both thumbs up. The progress of his disease, however,
caused him to relocate to the dry heat of Kerrville two years later. In his
music he introduced a plaintive wail that he called the "blue yodel," which
was widely imitated by a succession of country stars. During his four final
years in Texas he continued to record. Frequently referred to as the Father of
Country Music, Rodgers was the first person inducted into the Country
Music Hall of Fame in Nashville; the vote was unanimous.

SIXTY-FOUR

MORE FERGUSONS, AND WORSE

THE MOODYS' TENURE IN THE GOVERNOR'S MANSION had prolonged a tiff over a large greenhouse on the southwest grounds. When Ma Ferguson enlarged the structure during her husband's term, she had her name cast in concrete over the door. When she returned as governor in 1925 she was infuriated to discover that her name had been removed by either Hobby or Neff, and had it reinstated. It was said that when Mildred Moody was asked whether she would also obliterate the Ferguson name from the greenhouse, she refused with a comment that she wanted to do nothing to provoke them into making another run. It was a vain hope; in the 1932 primaries Ma Ferguson lay in ambush for Sterling.

"Two years ago you got the best governor money could buy," she proclaimed. "This year you have an opportunity to get the best governor patriotism can give you." It was blarney that a suffering public was eager to embrace. Jane Y. McCallum, the secretary of state appointed by Moody and continued by Sterling, was not shy about her sentiments in the race, publishing figures showing that during the final month of her first term, Ferguson's infamous liberality with pardons had freed 127 moonshiners, 124 robbers, 133 murderers, and 33 rapists.

Occupied with state affairs while going broke from neglecting his own, Sterling did not campaign until the final month before the primary, and that proved his undoing. Ma Ferguson gained her second term by fewer than 4,000 votes out of nearly a million cast, while Franklin Roosevelt and John Nance Garner crushed Hoover across the country. Garner had represented Uvalde in Congress for fifteen terms, the last one as Speaker of the House. Garner's capacity for making friends was evidenced in his first run for elective office, for Uvalde county judge in 1893; first he defeated his opponent, Ettie Rheiner, and then he married her. Once in Congress he lubricated his friendships with a free flow of bourbon, and over three decades built up a stock of goodwill that, as congressional point man for the coming blizzard of legislation, FDR would find invaluable.

Ferguson took office just as the state of the state was about to reach one of its historic lows. For decades farmers had been responding to good years by increasing their acreage, which depressed prices and ruined their own market. Wheat production, for instance, tripled during the twenties until that market collapsed in 1931. Introduction of the mechanized tractor only increased the farmers' ambitions; near Plainview in 1929, on one new factory farm alone, over 35,000 acres were plowed, and across the Panhandle in the last half of the twenties, a land area nearly the size of Massachusetts was furrowed, the tough, moisture-conserving prairie sod turned under and the bare dirt exposed to the elements to receive crops that, suddenly, never came. The stage was set for a climatic disaster of catastrophic proportions. Beginning in 1932 the spring rains failed repeatedly until the soil was parched a yard deep, and then the wind began to blow. What resulted became known as the Dust Bowl.

In minor dust storms the surface grit was lifted by strong prevailing winds, but in the great storms, electrostatic tension between hot air and an advancing cold front lifted dust more than a mile in the air, creating terrifying, boiling walls of dirt that swallowed whole towns at a time, reduced visibility to zero, and soiled the interior of homes no matter how carefully doors and windows were sealed. The denuded farms fed these storms helplessly, which increased in number from 22 in 1934 to 40 in 1935, 68 in 1936, and 72 in 1937 before the cycle began to subside. Pampa balladeer Woody Guthrie, long before he became famous, wrote his song "So Long, It's Been Good to Know You" in awe of a 1935 dust storm that convinced some Panhandle residents that doomsday had come, and there was only time to say good-bye. The song became an anthem for the thousands of prairie farmers who packed up and left. As banks foreclosed on worthless farms with houses half-obscured behind banks of dust, as many as one-third of all the farmers on the Staked Plains joined the caravan of "Okies" and others, many headed for migrant work in California. It was a tragedy documented by John Steinbeck in his novel *The Grapes of Wrath*, which was as savage in its attack on the capitalist system, with its bankers and cops and strikebreakers, as it was sensitive to the plight of environmental refugees.

This was one occasion where the Tejano immigrant workers and farmers had an advantage over their Anglo counterparts. While displaced white victims of the Dust Bowl headed for California, displaced Hispanics had the additional option of seeking better times south of the border, which several hundred thousand of them did. Another response, when the glutted immigrant labor market was exploited, was to strike, and in 1938 the largely Mexican pecan shellers, led by Emma Tenayuca, formed a union and struck for better wages than the nickel an hour they had been getting.

Federal aid began to arrive, but not before one dust storm in May 1934 blew all the way to Washington, D.C., darkening the skies during a hearing by a congressional committee to debate the seriousness of the drought in the West. Amarillo became the headquarters of the relief effort, and with complex coordination among the alphabet soup of the New Deal—the FSA, the AAA, the WPA, the CCC—busted farmers were given jobs building stock tanks, ranchers received emergency feed loans, and the Soil Erosion Service began trying to stabilize the landscape. Even after the expenditure of more than half a billion dollars, it still took the return of rain at the end of the decade to bring the Plains back to normal. By then, cotton acreage had fallen by half (partly the result of federal policy to stabilize prices by limiting production), and Texas farms had lost about a third of their value.

Texas politicians responded to the New Deal with schizophrenia. Republicans—bankers, investors, and corporate executives—in Texas and around the country despised Roosevelt with a venom reserved for a man who was seen as a traitor to his wealthy class. Texas conservative Democrats supported FDR at first, but became more gun-shy the larger the federal bureaucracy became. Eventually they reached a kind of accord with the Republicans, but they willingly cashed and spent all the federal checks that arrived, and made certain that the heavily muscled Texas congressional delegation procured a disproportionate share of all federal relief. Marvin Jones of Amarillo chaired the House Agriculture Committee, where he secured passage of the Emergency Farm Mortgage Act, the Agricultural Adjustment Act, and Farm Credit Act, among others. Brenham's James Buchanan chaired the all-important Appropriations Committee, and Garner's own well-groomed prize pupil, Sam Rayburn of Bonham, assumed many of Cactus Jack's old powers and eventually sat in the Speaker's chair. Rayburn was a key player in reforming the stock market to prevent any repeat of the crash, and in utilities regulation. Among these and four other powerful Texas committee chairmen, they brought pork home to Texas throughout the New Deal at least 30 percent above the national per capita average.

It was Ma Ferguson who was responsible for the dispensing of federal relief in Texas, and with Farmer Jim's desk once again next to hers, they gave in to their apparently genetic predisposition to corruption. Reconstruction Finance Corporation money was deposited in pet banks and a crony named Lawrence Westbrook was made director of the Texas Relief Commission, to oversee disbursements to local county boards, also staffed with Ferguson soldiers. That whole game was shut down by an investigation by the state senate in 1934, but an even worse scandal plagued the Texas Rangers. Ma fired the whole force for having supported Sterling, and replaced them with a small army of over 2,300 "special" Rangers, many of them thieves and thugs. In some instances, their raids on stills and gambling halls resulted not in destruction of the contraband, but in the Rangers actually taking over the business.

This much, at least, of the Ferguson travesty was obviated by ratification in December 1933 of the Twenty-first Amendment, making alcohol legal again. Thousands of moonshiners were now honest citizens again, but the contempt for law so evident on the part of the state administration only encouraged those whom the times had thrown onto their own resources anyway to turn to crime. Living by their wits and their firepower, gangs of outlaws such as those of "Machine Gun" Kelly, and Bonnie Parker and Clyde Barrow, enjoyed a heyday. The latter became the most notorious, he a fifth-grade dropout from Teleco, she an 85-pound wildcat from Dallas. Beginning in spring of 1932, operating either alone or with various accomplices whom they took in, such as Barrow's brother and sister-in-law, and Ray Hamilton, who had been his lover in prison, they embarked on a more or less continuous crime spree. They robbed, sometimes killing their victims or capriciously letting them go free, shooting cops in cold blood. ("Why, look-a-there," Bonnie said after shotgunning a prostrate highway patrolman, "his head bounced just like a rubber ball.") With the Rangers in disarray, it was the director of the state prison system, Lee Simmons, who coaxed Frank Hamer out of another retirement to track the pair.

Working alone, since he didn't know who could be trusted, Hamer trailed them for months. "I learned the kind of whiskey they drank," he wrote, "what they ate, the color, size, and texture of their clothes." Barrow was a master fugitive, reeling off as much as a thousand miles a day on confusing back roads. Hamer finally got one of the gang members to turn on them and set up an ambush with several trusted deputies, at the pair's mail drop in the northwest corner of Louisiana. Allegedly spurning a chance to surrender, Bonnie and Clyde died in a hail of bullets, their riddled car becoming a traveling tourist attraction.

Far less violent than the exploits of Bonnie and Clyde, but equally famous in its way, was a brothel in the town of La Grange, situated about equidistant from San Antonio, Austin, and Houston. Founded in 1844, this outpost of the world's oldest profession was surely one of the oldest continuously operating businesses in Texas. Both the La Grange city marshal and the Fayette County sheriff, two brothers named Loessin, regularly presented the issue of the madam, whose assumed name was Jessie Williams, to a grand jury, but they were concerned only that her girls get frequent medical exams. Before the Depression basic service, which was called a "four-get" (get up, get on, get off, get out), cost three dollars. When times got tough Miss Jessie halved that rate, but when customers still had trouble finding the cash, word got around that she would accept a chicken as the base fee. Thus was born the legendary Chicken Ranch. In addition to lowering her rates, she also supported local charities, and spread her own purchases fairly among the other local merchants. These were all sound New Deal principles, and indeed, Miss Jessie tolerated no criticism of Franklin Roosevelt in her establishment. She also tolerated no Negroes—and no kinky stuff; former doughboys who learned about varietal sex acts from women in France were doomed to disappointment. One veteran recalled trying to coax extra service from one girl who, sadly for him, was known as Deaf Eddie, and Miss Jessie overheard them. "She come acrashin' inta there," he recalled, "hittin' me with a big iron rod and hollerin'." His visitation privileges were suspended for a month.

Whether because she wished to honor the two-term tradition, or because she figured her record would attract more scorn than sympathy, Ma Ferguson decided not to run again in 1934. She was succeeded by the attorney general, Jimmy Allred, who was only thirty-five but lacked nothing in self-confidence. Born to poverty in Bowie, he served in the navy in the Great War, calmly asserting to shipmates that when he returned to Texas he would become governor. He served as an anti-Klan protégé of Pat Neff, who made him a DA. As attorney general beginning in 1930, he gained notice for his attempts to limit corporate domination of the legislature. Two positions he outlined while running for governor were a graduated tax on large chain stores, to improve the competitive ability of local merchants, and his opposition to a state sales tax, which would fall disproportionately on the poor. It was under Allred's oversight that the bulk of federal New Deal aid poured into the state, which he routed into the appropriate bureaucracies: $109 million from the Public Works Administration; $110 million from the Federal Emergency Relief Administration, from which nearly 300,000 Texans were kept afloat; $103 million from the Home Owner's Loan Corporation to stave off foreclosures; $178 million from the Works Progress Administration; additional jobs and money from the Civilian Conservation Corps, which employed 110,000 young bachelors who were required to send $25 of their $30-per-month wage home to their families; the Civil Works Administration; the National Youth Administration; and a host of farm aid programs.

It was not just the strong of back who gained employment; artists and eggheads got federal jobs, too. Painters in need covered public buildings and post offices with murals; photographers documented the hard times, and the great Dorothea Lange snapped some of her most unforgettable images in Texas. Folklorists traveled the back roads, recording traditional ballads and stories. The historical record that they left is priceless, but the make-work aspect of it was undeniable, and in some programs the efforts of unqualified workers produced spotty results. The ambitious Texas Historical Records Survey was undertaken in 1935 to systematize and catalog literally millions of public documents to make them more accessible to historians. Although guided by able professionals, one of whom subsequently became the Librarian of Congress, the clerks were often in over their heads and they left as much undone by the end of the program as they accomplished. But what they did complete was enough to allow a checklist of early Texas newspapers to be compiled, and bibliophile Thomas W. Streeter used their data to produce a reference catalog of early Texas imprints that is still in use.

In all, the New Deal bailed Texas out of the Depression with nearly $1.5 billion in direct aid. While that money did little to stimulate the domestic economy to right itself, the bridge it provided from one stable time to the next kept Texas and the nation from sliding into an irrecoverable decline. Its only dark stain was the discrimination that left most black and brown Texans to shift for themselves. Another population that suffered were tenant farmers, who often received little or none of the payments that farm owners received to take their land out of production; these were forced into the growing crowd of urban unemployed, or became hobos.

Texas' consciousness of its history, which had been growing since the turn of the twentieth century, meshed nicely into the make-work relief projects of the New Deal when it came time to celebrate the hundredth anniversary of Texas independence in 1936. Competition among Texas cities to host the world's fair–like Centennial Exposition was bruising. When Dallas got the nod with a $10 million local incentives package, history buffs in Houston were so upset they published a small book of blank pages outlining Dallas' contribution to the revolution. Houston made do with construction of a gigantic concrete obelisk at the site of the Battle of San Jacinto. Financier Jesse H. Jones, always an energetic Houston backer, got federal aid for the $1.5 million cost by promising that it would not be taller than the Washington Monument. He did conveniently leave the 34-foot Lone Star at the summit out of his calculations, under which the spire topped the Washington Monument by fifteen feet. Austin got into a controversy with its own salute to the centennial, a 27-story limestone tower on the University of Texas campus to house the main library, surmounted by a clock and carillon. Faculty member J. Frank Dobie, a folklorist, author of *Coronado's Children,* and a state literary lion, carped that the money would be better spent on teachers and programs. Frustrated that the funds were legally limited to expenditures for physical plant, Dobie referred to the vaguely phallic-looking structure as the last erection of an impotent administration, and lost his job.

As the economy began to recover, Texans' attention was snatched by an unexpected tragedy. In the boomtown of New London in the heart of the East Texas field, the new high school boasted no fewer than seven producing oil wells on its campus, making it one of the richest districts in the nation. To save a little money in its construction, contractors allowed gas-fired steam radiators to empty into the walls, instead of venting them into flues. When gas started leaking it permeated the entire structure—under the floors and in the walls and crawlspaces. On Monday, March 18, 1937, there was a shattering explosion; the red tile roof lifted into the air as walls and windows blew out, then crashed down into the debris. After survivors were rounded up—one was blown two hundred feet and had amnesia—and body parts were fitted together, the death toll was 293, the worst school disaster in American history. "It's the old story," a consulting engineer told the inquest, "of saving a few dollars and endangering a thousand lives."

Thirteen candidates lined up to succeed Jimmy Allred as governor in 1938, including Pa Ferguson, who was attempting yet another comeback. In the primary, Texans did have an exceptional candidate in Ernest O. Thompson; as mayor of Amarillo he had strong-armed utility rate reductions for the people, and as railroad commissioner his artful interpreting of the regulations kept small wildcatters in the game, even while prorationing itself intrinsically favored the huge conglomerates. He could have made an outstanding governor. Unfortunately for Thompson, there was facing him on the primary ballot one of the most curious phenomena in the history of Texas politics. W. (for Wilbert) Lee O'Daniel was a flour salesman, born in Ohio and raised and worked in Kansas, relocated to Louisiana, and finally settled in Fort Worth in 1925 as manager of the Burrus Flour Mills. He was an adequate salesman, although unsophisticated when it came to advertising; all that changed when he discovered the power of radio. There was in Fort Worth a country musician named Bob Wills who had been playing local clubs while developing a new style that became known as Texas Swing, which combined musical elements of Appalachia, the cowboy era, and work songs of the black field hands. O'Daniel was offended by the band, which played in dance halls, and by their music, which included interjections of "Lord, Lord!" Wills also drank, which was even worse. However, when Wills hectored O'Daniel into sponsoring them on a radio show as the Light Crust Doughboys, sales of Burrus flour skyrocketed.

O'Daniel was soon doing the commercial advertisements himself, utilizing the running tagline "Pass the Biscuits, Pappy." He was also offering bits of homespun philosophy and homilies to the radio audience, and soon found himself a major celebrity. That was a tonic rubbed into his ego; he began cracker-barrel expositions on the subject of politics, a subject of which he understood virtually nothing, but as his bile rose against the political establishment early in 1938 he told his listeners that perhaps he should be in the primary for governor, and each one should mail him a penny postcard if they wanted him to enter the race. In short order he received more than fifty thousand postcards and Pappy O'Daniel, political phenomenon, was off and running.

The centerpiece of Pappy O'Daniel's campaign was an old age pension for all Texans of thirty dollars per month. He toured the state in an unreliable old bus with his family and his own band, now performing his own songs, maudlin horrors with titles like "The Boy Who Never Gets Too Big to Comb His Mother's Hair." Droves of people came to listen to him—8,000 in San Angelo, which was one-third of the entire town. O'Daniel raised his campaign expenses by sending his children through the crowds collecting contributions. In the primary balloting, O'Daniel polled over 573,000 votes, Thompson 231,000—not the last time that Texans would choose an affable novice with big empty promises over an experienced if somewhat austere veteran. Thompson confessed that he never saw O'Daniel coming. Rather, "the first thing I knew he passed all of us and left me with a cloud of flour dust in my eyes." Even with thirteen candidates in the field, O'Daniel avoided a runoff with 51.4 percent of the vote. Pa Ferguson's comeback bid fell flat; he polled only 3,800.

O'Daniel held his inauguration in the University of Texas football stadium, a raucous affair serenaded by dozens of different bands. His gubernatorial record is easy to summarize. He accomplished virtually nothing; the legislators were appalled by him, and while they did pass a state old-age pension, they passed no appropriation to pay for it—the ultimate show of Texas lawmakers' disdain. Undeterred, O'Daniel ran for reelection in 1940, with a campaign card touting the lyrics of his song "My Million Dollar Smile" and all one needed to know about his political philosophy:

My Platform:
THE TEN COMMANDMENTS
My Motto:
THE GOLDEN RULE
My Slogan:
LESS JOHNSON GRASS AND POLITICIANS
MORE SMOKESTACKS AND BUSINESS MEN
My Tax Plan:
THE ONE THE LEGISLATURE PASSES

The earnest Ernest Thompson was again his main opponent, but he never had a chance. Typical of his effort was a rally in Greenville, to which almost nobody came; when asked why, he said disgustedly, "I don't yodel." Ma was the designated Ferguson in this primary, but she polled only 100,000 votes to Thompson's 256,000. O'Daniel passed them both, said Thompson, like a freight train passing a tramp, with 645,000.

Morris Sheppard died on April 9, 1941, having served longer in the Senate than any other Texan, thirty-eight years. Governor O'Daniel, who desired the seat for himself, appointed Andrew Jackson Houston, almost eighty-seven years old, superintendent of the San Jacinto Battlefield and only surviving child of Sam Houston, to fill it temporarily. It was a brilliant if cynical publicity stunt. Against the wishes of his spinster daughters, the elderly Houston made the trip to Washington, entered the Senate as its second-oldest member in history, attended a committee meeting, announced his support for O'Daniel, and died two days before the special election.

In his run for Sheppard's Senate seat, the governor was opposed by twenty-six others who wanted the job; his most dangerous rival proved to be Lyndon Baines Johnson, a native of Johnson City, the seat of Blanco County in the Hill Country fifty miles west of Austin. Born to humble circumstances in 1909, his résumé included a stint teaching poor Tejanos in the Brush Country town of Cotulla, which imbued him with a deep empathy for the poor. He then spent four years as administrative assistant to "Cowboy Congressman" Richard Kleberg of the King Ranch, and began weaving a web of Washington contacts. He married well when he wed Claudia Alta Taylor in 1934, whom he renamed Lady Bird to match his own initials. She not only had enough money to make them independent, she had the brains, patience, and discretion to serve as an effective political wife. Opportunity knocked at Johnson's door when Jimmy Allred introduced him to President Roosevelt on a Gulf fishing trip. The fast-talking young Johnson hitched a ride back to Washington on FDR's train, and emerged as director of the National Youth Administration in Texas, which he quietly integrated to bring New Deal boon to the ethnic population. In 1937 he ran for and won an open congressional seat, and three years later, not to make too fine a point of his relationship with Roosevelt, announced his candidacy for the U.S. Senate from the White House. Johnson outspent O'Daniel six dollars to one, and by midnight after the election led him by some three thousand votes. Four days later, though, after late boxes were tallied with improbably huge margins for O'Daniel, Johnson lost by 1,300. It was a lesson that LBJ never forgot.

When Pappy O'Daniel was elevated to the federal Senate, even Texas' Democratic wags had to admit their contentment; just to get him out of the state would improve the political climate. Sheppard's unexpired term was up the next year, and O'Daniel had to stand for reelection in the primary against both Dan Moody and Jimmy Allred, both former boy wonder governors who remained very popular. O'Daniel beat them back, but with a small margin; his popularity continued to decline during his full term, during which one historian famously noted that no proposal he introduced ever got more than four votes. He retired from politics in 1948 as empty-headed as he had entered, but he left as an undefeated heavyweight. He attempted two comebacks in the fifties, ranting about the Communist influence behind racial desegregation, but once gone, he stayed gone. Although the center plank of his platform in running for governor had been old-age pensions, O'Daniel in the Senate was a consistent and vocal foe of Roosevelt and the New Deal. On this point if no other he was in accord with much of the Texas congressional delegation. In the early years of the New Deal Texas politicians went along with it, partly because the condition of the country seemed to require some extraordinary effort. They were also relieved because Roosevelt, rather than acting like the socialist many had feared, retained Hoover's director of the Reconstruction Finance Corporation, the enormously powerful Houston financier Jesse H. Jones. FDR lost the support of the Texas delegation one by one, partly over the growing national dependency on federal relief, and even more over FDR's attempt to cleanse Congress of anti–New Deal Democrats, including eight Texans, among them Kleberg and the archconservative Martin Dies from Southeast Texas. The last thread tore when the president dumped John Nance Garner as vice president when he ran for a third term, scalding Texans who expected FDR to retire and Cactus Jack to have an easy waltz into the White House in 1940. The average citizens perceived a clearer picture, however. Roosevelt was widely venerated, and despite how much the Texas political establishment had come to loathe him, Texans approved of his third term, by a vote of 905,000 to 211,000. After the election, the thorny puzzle of how to wrest control of the Democratic Party away from Roosevelt and his liberals was the issue front and center for most Texas politicians, but then the whole question was sidelined by events in Hawaii on December 7, 1941.

SIXTY-FIVE

TEXAS AT WAR, AGAIN

LONG BEFORE PEARL HARBOR, ABHORRENCE OF GERMAN national socialism was widespread, even to the point of joining foreign services to fight it. Numerous Texas pilots had already left for the Royal Canadian Air Force for volunteer service in Europe, and still others had joined the "Flying Tigers" of Claire Lee Chennault, a native of Commerce in Northeast Texas and one of America's most distinguished flying officers and instructors. Deaf and difficult, he was pushed into retirement in 1937, but became an advisor to Chiang Kai-shek and formed a volunteer air force, the "Flying Tigers," to fight on behalf of the Chinese.

The day after Pearl Harbor, President Roosevelt addressed the Congress and asked for a declaration of war. It was Texas Senator Tom Connally, chairman of the Foreign Relations Committee, who introduced the resolution. According to the War Department, no other state contributed a larger portion of its manpower to the war, as 728,000 Texas men donned a uniform during the next four years. Twenty thousand of them were Aggies—students or graduates of Texas A&M University—and nearly three-quarters of the Aggies were officers, including thirty-nine generals and one admiral; six Aggies returned with Medals of Honor.

The German Texans in the Hill Country did not suffer any repeat of the browbeating they took in 1917. The disdain under which they lived from antebellum times because of their opposition to slavery had finally dissolved into the past, and the emphasis now was on common purpose and unanimity. That did not apply, however, to Texans of Japanese descent. For them, owing to Pearl Harbor, Texas' assumption of a war footing demonstrated a resurgence of our historic xenophobia, which in the case of Japanese Texans had already been building for many years. In the early part of the century Japanese immigrants were welcomed as a boost to the rice industry, but as time passed the experience soured for them. When they succeeded they were seen as a threat, and when they failed they were seen as a nuisance. Once rice commodities took a dive after World War I, the Japanese diversified into citrus growing and truck farming, which dispersed them into an unwelcoming society, and then their numbers were increased by Japanese seeking to escape ethnic hatred in California. Three years before the U.S. Congress shut the door to further Japanese immigration in 1924, the Texas legislature barred Japanese residents from buying or even leasing more land than they already occupied.

After Pearl Harbor, the manicured Japanese Tea Garden in San Antonio suddenly became the "Chinese" Tea Garden, and the family that had tended it for twenty years was thrown out of its house. Shortly after America entered the war, the Justice Department fenced off three internment camps in Texas: a converted minimum-security women's prison at Seagoville, near Dallas; a former Civilian Conservation Corps camp at Kenedy, between San Antonio and Corpus Christi; and a Farm Security Administration migrant labor camp at Crystal City, in the Brush Country, which became the largest camp administered by the Immigration and Naturalization Service. While these camps housed some Japanese-Americans from Hawaii and the West Coast, they took in mostly Axis nationals from Latin America, the countries of which were U.S. allies in the war but had no internment facilities of their own. Many Japanese Texans were rounded up and questioned, but they were not seen as a threat and were not imprisoned for the duration of the war. Instead, many enlisted in the celebrated 442nd Regimental Combat Team and won individual and unit citations fighting in Europe.

In addition to the 728,000 men, 12,000 Texas women also served in World War II, more than from any other state. Most prominent among them was Oveta Culp Hobby, the wife of Texas' World War I governor, commander of the Women's Army Auxiliary Corps (WAACs), and the first woman in the army to attain the rank of colonel. Born in Killeen in 1905, she early demonstrated her withering intelligence and no-nonsense discernment; at age five she was asked to take the WCTU temperance pledge but she declined. She didn't care to drink, she said, but when she grew up, she might. In sixth grade she entered a spelling bee to win a Bible that was the prize, announcing to the teacher, "You might as well write my name in it right now." She won. She lost school days at fourteen when she accompanied her father to Austin when he was elected to the legislature; she was trading in classes for real experience. She went on to attend Mary Hardin Baylor College in Belton. From 1925 to 1931 she was the parliamentarian of the Texas House of Representatives, when she moved to Houston to become assistant to the city attorney. There she renewed her acquaintance with Will Hobby, now fifty-three and publisher of Governor Sterling's *Houston Post;* they had met twelve years earlier, when Oveta was fourteen and her father was in the legislature. Hobby had been widowed since his first wife and first lady, Willie

Cooper, died in 1929, and he married Oveta in February 1931. She became an indispensable part of the *Post*'s operation, as well as undertaking a long list of charitable and civic responsibilities.

Will and Oveta Hobby added a radio station to their newspaper interests, and she went to Washington in June 1941 for meetings with the Federal Communications Commission. At the request of Generals David Searles and George C. Marshall (and with Hobby's agreement) she became head of the Women's Interest section of the army's public relations bureau. Immediately after Pearl Harbor, the army was showered with letters, ten thousand a day, from women asking what they could do to serve. Marshall asked her to design a Women's Army Auxiliary Corps, survey similar units in European armies with suggestions of how they might be improved, and provide a list of women who might command it. When she completed her report, Marshall ignored the list and asked her to take command. She agreed, but the army brass quickly discovered that she had no intention of enlisting women to bake cookies. She demanded, and got, a list of 239 specific tasks—meaningful jobs, from folding parachutes to the air warning service—which women would be rated for. She knew perfectly well what asses officers can be, and when the regulation was promulgated that WAACs who became "pregnant without permission" would receive dishonorable discharges and lose their benefits, Hobby bridled. When she insisted that the fathers receive the same treatment, the rule was modified to honorable discharge with benefits. She designed the no-nonsense uniforms—no lingerie, no pleated skirts, topped with trim and sensible "Hobby hats." She declined to come and go through the rear door of the officers' club, and generally battled the army command to a standoff, although she maintained, ladylike, that she never had to fight, really, for such progress. The WAACs became so integral to the army's operation that the word "auxiliary" was finally dropped from the name in 1943; Oveta Hobby resigned command of the WACs in 1945 with a Distinguished Service Medal.

The mindless discrimination that Hobby had to overcome was displayed even more vividly to the Women's Air Service Pilots (WASPs). With male fliers needed for combat, the idea was floated to have women perform domestic flying needs, such as ferrying new planes from the manufacturers to the various air bases. As with the black airmen training in Tuskegee, Alabama, unsympathetic officers tried to make it as difficult as they possibly could. The first women in the program were required to already be licensed pilots, and were sent to train at the Houston Municipal Airport. Because the program was experimental it was not actually taken into the military; hence when the cadets arrived in Houston they found no accommodations, no transportation, and often not even any food. Then the program was installed at Avenger Field, near Sweetwater, in the middle of nowhere fifty miles west of Abilene. The cadets were required to pay their own expenses to get there (and home, if they washed out) and to pay room and board to share barracks with scorpions and rattlesnakes. Four in ten did wash out. Nevertheless, the 1,074 women who graduated flew 60 million domestic miles for the military, ferrying, deploying, and test piloting planes repaired from battle damage. Thirty-eight were killed in crashes. A bill in 1944 that would have adopted the program into the military was defeated after lobbying by male civilian pilots, and not until 1977 did the WASPs receive recognition and veterans' benefits.

Oveta Hobby was as conservative a Texan as they come, but she had a sensitive spot when it came to racial discrimination and as an editor at the *Houston Post* she made sure to include news of relevance to the African-American community. In organizing the WAAC, though, she did not buck the army's policy of segregation, and two of the twenty-seven WAAC units were for black women. The fact that black servicemen were relegated to cooking and janitorial tasks did not stifle news that some displayed extreme valor overseas. One of the first stories out of Pearl Harbor was of the heroism of Doris Miller, a mess attendant on the battleship *West Virginia*. His ship was already doomed from being torpedoed six times and hit by two bombs, when the neighboring *Arizona* blew up and showered her with flaming debris. Miller rushed to the main deck, where he carried the mortally wounded captain to shelter. He then took control of an unoccupied machine gun and began firing at the attacking Japanese. Subsequent publicity drives credited him with shooting down between two and five planes, but Miller himself only said that he thought he hit one. His actions nevertheless were enough to earn him a Navy Cross. He subsequently served in the cruiser *Indianapolis*, and was still a mess attendant when he was killed in the sinking of the carrier *Liscombe Bay* in 1943.

Despite the menial tasks that African-American servicemen were relegated to, "Dorie" Miller was not the only black Texas sailor to win high distinction. During the battle for Guadalcanal, mess attendant first class Leonard Roy Harmon was killed onboard the cruiser *San Francisco* while shielding a wounded sailor with his body. He was posthumously awarded the Navy Cross, and the following year he became the first black American to have a ship named after him, with the launching of the destroyer escort USS *Harmon*. The USS *Miller* followed.

If there was one theater of the war where heroism was needed, it was the Pacific. The Japanese pounce on Pearl Harbor coincided with their attacks on British, French, and Dutch colonies as well. Their conquest was so rapid that isolated Allied naval units were trapped behind their line of advance and left to fight as best they could. One such ship was the heavy cruiser *Houston*, which was one of FDR's favorite ships; he had taken two long cruises on her, and she was a vessel, along with the *Texas*, in which the people of the state took a particular interest. She hurriedly formed a joint task force of British, Australian, American, and Dutch warships to oppose the Japanese takeover of the resource-rich Dutch East Indies. In weeks of sharp action in early 1942, the Japanese claimed to have sunk the *Houston* so many times she became known as the Galloping Ghost, and indeed she lost fifty-five men on February 4 when a bomb hit the after eight-inch gun turret, but the ship was saved. The *Houston* and the Australian *Perth* were the only Allied cruisers to survive a brutal defeat off Bali on February 19.

They refueled at Jakarta and received orders to attempt an escape from the area around the west end of Java. Putting to sea, they chanced across a Japanese landing at Banten Bay and attacked with guns blazing on the night of February 28, sinking or disabling a number of ships, but it was suicidal. The landing was covered by an overmatching force, including the *Mikumi* and *Mogami*, two of the largest and most modern cruisers in the Japanese fleet. *Houston* trained her two remaining main battery turrets one to starboard and one to port and fought to the last. Only 360 of the crew of 1,015 survived, and 75 of them died in prison camps in the following three and a half years. *Houston*'s captain, A. H. Rooks, was awarded a posthumous Medal of Honor, and the crew was given a Presidential Unit Citation, one of only three awarded to cruisers in World War II.

Also lost with Java was a battalion of the 36th (Texas) Division of National Guard, which had been mobilized in November 1941 and sent to the Pacific. They docked in Pearl Harbor and left again, hearing news of the attack a week later. The unit was the 2nd Battalion of the 131st Field Artillery, and they were sent in secret on the Dutch steamer *Bloemfontein* to defend an airfield on Java. When the Japanese overran the island, they were compelled to surrender on March 10. They became known as the Lost Battalion, as the U.S. government kept mum about their fate, even as they were herded into forced labor camps to work on the Burma-Thailand Railroad—later fictionalized into building a bridge over the Kwai River.

In the early months of the war almost all the news from the Pacific was bleak, but Roosevelt's choice for commander in chief of that theater was one of the unlikeliest, and shrewdest, of his career—Chester Nimitz, from a German family in Fredericksburg, a place where the deepest water was the fishing holes in the Pedernales River. His career was one of the most varied in the navy, having seen duty on almost every kind of warship, and his loyalty to the service was extraordinary. As a young commander he could have left the navy rather than be court-martialed for running his destroyer aground, but he took his medicine and returned to duty. He lost part of a finger while studying a diesel engine at too close quarters, but mastered the machines so completely that a private manufacturer offered him ten times his navy salary to enter the private sector. He refused. At home ashore, where he designed a naval ROTC curriculum and became the ranking member of the Board of Submarine Design, or at sea, where by 1938 he was commander of the heavy cruiser *Augusta,* he was an extraordinary thinker.

Nimitz had not only predicted a Japanese sneak attack fifteen years before it occurred, he also foresaw that American naval officers on active command in the Pacific would be made scapegoats for the national lack of preparedness. He confided to his son that he intended to remain at a desk, stateside, until after the war began. Indeed, he refused the command at Pearl Harbor, which went instead to Admiral Husband Kimmel, whose career was ruined when the Japanese did attack and the navy pinned the scope of the disaster on him. Roosevelt, who spent eight years as assistant secretary of the navy in the Wilson administration, and whose shrewd eye for talent was legendary, jumped Nimitz over twenty-eight ranking admirals to take command of the shattered remnants of the Pacific fleet.

There the realities of the situation—his battleships sunk or disabled and with only four aircraft carriers—compelled Nimitz to deploy his few big guns in support of carrier task forces, which was the first basic redesign of the naval battle fleet since Nelson. In the opening months of the war, Nimitz bought strategic victories with tactical defeats in the battles of the Coral Sea and the Solomon Islands. He also had the good sense to retain Kimmel's staff, including a key codebreaker who surmised, on the thinnest evidence, that the next enemy strike would be at Midway. Leaving Hawaii itself without an effective defense, Nimitz deployed his weakened forces to ambush the Japanese there, a gamble that paid off with the sinking of four enemy fleet carriers and halting Japanese expansion only six months after Pearl Harbor.

With a gambler like Nimitz commanding the Pacific Theater, it's no surprise that the most decorated sailor in the war served under him, and was a fellow Texan, Lieutenant Commander Samuel David Dealey of Dallas, nephew of George B. Dealey of the *Dallas Morning News*. For him the war got personal in a hurry, with the sinking of the dreadnought *Nevada* at Pearl Harbor, a ship on which he had served, and with the death of his best friend on the destroyer *Reuben James,* sunk by a U-boat near Iceland. After months of waiting, Dealey learned he was to be given charge of the new submarine *Harder,* and when given the commander's traditional prerogative of where to place the deck gun, forward or abaft of the conning tower, answered, "Forward, of course. Whom are we running away from?" In four cruises he sank fifteen Japanese vessels, before being given the job in June 1944 of fetching British and Australian commandos from the north coast of enemy-held Borneo.

What made Dealey remarkable was his penchant for attacking destroyers, whose principal purpose is the destruction of submarines. Dealey realized that the Japanese navy was glutted with big powerful capital ships, but that their destroyer screens were inadequate. Sink their destroyers, he reasoned, and the big ships would be at the mercy of American submarines. This was a view completely against conventional wisdom, but Nimitz was not about to contradict someone with so much fight in him. Dealey sank two Japanese destroyers on his way to Borneo—the second of which he lured in by leaving his periscope up as bait—and rescued the commandos, who had been operating in constant danger for two years. In retiring through the Sibutu Passage, Dealey attempted to carry out one other assignment, which was to survey the Japanese fleet anchorage at Tawi-Tawi, but he was forced to submerge when lookouts sighted not one but two picket destroyers. Rather than run silent and sneak away like any sensible commander, Dealey calmly plotted a firing solution and sank them both with one salvo of four torpedoes as they crossed his bow. Thinking himself under attack by a huge force of submarines, Admiral Soemu Toyoda sortied his three battleships, four cruisers, and only eight destroyers, abandoned the Tawi-Tawi anchorage, and sailed straight into the Battle of the Philippine Sea, and a crippling defeat. As they left the harbor, the *Harder* was sighted and one destroyer peeled off to attack, which Dealey dispatched by firing two torpedoes zero angle on the bow—down the throat. The destroyer blew up as Dealey dived under her, the concussion rocking the sub severely. Subsequently they endured a three-hour depth-charging so relentless that at one point, one of the Australian commandos sidled up to Dealey and said, "I say, old man, would you mind taking us back to Borneo?"

The *Harder* was lost with all hands on her sixth cruise, the crew having earned two Presidential Unit Citations, and Dealey having earned, among other decorations, a Navy Cross with three gold stars, a Silver Star, a U.S. Army Distinguished Service Cross pinned on him by Douglas MacArthur, and the Congressional Medal of Honor.

Atlantic operations were slower to take shape. They began with the invasion of North Africa, at which a Texas icon from the previous world war resurfaced. At the time of her launch, the battleship *Texas* was the most powerful afloat; now she was a wallowing antique, her reciprocating steam engines too slow to keep up with the turbine-powered fleet. Her Pacific sisters, however, lay on the bottom of Pearl Harbor, and the new third-generation super-dreadnoughts were still at the builders, so she was still every inch a capital ship. *Texas* had been extensively rebuilt during the war, a torpedo blister added to her hull, massive tripod masts and antiaircraft batteries added to her superstructure. Oddly enough, throughout World War I her main battery had never come into action, but off the coast of Morocco the muzzle caps were yanked off the fifty-foot barrels and the fourteen-inch guns roared to life. After North Africa the *Texas* entered the Mediterranean to support the landings in Italy and southern France. The accuracy of her gunnery crews had been honed by years of pressure as a flagship in the peacetime Navy, and during the Italian campaign, *Texas* ranged up and down the coast in fire support. Despite the doubts of navy-scoffing army officers, she saved countless dogfaces' lives by laying 1,400-pound shells (accurately referred to as "haymakers") spot on Axis fortifications and gun emplacements.

Texas materialized again off the coast of Normandy on June 6, 1944, and soldiers waiting on a troopship three-quarters of a mile away felt the concussion of her ten-gun broadsides in support of the landings. After the beachhead was established, *Texas* engaged German shore batteries, many of which emplacements mounted old eleven-inch naval rifles, the standard armament of the German navy in World War I and possibly the most accurate large gun in that conflict. On June 25 *Texas* fought a three-hour duel against one shore battery. She maneuvered warily and was straddled numerous times before taking an eleven-inch hit in the conning tower; the hit shattered the wheelhouse, wounding thirteen and killing one, the only fatality of her career. She regained her steering ability and finished the fight, before heading into the Mediterranean to support landings in southern France in August.

One of the Texans wading ashore under the *Texas'* guns there was a baby-faced son of a tenant farmer from Farmersville, northeast of Dallas. His name was Audie Murphy, and his family had experienced the full brunt of the Depression. Picking cotton, living occasionally in boxcars, galled at having to accept charity even from teachers when he was able to go to school, Murphy grew up resentful. "Every time my old man couldn't feed the children he had," he said once, "he got him another one." There were nine, not counting three who died young. He was also a crack shot, having grown up hunting rabbits and squirrels. Only five feet seven inches and 130 pounds, he enlisted at Greenville as soon as he turned eighteen in June 1942. Fighting his way through North Africa, Sicily, Italy, and then France, this unlikely boy was thrice wounded, promoted to lieutenant on the battlefield, and accumulated every decoration for bravery in the gift of the Army, culminating in his single-handedly stopping a German armor-led assault near the French town of Holtzwihr on January 26, 1945.

After a three-day action that disabled both his tank destroyers and left only thirty survivors in his company, he was ordered to hold a forest position and wait for reinforcements (they never arrived). When the Germans counterattacked with two hundred men behind six tanks, Murphy leaped onto a burning tank destroyer (whose ammunition was likely to explode at any moment) and held them off with the .50-caliber machine gun. Calling in artillery strikes virtually on his own head, Murphy was asked how close the enemy was to his position and he shot back, "Hold the phone, I'll let you talk to one of the bastards!" Wounded by shell fragments from two hits on his destroyer, Murphy killed about fifty of the Germans before they retreated. Informed in May that he had won the Medal of Honor, Murphy wrote his sister that the accolade accrued five more points toward getting to come home.

Civilian life was a tough adjustment for Murphy, however. In 1949 he published a memoir entitled *To Hell and Back*, which became a national best-seller and then a successful motion picture, with Murphy playing himself, reliving the horror of the Holtzwihr assault. Eventually he appeared in more than forty films, and while there have been worse actors in Hollywood, and while Murphy gained a measure of success also as a writer and composer, he often found it difficult to live with his violent memories. Most biographical sketches of him discreetly omit mention of his subsequent terrors of nightmares and nervous reactiveness, his struggle with alcohol, and other symptoms of severe post-traumatic stress. He was killed in a plane crash in Virginia in 1971, a few days short of his forty-seventh birthday, and was buried with full military honors in Arlington National Cemetery.

Other Texas units distinguished themselves in Europe. While one battalion of the 36th (Texas) Division's 131st Field Artillery was lost in Java, most of the rest of the unit saw action in the Atlantic Theater. They participated in the landing at Oran, Algeria, and were the first ashore at Salerno, and thus the first Americans to land on mainland Europe. (As often happened with war journalism, the correspondents who filmed the invasion needed some retakes, which were staged without benefit of enemy fire. That was why home viewers of exciting newsreels saw their Texas Division storming into Italy with goofy grins on their faces.) After Normandy, they fought through Italy, France, and Germany, suffering 4,000 dead, 19,000 wounded, and 4,300 missing, but in return accounting for 175,000 prisoners taken. The 90th "Texas-Oklahoma" Division, the Tough 'Ombres, were mobilized after the T-Patchers. Their first action was on D-Day, then through the Ardennes and across the Rhine, taking a total of 18,000 casualties.

Many other Texans who served in World War II acquitted themselves with extraordinary heroism, including Medal of Honor recipient John Cary Morgan, an oil field roughneck from Vernon. As the copilot of a crippled B-17, whose pilot was crazed by a head wound and with interphone communication with the rest of the crew broken, he kept the plane in formation for two hours and completed a crucial bombing run—an exploit that was the basis for the novel *Twelve O'Clock High!* James Earl Rudder, from the village of Eden near San Angelo, led the 2nd Ranger Battalion in scaling hundred-foot cliffs facing the Normandy beaches. Himself twice wounded leading a unit that took 50 percent casualties, he survived to become president of Texas A&M. Macario García of Sugar Land, near Houston, became one of five Tejanos to earn Medals of Honor when he cleaned out two German machine gun nests. After he returned home he made news again, for being refused service in a restaurant because he was Hispanic.

The war made political careers, too. Lyndon Johnson managed to get some flying time in the Pacific, as he helped Washington brass plot strategy for that theater. When Pappy O'Daniel left the Governor's Mansion for the Senate, the lieutenant governor elevated to fill the vacancy was Coke Stevenson, the last of the Texas governors to have come from a log cabin, and a future nemesis of Johnson's. Born near Mason at the northern edge of the Hill Country in 1888, he and his family later relocated to Junction, and Stevenson early supported himself driving a freight wagon, educating himself (after rudimentary schooling) by the light of campfires. He entered banking by starting as a janitor and working up to cashier; he read for the law and passed the bar. He came to be Junction's leading citizen, with a hand in the drugstore, the hardware store, the car dealership, the newspaper, and the movie theater. Between 1914 and 1921 Junction's citizens made him county attorney and county judge, before sending him to the state house in 1928. He served two terms as speaker of the house before being elected lieutenant governor in 1938, and succeeded O'Daniel as governor on August 4, 1941. Elevation was soon accompanied by heartbreak, however, as he converted the mansion library into a sickroom for his wife Fay, who was terminally ill and unable to climb stairs. He rose at six, made his own breakfast, drove himself to the capitol, worked all day, and turned the lights out when he left. Hard work and thrift had gotten him where he was, and he believed that all would come right if Texas just followed his example.

O'Daniel's regime had left Texas about $25 million in debt. It was a serious enough deficit that the federal government began threatening to withhold its pension contributions unless something was done to generate state revenue. Conservative beyond what any had yet imagined, Stevenson's response instead was to cut spending to the point of the state withdrawing from even its most basic responsibilities. Institutions for the deaf and blind fell into disrepair and disrepute; state judges not only did not get the raise they asked for, the governor let vacancies on the benches lie fallow, increasing the workload of the remaining jurists. Shrilly attacked by New Dealers, Stevenson smiled sardonically, smoked one of his 150 pipes, and gained the nickname of Calculatin' Coke. "Blessed is he who sayeth nothing," ran his principal beatitude, "for he shall not be misquoted." What he was waiting on was for the hated feds to spend more money in Texas, and come for the oil and cotton and beef that a war effort was sure to require.

He was not disappointed. Prewar preparedness spending, thanks to the powerful muscle in Congress, amounted to some $600 million. Texas now held more than half of all proven oil reserves in the country, and while the war was usually thought of as one fought overseas, German U-boats occasionally brought the conflict right up to the Gulf coast, torpedoing freighters and tankers within sight of the beach. The fear of commando strikes on the massive petroleum complexes in Southeast Texas was very real, and coastwatching was vigilant. FDR's Interior Secretary, Harold Ickes, foresaw this, and had been trying for two years to get a secure pipeline built from Texas to refineries in the East, but without success. With the reality of war, construction of the so-called "Big Inch," a 24-inch pipeline laid in a four-foot deep trench from Longview in the East Texas oilfield to Illinois and thence Pennsylvania and New York, began in August 1942. Amazingly, the first Texas crude reached Illinois only six months later, and distribution lines to the East Coast were finished six months after that. A few months later approval was given to construct a 20-inch pipeline—the "Little Big Inch"—to carry refined products such as gasoline from refineries near Houston to the East Coast, and it was finished in only fourteen months. Both completed at a cost of $140 million, by the end of the war the two pipelines had carried a staggering 350 million gallons of Texas petroleum and products.

One economic measure, value added by manufacturing, quadrupled in Texas during the course of the war, and while the New Deal had kept thousands from starving or losing their homes, it was war spending that in fact ended the Depression. Convair, General Dynamics, and North American Aviation employed some sixty thousand workers in Dallas and Fort Worth to crank out B-24 "Liberator" bombers and then B-36s. A large percentage of them labored in the mile-long assembly building at the Vultee Aircraft Corporation plant at Carswell. Ammunition was made in Texarkana, Daingerfield sprouted a steel mill, and a gigantic tin smelter was put into operation at Texas City. The Houston Ship Channel proved its worth in ways unexpected during its dredging, as Brown Shipbuilding slipped some three hundred sub chasers, minesweepers, landing craft, and destroyer escorts into Green's Bayou—a waterway so narrow that the vessels were launched sideways. Concrete barges were produced by San Jacinto Shipbuilding Corporation, and on the ship channel more than two hundred workhorse freighters known as Liberty Ships were assembled by Todd Shipyards. Of the twenty thousand workers, the supervisors were the only ones who understood naval architecture, but standardized blueprints and mass production kept crucial convoys supplied. In all, nearly four dozen companies in the Houston area alone held defense contracts. It was all funded of course by vast federal deficit spending, but it allowed Stevenson and other anti-Roosevelt conservative Democrats to preside over a full economic recovery in the state.

Texans on the home front did all that was required of them; they bought bonds, planted victory gardens, held drives for scrap metal, and accepted most of the federally mandated ration system—except on the commodity of gasoline, a conflict that Coke Stevenson energetically took up with the authorities. Planners had determined the gasoline ration—three gallons per week for a nonfarm household—without reckoning the vast distances that had to be covered in Texas. Stevenson jawboned an informal compromise, under which local ration boards issued higher-priority cards to Texas rural families. More serious trouble loomed when federal rubber czars criticized Texans for putting wear on their tires in traveling to high school football games. At this Stevenson threatened to activate the Texas Rangers against the feds, as not even for a war do you interrupt high school football. (Interior Secretary Ickes was adamant, accusing Stevenson of cladding himself "in the outer garments of patriotism and the underwear of self-interest." All it did was make Calculatin' Coke more popular.)

Not all the federal ramp-up was welcome in Texas, as for instance when three hundred farm and ranch families were evicted from their land near Killeen to establish an antitank training ground. Named for Texas Confederate general John Bell Hood, it later became the principal tank school as well as the largest military installation in the United States. The war effort also caused considerable dislocation and social upheaval. The desertion of rented farms by tenants that began with farm owners keeping for themselves their AAA subsidies to limit planting continued as tenant farmers headed toward cities for work in war production. With men in the service, women entered the workforce, proving their capability in formerly male-only jobs from aircraft construction to shipbuilding. While this was celebrated in the song "Rosie the Riveter," men returning from the war would find it difficult to convince all these newly independent women to return to the kitchen in peacetime.

Race relations occasionally demonstrated the fragility of the peace at home. Stevenson was as conservative on social issues as he was on fiscal ones, strong-arming no-strike guarantees from labor unions during the war, and carrying on with benign neglect of growing racial tension. When an African-American named Willie Vinson was dragged from a hospital and lynched in August 1942 for the alleged assault of a white woman, Stevenson defended his decision not to intervene by saying that anyone, not just a black, would have been lynched for it. More than a quarter of a million African-American Texans registered for the draft and about a third of them served, receiving inferior training in segregated installations. At Camp Wolters near Mineral Wells, black troops had enough of being denied use of recreational facilities and built their own. Some facilities for them were prepared in Texas through the Negro War Recreation Council, such as a rec hall in Austin named for Doris Miller.

Things were tougher in the civilian sector, because the crushing need for workers in the defense plants sometimes resulted in blacks performing skilled tasks previously reserved for whites, and cities unprepared for the influx of laborers could not always provide separate facilities. One case in point was Beaumont, where the situation was sharpened by food shortages, because the city's ration allotments were based on its prewar population, and did not factor in the tide of twenty thousand who swept in during 1942 to work in the shipyards and refineries. Tensions were particularly high in

Beaumont because the local Ku Klux Klan was organizing a rally to compete with a planned Juneteenth celebration by the black community. After two alleged assaults of white women by black men, mobs totaling three to four thousand surged through black neighborhoods, pillaging a hundred black households and killing three men. With both the governor and lieutenant governor out of the state, the president pro tempore of the state senate ordered in nearly two thousand state troops, guardsmen, and Texas Rangers, but the event had already subsided. More than two hundred were arrested and held on the county fairgrounds, but only a couple dozen were recommended for trial. Governor Stevenson floated above the racial discord, seemingly satisfied that people worked out a good solution to shortages when white citizens purchased ration tickets from blacks and Hispanics who could not afford the goods anyway.

When the war finally ended, Texas celebrated along with the rest of the country. Oveta Culp Hobby was asked to help plan victory festivities. She said she would be pleased to do so, provided that all veterans who served, regardless of color, would be welcome to participate. The planners demurred rudely, prompting an equally rude appearance by her husband on her behalf, whose own record on race relations when he was governor had been somewhat problematical. Admiral Nimitz came home to a hero's welcome in dry, rocky Fredericksburg. When he had left for the Naval Academy at the turn of the century, his high school math teacher had advised against it until he got his high school diploma. He told her not to worry; he would come home one day as an admiral. The highlight of his visit was receiving his high school diploma—from her.

Texans, like all Americans, were ready to get on with their lives, but other small acts of closure occurred during the following years. Twenty-one prisoner-of-war camps located in the state had to be emptied and the inmates repatriated. The Crystal City camp for interned civilians finally closed in November 1947, the last INS facility of its kind to shut down. Its largest single group of inmates were Peruvian Japanese deported at the beginning of the war. Their detention was lengthened because Peru refused to accept them back, their removal having been an issue more of ethnic cleansing than security to begin with. Some were allowed to stay in the United States; most were sent, to their grief and fright, to Japan. Most of the many other federal wartime camps and installations closed, some recycled into other, new uses, and others given up to dry rot and tumbleweeds.

In a final ceremony of closure, in 1948 the USS *Texas* was presented to the state as a memorial. After Normandy she had returned to the yard for refitting with new gun liners and then was sent to the Pacific, where she fired more than nine hundred main-battery rounds into Iwo Jima and more than two thousand rounds into Okinawa. With Japan crumbling and the new U.S. battleships on line, *Texas* was finally allowed to stand down. Battleships much newer than she had already gone to the breakers, and within a few years the "Mighty T" was the only surviving dreadnought to have fought in both world wars. Rather than see her scrapped, Texans towed her to an appropriate slip at the San Jacinto battlefield, next to the oak grove that sheltered Sam Houston's army, her forward 14-inch turrets trained toward Santa Anna's line. Here visitors could experience, it was hoped, the alpha and the omega of Texans in war.

SIXTY-SIX

CLIMBING JACOB'S LADDER

AS TEXAS' WARTIME ECONOMY REVERTED TO CIVILIAN manufacture, the chemical industry of Southeast Texas had a huge job to perform. Thousands of tons of ammonium nitrate that had been produced for bombs and naval shells were now recycled instead into fertilizer. On April 16, 1947, the French steamship *Grandcamp* lay moored at the dock in Texas City, between Galveston and Houston, loaded to transport the much-needed fertilizer to war-ravaged farms in Europe. Just after 8:30 A.M. an alarm that the ship was burning was called in to the Texas City Fire Department, which responded with all four of its trucks. The fire spread and smoke poured from the stricken vessel, as thousands of spectators gathered to watch, unaware of the volatility of fuel oil and fertilizer. At 9:12 the *Grandcamp* blew up in a shattering explosion that was felt in Port Arthur, seventy-five miles away. All twenty-six firemen were killed and their equipment destroyed. The death toll was appalling—the exact number unknown but close to 600, including about 180 listed as missing who were blown to pieces or incinerated, and 63 bodies that could not be identified. Thousands were injured. The entire dock area was leveled, either by the blast or by the fifteen-foot wall of water created by the concussion. The nearby Monsanto chemical plant was wrecked, and between the blast and the flaming debris that rained on the rest of the city, at least a thousand structures were destroyed or damaged. The explosion also set afire the nearby SS *High Flyer*, which like the *Grandcamp* was laden with ammonium nitrate. She was towed a hundred feet from the dock before being left to burn; she blew up at one the next morning, taking a third ship, the *Wilson B. Keene*, with her.

The Red Cross moved in to coordinate relief and treat the injured, but with no water pressure or electricity, it took thousands of volunteers days to put out the fires. Local residents, stunned by the disaster, were unwilling to bury the sixty-three unidentified corpses in a mass grave. As Texas City had no public cemetery, a committee quickly purchased a two-acre tract, and a funeral, interracial and interfaith, was conducted on Sunday, June 21, with the bodies buried in caskets donated by funeral homes in nearly thirty cities. It took three years to rebuild Texas City, but the legal wrangling went on for a decade and a half. Three thousand resulting lawsuits were not put to rest until a $16.5 million special appropriation from Congress settled all claims against the government in 1956. The French government, which owned the *Grandcamp*, was not exonerated until a Supreme Court decision in 1962.

The gruesome events in Texas City seemed to signal a whole era in which Texas just couldn't seem to put a foot right. War had always given Texans purpose, but peace, whether in 1836, 1865, 1918, or 1945, always seemed to generate a struggle to craft a new identity. The era after World War II was the most snarled yet, first because things changed so fast. The exodus from the farms during the Depression, followed by the jobs boom during the war, transformed Texas into a majority urban population for the first time. During the course of the war some half million Texans sought work in war production in the cities, and according to the 1950 census, stayed there. Many traditional privileges—of race, of wealth, of political position—came under assault. The ferocity with which the Texas establishment fought to maintain mastery of the economy and the political landscape seemed continually tied, either directly or tenuously, to race. Even when not debated openly, it was the elephant in the parlor of every political discussion.

The easiest postwar task and the one most heartily tended to was easing the transition of veterans back into civilian life. Of the nearly three-quarters of a million Texans who served in World War II, 23,000 had been killed. The huge remaining number of survivors came streaming home, and the state passed bills to exempt veterans from the poll tax, renew their driver's licenses without examinations, and provide free tuition at state colleges. Appropriately for Texas, whose revolutionary veterans had received land bounties from the Republic, the largest new program involved real estate. The public domain had been granted off or sold long ago, but in 1946 a constitutional amendment passed creating a Veterans Land Board, authorized to issue $25 million in bonds to buy land and resell it in parcels of a minimum of twenty acres to veterans at low interest on forty-year notes. Expanded in the following decades to much larger sums and to include veterans of later wars, the VLB eventually redistributed some 4.5 million acres in mostly small plots to some 130,000 veterans.

Predictably, the inclusion of veterans of color proved problematical, and the dispensation of land nearly derailed in a major scandal. In the fall of 1954 Roland Towery, the manager of the newspaper in Cuero, a sleepy town on the Guadalupe River northwest of Victoria that had previously been known principally for its annual roundup of turkeys, investigated a report that black men were being hosted after hours at the local country club. What developed was that poor, semi-literate black veterans were being fêted at the club and duped by land shills into applying for VLB acreages, of which they were unaware until they began receiving duns for the mortgage payments. After a year's inquiry, Towery copped a Pulitzer Prize for local affairs investigation, and Texas Land Commissioner Bascom Giles served three years in Huntsville for the illegal use of public funds. He was the first Texan elected to statewide office to serve time for crimes committed during his term.

The VLB scandal was a small sideshow, however, compared to the so-called Tidelands Controversy, because of which Texas' relations with the federal government reached their lowest point since the boundary dispute was settled in 1850. Indeed, the roots of the conflict tapped straight back to annexation in 1845, and revealed a political chemistry only slightly less volatile than the fuel oil and nitrate that destroyed Texas City. Because of Texas' origin as a Spanish province, she had then, and had subsequently as a Mexican province and independent nation, claimed territorial waters not to three miles but to three leagues (10.35 miles). This was recognized by the United States at the time of admission, and again in the Treaty of Guadalupe-Hidalgo of 1848 and the Gadsden Treaty of 1853. More than fifty decisions by the U.S. Supreme Court had cited Texas' title to land between the low-tide line and the three-league limit. Texas began issuing mineral leases on offshore parcels, which generated millions of dollars that were dedicated to school funds. With the discovery of offshore oil, however, hundreds of drillers applied for leases under federal law, overlapping but without regard to the state leases. The federal government in 1946 filed suit against several coastal states (whose title to tidelands had also never been questioned, even without having the unique national history of Texas) in an attempt to appropriate the marginal sea area to federal ownership.

In that same year Texas elected another in its series of wunderkind attorneys general in Price Daniel, who at thirty-six had already been speaker of the state house before becoming the youngest state AG in the country. In that post he first gained notice for a largely successful assault on racketeering, which had been quietly prospering since the end of Prohibition. Once the tidelands issue came to the fore he mounted a vigorous legal and political defense of the state's position, and the legal history was so clear it didn't seem that he could lose. However, after a convoluted series of cases, Texas and the other coastal states lost their tidelands to national seizure, based not on any superior claim but on the "paramount right" of the federal government to protect its territory from foreign aggression. It was a stunning piece of judicial legislation.

Texas responded by muscling a bill through the Congress restoring its tidelands. The bill was vetoed by President Truman, then the next year passed again and vetoed again, to the growing ire of Texans generally, but especially conservative Democrats who hated Truman anyway. In the 1952 presidential election the Republican nominee was World War II hero General Dwight Eisenhower, whom the state warmly espoused for having been born in Denison, although he had moved away as an infant. He vowed to sign the tidelands back over to the states if he was elected. The Democratic nominee, Adlai Stevenson of Illinois, honorably if suicidally upheld the right of federal ownership.

In citing national security as a rationale for gifting the tidelands to the federal government, the Supreme Court was reacting to the spirit of the times, which was nationwide paranoia on the subject of a feared Communist takeover of the country. Fueled by a new war in Korea among other international hot spots, and also in good measure by grandstanding at home, the mood of the country reached chronic, midlevel terror. Texas fielded a couple of major players in the so-called Red Scare, one in the person of Martin Dies, firebrand representative of the 2nd District in the southeast corner of the state. Filling the chair once occupied by his father, Dies entered Congress as its youngest member, and became chairman of the House Un-American Activities Committee when it was created in 1938, where he staged theatrical hearings. His use of the spectre of Communism to attack his real targets—the New Deal and organized labor—alternately thrilled and embarrassed the rest of the membership. In 1944 the Congress of Industrial Organizations mobilized a formidable effort to unseat him, but Dies did not run. He returned to Congress in 1952 in a special at-large election, but the House leadership had had enough of his medicine show and railroaded him away from his old HUAC chair. He faded from public service after two failed tries for the Senate, maintaining to the end that Communists lurked everywhere.

If Martin Dies was one of the principal criers of the Red Scare, Texas' other major player in it was one of its principal victims, entertainer and humorist John Henry Faulk. Born in Austin, the son of Methodist freethinkers who hated racism, Faulk attended the University of Texas and wrote his master's thesis on African-American sermons. Through his fascination with folklore he gained the friendship of John Lomax, who introduced him to the world of New York entertainment. There Faulk's natural gift of humor and storytelling netted him a series of jobs on radio, culminating in his popular *John Henry Faulk Show*, a variety venue that ran for six years on WCBS radio. Active in his union, the American Federation of Television and Radio

Artists, Faulk took part in a leadership struggle, and found himself black-listed as a Communist. With money advanced by famed journalist and CBS vice president Edward R. Murrow, Faulk opened a five-year legal battle to restore his good name. If the incident had happened earlier in the Red Scare era he doubtless would have failed, but after the exposure of McCarthyism, he was fully vindicated when a jury awarded him a libel judgment of $3.5 million. It was more money than he had sought, and was the largest libel judgment ever given up to then, but between legal fees and the company's depleted assets, he remained in dire financial straits. After publication of his memoir, *Fear on Trial*, he remained a vivid spokesman for the First Amendment, and didn't return to folksy humor until he became a regular on the television show *Hee Haw*. After his death the city of Austin named its central library after him.

The Tidelands Controversy had less to do with race than with the maintenance of Texas' state, and formerly national, prerogatives. The same cannot be said for the Red Scare, as Texas conservatives found it easy to believe that African-Americans and organized labor were fronts for sinister, bomb-throwing Bolsheviks. The contribution that African-Americans in Texas made to the war effort led many of them into some expectation that greater political and social justice might follow, but it was slow going. Lynching had declined, thanks in part to the whites-only Association of Southern Women for the Prevention of Lynching, begun by Jessie Ames, which had boasted over a hundred chapters and some four million members by the late 1930s. The Texas wing, led by Sallie L. Hanna of Dallas, wrested pledges from gubernatorial candidates to work for the end of lynchings, and they kept the issue in such public view that by 1942 the association began to disband in the belief that their aims had been accomplished. There was one lynching in 1942, but that followed six years without a single reported case.

Their optimism was still premature, however, as wartime pressure strained race relations in unexpected ways, as was learned in the Beaumont race riot of June 1943. Politically, Texas blacks lost ground in the 1935 case of *Grovey v. Townsend*, which erased earlier gains by declaring the Democratic Party a private organization that could establish its own membership standards. After World War II, however, people of conscience of all races wanted to believe the wartime propaganda about American values, and the Houston NAACP filed suit on behalf of Lonnie Smith, a black dentist who had been prevented from voting in a Democratic primary. Argued before the Supreme Court by Thurgood Marshall, *Smith v. Allwright* resulted in a monumental victory in 1944, outlawing whites-only primaries and overturning all previous decisions to the contrary. By 1947 more than 100,000 Texas blacks registered to vote, a number that would have been much higher had not the white power structure resorted to cruder intimidation than the law.

Very active in the waging of *Smith v. Allwright* was the Houston NAACP's longtime executive secretary, Christia Adair, who had first tried to vote in Kingsville after the campaign for woman suffrage. In subsequent years, she was grilled by Houston police who wanted access to the NAACP membership roster. She stiffed them and was again upheld by the Supreme Court. Fired by the fuel of righteousness, she played important roles in desegregating Houston's library, airport, city buses, and even department store dressing rooms. Although the Texas Democratic Party remained hostile to her well into the 1960s, she served as precinct judge and absentee-voting clerk for decades further. She was ninety-six when she passed away in 1989.

To say that the Democratic Party in Texas was outraged by the decision in *Smith v. Allwright* would be a vast understatement. At the state convention in 1944, conservatives tried to make condemnation of the case a test oath. The state's eroding corps of liberals, New Dealers, and those loyal to the national administration even through their misgivings, refused to go along, and the party split. The racist faction, calling themselves the "Texas Regulars," began looking for allies on the Republican side of the aisle. The governor, Calculatin' Coke, saying nothing, gave the impression of being an honest broker and got himself massively reelected, with 84 percent of the vote in the primary. The combination of Stevenson's parsimony and the boom of the wartime economy provided the state a budget surplus, and therefore few pressing issues for the 1946 campaign. The two principal candidates of the fourteen in the field fit the script perfectly: Beauford Jester, a hammy conservative from Corsicana, lately in office as railroad commissioner, and Homer Rainey, a former president of the University of Texas, who had been deposed by conservative regents for various liberal sins. Rainey put together the first effective coalition of progressives, union members, and minorities, and led in the early polls. However, he also advocated a tax on natural resources, which set the oil money against him, especially running against a popular railroad commissioner. Labor also figured in the election, as ill-timed strikes in Fort Worth and Waco cost Rainey further popularity, and Jester beat him going away in the runoff.

As governor, Jester pursued a moderate program, increasing aid to eleemosynary institutions, equalizing public school funding with the Gilmer-Aikens Law, which also standardized the nine-month public school year, and improving in-state transportation with funding for the farm-to-market road system. Jester shored up his conservative support with anti-labor legislation, including so-called right to work laws, which mollified the establishment enough that in the 1948 election, they were overborne to follow Jester's advice, hold their noses, and support the renomination of Harry Truman. The Texas Regulars, however, bolted, and marching behind Pappy O'Daniel and Martin Dies, they formed a Texas battalion of Dixiecrats who nominated Strom Thurmond of South Carolina on a segregationist ticket. The size of Truman's triumph in Texas, though, spoke volumes about Texas Democrats who remained grateful for the New Deal's pulling them back from ruin.

The real fireworks in the 1948 election was in the Texas race for the U.S. Senate seat being vacated by Pappy O'Daniel. Coke Stevenson should have been a shoo-in, but he received an unexpectedly vigorous challenge from that troublesome New Deal congressman, Lyndon Johnson. While Stevenson progressed across the state in his Plymouth, buying gasoline only five gallons at a time to stop and speak at the filling stations, Johnson hopscotched in a helicopter, speaking to as many as five rallies in a day—118 towns in less than three weeks—each one organized in advance by a capable aide, a former University of Texas student body president named John Connally. Johnson's political nimbleness turned one liability into an asset. Texas labor, astonishingly, endorsed Stevenson despite his record, because Johnson had supported the Taft-Hartley Act, which contained elements both favoring and regulating labor. Calculatin' Coke, observing his famous beatitude, said nothing, until cornered by pro-Johnson reporters to explain himself. LBJ then showered the state with copies of Stevenson's fumbling dodge of a reply. By election day Stevenson and Johnson were running dead even.

There was a story, regrettable only in that it cannot be proven, that on election night as the cliffhanger progressed, Johnson telephoned Archer Parr, the Duke of Duval County, where Johnson was supposed to run very well, and asked how many votes he had. "Well, Lyndon," Parr was said to have answered, "how many do you need?" (Parr's facility with ballots was legendary, and Calculatin' Coke himself had depended on him multiple times before. The story was that Parr was now annoyed with Stevenson for passing over one of his lieutenants for a state job.) Whether or not such an exchange actually took place, Duval County announced that it would be submitting amended returns, and a week and a half after the election the late ballots were tallied, giving Stevenson 40 votes, and Johnson 4,622, handing Johnson the election by 87 votes. Stevenson challenged the result both in the courts and in the Senate, despite the fact that the precincts where he enjoyed a safe majority probably would not have withstood much auditing, either. Taking ex-Ranger Frank Hamer to South Texas, Stevenson found rock-solid proof of fraud in Jim Wells County, but the Democratic Election Committee, amid fisticuffs and a heart attack, sustained the result by a single vote.

Although the Texas political establishment squinted at Johnson's New Deal sympathies, Stevenson's challenge faltered because the veteran representative during his dozen years in the House had tended his constituency too well, and made too many friends, for the bitter ex-governor to find many allies in his bid to nullify the election. Indeed the most accurate summary of the 1948 Senate contest is probably the same as was said by the most astute observers at the time: that Johnson had merely "out-stolen" the vote from Calculatin' Coke. Thus "Landslide Lyndon," as he was suddenly known, tiptoed into the Senate and had the chance to become the LBJ of legend.

The victory achieved by the NAACP in *Smith v. Allwright* in 1944 invigorated an organization whose membership had vacillated for decades; by 1949 there were some 30,000 members, and they were emboldened to extend their effort into the volatile area of school desegregation. Heman Sweatt was a thirty-three-year-old substitute mail carrier in Houston, a city to which he had returned after attending Wiley College in Marshall, and teaching school for a time in the town of Cleburne, south of Fort Worth. He was well known in Houston NAACP circles, having been acquainted with both Richard Grovey and Lonnie Smith of the whites-only primary cases. As the local secretary of the National Alliance of Postal Employees, he prepared grievances against the systematic discrimination suffered by black mailmen, an experience that left him with the desire to go to law school. NAACP leaders sensed an opportunity. The reigning Supreme Court doctrine permitted school segregation, provided that the education offered to blacks was comparable to that which was enjoyed by whites: separate but equal, although equality did not have to be, and never was, exact or even close. (Governor Jester, who opposed integration, had to importune the University of Texas to admit a black student to its medical school on the grounds that there was no medical school for Negroes in the state; the university complied reluctantly in 1949.) Texas, the NAACP was counting on, had no law school at all for blacks.

Under the eye of NAACP strategists, Sweatt applied to the University of Texas School of Law, was turned down, and filed suit in May 1946. The university had a capable strategist of its own, defended in the suit by Attorney General Price Daniel. UT won a six-month continuance from the state district court, during which time they slapped together a "law school" for blacks in a house between the university and the state capitol. With the university's good intentions thus proven, the NAACP's case lost both at trial and on appeal, while Sweatt's life became a nightmare of vandalism and death threats that resulted in his suffering from ulcers and a heart attack. The U.S. Supreme Court eventually granted certiorari and heard the case, and in 1950 the monumental *Sweatt v. Painter* decision overturned the longstanding separate but equal doctrine. Sweatt was enrolled in the University of Texas Law School, but with both his health and his marriage wrecked, he soon left and pursued a career instead with the NAACP and National Urban League.

It was well that civil rights advocates celebrated the milestone of *Sweatt v. Painter*, because things were about to take a turn for the worse. Governor Beauford Jester died of a heart attack while entrained for a speech in Beaumont on July 11, 1949, and the office was assumed by the lieutenant governor, Allan Shivers. He had begun political life as a moderate and still showed flashes of it, as when he called for increased taxes to pay for Jester's programs to catch up from the neglect of the Stevenson years. Once ensconced in office, he transformed into a forceful advocate for conservative values—the kindest thing he could say about integration was to express his belief that "blacks do not want to go to school with whites." He also knew how to amass power, having gotten state senate rules changed during his term as lieutenant governor to hand him the right to make committee appointments. Shivers was also far less loyal to the national Democratic organization than Jester had been. Disgusted with the Truman administration over the Tidelands issue and their civil rights initiatives, Shivers openly backed Eisenhower for president in 1952—support to which he gave muscle by expunging dissenters from the executive committee of the state party, and with a legislative bill to permit "cross-filing," or letting candidates run in both party primaries.

Undeterred by the cooling climate, the Texas NAACP determined to try to build on their recent court gains. Technically, *Sweatt v. Painter* did not outlaw school segregation per se, but it made separate equality so hard to establish that once the door was open to some cases, all knew that the door must remain open. The NAACP set its sights on integration of the public schools, and that proved to be the greatest challenge yet. After the 1954 *Brown v. Board of Education* case set the precedent (filed by Thurgood Marshall, who had also represented Heman Sweatt), many Texas school districts began to quietly integrate, especially those in West Texas. Perhaps the first to desegregate were schools in the town of Friona, near the New Mexico line southwest of Amarillo, where the advantage of enrolling black students soon made itself felt—in sports. Where local athletes triumphed, hearts and minds were sure to follow, and racial progress was aided by solicitude for the welfare of star performers.

Another West Texas school reached a milestone at the college level, when in 1966 Texas Western University in El Paso (now the University of Texas at El Paso) won the NCAA basketball championship with a team of all-black starters, defeating an all-white team from the University of Kentucky by a score of 72–65. In the public consciousness, the event did not register as the kind of social thunderclap that it really was, first because the game was played during bloody riots in the Watts section of Los Angeles, and second because NCAA championships at that time were not nationally broadcast. Throughout college basketball, however, other programs followed the lead of Texas Western Coach Don Haskins in recruiting superior minority players from the inner cities of the industrial Northeast. Perhaps because colleges are supposed to be centers of progressive thinking anyway, integration of black students onto Texas campuses actually occurred with little legal opposition, although there were some unpleasant incidents at Lamar State in Beaumont and West Texas State Normal College in Canyon.

Public school desegregation was a tougher sell in Central and East Texas than on the high plains. One holdout was the town of Mansfield, whose school district numbered about 700 white students, and 60 blacks who were bused to a black school in Fort Worth about twenty miles to the northwest. Citing *Brown v. Board*, the Texas NAACP filed suit in federal court and quickly won, making the Mansfield school district the first in Texas to be constrained with a federal court order to integrate. The school board moved to obey, but at the opening of the 1956 school year, several hundred angry whites surrounded Mansfield High School, with the tacit acceptance of the city police chief and the mayor. The segregationists cowed the county sheriff and set up roadblocks to prevent anyone they suspected of being black sympathizers from entering the town. Governor Shivers sent Texas Rangers to keep order—by enforcing segregation and seeing to it that the black students continued to be bused to Fort Worth. Appeal was made to the federal government, but President Eisenhower, facing a reelection campaign in which he needed Texas support, did not involve himself. (He had less success ducking a similar situation in Little Rock, Arkansas, the following year, after being safely returned to the White House.) The Mansfield school district successfully defied the federal integration order, and Mansfield schools did not integrate until 1965.

By 1956 about 120 Texas school districts had admitted black students, over vocal white opposition, and in 1957 the Texas legislature took up the issue. A series of bills, backed by Shivers, reinstituted legal sanction for segregation. Only a couple of them passed: one that shut off state aid to districts that integrated without a popular referendum, and another that shut down any school at which national guard or federal troops were posted. The provisions would have been much worse, but for a marathon filibuster in the state senate by a junior member, Henry B. González of San Antonio, the first Hispanic to sit in the modern senate. "Did you know that Negroes helped settle Texas?" he demanded, "that a Negro died at the Alamo?" He held the floor for twenty-two hours, still a record for that chamber, until Shivers' senate allies gave up on most of their resegregation package. As the first Hispanic to sit on the San Antonio City Council in generations, González had already been instrumental in integrating that city's public swimming pools.

González' rise to prominence came after a decade of steady progress for Tejanos. Unequal treatment from the veterans' department led to the founding of the G.I. Forum of Texas in Corpus Christi in 1947. The following year, a funeral home in Three Rivers refused to allow services to be conducted for a Tejano veteran, Felix Longoria. That row subsided when Lyndon Johnson arranged for his burial with honors in Arlington National Cemetery, but it was now apparent that Mexican-Americans were in a legal limbo: their status as Caucasians had been affirmed by the courts early in the century, but de facto discrimination took place against them anyway, and they had no legal recourse as a protected class, as African-Americans did. This was remedied in the case of *Hernández v. State of Texas*, which extended them protection from discrimination without need of a color distinction. In that same year, 1954, Hispanics were allowed to sit on Texas juries, and their political activity increased. Henry B. González served with distinction in the state senate, and his reelection in 1960 was by such a large margin that it affected the national election.

SIXTY-SEVEN

A FLOWERING OF TEXAS LETTERS

OPPOSITION TO CIVIL RIGHTS WAS THE MOST VISIBLE front in the campaign by the conservative establishment to enforce a social paradigm, but it was not the only front. Almost as well known at the time was their distaste of intellectuals and academics, who prompted students to think critically. Pappy O'Daniel may have been a national laughingstock, but there was one of his policies that Coke Stevenson continued with approval: using his appointment power to name conservative regents over the University of Texas as old terms expired. In 1942 this largely new Board of Regents forced the university's president, Homer Price Rainey, to fire some economics professors who voiced support for the New Deal, and others who had the nerve to defend labor unions. Then they banned John Dos Passos' book *USA*, which had been placed on a reading list in the English Department, and tried but failed to get the offending teacher fired. By 1944 the O'Daniel-Stevenson regents comprised a majority, and fired Rainey himself for the offense of complaining about them at a faculty meeting.

Rainey, who had been engaged by Jimmy Allred and had once enjoyed the support of a progressive phalanx of regents, did not go quietly into the night. Students poured onto the campus malls in protest, 8,000 of them marching silently to the Governor's Mansion. As the stink worsened the regents had to come up with ever more creative reasons for his sacking, culminating in a charge that he had allowed the school to become a "nest of homosexuals." The legislature became involved, and at one hearing in the capitol, a weary lawmaker asked one witness, "Any other dirty little thing about the university you want to volunteer?" Rainey was cleared of any charges but not reinstated, and the American Association of University Professors sanctioned UT for nine years to warn potential teachers that it was a dangerous place to work. Rainey, for his part, continued his battle in a run for governor in 1946. He had the social credentials for it—as an ordained Baptist minister, an army veteran, and a former Texas League baseball pitcher, but he was unable to overcome the stain of also being an intellectual and was clobbered in the primary by the glad-handing Beauford Jester.

Out of such stony soil bloomed what is called the Golden Age of Texas

Letters. This overstates the case somewhat, but undoubtedly it was a time when Texas writers gained national and even international reputations. First in line was Katherine Anne Porter, who when she presented a lecture at the University of Texas in 1958 imagined that she had returned home in triumph. She was born in the former Comanche heartland of Indian Creek, near Brownwood, in 1890, was raised by her grandmother in the little town of Kyle, near San Marcos, and attended finishing school in San Antonio. After a grueling stint in Victoria, teaching elocution and dancing to girls from her rented room, she married at sixteen. She was divorced five years later and left Texas to pursue a literary career. Wherever she lived—Chicago, New York, Mexico, New Orleans, Hollywood, brief stays back in Texas—she labored to make ends meet with her writing. Much of her early work was set in Texas. When the Texas Institute of Letters was established, she hoped to receive their first literary award for *Pale Horse, Pale Rider*, but the award went instead to J. Frank Dobie.

Dobie, born in 1888, became the elder statesman of a triumvirate of Texas writers who were as famed for their camaraderie as for their work. From his beginnings in the brush country between San Antonio and Corpus Christi, at age sixteen he deserted the ranch on which he was born, and lived with his grandparents in the town of Alice so he could attend high school. He went on to earn a B.A. at Southwestern University in Georgetown and an M.A. from Columbia, and while he spent most of his youth fleeing from the intellectual limitations of his early years, yet he adored the ideal of the Texas rural life and dedicated his career to preserving and interpreting the life of the cowboy. After acquiring his M.A. from Columbia, he served two decades as secretary of the Texas Folklore Society, won a Literary Guild Award for his second book, *Coronado's Children*, in 1931, and achieved such a reputation that the University of Texas accorded him the unprecedented honor of hiring him as a full professor without having a Ph.D. Once he became known as an incorrigible he took a leave of absence during the war and went abroad. Teaching in London and Cambridge and on the Continent gave Dobie a taste of what real academic excellence was, which sharpened his disgust over the firing of Homer Rainey and prompted Governor Stevenson to mark him as a "troublemaker." The school got rid of him. The university's loss was the world's gain, as Dobie wrote virtually nonstop until his death in 1964, a literary lion who put the Texas heritage on the world stage after being disgraced by oafs at home.

The second member of the trio was the historian Walter Prescott Webb, who gained academic notice when he first propounded that "the West cannot be understood as a mere extension of things Eastern." Much to the contrary, the westward roll of American settlement came to a crashing halt when it arrived at what was then known as the Great American Desert. In *The Great Plains,* Webb pointed out that technology had to catch up: the natives could not be bested until the advent of repeating firearms, the prairies could not really be made productive until the arrival of barbed wire, and farming had to await irrigation. It was a natural thing to occur to a deep thinker who, in his childhood, had been uprooted from a lush farm near the Louisiana border and transplanted in the barren rocky screes of Ranger, east of Abilene. He was the same age as Dobie, and like Dobie escaped his circumstances, in his case with the help of a mentor, New York toymaker William Hinds, who took an interest when Webb, in his boyhood, wrote a magazine editor for advice on how to become a writer. And like Dobie, the University of Texas bent its rules for him, placing him on the history faculty despite his having taken his Ph.D. in their own program. Webb produced a large and popular history of the Texas Rangers—an expansion of his master's thesis—and *Divided We Stand,* a criticism of the extent to which he believed the South had become economic colonies of Northern corporations. He gained further prominence with *More Water for Texas,* espousing conservation of natural resources, and held numerous fellowships and presidencies before he was killed in a car crash the year before Dobie died.

The third member of Dobie's triumvirate was a naturalist, Roy Bedichek, older than Webb and Dobie by a decade and the last to establish a reputation. In fact it was only at their insistence that Bedichek secreted himself at Webb's Friday Mountain Ranch southwest of Austin to write *Adventures with a Texas Naturalist* in 1947, followed by the prizewinning *Karankaway Country* three years later. At Dobie's small ranch, Paisano, near Webb's, the three would perch on Philosopher's Rock in Barton Creek, drink whiskey, and wax literary. Luxuriating in his eccentricity, Dobie loved working by a fireplace, and had window air conditioners installed so he could warm by the fire during the scorching summers. Less known of Dobie was his fascination with bathroom graffiti, and for years his buddies Webb and Bedichek scoured public restrooms for folk wisdom, which they passed to Dobie on slips of paper that he hoarded in a shoebox until his death.

Ironically, it was the writer who brought the Paisano trio to public attention who was himself probably the most worthy to inherit Katherine Anne Porter's mantle of national merit. William A. Owens was born into a family of sharecroppers in the Northeast Texas hamlet of Pin Hook, near Paris, in 1905. He began his career as a folklorist, but achieved wide acclaim for resurrecting the history of a mutiny that took place on the slave schooner *Amistad*, which was published in 1953. His greatest fame came with a memoir of his hardscrabble youth, *This Stubborn Soil*, followed shortly by *Three Friends*, his tribute to Webb, Dobie, and Bedichek. His later writings included pleas for racial harmony, and an American bicentennial salute, *A Fair and Happy Land*. In a lifetime of both celebrating his roots and fleeing the limitations of his native culture (a theme repeated in the lives of both Porter and Dobie), he was revered as a teacher as well as an author, and rose to the pinnacle of his profession. He died as the dean emeritus of the School of Creative Writing at Columbia University.

Owens' concern for racial and ethnic justice was echoed by one of Texas' most successful poets of the era, Fania Kruger, a Russian Jewish immigrant whose visions of ruthless pogroms were burned into her memory during her childhood in the Crimea. Her work won major awards from the New York City Writer's Conference and the Poetry Society of America. Kruger had ample opportunity to appreciate the opportunities afforded immigrants in America. Her husband and fellow Russian Jew, Sam Kruger, started a successful jewelry business; her sister-in-law married into another family of gem merchants named Zalefsky, and it was Sam Kruger who financed the venture that evolved into a diversified retail giant, the Zale Corporation. Fania's mother-in-law, by contrast, whom the family was unable to rescue from Russia, starved to death.

The end of Katherine Anne Porter's Texas affiliations were sad. She had moved away before she was thirty, and for the next sixty years returned only for brief sojourns. Eventually she taught at Stanford, William and Mary, and the University of Michigan. Over the years Porter received the Pulitzer Prize, the National Book Award, and a Gold Medal from the National Institute of Arts and Letters, yet she never ceased craving recognition from her home state. Having heard a rumor that the University of Texas intended to name a new library after her, she commissioned a large photographic portrait of herself to grace it. So bitter was her disappointment when the story proved untrue that she left Texas with an oath never to return, and bequeathed her papers to the University of Maryland at College Park, near where she died in 1980.

While Dobie, Webb, and Bedichek are customarily recited as the Golden Age of Texas letters, other scholars and writers of merit were working the same territory. As the historian Webb was formulating deep theories and being invited to teach at Oxford and London, J. Evetts Haley was preserving the Texas story closer to home, husbanding primary sources before they were lost. Born in Belton but most closely identified for many years with West Texas Normal College (now West Texas A&M University) in Canyon, he was twenty-four when he met Charles Goodnight, and interviewed the grizzled pioneer rancher extensively. His biography of Goodnight was preceded by a history of the XIT Ranch, and followed by extensive publications on the frontier era. Haley was a better narrative chronicler than Webb, but he lacked Webb's probity. Later in life his frequent dabbling in politics—including a run for governor as a segregationist in 1956, production of the controversial *A Texan Looks at Lyndon* in 1964, and ending his long relationship with the college in Canyon when it admitted black students—tarnished an otherwise enviable reputation.

As a spinner of Texas stories, Fred Gipson, born on a farm near Mason, was in no wise inferior to Dobie. His *Hound-Dog Man, Old Yeller,* and numerous other books brought him fame, awards, the presidency of the Texas Institute of Letters, and a grave of honor in the State Cemetery, near Webb and Dobie. As this generation began to pass—Bedichek died in 1957, Webb in 1963, Dobie in 1964, and Gipson in 1973—their market share if not their shoes began to be filled by Ben K. Green, a self-taught veterinarian from another Northeast Texas village, Cumby, in Hopkins County.

Perhaps the greatest current exponents of Texas' dual heritage of Old South and Old West, respectively, are Horton Foote of Wharton, author of *The Trip to Bountiful,* and Western novelist Elmer Kelton of San Angelo, seven-time winner of the Spur Award from the Western Writers of America for such tales as *The Good Old Boys, The Day the Cowboys Quit,* and *The Time It Never Rained,* set in the vastness of West Texas. Kelton's exquisite style develops the themes of a love of liberty and a suspicion of authority which tap deep into Texas' heritage, and it also reflects the very current hostility of the "sagebrush rebellion."

SIXTY-EIGHT

ASSASSINATION, WAR, AND ANTIWAR

IF DWIGHT EISENHOWER THOUGHT THAT RECEIVING THE support of Texas' conservative Democrats in 1952 meant that they were now his friends, the Shivercrats quickly disabused him of that notion. The deal that they offered him with the cross-balloting measure was to guarantee that he would carry Texas if he would disavow any intent to stretch coattails down the ballot. Their disdain for Republicans was all that it had ever been; they had merely come to despise liberal Democrats even more. When Eisenhower's camp signed off on the deal, Texas Republicans, who had been looking forward to what could have been their most bountiful election in history, were crestfallen. County conventions met in confusion, and some "Old Guard" Republicans who had taken their lumps for decades, and who regarded Eisenhower as a foreign vessel flying a flag of convenience, threatened to split off and form a conservative Republican Party loyal to Ohio Senator Robert A. Taft to prove that they could be even further to the right than Shivers.

After nearly a century, however, as the perennial and sometimes laughable minority party, Republicans in Texas learned how to sacrifice for the greater good. Friendly but earnest cocktail parties were given, feelings were soothed, and the Republican Party listed statewide Democratic candidates on their primary ballots. Fearing a repeat of the Truman victory in 1948, that the people would vote Democratic despite being told to do otherwise, Texas power brokers and especially oil and business money—Sid Richardson, Hugh Roy Cullen, William P. and Oveta Hobby—ponied up a fortune in aid for Ike, but also for Democratic conservatives down-ballot. On election day, Texas went for Eisenhower, and state Republican candidates who bothered to run grinned and quaffed their hemlock one more time.

What Eisenhower had to work with in a Democratic-controlled Congress was essentially a Texas-controlled Congress. Sam Rayburn, bald and courtly and efficient, continued as Speaker of the House, and his protégé Lyndon Johnson, still walking the tightrope between his New Deal beginnings and the conservative Texas reality, quickly advanced to become Majority Leader in the Senate. Texans also held the reins of key committees, so for

Ike, governing successfully largely meant keeping Texas happy—hence his ducking the federal court order to integrate the public schools in Mansfield. (The political shrewdness of that stance became apparent the following year, when Texas conservatives vented their spleen on him when he did send troops to let black children into the high school in Little Rock, Arkansas.) Only four months into his term, he signed quitclaim papers reverting the tidelands and their petroleum back to the states.

Allan Shivers ran for an unprecedented third term as governor, but he almost lost to a new gadfly in the person of a jolly, unrepentant New Deal liberal, Judge Ralph Yarborough of Austin, a native of the town of Chandler just west of Tyler. He had been named assistant attorney general in 1931, and the cases he won against major oil companies safeguarded billions in future income for Texas schools. He was an old-time campaigning road warrior, gifted with a phenomenal memory for faces and events, a wealth of personal charm and ebullience, and a sarcastic wit that was the bane of the pompous. Yarborough had opposed Shivers in 1952 and gotten run over. Now, however, Yarborough questioned how the Veterans Land Board scandal could have occurred without Shivers' knowledge when the governor sat right there on the board of directors, and questioned whether two major scandals in one administration could be a coincidence. Shivers answered that Yarborough was supported by labor union racketeers and Communists, and—dropping his political atom bomb—that he supported mixing of the races. The old formula was still enough to get Shivers reelected, but just barely.

Yarborough tried again for the Governor's Mansion in 1956, this time running against Senator Price Daniel, and lost by a hair's breadth. Daniel, however, had resigned from the U.S. Senate after winning the nomination for governor, necessitating a special election to fill the unexpired last year of his term. Thinking to save the cost of a probable runoff, the legislature provided that the primary might be won merely by a plurality, rather than a majority. With the winner taking all in one election, and with the conservative vote splintered among numerous candidates, Yarborough finally won a statewide election. The accidental senator went to Washington with only 38 percent of the vote and the blessing of J. Frank Dobie, who called him "perhaps the best-read man that Texas ever sent to Washington." He arrived in time to support the Civil Rights Act of 1957—one of only five senators from the South to do so.

Yarborough's success in finally winning a high office left Texas liberals jubilant. In Houston they quickly organized a sort of party-within-the-party, called "Democrats of Texas," and had the effrontery to pass a slate of demands on the state party: loyalty to the national party, more respect for the liberal wing in state matters. The conservatives took little notice, but the "DOT" was organized enough to carry Yarborough to a second victory in the regular election for his seat in 1958. In Daniel's three gubernatorial terms of moderately conservative government, he cultivated good relations with the legislature, and only twenty of his more than 150 major legislative initiatives were turned down. The most lasting contribution was the construction of the Texas State Library and Archives Building east of the capitol, a project to which Daniel gave the closest oversight.

Lyndon Johnson suffered a serious heart attack in 1955, but after his recovery, he was a formidable candidate for president in 1960. Rayburn was backing him, and the Texas legislature made straight the road before him, altering the primary date and changing the rules to allow him to run both for senator and president. His likeliest opposition came from a man who could hardly have been more his opposite, Senator John F. Kennedy of Massachusetts—young, handsome, rich, flashy, funny, a war hero, married to society beauty Jacqueline Bouvier, and a man whom LBJ considered in every particular to be his inferior. After the primaries and into the convention, however, it was obvious that Kennedy must win. For many reasons, including geographical balance and the fact that Kennedy's short stint in the Senate convinced him that Johnson would make his presidency a nightmare if the Texan remained in command of the Senate, the Boston liberal offered Johnson the second spot on the ticket. Torn over whether to accept the vice-presidential nomination, Johnson turned to an early mentor, John Nance Garner, who spent eight contentious years in that office under FDR, and now past ninety was living in retirement in Uvalde. The vice presidency, he told Johnson, wasn't worth a bucket of warm piss, a remark that was quickly bowdlerized for the press into a "pitcher of warm spit"—not an expression that he would have recognized. (The fact that Ettie Garner burned all of Cactus Jack's personal notes and papers after he died doubtless cleansed the record of many other similarly colorful assessments, but that is history's loss.)

At home, Johnson had paid up his conservative dues by siding with the Shivers-Daniel faction to undercut Senator Yarborough, even while courting Yarborough in Washington and voting with him on key issues. Somehow—and it was his genius—Johnson kept both sides mollified. What saved the Kennedy-Johnson ticket in Texas was San Antonio's state senator Henry B. González, who was reelected with such a margin that his coattails reached up the ballot, not vice versa. He had been a key figure in organizing Viva Kennedy–Viva Johnson clubs in the Hispanic community, which delivered a stunning 91 percent of their vote for the Democratic ticket—accruing certainly more than the margin of 46,000 votes by which Kennedy carried Texas. Two years later González advanced to Congress, where he served eighteen terms as the tireless champion of the underprivileged.

Kennedy appointed Johnson's onetime aide John B. Connally as secretary of the navy. The post raised some eyebrows, for although Connally was a former lieutenant commander, he had also become tied to Houston oil magnate Sid Richardson and was now to become the world's largest purchaser of naval fuel oil. Connally resigned from the job in 1962 to make a run for governor. In that race, Price Daniel announced for a fourth term, and in the early going Connally enjoyed only 4 percent support in the polls. After more than two decades at the side of Lyndon Johnson, however, the things that Connally didn't know about politics weren't worth knowing, and he was able to capitalize on Daniel's unaccustomed unpopularity over a sales tax that Daniel himself hadn't wanted and had let become law without his signature.

On January 15, 1963, Connally was sworn in as Texas' thirty-ninth governor. Nonetheless, the 1962 election was the first to provide meaningful hope to Texas Republicans. With the Eisenhower accord no longer in effect from conservative Texas Democrats, some began switching parties, and the man Connally defeated in the general election, Jack Cox, had started as a Democrat, and polled a very respectable 46 percent against Connally. While Allan Shivers, who by now was a Republican in all but name, supported Nixon and lost, the Texas Republicans actually triumphed in the special election to fill Johnson's vacant Senate seat. The lucky man was John Tower, a native of East Texas and government teacher at Midwestern University in Wichita Falls. He was bright—he had a master's degree from the London School of Economics—and it didn't hurt his bid that his Democratic opponent, William Blakely, who had been appointed to Johnson's seat as interim senator, was a boring and snakebitten campaigner.

Still smarting from his humble beginnings—he had plowed fields barefooted behind a mule on the farm near Floresville where he was born—Governor Connally nursed an ambition to be accepted by intellectuals. He increased teacher salaries and funding for research libraries and higher education, which he financed by raising taxes, and he oversaw the creation of the Texas Historical Commission, the Texas Commission on the Arts, and the Institute of Texan Cultures, which premiered at a space-age world's fair in San Antonio called the Hemisfair in 1968.

As controversial as he was at home, Yarborough's intelligence, passion, and effectiveness in the Senate began to draw him a national following, not just old New Dealers but new Kennedy liberals as well. The Texas Democrats, by contrast, began to rally around Connally. Mindful that he had only barely carried Texas in 1960, President Kennedy scheduled a trip to the state late in 1963, intending to let his glamorous wife Jacqueline win public hearts while he tried to smooth feathers and perhaps reunite the state party, and also acknowledge the role that Tejanos had played in his election. (He had already kept one campaign promise, to appoint a Hispanic ambassador to a Latin American country.) After a brief visit to San Antonio to dedicate the School of Aerospace Medicine on November 21, he and the first lady flew to Houston for a testimonial dinner and then attended the LULAC Director's Ball (to the delight of the Mexican-American community) before flying to Fort Worth to spend the night. After addressing the Chamber of Commerce in the morning there was a short flight to Dallas and what he feared would be a frosty reception.

Despite his stand during the Cuban missile crisis, Texas conservatives loathed him for being, in their minds, soft on Communism, for beating Johnson, and in general for being a Massachusetts liberal. There was also a recent issue that galled them particularly—Texas war hero General Edwin Walker, who had led elite commandos in Italy and now was commanding the 24th Infantry in Germany, had been dressed down by the secretary of defense and resigned from the service for distributing John Birch Society literature among his soldiers. Walker now lived in Dallas, flying the American flag outside his house upside down, and writing right-wing doggerel. As Kennedy's motorcade was put together at Love Field, the presidential car was shared by Governor and Nellie Connally; the vice president and Lady Bird would share the second car with Ralph and Opal Yarborough. The parade would wind through downtown before returning north to the Trade Mart for a noon luncheon speech. "Mr. President," Nellie Connally shouted above the thunder of cheers, "you can't say that Texas doesn't love you now!" The cars turned onto Elm Street, passing by a nondescript brick warehouse, the Texas School Book Depository. Rifle shots cracked, and history changed.

Back aboard Air Force One, flanked by Lady Bird and a blood-spattered Jacqueline Kennedy, a grim Johnson was sworn in as the 36th president of the United States by Dallas judge Sarah T. Hughes. She, coincidentally, had been appointed to the federal bench two years before by Kennedy, who acquiesced to powerful Texas lobbying by Johnson, Rayburn, and Yarborough, and over the objection of his brother, U.S. Attorney General (and Johnson enemy) Robert Kennedy.

The most difficult problem that Johnson inherited from Kennedy was what to do about America's growing involvement in Vietnam, a conflict that began as a nationalist struggle against French colonialism, but had since become a point of Cold War contention. Johnson committed more and more U.S. forces to the quagmire and just as increasingly hamstrung his presidency. When Lyndon Johnson was nominated for a second term in 1964, he won in a landslide against Senator Barry Goldwater of Arizona. Within a couple of years, though, in much of the country, Johnson was vilified for his conduct of the war, to an extent that elements of his "Great Society," such as Medicare, Head Start, and the Civil Rights Act, could not counter. Escalation of the Vietnam War had a dramatic impact on the economies of several Texas cities. One example was the community of Hurst, in Tarrant County northeast of Fort Worth; its population had numbered in the dozens, partly supported during Prohibition by surreptitious whiskey stills in the Trinity River bottoms. Bell Aviation opened a helicopter plant in the early fifties, and it became the town's largest employer. In the late sixties production mushroomed to fill Pentagon orders for Huey gunships, until at its height the plant employed more than 11,000 workers.

Even aside from the benefits of a renewed war economy, the war was popular almost everywhere in Texas. The youth movement that grew elsewhere, in part in opposition to the war, was limited to the University of Texas. Young people who wanted to share in the questioning voice of their generation needed to find safer places to do it—as did a singer named Janis Joplin. Born in 1943 to a middle-class family in Port Arthur, she grew up bright and artistic. She worked hard to become a painter but grew discouraged from lack of recognition. In her teens she was drawn into what little beat culture there was in Southeast Texas, and quickly espoused their rejection of middle-class values. Her onetime friends felt confused and betrayed by this; she was unpopular and even ridiculed by the time she graduated in 1960 from Port Arthur's Jefferson High School. Seeking to replace friends with an audience, she began singing in local coffee houses.

At first her music was derivative, imitating performers from Joan Baez to Odetta, with a heavy absorption of Bessie Smith. She left to attend the University of Texas, and in Austin she became a favorite performer at a roadhouse called Threadgill's. Austin was more progressive than Port Arthur, but when university frat boys named her Ugliest Man on Campus she headed for San Francisco, where the lifestyle nearly killed her. Sent home to recuperate, she tried to adjust to life in Port Arthur but found it hopeless. Back in San Francisco with the band Big Brother and the Holding Company, she adopted the blues mama persona and "sang hard," as she called it, for the first time. She immersed herself in her music, alternating her trademark hard-driving rock with heart-wrenching blues ballads. She generated shock waves at the 1967 Monterey Pop Festival and in an album the following year, which led to outward stardom. Throughout her brief career, however, Joplin was the victim of an inner war between her keen intelligence and her corrosive insecurity. She returned to Port Arthur for her tenth high school reunion in July 1970—an odd kind of triumph in which she was eyed and in a way admired by many who recoiled from her life of drugs, sexual experimentation, and music they didn't understand. Few were surprised when she died of an overdose three months later.

If Texas mainly avoided the counterculture of the sixties, it was nonetheless affected by the religious revival centered among the youth that began in that decade. Charismatic leaders, some sincere and some not, spoke in the new vernacular and replaced staid hymns with Jesus-oriented rock music. It was a medium ripe for the growth of cults, perhaps the most notorious of which was the Children of God, a California group that fled what they believed would be an apocalyptic earthquake, and got permission to settle on a 425-acre farm about twenty miles north of Stephenville that was owned by a nondenominational ministry. Urged to give up their material possessions and forsake contact with their families, they took biblical names for themselves and divided commune chores among work groups named for the twelve tribes of Israel. They evangelized the University of Texas campus wearing sackcloth and ashes in 1970, but during the following year they were broken up when the owners of their property got wind of their permissive sexual practices including, reportedly, orgies and what the Children called "flirty-fishing," or perhaps more appropriately, "f-ing," using their youthful charms to attract new members. Dispossessed of their farm, many took refuge with communes of the same group in other states.

The most memorable campus event in Austin in the sixties was neither political nor religious. Rather, it was the terrible morning and midday of August 1, 1966, and one of the worst mass murders in American history. At first glance Charles Whitman offered no hint of the angst of his generation. He was as clean-cut as the times could have required, handsome, his blond hair clipped in a short crew cut. He was a product of Catholic schools in Lake Worth, Florida; he had been an Eagle Scout and a Marine. In the service he passed his officer training exams and was sent to study engineering at the University of Texas, but plagued by bad grades, he first left school and then was discharged from the Marines. He reentered UT twice, and in the spring 1966 semester sought psychiatric evaluation at the school's health center, but he did not keep his follow-up appointments. On July 22, accompanied by his brother, he visited the UT tower, whose lower floors housed administrative offices, and above them, story after story of stacks and carrels of the graduate library. They reached the tourist perch of the observation deck on the twenty-eighth floor, a narrow walk that encircles the clock tower and belfry, which offered a commanding view from more than 230 feet above the campus, before departing.

Whitman was a marksman and owned five guns, which in Texas was regarded with approbation. Without hint of trouble, Whitman awoke early on the morning of August 1, killed his wife, then went to his mother's apartment and killed her. He visited a gunshop and purchased a shotgun, along with a grab bag of ammunition for the rest of his arsenal. Shortly before noon he arrived at the tower, lugging a heavy footlocker packed with firearms, ammunition, and provisions. On the twenty-eighth floor he clubbed the receptionist to death, and shot four people who were ascending the stairs, of whom two died. Whitman then began shooting outside, firing over the rail and through the water spouts, picking off students on the south mall, and shoppers on the Guadalupe Street "drag," dropping human targets at astounding ranges. Over the next two hours, he killed ten more people and wounded thirty-one, one of them mortally, before police gained entry onto the deck and ended his life in a hail of bullets. At the autopsy it was discovered that Whitman had a walnut-sized tumor in his brain, which led to acrimonious debate whether he had been responsible for his actions.

The protests of the sixties also brought an increasing consciousness of ecological degradation around the country. Texans had spent most of five generations trying to wring a living out of the land, and they associated environmentalism with flower children and other nonsense. Neither of Texas' two great economic pillars—cattle and oil—could be described as environmentally friendly. (Palmetto State Park near Luling, for instance, was set aside in 1933 mostly to preserve sulfurous hot springs, which dried up after extensive drilling lowered the water table.) Further, Texas had also never enjoyed the massive acreage of national parks and forests that other Western states had because it had kept its public domain, and there were no large federal tracts to reserve. Conservation of nature was a pet concern, however, of Texas' maverick Senator Yarborough.

One of his main goals was to preserve part of Padre Island, the longest sand beach in the United States and host to more than six hundred plant species, some of them unique. Efforts to save it dated to the 1930s, when a bill to establish a state park there was vetoed by Governor Allred because, he believed, the state already owned some of the land. The courts said otherwise, the controversy led to a flurry of waterfront buying by investors and developers, and the momentum to establish a park was lost. Yarborough seized upon Eisenhower's endorsement of a ten-year expansion plan for the national park system to place a Padre Island National Seashore in the works. Investors and resort developers opposed him every step of the way, and their lawsuits required acquisition of most of the land by condemnation, increasing the cost fivefold to over $23 million, and making Yarborough a virtual bogeyman to private property advocates. But the park was eventually dedicated in 1968, was quickly acknowledged as one of the jewels of the national park system, and commenced providing a continuous boon to coastal tourist industry.

A much easier time was had in reserving Guadalupe Mountains National Park in the Trans-Pecos, an upraised fossil coral reef pairing spectacular scenery, including Texas' highest mountain peak, with delicate ecology. Aware of the area's unique natural heritage, one of the principal landowners, petroleum geologist William C. Pratt, donated over five thousand acres to the park and was instrumental in getting his neighbor, J. C. Hunter Jr., to sell more than seventy thousand acres. What opposition there was fell apart when test wells discovered no oil to fight over.

The keystone of Yarborough's conservation effort, and his last and greatest fight in his waning Senate years, was the preservation of part of the Big Thicket, a dense tangle of swamp and forest in the southeast corner of the state. Owned mostly by large timber companies whose logging had reduced its area by over 90 percent, from 3.5 million acres to about 300,000, the Thicket harbors species that are relics from the last Ice Age, including carnivorous plants, forty species of orchids, and a vast bird list that may still include a remnant population of the enormous ivory-billed woodpecker. Lobbying by big timber companies managed to delay consideration of a Big

Thicket National Park for years, unintentionally aided by infighting among citizen groups who were advocating it. By logging frenetically during the tactical delays, the lumber concerns managed to limit the size of the park to a fraction of what was once envisioned, and less than what was needed to protect the fragile ecosystem. And instead of a single large bloc of wilderness, they managed to hold it to a patchwork of smaller parcels, which they euphemistically touted as a "string of pearls." (Not without reason was the area's congressman nicknamed "Timber Charlie" Wilson.)

Yarborough had help, however, largely in the person of maverick local newspaper editor Archer Fullingim of the *Kountze News*, who took on the timber companies and kept the issue alive among the residents who otherwise would have had little alternate source of information. (He was also known nationally as the first journalist to coin the epithet "Tricky Dicky" in reference to Richard Nixon.) Once established, however, the National Park Service recognized its stature with an entirely new classification, the Big Thicket National Biological Preserve. Land acquisition still creeps along, totaling 97,206 acres as of fiscal 2004, but enough to have been recognized by the United Nations as a biosphere reserve of world importance.

The sixties were also a time when the state parks system began to expand to a system befitting the state. From the time Governor Pat Neff gave his family farm to the people of Texas for their first state park, that system had limped along as one of the smallest and weakest-run in the nation. Texas had less acreage set aside for parks than Maine, and what parks existed were mostly small and geared toward intensive recreation—swimming pools, golf courses, and the like. For many years the largest state nature park was Palo Duro Canyon at about 15,000 acres, but it was still marred by a cable lift, miniature railroad, and summer musical theater. Meaningful expansion began in 1967 with the passage of a $67 million bond package for land acquisition. Some of the parks purchased with these funds have become among the most popular in the system, such as 5,000-acre Pedernales Falls near Johnson City.

Texans supported their senator-turned-president's foreign policy, but they did not follow his lead on domestic policy, especially civil rights for blacks. It would have been the easiest thing in the world for Johnson to have used the monolithic opposition of Southern senators as an excuse to scrap the Civil Rights Act of 1964. Instead, he drew upon every reserve of his flattering, hectoring, and arm-twisting powers of persuasion to secure its passage. He then took on a black protégée, a young woman from Houston named Barbara Jordan. A poor woman of large frame, stentorian voice, and flame-throwing intelligence, a product of Houston's disintegrating Fourth Ward, she graduated from the not-so-equal but very separate Texas Southern University. Rather than endure the distractions of the recently integrated University of Texas Law School, she took her jurisdoctorate at Boston University, where she perfected a mesmerizing speaking style grounded, rather like Sam Houston's had been, in a large and precisely used vocabulary. She taught at Tuskegee for a year before returning to Houston. She practiced law out of her parents' home because she couldn't afford to open an office, and failed in two attempts to run for a seat in the Texas senate.

A strong liberal bloc in that body then challenged the rules. Led by Oscar Mauzy of Dallas and others, the group forced a change in election procedure to single-member districts. That, plus the Supreme Court's striking down the payment of poll taxes, helped the campaigns of minority candidates such as Joseph Lockridge of Dallas and Curtis Graves of Houston, who were elected in 1966 to become the first blacks to sit in the state house since before the turn of the century. Joining them in the state senate that year was Barbara Jordan. Mauzy also believed that, while *Sweatt v. Painter* desegregated the university law school, that was insufficient progress and they should actively recruit minority students, and women as well.

Barbara Jordan's career in the Texas senate did not begin smoothly. She endured repeated slights, and several colleagues referred to her, usually behind her back, as "the washerwoman," or "Mammy." Wise as well as intelligent, Jordan worked hard, politicked deftly, and made believers out of those who mocked her; after election to her third term she was chosen—unanimously—as president pro tempore of the senate. She then moved on to the U.S. House of Representatives, where her eloquence during the 1974 Watergate hearings moved the nation. She was the first woman to keynote a Democratic National Convention, in 1976. After three terms in Congress, as her health began to prematurely decline, she left politics to teach at the Lyndon B. Johnson School of Public Affairs at UT.

SIXTY-NINE

CHANGES, FASTER AND FASTER

JUST AS LYNDON JOHNSON DECLINED TO RUN FOR A SEC-
ond term in 1968, John Connally retired from the Texas governorship the
same year, sparking a thirteen-way free-for-all to replace him. The candidate
who emerged victorious was the two-term lieutenant governor, Preston
Smith, an erstwhile theater owner from Lubbock. An uninspiring leader
who drew most of his support from rural areas, Smith kept a low profile and
left the legislature to stronger hands: house speaker Gus Mutscher, and an
up-and-coming lieutenant governor for whom a national career was predicted, Ben Barnes, whose curly blond hair helped make him a new political
Golden Boy. Smith's two terms were relatively nondescript, the major story
of those years being the fall of Ralph Yarborough from the U.S. Senate. After
two full terms, he was opposed in 1970 by Rio Grande Valley rancher Lloyd
Bentsen, who entered the race backed with enough conservative money (a
good deal of it his own) to send Texas' last happy liberal into retirement.

A much bigger story erupted two years later, in an unprecedented scandal. One Frank Sharp (appropriate name), Houston banker and insurance
executive, found his empire in trouble, and determined to seek relief from
the legislature in the form of a craftily worded bill that would have the effect
of exempting his bank from scrutiny. In consideration, he had $600,000 to
lend from his bank to key lawmakers, including Smith, Mutscher, and others. They could use the money to purchase stock in Sharp's own National
Banker's Life Insurance Company, stock whose value Sharp would make
sure became inflated, allowing the officials to sell at a profit. Incredibly,
Mutscher and others bought it. The entire scheme was busted wide open;
after trial, Speaker Mutscher, Representative Tommy Shannon of Fort
Worth, and Mutscher aide Rush McGinty were convicted of conspiracy to accept a bribe in March 1972 and sentenced to probation for five years. The
larger fallout was political, as the prosecutor let it slip that Preston Smith
had been named as an unindicted co-conspirator.

The Democrats charged that the entire affair was one of Richard Nixon's
infamous dirty tricks, but the accusation rang hollow when one prominent
Texas Democrat who supported Nixon, Will Wilson, lost his high-profile job

at the Justice Department when his own ties to Frank Sharp became known. John Connally now joined the file of Democrats who crossed the aisle, founded the Democrats for Nixon in 1972, and was rewarded with the Treasury portfolio. Claiming his innocence and pointing out that he had in fact vetoed the bill that would have benefited Sharp, Preston Smith announced for reelection to a third term as governor.

His principal opponent was Uvalde land baron Dolph Briscoe, a four-term legislator and a past president of the Southwestern Cattle Raisers Association. But then a ringer appeared in the primary, in the form of a feisty Corpus Christi educator and liberal state representative named Frances "Sissy" Farenthold. She was the beneficiary of nearly two decades of progress for Texas women, which included their growing economic independence, with steady increments in the number of women employed outside the home. Women enjoyed a growing sense of political awareness, first being allowed to serve on juries in 1954, and after 1966 the presence of the National Organization for Women led to more political ferment than at any time since suffrage days. Texas women now also boasted a simple hefty demographic, as they outnumbered Texas men for the first time in 1960. Farenthold finally was able to ride a crest of support for an equal rights amendment to the state constitution, which passed in 1972.

To no one's surprise, Preston Smith was humiliated with a tiny percentage of the vote, but to everyone's surprise, Sissy Farenthold forced Briscoe into a spirited runoff. She lost, but observers enjoyed the contest. Such was the ire of the voters in the 1972 election that half of the entire state house of representatives was either shamed into retirement or defeated at the polls— a housecleaning that was unprecedented in Texas history. The sitting lieutenant governor, Ben Barnes, who was not implicated in the Sharpstown scandal, was nevertheless thrown out with the rest of the rascals, unseated by William P. Hobby Jr., son of Texas' World War I–era governor. He was considered a moderate reformer and held the job for eighteen highly respected years.

As governor, Briscoe smiled a lot but did rather little, but then, he didn't have to. The industrial component of Texas' economy entered a rapid and muscular expansion, and while Briscoe adopted a no-new-taxes mantra, the state budget, which doubled during his tenure, was paid for by the same rate on a swelling tax base. Also under Briscoe, the length of the gubernatorial term was doubled to four years, elections to be held in the biennium alternate from presidential elections. Thus Briscoe served six years by being reelected only once in 1974.

One aspect of the economic boom was a stunning increase in immigration from outside the state. From a 1970 census figure of 11.2 million, Texas grew to 14.2 million in 1980, about half of that increase accounted for by immigration. Half a million arrived in the first half of the seventies, a million more in the second half, and another million in the eighties. People who spoke with a Texas drawl almost became minorities in their own cities, and these outsiders brought with them beliefs and loyalties often different from the traditional Texan's.

This shift set the stage for equally huge political changes. Briscoe, desiring to become the first Texas governor to serve for ten years, announced for a third term in 1978. The voters in the Democratic primary, however, preferred the attorney general, John Hill, who was vigorously backed by the teachers' organizations. The Republican opposing him was an abrupt and snarly Dallas oilman named William Clements, a political outsider who financed much of his $7 million campaign with his own checkbook. While in former days it would have been an easy win for Hill, Clements was able to draw on that vast new pool of Texas residents who felt no particular loyalty to the Texas Democratic tradition and stunningly, he became the first Republican governor of Texas since Reconstruction.

With 80 percent of the population now living in cities, it became harder and harder for those born on the land to stay on it. By 1980 the farm population had shrunk to only 215,000, less than 15 percent of what it was at the end of World War II, and the number of farms declined by more than half. As family farms failed, the land was acquired by corporate agribusinesses, and the size of the average farm more than doubled in the same period, to about 700 acres. Cotton and cattle continued to predominate, but the eighties saw the beginnings of an extraordinary diversification.

In finding creative ways to stay on the land, some looked to history. The first wine grapes in Texas were grown by Franciscan friars near El Paso beginning in 1662, and it became known over the centuries that the state's myriad soils and climates would support a variety of grapes. Before Prohibition put them out of business, Texas had twenty commercial wineries. Farmers were slow to return to that crop, partly because experimental plots planted in the 1950s in South Texas were destroyed by Pierce's disease, but from the seventies on, dogged planters brought viticulture back to Texas, and eventually grapes came to be grown in more than two hundred commercial vineyards, supplying at least part of the need of about fifty wineries.

Owners of some large spreads began stocking exotic game; others excavated ponds for commercial catfish production, the latter becoming a thriving industry. (Some other attempts at agricultural diversification proved faddish, such as ostrich farming, which peaked at 80,000 birds before imploding.) Organic farms, usually small and intensively worked, began to have an impact on the agricultural economy. Ever since the introduction of large-scale pesticide spraying in the twenties, some people who were regarded as eccentric doubted the safety of such products. As time passed and pests became resistant to eradication, some crops such as Texas spinach from the Rio Grande Valley, which is a major source for the U.S. supply, could not feasibly even be grown without chemical treatment. Nonetheless, consumer demand for wholesome meat and produce led to the establishment of a major grocery chain, Whole Foods Markets, headquartered in Austin. The advent of bovine encephalopathy, so-called mad cow disease, fatal to humans if ingested in infected meat, only strengthened the movement to organics. In 2004 the first and only case of the disease in a Texas cow surfaced, but it was determined that no part of the animal had been sold for human consumption. Nevertheless, the extraordinary incubation period of the disease, which could allow the virus to lurk in the commercial meat supply for up to seven years, has made organic products that much more attractive.

One unforeseen result of the decline in agriculture in the Valley, which was occasioned by droughts, frosts, and market factors, has been the return of wilderness. In the centuries before development, the Rio Grande jungle was the northernmost limit of the Central American forest, featuring tropical birds and exotic hardwoods such as ebony. During the decades of clearing, the natural cover was bulldozed into windrows and burned almost to extinction. In the entire hundred miles of the lower Valley, only 2,500 acres survived in three scattered parcels: the Bentsen–Rio Grande State Park, a hundred-acre island owned by the National Audubon Society in the mouth of the Rio Grande, and the largest tract, the 1,900-acre Santa Ana National Wildlife Refuge, often referred to as the jewel of the federal refuge system. Recognizing the drastic loss of habitat and the endangered status of many of its species, federal authorities began acquiring land in 1979 for a string of refuges to restore an adequate stretch of Rio Grande jungle to its former vitality. More Valley farmland went up for sale than federal planners imagined. As parcels were acquired, the families who sold the land were often hired to restore it to its natural condition. As a result, what was once one of the most endangered ecosystems in North America is now one of the best protected. In 1999, after a federal investment of $80 million, the first seven new refuges totaling some 90,000 acres were opened to the public. They embrace coastal marsh, riverine jungle, brush country, and such historic sites as the Palmito Ranch battleground, where the last land battle of the Civil War was fought, and the Sal del Rey, a brine lake that supplied salt to conquistadores and the Confederacy. Plans are proceeding to round out the Lower Rio Grande Valley National Wildlife Refuge with the purchase of an additional 42,500 acres. The hope is that what the Valley loses in competitive agriculture, it will gain in tourism. A different program of land acquisition has been the Balcones Canyonlands National Wildlife Refuge of 22,000 acres on the western outskirts of Austin, intended for the protection of various endangered species.

When Ronald Reagan won the presidency in 1980, he carried Texas by an enormous margin, and during the increasingly conservative 1980s, Texas progressives found themselves under siege and having to defend the most basic public policy grounds of a social safety net. Henry B. González was one; during his decades in Congress he rose steadily through the ranks of seniority until he sat as chairman of the powerful Banking Committee. During the headlong rush to deregulate the savings and loan business, González warned that the S&Ls would collapse, and sure enough the industry imploded, costing the American public a rescue of several hundred billion dollars. His oratory was still angry and piquant, but most newly elected Texans were now conservative Republicans, such as Phil Gramm, elected in 1984 to replace John Tower in the Senate. Most of the new guard were relieved when González finally retired, but not before he warned that Mexican banks were not equipped to deal with the North American Free Trade Agreement. No one took him seriously until the peso collapsed.

In 1982 Clements was unseated by another attorney general, Mark White, despite an expenditure nearly double that of his first campaign. Clements had alienated Hispanic voters by endorsing resumption of a "bracero" guest-worker program similar to what was employed during World War II. White, by contrast, had the teachers' organizations solidly behind him, with promises of higher pay and reforms in the system. White's four years in the mansion were difficult, for in the true sign of a moderate, he was often too liberal for the conservatives and too conservative for the liberals. He did give consumers input to the Public Utilities Commission, but his education reform backfired with its so-called No Pass, No Play provision, which denied students participation in extracurricular activities if their grades fell too low. In a state where family life revolves around high school football, penalizing athletes courted political suicide. White also had the bad luck to preside over the collapse of the boom years. Oil prices fell to less than ten dollars per barrel, evaporating the tax base and putting the state in a severe bind. Seeking reelection in 1986, White had to face Clements again, and this time Clements beat him.

The most important event of Bill Clements' second term was the election of George Bush to the presidency. Son of a Connecticut senator who had come to Texas to enter the oil business, Bush was a former House member who built up an extensive résumé in federal service before spending eight years as Reagan's vice president. Clements' term was also marked by a landmark federal lawsuit in which the state prison system was placed under court supervision until it corrected barbarous inadequacies. In retrospect, Clements was not as bad a governor as he was made out to be by delicate people who were put off by his sour demeanor. He had a good record of minority appointments and his legislative program was lean but moderate, although largely ignored by the legislature, many of whose members entered into a state of denial over Texas electing its first Republican chief executive since E. J. Davis. His most lasting legacy was an exhaustive, three-year renovation of the Governor's Mansion.

In 1990 Texans elected their second female governor, Ann Willis Richards, a former Travis County commissioner and two-term state treasurer. Most famous for her white bouffant hair, she was also noted for her rapier wit and skill at storytelling, both delivered in a nasal twang redolent of her Waco roots. She was a recovering alcoholic who had been dry for fifteen years, indicating a strength of character that made her one tough cookie politically. Then too, Richards had the advantage of campaigning against a Republican nominee, Midland oil millionaire Clayton Williams, who was a political novice and campaign bumpkin. Like the retiring Governor Clements, Williams had engineered his nomination with an enormous influx of his own money. To 51 percent of the electorate, Williams' tasteless remarks about his misspent youth (going across the border to "get serviced") and rape (that once a woman sees it's inevitable, she should "sit back and enjoy it") were unacceptable, and Ann Richards squeezed into the Governor's Mansion with a bare victory.

In the 1992 presidential election, Texans preferred their pseudo-native George Bush, seeking reelection, over challenger Bill Clinton of Arkansas, but just barely, 2.5 million to 2.3 million. That margin would have been wider, however, without the candidacy of an eccentric business whiz from

Dallas, Ross Perot, who polled 1.3 million. Although Clinton unseated Bush and won the presidency, Republican gains in the state legislature and an unmistakable conservative shift in Texas generally prompted a matching rightward shift in the Richards administration. Before long, however, all eyes were on Texas for a vastly different reason.

Texas' long pairing of fervent religious faith with theological naïveté, and of contempt for the government with the love affair with firearms, were dangerous ingredients that needed only the right spark to touch off a lethal conflagration. That catalyst was born Vernon Wayne Howell in Houston on August 17, 1959. After a troubled and unsettled childhood, Howell became enthralled with the teachings of the Seventh-Day Adventist Church, to which his family belonged. Enamored of the mysteries of the Book of Revelation, he fancied that he had unlocked its secrets and been anointed to deliver its message. Calling himself by the new name of David Koresh, he assumed leadership of an Adventist splinter group on a property ten miles east of Waco at a place they called Mount Carmel. There about a hundred of his followers, when not listening to his high-volume harangues that garbled the Bible with assault rifles and explosives, made their living and built a residential compound. It was soon elaborated into a complex of frame structures clustered about a four-story watchtower, a concrete bunker where the arms and ammunition were stored, and a school bus buried in the ground as a final refuge against some mysterious future assault.

In August 1989, Koresh claimed to have received the Revelation of the New Light, anointing him, not as Christ reincarnate, but as an imperfect messiah. Flawed or not, he claimed dominion over all the women in the sect. The men who remained were enjoined to celibacy, as Koresh began impregnating their wives and daughters, having sex with girls as young as twelve. In a short time he fathered twelve children, in addition to the two he had with his wife and three with his sister-in-law. He began referring to Mount Carmel as "Ranch Apocalypse." Accounts of child sexual abuse led to inquiries by child protection services; further reports of the stockpile of illegal weapons and explosives generated interest on the part of the Federal Bureau of Alcohol, Tobacco, and Firearms. As their demands for information became more insistent, Koresh's preaching became more rabid. His defiance led to the property being surrounded with a military perimeter, with federal agents employing sleep deprivation and other antihostage tactics. After weeks of fruitless negotiations, federal authorities attempted an incursion into the fortified compound, resulting in an eruption of gunfire and the deaths of four ATF agents. With the feds more determined than ever, on

April 19, 1993, an armored vehicle punched through a wall to place tear gas. Koresh and his followers touched off incendiaries and the compound quickly became a raging inferno. The charred remains of eighty-two Branch Davidians, including twenty-two children, Koresh and most of his extended "family," were found in the debris. Forensic examination showed that most had been murdered or committed suicide.

It was a tragedy, and a cautionary tale of what can happen when groups combine faith, ignorance, hate, and guns. Governor Ann Richards had had nothing to do with it, but her position as a Democratic governor in an increasingly Republican state accelerated the political transformation. Clinton had tapped Texas Senator Lloyd Bentsen to serve as his treasury secretary, and that chair was won by Republican Kay Bailey Hutchison, a former University of Texas cheerleader who had gone on to a career as a journalist and legislator before succeeding Richards as state treasurer. Her husband, Ray Hutchison, had run for governor back in the days when being a moderate Republican was politically acceptable. The following year Ann Richards stood for reelection, and to oppose her the Republicans chose George W. Bush, son of the former president. He had never held political office, surviving various failures in the oil business to become managing partner of the Texas Rangers professional baseball team.

On paper he was no match for the gregarious, storytelling Richards, who in the second half of her term ran to the right as hard as she could. She signed death warrants with alacrity and vastly increased the capacity of the Texas prison system; she even signed a bill allowing Texans to carry concealed handguns. In seeking to embrace conservatives who would never hug her back, Ann Richards alienated the coalition of minorities, progressives, and educators who had elected her the first time. She forgot a cardinal rule of Texas politics: Dance with the one who brung you. As the election neared, her aides and supporters were perplexed at her apparent disinterest in the campaign, after she had made a career of being a live wire. Perhaps she sensed that with the recent influx of at least three million non-Texan voters, many of them from the conservative Midwest and West, and many of them with preexisting loyalties that had nothing to do with Texas, she didn't have a chance. And Bush, unlike Clayton Williams, ran an intelligent, effective, no-mistakes campaign. His heavily accented Spanish was acceptable if not fluent, and his linguistic efforts siphoned Hispanic support away from the Democrats who had come to take the brown vote for granted. He ran as a conservative, but not as an ideologue—a stratagem that had stood his father well. On election day the Bush scion beat Richards with a comfortable 53 percent majority. She need not have taken the defeat personally, though, for the only positive result the Texas Democrats could take away from the 1994 election was that they kept control of the legislature—although with only a three-vote majority in the state senate. Both U.S. Senate seats were now in Republican hands for the first time since Reconstruction. The GOP swept all three seats on the powerful railroad commission, claimed a majority on the state supreme court, and gained two seats in the federal House.

AFTERWORD

In 2000, halfway through his second term as governor, George W. Bush was elected president of the United States. He was succeeded in the mansion by the lieutenant governor, Rick Perry, a onetime agriculture commissioner from the high plains. The state election that year resulted in split control of the state capitol between the Republican senate and Democratic house. This gain for the GOP was only a prelude to a spectacular sweep two years later, when they captured every statewide office—including Perry's election in his own right—every chair on the state supreme court, and majorities in both the state house and senate for the first time since Reconstruction.

With Bush's reelection in 2004, Texas surpassed California as the locus of reigning political philosophy, with more years of national leadership in the White House than any other state. The Texas style of minimal government with an emphasis on law and order has become the national norm. This has marked a gravitational shift in the Republican Party as well. Once divided between Northeastern moderates and a libertarian wing anchored by Western Goldwaterites, the party is now firmly Texanized with a focus on social conservatism. In this guise the party has captured more and more state legislatures, with Texas in the surprising political role as the new California.

Yet in Texas, as nationally, there have been signs of strain, reflected not least in an increasing ethnic polarity. In the 2003 legislature, for instance, of 19 Republican state senators, all were white, but of 12 Democratic state senators, all but 3 were Hispanic or African-American. Of 88 Republicans in the state house, 86 were white, 2 were Hispanic; of 62 Democrats, only 20 were white. This has occurred during a third wave of immigration, still incoming, whether high-tech white-collar from the Midwest or *indocumentados* from Latin America, that has pushed Texas inexorably into the status of urban colossus. The number of Texans has now passed 20 million, double the number that Sam Houston once extravagantly boasted that the land could support. Three of the United States' ten largest cities are in Texas, and there are more than two dozen metropolitan areas with populations of

100,000 or more each. Of America's ten fastest-growing major counties, half are in Texas; the Austin area alone has doubled in size in twenty years, from half a million in 1980 to more than a million today.

And Texas is an urban colossus facing significant challenges for which its history may not have prepared it. Some of them are economic, beginning with the accelerating decline of the oil industry. From a 1960 production of 1.2 billion barrels, output peaked in 1972 with 1.3 billion. By 1988 this slackened to 700 million barrels, and by 2001 only 379 million barrels. Proven reserves in 1960 stood at 15 billion barrels, but shrank to only 5 billion in 2001, a year in which almost as many wells were plugged (8,023) as were drilled (8,080). Most telling of all, in memory of hundred-foot-tall gushers of crude a century ago, the average well, which produced 22 barrels per day in 1948, in 2000 bubbled out only 4 barrels per day. Despite offsets from new exploration both in the Gulf and on land, the oil tap is slowly but surely being shut off.

The downsizing of the oil patch will be dwarfed by a coming competition for the most basic element, water, which has come in shorter and shorter supply with increased population, usage, and pumping from sinking aquifers. Texas water law is governed by the frontier doctrine of "capture": my land, my well, my water, no matter what effect the pumping could have on one's neighbors. Texas groundwater has become the target of corporate arbitrageurs, who have been buying up vast acreages of water rights from poor dirt farmers, aiming to pump in volume and sell the water to thirsty cities such as El Paso and San Antonio, the latter depending on wells for its entire supply. This is a particularly sobering prospect on the Staked Plains, where the Ogallala Aquifer has already been falling at some four feet per year. About the only town that has taken steps to provide for a future after irrigation is Andrews, near the New Mexico line about a hundred miles southwest of Lubbock. In 2005 that community preserved future jobs and income by opening a dump to receive the nation's nuclear waste—a bleak vision of life after water on the Staked Plains.

Other challenges will be social. Texas ranks last among the fifty states in per capita public expenditures, and forty-ninth—ahead of Colorado—in per capita tax rate. The laissez-faire attitude of the frontier has never entirely disappeared, and the economic results have been predictable: booms of population and wealth go hand in hand with extreme need. Texas ranks forty-ninth in water quality and fiftieth in medical insurance for children. It ranks first in the rate of teen pregnancy, and infant mortality has been rising for five years. The 2005 legislature failed both in regular session and in two spe-

cial sessions to repair a public school finance system that was declared unconstitutional, and Texas continues to rank last among the states in the rate
of high school graduation.

Still other challenges for the coming years will be legal and political, with
racial justice first on the list. One case that gained sensational national attention originated in Tulia, a Panhandle town of 5,100 people fifty miles
south of Amarillo. In January 1998, an officer of the Panhandle Regional
Narcotics Task Force, working alone for months, "cracked" a dangerous
drug ring in Tulia, resulting in July 1999 in the arrests of forty-six people, all
of them black or with ties to the black community—about 10 percent of the
town's entire African-American population. The first few trials resulted in
draconian sentences, from forty to ninety years, based solely on the officer's
testimony, without field notes, video, or audio tapes, and despite the fact
that no money or drugs were seized. Even when prosecutors were forced to
dismiss some cases once it was proven that the defendants were not even in
town at the time of their alleged offenses, they still declined to link those
dismissals to the officer's credibility in the remaining cases. After seeing
their neighbors and relatives sentenced, the rest of the Tulia defendants
sought plea bargains ranging up to twenty years rather than face the full
stretch. The Texas Narcotics Control Program gave the investigating officer
its coveted Outstanding Lawman of the Year award.

In September 2001, as the Tulia convicts sat in prison, the Legal Defense
and Education Fund of the NAACP retained lawyers who quickly unmasked
the whole game. The Texas Court of Criminal Appeals began ordering new
hearings and assigned a retired state district judge to preside. Relocating to
Tulia, his inquiry screeched to a halt when county prosecutors conceded all
points, agreed not to retry the cases if they were overturned, and themselves
turned on the rogue officer, who was indicted for felony perjury. He was
given ten years probation, while the Tulia defendants accepted a $6 million
civil settlement for their treatment.

Both the strengths and weaknesses of the Texas judicial system are seen
at their most sobering, and final, in capital cases. Texas' last public hanging
took place on July 30, 1923, when 10,000 people in Waco turned out to see
a black man named Roy Mitchell, a mass murderer, get his neck stretched.
When the state government took over the capital function from the various
counties soon after, voltage was selected over the noose as the mode of dispatch, and the electric chair in Huntsville, "Old Sparky," was scheduled to
be broken in with five executions on one day: November 8, 1924. Some
weeks before that date the warden of the "Walls" unit, who would have

thrown the switch, resigned. "A warden can't be a warden and a killer, too," he said. "The penitentiary is a place to reform a man, not kill him."

Reformers then as now hold a minority view, and after what was considered an annoying hiatus during which the Supreme Court held capital punishment unconstitutional until better procedures were developed, Texas resumed executing the condemned in December 1982. Old Sparky, whose jolt was renowned for popping eyeballs right out of their sockets, was retired in favor of a gurney on which to administer a lethal injection of barbiturates. By the end of 2004, some 336 convicts had been killed—the most of any state in the nation—after an average wait of sixteen years. And 452 remained on death row, also the most in the nation. Of that 452, exactly one was a white man convicted of killing an African-American, fueling the argument that the death penalty fell disproportionately upon minorities and the poor. The fallibility of capital sentences was also demonstrated with the release of eight men from death row after DNA evidence showed them to have been falsely convicted. (Late in 2005 facts developed, which were not seriously contested, showing that in 1993 Texas did in fact execute an innocent man named Ruben Cantu for a San Antonio murder.) In 2004 and 2005 the U.S. Supreme Court intervened to reverse Texas death sentences no fewer than four times, on such issues as putting juveniles and the mentally retarded to death, or going forward with executions after revelations of egregious trial-rigging by police and prosecutors.

This accumulating consternation appeared to have its effect in 2004. Twenty-three convicts were executed during the year, still the most of any state in the nation but off the previous pace, and Texas juries condemned only twenty-two defendants, the smallest annual cull in more than two decades. The 2005 session of the legislature passed a law giving Texas juries the option to consider life without parole as an alternative to a death sentence. Another important criminal law reform to come out of 2005 was the requirement that all inmates in the Texas prison system be required to submit DNA samples for inclusion in the state database.

On an entirely different legal front, a growing gay rights movement has been making itself felt. In 1973, the year in which the American Psychiatric Association removed homosexuality from its *Diagnostic and Statistical Manual* of mental illnesses, Texas' sodomy statute was rewritten to legalize varietal sex acts for heterosexuals, but it recriminalized them for homosexuals. The law was rarely enforced. In 1998, however, a mischievous phone call led Houston police to a residence on a false report of a disturbance by an armed man. They entered the house and found two men having sex; the pair were arrested, jailed, and later fined. The case became a national issue when it reached the Supreme Court as *Lawrence v. Texas,* in which a 6–3 majority overturned its own recent precedents and declared that private sexual conduct between consenting adults was protected by the Constitution. Both supporters of the decision and those who were horrified by it agreed that the legal ground rules for sexuality are now profoundly different. During the 2005 session the legislature responded by passing an amendment to the state constitution, later overwhelmingly ratified by the voters, barring recognition of same-sex relationships even if they are legal in other states.

Of all the issues facing Texas today, one overarches—economically, politically, and socially—and sets a context for all other dilemmas: the dramatic, and accelerating, re-Hispanization of Texas. Driven by poverty and overpopulation in Latin America in general and Mexico in particular, encouraged by the Mexican government which issues desert survival kits to those about to slip into the United States, accelerated by NAFTA, and welcomed by advocacy groups within Texas, it is all but certain that within a generation the state will be predominantly Hispanic.

Lacking any realistic chance at legal arrival in the United States, many immigrants turn to professional smugglers known as "coyotes," some of whom extort exorbitant sums and then strand their cargo in isolated and dangerous circumstances. In the deadliest single instance of smuggling gone bad, in May 2003, one of a ring of fourteen coyotes drove a tractor-trailer rig north from the border bound for Houston, crammed with seventy hapless immigrants in the back. After they began dying of heat, the driver abandoned the rig at a Victoria truck stop; by the time the doors were forced open, seventeen were dead and two more died later. The ringleaders faced up to life in prison and the driver faced capital charges. *Indocumentados* who do elude capture face a life in a shadow economy; they come to work, and no one denies that Hispanic immigrants work hard, but being illegal, they are often victims of abuses on the job that other workers are not subject to, and they often have no recourse to police or other social services without drawing attention to themselves and their status. There are large numbers of legal Latino immigrants as well, and the cultural impact of both legal and undocumented residents is enormous. In addition to the positive cultural diversity comes ethnocentrism, which has an even longer history than that of Anglos, and a portion of the drug trade that flourishes in northern Mexico. The city of Laredo, directly across the Rio Grande from its Mexican sister city of Nuevo Laredo, is the terminus of Interstate Highway 35, the carotid artery for Mexican drugs entering the United States. Homicides and kidnappings of U.S. citizens have been an increasingly serious problem.

Writing in *The Life of Reason* in 1905, the Spanish-American philosopher George Santayana maintained, "Those who cannot remember the past are condemned to repeat it." Texans, both Hispanics in the age before Stephen F. Austin and Anglos of the Republic and frontier eras, have never done well with pluralism. Whether they can now draw on their long heritage of individualism and adaptability to coexist contentedly in a multinational condominium is concealed in a future that none can divine.

SELECTED SOURCES
AND FURTHER READING

ABBREVIATIONS

BOOK PUBLISHERS

EP	Austin or Burnet, Texas: Eakin Press
LSUP	Baton Rouge: Louisiana State University Press
PPHS	Canyon, Texas: Panhandle-Plains Historical Society
SMUP	Dallas: Southern Methodist University Press
TAMUP	College Station: Texas A&M University Press
TCUP	Fort Worth: Texas Christian University Press
TMM	Austin: Texas Memorial Museum
TSHA	Austin: Texas State Historical Association
TWP	El Paso: Texas Western Press
UNMP	Albuquerque: University of New Mexico Press
UNT	Denton: University of North Texas Press
UOP	Norman: University of Oklahoma Press
USGPO	Washington, D.C.: U.S. Government Printing Office
UTP	Austin: University of Texas Press
VBJ	Austin: Von Boeckmann-Jones
YUP	New Haven, Conn.: Yale University Press

PERIODICALS

CO	Chronicles of Oklahoma
ETHJ	East Texas Historical Journal
JMAH	Journal of Mexican-American History
PPHR	Panhandle-Plains Historical Review
QTSHA	Quarterly of the Texas Historical Association
SHQ	Southwestern Historical Quarterly
WTHAY	West Texas Historical Association Yearbook

GENERAL TEXAS HISTORIES

Overarching histories of Texas are not as numerous as one might expect for such a heavily traveled subject. The more modern ones include Robert A. Calvert and

Arnoldo de León, *The History of Texas,* 2nd ed. (Wheeling, Il.: Harland Davidson, 1996); Randolph B. Campbell, *Gone to Texas: A History of the Lone Star State* (New York and Oxford: Oxford University Press, 2003), which is professional in tone but has made a place for itself on the trade shelf; T. R. Fehrenbach, *Lone Star* (New York: Macmillan, 1968); the excellent college text, Jesús F. de la Teja, Paula Mitchell Marks, and Ron Tyler, *Texas: Crossroads of North America* (Boston and New York: Houghton Mifflin, 2004); Rupert Richardson, *The Lone Star State,* 2nd ed. (Englewood Cliffs, N.J.: Prentice Hall, 1958) and 7th edition in 1997. Both editions were used here, in order to contrast what Dr. Richardson actually wrote with what subsequent editorial committees have politically corrected since his death, some of which would doubtless mortify him.

There are also older Texas histories, less interpretive but more documentary in nature, and therefore useful if read cautiously. These include Dudley G. Wooten, *A Comprehensive History of Texas, 1685–1897,* 2 vols. (Dallas: Texas History Co., 1898) and Louis J. Wortham, *A History of Texas from Wilderness to Commonwealth,* 5 vols. (Fort Worth: Wortham-Molyneaux Co., 1924). Preceding them was Henderson Yoakum, *History of Texas from Its First Settlement in 1685 to Its Annexation to the United States in 1846,* 2 vols. (New York: Redfield, 1855), which remains interesting for its extensive quotations from documents, many of which were lent to Yoakum by Sam Houston from his personal papers and some of which have since been lost. A volume of annotated documents covering Texas history from 1528 to 1961, surprisingly interesting considering the format, is Ernest Wallace and David M. Vigness, eds., *Documents of Texas History,* 2nd ed. (Austin: Steck Co., 1963).

Mention must also be made of Ron Tyler, editor in chief, *The New Handbook of Texas,* 6 vols. (TSHA, 1996). The fact that this huge work was compiled by literally thousands of volunteer contributors makes the scholarship uneven from one article to another, but it is an indispensable portal to every aspect of Texas history. It has the advantage of being available online, at www.tsha.utexas.edu/handbook/online.

Although I chose not to begin this history with primordial ooze, there is a unique natural history of Texas, Robin W. Doughty, *Wildlife and Man in Texas: Environmental Change and Conservation* (TAMUP, 1983).

BOOK ONE: GOLD AND SOULS

General overviews of the Spanish period in Texas begin with classics that still bear currency: Hubert Howe Bancroft's *History of the North Mexican States and Texas,* 2 vols. (San Francisco: History Co., 1884, 1889) and Herbert E. Bolton's *The Spanish Borderlands* (YUP, 1921) and *Spanish Exploration in the Southwest* (New York: Barnes & Noble, 1952). They have given rise to good modern efforts such as David Vigness, *Spanish Texas, 1519–1810* (Boston: American Press, 1983) and Donald E. Chipman, *Spanish Texas, 1519–1821* (UTP, 1992). Elizabeth A. H. John, *Storms Brewed in Other Men's Worlds: The Confrontation of Indians, Spanish and*

French in the Southwest, 1540–1795 (TAMUP, 1975) is reader-friendly despite its intimidating size. The development of the vaquero culture is readably treated in Jack Jackson's *Los Mesteños: Spanish Ranching in Texas, 1721–1821* (TAMUP, 1986); see also Andrés Tijerina, *Tejano Empire: Life on the South Texas Ranchos* (TAMUP, 1998) and in shorter length, Odie B. Faulk, "Ranching in Spanish Texas," *Hispanic American Historical Review* 45 (1965). Armando Alonzo, *Tejano Legacy: Rancheros and Settlers in South Texas, 1734–1900* (UNMP, 1998) carries the examination to a later period. A welcome attempt to put real people to so many names is Donald Chipman and Harriett Denise Joseph, *Notable Men and Women of Spanish Texas* (UTP, 1999).

Of general works on Native Americans in Texas, probably the most consulted, for good reason, is W. W. Newcomb's *The Indians of Texas from Prehistoric to Modern Times* (UTP, 1961, rev. ed., 1974) cited in short form hereinafter. It largely supplanted the long-used Mary Jourdan Atkinson, *The Texas Indians* (San Antonio: Naylor Co., 1935). More recent is the very able Paul H. Carlson, *The Plains Indians* (TAMUP, 1998).

1. SMILING CAPTORS

Fanny Bandelier's long-serving 1905 translation of Cabeza de Vaca, *The Journey of Alvar Nuñez Cabeza de Vaca* (reprint, Chicago: Rio Grande Press, 1964), and other later translations such as Cyclone Covey's *Cabeza de Vaca's Adventures in the Unknown Interior of North America* (New York: Collier Books, 1961) have been largely supplanted by the far more annotated Alex D. Krieger, *We Came Naked and Barefoot: The Journey of Cabeza de Vaca Across North America* (UTP, 2002). The extensive bibliography in the latter volume will steer the reader to the many related books and articles, although separate reference should be made to Donald E. Chipman, "In Search of Cabeza de Vaca's Route Across Texas: A Historical Survey," *SHQ* 91 (1987). A modern take on his experience is Nancy P. Hickerson, "How Cabeza de Vaca Lived with, Worked Among, and Finally Left the Indians of Texas," *Journal of Anthropological Research* 54 (1998). New light on the possible trail of his journey was provided by Donald W. Olson et al., "Piñon Pines and the Route of Cabeza de Vaca," *SHQ* 101 (1997).

Karankawa Indians are ably and readably examined, as are all major native groups in Texas, in W. W. Newcomb, *The Indians of Texas*. Study of the Karankawa Indians may begin with Robert A. Riklis, *The Karankawa Indians of Texas* (UTP, 1996). Earlier studies are still useful, such as Albert S. Gatschet, *The Karankawa Indians: The Coast People of Texas* (Cambridge, Mass.: Peabody Museum, 1891), and Richard P. Schaedel, "The Karankawa of the Texas Gulf Coast," *Southwestern Journal of Anthropology* 5 (1949). See also Lawrence E. Aten, *Indians of the Upper Texas Coast* (New York: Academic Press, 1983).

2. THE CITIES OF GOLD

For a general history of this early period, see Juan Bautista Chapa, *Texas & Northeastern Mexico, 1630–1690* (UTP, 1997). George Parker Winship, *The Coronado Ex-*

pedition, 1540–1542 (USGPO, 1896, as Smithsonian Institution, 14th Annual Report, part 1) guided most subsequent study. Useful among its descendants are George P. Hammond and Agapito Rey, *Narratives of the Coronado Expedition* (UNMP, 1940); Arthur Grove Day, *Coronado's Quest: The Discovery of the Southwestern States* (Berkeley: University of California Press, 1940); and Herbert Eugene Bolton, *Coronado: Knight of Pueblos and Plains* (UNMP, 1949). His possible route is picked apart in detail in J. W. Williams, "Coronado: From the Rio Grande to Concho," in *SHQ* 63 (1959). For a short and readable summary see George P. Hammond, *Coronado's Seven Cities* (Albuquerque: U.S. Coronado Exposition Commission, 1940). Coronado's downfall is recounted in Richard Flint, *Great Cruelties Have Been Reported: The 1544 Investigation of the Coronado Expedition* (SMUP, 2002).

The Wichita Indians discovered by Coronado, and whose range extended down into central Texas, are sketched in W. W. Newcomb's *The Indians of Texas.* He wrote a more extensive study in *The People Called Wichita* (Phoenix: Indian Tribal Series, 1976), and also co-authored, with Robert Bell and Edward B. Jelks, *Wichita Indians* (New York: Garland, 1974). Wichita culture is also treated in Edward S. Curtis, *The North American Indian,* vol. 19 (Cambridge, Mass.: Harvard University Press, 1930) and George A. Dorsey, *The Mythology of the Wichita* (Washington, D.C.: Carnegie Institution, Publication No. 21, 1904). Their history is discussed in three articles by Elizabeth Ann Harper: "The Taovayas Indians in Frontier Trade and Diplomacy, 1719–1768," *CO* 31 (1953); a similar title for the years 1769–79 in *SHQ* 57 (1953); and for the years 1779–1835 in *PPHR* 26 (1953). A more recent interpretation is F. Todd Smith, *The Wichita Indians: Traders of Texas and the Southern Plains* (TAMUP, 2000).

3. SO BESET WITH HARDSHIPS

Not even the projected route of Coronado has bedeviled scholars more than that of Moscoso. The October 1941 issue of the *SHQ* was in large part devoted to it. Therein, Rex Strickland's conclusion ("Moscoso's Journey Through Texas," at p. 135) that the journey ended at the Trinity stands near J. W. Williams' conclusion ("Moscoso's Trail in Texas," at p. 140) that he reached the Brazos in the Crosstimbers near present Palo Pinto. Strickland probably has the better argument, as has been accepted by later general accounts such as Calvert and De León, *History of Texas,* map at p. 11. Each reached his conclusion with convoluted extrapolations from the two original, or near original, accounts: the "Relation" by Luys Hernández de Biedma, and the "True Relation of the Hardships" set down by the Fidalgo of Elvas, both contained, conveniently, in Edward Gaylord Bourne, *Narratives of the Career of Hernando de Soto in the Conquest of Florida* (New York: Allerton Book Co., 1922). A later attempt at disentangling the possibilities is James E. Bruseth and Nancy A. Kenmotsu, "From Naguatex to the River Daycao: The Route of the Hernando de Soto Expedition Through Texas," *North American Archeologist* 14 (1993).

The Caddo Indian culture is synopsized in W. W. Newcomb, *The Indians of*

Texas. Texas A&M University Press has dominated the field in more expansive treatments, with Vynola B. Newkumet and Howard L. Meredith's *Hasinai: A Traditional History of the Caddo Confederacy* in 1988; Timothy K. Perttula's *The Caddo Nation: Archaeological and Ethnohistoric Perspectives* in 1992, and F. Todd Smith's *The Caddo Indians* in 1995. See, however, Cecile Elkins Carter, *Caddo Indians: Where We Come From* (UOP, 1995) and David La Vere, *The Caddo Chiefdoms: Caddo Economics and Politics 700–1835* (Lincoln: University of Nebraska Press, 1998). See also William B. Glover, "A History of the Caddo Indians," *Louisiana Historical Quarterly* 18 (1935). A portal into the more scientific record of their culture is John R. Swanton, *Source Material on the History and Ethnology of the Caddo Indians* (USGPO, 1942 as Smithsonian Institution, Bulletin 132 of the Bureau of American Ethnology).

4. IMPERIAL COMPETITION

The history of the El Paso area is treated generally in W. H. Timmons, *El Paso: A Borderlands History* (TWP, 1990). A good biography of Oñate is Marc Simmons, *The Last Conquistador: Juan de Oñate and the Settling of the Far Southwest* (UOP, 1991).

La Salle's gerrymandering of the Mississippi River to secure financing for his Gulf expedition is rather convincingly treated in Louis de Vorsey Jr., "The Impact of the La Salle Expedition of 1682 on European Cartography," in Patrick K. Galloway, ed., *La Salle and His Legacy: Frenchmen and Indians in the Lower Mississippi Valley* (Jackson: University of Mississippi Press, 1982), which also treats several collateral issues. The politics of it is more generally dealt with in Henry Folmer, *Franco-Spanish Rivalry in North America, 1524–1763* (Glendale, Calif.: Arthur H. Clark Co., 1953). The Minet diary, the debriefing of the Talon children after the massacre of the surviving holdouts at Fort St. Louis, and other aspects of the La Salle story are located in Robert S. Weddle, ed., *Three Primary Documents: La Salle, the Mississippi, and the Gulf* (TAMUP, 1987). See also by Weddle, *The French Thorn: Rival Explorers in the Spanish Sea, 1682–1762* (TAMUP, 1991); *Wilderness Manhunt: The Spanish Search for La Salle* (UTP, 1973); and *The Wreck of the* Belle, *The Ruin of La Salle* (TAMUP, 2001).

5. SOULS WITHOUT GOLD

The classic study of the local natives is Herbert E. Bolton, *The Hasinais: Southern Caddoans as Seen by the Earliest Europeans* (reprint UOP, 2002). See also William C. Auster, *Spanish Expeditions in to Texas, 1689–1768* (UTP, 1995). The first effort to Christianize the natives is covered in an overarching history of the period, Carlos E. Castañeda, *Our Catholic Heritage in Texas*, 7 vols. (VBJ, 1936–58), which is also the best secondary source on the establishment of the eastern missions.

6. LOVE AND BOOTY

St. Denis was a focus of the first volume (1898) of the *QTSHA*, including Edmond J. P. Schmitt, "Who Was Juchereau de St. Denis?" and Lester G. Bugbee,

"The Real St. Denis." Much more complete is Ross Phares, *Cavalier in the Wilderness: The Story of the Explorer and Trader Louis Juchereau de St. Denis* (LSUP, 1952). The general importance of San Juan Bautista is laid out in Robert S. Weddle, *San Juan Bautista: Gateway to Spanish Texas* (UTP, 1968). Captain Ramón's own thoughts are preserved in Paul J. Foik, "Captain Don Domingo Ramón's Diary of His Expedition into Texas in 1716," in *Wilderness Mission: Preliminary Studies of the Texas Catholic Historical Society II* (Austin: Texas Catholic Historical Society, 1999). The complicated dynamics of the relationships are parsed in David La Vere, "Between Kinship and Capitalism: French and Spanish Rivalry in the Colonial Louisiana-Texas Indian Trade," *Journal of Southern History* 64 (1998).

7. THE EMPTY QUARTER

8. MISSION LIFE

Herbert E. Bolton provides an overview of provincial affairs and government in *Texas in the Middle Eighteenth Century: Studies in Spanish Colonial Administration* (reprint, UTP, 1970). Bolton gives a good account of the services of Mézières in *Athanase de Mézières and the Louisiana-Texas Frontier, 1768–1780*, 2 vols. (Cleveland: Arthur H. Clark, 1914), which picks up where William C. Foster, *Spanish Expeditions into Texas, 1689–1768* (UTP, 1995) leaves off. The early history of San Antonio is covered in Jesús F. de la Teja, *San Antonio de Béxar: A Community on New Spain's Northern Frontier* (UNMP, 1995). The aftermath of the Chicken War is chronicled in Eleanor C. Buckley, "The Aguayo Expedition into Texas and Louisiana, 1719–1722," *QTSHA* 15 (1911). Robert S. Weddle, *The San Saba Mission: Spanish Pivot in Texas* (UTP, 1964) is the place to begin in studying that installation, but still useful are long-ago articles by William E. Dunn, "Apache Relations in Texas, 1718–1750," *SHQ* 14 (1911) and "The Apache Mission on the San Saba River," *SHQ* 17 (1914). The immensely capable De Croix is examined in Alfred B. Thomas, *Teodoro de Croix and the Northern Frontier of New Spain* (UOP, 1941). The common soldier's life is portrayed in Odie and Laura Faulk, *Defenders of the Interior Provinces: Presidial Soldiers on the Northern Frontier of New Spain* (Albuquerque: Albuquerque Museum, 1988).

For a long-term view of one installation, see Kathryn Stoner O'Connor, *Presidio La Bahia del Espiritu Santa de Zuniga, 1721–1846* (VBJ, 1966). Rare looks at social history of the era are Oakah L. Jones Jr., *Los Paisanos: Spanish Settlers on the Northern Frontier of New Spain* (UOP, 1979) and Light T. Cummins, "Church Courts, Marriage Breakdown, and Separation in Spanish Louisiana, West Florida and Texas," *Journal of Texas Catholic History and Culture* 4 (1993). Glimpses of the near end of the era are J. Autrey Dabbs, "The Texas Missions in 1789," in *Preparing the Way: Preliminary Studies of the Texas Catholic Historical Society III* (Austin: Texas Catholic Historical Society, 2000) and Benedict Leutenegger, ed., and Marion A. Habig, "Report on the San Antonio Missions in 1792," *SHQ* 77 (1974).

9. AMERICANS

For biographies of two principal filibustering players, see James Ripley Jacobs, *Tarnished Warrior: Major-General James Wilkinson* (New York: Macmillan, 1938) and Maurine T. Wilson and Jack Jackson, *Philip Nolan and Texas: Expeditions to the Unknown Land* (Waco: Texian Press, 1987). See more generally Jack D. L. Holmes, "Showdown on the Sabine: General James Wilkinson vs. Lieutenant-Colonel Simón de Herrera," *Louisiana Studies* 3 (1964) and Harris G. Warren, *The Sword Was Their Passport* (LSUP, 1943). Further perspective on the Neutral Ground is in Patrick J. Walsh, "Living on the Edge of the Neutral Zone: Varieties of Identity in Nacogdoches, Texas, 1773–1810," *ETHJ* 37 (1999) and Charles W. Hackett, "The Neutral Ground Between Louisiana and Texas, 1806–1821," *Louisiana Historical Quarterly* 28 (1945). Conditions are described in Nettie L. Benson, "A Governor's Report on Texas in 1809," *SHQ* 71 (1968).

10. GREEN FLAG, RED BLOOD

11. STRANGE BEDFELLOWS

Further reading for these chapters would have to include Felix D. Almaráz, *Tragic Cavalier: Governor Manuel Salcedo of Texas, 1808–1813* (UTP, 1971); Frederick C. Chabot, ed., *Texas in 1811: The Las Casas and Sambrano Revolutions* (San Antonio: Yanaguana Society, 1941); Julia K. Garrett, *Green Flag over Texas: A Story of the Last Years of Spain in Texas* (New York: Cordova Press, 1939); Ted Schwartz, *Forgotten Battlefield of the First Texas Revolution: The Battle of the Medina, August 18, 1813* (EP, 1985); and Mattie Austin Hatcher, ed., "Joaquín de Arredondo's Report on the Battle of the Medina," *SHQ* 11 (1908). The complex machinations of filibustering are the subject of Ed Bradley, "Fighting for Texas: Filibuster James Long, the Adams-Onís Treaty, and the Monroe Administration," *SHQ* 102 (1999). See also Odie B. Faulk, *The Last Years of Spanish Texas* (The Hague: Mouton, 1964). The melancholy tale of Napoleonic refugees is told in Kent Gardien, "Take Pity on Our Glory: Men of Champ d'Asile," *SHQ* 87 (1984) and the romantic enigma who helped ruin their scheme is biographized in Jack C. Ramsay, *Jean Lafitte, Prince of Pirates* (EP, 1996). The classic study of the crumbling of Spanish isolationism is Mattie Austin Hatcher, *The Opening of Texas to Foreign Settlement, 1801–1821* (reprint, Philadelphia: Porcupine Press, 1976).

BOOK TWO: FROM EMPRESARIOS TO INDEPENDENCE

The largest collection of Texas revolutionary documents is collated in John H. Jenkins, *Papers of the Texas Revolution* (Austin: Presidial Press, 1973), which must be used with caution because it is rife with typographical errors, owing to Jenkins' lack of enthusiasm for copyediting.

12. A CONNECTICUT YANKEE IN KING FERDINAND'S COURT

About the only commendable biography of Moses Austin is David B. Gracy II, *Moses Austin: His Life* (San Antonio: Trinity University Press, 1987). The Austins in the pre-Texas years are also treated in Charles A. Bararisse, "Why Moses Austin Came to Texas," *Southwestern Social Science Quarterly* 40 (1959); and Robert L. and Pauline H. Jones, "Stephen F. Austin in Arkansas," *Arkansas Historical Quarterly* 25 (1966). The political context of approving the Austin colony is covered in Felix D. Almaráz, "Governor Antonio Martínez and Mexican Independence in Texas: An Orderly Transition," *Permian Historical Annual* 15 (1975). More can be gleaned from Virginia H. Taylor, trans. and ed., *The Letters of Antonio Martínez, Last Governor of Texas* (Austin: Texas State Library, 1957) and Fane Downs, "Governor Antonio Martínez and the Defense of Texas from Foreign Invasion, 1817–1822," *Texas Military History* 7 (1968). For accounts of life in San Antonio during this period, see Jesús F. de la Teja and John Wheat, "Béxar: Profile of a Tejano Community," *SHQ* 89 (1983).

13. THE YOUNG EMPRESARIO

Study of Stephen F. Austin should begin with Gregg Cantrell, *Stephen F. Austin: Empresario of Texas* (YUP, 1999). This prize-winner largely supplanted the long-relied-on Eugene C. Barker, *The Life of Stephen F. Austin, Founder of Texas, 1793–1836* (reprint, TSHA, 1949). Cantrell is more analytical and objective, but Barker is longer, more detailed and documentary, and still useful. Voluminous primary documentary material on the Austins is available through Barker, ed., *The Austin Papers*, vols. 1 and 2 (USGPO, 1924, 1928) and vol. 3 (UTP, 1927), and Austin's own impressions in Stephen Fuller Austin, "Journal of Stephen F. Austin on His First Trip to Texas, 1821," *QTSHA* 7 (1904). For other views, see George L. Hammeken, "Recollections of Stephen F. Austin," *SHQ* 20 (1917). Austin's recognition of bachelors as constructive "families" was noted in Lester G. Bugbee, "The Old Three Hundred," *QTSHA* 1 (1897).

The same article also discusses individual topics concerning the early days of Austin's colony, as does his "What Became of the Lively?" in *QTSHA* 3 (1899); the lost ship is also discussed in W. S. Lewis, "The Adventures of the 'Lively' Immigrants," in the same number as the latter. See also Gregg Cantrell, "The Partnership of Stephen F. Austin and Joseph H. Hawkins," *SHQ* 99 (1995). Austin's land commissioner and major domo is chronicled in Charles A. Baracisse, "Baron de Bastrop," *SHQ* 58 (1955).

14. PELTS PASSED CURRENT

The story of the Austin family compound, with plans of the house that Stephen Austin designed for his kin, is told in Marie Beth Jones, *Peach Point Plantation: The First 150 Years* (Waco: Texian Press, 1982).

Many books have assembled short biographies of women on the Texas frontier. Perhaps the first, and still worth reading, is Annie Doom Pickrell, *Pioneer*

Women in Texas (Austin: E. L. Steck & Co., 1929), which has become a staple of the rare and collectible books trade. Embracing a period from the Old Three Hundred to modern times is Ann Fears Crawford and Crystal Sasse Ragsdale, *Women in Texas: Their Lives, Their Experiences, Their Accomplishments* (EP, 1982). Departing a bit from the standard recitative canon is Francis Edward Abernethy, ed., *Legendary Ladies of Texas* (Nacogdoches: Texas Folklore Society, 1981). See also Fane Downs, " 'Tryels and Trubbles': Women in Early Nineteenth Century Texas," *SHQ* 90 (1987) and Paula Mitchell Marks, *Hands to the Spindle: Texas Women and Home Textile Production* (TAMUP, 1998).

First-person accounts of everyday life in the early period of Anglo settlement are numerous and illuminating, none more so than Noah Smithwick, *The Evolution of a State, Or, Recollections of Old Texas Days* (Austin: Gammel Books, 1900). See also W. B. Dewees, *Letters from an Early American Settler of Texas* (reprint, Waco: Texian Press, 1968); Dilue Rose Harris, "Reminiscences of Mrs. Dilue Harris," *SHQ* 4 (1900, 1901); and J. H. Kuykendall, "Reminiscences of Early Texans," *QTSHA* 6, 7 (1903).

Specific Topics: Edwin P. Arneson, "The Early Art of Terrestrial Measurement and Its Practice in Texas," *SHQ* 29 (1925); Eugene C. Barker, "The Government of Austin's Colony," *SHQ* 21 (1918); Max Berger, "Stephen F. Austin and Education in Early Texas," *SHQ* 48 (1945); M. M. Kenney, "Recollections of Early Schools," *QTSHA* 1 (1898).

15. GONE TO TEXAS

16. A FINGER IN THE DIKE

The letter from Wayne County, Tennessee, is preserved in the Sam Houston Papers at the Catholic Archives of Texas, in the diocese chancery in Austin. A long-needed and well-done family history of the De Leóns was put forward by Ana Carolina Castillo Crimm, *De León: A Tejano Family History* (UTP, 2003).

The two essential books are Ohland Morton, *Terán and Texas: A Chapter in Texas-Mexican Relations* (TSHA, 1948); Manuel de Mier y Terán, *Texas by Terán: The Diary Kept by General Manuel de Mier y Terán on His 1828 Inspection of Texas*, edited by Jack Jackson, translated by John Wheat (UTP, 2000). An earlier study is Alleine Howren, "Causes and Origin of the Decree of April 6, 1830," *SHQ* 16 (1913).

17. ALMOST A BLACK COLONY

It is regrettable that Benjamin Lundy has received little attention from scholars. The only biography is Merton L. Dillon, *Benjamin Lundy and the Struggle for Negro Freedom* (Urbana: University of Illinois Press, 1966). Lundy's own memoir is Benjamin Lundy, *The Life, Travels and Opinions of Benjamin Lundy, Including His Journeys to Texas and Mexico*, compiled by Thomas Earle (Philadelphia: W. D. Parris, 1837), made accessible in reprint (New York: Negro Universities Press, 1969), (New York: A. M. Kelley, 1971). His relationship with Colonel Almonte is covered in *Almonte's Texas: Juan N. Almonte's 1834 Inspection, Secret Report & Role in the 1836 Campaign*, edited by Jack Jackson, translated by John Wheat (TSHA, 2003), a multiple prize-winner.

18. FLASHPOINT DOUSED

On this topic there are sharply contrasting differences between the traditional, pro-Anglo historical treatment, for which see Edna Rowe, "The Disturbances at Anahuac in 1821," *QTSHA* 6 (1903), and the more modern revisionist viewpoint sympathetic to Bradburn, for which see Margaret Swett Henson, *Juan Davis Bradburn: A Reappraisal of the Mexican Commander at Anahuac* (TAMUP, 1982).

19. SAM HOUSTON, LATE OF TENNESSEE

The latest biography of this legendary figure is James L. Haley, *Sam Houston* (UOP, 2002) but useful reference can still be made to three earlier ones that have stood the test of time: Marquis James, *The Raven* (1929; reprint, UTP, 1988); Llerena Friend, *Sam Houston: The Great Designer* (UTP, 1954) and Marion K. Wisehart, *Sam Houston: American Giant* (Washington, D.C.: Robert B. Luce Inc., 1962). A much shorter, but perceptive and well-balanced account, is Randolph B. Campbell, *Sam Houston and the American Southwest* (New York: HarperCollins College Publishers, 1993). Houston's papers are scattered widely, although hundreds were published in Eugene C. Barker and Amelia W. Williams, eds., *The Writings of Sam Houston, 1813–1863*, 8 vols. (UTP, 1938–43). The principal repositories for his papers are the University of Texas, the Texas State Library and Archives, and the Catholic Archives of Texas, all in Austin; Rice University in Houston, the Sam Houston Memorial Museum in Huntsville, and the Sam Houston Regional Library and Research Center in Liberty.

20. THE QUIET BEFORE THE STORM

21. COME AND TAKE IT

Much understanding of the 1834 to 1835 period will be reordered as the historical community absorbs *Almonte's Texas*, cited above. The most detailed chronology of the revolution is Stephen L. Hardin, *Texian Iliad: A Military History of the Texas Revolution, 1835–1836* (UTP, 1994); the more recent William C. Davis, *Lone Star Rising: The Revolutionary Birth of the Texas Republic* (New York: Free Press, 2004) gives more political context, although the major effort to belittle the role of Sam Houston is disproportionate. More balanced and covering a wider span of time (but therefore less detailed), and making more of an effort to see the revolution in the context of American history, is H. W. Brands, *Lone Star Nation: How a Ragged Army of Volunteers Won the Battle for Texas Independence—And Changed America* (New York: Doubleday, 2004). Useful reference can still be made to Paul D. Lack, *The Texas Revolutionary Experience: A Political and Social History* (TAMUP, 1992). Elijah Bailey's letter to the Robertson Colony is in the Texas State Archives, Domestic Correspondence of the Secretaries of State.

22. WHO WILL GO WITH OLD BEN MILAM?

23. PRETENDED GOVERNMENT

24. I AM DETERMINED TO DIE LIKE A SOLDIER

Alwyn Barr, *Texans in Revolt: The Battle for San Antonio, 1835* (UTP, 1990) can be paired with Lois A. Garver, "Benjamin Rush Milam," *SHQ* 38 (1934–35) for an introduction to the siege of Béxar. The best source to consult on what passed for a government is still Eugene C. Barker, ed., "The Journal of the Permanent Council," *QTSHA* 7 (1904). The principal biography of Travis is Archie P. McDonald, *Travis* (Austin: Jenkins Publishing Co., 1976).

25. THE NEW NATION

For a précis of the convention that declared independence, with biographical synopses of those attending, no one has yet topped Louis Wiltz Kemp, *The Signers of the Texas Declaration of Independence* (Houston: Anson Jones Press, 1944). The goings-on at the convention were recorded in Paul D. Lack, ed., *The Diary of William Fairfax Gray from Virginia to Texas, 1835–1837* (Dallas: De Golyer Library, 1997).

26. BRILLIANT, POINTLESS, PYRRHIC

27. HOW DID DAVY DIE?

William C. Davis' triple biography, *Three Roads to the Alamo: The Lives and Fortunes of David Crockett, James Bowie, and William Barret Travis* (New York: HarperCollins, 1998) is a fine beginning point on the lives of these three principals, despite some minor errors that were pounced on, perhaps unfairly, by buffs of the minutiae. The incendiary device that has fired nearly a generation of passionate examination of the Alamo was José Enrique de la Peña, *With Santa Anna in Texas: A Personal Narrative of the Revolution* (TAMUP, 1975). The latest entries into this melee over the Alamo are by the brilliant deconstructionist, James Crisp, *Sleuthing the Alamo: Davy Crockett's Last Stand and Other Mysteries of the Texas Revolution* (New York: Oxford University Press, 2004); and by Alamo curator Richard Bruce Winders, *Sacrificed at the Alamo: Tragedy and Triumph in the Texas Revolution* (Abilene, Texas: McWhiney Foundation Press, 2004). Recent years have also brought the well-done Randy Roberts and James S. Olson, *A Line in the Sand: The Alamo in Blood and Memory* (New York: Free Press, 2001); Thomas Ricks Lindley, *Alamo Traces: New Evidence and New Conclusions* (Dallas: Taylor Trade Publishing, 2003), which is basically an indictment of previous scholars; Ron Jackson, *Alamo Legacy: Alamo Descendents Remember the Alamo* (EP, 1997); Todd Hansen, ed., *The Alamo Reader: A Study in History* (Harrisburg, Pa.: Stackpole Books, 2003); less angry and more synoptic is Bill Groneman, *Eyewitness to the Alamo* (Plano, Texas:

Republic of Texas Press, 2001). Very useful is Timothy M. Matovina, *The Alamo Remembered: Tejano Accounts and Perspectives* (UTP, 1995). Some classics of previous years have not lost their luster, such as Lon Tinkle, *Thirteen Days to Glory: The Siege of the Alamo* (New York: McGraw-Hill, 1958). See also Richard G. Santos, *Santa Anna's Campaign Against Texas* (Salisbury, N.C.: Documentary Publications, 1982); and Richard G. Flores, *Remembering the Alamo: Memory, Modernity, and the Master Symbol* (UTP, 2002).

28. THE ILL-FATED FANNIN

29. YOU MUST FIGHT THEM

One history of the debacle on the Coleto is Craig H. Rowell, *Remember Goliad! A History of La Bahía* (TSHA, 1994); see also Jakie L. Pruett and Everett B. Cole, *Goliad Massacre: A Tragedy of the Texas Revolution* (EP, 1985); Harbert Davenport, "Men of Goliad," *SHQ* 43 (1939); and Ruby C. Smith, "James W. Fannin, Jr., in the Texas Revolution," *SHQ* 23 (1919). Several memoirs of common soldiers fighting the Runaway Scrape are collated in Eugene C. Barker, "The San Jacinto Campaign," *SHQ* 4 (1901). See also S. F. Sparks, "Recollections of S. F. Sparks," *SHQ* 12 (1908). Juan Seguín's revolutionary gallantry and subsequent melancholy history come through in Jesús F. de la Teja, ed., *A Revolution Remembered: The Memoirs and Selected Correspondence of Juan N. Seguín*, 2nd ed. (TSHA, 2002).

30. THE BATTLE OF SAN JACINTO

The latest lengthy treatment of the battle at San Jacinto is also perhaps the best: Stephen L. Moore, *Eighteen Minutes: The Battle of San Jacinto and the Texas Independence Campaign* (Dallas: Republic of Texas Press, 2004). Still useful, however, is Frank X. Tolbert, *The Day of San Jacinto* (New York: McGraw-Hill, 1959). Capsule biographies of the participants are the major component of Sam Houston Dixon and Louis Wiltz Kemp, *The Heroes of San Jacinto* (Houston: Anson Jones Press, 1932). Kemp also coauthored a readable little pamphlet with Ed Kilman, *The Battle of San Jacinto and the San Jacinto Campaign* (n.p., 1947). The only contemporary reference to the role that Emily West may have played in Santa Anna's defeat was what Sam Houston imparted to William Bollaert, most readily found in W. Eugene Hollon and Ruth Lapham Butlers, eds., *William Bollaert's Texas* (OUP, 1956).

BOOK THREE: FROM NATION TO STATE

31. INDEPENDENCE AND THE SOUTHERN CONSPIRACY

The movements of the Mexican army after the loss at San Jacinto are wonderfully sleuthed in Gregg J. Dimmick, *Sea of Mud: The Retreat of the Mexican Army After San Jacinto, An Archeological Investigation* (TSHA, 2004). Benjamin Lundy's screed that delayed the annexation of Texas for several years is "By a Citizen of the United States," *The War in Texas* (Philadelphia: Merrihew & Gunn, 1837). The Dillon biography of Lundy is cited in Chapter 17, above. The classic political study of the opening years of the Texas Republic is Joseph Milton Nance, *After San Jacinto: The Texas-Mexican Frontier, 1836–1841* (UTP, 1963).

32. A NEW COUNTRY, A NEW CITY

33. POET AND PRESIDENT

34. THE SANGUINARY SAVAGE

The classic social history of the Republic era is William Ransom Hogan, *The Texas Republic: A Social and Economic History* (UOP, 1946). See also John Edward Weems, *Dream of Empire: A Human History of the Republic of Texas, 1836–1846* (New York: Simon & Schuster, 1976).

This example of Mirabeau Lamar's poetic efforts is the "Birthday Acrostic," 1838, in the Special Collections of the University of Texas at Arlington Libraries; his career in general and administration in particular are abundantly documented in C. A. Gulick, Jr., et al., eds., *The Papers of Mirabeau Buonaparte Lamar*, 6 vols. (Austin: Von Boeckmann-Jones, 1921–27).

The ill-fated Santa Fé scheme is covered in Paul N. Spellman, *Forgotten Texas Leader: Hugh McLeod and the Texan Santa Fé Expedition* (TAMUP, 1999). A colorful first-person account is Thomas Jefferson Green, *Journal of the Texian Expedition Against Mier* (New York: Harper & Bros., 1845). See also Thomas Falconer, *Letters and Notes on the Texan Santa Fé Expedition* (New York: Dauber & Pine Bookshops, 1930).

Indian raids of this era were chronicled unsympathetically by a scalped survivor in Josiah Wilbarger, *Indian Depredations in Texas* (Austin: Hutchings Printing House, 1889), a book now largely disused in favor of others more politically correct. The travails of the Texas Cherokees are treated in Mary Whatley Clark, *Chief Bowles and the Texas Cherokees* (UOP, 1971) and Dianna Everett, *The Texas Cherokees: A People Between Two Fires, 1819–1840* (UOP, 1990). See also Charles Sterne's memoir, manuscript in the Texas State Archives. The only book-length treatment of the Linnville raid and the Battle of Plum Creek is the well-researched Donaly E. Bryce, *The Great Comanche Raid: Boldest Indian Attack of the Texas Republic* (EP, 1987). See also Robert Hall's remembrance of the Plum Creek fight in Brazos [pseud.], *The Life of Robert Hall* (Austin: Ben C. Jones & Co., 1898). Contemporary sensitivity to the issues faced by Native Americans has been raised an order of magnitude in the works of Gary Clayton Anderson, for instance, *The Indian Southwest, 1580–1830: Ethnogenesis and Reinvention* (UOP, 1999). His points are well taken, but for a reality check one might consult, for instance, Carl Coke Rister, *Comanche Bondage* (1955; reprint, Lincoln: University of Nebraska Press, 1989). The classic study remains Rupert Richardson, *The Comanche Barrier to South Plains Settlement* (Glendale, Calif.: Arthur H. Clark Co., 1933).

Although organized some years before, the Texas Rangers come into their own as a fighting force during this period. Robert M. Utley's prize-winning *Lone Star Justice: The First Century of the Texas Rangers* (New York: Oxford University Press, 2002) is the latest interpretation in a genre spanning back to Walter Prescott Webb, *The Texas Rangers: A Century of Frontier Defense* (Boston: Houghton Mifflin, 1935).

35. RETRENCHMENT

36. THE ANNEXATION QUICKSTEP

A delightful memoir of Texas affairs during the Washington-on-the-Brazos period is Jonnie Lockhart Wallis with Laurance L. Hill, *Sixty Years on the Brazos: The Life and Letters of Dr. John Washington Lockhart* (reprint, New York: Argonaut Press, 1930). Minutes of Sam Houston's 1843 treaty council with the Brazos Indians were taken by his private secretary, now in the Washington Miller papers at the Texas State Archives in Austin. The Mexican reaction to the excesses of the Lamar government's expansionism is provided in Sam W. Haynes, *Soldiers of Misfortune: The Somervell and Mier Expeditions* (UTP, 1990).

A highly colored and colorful look at Texas politics and annexation is Anson Jones, *Memoranda and Official Correspondence Relating to the Republic of Texas, Its History and Annexation* (reprint, Chicago: Rio Grande Press, 1966), useful for its documentary inclusions, but caution must be used in assessing its notes and endorsements, which over time most clearly show Anson Jones not illuminating the history, but rather losing his mind. Many details of the diplomatic faro can be ferreted out of George P. Garrison, ed., *Diplomatic Correspondence of the Republic of Texas*, 3 vols. (Washington, D.C.: Annual Reports of the American Historical Association, 1907–08). The progress of the contest from the French perspective can be gained from *Alphonse in Austin*, edited and translated by Katherine Hart (Austin: Encino Press, 1967), and *The French Legation in Texas*, edited and translated by Mary Nicholls Barker (TSHA, 1971); and from the British side in the various installments of E. D. Adams, ed., "British Correspondence Concerning Texas," *SHQ* 15–21 (1912–1917).

37. NOTHING WANTING, NOTHING TOO MUCH

The German experience in Texas is richly documented in a number of primary sources, including Caroline Ernst von Hinüber, "Life of German Pioneers in Early Texas," *QTSHA* 2 (1899), and Minetta Altgelt Goyne, *Lone Star and Double Eagle: Civil War Letters of a German-Texas Family* (TCUP, 1982). A first-person rendering of their early hardships is Rosa von Röder Kleberg, "Some of My Early Experiences in Texas," *QTSHA* 1 (1898).

Scholarly treatments to consult include Rudolph L. Biesele, *The History of the German Settlements in Texas, 1831–1861* (VBJ, 1930); Walter Struve, *Germans and Texans: Commerce, Migration, and Culture in the Days of the Lone Star Republic* (UTP, 1996); Don Hampton Biggers, *German Pioneers in Texas* (Fredericksburg, Texas:

Fredericksburg Publishing, 1925); Glen G. Gilbert, *Linguistic Atlas of Texas German* (UTP, 1972); Gillespie County Historical Society, *Pioneers in God's Hills*, 2 vols. (Austin: VBJ, 1960, 1974); Terry G. Jordan, "The German Element in Texas: An Overview," *Rice University Studies* 63 (1977); Jordan, *German Seed in Texas Soil: Immigrant Farmers in Nineteenth Century Texas* (Austin: UTP, 1966); Jordan, "The German Settlement of Texas after 1865," *SHQ* 73 (1969); Glen E. Lich, *The German Texans* (San Antonio: Institute of Texan Cultures, 1981); Lich and Dona B. Reeves, eds., *German Culture in Texas* (Boston: Twayne, 1980); Moritz Tiling, *History of the German Element in Texas* (Houston: Rein & Sons, 1913); Chester William and Ethel Hander Geue, eds., *A New Land Beckoned: German Immigration to Texas, 1844–1847*, enlarged ed. (Waco: Texian Press, 1972); and Carl Wittke, *Refugees of Revolution: The German Forty-Eighters in America* (Philadelphia: University of Pennsylvania Press, 1952). The career of a leading German artist is recounted in James Patrick McGuire, *Herman Lungkwitz: Romantic Landscapist on the Texas Frontier* (UTP, 1983).

38. THE STATE OF TEXAS

39. LIFE IN THE LONE STAR STATE

A marvelous history of the Governor's Mansion, including political synopses of the administrations, is Jean Houston Daniel, Price Daniel, and Dorothy Blodgett, *The Texas Governor's Mansion: A History of the House and Its Occupants* (Austin: Texas State Library and Archives Commission, 1984).

Much of what William Ransom Hogan wrote in his classic social history of the Republic era, *The Texas Republic: A Social and Economic History* (UOP, 1946), remained true after statehood. Some wonderful glimpses of frontier social history are also contained in the underrated Wayne Gard, *Rawhide Texas* (UOP, 1965). The cotton culture is the subject of Elizabeth Silverthorne, *Plantation Life in Texas* (TAMUP, 1986). An interesting newer perspective is in Mark M. Carroll, *Homesteads Ungovernable: Families, Sex, Race, and the Law in Frontier Texas, 1826–1860* (UTP, 2001). A keenly observant outsider's view of life in Texas in early statehood is Frederick Law Olmsted, *A Journey Through Texas, Or, A Saddle-Trip on the Southwestern Frontier* (reprint, UTP, 1978). The life of a leading early Texas missionary is chronicled in Laura Fowler Woolworth, *Littleton Fowler, 1803–1846* (Shreveport, La., n.p., 1936).

40. STILL MORE FIGHTING

Sul Ross' raid on the Nocona Comanche camp is recounted in Rupert N. Richardson, ed., "The Death of Nocona and the Recovery of Cynthia Ann Parker," *SHQ* 46 (1942). Quanah Parker maintained that Peta Nocona was not killed in the Sul Ross raid, a point of view adopted by his most recent biographer in William T. Hagan, *Quanah Parker: Comanche Chief* (UOP, 1993). The valiant career of Agent Neighbors is chronicled in Kenneth F. Neighbours, *Robert Simpson Neighbors and the Texas Frontier, 1836–1859* (Waco: Texian Press, 1975).

41. SLAVERY AND SECESSION

An outstanding study of slavery in Texas is Gregg Cantrell, *An Empire for Slavery: The Peculiar Institution in Texas, 1821–1865* (LSUP, 1989). See generally also Walter Buenger, *Secession and the Union in Texas* (UTP, 1984). For the personal viewpoint of an ardent secessionist, see "The Diary and Letters of William P. Rogers, 1846–1862," *SHQ* 32 (1929). Many of Rogers' papers are at the Center for American History at the University of Texas. Also of interest is Earl Wesley Fornell, *The Galveston Era: The Texas Crescent on the Eve of Secession* (UTP, 1961). For a remarkable and minute study of how the town of Marshall and the surrounding area weathered slavery, the Civil War, and Reconstruction, see Randolph B. Campbell, *A Southern Community in Crisis: Harrison County, Texas, 1850–1880* (TSHA, 1983).

42. A LITTLE TERROR

43. THE WAR IN TEXAS

Witnesses relating the Great Hanging include Sam Hanna Acheson and Julia Ann Hudson, eds., *George Washington Diamond's Account of the Great Hanging at Gainesville, 1862* (TSHA, 1963), and L. D. Clark, ed., *The Civil War Recollections of James Lemuel Clark* (TAMUP, 1984). See also "Disaffection in Confederate Texas: The Great Hanging at Gainesville," *Civil War History* 22 (1976), and David Pickering and Judy Falls, *Brush Men and Vigilantes: Civil War Dissent in Texas* (TAMUP, 2000).

See also two books by Ralph A. Wooster, *Texas and Texans in the Civil War* (EP, 1996) and *Lone Star Generals in Gray* (EP, 2000); and Evault Boswell, *Texas Boys in Gray* (Plano: Republic of Texas Press, 2000). The border angle is surveyed in two books by Jerry Thompson, *Vaqueros in Blue and Gray* (Austin: Presidial Press, 1976) and *Mexican Texans in the Union Army* (TWP, 1986). Donald S. Frazier, *Blood & Treasure: Confederate Empire in the Southwest* (TAMUP, 1995) relates the ill-advised gambit into New Mexico. For the fall and rise of Galveston, see Robert M. Franklin, *The Battle of Galveston* (Galveston: Galveston News, 1911). *The Official Records of the Union and Confederate Navies in the War of the Rebellion* (USGPO) details naval actions off the Texas coast, and the Union defeat at Sabine Pass is recounted in Andrew Forest Muir, "Dick Dowling and the Battle of Sabine Pass," *Civil War History* 4 (1958); Alwyn Barr, "Sabine Pass, September 1863," *Texas Military History* 2 (1962); and Frank X. Tolbert, *Dick Dowling at Sabine Pass* (New York: McGraw-Hill, 1962).

Of regimental histories, see Joseph E. Chance, *The Second Texas Infantry: From Shiloh to Vicksburg* (EP, 1984); and Jerry Thompson, ed., *Civil War in the Southwest: Recollections of the Sibley Brigade* (TAMUP, 2001). The 8th Texas Cavalry is chronicled in James Knox Polk Blackburn, *Reminiscences of Terry's Texas Rangers* (reprint, Austin: Ranger Press, 1979); and Thomas W. Cutrer, ed., " 'We Are Stern and

Resolved': The Civil War Letters of John Wesley Rabb, Terry's Texas Rangers,"
SHQ 91 (1987).

44. FORTY ACRES AND A MULE

45. SCALAWAGS AND CARPETBAGGERS

For a general racial history see Alwyn Barr, *Black Texans: A History of African-Americans in Texas* (UOP, 1996). For a focus on this era, see by the same author *Reconstruction to Reform: Texas Politics, 1876–1906* (UTP, 1971) and Gregg Cantrell, "Racial Violence and Reconstruction Politics in Texas, 1867–1868," *SHQ* 93 (1990). Union oversight is examined in Barry Crouch, *The Freedmen's Bureau and Black Texans* (UTP, 1992). For a modern take on the end of Reconstruction see Carl Moneyhon, "Edmund J. Davis in the Coke-Davis Election Dispute of 1874: A Reassessment of Character," *SHQ* 100 (1996). Examination of black leadership is the focus of Merline Pitre, *Through Many Dangers, Toils, and Snares: The Black Leadership of Texas, 1868–1900* (EP, 1985) and see generally Lawrence D. Rice, *The Negro in Texas, 1874–1900* (LSUP, 1971).

BOOK FOUR: CATTLE EMPIRE

46. CLEARING THE PLAINS

As readable as it is reliable, and with a comprehensive bibliography of works up to that time, the standard treatment of the eviction of the Indians in post–Civil War Texas is William H. Leckie, *The Military Conquest of the Southern Plains* (UOP, 1963). The remarkable story of the Kiowa chief Striking Eagle's Talons, or Kicking Bird, is told in Morris F. Taylor, "Kicking Bird: A Chief of the Kiowas," *Kansas Historical Quarterly* 38 (1972). A sensitive and able discussion of the Kiowas from first white contact through the reservation days is Stan Hoig, *The Kiowas & The Legend of Kicking Bird* (Boulder: University Press of Colorado, 2000). Reference can still be made to the more anthropological Mildred P. Mayhall, *The Kiowas* (UOP, 1962). The event that nearly cost General Sherman his life was considered in detail in Benjamin Capps, *The Warren Wagontrain Raid* (New York: Dial Press, 1974) but considerably revised in Charles M. Robinson III, *The Indian Trial: The Complete Story of the Warren Wagon Train Massacre and the Fall of the Kiowa Nation* (Spokane: Arthur H. Clark Co., 1997). Background on soldiers' life in the frontier forts is in Robert Wooster, *Soldiers, Suttlers, and Settlers: Garrison Life on the Texas Frontier* (TAMUP, 1987). Life on one such post is examined in Allen Lee Hamilton, *Sentinel of the Southern Plains: Fort Richardson and the Northwest Texas Frontier, 1866–1878* (TCUP, 1988).

47. BUFFALO DAYS

48. THE RED RIVER WAR

The evolution of the buffalo hunter culture is chronicled in E. Douglas Branch, *The Hunting of the Buffalo* (New York: D. Appleton & Co., 1929) and later in Frank H. Mayer and Charles B. Roth, *The Buffalo Harvest* (Denver: Sage Books, 1958) and Wayne Gard, *The Great Buffalo Hunt* (New York: Alfred A. Knopf, 1959). The pivotal role played by the Mooar brothers in starting the hide business can be found in Josiah Wright Mooar, "The First Buffalo Hunting in the Panhandle," *WTHAY* 5 (1930); Mooar, "Buffalo Days," edited by James Winfred Hunt, *Holland's Magazine* 52 (Jan.–April 1933); and a biography, Charles G. Anderson, *In Search of the Buffalo: The Story of J. Wright Mooar* (Seagraves, Texas: Pioneer Book Publishers, 1974). The exploits of other prominent buffalo hunters include Olive K. Dixon, *The Life of "Billy" Dixon* (Dallas: P. L. Turner, 1927) and Richard O'Connor, *Bat Masterson* (Garden City, N.Y.: Doubleday, 1957). A photographic expedition on to the buffalo plains is recounted in Wayne Gard, "How They Killed the Buffalo," *American Heritage* 7 (1956).

The desperation of the Plains Indians' circumstances was fully reported by the Quaker agents to their headquarters, and quoted in James L. Haley, *The Buffalo War: The History of the Red River Indian Uprising of 1874–1875* (Garden City, N.Y.: Doubleday, 1976), which is still the standard general work to see on the Red River War. A good summary of the attack on Adobe Walls is G. Derek West, "The Battle of Adobe Walls," *PPHR* 36 (1963) and the revelation of the true story of the "cracked" ridgepole in Hanrahan's saloon is in Mooar, "Buffalo Days." An accounting of native participants is given on a monument at the site, and in Rupert N. Richardson, "The Comanche Indians at the Adobe Walls Fight," *PPHR* 4 (1931). The battle as it was illuminated by excavations at the site is in T. Lindsay Baker and Billy R. Harrison, *Adobe Walls: The History and Archaeology of the 1874 Trading Post* (TAMUP, 1986). A feel for the progress of the Red River War in its paper trail is given in Joe F. Taylor, ed., *The Indian Campaign on the Staked Plains, 1874–75: Military Correspondence from the War Department Adjutant General's Office, File 2815-1874* (PPHS, 1962). An example of a memoir from this conflict is Ed Carnal, "Reminiscences of a Texas Ranger," *Frontier Times* 1 (1923).

49. CATTLE EMPIRE

Classic histories of individual ranches include W. M. Pearce, *The Matador Land and Cattle Company* (UOP, 1964); J. Evetts Haley, *The XIT Ranch of Texas* (1929; reprint, Norman: University of Oklahoma Press, 1953). Goodnight and the JA are chronicled best in J. Evetts Haley, *Charles Goodnight, Cowman and Plainsman* (Boston & New York: Houghton Mifflin Co., 1936) and H. T. Burton, "A History of the JA Ranch," *SHQ* 31 (April 1928). A recent history of the King Ranch, concise, readable, and of merit for not being authorized and monitored, is Don Graham, *Kings of Texas: The 150-Year Saga of an American Ranching Empire* (New York:

John Wiley & Sons, 2003). For the economics of drovering, see Jimmy M. Skaggs, *The Cattle-Trailing Industry: Between Supply and Demand, 1866–1890* (Lawrence: University Press of Kansas, 1973).

The paradigmatic cowboy memoir is probably Charles A. Siringo, *A Texas Cowboy; Or, Fifteen Years on the Hurricane Deck of a Spanish Pony* (New York: J. S. Ogilvie, 1886). For a particularly telling and wide-ranging cowboy memoir, see E. C. Abbott and Helena Huntington Smith, *We Pointed Them North: Recollections of a Cowpuncher* (New York: Farrar & Rinehart, 1939). Equally salient is Frank S. Hastings, *A Ranchman's Recollections: An Autobiography in Which Unfamiliar Facts, etc.* (Chicago: Breeder's Gazette, 1921). See also Jim and Judy Lanning, eds., *Texas Cowboys: Memories of the Early Days* (TAMUP, 1984) and John C. Dawson Sr., *High Plains Yesterdays: From XIT Days Through Drouth and Depression* (EP, 1985). Joe B. Frantz and Julian Ernest Choate, *The American Cowboy: The Myth and the Reality* (UOP, 1955) attempts a true relation.

The sheep wars are covered in T. R. Havins, "Sheepmen-Cattlemen Antagonisms on the Texas Frontier," *WTHAY* 18 (1942) and Roy Holt, "The Woes of a Pioneer Sheepman," *Sheep and Goat Raiser* 21 (1940). A good introduction to the fencing conflict is the ever-readable Wayne Gard, "The Fence Cutters," *SHQ* 51 (1947), and see also Roy Holt, "Introduction of Barbed Wire into Texas and the Fence-Cutting War," *WTHAY* 6 (1930).

50. THE POPULIST MOVEMENT

51. LIFE BY MAIL ORDER

The economic changes of this period are examined in John Stricklin Spratt, *The Road to Spindletop: Economic Change in Texas, 1875–1900* (SMUP, 1955) and Vera Lee Dugas, "Texas Industry, 1860–1880," *SHQ* 59 (1955). See further J. Evetts Haley, "The Grass Lease Fight and Attempted Impeachment of the First Panhandle Judge," *SHQ* 38 (July 1934) and Ruth A. Allen, *The Great Southwest Strike* (UTP, 1942). Roscoe Martin, *The People's Party in Texas* (UTP, 1933) is a good synopsis of the political movement. See also Robert C. McMath, *Populist Vanguard: A History of the Southern Farmer's Alliance* (Chapel Hill: University of North Carolina Press, 1975). The articles by Ralph Smith provide succinct views of "The Co-operative Movement in Texas, 1870–1900," *SHQ* 44 (1940); "The Farmer's Alliance in Texas, 1875–1900," *SHQ* 48 (1945); and "The Grange Movement in Texas, 1873–1900," *SHQ* 42 (1940).

A representative ad for Radam's Microbe Killer is contained in the Austin *American* of November 29, 1887. See also Gene Fowler, "Livers and Land," *Texas Highways,* June 2003. For development of the spa at Mineral Wells see Gene Fowler, *Crazy Water* (TCUP, 1991) and Mary Whatley Clarke, *The Palo Pinto Story* (Fort Worth: Manney, 1956).

For the career of Joe Henry Eagle see *Biographical Directory of the American Congress.*

52. FINAL RAIDS

The lamentable saga of the displaced Kickapoos is recounted in Arrell M. Gibson, *The Kickapoos, Lords of the Middle Border* (UOP, 1963) and Felipe A. and Dolores L. Latorre, *The Mexican Kickapoo Indians* (UTP, 1976). The clash with Confederates is best covered in William C. Pool, "The Battle of Dove Creek," *SHQ* 53 (April 1950), and the Mackenzie raid in Ernest Wallace, *Ranald S. Mackenzie on the Texas Frontier* (Lubbock: West Texas Museum Association, 1964), and Charles M. Robinson III, *Bad Hand: A Biography of General Ranald S. Mackenzie* (Austin: State House Press, 1993).

Kiowa informants gave their version of their last raid into Texas in Wilbur Nye, *Carbine and Lance* (UOP, 1937) and of Big Bow's recovery of his stolen stock in Nye, *Bad Medicine & Good: Tales of the Kiowas* (UOP, 1962).

53. FORT DAVIS: WESTERN ANCHOR

The essential reading on this topic includes William H. Leckie and Shirley A. Leckie, *Unlikely Warriors: General Benjamin H. Grierson and his Family* (UOP, 1984); Barry Scobee, *Old Fort Davis* (San Antonio: Naylor, 1947); and Frank M. Temple, "Colonel B. H. Grierson's Administration of the District of the Pecos," *WTHAY* 38 (1962). The best examination of Victorio is Dan L. Thrapp, *Victorio* (UOP, 1974).

54. LAW VS. OUTLAW

A local account of the trouble in Richmond is Pauline Yelderman, *The Jay Birds of Fort Bend County* (priv. pr., 1981). For individual portrayals, see John Wesley Hardin, *The Life of John Wesley Hardin* (Seguin, TX: Smith & Maine, 1896); Paul Adams, "The Unsolved Mystery of Ben Thompson," *SHQ* 48 (1945). C. L. Sonnichsen, *Roy Bean, Law West of the Pecos* (UNMP, 1986 repr.) is a good introduction to that figure; his foray into boxing management is chronicled in Luke Brite, "The Bob Fitzsimmons-Peter Maher Fight," *Password* 10 (1965).

55. POLITICAL EVOLUTION

The 1876 Constitution so weakened the governorship that it is misleading to chronicle Texas history by their tenures as though they had real power. History must be arranged somehow, though, and several writers have found this as convenient a way as any. The least pretentious, as well as the most fun and revealing because of its eyewitness nature, is Norman G. Kittrell, *Governors Who Have Been and Other Public Men* (Dallas: Dealey-Adey-Elgin, 1921). Others have included James T. Deshields, *They Sat in High Places: The Presidents and Governors of Texas* (San Antonio: Naylor Co., 1940); Ross Phares, *The Governors of Texas* (Gretna, La.: Pelican Publishing Co., 1987), which is notable for its capsules of royal Spanish governors; and perhaps the most serious of that genre, Kenneth E. Hendrickson Jr., *The Chief Executives of Texas, from Stephen F. Austin to John B. Connally, Jr.* (TAMUP, 1995). June Rayfield Welch, *The Texas Governor* (Dallas: G. L. A.

Press, 1977) seems to have been the only one to produce a companion volume, *The Texas Senator* (Dallas: G. L. A. Press, 1978).

Among memoirs of the period, the most readable and entertaining is Francis R. Lubbock, *Six Decades in Texas: Memoirs of Francis Richard Lubbock,* edited by C. W. Raines (Austin: B. C. Jones, 1900).

Kingmaker E. M. House is examined in Charles E. Neu, "In Search of Colonel Edward M. House: The Texas Years, 1858–1912," *SHQ* 93 (1989). House's protégé, Jim Hogg is biographized by Robert C. Cotner, *James Stephen Hogg: A Biography* (UTP, 1959) and Paul Louis Wakefield, *James Stephen Hogg: A Biography, 1851–1906* (Austin: Texas Heritage Foundation, 1951). See also C. W. Raines, ed., *Speeches and State Papers of James Stephen Hogg* (Austin: State Printing Co., 1905). For other key figures see Robert L. Wagner, *The Gubernatorial Career of Charles Allen Culberson* (Austin: n.p., 1954) and Ben Procter, *Not Without Honor: The Life of John H. Reagan* (UTP, 1962).

56. GOD GOES PRIMITIVE

Religious development in Texas is richly documented. See Carter Boren, *Religion on the Texas Frontier* (San Antonio: Naylor, 1968), and Samuel S. Hill, ed., *Encyclopedia of Religion in the South* (Macon, Ga.: Macon University Press, 1984). The standard works on the Baptist ascendancy are James Milton Carroll, *A History of Texas Baptists* (Dallas: Baptist Standard, 1923), Robert A. Baker, *The Blossoming Desert: A Concise History of Texas Baptists* (Waco: Word, 1970), and Zane Allen Mason, *Frontiersmen of Faith: A History of Baptist Pioneer Work in Texas, 1865–1885* (San Antonio: Naylor, 1970). The other, less attractive, side of the Baptist coin is chronicled in Charles Carver, *Brann the Iconoclast* (UTP, 1957). The Methodist saga is detailed in Walter N. Vernon et al., *The Methodist Excitement in Texas* (Dallas: Texas United Methodist Historical Society, 1984), and the dissenters in "The Burning Bush," *SHQ* 50 (January 1947), and Timothy Smith and W. T. Purkiser, *Called into Holiness: The Story of the Nazarenes,* 2 vols. (Kansas City, Mo.: Nazarene Publishing House, 1962, 1963). For Campbellite history see Stephen Daniel Eckstein, *History of the Churches of Christ in Texas, 1824–1950* (Austin: Firm Foundation Press, 1963) and R. L. Roberts, "Expansion of the Church of Christ in West Texas, 1870–1900," *WTHAY* 53 (1977). See also Joe Evans, *Bloys Cowboy Camp Meeting* (El Paso: Guynes Printing Co., 1959).

57. GAINING CULTURE

Oscar Wilde's capers through Texas are recounted in Dorothy McInerney et al., "Oscar Wilde Lectures in Texas," *SHQ* 106 (April 2003).

The great hurricane of 1900 is related in Patricia Bellis Bixel and Elizabeth Haynes Turner, *Galveston and the 1900 Storm* (UTP, 2000) and Erik Larson, *Isaac's Storm: A Man, A Time, and the Deadliest Hurricane in History* (New York: Vintage Books, 2000).

BOOK FIVE: OIL EMPIRE

58. EARLY GUSHERS

Authoritative and readable, an excellent introduction to the petroleum era is Roger Olien and Diana Davids Olien, *Oil in Texas: The Gusher Age, 1895–1945* (UTP, 2002). See also Robert W. McDaniel and Henry C. Dethloff, *Pattillo Higgins and the Search for Texas Oil* (TAMUP, 1989) and Judith Walker Linsley, Ellen Walker Rienstra, and Jo Ann Stiles, *Giant Under the Hill: A History of the Spindletop Oil Discovery at Beaumont, Texas, in 1901* (TSHA, 2002). Still classic is Carl Coke Rister, *Oil! Titan of the Southwest* (UOP, 1949). A first-person account by one of the Spindletop principals is Anthony F. Lucas, "The Great Oil Well Near Beaumont, Texas," *Transactions of the American Institute of Mining Engineers* 31 (1902). A telling vignette of life in an early boomtown is Charlie Jeffries, "Reminiscences of Sour Lake," *SHQ* 50 (July 1946).

59. A NEW CENTURY

The remarkable Rabbi Cohen was biographized in A. Stanley Dreyfus, *Henry Cohen: Messenger of the Lord* (New York: Bloch, 1963), and Monsignor Kirwin in George T. Elmendorf, *Memoirs of Monsignor J. M. Kirwin* (priv. pub. 1928). For the growth and decline of city government by commission, see Bradley Robert Rice, *Progressive Cities: The Commission Government Movement in America, 1901–1920* (UTP, 1977). The commercial ascent of Houston over Galveston is covered in R. M. Farrar, *The Story of Buffalo Bayou and the Houston Ship Channel* (Houston: Houston Chamber of Commerce, 1928); see more generally Marilyn M. Sibley, *The Port of Houston* (UTP, 1968). Governor Campbell's greater progress toward reform is outlined in Janet Schmelzer, "Thomas M. Campbell, Progressive Governor of Texas," *Red River Valley Historical Review* 3 (1978). His, Colquitt's, and others' tenures are discussed in Lewis L. Gould, *Progressives and Prohibitionists: Texas Democrats in the Wilson Era* (UTP, 1973).

60. VALLEY OF THE SHADOW

Conflicts in the changing demographics of the Valley are discussed in Kenneth L. Steward and Arnoldo de León, *Not Room Enough: Mexicans, Anglos, and Socioeconomic Change in Texas, 1850–1900* (UNMP, 1993). The issues are if anything laid out more starkly in Arnoldo de León, *They Called Them Greasers: Anglo Attitudes Toward Mexicans in Texas, 1821–1900* (UTP, 1983). This era is also the beginning point for Guadalupe San Miguel Jr., *Let All of Them Take Heed: Mexican Americans and the Campaign for Educational Equality in Texas, 1910–1981* (UTP, 1987). The most frequently cited work on Gregorio Cortez, although rendered by a folklorist, with attendant factual subjectivity, has been Americo Paredes, *With A Pistol in His Hand: A Border Ballad and Its Hero* (UTP, 1958). A more documented account is Richard J. Mertz, "No One Can Arrest Me: The Story of Gregorio Cortez," *Journal of South Texas* 1 (January 1974).

The latest word on the Plan de San Diego has been the very detailed Charles H. Harris III and Louis R. Sadler, *The Texas Rangers and the Mexican Revolution: The Bloodiest Decade, 1910–1920* (UNMP, 2004). Reference should still be made, however, to Benjamin Heber Johnson, *Revolution in Texas: How a Forgotten Rebellion and Its Bloody Suppression Turned Mexicans into Americans* (YUP, 2003); Glenn Justice, *Revolution on the Rio Grande* (TWP, 1992); Don M. Coerver and Linda B. Hall, *Texas and the Mexican Revolution: A Study in State and National Border Policy, 1910–1920* (San Antonio: Trinity University Press, 1984); James Sandos, *Rebellion in the Borderlands: Anarchism and the Plan of San Diego* (UOP, 1992) and Charles C. Cumberland, "Border Raids in the Lower Rio Grande Valley—1915," *SHQ* 57 (January 1954). Its conditional antecedents can be studied in Manuel Gamio, *Mexican Immigration to the United States* (Chicago: University of Chicago Press, 1930) and Emilio Zamora, *The World of the Mexican Worker in Texas* (TAMUP, 1993). See more generally F. N. Samponaro and P. L. Vanderwood, *War Scare on the Rio Grande* (TSHA, 1992).

61. INTELLIGENT PATRIOTISM AND FLYING MACHINES

Most of the essential politics of this period can be read in Lewis L. Gould, *Progressives and Prohibitionists: Texas Democrats in the Wilson Era* (UTP, 1973). A longer political span is covered in Seth McKay, *Texas Politics, 1906–1944* (Lubbock: Texas Tech University Press, 1952). Ferguson's successor is treated in James Anthony Clark and Weldon Hart, *The Tactful Texan: A Biography of Governor Will Hobby* (New York: Random House, 1958). One aspect of Texas war production is portrayed in Richard W. Bricker, *Wooden Ships from Texas: A World War I Saga* (TAMUP, 1998). That Reddin Andrews, the Baptist preacher and socialist, was not far from the pulse of his constituency, can be studied in James R. Green, *Grass-Roots Socialism: Radical Movements in the Southwest, 1895–1943* (LSUP, 1978). See by the same author "Tenant Farmer Discontent and Socialist Protest in Texas, 1901–1917," *SHQ* 81 (1977).

62. FLAPPERS AND FERGUSONISM

Probably the ablest study of the politics of this era is Norman D. Brown, *Hood, Bonnet, and Little Brown Jug: Texas Politics 1921–1928* (TAMUP, 1984). A good look at the autocratic fiefdoms in south Texas is Evan Anders, *Boss Rule in South Texas: The Progressive Era* (UTP, 1982). A good biography of Ma Ferguson is May Nelson Paulissen and Carl McQueary, *Miriam: Miriam Amanda Ferguson of Bell County, The Southern Belle Who Became the First Woman Governor of Texas* (EP, 1995). Texas Ranger Captain Frank Hamer was biographized without much criticism in John H. Jenkins, *I'm Frank Hamer: The Life of a Texas Peace Officer* (Austin: Pemberton, 1957). The role of Rangers more generally in keeping order is seen in Ben H. Procter, *Just One Riot: Episodes of Texas Rangers in the Twentieth Century* (EP, 1991).

Among works on the advancing role of women are Walter Harris, "Margie E. Neal: First Woman Senator in Texas," *ETHJ* 11 (Spring 1976) and Jacquelyn Dowd Hall, *Revolt Against Chivalry: Jessie Daniel Ames and the Women's Campaign Against Lynching* (New York: Columbia University Press, 1979).

63. SO LONG, IT'S BEEN GOOD TO KNOW YOU

64. MORE FERGUSONS, AND WORSE

The oft-overlooked importance of Garner to FDR's rise to national power is re-covered in Norman D. Brown, "Garnering Votes for 'Cactus Jack': John Nance Garner, Franklin D. Roosevelt, and the 1932 Democratic Nomination for Presi-dent," *SHQ* 104 (2000). The Great Depression and the coming of the New Deal in Texas are treated in James Smallwood, *The Great Recovery: The New Deal in Texas* (Boston: American Press, 1983); Donald W. Whisenhunt, *The Depression in Texas: The Hoover Years* (New York: Garland, 1983); James Wright Steely, *The Civilian Conservation Corps in Texas State Parks* (Austin: Texas Parks and Wildlife Depart-ment, 1986); Lionel V. Patenaude, *Texans, Politics, and the New Deal* (New York: Garland, 1983); Robert L. Reid, *Picturing Texas: The FSA-OWI Photographers in the Lone Star State, 1935–1943* (TSHA, 1994); David L. Smiley, "A Slice of Life in De-pression America: The Records of the Historical Records Survey," *Prologue, The Journal of the National Archives* (Winter 1971). Hoover's brains behind the Recon-struction Finance Corporation, retained by Roosevelt, is biographized in Bas-com N. Timmons, *Jesse H. Jones* (New York: Holt, 1956). For Texas' most colorful political figure of the time, see Seth Shepard McKay, *W. Lee O'Daniel and Texas Pol-itics, 1938–1942* (Lubbock: Texas Tech University Press, 1944). The recovery program's impact on one city is examined in Roger Biles, "The New Deal in Dal-las," *SHQ* 95 (1991). How the bad times affected different ethnicities is exam-ined in Julia Kirk Blackwelder, *Women of the Depression: Caste and Culture in San Antonio, 1929–1939* (TAMUP, 1984). An urban view is offered in Robert C. Cot-ner, et al., *Texas Cities and the Great Depression* (Austin: Texas Memorial Museum, 1973).

Works on the great Western drought include Donald Worcester, *Dust Bowl* (New York: Oxford University Press, 1979); Paul Bonnifield, *The Dust Bowl: Men, Dirt and Depression* (UNMP, 1979); and R. Douglas Hurt, *The Dust Bowl: An Agri-cultural and Social History* (Chicago: Nelson-Hall, 1981). Woody Guthrie's hum-ble roots, later fame, and tragic decline are chronicled in Joe Klein, *Woody Guthrie: A Life* (New York: Knopf, 1980). For a more general music history, see Larry Willoughby, *Texas Rhythm and Texas Rhyme: A Pictorial History of Texas Music* (Austin: Texas Monthly Press, 1984). For Texas' 1936 birthday celebration, see Kenneth B. Ragsdale, *The Year America Discovered Texas—Centennial '36* (TAMUP, 1987). For a history of the state fair that includes earlier years, see Nancy Wiley, *The Great State Fair of Texas* (Dallas: Taylor Publishing Co., 1985).

65. TEXAS AT WAR, AGAIN

For the Texas war effort, see James Lee Ward, et al., eds., *Texas Goes to War* (UNT, 1991) and Robert L. Wagner, *The Texas Army: A History of the 36th Division in the Italian Campaign* (Austin, n.p., 1972). For POW camps in Texas, see Arnold P. Krammer, "When the Afrika Korps Came to Texas," *SHQ* 80 (1977). The Peruvian interns are treated in C. Harvey Gardiner, *Pawns in a Triangle of Hate: The Peruvian Japanese and the United States* (Seattle: University of Washington Press, 1988).

More on Texas' flinty wartime governor is in Booth Mooney, *Mr. Texas: The Story of Coke Stevenson* (Dallas: Texas Printing Co., 1947). For other Texas figures in the war, see Harold B. Simpson, *Audie Murphy, American Soldier* (Hillsboro, Texas: Hill Junior College Press, 1975) and Don Graham, *No Name on the Bullet: A Biography of Audie Murphy* (New York: Viking Penguin, 1989); E. B. Potter, *Nimitz* (Annapolis, Md.: Naval Institute Press, 1976) and Frank A. Driskill, *Chester W. Nimitz, Admiral of the Hills* (EP, 1983).

66. CLIMBING JACOB'S LADDER

Accounts of the disaster at Texas City include: American National Red Cross, *Texas City Explosion, April 16, 1947* (Washington, D.C.: Red Cross, 1948); Ron Stone, *Disaster at Texas City* (Fredericksburg, Texas: Shearer, 1987); and Elizabeth Lea Wheaton, *Texas City Remembers* (San Antonio: Naylor, 1948).

The controversy of the ownership of the tidelands from an effective advocate's point of view is Price Daniel, *Sovereignty and Ownership in the Marginal Sea and Their Relation to Problems of the Continental Shelf* (Austin, n.p., 1950). For a larger context one can see Ernest R. Bartley, *The Tidelands Oil Controversy: A Legal and Historical Analysis* (UTP, 1953). The hysteria over communist infiltration is logged in Don E. Carleton, *Red Scare: Right-Wing Hysteria, Fifties Fanaticism, and Their Legacy in Texas* (Austin: Texas Monthly Press, 1985). The long reign of the Speaker of the House is chronicled in Anthony Champagne, *Congressman Sam Rayburn* (New Brunswick, N.J.: Rutgers University Press, 1984) and Dorsey B. Hardeman and Donald C. Bacon, *Rayburn: A Biography* (Austin: Texas Monthly Press, 1987). The emergence of the Republican Party is covered in the insightful and interview-enhanced Roger M. Olien, *From Token to Triumph: The Texas Republicans Since 1920* (Dallas: SMUP, 1982). For coverage reaching back earlier see Paul Casdorf, *A History of the Republican Party in Texas* (Austin: Pemberton Press, 1965), or project forward with John R. Knaggs, *Two Party Texas: The John Tower Era, 1961–1984* (EP, 1986).

For civil rights issues, see James A. Burran, "Violence in an 'Arsenal of Democracy,' " *ETHJ* (1976); Jacquelyn Dowd Hall, *Revolt Against Chivalry: Jessie Daniel Ames and the Women's Campaign Against Lynching* (New York: Columbia University Press, 1979); Alecia Davis, "Christia V. Adair: Servant of Humanity," *Texas Historian* (September 1977); Michael L. Gillette, "Blacks Challenge the White University," *SHQ* (October 1982); Darlene Clark Hine, *Black Victory: The*

Rise and Fall of the White Primary in Texas (Millwood, N.Y.: KTO Press, 1979); and Alwyn Barr and Robert A. Calvert, eds., *Black Leaders: Texans for Their Times* (TSHA, 1981). The story of the Texas Western basketball championship is recounted in Frank Fitzpatrick, *And the Walls Came Tumbling Down: Kentucky, Texas Western, and the Game That Changed American Sports* (New York: Simon & Schuster, 1999). The Felix Longoria matter is handled in context in Carl Allsup, *The American G.I. Forum: Origins and Evolution* (UTP, 1982).

67. A FLOWERING OF TEXAS LETTERS

Reading on Katherine Anne Porter should begin with Joan Givner, *Katherine Anne Porter: A Life* (New York: Simon & Schuster, 1982), and then more particularly Clinton Machann and William Bedford Clark, eds., *Katherine Anne Porter and Texas: An Uneasy Relationship* (TAMUP, 1990). The book that brought the Dobie-Webb-Bedichek triumvirate to public notice was William A. Owens, *Three Friends: Roy Bedichek, J. Frank Dobie, and Walter Prescott Webb* (Garden City, N.Y.: Doubleday, 1969), but he was preceded by Ronnie Dugger, *Three Men in Texas: Bedichek, Webb, and Dobie* (UTP, 1967). Some of Ben K. Green's most popular collections of stories, published by Knopf, include *Horse Tradin'* (1967), *Wild Cow Tales* (1969), *Village Horse Doctor: West of the Pecos* (1971), and *Some More Horse Tradin'* (1972). Green's sometimes disconcertingly candid correspondence with Knopf's legendary editor Angus Cameron is in the Special Collections of the University of Texas at Arlington Library.

68. ASSASSINATION, WAR, AND ANTIWAR

A general political survey of this and the following period is in George N. Green, *The Establishment in Texas Politics* (Westport, Conn.: Greenwood Press, 1979).

The obvious beginning point to wade into the Kennedy killing is *Report of the President's Commission on the Assassination of President John F. Kennedy* (USGPO, 1964). Jim Marrs, *Crossfire: The Plot That Killed JFK* (New York: Carroll & Graf, 1989) is one of countless entradas into the parallel universe of conspiracies. Of that other incident from the '60s that all Texans remember, see William J. Helmer, "The Madman in the Tower," *Texas Monthly* (August 1986). The Center for American History on the UT campus also has an extensive vertical file on the subject.

For specific figures, see Sam Kinch Jr. and Stuart Long, *Allan Shivers: The Pied Piper of Texas Politics* (Austin: Shoal Creek Publishers, 1974); Dan Murph, *Texas Giant: The Life of Price Daniel* (EP, 2002); James Reston, *The Lone Star: The Life of John Connally* (New York: Harper & Row, 1989); and Ann Fears Crawford and Jack Keever, *John B. Connally: A Portrait in Power* (Austin: Jenkins Publishing Co., 1973). Connally's liberal bugbear is lionized in William G. Phillips, *Yarborough of Texas* (Washington, D.C.: Acropolis Books, 1969) but not biographized until Patrick Cox, *Ralph Yarborough: The People's Senator* (UTP, 2001). Of the earlier biographies of Lyndon Johnson, see Paul Conkin, *Big Daddy from the Pedernales: Lyndon Baines Johnson* (Boston: Twayne Publishers, 1986) and Robert Dallek, *Lone*

Star Rising: Lyndon Johnson and His Times (New York: Oxford University Press, 1991) and Doris Kearns, *Lyndon Baines Johnson and the American Dream* (New York: Harper & Row, 1976); each have commendable points. The Robert Caro trilogy about him, *The Years of Lyndon Johnson,* all published by Knopf, include *The Path to Power* (1982), *Means of Ascent* (1990), and *Master of the Senate* (2002). The controversy surrounding these books has been needless, for their aim has not been to defame LBJ, but to provide a narrow-focus study just of the acquisition and dispensation of power, nothing more. Interpretations of Janis Joplin include Myra Friedman, *Buried Alive: The Biography of Janis Joplin* (New York: Harmony Books, 1992) and Ellis Amburn, *Pearl: The Obsessions and Passions of Janis Joplin: A Biography* (New York: Warner, 1992).

69. CHANGES, FASTER AND FASTER

For a summary of Governor Smith see Donald Walker, "Governor Preston E. Smith," *WTHAY* 75 (1999). Sharpstown is the principal subject of Charles Deaton, *The Year They Threw the Rascals Out* (Austin: Shoal Creek Publishers, 1973) and Sam Kinch Jr. and Ben Procter, *Texas Under a Cloud* (Austin: Jenkins Publishing Co., 1972). Some sense of the changing agricultural demographic can be gained from Mark Friedberger, "Mink and Manure: Rural Gentrification and Cattle Raising in Southeast Texas, 1945–1992," *SHQ* 102 (1999). See also Bruce J. Schulman, *From Cotton Belt to Sunbelt: Federal Policy, Economic Development, and the Transformation of the South, 1938–1980* (New York: Oxford University Press, 1991).

William P. Clements has not proven to be a great attraction for biographers, but if you can bear to pick up a book with such a title, see Carolyn Barta, *Bill Clements: Texian to His Toenails* (EP, 1996). The 1990 gubernatorial contest is the center of Sue Tolleson-Rinehart and Jeanie R. Stanley, *Claytie and the Lady: Ann Richards, Gender, and Politics in Texas* (UTP, 1994). See more generally Celia Morris, *Storming the Statehouse: Running for Governor with Ann Richards and Dianne Feinstein* (New York: Scribner's Sons, 1992), and Richards tells her own story in Ann Richards, *Straight from the Heart: My Life in Politics and Other Places* (New York: Simon & Schuster, 1989). Another biography is Mike Shropshire, *The Thorny Rose of Texas: An Intimate Portrait of Governor Ann Richards* (Secaucus, N.J.: Carol Publishing Group, 1994). Feelings about George W. Bush still run so high that truly objective books are scarce. From the squinting left there is Paul Begala, *Is Our Children Learning: The Case Against George W. Bush* (New York: Simon & Schuster, 2000) and Molly Ivins and Lou Dubose, *Shrub: The Short but Happy Political Life of George W. Bush* (New York: Random House, 2000). From the equally approving right there is Stephen Mansfield, *A Charge to Keep: The Faith of George W. Bush* (New York: Tarcher, 2003) and Carolyn B. Thompson and James W. Ware, *The Leadership Genius of George W. Bush* (New York: Wylie, 2003).

The importance of irrigation on the Llano Estacado is plain from Donald E. Green, *Land of the Underground Rain: Irrigation on the Texas High Plains, 1920–1970* (UTP, 1973). The investigating narcotics officer in the Tulia case was indicted for perjury, not for statements made during the trials, on which the statute of limitations had run, but for false statements made during the subsequent inquiry. The jury recommended seven years probation; the judge increased it to ten years. The entire Tulia affair is detailed in Nate Blakeslee, *Tulia: Race, Cocaine, and Corruption in a Small Texas Town* (New York: PublicAffairs, 2005).

Hispanic immigration has ignited as much scholarly debate over its meaning and implications as it has grassroots apprehension. Contrast, for example, the rather foreboding Samuel P. Huntington, *Who Are We? The Challenges to America's National Identity* (New York: Simon & Schuster, 2004) with the polarimetrically sunny Marco Portales, *Latin Sun, Rising: Our Spanish-Speaking U.S. World* (TAMUP, 2005), which bases some of its genial findings on the very traits that Huntington finds so alarming.

INDEX

Aberdeen, Earl of, 249, 380
Abilene, Texas: founding of, 388
ab initio question, 327, 330
Abraham, Nahim, 394
Adair, Christia, 478, 524
Adair, Elbert, 478
Adair, John George, 379–80
Adams, John Quincy, 203, 204, 246, 247, 252
Adams-Onís Treaty (1819), 62
Adelsverein. *See* German communities
Adobe Walls, 353–54, 355–58, 359, 361, 362, 376, 400
Aesthetic Movement, 433
agents, Indian, 342–43, 354, 401, 405–6, 435
Agricultural Adjustment Act (AAA), 495, 516
agriculture, 47, 548–49. *See also* cattle; cotton; farmers/farming; ranching
Agua Dulce: battle at, 143
Aguayo, Marquées de San Miguel de (José de Azlor), 41–42, 47, 48
Ahto-tain-te (White Cowbird) (Kiowa), 401
Ahumada, Mateo, 92, 93
airplanes, 469–71
Akokisa Indians, 39
Alamán y Escalada, Lucas, 97
Alamo: Battle of the, 152–53, 154–61, 162–67; Blacks at, 529; causes of deaths at, 162–67; Cos' troops at, 127, 132, 133; courage of defenders at, 167; fall of, 152, 159–61, 179, 374; filibusters as defenders of, 164; founding of, 40; and Houston, 139, 144, 154, 157, 160, 167, 168–69, 179; Houston's orders to Bowie about, 139, 144,

169; initial skirmishes at, 130–31, 133; as legend, 162; McKinley speech at, 450; Mexican casualties at, 160, 161; Neill as commander at, 142, 143, 144, 145; questions about, 162–67, 168; remembering the, 188, 198; revenge for, 165, 192; Santa Anna arrives at, 146–47, 152; schisms at, 145; scholarly studies about, 155; Texans' cause for fighting at, 168; Texans' reactions to fall of, 152, 168–69, 170, 179, 188, 189, 192; Texas reinforcements for, 143–45, 146–47, 154, 156, 157, 158; Travis as commander at, 145–47; Travis' letter from, 146–47
Alarcón, Martín de, 40
Alazán Creek, 58, 132
Albuquerque, New Mexico, 13, 304
Alcaraz, Diego de, 10
Alderton, Charles, 398
Alexander, Robert, 278
Allen, Augustus C., 212, 215
Allen, Charlotte, 212
Allen, John K., 212
Allred, Jimmy, 497, 499, 502, 530, 543
Almonte, Juan, 100, 117–19, 154, 160, 161, 166, 183, 184, 188, 197, 200, 208
Alpine, Texas, 415
Althaus, Christian, 275–76
Althaus, Elizabeth, 275–76
Alt-Leiningen, Count of, 255–56
Alvarado, Hernando de, 13
Alvarez, Francisca, 176
Alvarez de Pineda, Alonso, 3–4
Alvarez de Toledo, José, 56, 58–59
Alvord, Henry, 347–48

589

Point Bolivar, 63
Polish immigrants, 271
political contributions, 453
political parties: during Republic of
    Texas, 218. *See also specific party*
Polk, James Knox, 149, 248, 249, 263,
    264, 266
poll taxes, 466, 520
Ponce de León, Juan, 17
Ponton, Andrew, 121, 122, 123
Poor Buffalo (Kiowa), 364
Pope, John, 358, 365–66
Popé (Pueblo chief), 27
Populist Movement, 383–92, 451
Port Arthur, Texas, 540, 541
Porter, David Dixon, 311, 316
Porter, Katherine Anne, 531, 532,
    533
Portilla, José Nicolás de la (El Indio),
    175–76, 177, 200
Potter, Robert, 150, 168, 183, 200
Pratt, William C., 543
Presbyterians, 85–86, 280, 297, 425
presidency, Texas: ad interim, 171,
    182–83; first elections for, 201–2;
    salary of, 236; terms of, 218. *See
    also specific person*
President's House, 268
presidios, 9, 41, 43, 44, 49, 50, 55. *See
    also specific presidio*
Pretti, Nicolas, 34
Price, Sterling, 307
Price, William Redwood, 361, 365
priests, 11–12, 26, 27, 34–37, 41, 43,
    47, 48, 49, 84. *See also
    missionaries; specific person*
Prison Commission, 480
prison farms, 317
prison system: court supervision of,
    551; and death
    penalty/executions, 553, 557–58;
    in early 20th century, 448, 453,
    454, 464, 478, 480, 484; fire in,
    448; Indians in, 401, 402; in late
    19th century, 401, 402, 432; in
    1980s, 551; pardons for people in,
    483, 493; rebuilding of, 448;
    reform of, 478, 484
prisoner-of-war camps, 517

progressives, 385, 389–91, 419,
    421–24, 435, 448, 449, 452–54,
    524, 550, 553
Prohibition: bootlegging during, 480;
    in early 20th century, 454, 462,
    463, 467, 468, 472, 474–76, 480;
    and Houston, 432; and
    immigrants, 432; in late 19th
    century, 422, 424, 425, 432; and
    moonshining, 474–76, 496, 540;
    in 1930s, 490; and racketeering,
    475; and religion, 432; repeal of,
    496; in Republic of Texas, 432;
    and Texas Rangers, 474, 475–76;
    and womens' issues, 476, 478. *See
    also* Woman's Christian
    Temperance Union (WCTU)
prostitution, 496–97
Pryor, Charles, 296–97
Public Utilities Commission, 550
Public Works Administration, 497
"Publius," 233–34
Pueblo Indians, 12, 23–24, 26, 27
Pullman Strike, 423
pure food and drug laws, 453
Putnam (girl), 228

Quahadi Indians, 340, 341, 343, 346,
    348, 350, 355, 356, 369, 372, 400,
    402
Quakers, 342–43, 350, 354, 405–6
Quanah Parker (Quahadi), 341,
    355–56, 357, 369, 375, 400, 402
Quanah, Texas, 359, 401
Quantrill, William Clarke, 301
Quivira story, 13, 14, 15, 25, 26

race relations: in antebellum years,
    300; and challenges facing Texas,
    557–60; and citizenship, 455; in
    early 20th century, 452, 478–79,
    481–82, 485–86; and education,
    526–29; and electoral system,
    452; in films, 492; and Hispanics,
    253, 414–15, 456, 472, 513, 529,
    555, 559–60; in late 19th century,
    413–14; in 1950s, 502; and
    post–World War II years, 520,
    526–29; in Reconstruction,

ABOUT THE AUTHOR

James L. Haley grew up in Fort Worth, Texas, and currently lives in Austin. He is the author of several books of history, including *The Buffalo War, Apaches,* and *Sam Houston,* which won nine historical and literary awards.